Working in a Global Era

Working in

a Global Era

Canadian Perspectives edited by Vivian Shalla

CANADIAN SCHOLARS' PRESS   •   TORONTO

Working in a Global Era: Canadian Perspectives
edited by Vivian Shalla

First published in 2006 by
Canadian Scholars' Press Inc.
180 Bloor Street West, Suite 801
Toronto, Ontario
M5S 2V6

www.cspi.org

Canadian Scholars' Press gratefully acknowledges financial support for our publishing activities from the Government of Canada through the Book Publishing Industry Development Program (BPIDP) and the Government of Ontario through the Ontario Book Publishing Tax Credit Program.

Library and Archives Canada Cataloguing in Publication

Shalla, Vivian, 1959-
   Working in a global era : Canadian perspectives / Vivian Shalla.

Includes bibliographical references.
ISBN 1-55130-290-X
1. Labor--Canada—Textbooks. 2. Labor movement—Canada—Textbooks. 3. Globalization—Economic aspects—Canada—Textbooks. I. Title.

HD8106.5.S43 2006   331'.0971   C2006-900058-1

Book design and composition: George Kirkpatrick

06   07   08   09   10   5   4   3   2   1

Printed and bound in Canada by Marquis Book Printing Inc.

Canadä

CONTENTS

PREFACE

A FEW YEARS AGO, when I began teaching a course on work in a global era, I was frustrated at the limited number of textbooks or readers that focused more specifically on the transformation of work in the Canadian context. I found students to be thirsty for knowledge about what was happening to work in Canada even though they remained very curious about the impact of globalization and economic restructuring on the transformation of work in other parts of the world. They wanted to know what would be happening to them once they engaged more permanently with the world of paid work. They also wanted to make more sense of the lives, dreams, accomplishments, and disappointments of their parents, most of whom were part of the Canadian labour force or who were trying to get a foothold in the labour market in Canada. They also were interested in how work in Canada could be linked to broader global structures and processes. This collection of articles is meant to help fill a gap in the literature on work in Canada. The topics relate to realities that are encountered throughout the world, but, for the most part, the articles deal with the expression of these realities in the Canadian context.

This book is also about critical perspectives on work and its transformation. I discovered early on in teaching courses on work in a global era that students were very open to critical perspectives on work. While they may not have always felt comfortable with some of the critical analyses that were being presented to them, they found these interpretations intriguing and, for many, these non-mainstream and non-common sense explanations of social reality seemed to make quite a bit of sense. What is more, over the past few years, many students who have signed up for the course on work have told me of the deep satisfaction they have felt in debating topics about work with their friends and families, especially their parents, and of being able to hold their own in discussions when adopting critical positions about the changing world of work. A student recently recounted to me that she had had a vigorous and very heated debate with her parents about the growing precariousness in the labour market and how that process put women at greater risk and deepened polarization and social exclusion. Her parents, she observed with a twinkle in her eye, had no choice but to eventually concede that her solid arguments had a ring of logic that they had chosen to disregard in the past. In itself, that is sufficient reason to continue exploring critical perspectives on work. This collection of articles presents a range of critical outlooks on work in Canada.

This book would not be in the hands of students interested in work in a global era without the help of Megan Mueller of Canadian Scholars' Press. Megan encouraged me to put this book together and was patient with the various other demands on my time during a very trying period. For that, I am very grateful. I would also like to thank Wallace Clement who believed that this collection was a great idea and has continued to cheer me on from afar.

A Note from the Publisher

Thank you for selecting *Working in a Global Era* edited by Vivian Shalla. The editor and publisher have devoted considerable time and careful development (including meticulous peer reviews) to this book. We appreciate your recognition of this effort and accomplishment.

Teaching Features

This volume distinguishes itself on the market in many ways. One key feature is the book's well-written and comprehensive part openers, which help to make the readings all the more accessible to undergraduate students. The part openers add cohesion to the section and to the whole book. The themes of the book are very clearly presented in these section openers.

The general editor, Vivian Shalla, has also greatly enhanced the book by adding pedagogy to close and complete each section. Each part ends with critical thinking questions pertaining to each reading, detailed annotated recommended readings, and annotated related websites.

INTRODUCTION

OVER THE COURSE of the past few decades, the world of work has been undergoing rapid and profound transformation. This transformation has occurred within the broader context of globalization, economic restructuring, and fundamental shifts in public policy. While few people around the world have been left untouched by these changes, this book focuses mostly on the Canadian experience, situating it within global structures and processes.

The book brings together a collection of articles that adopt a critical approach to work and its transformation. The articles are critical in three ways. First, they challenge widespread assumptions about key issues pertaining to work in a global era. Second, they critically assess explanatory frameworks that have attempted to account for the transformation of work. And third, they are critical of the direction work is taking and of the ways the livelihoods of working people and their families are being degraded and shattered. Most of the articles, however, offer hope for better worlds of work.

Section I, "Understanding Globalization," helps to situate transformations in the world of work and begins to debunk some of the widely held assumptions about globalization. In Chapter 1, Gary Teeple examines a number of themes to demonstrate that globalization, which is both an economic and political process, is fundamentally capitalism seeping into, and connecting, all parts of the globe. Chapter 2, by Linda McQuaig, challenges the widespread belief that, in the face of globalization, democratically elected governments have become powerless to make decisions that might frighten away corporate investors.

Section II, "Post-Fordism at Work," focuses on some of the major changes that have occurred in the workplace since the 1970s, and locates workplace redesign in an increasingly competitive global economic context. In Chapter 3, Wayne Lewchuk and David Robertson assess the new methods of work production implemented by auto manufacturers, and conclude that these methods have not lived up to their promise of bringing significant improvements to vehicle assembly workers' overall jobs. In Chapter 4, Bonnie Fox and Pamela Sugiman also take a critical look at new systems of work organization, but shift their focus to clerical work. They find that managerial practices are complex, yet often unplanned, and that workers' actions and reactions influence workplace dynamics, thereby making the outcome of new systems of work organization uncertain.

Section III, "Precariousness in the Labour Market," focuses on the changing nature of labour markets and employment relationships in the post-industrial economy. Chapter 5, by Cynthia J. Cranford, Leah F. Vosko, and Nancy Zukewich, examines the complex links among gender, forms of employment, and dimensions of precarious employment. Their analysis clearly shows that employment norms are being feminized, and that while women continue to be more disadvantaged, many men are losing out in an increasingly precarious labour market. In Chapter 6, Vivian Shalla uses a case study of the contracting out of work in the Canadian airline industry to explore the changing nature of employment in the service sector. She finds clear evidence of employment relationship degradation, but notes that workers' struggles help minimize precariousness.

Section IV, "Working in the Free-Trade Zones of the North and South," focuses on economic development strategies in Third World countries and underdeveloped regions of First World countries, and the impact of these strategies on local labour markets. Chapter 7, by Naomi Klein, analyzes the mushrooming of free-trade zones in the developing world, locating this trend within broader global structures and labour-shedding practices of mega-corporations. Her discussion of the working and living conditions in free-trade zones exposes the limitations of this development strategy. In Chapter 8, Ruth Buchanan shifts our attention to similar development strategies in New Brunswick, Canada. She explores the role of local governments, multinational corporations, and workers in shaping the call centre industry, thereby highlighting the dynamic relationship between global economic restructuring and local cultures and histories.

Section V, "Unfree Labour: Migrant Workers and Citizenship," takes an in-depth look at labour migration from the poorest to the richest regions of the world as an integral dimension of an increasingly globalized economy. Chapter 9, by Donna Baines and Nandita Sharma, examines how Canada makes use of citizenship to selectively provide migrant workers with access to resources and privileges. They demonstrate how this practice increases the employment and social vulnerability of migrant workers. In Chapter 10, Daiva K. Stasiulis and Abigail B. Bakan discuss the problems faced by migrant women from Third World countries who come to Canada to take on jobs as domestic workers. Their analysis lays bare the unequal rights of the citizen employer and the non-citizen worker, and points to how foreign domestic worker policies help perpetuate the general condition of women's oppression.

Section VI, "Neo-Liberalism and the Dismantling of the Welfare State," addresses the neo-liberal attack on the Keynesian welfare state over the past few decades. Chapter 11, by Stephen McBride, emphasizes the significance of national factors, and especially decisions by governments, in explaining the shift towards neo-liberalism. He highlights how this paradigm shift has left workers and their families more insecure. In Chapter 12, Jane Pulkingham and Gordon Ternowetsky analyze the process of state retrenchment in Canada and demonstrate that the adoption of a series of policies and programs has resulted in the federal government abandoning its responsibility for the collective well-being of its citizenry.

Section VII, "Education, Training, and Skills in a Knowledge-Based Economy," challenges the widely held assumption that a highly trained and highly skilled workforce is increasingly required for the purported knowledge-based economy. Chapter 13, by David Livingstone, focuses on the complex relationship between training and employment, unearthing some of the contradictory and tenuous links between formal education attainment and the type and quality of jobs available. In Chapter 14, Alan Sears explores education reforms introduced by the Ontario government in the 1990s, which aimed to produce a more compliant workforce willing to take jobs in lean workplaces. The article concludes that the nurturing of a culture of obedience does not contribute to the generic or critical-thinking skills supposedly required by the knowledge economy.

Section VIII, "The Labour Movement in Transition," takes a close look at the weakening of the Canadian labour movement over the past three decades in the wake of neo-liberal globalization. Chapter 15, by Leo Panitch and Donald Swartz, documents the sustained attack by federal and provincial governments, regardless of their political inclinations, on the rights and freedoms of workers and their unions. Woven through the article is an analysis of the labour movement's struggle to resist these attacks. In Chapter 16, Sam Gindin and Jim Stanford discuss the challenges that a weakened Canadian labour movement continues to face in the current economic and political climate. The book's concluding article nevertheless strikes a note of optimism about the labour movement's potential to become a leading agent of progressive and transformative change.

Section I

Understanding Globalization

THE OPENING SECTION of the book introduces students to some of the key concepts related to globalization and to debates about the meaning and reality of globalization. The two articles in this section are intended to provide students with a wider context for analyzing the ways in which workers, and especially workers in Canada, encounter, experience and react to transformations in the world of work. Situating the major changes that have occurred in the world of work over the past few decades within broader global economic, social and political structures, processes and relations leads to a better understanding of these changes. Underlying both articles is the premise that globalization and Canada's insertion into global processes cannot be conceptualized or discussed without seriously taking into account power relations and agency.

The first article in this collection is taken from the revised edition of Gary Teeple's book *Globalization and the Decline of Social Reform* in which he seeks to demonstrate that globalization represents the triumph of capitalism on a world scale. The author critically assesses two main arguments put forth by skeptics of globalization who believe a) that no fundamental and major changes have occurred in the world economy over the past three decades that warrant the use of the term globalization; or, b) that globalization merely represents an ideological concept used by those in power to demand concessions from subordinate classes. Teeple focuses on various themes to substantiate his claim that globalization is both a palpable reality and an ideological construct that maintain and deepen power relations. These themes include qualitative and quantitative global economic shifts, the technological revolution, the transformation of systems of production, the dominance of transnational corporations, the creation of a global market, the weakening of the sovereignty of national governments and the consolidation of bodies of supranational governance, and structural adjustment policies and the deepening of inequalities between the North and the South. Teeple argues that it is important to develop a clear analysis of both the concept and reality of globalization to provide the tools necessary for progressive groups to mount an effective resistance and develop alternatives to the global economic and political developments that have served the interests of a small, but powerful, minority.

Linda McQuaig's article is taken from her book *The Cult of Impotence: Selling the Myth of Powerlessness in the Global Economy*. The author questions the widespread belief that, in our increasingly globalized world, democratically elected governments have limited power to resolve economic and social problems such as unemployment, poverty and homelessness, or to invest heavily in popularly supported social programs such as health care and education. She challenges the dominant view that the processes of technological change and globalization have inevitably and fundamentally changed the way things can be done, thereby eliminating the democratic options that existed in the golden years of postwar economic growth. McQuaig's analysis of budget decisions made by the Canadian government in the mid- to late-1990s reveals that the constraints imposed on nation-states in the global economy are exaggerated, and governments have more room to manoeuvre than we have been led to believe. The author is aware of the increased power that major international investors have garnered over the past few decades to pursue their own self-interests. She highlights, however, some of the contradictions inherent in arguments that global financial players will withdraw much-needed capital if their demands are not met, a situation that would leave Canadians in even more difficult circumstances and force them to contend with worsening social ills. For McQuaig, decision-making and real choices by political leaders underlie the relinquishing of power to private interests and global financial markets. She concludes that governments have not lost their sovereignty in the global marketplace and are therefore not impotent to implement changes that respect the wishes and support the aspirations of the majority of citizens.

CHAPTER 1

A Critique of the Sceptics

Gary Teeple

IN LITTLE MORE than a decade an enormous literature on the subject of globalization has appeared. Yet, despite the wide exploration of this concept, there is little consensus as to its meaning. Indeed, there is no small amount of scepticism as to its empirical referent and there is much criticism surrounding its use—especially on the left of the political spectrum.

A great deal rests on demonstrating that there is a reality to globalization and on grasping the nature of that reality. Since the early 1970s, much of the intellectual and organizational disarray in the movements of subordinate classes and other groups has been a product of the radical changes brought about by globalizing capital, transformations that have seemingly overturned all former certainties. Class structures and legal and political systems of the recent past are undergoing more or less rapid modification; and the critical theories and objectives of the left have all come into question. As a consequence, resistance and alternatives to current economic and political developments are necessarily being rethought,

but their success can only come with an understanding of just what it is that is happening.

Without a clear analysis of globalization there can be no effective resistance. It is crucial, then, to clarify the concept and the reality underlying it; and part of this task can be done by addressing some of the criticisms made of it.

Globalization as Mere Rhetoric

Some critics of the concept of globalization dismiss it as not reflective of real or significant change in the world economy; we must therefore begin our discussion here, at the very least to make some important distinctions. If we cannot go beyond the claim that the concept of globalization is empty of content, the discussion stops and we are left with a vision of a world of nation-states and their attendant concepts.

A common criticism of globalization makes it out to be a merely ideological concept, a sort of instrument of the powers that be to demand concessions from subordinate classes. As one sceptic observed, "The 'globalization thesis' here became a powerful tool to beat upon socialists, welfare statists, nationalists and so on."[1] A non-sceptic refers to the same point: "In much of the Left's anti-globalization writing, globalization is seen as an ideology that is sapping the working class of its power ('paralysed by the bogeyman of globalization'); it serves to quash the 'socialist project,' and play into the hands of a resurgent capitalist class."[2] Another critic goes further, asserting that the "idea itself is suspect"; it is simply an attempt to find "an alternative to the existing Marxist vocabulary."[3] There is little question that corporate and political leaders have used the idea that "there is no alternative" to the current trends in these ways, but we must make a distinction between the political use of the term "globalization" and its conceptualization of a reality. This is perhaps a small point, but apparently necessary to make: a critique and rejection of the ideological use of a concept should not lead to the dismissal of its possible reference to a reality.

The notion that globalization is but an ideology connected with large corporations and compliant politicians and academics has led some writers to the conclusion that as mere ideology it can be countered by similar means. In other words, if the phenomenon is simply ideological it will be enough to change the ideological perspective of those in power or at least to resist only on the ideological plane. But even if globalization were merely an ideological weapon without real content, it is no longer clear that any ready counter-ideational weapon is at hand. All the previous givens about the welfare state, about socialism in the nation-state, about the contradiction between national capitalist and working classes, and about the nature of the national state and national mar-

kets are being transfigured; they are no longer the same as they were even a short generation ago. Similarly, in the Third World the previous contradictions between centre and periphery no longer hold. The meaning of imperialism, furthermore—when applied to a country or organization in the age of transnational corporations, globalized production, distribution and consumption, and supranational agencies and regulations—is no longer clear.

The sceptics not infrequently point to the rhetorical promotion of globalization as a "recipe for prosperity,"[4] and rightly show that except for a minority this claim is patently false. Numerous studies, national and global, show that globalization has brought more or less rapidly increasing disparities in wealth everywhere. One of them concludes, "Global integration is among the main causes of rising inequality and poverty in any nation-state."[5] Little counterevidence has been offered. Just because the process itself does not bring benefits for all as claimed, however, is again no reason to dismiss the concept, along with its purported "promise" and theologue-like advocates.

As a variation on this theme, there are those who have argued that something is indeed happening, but whatever it is, it is not globalization. In this vein, the book-length treatment of the issue by Paul Hirst and Grahame Thompson contends with qualifications that globalization "is largely a myth," despite providing evidence for a certain reality behind the "myth."[6] Another study argues that far from being a new world in the making, globalization is about the old world order coming apart—as if the two could be separated.[7] The works by Hirst and Thompson and David Gordon are serious efforts to explore the empirical evidence for the phenomenon; but there are now too many authors and too much evidence pointing to pervasive qualitative global shifts to suggest that globalization is merely a myth. The debate can only be about how to understand and characterize it and what to do about it; it can no longer be about whether or not it is happening.

Nothing New—Plus ça change ...

Given that the rhetorical use of the concept does not deny the underlying reality of new global conditions, the question that follows for the sceptics concerns the nature of that reality. A notable stream of criticism of the concept of globalization makes the case that it does not reflect any significantly new development and is in fact simply the continuing "logic of capitalism." One notable analyst, David Harvey, writes: "Certainly from 1492 onwards, and even before, the globalization process of capitalism was well under way." Paul Sweezy concurs: "Globalization is not a condition or a phenomenon: it is a process that has been going on for a long time, in fact ever since capitalism came into the world as a viable form of society four or five centuries ago." He adds that globalization has been "the always expansive and often explosive capital accumulation process."[8]

Ellen Meiksins Wood agrees: "What they are calling a new epoch may be just the basic logic of capitalism asserting itself again after the exceptional, anomalous moment of the postwar boom. They may call it globalization or postmodernity, but it is really capitalism." Earlier she had written, "The only concept we need to deal with this new reality is capitalism." W.K. Tabb reiterates: "The most significant features of what is called globalization have always been part of capitalist development, even

if the forms are different in different periods (including our own)."[9]

Such positions are widely accepted on the left and amount to saying that the present changes are but the continuation of the expansion of capitalism down through the ages, or that capitalism is capitalism is capitalism. At a high level of abstraction this is true enough, but truisms do not make us much wiser; they do not help to explain either the stages in capitalist world development or the present shift in this expansion to the global level. Few if any writers on globalization, moreover, have said that it is not capitalism; most would agree that it is a stage in the development of capitalism. The problem is to identify the defining characteristics of this particular stage as opposed to other stages.

These positions may well rest on a certain reading of Marx, who writes: "The world market itself forms the basis for this [capitalist] mode of production."[10] But this says nothing about the stages of development of capitalism or its world market; it merely points to a necessary relationship. In the same vein, we can say that a social system is the precondition for the individual human, but this does not bring us any closer to an explanation of the stages of human social development.

If not derived from Marx, these positions seem implicitly to assume Immanuel Wallerstein's notion of a "world-economic system."[11] Yet in this concept he has reified an international capitalist trading system, given it an autonomous reality separate from the historically developing national capitals that have constituted its parts. The assertion of an independent reality for the world economy is to hypostatize the market, to give it a life outside of its actors. It is, in other words, to grasp only one side of a relationship, to miss the very dependency of this market on the competing national capitalist/managerial classes, corporations, and states that are/were its embodiment. The effect of positing the "world-economy" as an independent variable stretching forward from the 16th century is to impede an understanding of distinct stages in its growth, of its relation to its member nations, and of the transition from nationally based capital to capital increasingly free from or indifferent to national interests.

The point is that there is no such thing as capitalism pure and simple. Only in the most general, abstract sense is capitalism the same phenomenon down through the ages. If its fundamental characteristics are commodity production, production for profit, corporate private property, social labour, a world market, and the law of value, none of this says anything about the developmental stages of these characteristics or about how any of these elements manifest themselves in a given age or country. Similarly, there is no such thing as an independent world market, except as an abstraction. Just as there is no society without its constituent members, so too is there no market without its member capitals, and no international market without nation-states.[12] And just as the history of capital evolves through many qualitatively distinct stages, so too does the corresponding world market.

Prior to the 1970s, capital was largely national in character and the world market was still more or less international, a trading system by and large framed by international relations. Only with the current process of globalization is there the actual establishment of "self-generating"[13] capital at the global level, in the form of the transnational corporation (TNC), where the national character is of little consequence. Only now has capitalism become independent of its previous political and economic restric-

tions and developed a reality as self-generating capitals, as a system *sans* nationality. In all previous stages, capitalism had national characteristics, a national bourgeoisie, and its own specific history. Contra Wallerstein, national capitals always produced a fractious, warring, international system rather than an integrated, coherent one. After the early 1970s, however, globalization became the growing realization of Wallerstein's "capitalist world-economy," that is, as a world market in transition—on the way to becoming a unified, unfettered global trading system.

Global capital has no national bourgeoisie and no national allegiances; it has declining national characteristics and increasingly the characteristics of capital per se, as framed by the current global conditions. Its history begins after World War II with the creation of a supranational framework for the global market. Just as the national market was created by eliminating trade barriers over a certain territory in the bourgeois revolutions of the 18th and 19th centuries, so too the global market is being created by the systematic reduction of national trade barriers worldwide. In this way the global market is qualitatively different from the national capitalisms and the international systems of the previous eras. Historically, the world market evolved through stages marked by the growth in the relations of its constituents, namely, national states and national corporations; now there is movement towards a global market, and its members are TNCs.

In every stage in the development of capitalism, its fundamental characteristics appear in different ways, in strikingly different class structures and relations, labour processes, social, political, and legal relations, and organizations representing labour and capital. The differences between the stages such as "manufacturing," "large-scale industry," and Fordism, for example, represent nothing less than transformations of the whole of "society"—with profound differences in the manifestations of the contradictions of capitalism. To call it all capitalism is to add nothing. In fact, that view hinders the analysis of transformed conditions of accumulation and the new social, political, and legal landscape that accompanies them. It is one thing to argue that globalization is *not* a new stage of development and that there is *no* new regime of accumulation; but to say that it is all just capitalism is merely an empty truism intended only to dismiss.

To make the case that what the world is experiencing now is nothing new, some sceptics point to the period between 1870 and 1913 as a time of similar or greater international economic integration than the present. Over those decades labour migration from Europe to North and South America, it is argued, was unprecedented; citizenship was granted easily to immigrants; capital mobility and profit "repatriation" were more or less unrestricted; exports grew faster than domestic production; the gold standard governed foreign exchange; a free-trade philosophy dominated international relations. Yet, even if we accept these points (though most are open to debate), we can see that the critics miss out the significance of the event that brought the period to a close. If the international integration of that era amounted to globalization, then the meaning of World War I is not at all clear.

Undoubtedly, that period was a time of extensive international economic integration, but the integration took the form of the expansion of national capitals. It was the age of "nation-building," or the consolidation of the domestic market, and of the extraterritorial extension of the national market character-

ized by colonization and imperialism. Both the First and Second World Wars represented the limits of an *international* expansion that took the shape of the near destruction of much of the world due to the contradiction between the form and content of capital at a certain stage in its development. Globalization has nothing to do with the expansion of territorially exclusive markets; it is about making the world into one market.

The sceptics who deny that the present era is any different are missing a key characteristic of the phenomenon. Globalization can be described as the unfolding resolution of the contradiction between ever-expanding capital and its national political and social formations. Until the 1970s the history of capitalism had been the history of the nation-state; and the expansion of capital came always in the form of national capital—capital with particular territorial and historical roots. This development was characterized by colonial conquest and conflicts between nations, culminating in the two world wars. By the 1970s, however, capital was expanding in the form of, simply, the corporation; ownership corresponded less and less with national geographies. Just as at one stage capital had to create a national state and a defined territory in order to come into its own, now in the form of the TNC it has to remove or transform this "shell" to create institutions to ensure and facilitate accumulation at the global level. The national history of capital has come to a close, and the history of the expansion of capital *sans* nationality has begun.

Technological Revolution

Aside from the matter of the postwar construction of a global market framework, a significant part of the case for globalization as a "new reality" has rested on the perceived technological revolution based on the coming of microelectronics, computers, and biotechnology, and their applications from the early 1970s. One of the main critics of the so-called globalization thesis, Ellen Wood, takes issue with the argument:

> So what is new about this so-called new economy is not that the new technologies represent a unique kind of epochal shift. On the contrary, they simply allow the logic of the old mass production economy to be diversified and extended. Now, the old logic can reach into whole new sectors, and it can affect types of workers more or less untouched before.[14]

Wood argues here that, first, there has not been a significant or qualitative change in technology sufficient to talk about an "epochal shift" or "historic rupture"; and, second, given that there are new technologies, they only advance "the old logic" of cheapening production and increasing managerial control. The second point is a non-point: given that technological change under capitalism in general has been brought about for these reasons, what we have here is a *non sequitur*—that technological change contains capitalist logic has no specific bearing on whether or not it brings into being a new stage in capitalist development.

The first point, however, calls for more examination. Published criticisms of the argument for globalization do not often address the question of the technological aspect of the shift, in theory or in practice, but it is here that the crux of the differences lies. Because most of the critics are on the left, it is not unfair to borrow from Marx to map out conceptually

why there is a transition from one stage of development to another. On the level of the mode of production, referring to broadly coherent systems—that is, communal, Asiatic, slave, feudal, or capitalist—Marx saw the *differentia specifica* as resting in the nature of the labour process, that composite of purposeful work, "raw" materials, and the instruments of production. To differentiate modes of production at this level of abstraction, however, does not address the need to differentiate historical changes within them.

The stages of development in the history of capitalism are characterized by significant changes in class structure, government systems, ideologies, and so on. These stages, as Marx argues in several places, are similarly delineated by transformations in the labour process, principally in the instruments of production. Hence, the shift in capitalism between "manufacturing" and "large-scale industry"— the only two stages that Marx discussed and could have known about—is laid at the feet of the coming of the machine.[15] And it is the introduction of machinery that Marx argues as transforming the relations of production and exchange within a given social formation and causing the shift in regimes of accumulation. The class structure, its mediating mechanisms, the state, ideologies, the works—are all more or less revolutionized in the process.

When the scientific and technological changes of the late 19th century brought new sources of energy, new branches of industry, and new means of communication, the stage was set for a transformation in the labour process of the day. The coming of Fordism in the first decades of the 20th century rested on these developments and can be demarcated by major shifts in the labour process. "Scientific management" transformed the organization of labour at the point of production, the assembly line revolutionized the instruments of production, and science transformed the material of labour. There followed a consequent transformation in the structure of the capitalist and working classes, along with the rest of the social formation. Mass production ushered in "mass" society with the rapid growth in proletarianization and the ability to satisfy and expand needs as never before via commodity production.

The 1940s and 1950s ushered in another stage—advanced Fordism—in which the wartime advances in science and technology and their subordination to capital grew in an unprecedented way. For the first time in history, scientific and technological innovation became central to the labour process; and capital accumulation became more than ever dependent on research and development. As in previous shifts, major social changes took place. The class structures and social and political relations were more or less transformed;[16] increased productivity allowed for the laying of the economic basis for the Keynesian welfare state, and also made necessary the first genuinely supranational experiment in governance. It was not for no reason that in the aftermath of World War II there was talk of a "new world order."

The same argument underlies the so-called globalization thesis. With the coming of computer technology and its many applications in the early 1970s, a veritable revolution in the labour process began to take place.[17] In this case, however, each of its three components was transformed in a very short time. Unlike any previous instruments of production, the computer and its applications made the robotization or automation of every conceivable aspect of work a real possibility: they possessed the potential for minimizing and even eliminating human beings at the point of production, distribution, or communication. The raw material of the process, moreover, became less the existing forms of nature than the elemental building blocks. Increasingly, unlike any earlier period, the product of the process became wholly or partially synthetic. More than just transforming the labour process, the computer allows scientific and technological change to develop into what can only be deemed a permanent technological revolution. With the vast increase in productivity and "flexibility" stemming from this transformation, the entire structure of production, distribution, and consumption moves to the global plane, increasingly indifferent to national considerations except to overcome them as impediments to commerce. And more, there is in the computer the potential for the elimination of all the divisions of labour that previously determined the history of our social relations.[18]

The transformation of the national relations of production and the political shell, a result of this revolution in the labour process, is now evident everywhere. National class structures and agencies, the labour and capital markets, systems of government, culture, family, precapitalist social formations, and the nation-state and its political geography all come into question. All face the process of disintegration and reconstitution in new forms.[19]

From this perspective, it can be seen that the concept of globalization actually refers to the consequences of the transformation of the labour process. It refers to the growing denationalization of capital and to the expanding supranational regime of accumulation, and is therefore not an appropriate label for characterizing the material basis of the distinctive era that we have entered. Similarly, the concepts of lean production, "just-in-time," flexible manufacturing, and even biotechnology all point to consequences of the new labour process and not to its foundation in computers. We have entered *the age of the computer* with unprecedented and comprehensively revolutionary consequences.[20] Yet it is still an age based on a capitalist mode of production with all of its contradictions, albeit in new forms and at new levels. It is unquestionably a new world, but one that the sceptics do not acknowledge.

The Transnational Corporation and the Global Market

The TNC is the chief carrier and user of the new technology in all spheres of the economy; and as the corporate embodiment of this technology, it is the TNC and its demands that become the central motive for the systematic changes to the nation-state as we have known it. The new technology makes national relations of production, and corresponding political, legal, and ideological structures, all reflecting the national character of capital, seem increasingly redundant, antiquated, and even antagonistic in relation to its powers to reduce the dimensions of time and space. But the sceptics challenge the very concept of the TNC.

Before their objections are addressed, we should attempt a definition. The TNC is a corporation whose productive and distributive capabilities span the jurisdiction of many nations, minimizing its national character, and for which national labour, consumer, and capital markets have more or less lost meaning, except to take advantage of their differences or impose harmonization. Its location and decisions are based on global market considerations and not national ones. While its management and

ownership need not be transnational, they are indeed transnational in outlook, objectives, and interest. In principle if not in practice, the TNC stands as a contradiction to national sovereignty; that is, its interests are served better by a supranational, and not national, regulatory framework. This is not to say that it does not remain a national legal entity or no longer operates within national regulatory regimes; there is at present no alternative to certain national delimitations. Essential to this definition, however, is an established and growing coherent and comprehensive transnational regulatory regime and rapid national harmonization with it.[21]

Drawing on these characteristics, globalization can be defined as the arrival of "self-generating capital" at the global level: that is, capital as capital, capital in the form of the transnational corporation, increasingly free of national loyalties, controls, and interests. This is not to be understood as the mere internationalization of capital, which assumes a world of national capitals and nation-states, but as the supersession by capital of the nation-state as its historically necessary but now redundant social and political framework. It is a process in which the main actors become the TNCs and all the circuits of capital become global in nature, with a distinct global framework; and the national economy—and its associated borders, policies, and programs—becomes a fetter.

No corporation, national or transnational, stands on its own; there are always many, and they always develop in relation to a market. Although the firm or corporation is not often grasped in this way, the market is always a necessary component of its definition. Prior to the preeminence of the TNC, the market had both national and international dimensions. The national market was by and large a politically unified economic union without significant barriers; and the international market was a system characterized by multilateral and bilateral agreements and treaties, foreign exchange rates and mechanisms, imports and exports between national jurisdictions, trade barriers and wars, international loans and debts, and diplomacy and warfare between nations. The last significant war between capitalist nations was World War II,[22] and in its immediate aftermath there began the process to transform the inter national market into a transnational or global one. This is the historical significance of the formation of the United Nations (UN), the Bretton Woods agreement, and the General Agreement on Tariffs and Trade (GATT). They comprised the first systematic attempt to end the hitherto international market and provide the institutional beginning, the "core enabling framework," for globalization: the staged and negotiated process of creating a single, unified, global market without significant national barriers. In the early stages of development the framework provided the precondition for the rise of the multinational corporation; at a later stage in the reduction of national barriers, in the early 1970s, it became the precondition for the TNC and its growing employment of computer-based technology.

Given this transformation of the market, globalization may be seen as the shifting of the main venue or site of capital accumulation from the national to the supranational or global level. This shift, captured in the phrase "the end of (political) geography," implies the realization of a global market as such, which requires the establishment of administrative bodies at the global level and a transformation or harmonization of national relations of production that have become barriers to the global accumulation of capital.

The global market and the TNC, then, are qualitatively different from the prewar and postwar international market and multinational corporations (MNCs). The global market has been constructed through the systematic dismantling of national barriers to trade and investment and by the creation of supranational regulatory agencies to advance and maintain the emerging global system. National and regional markets become merely the component parts of the global market, and their specificity declines in relation to the realization of the global. In tandem with these developments, the TNC expands its global assets, sales, employment, perspective, ownership, and management. Both market framework and TNC develop in a reciprocal relationship; with the staged systematic diminution of national barriers comes an increase in transborder operations, a growing preponderance of foreign direct investment over commodity trade, and large numbers of transnational corporate mergers and takeovers, joint ventures, share agreements, cartels, and oligopolies. The degree to which all this is realized challenges the sovereign economic powers of the national state.

The sceptics are reluctant to use the concept of TNC and prefer the label MNC. The most thorough critiques to date, by Hirst and Thompson and Linda Weiss, use MNC throughout their book-length works, and they even convert the label TNC to MNC without argued justification when citing statistics designated "TNC" from the UN Centre on TNCs and other sources.[23] What is at issue is the reality of the TNC, and this cannot be addressed by evading the concept in order to retain a vision of a world of nation-states and nationally based MNCs. Several of the sceptics also seek to minimize not only the reality but also the size and number of TNCs,[24] but without providing the appropriate evidence. As long ago as 1974 the UN Centre on TNCs began to report extensively on the size, growth, and operations of TNCs. In the early 1990s the Centre estimated that there were about 37,000 TNCs and that they controlled about one-third (and rising) of all the private-sector assets in the world.[25] Other studies by the World Bank, the International Monetary Fund (IMF), and the Organization for Economic Cooperation and Development (OECD) all reiterate the existence, size, and economic significance of TNCs. One writer points out, "The number of these [TNCs] based in 14 major developed home countries more than tripled ... from 7,000 in 1970 to nearly 24,000 in 1990. The total number of foreign affiliates stands at 200,000, a dramatic acceleration over the 3,500 manufacturing affiliates established between 1946–61."[26] The *World Investment Report* for 1998 states: "In 1997, the value of international production, attributed to some 53,000 TNCs and their roughly 450,000 foreign affiliates, was $3.5 trillion as measured by the accumulated stock of foreign direct investment (FDI), and $9.5 trillion as measured by the estimated global sales of foreign affiliates."[27]

The assets and revenues of the largest TNCs are greater than the gross domestic product (GDP) and tax revenues of the majority of nation-states; and the enormous size, pervasiveness, and power of TNCs are sufficient to raise the question of the very meaning of the "national economy." Although for the most part economic measures and statistics collected remain largely national, this condition reflects a certain "institutional lag" and belies a changing reality. If a national economy implies a national capitalist class and interests, those elements can hardly be said to exist today with

any significant degree of effect and integrity, with the possible but declining exceptions of the United States, Japan, and Germany. TNCs dominate in most spheres of most national economies; and given the extensive "import penetration," increasing affiliations, intracorporate trade, intercorporate collaboration, and foreign direct investment, TNCs make the possibilities for persisting national economies increasingly dubious.

The sceptics also appear to have a preference for the concept of the international market rather than the global, again suggesting a reluctance to admit to the changing nature of the world market. The emergence of the global market is now far advanced and is qualitatively different from what is meant by the international market. The evidence of an emerging transnational economy is overwhelming. Hardly a single country is not at present a member of one or another trade zone or customs union. The progressive economic integration that accompanies such unions, along with membership in GATT (now the World Trade Organization (WTO)), makes the idea of persisting national economies in an international market appear to be an exercise in nostalgia. In Europe, moreover, the replacement of national currencies with the Euro signals the consolidation of the European economy and the end of the national economy in any significant sense in Europe. Much of the rest of the world has already embraced the reality of "dollarization" or currencies "pegged" to the dollar. And the dollar increasingly dominates as a foreign reserve currency, bringing the world closer to a single currency in trade and investment. Indeed, the degree of global interfirm collaboration and intrafirm trade is sufficient in some economic sectors even to foresee an eclipse of the market and its replacement by corporate planning—a form of "central planning," but for profit.

As a counter to the concept of the TNC and rationale for using MNC, several critics raise the question of a "home base" for the "footloose" MNC.[28] They suggest that most corporations have a "home base," which in itself is an indication of less "transnationality." They do not consider, though, the meaning of the home base. If the case can be made that it refers to national interests, then, indeed, they have added to the argument against the idea of globalization. Having a home base in itself, however, is neither here nor there; it indicates nothing about national as opposed to global interests. Indeed, it would be odd for a corporation not to have a home base. Similarly, the nationality of ownership and management is no indicator of corporate national interests. Moreover, as more corporations develop a "virtual" existence, as many financial institutions have already done, the existence of a home base and nationality of management become meaningless. The rapidly growing "electronic economy," moreover, attaches no significance to nationality or the notion of a home base.[29]

One of the hallmarks of the global economy is the vast and growing movement of equity capital or foreign direct investment (FDI); its significance lies in its connection with ownership and control and the decline of the integrity of national economies. The 1998 *World Investment Report* makes the point rather directly:

The ratio of inward and outward FDI stocks to global GDP is now 21 percent; foreign affiliate exports are one-third of world exports; and GDP attributed to foreign affiliates accounts for 7 percent of global GDP. Sales of foreign affiliates have grown faster than world exports of goods and services, and the ratio of the volume of world inward plus outward FDI stocks to world GDP has grown twice as fast as the ratio of world imports and exports to world GDP, suggesting that the expansion of international production has deepened the interdependence of the world economy beyond that achieved by international trade alone.[30]

To counter the idea of globalization the sceptics must find a way of diminishing the obvious significance of foreign direct investment. To do this they make several distinctions within FDI; they argue, for instance, that aggregate data on FDI do not tell the whole story.[31] Some of them suggest that non-manufacturing investments have a higher rate of growth than do manufacturing investments. Even if this is the case, it is a non-issue; such a shift might be expected when manufactured goods and key services are already largely controlled by transnational oligopolies and cartels. The issue is the degree of non-national control and/or ownership over a corporation. Another distinction the sceptics make is between FDI and portfolio capital, which would be a significant point to make if capital were still national in character. But the Eurodollar market has been in existence for a long time now and represents the more or less complete integration of the world's capital markets, outside the control of individual national governments or central banks. The distinction the sceptics make is not significant in the context of the global capital market.

Another point that sceptics make concerns the high degree of FDI that goes into mergers and acquisitions (M&As), suggesting that investment in "existing ventures" rather than new ones is somehow less globalizing. Such a trend would be precisely what would be expected with globalization; it marks the concentration and centralization of capital through competition at the global level. If anything, the rapid progress of M&As is a strong indicator of growing TNC control. The 1998 *World Investment Report* states, for instance:

> Worldwide cross-border M&As, mostly in banking, insurance, chemicals, pharmaceuticals and telecommunications, were aimed at the global restructuring or strategic positioning of firms in these industries…. Valued at $236 billion, majority-owned M&As represented nearly three-fifths of global FDI inflows in 1997, increasing from almost half in 1996…. One outcome is a greater industrial concentration in the hands of a few firms in each industry, usually TNCs.[32]

The problem for the sceptics is that FDI has continuously been greater than the growth of GDP and trade, bringing more and more economic activity under the control of TNCs, and that, furthermore, FDI statistics do not reveal the actual degree of global corporate inter-penetration. TNC collaboration in research, marketing, and production continues to expand[33] and intracorporate trade is increasing as a proportion of all trade. Investments in the world stock and financial markets are close to being fully integrated; food production and distribution of major staples are highly monopolized by a handful of TNCs;[34] industrial manufacturing of appliances, vehicles, airplanes, computers, telecommunications, clothing, and arms is dominated by the TNCs; and mergers and acquisitions continue to grow.[35] By most accounts, the TNC and the global market have arrived; and the adoption of neo-liberal policies and the expansion of TNCs develop in tandem. The global market is so integrated in so many spheres that it is no longer possible to identify or measure nationality in some industries in a meaningful way.[36]

Global Governance

The institutions of the postwar rapprochement—the United Nations, the IMF and the World Bank, and GATT—constituted the "core enabling framework" that would underlie the coming of a genuinely global market as such, distinct from an international one. The TNCs that grew in response then required further continuous transformation of the previous international system of nation-states. The whole postwar period down to the present day has seen the continued expansion of this framework for the global market with the progressive removal of national barriers to trade and investment, the creation and consolidation of global oversight and enforcement agencies, the freeing of currencies from national control, and a system of global security.

Despite the growth of this framework, historically novel because it operates at the global level, the sceptics are reluctant to admit to its significance. One of them writes: "The world shows almost no signs of moving from a high level of economic globalization towards the formation of a serious global state."[37] It is not clear what a "serious global state" is, but it is not possible to have global economic integration without a governing framework, and there can be no doubt that a comprehensive, albeit multilayered, institutional framework has been set in place to govern the global activity of corporations. It is of course for capital only; it is a system for governing economic relations without any means of "access" by subordinate classes and groups.

While it is not possible to determine precisely the relative significance of the given parts of the system, it is clear that they are united in their underlying principles and operate within a certain division of labour in global governance. They are not without their internal and cross-institutional disputes, reflecting vestigial national or regional interests and intrasector and intracorporate conflicts. But such contradictions within the global framework do not belie its role as the emerging system of governance at the global level; and they did not prevent its rapid expansion, particularly after 1970.[38]

The rise of global governance can be understood by analogy to the rise of the nation-state in that many national economies were unified and made coherent in the same way. Numerous and disparate sub-national territorial units were often first brought together as customs unions of various sorts, frequently with mainly bureaucratic supervision; and then, only later, were broader political mechanisms added to give voice to and mitigate growing and changing class interests. Governance of the nation-state, nevertheless, was and remains first and foremost the administration of economics. In this sense, the growth after World War II of a supranational enabling framework for capital at the global level has been no different.

While there may be disagreement about the hierarchy of authority, or the division of labour, amongst these levels and agencies, there is certainly considerable agreement about the main components of supranational governance. Certain broad policy matters are determined by the heads of the major national governments in the G-3/7/8 forums.[39] Several pivotal agencies (such as the UN, WTO, IMF, World Bank, OECD, and the Bank of International Settlements (BIS)) staffed in part by government appointees play a significant role in supranational regulation, policy formation, standardization, and credit facilitation. State membership in common markets or trading blocs (such as the European Union (EU), the North American Free Trade Agreement (NAFTA), and MERCOSUR [*El Mercado Comun del Sur*]) goes a long way to create supranational control over the economic. Multilateral agreements (such as Organization of the Petroleum Exporting Countires (OPEC), and United Nations Conference on Trade and Development (UNCTAD) commodity agreements for key staples) also diminish national powers over the production and distribution of major commodity exports. The growth of international law after World War II, moreover, provides another level of supranational governance. Not least, since 1945 the growth of an international regime of individual and "human" rights has increasingly allowed national sovereignty to be challenged by "rights" defined at the supranational level.[40] If these are the main layers of global governance, the mechanisms of enforcement and advancement of the rule of capital should be added; UN peacekeeping operations, the North Atlantic Treaty Organization (NATO), and several bilateral and multilateral military pacts, as well as mercenary operations, complete the global system.

One can talk of such governance only after World War II.[41] It is still an evolving system whose parts are coherent in principle though somewhat disparate in origin and function. It can be understood as levels of administrative agencies and institutions controlling, directing, regulating, and facilitating the activities of TNCs and the shape of the growing global market. Although not without differences and conflicts, it is comprehensive and united in principle and through subordination to the U.S. government. It has been labelled "governance without government,"[42] which is meant to imply an authoritative administrative apparatus without the political and legal legitimacy of an elected government purportedly responsible to its citizenry.

That the U.S. government has tended to play a dominant role in all these agencies at all levels is not strictly an example of national control. To be sure, there has been an active element of national interest, but more importantly this role is a consequence of the U.S. position as the world's dominant capitalist power and so the initiator and "overseer" of the global enabling framework. This position in turn is a consequence of a series of historical junctures, in particular the outcome of World War II and the end of colonialism that allowed for the initiation of this framework. China's shift to the "capitalist road" and the demise of the Unon of Soviet Socialist Republics (U.S.S.R.), furthermore, opened the way for the entire globe in effect to be subordinated to the U.S.-dominated capitalist market and framework, ended any significant resistance or alternatives to the market by states representing socialized property relations, and left the United States unchallenged militarily.

The development of a global framework for transnational capital required it to be secured, defended, and advanced, while socialism had to be contained. Where peaceful maintenance of, or transition to, capitalism could be obtained, diplomatic or other non-violent means could be employed. Where there has been resistance to capitalist property relations, military or police actions have been used. In these cases, the United States (and other powers) employed unilateral interventions, bilateral and multilateral military pacts, the UN peacekeeping operations, economic blockades, and the arms race, as well as a variety of covert means. Underlying the establishment of the global enabling framework during the whole of the postwar period to the present was the principle of *Machtpolitik,* and its chief proponent has been the U.S. government and the military-industrial complex, whose interests are served both as capital in general and a particular sort of capital.[43]

Role of the National State: "Convergence" versus "State Capacity"

Despite the emergence of a distinctly global framework for capital and the dominance of TNCs in every major economic sphere, the national state has by no means disappeared. Given this, there are many who would make an argument for a world of viable nation-states, of states, that is, with "varieties of state capacities" or persisting "national priorities" and significant remaining powers in the face of global capital and its supranational representatives.[44] Others, more circumspect, would admit conflict between the three hegemons, the United States, Japan, and a German-led Europe,[45] with the rest of the world subordinated in one way or another to those powers. Contrasted to these positions is the argument that globalization brings with it an inexorably progressive transnational "convergence."[46] We would argue that the issue is not one or the other, but that in this current interregnum between two eras we are confronting the transition from national interests to global convergence. What lies at the heart of these different views, however, are the implicitly conflicting views on the nature of the state.

Underlying the view of convergence is the notion that with the rise to power of the modern capitalist class, the modern national state was born. It comprises the machinery of government that embodies the property relations of this class and mediates class relations and conflict with other classes and strata embodying different forms of property. The character of the state, it follows, changes with the changing class structures, which in turn reflect the level of capital accumulation and development of technology. Besides representing this formation of capital and its consequent class relations, the state has no specific content of its own. The very existence of the state is relative to the demands of capital accumulation and to the character of class conflict; it exists only in relation to its civil society and is defined in terms of this relation.

When at different stages of development the capitalist class pursues its interests outside the nation-state, the state similarly extends its policies and security as "national" policies, hence colonialism and imperialism. But when the assets, production, sales, and employees of corporations have become increasingly transnational, and so too their interests, then national policies must be circumscribed, subordinated, eliminated, or asserted as transnational, as "universal." The degree of persistence of national policies and the degree of their subordination to universal policies are largely determined by the amount, ownership, and control of nationally accumulated and productive capital. From this point of view, the role of the national state principally follows the development of the capital whose interests it represents (mitigated by national class conflict). And when this capital expands as transnational capital, the state must also adopt transnational policies, which are determined in global forums and reflect the contradictions of capital at that level. This perspective conflicts

with those who want to make states into the "authors" of globalization or globalization into a product of state strategy.[47]

Underlying the view of persisting "state capacities" is a state-centric notion of the relative autonomy of the state, with a stress on the side of autonomy. It is largely a vision of the state as an independent variable, hence the description of a state as "strong," "weak," "catalytic," or "competitive,"[48] as if the state itself were the source of these characteristics rather than the capitalist class or class relations it represents. The focus on the state as actor suggests that it has interests of its own, other than the merely bureaucratic. Its ability to act appears to be without reference to the characteristics of the capitalist class and the contradictions that define its civil society. The view ignores or evades the question of the origin of the interests of the state.

From this perspective there appear to be political means to counter the effects of globalization. Examples of Asian economic development are often offered.[49] The "state-led path to development" taken by the "Four Tigers" of Southeast Asia and Japan are pointed to as instances of state-induced national economic success, as if the role of the state were independent of its own civil society and the larger world market. The problem is that, in general, it is in the nature of capitalism that the state is employed by national capital to further its own ends. It is a question of how it is done, the degree and character of the involvement; but it is never a question of the state having its own agenda—except when political decisions become pre-eminent, as under fascism or socialism, albeit propounded in different ways and for different reasons.

Representative of this same perspective is the position that sees globalization (or aspects of it) as "reversible." One writer on finance argues that the reasons for "financial liberalization" were specific in time and place and are now changing, opening the possibilities for a reassertion of national control; and that the crises in the financial markets in the 1980s fostered an interest in a return to national control for the sake of stability. He concludes that this reasoning is a "challenge [to] the argument that the globalization of financial markets is irreversible."[50] Unfortunately, no aspect of the speculated "reversal" has come about; if anything, financial liberalization expanded enormously in the 1990s. Deregulation of these markets has now been carried out more or less across the world, global bond and equity markets are firmly established and joined electronically, the majority of industrial nations now accepts the Euro as a single currency, the largest reserve currency remains the U.S. dollar, and the "dollarization" of the rest of the world continues apace. Very few financial analysts would not agree that the world's financial markets are irretrievably integrated.[51] Not only is the possibility of a reversal in the structure of the global financial markets implausible, but also the power of these markets over national governments is greater than ever.

These are quintessentially political views; they arbitrarily assign a certain primacy and independence to political actions by the state without an attempt to account for these actions by identifying the source of state interests. They lend themselves to the view that globalization is really "internationalization";[52] and they obscure the possibilities of a supranational existence beyond the nation-state. They also want to make globalization into "a politically rather than a technologically induced phenomenon."[53] In other words, the acceptance of the demands of the global market,

"willingly or unwillingly," is still a determination by the state. They try, moreover, to outline several possible strategies or policy options the state can choose to follow, without seeing that the idea of choice obscures what are merely certain optional arrangements for the most advantageous integration into the global economy.[54] Such possibilities are to be expected in the transition from an international to a global system, but they do not point to a national strategy for confronting global demands.

Such perspectives do not admit that an enormous proportion of world capital, especially finance capital, no longer has national or domestic interests and has for several decades worked to create a system of supranational administrative structures, including the political independence of central banks. The growth of these agencies for capital at the global level cannot but gradually usurp and subordinate the role and powers of the national state; and this because such structures represent the largest and most powerful capitals that have penetrated, with minor exceptions, all the world's national economies. As a consequence, the national state is subsumed in larger political and/or economic units (EU, NAFTA, MERCOSUR, among others); and, moreover, it adopts under pressure or for ideological reasons the neo-liberalism of the global market.

State counterpositions and policies can only be sustained under the circumstances of a relatively independent capitalist class, or defiant or well-organized subordinate classes. Even so, such positions can generally be maintained only as secondary to the primacy of the most powerful sector of capital, be it national or transnational. The present role of the state can only be to follow the interests of its capitalist class—mitigated in its policies by the necessity to take into some account counterforces within its jurisdiction. For the most part, the direction of the contemporary state follows the lead of globalizing capital, and its relative autonomy is prescribed by new contradictions at the global and national levels. To put this point another way: state sovereignty rests on the relative coherence of a national bourgeoisie, but with its transfiguration into TNCs a relative shift in sovereignty occurs from the national state and bourgeoisie to the supranational framework and the TNC.

These developments should not be seen as merely the "restructuring" of the national state but as the redefinition of the state because its original definition was the political expression of a national bourgeoisie and its subordinate classes. This is not to say that the national state apparatus will disappear in the near future—only that it will be subordinate to the demands of an increasingly integrated global system. There continue to be important roles for it to play. (In this sense the state is not powerless, but it is if one is suggesting a persisting capacity for independent counter-hegemonic activity.) One of the state's key tasks will be to facilitate the harmonization of national with global policies; another will be to build more of the infrastructure for global processes; a third will be to promote the accumulation of global capital; and domestic social control will also be an obligation. But while the state was once the monopoly of the "whole" in the face of civil society at the national level, it is now a "part" of the global civil society, with only weighted voting rights in its relation to supranational governing structures. Once the embodiment of national corporate property rights, the state must increasingly harmonize those rights with global corporate rights, and in the process transform itself.

The North–South Divide, or the Core and Periphery

On the question of globalization and the Third World, sceptics frequently point to world trade statistics showing that the largest share of trade and investment continues to be within the industrialized world. The persistence of these patterns is said to be "inconsistent with a globalization tendency."[55] The fact that FDI remains "highly concentrated" in the industrial nations and limited in the Third World is another reason, argue some, that globalization is "largely a myth."[56]

A focus on aggregate data for trade and investment flows, however, never reveals the entire picture. The value of imports and exports might remain relatively stable, while the volumes might see large increases due to radical currency devaluations in Third World countries. The composition of the capital invested and its purpose and destination, moreover, changed considerably in the 1980s and 1990s. Even the meaning of national statistics is open to question given the substantial and growing amount of intracorporate trade. Above all, the use of trade and investment statistics does not address the changing nature of the relation between North and the South.

The continued use of the concepts of internationalization and MNCs in the context of the North-South divide implies the persistence of one or another "development model" for the Third World. The view remains that, although exploited by industrial nations, the "developing" nation-states still retain domestic markets and the potential for independent economic growth. This argument ignores the effects throughout the "undeveloped" world of years of growing indebtedness,[57] of decades of aid programs intended to modernize, and of the widespread enforcement of structural adjustment policies (SAPs) beginning in the 1970s. By the 1980s, in the words of one observer, "a *substantial change* in the dependency relationship between the South and the North" could be seen.[58]

As neo-liberal policies for the Third World, the SAPs are the policy side of globalization imposed progressively with every new loan or foreign exchange crisis. The consequences have changed the character of dependency for the Third World. They have effectively ended state-led national development strategies.[59] The "import-substitution model" for industrialization, for instance, that once held a certain promise for independent development, has all but been eclipsed. The SAPs have eliminated protectionist measures and the domestic market "as a factor in development"[60] and have gone far to transform the "unit of development" from the nation-state to free-trade zones, local areas or cross-national regional markets. Continued trade policy discrimination by the industrial nations against the Third World at the global level has consolidated these developments.

There are many examples of this transformation of the Third World.[61] Chile might well have been the first significant case in which the policies of state intervention for national development were brutally replaced in a coup d'etat with policies promulgated by military intervention for the benefit of the TNCs. Here, the role of the U.S. government as guarantor of the global enabling framework was to become plainly visible, but there are numerous instances of U.S. unilateral intervention to end national strategies around the world, particularly throughout Latin America. Moreover, the so-called "Asian crisis" that peaked in 1997–98 presented the opportunity, taken through the IMF and World Bank, to undermine certain Asian national development strategies, par-

ticularly in Korea and Thailand.[62] Even the suggested Japanese solution to the crisis to establish a regional development strategy was nipped in the bud, and Japan too was forced by the circumstances to revamp many of its protectionist policies.

Besides ending in general the possibilities for national development, the imposition of SAPs opened the possibilities for TNCs to increase Third World dependency by integrating food production, distribution, and consumption into a global system. This deepening of dependency is being accomplished in part through the increased capitalization, subsidization, and vertical integration of food production and distribution in the industrial countries, making ever cheaper food staples available for export.[63] A more significant means, however, is the transformation and use of property rights over the genetic makeup of plants and animals and humans. The patenting of life forms means that the reproduction of plants and animals that constitute the world's food supply is placed into the hands of a few large TNCs, a shift that amounts to the "corporate enclosure of the genetic commons." This enclosure is affirmed in certain agreements in the WTO and the Convention on Biological Diversity that legalize and codify the right to patent the plant and animal resources of the world and furthermore "restrict the ability of governments to control and regulate the process."[64] It is the most complete and profound mechanism ever devised for economic dominance, allowing corporate private property to be the direct means of control over the world's population. The use of food as a weapon has a long history, but never on the global scale, or so completely, or in such an apparently legitimate or legal way, as is now occurring.

For the Third World the implications of

these means of creating increasing global dependency on global sources is the destruction of independent food supply and distribution, of entire ways of life, and of the livelihood for many millions, as well as a massive increase in migration and urbanization. For the world as a whole, they contribute to the growth of the global capitalist labour market and so-called "industrial reserve army," increased pressure to level wages, further ecological destruction, and the standardization and adulteration of food supply, among other consequences.

In effect, this changing relationship between North and South marks the "end of the Third World" in the sense that we are witnessing the end of national development strategies for Southern countries and their direct subordination to the TNCs through the transformation and globalization of property rights, enforced by a supranational regulatory regime. SAPs signal the end of the possibility for independent economic development and the demise of Third World nations as national characters on the world stage—before they got to play anything but a minor role. Still, the industrial nations face much the same fate. Many of them have already subordinated their national independence to the demands of a transnational (or at least regional) economy in the European Union and NAFTA. The process of globalization subordinates all economies to an increasingly unified single economic process.

Endnotes

1 Harvey, D. 1995. "Globalization in Question." *Rethinking Marxism*, 8, 4 (Winter). p. 10.

2 Davis, Jim. 1998. "Rethinking Globalisation." *Race and Class*, 40, 2/3. p. 45.

3 Petras, James. 1999. "Globalization: A Socialist Perspective." *Canadian Dimension* (February). pp. 12–13. According to Petras:

"The globalization idea itself is suspect. In its most widely expressed usage, it argues for a universal incorporation to the world marketplace and the spread of benefits throughout the world. The empirical reality is neither universal incorporation nor the spread of benefits ... the globalist concept of interdependence is far less useful in understanding the world than the Marxist concept of imperialism....

The rise of 'globalist ideology' is found originally in the business journals of the late 1960s and early 1970s. The major expansion and conquest of markets by the multinationals was described as globalization by business journalists searching for an alternative to the existing Marxist vocabulary, since they sought to present the process in a favorable light.... What emerged from the academic recycling of the concept was 'globaloney': the embellishment of the concept by linking it to what was called the third technological revolution and imputing to it a historical inevitability and degree of interdependence that was remote from reality....

The ascendancy of imperialism is directly related to the circulation of the globaloney discourse and the eclipse of the revolutionary paradigm."

4 Wolf, M. 1997. "Global Opportunities." *Financial Times,* May 6. He writes: "Rather than damaging wages and throwing people out of work in advanced countries, globalization has been a force for prosperity in much of the world."

5 Kim, K.S. 1998. "Global Economic Integration: Issues and Challenges." In J-R. Chen (ed.). *Economic Effects of Globalization.* Aldershot, Eng.: Ashgate, p. 133. A recent report from the World Bank makes the same point: "World Bank Says Poverty Is Increasing," *The New York Times,* June 3, 1999.

6 Hirst P., and G. Thompson. 1997. *Globalization in Question.* Cambridge: Polity Press.

7 Gordon, D. 1988. "The Global Economy. New Edifice or Crumbling Foundations?" *New Left Review,* 168.

8 Harvey, D. 1997. "Globalization in Question." p. 2; Sweezy, Paul. 1997. "More (or Less) on Globalization." *Monthly Review* (September), pp. 1, 4.

9 Wood, E.M. 1998. "Capitalist Change and Generational Shifts." *Monthly Review* (October). p. 8, and (the earlier reference) 1996. *Monthly Review* (July/August). p. 38; Tabb, W.K. 1999. "Progressive Globalism: Challenging the Audacity of Capital." *Monthly Review* (February), p. 1.

Such statements seem to be repeated everywhere. See Kagarlitsky, B. 1999. "The Challenge for the Left: Reclaiming the State." In L. Panitch and C. Leys (eds.). *The Socialist Register 1999: Global Capitalism vs. Democracy*. Halifax: Fernwood Publishing. He writes (p. 296): "Globalisation is nothing qualitatively new in the history of bourgeois society. Capitalism was born and grew to maturity as a world system."

10 Marx, K. 1967. *Capital,* vol. 3. New York: International Publishers, p. 333.

11 Wallerstein, I. 1976. "Theoretical Reprise." In *The Modern World-System: Capitalist Agriculture and the Origins of the European World-Economy in the Sixteenth Century*. New York: Academic Press. For another clear statement of his argument, see Wallerstein, I. 1983. "Three Instances of Hegemony in the History of the Capitalist World Economy." *International Journal of Comparative Sociology,* 24.

12 If we must make the case with Marx: "It is otherwise on the world market, whose integral parts are the individual countries." Marx, *Capital,* vol. 1, p. 702.

13 Palloix, C. 1977. "The Self-Expansion of Capital on a World-Scale." *Review of Radical Political Economics,* 9, 2 (Summer).

14 Wood, E. 1996. "Modernity, Postmodernity, or Capitalism?" *Monthly Review* (July/August), p. 35.

15 Marx, *Capital,* vol. 1, pp. 504ff.

16 The postwar expansion of the social sciences was primarily concerned with these changes; and the rapid growth of university training in science and technology reflected corporate demands.

17 For a good review of these issues, see Davis, J., T. Hirschl, and M. Stack (eds.). 1997. *Cutting Edge: Technology, Information Capitalism and Social Revolution*. London: Verso.

18 A cautionary note on "technological determinism" should be introduced here. These scientific and technological changes take place in the context of the capitalist mode of production; they are changes whose impulse is the extraction of greater surplus value by increasing the subordination of knowledge and skill and labour power, not to mention the forces of nature itself, to capital.

19 Overbeek, H. and K. van der Pijl. 1993. "Restructuring Capital and Restructuring Hegemony." In Overbeek (ed.). *Restructuring Hegemony*. This article does not make the case as broadly as made here, but it goes part of the way.

20 Some debate has taken place on these issues. See Morris-Suzuki, T. 1984. "Robots and Capitalism." *New Left Review,* 147 (September/October); Steedman, I. 1985. "Robots and Capitalism: A Clarification." *New Left Review,* 151 (May/June); and Morris-Suzuki, T. "Capitalism in the Computer Age." In Davis, Hirschl, and Stack. *Cutting Edge*.

21 Hu, Y.-S. 1992. "Global or Stateless Corporations Are National Firms with International Operations." *California Management Review,* 34. This critical review of the definition of the TNC misses the point in that there is no alternative to the national legal delimitation of the corporation at the present time, but this does not mean that its operations and interests are any less transnational. In a more quantitative way, the TNC may be defined by means of "the index of transnationality," as employed by UNCTAD, which is "calculated as the average of three ratios: foreign assets to total assets, foreign sales to total sales, and foreign employment to total employment." There are many shortcomings to the index, but it does provide a certain measure of "transnationality," and a means to follow trends and make comparisons. UNCTAD, *World Investment Report 1998: Trends and Determinants* (Geneva, 1999), p. 4.

22 The Gulf War in 1991 and the war in Serbia in 1999 are good examples of the end of diplomacy or the end of war between nations (no more "formal declaration") and the rise of "police actions" at the global level. They amount to the assertion of the right of the prevailing property relations at the global level, just as previously the formation of the nation-state required such assertion across "national" territory.

23 Hirst and Thompson. 1998. *Globalization in Question;* Weiss, L. 1998. *The Myth of the Powerless State*. Cambridge: Polity Press.

24 See Weiss, *Myth of the Powerless State,* p. 185. "While laying claim to being 'global' is seen as a mark of respectability for the modern firm, the number of genuinely transnational companies is rather small." Hirst and Thompson, *Globalization in Question,* p. 195, write that "truly global TNCs are relatively few and that most successful multinational corporations continue to operate from distinct national bases."

25 Report of the Commission on Global Governance. 1995. *Our Global Neighborhood*. New York: Oxford University Press. p. 172.

26 Kozul-Wright, R. 1995. "Transnational Corporations and the Nation State." In J. Michie and J. Grieve-Smith (eds.). *Managing the Global Economy*. Oxford: Oxford University Press, p. 146.

27 UNCTAD, *World Investment Report 1998,* p. 1.

28 This case is best argued by Wade, R. 1996. "Globalization and Its Limits: Reports of the Death of the National Economy Are Greatly Exaggerated." In S. Berger and R. Dore (eds.). *National Diversity and Global Capitalism*. Ithaca, N.Y.: Cornell University Press. pp. 78–82. See also Weiss, L. 1997. "Globalization and the Myth of the Powerful State." *New Left Review*, 225 (September/October), p. 10; the same point is made in her book *Myth of the Powerless State*, p. 185.

29 Davidow and Malone. 1998. *Virtual Corporation;* European Commission, "The Need for Strengthened International Coordination." This document outlines the current stage of development of a regulatory framework for a "global electronic marketplace." See also International Finance Corporation, "The Net Effect on the Nation State," Winter 1999, a short paper on how the "electronic economy will force change within the nation state."

30 UNCTAD, *World Investment Report 1998*, p. 3; emphasis added.

31 Weiss, "Globalization and the Myth of the Powerful State," p. 10.

32 UNCTAD, *World Investment Report 1998*, p.10.

33 Alliances of many sorts but especially on technology are far advanced. See Gugler, P. and J. Dunning. 1993. "Technology-Based Cross-Border Alliances." In C. Relik (ed.). *Multinational Strategic Alliances*. New York: International Business Press; and Howells, J. 1990. "The Internationalization of R&D and the Development of Global Research Networks." *Regional Studies*, 24.

34 McMichael, P. and D. Myhre. 1991. "Global Regulation versus the Nation-State: Agro-Food Systems and the New Politics of Capital." *Capital and Class*, 43,2; and McMichael, P. and L. Raynolds. 1994. "Capitalism, Agriculture, and World Economy." In L. Sklair (ed.). *Capitalism and Development*. London: Routledge.

35 OECD. 1996. *Globalization of Industry*. Overview and Sector Reports. Paris.

36 Report of the Commission on Global Governance, *Our Global Neighborhood*, pp. 136ff.

37 Glyn, A. and B. Sutcliffe. 1992. "Global but Leaderless? The New Capitalist Order." In Miliband and Panitch (eds.). *Socialist Register 1992*, p. 93.

38 Hoefnagels, M. 1981. "Growth of International Organizations since 1945." In R. June and A. Grosse-Jutte (eds.). *The Future of International Organization*. London: Frances Pinter.

39 Bergesten C.F. and C.R. Henning. 1996. *Global Economic Leadership and the Group of Seven*. Washington, D.C.: Institute for International Economics; and Bayne, N. 1995. "The G7 Summit and the Reform of Global Institutions." *Government and Opposition*, 3, 4.

40 Sassen, S. 1998. "Towards a Feminist Analytics of the Global Economy." In S. Sassen, *Globalization and Its Discontents*. New York: The New Press, pp. 96–97. The partisan use of international law on human rights abuse or crimes against humanity by the U.S. and U.K. governments in Yugoslavia does not obviate the point made here: increasingly individuals and groups are challenging the sovereign rights of states on grounds of international law. The charges against General Pinochet in the late 1990s are a case in point.

41 Prior to that war, the only significant example of world government was the League of Nations. Despite being a multinational organization, it retained the principle of the primacy of national sovereignty. This contrasts with the United Nations, which was intended to be a supranational body whose principle was the primacy of certain "universals" superior to the sovereignty of national states. Similarly, the other bodies and agencies mentioned, in principle or in operation, assert a primacy over their members or "clients."

42 Rosenau, J.N. 1992. "Governance, Order and Change in World Politics." In J.N. Rosenau and E.-O. Czempiel (eds.). *Governance without Government: Order and Change in World Politics*. New York: Cambridge University Press.

43 The 1999 U.S./NATO offensive in Yugoslavia goes far to reveal the nature of police actions in securing a world open to capital penetration. See Klare, M.T. 1999. "U.S. Aims to Win on All Fronts." *Le Monde diplomatique* (May).

44 The general thrust of the argument by Hirst and Thompson, *Globalization in Question,* suggests such possibilities. See the critical review by Radice, Hugo. 1997. "The Question of Globalization." *Competition and Change*, 2.

45 Rude, C. 1997. "The End of the G-7 and Rising Imperialist Rivalry." *Monthly Review* (June), 51. Also p. 52: "Far from being powerless or irrelevant, the capitalist nation state, or more precisely, the conflict between the major capitalist nation states, is the reason for so much of the world economy's current instability."

46 For a good review of the "convergence" position, see Boyer, R. "The Convergence Hypothesis Revisited: Globalization But Still the Century of Nations?" In Berger and Dore (eds.). *National Diversity and Global Capitalism.*

47 Panitch, L. 1998. "'The State in a Changing World': Social-Democratic Global Capitalism?" In *Monthly Review* (October). He writes (p. 14): "States are the actual authors of globalization in so far as it is the changes they made in the rules governing capital movements, investment, currency exchange, and trade that permitted a new stage of global accumulation to come about." Making the rules of governance does not necessarily make one the "author" of those changes in the sense of being the independent actor, which is the implication here. National states do not willingly introduce neo-liberal reforms. Some are obliged to introduce them on pain of loss of credit, confidence, trade, and commerce, and some do so because they are acting in the interests of "their" TNCs.

48 Much is made of the "competition state," referring to state strategies as a means of encouraging transnational investment or seeking advantages for national capital in this global economy; but neither of these actions is to be confused with policies intended to maintain national integrity in the face of TNCs.

49 Weiss. "Globalization and the Myth of the Powerless State." She writes (p. 23), "As the advantages of the coordinated market economies continue to be highlighted, potential adapters of the Asian model are more likely to emerge—at least in the Asian region—than blind followers of the neo-liberal model of capitalism." No sooner was this published than the "Asian crisis" engulfed the region, bringing an end, among other things, to the so-called "Asian model," the "development state." What the author failed to see was the role of the global market, now visible in the "reconstruction" of these states, including the "reorganization" of Japan. The success of Japan was based on early initiatives in revamping mass production, access to the U.S. consumer market, export-driven production, protectionist policies and state assistance in capital accumulation, and reciprocal corporate shareholding. By the early 1990s all of this had begun to unravel. See Wood, C. 1994. *The End of Japan Inc.* New York: Simon and Schuster.

50 Helleiner, E. 1996. "Post-Globalization: Is the Financial Liberalization Trend Likely to Be Reversed?" In R. Boyer and D. Drache (eds.). *States against Markets: The Limits of Globalization.* London: Routledge, p. 204.

51 Among dozens of writers from the early 1980s, see Spero, J.E. 1990. "Guiding Global Finance." In P. King (ed.). *International Economics and International Economic Policy.* New York: McGraw-Hill.

52 Weiss. *Myth of the Powerless State,* p. 11: "Globalization, which I argue is more appropriately termed 'internationalization.'"

53 Weiss. "Globalization and the Myth," p. 23.

54 Palen, R., J. Abbot, and P. Deans. 1996. *State Strategies in the Global Political Economy.* London: Pinter. p. 5.

55 Weiss. "Globalization and the Myth of the Powerless State," p. 11.

56 Hirst and Thompson. *Globalization in Question,* p. 2.

57 Numerous books and articles discuss the Third World debt crisis. See, for instance, Payer, C. 1991. *Lent and Lost: Foreign Credit and Third World Development.* London: Zed Books; MacDonald, S.B., M. Lindsay, and D.L. Crum (eds.). 1990. *The Global Debt Crisis.* London: Pinter; and Schatan, J. 1987. *World Debt: Who Is to Pay?* London: Zed Books.

58 Cardoso, F.H. 1996. "North-South Relations in the Present Context: A New Dependency?" In M. Carnoy et al. (eds.). *The New Global Economy in the Information Age: Reflections on Our Changing World.* University Park: Pennsylvania State University Press, p. 157; emphasis in original.

59 Hoogvelt, A. 1997. *Globalization and the Postcolonial World.* Baltimore: Johns Hopkins University Press, p. 241.

60 Robinson, Wm. 1998–99. "Latin America and Global Capitalism." *Race and Class* 40, 2/3, p. 116.

61 Belli, P. 1991. "Globalizing the Rest of the World." *Harvard Business Review* (July–August).

62 Wade R. and F. Veneroso. 1998. "The Asian Crisis: The High Debt Model versus the Wall Street-Treasury-IMF Complex." *New Left Review,* 228 (March/April). For another view of the end of the "Asian model," see Bernard, M. 1999. "East Asia's Tumbling Dominoes: Financial Crises and the Myth of The Regional Model." In Panitch and Leys (eds.). *Socialist Register 1999.*

63 Lehman, K. and A. Krebs. 1996. "Control of the World's Food Supply." In J. Mander and E. Goldsmith (eds.). *The Case against the Global Economy.* San Francisco: Sierra Club Books.

64 Kimbrell, A. "Biocolonization." In Mander and Goldsmith (eds.). *The Case against the Global Economy,* p. 143. See also Biggs, S. 1988. "The Biodiversity Convention and Global Sustainable Development." In R. Kiely and P. Marfleet (eds.). *Globalisation and the Third World.* London: Routledge.

CHAPTER 2

Introduction to the Cult

Linda McQuaig

✱One can only call the political impact of "globalization" the pathology of over-diminished expectations. ✱
— PAUL HIRST AND GRAHAME THOMPSON

IT WAS JUST THE sort of irritating development that could ruin a perfectly good day.

For months now, things had been gradually falling into place. That is, things were looking more and more desperate. Not that anyone—particularly someone as high up the policy-making food chain as deputy finance minister David Dodge—liked to see the country in a desperate situation. But Dodge, along with just about everyone else in Ottawa's Finance department, knew that desperation, unfortunately, was a prerequisite for the kind of sweeping government action they had in mind.

So by late September 1994, it was hard for them not to be pleased by the evidence that the nation's finances were careering out of control. The ever-accumulating national debt—a juicy $40 billion added to its already grotesque size over the previous year!—surely made everything pretty clear. By this point, it didn't matter what platform the new Liberal government had been elected on. The numbers spoke for themselves, screaming a message of unsustainability. The country, bloated with debt, was tottering on a pair of too-high heels. A sudden gust of wind and the whole unwieldy form might topple over, reducing our once-proud nation to nothing but a writhing failure sprawled helplessly on the sidewalk for passers-by to gawk at and wonder: why was nothing done?

In his office, Paul Martin could be heard practising: "We are in hock up to our eyeballs … meet our target come hell or high water…." Gutsy stuff, to be delivered with bravado. Daniel in the lion's den. In only a few weeks, Martin was going to very publicly re-invent himself in two carefully planned televised broadcasts. No more deficit softie. Now, over the top, charge! Cape to the bull, shoulder to the wind. And the department could take at least some of the credit for helping him see the need for this full make-over.

Having seen it, Martin had become fanatical about doing it right, getting the message convincingly across to the public, which no one in Ottawa had yet succeeded in doing. So Martin's office was now constantly full of spin doctors showing him how to project his voice, move his hands, get the camera angle right. "Come hell or high water." Needs a little more edge in the voice. "Come *hell* or high water!" That's it. Forget your hands. Use your eyes. It was hard for David Dodge, peeking in from time to time, not to feel a little satisfaction. Here was the new, improved Finance minister, fresh from the department's intense deficit-immersion course, putting his own dramatic, earthy spin on the department's well-worn theme, managing through sheer performance to make it sound almost fresh. Everything was indeed falling into place.

And now this!

It goes without saying that the 13-page document that had just landed on David Dodge's desk was without merit.[1] Anything that came to such ridiculous conclusions had to be. So it wasn't that the document risked shaking his faith, undermining the certainty felt by Dodge and those beneath him in the Finance department that they were on the right track, doing what had to be done. At this point, the fear wasn't even that Martin himself might experience doubts and retreat into the kind of confused thinking he used to display when he was in opposition. No. There was little chance of that now. Martin had gone too far, the philosophical make-over that the department had led him through over the past year had taken too deeply. His new zeal was real. *Come hell or high water....* After you say that enough you start to believe in it. No. The danger wasn't Martin's straying off course. The danger was the public, which was less predictable.

Dodge read the irritating document again. No doubt about it, there was some material in

here that could easily confuse the public. Most troublesome was the suggestion that Canada's main problem was unemployment, not excessive government spending. The document noted that once full employment is achieved, "the budget gap of Canada vanishes." Not helpful. Indeed, this was the ultimate in dangerous, confused thinking. Such a view, if advocated by an editorial writer at a meeting of *The Globe and Mail* editorial board, would almost surely be enough to lead to a transfer to the Sports department. But the view was, nevertheless, infuriatingly popular with the public, who naively preferred to tackle the deficit by putting the country back to work rather than by substantially reducing the country's social programs. So with only five months to go before the department planned to bring down its crucial 1995 budget—in which social spending was to be cut to levels not seen in this country in fifty years—it was clearly not useful for the public to be exposed to this sort of thinking.

The biggest problem was the source. There were plenty of people out there saying this sort of thing. But they were mostly bleeding-heart softies, easily dismissed and ignored. This document, on the other hand, was from the head office of Goldman Sachs, one of the oldest and most respected Wall Street brokerage houses. The Opposition and the media would have a field day.

Draw up the bridge. Circle the wagons. Head them off at the pass. The department would have to be ready, and it would be. Extensive briefing notes had to be prepared for the minister to deal with questions about it in the House and in scrums with reporters outside.

After all the hard work of the past year, this could be just the kind of development that would get everything derailed. What was in the brains of those Goldman Sachs idiots anyway? Whose side were they on? Didn't they realize it was hard enough to orchestrate a sense of panic about the nation's excessive spending among the common people without Wall Street interfering, suggesting the nation's spending was *not* excessive? Sometimes it wasn't easy being deputy minister of Finance.

And, in truth, one couldn't entirely rule out the ultimate fear—that Martin himself could be derailed. God forbid. What if ... *We're in hock up to our eyeballs ... and the only solution is to put this country back to work!* You had to admit it sounded better, even if it was confused thinking.

The document had to be sent to the minister. But Dodge could weaken its impact by offering up his own harsh analysis of it. "Too sanguine a view," he wrote to Martin in a memo accompanying the Goldman Sachs report. "Could be used (misused) by those who object to the need for strong fiscal action."

* * * * *

Case Closed.

David Dodge's fears never materialized. Evidently, people looking for ways to derail Ottawa's spending cuts don't subscribe to Goldman Sachs's economic reports.

If there had been any doubt that Paul Martin would be hailed the white knight of Canadian public finance, it quickly evaporated in the warm aftermath of his February 1995 budget. Business and the financial sector were awed by the deep, deep spending cuts that everyone on Bay Street had long pushed for, but few believed they'd ever live to see. The flimsy parliamentary opposition tried to find a few flaws to rail against in TV clips, but did little to challenge the essential spending-must-be-cut thrust of the budget. The media seemed satisfied and generally reflected the view that Martin had had no alternative.

But it wasn't until October 1996 that the matter could really be put to rest. With the publication of *Double Vision: The Inside Story of the Liberals in Power,* two prominent media figures in Ottawa delivered their judgment, pretty well wrapping things up. The two authors, Edward Greenspon, *The Globe and Mail's* Ottawa bureau chief, and Anthony Wilson-Smith, Ottawa bureau chief for *Maclean's,* represented the two major national print media outlets in the country. And here they were teaming up to write the full story, as they saw it, not as their editors or publishers wanted it. Two independent, well-placed observers just telling it like it is.

At their book launch at the Ottawa press club, politicians mixed with journalists and bureaucrats, celebrating the publication of what appeared to be the definitive book on Ottawa in the 1990s. Like an account of some esteemed leader who rises to greatness after he sees the error of his ways, *Double Vision* is the story of Paul Martin's reckoning. Written with ample access to Martin and his closest advisers, the book is a kind of authorized biography of his conversion. It tells a tale of greatness in the making, of weakness overcome, of blindness that became vision. Paul Martin on the road to Damascus. Apocalypse Avoided.

That the country was to be fundamentally reworked, that hundreds of thousands of Canadians would lose their jobs in the wake of the cuts, that some of the poorest people would lose a major chunk of their income as a result of this conversion seemed outside the parameters of debate, as the party at the press club gathered steam. Indeed, with the publication of *Double Vision,* detailing the inside story of how Paul Martin found the courage to do what he had to do, it became clear that there was to be no debate.

Case closed.

* * * * *

What a difference a year makes. The end of 1997, a year after the release of *Double Vision*, and Canada is a very different place. The deficit, which loomed so huge on the national political scene, crowding out virtually every other issue, is now virtually gone. No longer careering out of control, the deficit is quickly careering into oblivion. Not since the Cold War evaporated almost overnight has there been such a sudden disappearance of a threatening enemy. Will pieces of the Fraser Institute's Deficit Clock soon become popular historical artefacts, like bits of barbed wire from the Berlin Wall?

By the time the Liberal government gets around to actually announcing the healthiness of the nation's finances in its Throne Speech in late September, the news has already trickled out. Indeed, for the previous six months, prominent Bay Street commentators have been openly marvelling at how quickly the deficit is shrinking. A new concept enters the political arena: fiscal surplus. All of a sudden, a major question has become: what do we do with the "fiscal surplus"? For the public, which for years has been trained only to think of getting by with less, the "fiscal surplus" doesn't immediately become a hot-button issue.

But it does with key opinion-makers, who are torn over the question. Whereas they had been pretty much of one mind in the past— government spending must be cut to reduce the deficit—they are now showing signs of disunity. Certainly, there is a strong consensus that previous levels of government spending must not be restored. But beyond this, there is much debate in government, business and media circles. The key questions being debated are: should the fiscal surplus go into debt reduction or tax reduction, and how quickly should the tax breaks be delivered?

One school of thought, represented by the Business Council on National Issues as well as the *Financial Post* editorial board, wants to see the crusade to reduce the annual deficit simply transferred to a crusade to reduce the nation's accumulated debt, with tax cuts to be delivered in the future.[2] Other prominent participants in the debate, such as *The Globe and Mail* editorial board and CIBC Wood Gundy chief economist Jeff Rubin, argue that we should let the debt gradually decline on its own; they want tax cuts and they want them now.[3]

Then there's Paul Martin, who talks of devoting 50 percent of future surpluses to restoring government spending (an idea frowned on by the financial elite), and splitting the rest between debt reduction and tax cuts. That certainly makes the Liberal government sound more socially progressive than those in elite circles. But it would be wrong to conclude from this that the government intends to restore spending. Indeed, Paul Martin's plan will do little to return government spending to anywhere near the levels it was at only a decade ago.

In the mid-1980s, spending on government programs amounted to more than 18 percent of our total national income.[4] By 1999, when Paul Martin's cuts are fully phased in, spending on government programs will have dropped to less than 12 percent of our national income—a drop of roughly one-third. Even if the Liberal government follows through with its promise to devote 50 percent of future surpluses to spending, the level of government spending will remain minimal. Depending on the formula the government uses to calculate its surpluses, program spending, four years from now, will amount to either 12.2 percent of national income or 11.7 percent— roughly the same as the historically low level to be reached in 1999.[5] In other words, the government fully intends to keep spending depressed to extremely low levels.

These calculations, by the way, are not the dreamchild of some social activist bent on ex-aggerating the size of the government's spending cuts. On the contrary, the calculations were done by John McCallum, chief economist at the Royal Bank of Canada, who wrote them up in a release that was widely distributed in the financial community in the fall of 1997. They fit with similar calculations done by experts at other leading financial institutions. And they also fit with calculations done by the Finance department. Paul Martin himself, in an interview, agreed they were "roughly" accurate.

But the numbers illustrate the extent to which the whole deficit-reduction process has changed the nature of how we divide up resources in this country. As Martin has noted, deficit reduction was achieved primarily through spending cuts; spending cuts have been seven times as large as tax increases.[6] Asked about this, Martin explained in the interview that the government felt it had no alternative. He pointed to the example of Sweden, which dealt with its deficit primarily by raising taxes. "And they got killed," he said. "The international marketplace descended upon them with a hammer. Their interest rates skyrocketed, and they had to back off totally .... The only way in which one was going to be credible was in fact to deal with this essentially by reducing spending."[7]

Yet even if Martin felt international financial markets left him no choice but to cut the deficit mostly through spending reductions,

this doesn't explain why he is not now planning to restore more of that spending. Once the deficit is gone, and we are no longer supposedly under the thumb of financial markets, why shouldn't a bigger portion of the fiscal surplus be directed back to spending—the area that took the biggest hit in the deficit-reduction crusade? But this is not what the Liberals are planning, which reveals that their interest in cutting government programs now goes beyond deficit reduction. They are presiding over a long-term redirection of our national income away from government programs. They are taking us much closer to the U.S. model, with lower taxes and smaller government.[8]

There's little evidence that this is what Canadians want. Donna Dasko, vice-president of Environics Research Ltd., says that Canadians continue to support strong social programs. An Environics poll in early 1997 found that when asked about what should be done with the fiscal surplus, 70 percent of Canadians said that their top priority was government programs— for job creation, health care and fighting child poverty. Surprisingly, only 18 percent of those polled favoured putting the extra money into debt reduction, and only 9 percent wanted to see it channelled into tax cuts—suggesting that ordinary Canadians have a very different set of priorities than do members of the financial elite. Indeed, Dasko says that polling done by Environics in the fall of 1997 shows that high unemployment far outranks all other issues as the biggest problem facing the country in the minds of most Canadians.

The massive government spending cuts of recent years were sold to a reluctant Canadian public on the basis that there really was no alternative. But now, presumably, there is an alternative. That's what we were told the whole deficit-reduction exercise was about—

regaining control over our destiny. And politicians even tell us that we've now achieved that. "Today, we're in a position where we can make our own decisions," a very pleased Paul Martin said on "Pamela Wallin" on CBC-TV's Newsworld in late October 1997.[9] Yet, even as we reach the promised land of deficit-free nirvana—the place where, we are told, the world will once again be our oyster and even the Finance minister claims we can make our own decisions—there are certain things we apparently still can't have, like jobs and social programs.

Case still closed.

* * * * *

From the outdoor café overlooking the shimmering water of Hamilton Harbour in Bermuda, the sun shines too brightly in the eyes of David Jones, making him squint.

Or is he squinting because the subject has turned to something so distasteful that his face has become contorted?

"If you inhibit cash flows, the alternative is war," says Jones, an affable, balding currency trader sipping a dark beer.

He is reacting to the notion of a tax on international currency transactions, that is, a tax on the $1.2 trillion a day that is traded on foreign currency markets around the world. The proposed tax, known as the Tobin tax, after Nobel Prize-winning economist James Tobin, would be set at a very low level—much less than 1 percent of the amount traded. But since the volume involved is so large, the tax could collect hundreds of billions of dollars in revenue each year. Some of the debate over the tax has focused on whether the money should be used exclusively to fund Third World development or whether some of it should be redirected back to the financially strapped treasuries of western nations, thereby creating a rare opportunity for society's high rollers to make a contribution to deficit reduction.

Before we start worrying about how to divide up the billions, there are a few problems. One is David Jones and the people whose money he trades. To them, the tax amounts to a restriction on the free movement of money. One of the reasons the $1.2 trillion floats around the world so effortlessly each day is that there are currently few restrictions on the movement of money. The major holders of capital in the world—chiefly the world's big commercial banks, large corporations and wealthy individuals, assisted by brokers like David Jones—can move money anywhere, anytime for no other purpose than to park it for a few days, hours—or minutes—where it can earn a slightly higher rate of interest. That slightly higher rate may be less than a cent on the dollar. But if you're moving $25 million, even for a few minutes, it adds up.

Clearly it's a lucrative business. In fact, this sort of trading is one of the reasons the Canadian banks—which are increasingly trading in this market—are reporting ever-rising profits. And traders like David Jones, who has brokered trading deals for CIBC and the TD Bank, have done nicely as well. In a good month, he can earn half a million dollars in brokerage fees. Perhaps it's not surprising he's not keen on a tax—even a little tax—on these capital flows. Perhaps he really does think that the only alternative is war.

But for the rest of us, such a tax might not be so bad. In fact, its real purpose isn't even to raise all those billions for world development. That's a secondary purpose. The real purpose is to slow down the flow of dollars around the world, to build a tiny little dike against the gushing torrent of free-flowing dollars, to, in

Tobin's phrase, "throw sand in the wheels" of our incredibly fluid capital markets.

The reason we might want to do this is because all this free-flowing capital is intimately connected to Paul Martin's conversion on the road to Damascus. As long as capital can whisk effortlessly around the world, shopping for the best terms, it can wreak havoc on national currencies, as we saw in Southeast Asia in the fall of 1997. It can intimidate governments into thinking they must do whatever it wants. This can leave a guy like Paul Martin feeling fearful, afraid that the economy he presides over will be "killed" when international markets descend "with a hammer." Indeed, this can leave a guy like Paul Martin willing to do pretty much what these markets say.

Over lunch at Toronto's Canoe restaurant at the top of the TD Bank Tower, amid much fashionable chrome and pewter and striking views of the city's harbour, another personable currency trader is explaining the ins and outs of currency markets. We talk market talk—of puts and calls and straddles, of covered shorts and naked shorts. He's personable—that is, until dessert arrives, and he's confronted with a question about the Tobin tax.

Yes, he's heard something about it, he explains, before launching into a mini-tirade about the utter stupidity of the tax. He doesn't argue that the only alternative is war, but otherwise seems just as furiously opposed to it as was the trader in Bermuda.

It's getting harder and harder to resist the feeling that there must be something to this tax.

* * * * *

An expert is holding forth earnestly on CBC Radio's "Sunday Morning."[10] It's pretty familiar fare, really. Dr. Ian Angell, professor

of information systems at the London School of Economics, is explaining how most of the working population will soon be redundant.

"Isn't there an economic cost to writing off the world's workers?" asks host Ian Brown.

The question suggests that Brown has bought the basic parameters of the debate: that we discuss only *economic* cost. Brown is asking: How does the unemployment of most of the world's population fit society's basic business plan? No one mentions *human* cost.

Still, the question doesn't suit Dr. Angell. Impatience is detectable in his voice.

"This requires a total rethinking of the institutions of the industrial age. You must throw them away," says Dr. Angell, trying to make things nice and simple for Brown to grasp. "All your thinking has to be different."

As the interview progresses, Brown becomes increasingly sceptical of what he's hearing. His questions reveal that he's struggling to see how all this unemployment helps ordinary people. Answer: it doesn't.

But that's not the issue. The issue is that it's the future. Globalization, technology, governments can no longer coddle their people, they must focus instead on getting their financial houses in order, lowering their deficits and their taxes, etc., etc.

An emboldened Ian Brown asks something about how people are to survive. Dr. Angell is getting a touch irritated with these repetitive questions about human needs. Brown just doesn't seem to get it. The point is that we're in a brand-new age, the information age. Technology and globalization have made all these questions about human needs irrelevant. That's part of yesterday's menu. Today we simply watch as the technological juggernaut rolls on, squashing our needs.

"Is this a world you look forward to?" asks

Brown, trying to make some sense of it all.

"That's neither here nor there," responds Dr. Angell.

"Is there some way we can stop this?" Brown asks anxiously. "Is there nothing we can do to avoid this dark future?"

That's when Dr. Angell snaps. "That question reflects the thinking of the machine age," he says curtly.

Hold it. Let's play that again slowly.

This line is more subversive than it first appears. It is perhaps as subversive a thought as it is possible to have. Dr. Angell is saying it's not just that we can't change things, *but we can't even think about the possibility of changing things;* to do so is to engage in old-style thinking.

So, it's not just that we're powerless to stop being pushed over the edge of the cliff in the new global world order. But to even try to prevent ourselves from being pushed over the cliff is a sign of regressive thinking.

The new way of thinking, as outlined by Dr. Angell, requires an acceptance of powerlessness, resignation to a world without solutions—a world of inaction and helplessness. That democratic impulse to assert one's rights must be contained, thwarted, rendered mute and inoperative.

Never mind the *democratic* impulse. It's actually the *human* impulse that's at stake here. The human impulse to act, to build, to create, to improve, to shape our lives, to use our brains to do better. It's called being alive.

It's just got to go.

* * * * *

"Imagine."

The word is half whispered. On the screen, we see a native girl of indeterminate age on a swing. Wistful. Dreamy. Free as the wind that blows in her face.

She is presumably imagining the possibilities, imagining a better world. Could she be thinking of change, improvement? Could she be thinking the *old way?* Perhaps a few weeks in a Dr. Angell re-education camp is needed.

But wait. This is a TV commercial for a bank. It's the Bank of Montreal, saying it is possible. Of course, it's never clear from the ad exactly what is possible. It seems to be suggesting that anything is possible. Surely that's the reason for choosing a young native girl for the part. We'd normally see the face of such a girl in the media only as part of a story about glue sniffing or teen suicide or young-runaway-turns-teen-stripper-and-ends-up-murdered-in-a-stairwell. But here, in the airbrushed world of the Bank of Montreal—or its hipper version, mbanx—this girl seems to be an inspired person, someone with limitless possibilities in front of her.

Surely if even someone like this—not an upwardly mobile white male in a suit, but a native female in a long skirt and cowboy boots—can have a dream, the possibilities out there for regular people must be truly endless.

And they are—when it comes to banking.

"At mbanx, we don't believe in limits," says the breathless prose in a print ad picking up the theme from the TV ad. "Your $13 monthly fee covers all your everyday banking needs and more. So go ahead and use any automated banking machine (ABM) on the Interac or Cirrus shared networks as often as you want. We won't charge you. Use your debit card. No charge. Call us any time. No charge. Do your banking on-line at mbanx.com. Our Internet service isn't just 'free for a limited time.' There's no activation charge. You just do it. No charge."

No wonder the native girl seems so blissed out. Imagine the possibilities. Why would anyone bother to sniff glue or commit suicide or get killed in a stairwell when there's a whole new wide world out there of ... debit cards, on-line shared networks, activation charges ... of, well, banking.

A black woman, pictured in the print ad, poses a question to those who are confused enough to still use other banks: "Do your remote banking services make you feel that way?"

M̲banx has an answer for that too. "At m̲banx, we see technology as something that links, not isolates. So, even though you may never see us, we're always here for you. In some ways, we're closer than any branch could be. And we guarantee you'll be satisfied with our service. Every time you call, you can speak with a portfolio manager whose job it is to know you, respect you, and make what you want happen...."

Is this banking or telephone sex? Is there a difference?

The ad continues: "Is there still stuff your bank won't let you do over the phone? Whether it's 3 in the morning or Sunday afternoon, you'll get simple point and click access to your day to day banking...."

Don't stop now....

As we delve deeper into the m̲banx philosophy, we see that there is nothing here Dr. Angell would have trouble with. As long as the native girl confines herself to imagining the banking possibilities that lie ahead, she is simply marvelling at the high-tech corporate world engulfing her. She is not trying to assert herself or work towards a better world.

But what if her mind were to stray from contemplating the wonders of modern banking to, say, contemplating the scope of Canada's unemployment problem? The unemployment story is just as dramatic, in its own way. Perhaps it doesn't have the immediate drama of moving money from a savings to a chequing account in the middle of the night or paying hydro bills through the Internet. Mostly, it seems to be about people feeling depressed and hopeless because they can't find work. Huge numbers of people. Virtually an army of people. This world is worth exploring for a minute, because, with its sense of hopelessness, it is the flipside of the ever-expanding dreamy world of the m̲banx commercial.

Sitting alone in their individual homes, depressed and angry and isolated, the army of the unemployed is difficult to visualize or relate to. Fortunately, however, Lars Osberg, an economist at Dalhousie University in Halifax, has come up with a graphic way to illustrate the size of this army and the enormous waste of its idleness.[11]

First, let's get a sense of the numbers involved. What we really want to measure is the number of *needlessly* unemployed people in Canada. In other words, there will always be people in between jobs, or people choosing not to work for now. If we include these people in our army, we will artificially inflate its size. In the interests of understating the size of our army, let's assume a fairly high level of transitional unemployment. In fact, let's just take the level of actual unemployment that existed in Canada in 1989, before the onset of the most recent recession. Back then, Canada's unemployment rate was 7.5 percent. If we simply consider the unemployment we've experienced *above this level* since then, we find that the additional number of unemployed people amounts to an average of roughly 450,000 a year.

One way to illustrate the size of this army and the waste of its idleness is to figure out what this army could have built, had it been working. Let's suppose that our army was put to work building something highly labour-intensive—something like, say, the great pyramids of ancient Egypt. It would be hard to imagine anything much more back-breaking and laborious than the construction of these massive tombs. Built more than 20 centuries before the birth of Christ, these colossal structures consist of enormous stone slabs installed on top of one another in symmetrical form. What makes the story so striking is the lack of technology or even basic tools involved. The massive stone slabs were cut from solid rock, dragged out of the quarry and hauled a considerable distance on wooden sleds—without even the use of a wheel, which hadn't yet been invented. In an advance that no doubt seemed terribly sophisticated at the time, water was poured over the paths to lubricate the route and reduce the friction.

A recent analysis by Stuart Wier of the Denver Museum of Natural History calculated the sheer human energy involved in building the Great Pyramid in Giza in the twenty-sixth century B.C. under the reign of King Khufu. Writing in the *Cambridge Archaeological Journal,* Wier breaks it down fairly specifically. For instance, when the pyramid was just getting going, it would take about 2,840 men per day to work in the quarry, and some 5,540 to work in transport (that is, pulling the stones). As the pyramid got taller (it eventually reached the equivalent of a 48-storey building today), it took fewer quarry workers and more haulers—eventually some 6,870 a day. When the pyramid was 60 metres high, 2,380 men were needed for lifting. Wier calculates that it would have taken some ten thousand men—about one percent of the population of ancient Egypt—about 23 years to complete Khufu's resting place.[12]

How would the army of needlessly unemployed Canadians have fared in pyramid construction? With the use of tractors and cranes, the modern equivalent of pyramids could be built relatively quickly. But for the sake of illustration, let's assume that the army of needlessly unemployed Canadians was busy building pyramids with the same technology that was available back in the twenty-sixth century B.C. No motors, no pulleys, no wheels. Just wood sleds, a little water and a great deal of lifting. Let's even assume that the Canadian pyramid workers get to work a comfortable Canadian schedule—a five-day work week, statutory holidays, a month's vacation—which would presumably slow things down from the Egyptian pace. Still, Osberg calculates that the army of needlessly unemployed Canadians could have built no fewer than seven pyramids since 1990 and be well on their way to completing their eighth.

Of course, the more significant question to consider is what could have been accomplished had they instead used modern technology and built something more useful than a tomb for a dead king. What if they'd built housing or highways, cleaned up the Great Lakes or operated day-care centres, or worked in the Canadian aerospace industry?

Imagine.

*   *   *   *   *

This book is about possibilities. It is about exploring the real limits of what is possible and what isn't in this age of the global economy. Is full employment possible? How about well-funded public health and education systems or a clean environment? Or is only all-night banking possible?

The dominant school of thought has become that of the naysayers, those who argue, essentially, that the market ultimately determines what is possible. It's an odd sort of situation we find ourselves in. The market offers us a giddy world of choice when it comes to consumer items: banking, cars, appliances, seat covers, bathroom fixtures, beer. Enter into any one of these consumer worlds, and one is confronted with a breathless array of possibilities. We can choose from hundreds of different car models, with thousands of options. Do we want a sedan or a hatchback, leather or plush seats, cruise control, anti-lock brakes, air conditioning, wrap-around stereo, coffee holders that flip out or pull down? What about telephone sets—do we want them to be cordless or plug-in, to beep with incoming calls or simply record them on an answering machine, to look like a fire engine or like the Star Trek spaceship? Or dental floss: do we want it waxed or unwaxed, mint or plain, thick or fine, floss or tape…. One could get dizzy if it weren't so exciting.

But when it comes to things that many people might consider more important—like whether we will have jobs, live in communities where water is drinkable, air breathable and no one will be left hungry or homeless—these things are apparently beyond our control. If we put in place policies that create the kind of society we apparently want, the market will move money out of the country, we are told. Thus, there are limits to what we can do in these areas. We have to stay within the dictates of the market. We have become captives of the marketplace.

It's interesting to note just how far we've moved outside the normal range of historical human experience. In his brilliant overview of world economic history, *The Great Transfor-*

mation, economic historian Karl Polanyi notes that the Industrial Revolution marked the first time in history that the notion of the private market was elevated to the central organizing principle of society. In earlier times, the market was only one of the forces around which society organized itself. Religion, family, custom, law, tradition were all considered more important. Now, if Dr. Angell and his ilk are to be believed, we've come to the point where not only has the market become the dominant force in our society, but its dominance is above reproach, above question. To suggest that we have a choice about what role the market will play in our lives is to fail to see that we've evolved to a supposedly higher plane—a plane where we now no longer have any choice about the market's power over our lives in areas that really matter, a plane where we are essentially impotent.

Thank God we've at least got all-night banking.

* * * * *

Nobody has made a more compelling case for our collective impotence than the authors of *Double Vision.* This very readable book, with its rich detail of inside information, provides a bird's-eye view of the story of Paul Martin's odyssey from a slightly confused believer in a jobs-and-growth strategy to a reluctant adherent of the ultimately-we-are-impotent school of thought. Its importance goes beyond its readability. Its impeccable sources give it an authoritative voice. And it ultimately, and enthusiastically, endorses the government's position—indeed, it suggests there was no alternative, that the harsh medicine was unavoidable. In a sense, it can be seen as the definitive statement of the position of the government—almost an official, authorized biography of the Liberal government. But, unlike the usual press releases that the government puts out extolling its positions, *Double Vision* fills the government's story with life and character and struggle.

Like all good stories, *Double Vision* presents a tale of moral dimensions, of right and wrong, of wise and foolish. It ultimately presents Paul Martin's conversion as a contest between, on the one hand, clear-thinking pragmatists who, ahead of their time, understand and accept the new powerlessness and, on the other, a team of woolly-headed, well-meaning but ultimately foolish bleeding hearts who keep naively clinging to the notion that governments can do a lot to improve the lives of their citizens. At the centre of this clash is Paul Martin himself, an affable but essentially empty vessel who gains greatness only by coming to accept the wisdom of the impotence-advocating pragmatists.

The woolly-headed bleeding hearts, led by the woeful Lloyd Axworthy but also including cabinet ministers Sheila Copps and Sergio Marchi, come across as an enormously pitiful bunch. Axworthy, then minister of Human Resources, is continually depicted as pale, besieged, confused, ineffective, stumbling, a "Liberal on his knees" as the chapter about him is titled.[13] Trudging on in his weak and incomprehensible attempt to reform the social safety net, Axworthy is seen as a well-meaning failure, one who subscribes to that fuzzy, warm-hearted belief that "having fought the good fight was as important as the outcome." As he shuffles ineffectually with his good intentions, he utterly fails to deliver, swept aside by the dynamic Paul Martin. "Martin, a powerful minister of finance with a head of steam and will of iron, ate the human resources minister for breakfast."

Arrayed against Axworthy and his motley crew of inept do-gooders are the pragmatists, the largely unsung advocates of impotence. Chief among them are David Dodge, deputy minister of Finance, and his senior staff, the "rationalists at Finance" who, to a man (and they all do seem to be men), are steeped in deficit obsession and seem to have been unable to sleep properly for years for all their worrying over Canada's credit rating.

Perhaps the most important of these pragmatists is Peter Nicholson, a former top adviser to Bank of Nova Scotia chairman Cedric Ritchie, who is brought into the department on special secondment and who becomes "an important figure in the Paul Martin story." Nicholson is bright, self-assured and talkative, with a Ph.D. in operations research. All summer long, through the hot days of July and August 1994, Nicholson conducts what amounts to an ongoing economics tutorial for Martin. In fact, Nicholson is not really an economist. But he makes up for that with his skill at numbers.

And what is the deficit besides a lot of big numbers? Nicholson is able to mesmerize Martin with the deficit's arithmetic of compound interest. It isn't that Nicholson is cold or callous. Indeed, he is a likeable, engaging man, a man not unlike the Finance minister himself. But Nicholson purports to know the limits of what the markets will allow; he knows "how unforgiving capital markets can be when they turn against you," as he said in a recent interview. He understands the true nature of impotence.

Double Vision essentially presents the notion that the government took the hard choices that were pragmatic and, ultimately, foresighted. We are reminded that Martin was a "humane and reluctant budget cutter" and that his goal in trashing social programs was ultimately to save them. The only alternative that is presented is the inept and clouded vision of Axworthy et al., who seem to be all heart and no brain. In *Double Vision,* anyone with brains sees the wisdom of the impotence school of thought. For instance, Judith Maxwell, a prominent economist and Martin adviser, doesn't let her well-known concern for social justice interfere with her conviction that everything must take a back seat to deficit reduction. Sure, she's socially concerned, but first comes the deficit.

The clear message is that there was no real debate within the Chrétien government. The confused utterings of the handful of socially minded Liberals were soon revealed for the sophomoric impracticality that they were and were shunted aside. More important, the message is that there was no real alternative, that it was either modern pragmatism, grounded in economic and fiscal reality and a firm understanding of the arithmetic of deficits, or bleeding-heart confusion, which wouldn't be able to distinguish arithmetic from ballroom dancing.

Yet, curiously, there was one man in the upper ranks of the Liberal government—a member of the Chrétien cabinet—who fit in neither of these two camps. Like Nicholson, he was a whiz at numbers. But unlike Nicholson, he was trained in economics—even the economics of high finance, having obtained a Ph.D. in finance from the University of Pennsylvania. Moreover, he understood financial markets, having spent 26 years of his life in one of the top jobs on Bay Street, as chief economist and later senior vice-president of one of the Big Six banks. If anyone in the top circle of government ministers and advisers understood numbers, economics and the way markets actually operated, and how they reacted to government policies, it was this man.

Yet, despite his Bay Street pedigree, he

didn't side with the "pragmatists," and he didn't subscribe to the impotence school of thought. Indeed, he argued constantly with the "rationalists at Finance," disputing their assumptions and challenging their conclusions. At the cabinet table, he pushed for a less obsessive approach to deficit reduction, for placing a higher priority on bringing down unemployment. And he fought for these things not out of some mushy sentimentality but with strongly grounded economic arguments. His very presence was a challenge to the notion that the only choice was between economic pragmatism and bleeding-heart foolishness. Rather, he made a compelling case for the deeply subversive view that there was a realistic alternative—an economically viable alternative.

Oddly, he never appears in *Double Vision.*

* * * * *

If a group of left-wing activists were trying to devise a convincing scenario for a corporate conspiracy, it would have been hard to come up with something better than the little gathering at the Ontario Club.

As news of the Multilateral Agreement on Investment (MAI) gradually trickled out of the Ottawa bureaucracy throughout 1997, anyone who had been involved in the earlier free trade and North America Free Trade Agreement (NAFTA) debates was highly suspicious. All across the country, small groups organized meetings to discuss this little-known treaty, which was being negotiated in Paris by representatives of the 29 nations that make up the Organization for Economic Co-operation and Development (OECD). One solution would have been for the Ottawa bureaucrats to release endless drafts of the proposed treaty in the hopes of boring the public into indifference. Instead, however, those handling the

MAI—assistant deputy minister of Industry Andrei Sulzenko and chief negotiator Bill Dymond—adopted the bizarre strategy of releasing very little information and assuring Canadians they had nothing to worry about, that the matter was in good hands.

To provide added assurance to the public, Sulzenko and Dymond even took their show on the road. They tried to set up a joint meeting with the University of Toronto's Centre for International Studies. Louis Pauly, the centre's director, was amenable, as long as the event was open to the public. The Ottawa team agreed, and pushed for a downtown location, easily accessible to the business community. Thus, the event, which attracted an eclectic mix of professors, protesters in Uncle Sam costumes, business executives and currency traders, took place in the unlikely setting of the Ontario Club, one of Bay Street's toniest haunts.

In their session, the Ottawa officials assured the audience that the MAI wasn't all that new; it simply built on terms that had already been established in earlier free trade treaties.[14] This was exactly what many in the room most feared. Indeed, the combination of the secretiveness of the presenters and the Bay Street location was enough to feed the conspiracy fantasies of all but the currency traders, who alone are likely free of conspiracy fantasies. (They *know* that the world operates in their interest; that's not a conspiracy, that's just the way things should be.) From a public relations viewpoint, however, the Ottawa team's event at the Ontario Club was easily a disaster.

Whatever form the final treaty takes, certain broad themes have emerged. As in earlier free trade treaties, the MAI is an attempt to provide private international capital-holders and corporations with certain rights. *Toronto Star* columnist Richard Gwyn suggested it was like a "charter of rights for absentee landlords"—with no responsibilities or obligations to accompany these rights.[15] In other words, the MAI is a one-way street in which capitalholders are given the power to challenge the laws of democratically elected governments and governments are given no reciprocal powers over them. This raises some interesting questions. For instance, will investors be able to challenge Canada's medicare system on the grounds that the government's monopoly in providing health care deprives them of their right to invest in the lucrative health-care field? The answer will be in the fine print of the MAI. But it does make one wonder why Canada is so gung-ho to get on board this train. As Gwyn puts it, "How necessary and productive and creative is it to be applying our talents and political energies to making the world safe for absentee landlords?"

One area of concern (among many) is whether the treaty will try to establish in international law the principle that capital must remain fully mobile, that governments cannot impose any restraints on this mobility. In reality, western governments currently impose very few restraints on capital mobility. But presumably enshrining this principle in international law could give it even more force. If so, ideas like the Tobin tax could be declared out of the question. Instead of simply languishing on the back burner, they could be removed entirely from possible consideration.

* * * * *

Are we really powerless in the global marketplace? Have governments truly lost their sovereignty in the face of globally wandering capital and wickedly clever currency traders? There are many who would have us believe this. Typical of this school of thought is Walter Wriston, former chairman of Citicorp, who writes, "The new world financial market is not a geographical location to be found on a map but, rather, more than two hundred thousand electronic monitors in trading rooms all over the world that are linked together. With the new technology no one is in control."[16] Wriston attributes this to the unstoppable forces of technological advancement: "[T]his new system was not built by politicians, economists, central bankers or finance ministers. No high-level international conference produced a master plan. The new system was built by technology."[17] Or as new-age guru Jeremy Rifkin puts it: "The Information Age has arrived. In the years ahead, new, more sophisticated software technologies are going to bring civilization ever closer to a near-workerless world.... The wholesale substitution of machines for workers is going to force every nation to rethink the role of human beings in the social process."[18] (What in the world does Rifkin mean when he talks of the need to "rethink the role of human beings in the social process"? Is Rifkin thinking we could perhaps remove human beings from the social process or assign them a more marginal role? What is the "social process" other than human society?)

While it sounds as if we're entering a brand-new, globalized techno-world, how much has really changed? Are we really in uncharted waters or just paddling through familiar waters in a fancy new boat, decked out with lots of new gadgets? In fact, the globalization of international finance is not a new phenomenon. It is rather a throwback to an earlier time. This is acknowledged by even enthusiastic advocates of the power of global markets, such as the well-known British magazine *The Economist.* In an article titled "Back to the Future," *The Economist* notes, "Capital is certainly more mobile now than it was two or three decades ago, but by some measures it was just as mobile before the first world war. In relation to the size of economies, net capital flows across borders then were much bigger than they are now.... The international bond market, too, was just as active at the start of this century as it is now.... Today's free-flowing capital fits with the long-term pattern."[19]

Let's follow a little further what *The Economist* has to say on this, because it is very revealing: "The anomaly is not, as many believe, the current power of global finance, but the period from 1930 to 1970 when, to various degrees, capital controls and tight regulation insulated domestic financial markets and *gave governments more control over their domestic economies* [italics added]." Indeed, it was in response to the devastating Depression, starting with the 1929 stock market crash, that governments around the world began to assert their power to bring footloose capital under some degree of democratic control. Immediately after the Second World War, they established a new international financial system that gave governments, for the first time, considerable power over financial markets. With governments, rather than markets, flexing their muscles, the result was an agenda more geared to popular wishes, such as full employment and social programs.

That early postwar period was, in many ways, the Golden Age. But now it is gone; full employment seems out of the question, no matter how much the public might like it, and social programs just keep shrinking, no matter how much the public seems to want them. The question is why. What has happened? Can this change really be attributed to the "globalization of financial markets" when, as it turns out, financial markets were just as global at the turn of the century?

It's true that the technology is dramatically different now—although perhaps not as different as we sometimes assume. At the turn of the century, there were no computers, but international transactions could be made almost simultaneously after the completion of the first transatlantic cable in the 1860s.[20] This wasn't as fast or comprehensive as computer technology, but it did make virtually instant international financial transactions possible. Computer technology has now made it possible to move money even more quickly. But does it follow that the faster movement makes it impossible to control money? On the contrary, there's a flipside to this computer wizardry that is almost always omitted from discussions about the new techno-world of global finance: *the very technology that makes it possible to move money more quickly than ever before also makes it possible to trace that movement more easily than ever before.* This is crucial to the issue of regulation. If the movement of money can be traced, it can be monitored and regulated. Eric Helleiner, a Canadian political scientist who specializes in global finance, says the case can be made that "[i]nformation technology strengthens rather than weakens state regulatory capacity in the financial sector."[21]

In other words, there is no reason—from a technological point of view—that international capital markets can't be regulated, as they were in the early postwar years. Indeed, if anything, it would probably be easier to regulate them now, because computers have made comprehensive tracking possible. The real problem, according to Helleiner and others, is not the technology but the unwillingness of governments to apply it to the task. Helleiner notes, "States have made little effort to use information technologies to control finance in the contemporary age." Interestingly, in the few instances where they have used it—such as in attempts to track money laundering by organized crime—the results have been impressive.

Which brings us to the key point of this chapter: the obstacles preventing us from gaining control over our economic lives have little to do with globalization and technology. The real obstacle is political. Governments have backed off from taking action to fight unemployment and provide well-funded social programs not because they lack the means but because they've chosen to render themselves impotent, powerless in the face of capital markets. The technological imperative turns out to be mostly a failure of will on the part of governments.

It might be useful to also draw attention quickly to one more important notion: namely, that the fundamental clash in economic policy debates today is much the same as it always has been. For all the changes in technology and the growing complexity of the language in our economic dialogue, the truth is that economic debate—and what is at stake—has changed surprisingly little. The essence of what's being debated remains fundamentally the same.

Here, then, is a shorthand version of the debate, to act as an easy guide in the coming chapters. There are basically two key items being continually fought over—whether money will be tight or loose, and how much government will redistribute resources, through social spending and taxation.

The first item, commonly referred to as "monetary policy," centres on how much a government will act to protect a nation's currency from inflation. Monetary policy is generally carried out by a nation's central bank, primarily through its power to influence interest rates in the country. If the central bank is primarily concerned with keeping inflation low, it will raise interest rates whenever it fears inflation. This will kill the inflation, but will also generally slow down the economy, throwing people out of work. Thus, a "tight" or "sound" monetary policy is generally favoured by those keen to protect the value of their financial assets from being eroded by inflation. (This is usually something of concern mostly to people with lots of financial assets—that is, rich people.) A "looser" money policy gives a higher priority to jobs, and therefore to keeping interest rates low. (This is usually favoured by people who are more concerned about having a job than about protecting the value of their financial assets—that is, most ordinary people.)

The second item, which comes under "fiscal policy," refers to how much the government will provide in social programs and who will bear the tax burden of paying for these programs. Since many social programs offer the largest benefits to those with the least resources and are financed by taxes paid by all, it is easy to see why high social spending is generally opposed by the well-to-do and favoured by the less well-to-do. Indeed, it is easy to see how society divides into opposing camps on these two issues. The rich generally benefit from tight money and low social spending. The non-rich—or the rest of society—generally benefit from looser money and higher social spending. The position favoured by the first camp has sometimes been identified as "right-wing," the second as "left-wing," although we could just as easily call them the "market" position and the "popular" position.

It has become fashionable to dismiss the very notion of such a debate. We are told the right/left split is no longer valid or relevant in the age of the global economy. While I have no attachment to labels like "right" and "left," I think the attempt to dismiss the labels is often also an attempt to reject the ideas behind them. It amounts to a denial of a real difference between the two positions, a denial that one position favours the rich while the other favours the non-rich. This attitude goes so far as to deny that there is any validity to the "left" or "popular" position; it even denies that looser money and higher social spending would actually benefit ordinary members of society. Such policies are being discarded, so the position states, not because the rich have managed to get their way, but because these policies are no longer relevant in the global marketplace, and they don't benefit ordinary people anyway.

Thus, in the global economy, there is only one valid position, and it is the position traditionally known as "right-wing." But now it's been stripped of that "right-wing" label, since there is no "left wing" any more to distinguish it from. This position is now simply called "pragmatic," "realistic," in line with the "realities" of the global marketplace. What used to be seen as "right wing" is now simply the reality. Policies that used to be clearly understood to favour the rich—policies that the rich have been pushing aggressively since time immemorial—are now presented as pragmatic and in everyone's interests.

The success of this position is reflected in the fact that a significant chunk of the public—including many who are far from rich—now believe that their interests lie in supporting the market agenda. In recent years, even social democratic parties, which purport to represent the common person, have keenly adopted the market agenda once they've attained power. Indeed, the spectrum of political debate has narrowed to the point that virtually any party in power these days seems to adopt it—despite the fact that the market agenda has delivered few concrete gains for ordinary people. While banks and stockholders have reaped handsome rewards, the economic well-being of the average Canadian has actually deteriorated over the past ten years, and most Canadians feel highly vulnerable about their future economic prospects.[22]

The willingness of the public to tolerate these deteriorating conditions has a great deal to do with the cult of impotence. It's not that people are glad to see themselves squeezed financially and their children unable to find jobs. It's not that they feel a quiver of pride at the thought of Canadian banks earning billions of dollars and being able to compete in the big leagues of international banking. It's rather that they feel powerless to do anything about this reordering of political power and wealth in the country.

This has some startling implications for democracy. A crucial difference between the current century and the last one has been the rise of mass democracy, creating the possibility that governments would act on behalf of the interests of the majority, not simply, as in the past, on behalf of the interests of the rich. This exciting democratic breakthrough explains much of what happened in the early postwar years. But now this possibility is being shut down. Policies from the "popular" agenda, such as full employment and generous social programs, are dismissed as out of date, impractical, no longer possible. Governments are seen as impotent to deliver them. Governments are apparently only able to deliver policies from the other agenda, the pragmatic one.

This has involved a massive selling job, convincing people that although governments technically may have the power to implement the "popular" agenda, they can't actually do so. Ultimately, the case for this democratic impotence rests on the awesome power of financial capital and its ability to flee from a country implementing these sorts of "popular" policies. It is essentially a threat, the promise of a final mechanism to force countries to do as financial markets want. But there is also a softer line of attack, a theoretical argument, which tries to make the same case by persuasion. The case—that governments are powerless to impose "popular" policies—thus rests on both the threat and the theory.

Endnotes

1   Dudley, William. 1994. "Budget Blues: Belgium, Canada, Italy and Sweden." *Goldman Sachs International* (Sept. 16).

2   Editorial. 1997. "Ignoring the Debt Leaves us Vulnerable in the Future." *Financial Post* (June 27).

3   Editorial. 1997. "The Deficit is Dead, Now Slay Taxes." *Globe and Mail* (May 5). See also Editorial. 1997. "Shed Unwanted Debt, Painlessly." *Globe and Mail* (May 20). Rubin, Jeff. 1997. "What Will Federal Budget Balances Look Like over the Next Mandate?" *Monthly Indicators*. CIBC Wood Gundy. Economics (May 7). Geddes, John. 1997. "Relief is Just a Mandate Away." *Financial Post* (March 22).

4   *Budget Plan*. 1996. Ottawa: Department of Finance. (March 6). Chart 1.4. p. 12.

5   McCallum, John. 1997. "Fiscal Dividend." Royal Bank of Canada (Sept. 30).

6   *Budget Plan*. 1995. Ottawa: Department of Finance. (Feb. 27), p. 9.

7   Some, of course, argue that it was high social spending that caused the deficit. For a rebuttal of this, see my *Shooting the Hippo: Death by Deficit and Other Canadian Myths*. 1995. Toronto: Viking.

8   Greenspon, Edward and Hugh Winsor. 1997. "Spending Increase Favoured, Polls Finds; Jobs, Health Care

Given Priority over Deficit-Cutting or Tax Reduction." *Globe and Mail* (Jan. 23), p. A1. In the fall of 1997, an Angus Reid poll, done in conjunction with *The Globe and Mail,* seemed to contradict the Environics finding, suggesting that debt reduction and taxes were the top fiscal goals of Canadians (Feschuk, Scott. 1997. "Cutting Debt, Taxes Top Canadians' List." *Globe and Mail* (Nov. 1). However, the nature of the questions asked in the Angus Reid poll might explain the result. Canadians were asked about their support for "spending more on government programs," which sounded like initiating new spending, something that worries many Canadians concerned about deficit problems in the future. When asked instead about *restoring* government programs, support seemed to be much stronger. As the *Globe* noted, "A solid majority—71 percent—said Ottawa should restore provincial funding that was cut as part of the deficit fighting campaign rather than embark on the creation of new drug-insurance or home-care programs, both of which have been cited as Liberal goals for the current mandate." Furthermore, the Angus Reid poll found that "55 percent also contended that the federal government caused too much pain across the country by cutting too deeply in its bid to eliminate the budget shortfall." Another poll that same month by Ekos Research Associates, done for the federal Human Resources Department, reinforced the Environics results, showing strong public support for spending the fiscal dividend on child poverty, unemployment and health care above debt reduction or cutting taxes. Edward Greenspon. 1997. "Ottawa Advised to Stress Welfare of Children." *Globe and Mail.* (Nov. 10). The *Globe* story quoted Ekos president Frank Graves criticizing the Angus Reid poll for failing to distinguish between different types of spending.

9   Martin, Paul. 1997. "Pamela Wallin." CBC Newsworld (Oct. 23), p. 11

10 Angell, Ian. 1996. Interviewed on "Sunday Morning." CBC Radio (Dec. 1).

11 Osberg, Lars. 1996. "The pyramiding costs of excess unemployment." Unpublished paper. Department of Economics. Dalhousie University, Halifax.

12 Wier, Stuart Kirkland. 1996. "Insight from Geometry and Physics into the Construction of Egyptian Old Kingdom Pyramids." *Cambridge Archaeological Journal* (Vol. 6), pp. 150–63.

13 Greenspon, Edward and Anthony Wilson-Smith. 1996. *Double Vision: The Inside Story of the Liberals in Power.* Toronto: Doubleday Canada.

14 Schmidt, Sarah. 1997. "Much ado about the MAI." *The Varsity* (Nov. 11).

15 Gwyn, Richard. 1997. "Investment deal a threat to our economic nationalism." *Toronto Star* (Nov. 23). See also "Oh, MAI!" *Left Business Observer* (#79, Sept. 29, 1997).

16 Wriston, Walter. 1992. *The Twilight of Sovereignty.* New York: MacMillan, p. 61.

17 *Ibid,* p. 59.

18 Rifkin, Jeremy. 1995. *The End of Work: The Decline of the Global Labor Force and the Dawn of the Post-Market Era.* New York: G.P. Putnam's Sons, p. xv.

19 "Back to the Future." *The Economist* (Oct. 7, 1995). See also, Hirst, Paul and Grahame Thompson. 1996. *Globalization in Question: The International Economy and Possibilities for Governance.* Cambridge, U.K.: Polity Press, pp. 26–31.

20 For an interesting discussion of the speed difference between telegraph and computer technology, see Wyrsch, Gerard. 1992. "Treasury Regulation of International Wire Transfer and Money Laundering: A Case for a Permanent Moratorium." *Denver Journal of International Law and Policy* (Vol. 20, No. 3, Spring), pp. 515–35. See also *op. cit, Globalization in Question.* p. 9; and Blinder, Alan S. and Richard E. Quandt. 1997. "The Computer and the Economy." *The Atlantic Monthly* (December).

21 Helleiner, Eric. 1999. "Sovereignty, Territoriality and the Globalization of Finance." In Smith, D., D. Solinger and S. Topik (eds.). *States and Sovereignty in the Global Economy.*

22 Fortin, Pierre. 1996. "The Great Canadian Slump." *The Canadian Journal of Economics* (Vol. 29, No. 4, Nov.). See also Sharpe, Andrew. 1997. *Perspectives on Federal Fiscal Policy in the 1990s and Beyond.* (Ottawa: Centre for the Study of Living Standards, Sept. 22).

SECTION I: UNDERSTANDING GLOBALIZATION

Critical Thinking Questions

Chapter 1: A Critique of the Sceptics, Gary Teeple

1. Discuss different definitions of globalization that you have encountered over the past few years. Has Teeple's article changed how you conceptualize globalization?

2. What evidence can be used to argue both for and against the existence of globalization as a real contemporary phenomenon?

3. Identify some of the consequences for Canadian workers that begin to emerge from Teeple's discussion of different dimensions of globalization. How can these negative outcomes be altered?

Chapter 2: Introduction to the Cult, Linda McQuaig

1. What are some of the key aspects of the cult of impotence? How has this cult been constructed?

2. Discuss how the cult of impotence affects the daily lives of Canadian workers and their families.

3. How can the cult of impotence that has taken hold in Canadian political circles be eradicated? What groups in society would resist the elimination of this myth of powerlessness?

Recommended Readings

Carroll, William K. 2004. *Corporate Power in a Globalizing World: A Study in Elite Social Organization.* Toronto: Oxford University Press. An exploration of the Canadian corporate network in the late 20th century and of the power it wields to both fundamentally shape the financial and political terrain in Canada and influence the reconfiguration of global capitalism.

Clarkson, Stephen. 2002. *Uncle Sam and Us: Globalization, Neoconservatism and the Canadian State.* Toronto: University of Toronto Press. An examination of the impact of North American free-trade agreements on the direction of Canadian governance and on various social, labour, environmental and cultural policies.

Held, David and Anthony McGrew (eds.). 2003. *The Global Transformations Reader: An Introduction to the Globalization Debate* 2nd ed. Oxford: Polity Press. A large collection of articles from different perspectives on various themes relating to globalization.

Petras, James and Henry Veltmeyer. 2001. *Globalization Unmasked: Imperialism in the Tenty-first Century.* Halifax: Fernwood Publishing. An analysis that connects globalization to new forms of imperialism, and starkly unveils the power of dominant classes to maintain and extend their power on a global scale.

Tabb, William K. 2001. *The Amoral Elephant: Globalization and the Struggle for Social Justice in the Twenty-First Century.* New York: Monthly Review Press. A critique of neo-liberal globalization that challenges arguments about science and technology as the foundation of the new economic order and points instead to political interests and decision-making.

Teeple, Gary. 2000. *Globalization and the Decline of Social Reform: Into the Twenty-First Century.* Aurora: Garamond Press. A detailed analysis of the rise and development of the Keynesian welfare state in the postwar period, and of its decline under neo-liberalism and globalization over the past three decades.

Related Websites

Canadian Centre for Policy Alternatives

http://www.policyalternatives.ca/

The Canadian Centre for Policy Alternatives is a progressive independent research institute concerned with issues of social and economic justice. It has produced numerous studies on topics related to globalization such as the North American Free Trade Agreement, the World Trade Organization, the World Bank and the International Monetary Fund.

Council of Canadians

http://www.canadians.org

The Council of Canadians is a citizens' watchdog organization that advocates for Canadian economic sovereignty. It runs national campaigns and publishes reports on various public policy topics, including Canada-U.S. relations.

Global Policy Forum

http://www.globalpolicy.org/globaliz/index.htm

The Global Policy Forum provides information on a broad range of issues that are addressed at the United Nations. The site includes a section on globalization that is broken down into several topics.

One World Action

http://www.oneworldaction.org/

One World Action provides assistance to organizations committed to strengthening the democratic process and improving people's lives in poor and developing countries. The website includes numerous publications on issues related to globalization.

World Social Forum

http://www.forumsocialmundial.org.br/index.php?cd_language=2

The World Social Forum provides a venue for critical discussions on neo-liberalism. The website includes a "Library of Alternatives" section that contains documents on issues pertaining to globalization.

Section II

Post-Fordism at Work

WORK SPECIALISTS FROM a variety of disciplines have been interested by significant changes to the workplace introduced by employers since the 1970s in a bid to remain competitive and profitable in the global order. Many have argued that this transformation can best be described as a shift from Fordist methods of work organization, which rely on rigid and standardized principles of scientific management and managerial control, to post-Fordist methods of work organization, which are based on flexibility, fluidity, and worker empowerment. Each article in this section of the book examines a type of Canadian workplace—one blue-collar, one white-collar—to assess the extent of changes that post-Fordist methods of production, variably labelled lean production, flexible specialization, Japanization, or total quality management, have brought to the structure and social relations of the workplace.

Wayne Lewchuk and David Robertson's article deals with the fundamental issue of worker empowerment in contemporary workplaces that have adopted lean production systems. The authors are critical of studies that accept the managerial perspective that these new methods of work organization are a significant improvement over Fordist methods of production because they have led to greater control and have enhanced the quality of worklife for workers. Lewchuk and Robertson are particularly interested in uncovering workers' own perceptions of their degree of empowerment under lean production systems. The article reports on data collected during the mid-1990s on vehicle assembly workers as part of a larger study that surveyed Canadian automobile workers employed by Ford, Chrysler, General Motors, and CAMI (a joint GM Suzuki initiative). Because these four car and truck manufacturers were at different stages in the transition to lean production when the research was conducted, the authors were able to provide a comparative analysis of worker empowerment in plants that are more advanced in their implementation of lean systems and in plants that have retained more traditional methods of work organization. Lewchuk and Robertson's analysis reveals that motor vehicle workers have not experienced empowerment. The majority surveyed were not able to modify their jobs, vary their pace of work, or leave their workstation to deal with personal matters. For the authors, the finding that perhaps most strongly contradicts arguments about the benefits of lean production is that workers in plants more advanced in implementing lean production techniques reported the least empowerment and the greatest increase in managerial control. Lewchuk and Robertson conclude that lean production does not seem to be a system geared towards eradicating the social and health problems commonly associated with Fordism, and may instead actually worsen them.

The contribution by Bonnie Fox and Pamela Sugiman also provides insights into dimensions of workplace transformation, but the focus is on the restructuring of the work of clerical employees in the billing department of a major telecommunications company in Toronto. The authors are critical of assumptions in the literature that managers tend to apply flexible specialization (or functional flexibility) and numerical flexibility to different parts of the labour force. Fox and Sugiman's detailed case study shows that, following the introduction of computer technology, management adopted various principles of total quality management, such as flattening the occupational structure, implementing employee incentive schemes, organizing workers into teams, introducing job rotation, and shifting certain managerial functions to workers. A concomitant shift also occurred in the employment structure whereby an increasing number of workers were hired on a part-time and temporary basis, and most of these workers were young and of diverse ethnic and racial origins. Fox and Sugiman's research reveals that while management strategies are used in combination in attempts to intensify control of the work process and of workers, these strategies are not always rational, well planned, consistent, or effective. Indeed, the combination of functional and numerical flexibility strategies, and workers' reactions to these managerial strategies, led to unexpected and contradictory outcomes. Fox and Sugiman's research highlights the complexity of workplace restructuring for worker–management relations, but also for relations among employees who are diverse in terms of gender, employment status, and ethnic and racial backgrounds. They conclude that workers have become more conscious of, and angry at, their exploitation because of the contradictions in their jobs, but that new divisions and growing tensions among workers serve to mediate these class-based relations.

CHAPTER 3

Listening to Workers:

The Reorganization of Work in the Canadian Motor Vehicle Industry[1]

Wayne Lewchuk and David Robertson

Introduction

SINCE 1994, THE CANADIAN Auto Workers (CAW) union has been the sponsor of one of the largest studies ever done on worker attitudes to work reorganization.[2] It represents the most recent chapter in a decade-long process during which the CAW developed one of the most uncompromising positions on work reorganization of any union in the industry.[3] It has openly challenged many of the trends in workplace reorganization, and in particular lean production systems, arguing they lead neither to more democratic workplaces nor to better working conditions.

The CAW has resisted the introduction of teams, contingent pay schemes, and job rotation where they are judged not in the interest of workers, and defended both the Annual Improvement Factor and the Cost of Living Agreements that were the cornerstones of the postwar labour truce. This chapter will examine what workers who assemble cars and trucks have to say about new models of work organization.[4]

The data are drawn from a benchmarking project which surveyed thousands of Canadian automobile workers employed by Ford, Chrysler, General Motors, and CAMI (a joint GM Suzuki initiative). Workers, all organized by the CAW, were asked a wide range of questions about their workload, health and safety conditions, empowerment, and relations with management. In what follows, only the data collected from the 2,424 vehicle assembly workers employed at nine different worksites are used. It provides a rare snapshot of what workers themselves think about their working conditions and their own degree of empowerment, and enables the chapter to cover the following areas.

First, the chapter reports what workers are

saying about their ability to make decisions that might influence their quality of worklife. Second, the chapter examines what it is like to work in plants organized according to the principles of lean production. Third, because the four companies are at different stages in the implementation of lean production practices, the chapter can compare empowerment in lean plants with that in more traditionally organized plants.

The methodology employed is a response to the increased use of benchmarking as a management tool for achieving what has come to be known as "world class" manufacturing practices.[5]

In a recent publication, *The Economist Intelligence Unit* defined benchmarking as "a process of continuous improvement in the search for competitive advantage. It measures a company's products, services and practices against those of its competitors or other acknowledged leaders in their fields."

Benchmarking provides concrete and detailed information about how one operation or aspect of a company's performance stacks up against similar operations at other workplaces anywhere in the world. The limitation of most benchmarking studies is that they rarely, if ever, ask workers about their working conditions, and more often than not they ignore one side of the production equation: the well-being of those involved in the operations. Benchmarks in some aspect of a company's operations, which can only be achieved through practices that undermine safety or lead to a deterioration in working conditions, are of questionable social value. The benefits of achieving "world class" manufacturing practice are minimal if the result is that excessive demands are put on workers' time

and energy to the point where workers can no longer fully participate in either family life or social life in general. The advantage of benchmarking studies that include the perspective of workers has been taken up by several other industrial unions (e.g.,United Steelworkers of America (USWA), Communiations, Energy, and Paperworkers Union of Canada (CEP), Union of Needletrades, Industrial, and Textile Employees (UNITE)) with the assistance of the Ontario Federation of Labour.[6]

The Work Organization Debate: Why Has Empowerment Become a Management Issue?

The negative social and health effects of the Fordist model of work organization have long been recognized. Workplace alienation became the rallying call of a new generation of post-1945 critics, but it was actually pre-World War I Ford managers who first appreciated the implications of the new model of work organization.[7] Conscious of a growing revolt among its workforce, management mounted an extensive campaign to convince its largely male workers that repetitive and monotonous work, stripped of most decision-making authority and planning responsibility, was still rewarding and manly.[8]

The recent work of Karasek and Theorell, which links low decision-making Fordist jobs with stress-related heart diseases, confirms what Detroit doctors in the 1930s already sensed: Fordist working conditions could be bad for your health.[9]

The "Ford flu" was defined as an illness brought on by the unique combination of heavy workloads, severe job insecurity, and limited control over the pace and rhythm of work. However, as long as the Fordist system was assumed to be a more efficient way of producing goods, the calls for change and for humanizing the labour process went largely unheeded.[10] It was widely accepted that boring and monotonous work was the price some people in society had to pay so that all could enjoy a higher standard of material well-being.

The recent competitive edge enjoyed by manufacturers based in Japan has led a growing number of analysts to reassess Fordism's assumed productive superiority. The Fordist production system is increasingly viewed as cumbersome, inefficient, unable to respond rapidly to changing consumer tastes, and wasteful of the creative potential of production workers.[11]

It is now widely believed that organizations will only survive if they implement more flexible forms of work organization that break down the rigid Fordist hierarchy of decision-makers and production workers. The lean production model is being promoted as a solution to these productivity problems. While there is much debate over exactly what constitutes a lean production system, the following four principles capture most of what is alleged to be unique about it:

1 design of products with an eye towards manufacturability;

2 use of more flexible machinery;[12]

3 reorganization of the manufacturing process to reduce inventories and improve product flows; and

4 reorganization of work to make better use of labour's knowledge of the production process.

Williams et al. have already made a convincing case that at least the first three of these characteristics are not unique to lean production, but were first put into practice by Henry Ford prior to 1920.[13] At best, Toyota rediscovered what had been forgotten in the West. The last characteristic, the better use of labour's knowledge, does mark a potential difference between Fordism and lean production. Womack et al. go so far as to claim that it is the main advantage of lean production in the search for improved productivity.[14]

The debate over lean production and worker empowerment is more than a debate over how to produce goods more efficiently. The promoters of lean production also see empowerment as a solution to the social and health problems associated with Fordism.

A model of work organization that is both more productive and reduces social and health problems would truly be an advance. Even the most ardent supporters of lean production are not suggesting that it fully reintegrates workers into the complex process of designing vehicles, selecting machinery, or coordinating the production process. But they are making claims that workers will have the authority to make decisions that directly affect how they work and, in the process, improve the quality of their work life. Given the global impact of the work of Womack et al., it is worth quoting them at some length:

> Most people—including so-called blue-collar workers—will find their jobs more challenging as lean production spreads.... [It] provides workers with the skills they need to control their work environment and the continuing challenge of making work go more smoothly.... Lean production offers

a creative tension in which workers have many ways to address challenges. This creative tension involved in solving complex problems is precisely what separated manual factory work from professional "think" work in the age of mass production ... By the end of the century we expect that lean-assembly plants will be populated almost entirely by highly skilled problem solvers whose task will be to think continually of ways to make the system run more smoothly and productively.[15]

Kenney and Florida have written about the introduction of lean production work organization in the United States. They are equally enthusiastic about the potential impact of lean production to involve workers in decision-making, although they are more guarded about its impact on the quality of working life. They write:

Japan is at the cusp of a new model of production organization that mobilizes workers' intelligence as well as physical skill.... The cornerstone of innovation-mediated production lies in the harnessing of workers' intelligence and knowledge of production.... The underlying organizational feature is the self-managing work team that enhances the functional integration of tasks.... The main objective of the Japanese system of work organization is to harness the collective intelligence of workers as a source of continuous product and process improvement.... Workers at the transplants, especially Honda and Toyota, have significant input into the design of their jobs.[16]

Evidence Supporting the Claims Made by Supporters of Lean Production

Those who put forward the hypothesis that lean production will enhance the quality of working life, or even give workers the authority to make decisions that might improve their jobs, are making statements of faith rather than tested propositions. While the social and health problems associated with Fordism are indisputable, the ability of lean production to correct these ills has yet to be shown. In fact, there is a growing body of literature that raises serious doubts about the alleged positive impact of lean production on the quality of working life.

Jane Parker and Mike Slaughter were among the first to raise these concerns.[17] Further studies of the Canadian CAMI plant, the Michigan Mazda plant, the British Nissan plant, and the Subaru-Isuzu plant in Indiana all contend that in many cases workers are worse off under lean production.[18]

In another study sponsored by the CAW, 1,670 workers employed at 16 different suppliers of automobile components were surveyed. It found no support for the hypothesis that lean production empowered workers or improved the quality of working life. If anything, the two lean plants scored significantly worse on many of the indicators of good working conditions, including empowerment.[19]

Workers at lean plants were significantly more likely to report that it was difficult to get time off from work or leave their workstation to go to the washroom. They reported that management had increased the level of surveillance over workers in the last two years. Compared with workers in traditionally organized Fordist plants, workers at lean plants were twice as likely to report having too little time for the work assigned and significantly more likely to say their work-pace was too fast, and that there were too few people to do the work.[20]

In another Canadian study, Colette Murphy and Doug Olthuis surveyed workers employed by a major parts supplier to CAMI. They concluded that in the CAMI department workers actually reported less cooperation between workers than in traditional departments, raising doubts about the potential of teamwork. They also reported that, while the quality of work life reported by CAMI workers was superior to that reported by welders working in traditionally organized departments, it was about the same as that reported by workers in other job classifications working in traditionally organized departments.[21]

Steve Babson surveyed 2,400 workers at the Mazda assembly plant in Flat Rock, Michigan. Far from finding that the organization of work at Mazda empowered workers, it would seem that, by design, Mazda management has created a system that tightly controls workers. The management rights clause in the collective agreement clearly establishes the company's exclusive right to "direct and control ... the methods, processes and means of handling work."[22]

Each worker is also provided with a Programmed Work Sheet that defines each job in minute detail, including the tasks to be performed, their sequence, and the number of seconds allotted for each task. Deviation from this planned worked sequence is discouraged, as consistency in following the Work Sheet is seen to ensure quality.[23] Babson concluded that, in a limited sense, the span of responsibility of Mazda workers had increased through their participation in the kaizen process.[24] However, rather than this allowing workers to

proactively control their work environment, participation was structured by managers in such a way that they, not workers, controlled the process. Babson concluded, "Where the MIT study sees a 'creative tension' that makes work 'humanly fulfilling,' many workers at Mazda experience tension, pure and simple."[25]

Garrahan and Stewart interviewed workers employed at Nissan's new assembly plant in Britain. Their research revealed that at Nissan the definition of skill, and the implied need to make decisions, had been turned on its head. Skill was defined as being able to do the job correctly, and that this was most likely if workers carefully followed the standard operations guidelines determined by management. Rather than exercising creativity, the essence of skill, workers were moulded into a reactive environment, responding to the needs of the line and technology.[26]

The plant makes use of teams, but they were not a mechanism through which workers could exercise some control over their work environment. Instead, "Teamworking ... is a process in which workers control one another's actions. It is this that gives to the autocratic internal regime a spurious air of employee participation and control in work. It is not, however, the kind of control that leads to employee empowerment at work, but rather to forms of self-control and peer control that inhibit individual development and control of work."[27]

Work Reorganization and the Quality of Worklife in Canadian Vehicle Assembly Plants

Research into the actual impact of lean production on worker empowerment and the quality of working life raises serious doubts about the rosy predictions of authors such as Womack et al. The remainder of this chapter will focus on the narrow question: do new forms of work organization enhance individual worker control over their immediate work environment in a way which allows them to enhance the quality of their working life?

The Canadian motor vehicle industry is dominated by American-based producers, although there has been a recent influx of Japanese assemblers. As a result of the 1965 Canada-U.S. Auto Pact, the Canadian automobile industry is fully integrated into the larger North American vehicle market. All of the plants in this study manufacture for a North American market, as distinct from a Canadian market. Over the last decade, the Canadian assemblers have also had to adjust to the changes associated with the passage of the Canada-U.S. Free Trade Agreement in 1989 and the North American Free Trade Agreement in 1993. Each of these agreements changed the rules regarding local content and duty remission, and further exposed Canadian assemblers to competitive pressures.

Management has responded by investing in new capital equipment, tightening up work practices, and experimenting with various forms of work reorganization.[28] Most of these changes have been guided by the philosophy of lean production. External to the workplace, all four companies have moved aggressively to rationalize their supplier base, force suppliers to cut costs, reduce the number of first-tier suppliers, rely on suppliers for more of the design and innovation function, and contract out major sub-components.[29]

Internal to the workplace, management has searched for ways to reduce buffers and work in progress, remove surplus labour, implement just-in-time (JIT) systems, promote continuous improvement, and make better use of worker

knowledge of the production process. The main interest of this chapter is the internal changes in work practices. Below, more detail is provided on the attempts at each company to internally reorganize, using the principles of lean production with a focus on differences between the four companies.

The system of lean production at CAMI, a joint venture of General Motors (GM) and Suzuki, is well known from the series of studies conducted by the CAW.[30] CAMI was a green field site which was intended to be a laboratory for the implementation of Japanese work systems in North America. Workers came to CAMI with the expectation that work would be different than in a traditionally organized Fordist assembly plant. They expected CAMI would offer a participative work environment and an opportunity to learn a number of jobs as a way of avoiding some of the negative effects of line work.

Workers were to have some control over how to design jobs. They were to do inspection, recommend product and process design changes, and improve job layouts as they worked on the job. The reality is different. Workers have little real power, and soon came to realize that kaizen led to workers speeding themselves up, rather than improving their quality of work life.

Workers are organized into "teams," but the teams have little authority. Most of the decisions are made in advance by industrial engineering. The plant is organized by the CAW and, as the result of a number of rounds of negotiations, including a recent strike, there are a number of practices designed to protect workers from autocratic managerial decision-making. The workplace that promised to give workers the right to design their own work has agreed to a union time study person to protect workers from unilateral management attempts to change their jobs. GM has made significant strides in converting its traditionally organized plants to operations based on the lean production philosophy. These changes began in the late 1980s under the name "Synchronous Manufacturing." GM documents openly refer to their drive to implement lean manufacturing. During the early 1990s, management moved aggressively to reduce staffing levels and maximize the use of available time. They promoted the use of Andon Boards for process control, pull systems to discipline the delivery of parts, material supermarkets, material card pull systems, visual line balancing processes (also referred to as the "wall"), just-in-time production, flexible work cells, and best people practices. The latter are supposed to involve employees in establishing the best practices for an operation. More often than not, it means speeding up the production process to meet the goals of loading jobs as close to 100% as possible and increasing the percentage of value-added time.

Chrysler has been less aggressive in pushing lean production in Canada, in part because the demand for its product at its largest Canadian facility, the Windsor Mini-Van plant, exceeds supply. This does not mean that Chrysler has been unaffected by the managerial interest in lean production. The Chrysler Operating System charts out a strategy to reorganize all Chrysler operations around the principles of lean production. For the time being, however, Chrysler has opted to move more slowly than GM or CAMI.

Management at Chrysler talk openly about the desire to "empower" the workforce, and one concrete step in this direction has been the reduction in levels of supervision over the last ten years. At Bramalea, a number of significant changes have been made. Management has made use of CORE groups. These consist of bargaining unit jobs, allocated by seniority, which help with product launches and working the bugs out of work-stations. They have also set up a system to facilitate Employee Assistance Requests, referred to as EAR cribs, which are supposed to take worker suggestions and implement them.

Management retains the right to vet suggestions and prioritize which ones should be pursued, leading to some conflict between using available EAR resources to make jobs better for workers versus using them to increase production and reduce the number of workers. Electronic monitoring also plays a role in increasing managerial control and increasing production, as does industrial engineering, which remains a critical management tool for setting work standards.

At the Chrysler Mini-Van plant in Windsor, the principles of lean production are being adopted slowly. Management has plans to change the culture of the plant and to shade the line between management and workers, but, given the solid market for mini-vans, there is no need to rush things. One person we interviewed argued, "In the 1960s, management forced their way to get where they wanted; they don't force any more. They win your heart and soul, they involve you more.... It is a different way of doing business."

There is a lot of talk about empowering workers, of letting the workers manage the place. "Working-together meetings" are held on a regular basis throughout the plant. Once a week, at the same time and in the same place, production workers, production coordinators, inspectors, supervisors and management come together to talk about problems and to allow management to communicate with shop floor workers.

Over 40 new communication centres are being constructed. Located directly on the shop floor, they are currently used as lunch areas. Each is located near a panel of information boards, each is equipped with a TV monitor, and it is not hard to see these as future team meeting locations.

At Ford, the push toward lean production is spelled out in the Ford 2000 program. However, the one Ford plant from which data are drawn for this chapter was also the least lean site we visited. Part of the plant was retooled in 1990, but much of the technology is of an older vintage. Cars are assembled on frames, using a drag line and doors on assembly. The kanban system[31] is not in use, kaizen is not practised, nor are there visual guides to help management keep track of production.

Reduction of the labour complement, while holding output constant, was still a management objective, as it was at plants that had adopted more of the lean management philosophy. The target for 1995 was the reduction of 167 workers out of a total workforce of 2,700.

Industrial engineering plays an important role in maintaining workloads. Process sheets are developed for each job and then externally determined time standards are applied to give a time for the job. Despite the minimal shift towards lean production, there were still changes. Management had backed off from its confrontational threatening approach to engage in what was described as a more cooperative style of problem-solving.

To some extent, all of the plants are lean. Externally, all companies are rationalizing their supplier bases and internally, all are experimenting with new forms of work organization. Having said this, there are two important qualifiers. First, some of the plants have been more successful in internally reorganizing the production process than others. We would argue that the CAMI and General Motors plants are the furthest along in implementing lean production, while the single Ford plant in the study has probably made the fewest changes. Second, none of the plants has adopted the human resource practices associated with lean production in Japan. Neither age-based nor merit-based pay systems have taken root in Canada. Nor are profit-sharing or bonus schemes employed.

The failure to make these changes does not reflect a lack of managerial interest in these policies. In the recent round of negotiations with the Big Three, management again pushed for their implementation but they were again rejected by the CAW and its members. Workers continue to be paid an hourly rate determined by the job they perform. At all plants, most job openings are allocated on the basis of seniority. Job rotation is only found at the CAMI plant, and teams are not very common.

Because many North American plants have not adopted the human resource practices of Japanese manufacturers, and because teams seem to have a less important role in North America, it has been suggested that North American plants are not really lean.[32] This creates a misleading impression of how lean production increases productivity. It suggests that, if only managers could be convinced to abandon traditional human resource methods and more fully implement lean principles, including teamwork and the blurring of lines of authority between managers and production workers, North American workplaces would be more productive and better places to work.

This ignores evidence to the contrary, at least as it applies to teams and other flexible human resource practices. In the Worldwide

Manufacturing Competitiveness Study, Oliver et al. followed a methodology similar to that used by the MIT researchers for *The Machine That Changed the World*.[33] This study, subtitled *The Second Lean Enterprise Report,* rather awkwardly found that high productivity was virtually uncorrelated with human resource policies intended to modify the attitude of workers towards their employers. They concluded: "The use of teams does not necessarily guarantee world-class performance, nor does their absence preclude it."[34]

The confusion over what makes a workplace lean can also be found in the recent work of Pil and MacDuffie, where lean work organization is equated with the implementation of flexible human resource practices.[35] Because Canadian plants have made less "progress" in adopting these practices than Japanese, or even American assemblers, Canadian plants are still described as Fordist. The problem with this analysis is that it fails to appreciate the subtle and nuanced changes in management practices taking place on shop floors, and the fact that the average Canadian plant has lower buffer stocks, higher productivity, and fewer quality defects than comparable American plants.[36]

The confusion as to what makes a workplace organization lean, and exactly what drives productivity in a modern manufacturing establishment, has been partially resolved by those trying to promote flexible human resources practices as the key. Oliver et al. concluded that success was based not on the innovative human resource practices found in Japan, but rather on process discipline and control.[37] This focus on control stands in sharp contradiction to the picture painted by supporters of lean production, who argue that authority will become more diffuse within the

organization and that workers will be empowered to improve their working lives. The Oliver study appears to argue quite the opposite. Successful lean plants are controlled plants; whether they empower workers is secondary.

Worker Views on Empowerment and the Quality of Working Life

The remainder of this chapter will analyze the responses from a survey of 2,424 workers employed in the Canadian vehicle assembly departments of CAMI, Chrysler, Ford, and General Motors. The data were collected during 1995.[38] Separate results are presented for direct production workers, most of whom work on the line or tend machines, and indirect production workers, many of whom are involved in material handling. The responses of male and female direct production workers are also reported separately.[39]

Caution, however, should be exercised in drawing conclusions from the comparisons of men and women in assembly plants, given the small number of women in some of the plants.[40]

It is important to place the debate over worker empowerment and lean production in context. As indicated above, not even the most ardent supporters of lean production are suggesting that this new system of work will result in a return to the level of worker empowerment enjoyed by skilled craft workers in the 19th century. There is, however, a strong suggestion that workers will participate in day-to-day problem solving, will have some influence over how they should perform their work, and through this will be able to enhance the quality of their working life. Hence the focus of this chapter is on day-to-day decisions over how and when work should be performed, rather than decisions over corporate policy, choice of technology, or product design.

Some of the questions are direct indicators of worker empowerment. Can workers change things they do not like about their jobs? Can they vary their work pace to conform to the changing rhythms of their bodies? Can workers leave their work-stations to go to the washroom or get time off work to attend to a sick child?

Other questions examine whether the work environment is conducive to workers' participating in decision-making, and provide indirect evidence of empowerment. Are workers so loaded with tasks that they have little time for anything else? How much of each day do they work as fast as they can just to keep up? How easy is it to communicate with other workers? Finally, we report responses to questions about training and whether management had increased performance monitoring. If workers respond that they have little authority to make decisions, are constantly working as fast as they can just to keep up, have little opportunity to communicate with other workers, and are monitored more closely, then the potential of lean production to enhance the quality of working life must be questioned. It would also raise doubts that empowerment is the driving force behind lean production plants producing more efficiently than traditional plants.

Table 3.1 provides some basic information on the characteristics of the workforces at the four companies. The only company that stands out as being different is CAMI, which employs more women, has a younger workforce, and has a greater percentage of direct production workers.

Direct Indicators of Worker Empowerment

A minimum level of empowerment would give workers some choice over how they work, the rhythm of work, and time off to attend to personal matters. This section of the chapter will look at four indicators of empowerment: 1) the ability to modify one's job, 2) the ability to vary the workpace, 3) the ability to leave one's workstation, and 4) the ability to get time off from work.

It is hard to conceptualize workers being empowered in a way that enhances the quality of working life unless they have some ability to change things they do not like about their jobs. As can be seen in Table 3.2, there is little evidence of worker empowerment at any of the four companies. Over 70 percent of all direct production workers at each company responded that it would be difficult to change things they did not like about their job. The differences between companies were relatively small, although workers at the two leanest

Table 3.1 Characteristics of Workforce by Company

	% Male	Average Age	% Direct Production Workers
General Motors	90	43	72
Chrysler	83	38	72
Ford	93	42	74
CAMI	77	33	80

companies, CAMI and GM, reported the greatest difficulty in changing things. This is exactly the opposite of what the proponents of lean production have argued.

Table 3.2 also looks at the responses of men and women working in assembly plants. Overall, women were marginally less likely to report that it was difficult to change things they did not like about their jobs, although the differences between men and women were relatively small. Given that, on average, women have much less seniority, just over eight years on average compared to almost 15 for male direct production workers, one might have expected women would have found it more difficult to change things they do not like about their jobs.

Table 3.2 also looks at the responses of indirect production workers who found it somewhat easier to change components of their jobs. The exception was CAMI, where indirects reported the least degree of empowerment. One of the surprising results of this research has been the extent to which indirect jobs, traditionally the job classifications into which older workers bid, have been negatively affected by new forms of work organization.

Another important indicator of empowerment is the ability to influence when work is done by varying the rhythm of work over the course of the day. Work by Karasek et al. has suggested that the ability to adjust workloads to the changing rhythms of one's body during the day is an important factor in reducing stress-related heart diseases. Overall, Table 3.3 does not indicate that recent work reorganization has resolved this problem for most workers, although there are some significant differences between companies and between direct and indirect workers.

While CAMI workers were the least likely to report they could modify their jobs, they were the most likely to report they could vary their workpace during the day. This may reflect the impact of job rotation within a team structure. Production workers at GM were the least likely to report they could vary their workpace. This is consistent with responses to other questions in the survey on workload. Almost 80 percent of direct production workers at GM reported their workload was too fast, and nearly 50 percent reported their workload was too heavy. GM workers were approximately twice as likely to report work was too fast or too heavy compared with direct production workers at the Ford assembly plant. The response of GM production workers suggests that a shift to lean production is not necessarily associated with more flexibility to control the rhythm of work over the course of a day.

Table 3.2 Workers Responding It Was Difficult to Change Things They Did not Like about Their Job (%)

	All Direct Production	Male Direct Production	Female Direct Production	All Indirect Production
Chrysler	72.02	74.55	60.19	66.39
GM	78.54	78.4	79.27	72.67
Ford	78.02	77.88	85.71	71.95
CAMI	79.76	81.82	72.22	90.48
TOTAL	76.22	77.18	70.05	70.84

Female direct production workers reported marginally less flexibility in adjusting the pace of work over the course of the day. The largest differences in male and female responses were found at Ford and Chrysler, the two companies that had made the least progress in internally reorganizing work practices. Not surprisingly, indirect production workers, who are much less likely to be machine-paced, reported significantly more flexibility in varying their workpace over the course of the day. However, nearly 50 percent of the entire sample of in-direct production workers still reported little flexibility in adjusting their work schedules. This is an indicator that, as lean production spreads, it ties even indirect workers to the as-sembly line's relentless control.

Tables 3.2 and 3.3 looked at two impor-tant aspects of empowerment as they pertain to working conditions: the ability to modify how work is done, and the flexibility to vary the rhythm of work. Another important aspect of worker empowerment is control over time itself, including the ability to leave a work-station to attend to personal matters such as going to the toilet, or getting time off work to attend to personal matters such as caring for a sick child or going to the doctor.

Table 3.4 examines the ability of vehicle assembly workers to find a relief replacement worker so they can leave their work-station to attend to personal matters such as going to the toilet. We look only at direct production work-ers, most of whom work on assembly lines and can only leave their work-stations if they find a relief worker. For almost two-thirds of the sample, it was difficult to find a relief worker to attend to personal matters. There was little

Table 3.3: Workers Responding They Could Vary Their Work-Pace a Little or Not at All (%)

	All Direct Production	Male Direct Production	Female Direct Production	All Indirect Production
Chrysler	55.56	53.86	62.86	44.67
GM	67.98	67.62	69.88	50.64
Ford	58.65	58.11	71.43	54.88
CAMI	51.76	50.00	55.56	38.1
TOTAL	61.48	60.78	65.45	48.56

Table 3.4: Workers Responding It Was Difficult To Find a Relief Worker So They Could Leave Their Workstation To Attend To Personal Matters Such As Going To the Toilet (%)

	All Direct Production	Male Direct Production	Female Direct Production
Chrysler	64.5	63.1	70.37
GM	62.1	62.78	57.32
Ford	57.56	56.95	71.43
CAMI	63.53	62.12	66.67
TOTAL	62.4	61.99	65.32

difference between companies, although workers at Ford, the least lean workplace, were also the least likely to report having difficulty finding a relief worker. Other than at GM, women found it marginally more difficult to find a relief worker so they could leave their workstation.

Table 3.5 examines the flexibility workers have in getting time off work to attend to personal matters. Here we see a major difference between companies. CAMI workers reported it was much more difficult to get time off, despite the fact that in the last year the market for the product CAMI manufactures had been relatively soft. Despite this lack of demand, CAMI workers work the second-most amount of overtime. Only Chrysler with its booming sales works more. GM direct production workers also reported it was relatively difficult to get time off, followed closely by Ford workers. Workers at Chrysler were the least likely to report having trouble getting time off when requested, even though Chrysler workers work more overtime than workers at any of the other companies.

A factor explaining inter-company differences around time off is differences in contract language. Workers at Ford, Chrysler, and GM are all entitled to personal paid absences, while in addition at Chrysler an agreement has been reached to allow temporary part-time employees to cover for absences between Fridays and Mondays. The CAMI contract lacks these provisions.

During interviews with workers at lean plants, it was not unusual to hear that management was less flexible in granting time off. At GM, management has been particularly aggressive in demanding changes to provincial legislation which would make it easier for management to demand workers work overtime. It is clear from Table 3.5 that, in this study, workers at lean production facilities have less flexibility in getting time off to leave the workplace.

Female direct production workers were marginally more likely to report they could get time off to leave the workplace to attend to personal matters. The gap between male and female workers was largest at CAMI. Indirect production workers also found it marginally easier to get time off work, and again the largest difference was between direct and indirect production workers at CAMI.

There is very little in Tables 3.2–3.5 to support the hypothesis that lean production can be associated with empowered workers who can influence the conditions of work.

Table 3.5: Workers Responding It Was Difficult To Get Time off Work To Attend To Personal Matters Such as Attending To a Sick Child (%)

	All Direct Production	Male Direct Production	Female Direct Production	All Indirect Production
Chrysler	18.66	18.49	18.87	19.33
GM	49.36	49.79	45.12	46.45
Ford	42.86	43.05	42.86	32.50
CAMI	83.53	86.36	72.22	70.00
TOTAL	39.23	39.84	34.55	35.49

Compared with workers at the other three companies, CAMI workers found it the most difficult to modify their jobs or get time off work. GM workers found it the most difficult to vary their work-pace. This suggests that either the shift to lean production has little to do with empowering workers, or that, if they are empowered, they do not have the authority to make changes that might improve the quality of their worklife.

The differences between men and women were relatively small, and sometimes to the advantage of women and sometimes men. Indirect production workers had marginally more control over how and when they worked, and enjoyed marginally more flexibility in getting time off work.

Indirect Indicators of Worker Empowerment

Other questions were asked about the work environment and whether it was conducive to workers' participating in decision-making. These questions provide indirect evidence of the potential for empowerment. Workers were asked whether they could do things other than the specific production tasks they were assigned during the day, whether they had to work as fast as they can just to keep up, and whether they could interact with other workers. Each of these are indicators of the degree to which the workforce has the potential for independent actions and can focus on matters other than the immediate tasks assigned.

Table 3.6 examines the potential for work-

Table 3.6: Workers Responding They Have Very Little or No Time during a Job Cycle To Do Things other Than the Assigned Tasks (%)

	All Direct Production	Male Direct Production	Female Direct Production
Chrysler	68.51	66.01	79.63
GM	84.47	84.42	85.54
Ford	67.23	66.37	85.71
CAMI	64.71	68.18	55.56
Total	75.45	74.82	80.27

Table 3.7 Workers Responding They Have To Work as Fast as They Can Half of Each Day or More So as not To Fall Behind (%)

	All Direct Production	Male Direct Production	Female Direct Production	All Indirect Production
Chrysler	57.52	55.78	65.74	55.33
GM	80.71	81.05	78.31	78.59
Ford	54.47	53.39	76.92	52.5
CAMI	52.38	56.06	38.89	66.67
TOTAL	67.48	67.34	68.92	66.41

ers doing things other than the work assigned during each job cycle. Most direct production workers are fully occupied by the work assigned during their job cycle. They find it difficult to find a moment when they might rest, or chat with another worker. This is especially the case at GM, where over 80% of workers said they had little if any free time during a job cycle.

On average, women were marginally more likely than men to say they had little free time during each job cycle, but there is no consistent pattern, with women workers at Chrysler and Ford indicating they were more fully occupied during their job cycles than those at CAMI who indicated they had marginally more flexibility.

Table 3.7 examines what portion of each day workers have to work as fast as they can just to keep up. Again, it is hard to imagine workers participating in decision-making or being empowered to improve the quality of their work life if they are so fully occupied that they have to work as fast as they can just to keep up. About two-thirds of those who responded indicated they had to work as fast as they can at least half of each day just to keep up; again, direct production workers at GM report being the most fully loaded.

Men and women, on average, reported working as fast as they can about the same amount each day, although there were some interesting differences between companies, with women at Chrysler and Ford reporting heavier workloads than men, while women at CAMI reported lighter loads.

When the question of workload was posed to indirect workers, there was little evidence that loads were lighter for them. At CAMI, indirect production workers reported working as fast as they can more often than direct production workers.

Table 3.8 examines whether workers can chat with one another outside of scheduled breaks. Again, it is hard to imagine a workforce of empowered workers who found it difficult to communicate with one another. Other than General Motors, the majority of workers found they were able to talk with other workers outside of breaks. The difference between CAMI and GM is surprising. While CAMI workers were the most likely to have this freedom, GM workers were the least likely. There was little evidence that men and women had different experiences in the plants.

The indirect indicators of potential worker empowerment tell a somewhat different story

Table 3.8: Workers Responding that Outside of Scheduled Breaks, They Can Rarely Talk with other Workers while Working (%)

	All Direct Production	Male Direct Production	Female Direct Production
Chrysler	36.35	34.77	43.52
GM	58.79	59.72	50.60
Ford	29.54	28.38	50.00
CAMI	25.88	25.76	27.78
TOTAL	45.15	45.14	45.29

than the direct indicators. GM workers were the most likely to be constrained by workload and had the least flexibility in communicating with other workers. CAMI workers, on the other hand, were marginally less likely to be constrained by workload and had the most flexibility in communicating with other workers.

Further analysis revealed an important link between flexibility in the work environment, defined as being able to do things other than the work assigned or communicate with other workers, and the ability to make decisions that might improve a worker's quality of working life.

Direct production workers who found it difficult to communicate with other workers outside of breaks were over 40 percent more likely to report that they found it difficult to change things they did not like about their jobs.

Direct production workers who had little time during the job cycle for tasks other than those assigned were almost 25 percent more likely to report that they found it difficult to change things they did not like about their jobs.

Other Indicators of Empowerment

A central assumption of the proponents of lean production is that this model of work organization creates the need for more skilled workers. This creates both the need for more cooperative relations between labour and management and an improved quality of working life. These new skills are either acquired through formal training, or are the by-product of having workers rotate over a range of jobs.[41]

Table 3.9 reports the results of a question which asked workers how long it would take to train someone to do their job. Here there seems to be a clear difference between the two plants that have been most aggressive in adopting the lean production philosophy. At GM, almost half of all workers, and at CAMI over half, responded it would take one week or more to train someone to do their job.

By contrast, at Ford and Chrysler, less than one-third of all direct production workers responded it would take a week or more. This suggests that the lean plants may make greater demands on their workers in terms of knowledge needed to perform a job adequately. There was also an important difference between the

Table 3.9: Percentage of Workers Responding It Would Take One Week or More To Train Someone To Do Their Job (%)

	All Direct Production	Male Direct Production	Female Direct Production	All Indirect Production
Chrysler	31.01	33.00	21.30	38.68
GM	46.33	48.30	30.12	56.55
Ford	36.71	36.49	42.86	47.56
CAMI	55.95	56.06	55.56	85.71
TOTAL	40.01	41.72	28.70	49.77

training needs of men and women. At both Chrysler and GM, women were significantly less likely to report they would need at least one week to train someone to do their job, while at CAMI the experience of men and women was similar.

This question was also asked of indirect production workers. Not surprisingly, indirects were more likely to report needing at least one week to be trained to do their job. The difference between direct and indirect production workers was particularly large at CAMI.

Table 3.10 examines the extent to which workers reported that managerial surveillance had increased in the last few years. The two leanest plants were much more likely to report increases in monitoring. This suggests that the lean model, far from providing a space where workers might act independently in their personal interest, is a system in which the range for autonomous action may actually be reduced.

The other two results of this table are that women are less likely to report that management has increased surveillance, and that indirect production workers report changes in monitoring similar to that reported by direct production workers.

Conclusions

This study has presented the results of a survey of over 2,000 Canadian motor vehicle workers working in plants at various stages in the transition to lean production. Overall, there was little evidence that motor vehicle workers were empowered. The majority found it difficult to modify their jobs, vary their work-pace, or leave their work-station to attend to personal matters.

For the most part, differences between men and women were relatively small. The majority of workers at the two companies most advanced in internally reorganizing work practices according to the lean production model, CAMI and General Motors, reported little potential for modifying working conditions or controlling the rhythm of work.

Finally, when we compared the two companies most advanced in implementing lean production with the two companies least advanced, we found that the lean plants often reported the lowest degree of empowerment and the greatest increase in monitoring.

The one finding that was consistent with lean predictions was that the workers at the two

Table 3.10 Workers Responding Management Monitors Their Work more Closely Compared with a Couple of Years Ago (%)

	All Direct Production	Male Direct Production	Female Direct Production	All Indirect Production
Chrysler	46.72	47.92	39.81	46.67
GM	78.83	79.52	73.49	79.17
Ford	48.32	48.43	50.00	51.85
CAMI	71.76	72.73	66.67	71.43
TOTAL	62.89	63.93	55.50	63.61

leanest companies also reported requiring the longest period to train someone to do their jobs.

Most of the results presented in this chapter contradict the predictions of the proponents of lean production, who have argued that this new model of work organization would empower workers and enhance the quality of working life. This raises a more fundamental issue: what is it that makes modern motor vehicle plants more productive than older plants? Issues such as capacity utilization, manufacturability and vintage of equipment almost certainly play an important role.

There is also evidence in this chapter that at lean plants managerial control of workers has actually increased. Direct production workers at lean plants continue to have little scope to change things they do not like about their jobs, often find it difficult to vary the rhythm of work, often find it difficult to get time off to attend to personal matters, and have a workload which leaves little time for resting during a job cycle.

These results are consistent with the work of other authors, such as Babson, Graham, Garrahan & Stewart, and Rinehart & Robertson et al., who make the case that workers in lean plants have less, not more control, over the quality of their work-life.

The various company documents intended to guide the shift to lean production may pay lip service to empowerment, but a careful reading suggests that the real focus is process control. At GM, lean production is synonymous with concepts of control, and standardization is evident from the list of operational definitions listed below, which were taken from a GM management document.

1. The Fixed Stop Position System ensures that the conveyance systems always stop in the same location.

2. Operation Footprints are defined as the standard measure of one job length.

3. Pull Systems are disciplined replenishment systems.

4. Material Supermarkets ensure that materials follow a standardized route.

5. Material Lightboard Systems ensure material replenishment at a predetermined reorder quantity.

6. Just in Time Production ensures that only what is needed, in the right quantity and at the right time, is produced.

7. Workplace Organization is defined as safe, clean and neat arrangements which provide specific locations for everything and eliminates anything not required.

8. Error Proofing is intended to make it impossible for parts, tools, equipment and fixtures to be used improperly.

Tighter process control is clearly the primary strategy for increasing output. Worker empowerment is not only irrelevant, but may also be counterproductive once a workplace is error-proofed and standardized. Rather than solving the social and health problems associated with Fordism, lean production may actually compound them.

Appendix: Survey Methodology

The study was made up of two components, a survey distributed to workers at each workplace involved in the study, and a site visit by one or more members of the research team. The site visit allowed us to inspect the production process and to interview members of the union executive. All workplaces assembling vehicles in Canada and organized by the CAW were originally included in the study. The Ford Oakville assembly complex had to be dropped due to a combination of funding problems and awkward timing.

The survey was distributed to approximately one out of every six production workers. Surveys were randomly distributed by local union members. Each person was asked to distribute 25 surveys to ensure an even distribution throughout the plant. Surveys targeted at different areas of the workplace and different shifts were pre-bundled by the research team, based on rough estimates of the proportion of people in each area of the plant.

Surveys were filled out by workers on their own time and were returned to their local union representative, or the union office, in unmarked sealed envelopes. Respondents were asked not to identify themselves on the survey. The surveys were returned to the national office of the CAW and then sent to McMaster University for coding and data analysis. Response rates from each workplace and for the study as a whole are reported below.

Table A.1: Response Rate (Assembly Plants)

	Population	Surveys Distributed	Surveys Returned	Response Rate
Chrysler				
Bramalea Assembly	2,600	450	305	67.8
Pillette Rd Assembly	1,700	270	206	76.3
Windsor Mini Van Plant	5,600	750	357	47.6
General Motors				
Oshawa Car Assembly Plant #1	2,841	450	335	74.4
Oshawa Car Assembly Plant #2	3,172	450	301	66.9
Oshawa Truck Assembly	3,600	450	107	23.8
Ste-Thérèse Assembly	2,841	450	382	84.9
Ford				
St Thomas Assembly	2,600	450	325	72.2
CAMI Car and Truck Assembly				
CAMI Car and Truck Assembly	2,500	550	106	19.3
TOTAL	27,454	4,270	2,424	56.8

Endnotes

1 The paper is based on a study conducted by the Canadian Automobile Workers in cooperation with faculty from McMaster University. We would like to thank the workers who took the time to fill in the survey as well as the many union representatives who assisted us. A number of people assisted in the development of the research instrument and the administration of the survey. We would like to thank in particular Bruce Roberts, Cara Macdonald, Dale Brown, Delia Hutchinson, Anne-Marie Quinn, Sonia Lowe and Linda Cantin for their contributions. We would also like to acknowledge the financial support of the Ontario Government through its Technology Adjustment Research Programme administered through the Ontario Federation of Labour.

2 To date over 7,000 members of the CAW and 50 different workplaces have been involved in these surveys. This paper relies only on the surveys collected from workers involved in the assembly of vehicles.

3 See CAW-Canada. 1990. *CAW Statement on the Reorganization of Work*; CAW-Canada Research Group on CAMI. 1993. *The CAMI Report: Lean Production in a Unionized Auto Plant*. Willowdale; CAW-Canada. 1993b. *Work Reorganization: Responding to Lean Production*; Rinehart, James, Christopher Huxley and David Robertson. 1997. *Just Another Car Factory? Lean Production and its Discontents*, Cornell.

4 This paper is based on earlier work published as Lewchuk, W. and D. Robertson. 1997. "Production Without Empowerment." *Capital and Class*, 63, pp. 37–64. The authors would like to thank the editors of *Capital and Class* for permission to use this material.

5 This same methodology was used by the authors of this paper in a study of parts manufacturers in Canada. See Lewchuk, Wayne and David Robertson. "Working Conditions under Lean Production: A Worker-Based Benchmarking Study." 1996. *Asia Pacific Business Review* (Summer), pp. 60–81.

6 See *Human Centred Benchmarking: Work Reorganization and the Quality of Work Life in the Clothing, Textile, Primary Textile, Box, Paper, Aluminum, Electrical and Electronic Products Sectors*. Report submitted to the Manufacturing Research Corporation of Ontario. August 1997, pp. 1–65. This report is available from the Ontario Federation of Labour.

7 Two of the classic works in this traditions are Blauner, Robert. 1964. *Alienation and Freedom*. Chicago; Chinoy, Eli. 1955. *Automobile Workers and the American Dream*. Boston. For a useful review of some of the older literature on this subject, see Nash, A. "Job Satisfaction: A Critique." 1976. In B.J. Widick (ed.). *Auto Work and Its Discontents*. Baltimore, pp. 61–88.

8 Lewchuk, Wayne. 1993. "Men and Monotony: Fraternalism as a Managerial Strategy at the Ford Motor Company." *Journal of Economic History*, vol. 53, pp. 824–56.

9 Karasek, Robert and Tores Theorell. 1990. *Healthy Work: Stress, Productivity and the Reconstruction of Working Life*. New York.

10 One of the few places where the social and health costs of Fordism were taken seriously was Scandinavia. For a discussion of the Volvo experiments, see Berggren, Christian. 1992. *Alternatives to Lean Production: Work Organization in the Swedish Auto Industry*. Ithaca.

11 Womack, James P., Daniel Jones and Daniel Roos. 1990. *The Machine That Changed the World: The Story of Lean Production*. New York, p. 13; See also MacDuffie, John Paul. 1995. *Human Resources Bundles and Manufacturing Performance*. ILRR; Adler, Paul S. and Robert E.Cole. 1993. "Designed for Learning: A Tale of Two Auto Plants." *Sloan Management Review*, vol. 34, pp. 85–94; Adler, Paul S. 1992. "The Learning Bureaucracy: New United Motor Manufacturing Inc." *Research in Organizational Behavior*, vol. 15, pp. 111–94.

12 Flexibility within the lean paradigm has a somewhat different meaning from flexibility as traditionally defined. It is much more than the opposite of dedicated, single-purpose machinery which many view as the hallmark of Fordism. While the ability to make different components is one aspect of flexibility, under lean production, flexibility also means lightweight machinery which can be easily moved, is equipped with quick connectors which are plug compatible, is soft wired and piped, and which is not anchored down. The flexibility to move equipment within a plant, or even remove it, has implication not only for adapting this equipment to new purposes but also to change the bargaining leverage of workers employed on this machine. Such flexibility empowers management at the expense of workers. General Motors. 1994. *Lean Manufacturing Operational Definitions*.

13 Williams, Karel et al. 1992. "Against Lean Production," *Economy and Society*, vol. 21, pp. 321–54. See also Williams, Karel et al. 1994. *Cars: Analysis, History, Cases*, Providence.

14 Womack, p. 14. Authors such as Marsh have raised concerns about how far the Japanese system has in fact actually gone in giving Japanese workers more power to make decisions compared with workers in North America. See Marsh, Robert M. 1992. "The Difference between Participation and Power in Japanese

Factories." *Industrial and Labor Relations Review,* vol. 45, pp. 250–57.

15 Womack et al., pp. 14 & 101–2.

16 Kenney and Florida. 1993. *Beyond Mass Production: The Japanese System and its Transfer to the U.S.* New York, pp. 9, 15–6, 106.

17 Parker, Mike and Jane Slaughter. 1988. *Choosing Sides: Unions and the Team Concept.* Boston.

18 CAW-Canada Research Group on CAMI. 1993. *The CAMI Report: Lean Production in a Unionized Auto Plant.* Willowdale; Fucini, Joseph J. and Suzy Fucini, *Working for the Japanese: Inside Mazda's American Auto Plant.* 1990. New York; Stewart, Paul and Philip Garrahan. 1995. "Employee Responses to New Management Techniques in the Auto Industry." *Work, Employment and Society* (September) vol. 9, pp. 517–36; Garrahan, Philip and Paul Stewart. 1992. *The Nissan Enigma: Flexibility at Work in a Local Economy.* London; Babson, Steve (ed.). 1995. *Lean Work, Empowerment and Exploitation in the Global Auto Industry.* Detroit; Green, W.C. and E.J.Yanarella. 1996. *North American Auto Unions in Crisis, Lean Production as Contested Terrain.* Albany.

19 Lewchuk, Wayne and David Robertson. 1996. "Working Conditions under Lean Production: A Worker-Based Benchmarking Study." *Asia Pacific Business Review* (Summer), pp. 60–81.

20 Lewchuk and Robertson. 1996. "Working Conditions under Lean Production," pp. 74 & 76.

21 Murphy, Colette and Doug Olthuis. 1995. "The Impact of Work Reorganization on Employee Attitudes Towards Work, the Company and the Union: Report of a Survey at Walkers Exhaust." In Christopher Schenk and John Anderson (eds.). *Reshaping Work: Union Responses to Technological Change.* Toronto, pp. 76–102.

22 Steve Babson. 1993. "Lean or Mean: The MIT Model and Lean Production at Mazda." *Labour Studies Journal,* vol. 18, p. 7.

23 Babson. 1993, p. 7.

24 Kaizen is a Japanese management concept that refers to continuous improvement. Kaizen is the process of searching out and eliminating waste, then deploying the resources made available to a more productive task.

25 Babson. 1993, p. 9.

26 Garrahan and Stewart. 1992, p. 61.

27 Garrahan and Stewart. 1992, p. 106.

28 For a review of trends in work practices in North American vehicle plants, see Kumar, Pradeep and John Holmes. 1996. "Continuity and Change: Evolving Human Resource Policies and Practices in the Canadian Automobile Industry." Kingston: Queen's University.

29 It is generally accepted that GM makes less use of contracting out than the other three companies. In the fall of 1996, the CAW won major concessions from the three North American based producers to limit the right to contract out jobs. This agreement was secured at GM only after a strike.

30 See Rinehart, James, Christopher Huxley and David Robertson. 1997. *Just Another Car Factory? Lean Production and its Discontents.* Cornell; CAW-Canada Research Group on CAMI. 1993. *The CAMI Report: Lean Production in a Unionized Auto Plant.* Willowdale.

31 Kanban is a central element of lean manufacturing. It is a process to manage the material flow of the production line.

32 See Abo, Tetsuo (ed.). 1994. *Hybrid Factory: The Japanese Production System in the United States.* Oxford.

33 Oliver, Nick et al. 1994. *Worldwide Manufacturing Competitiveness Study: The Second Lean Enterprise Report.* Anderson Consulting.

34 Oliver et al., p. 18.

35 Pil, Frits K. and John Paul MacDuffie. 1996. "Canada at the Cross-Roads: A Comparative Analysis of the Canadian Auto Industry." Unpublished.

36 Pil & MacDuffie, pp. 9, 14 & 16.

37 Oliver et al. p. 21.

38 Details of the research methodology can be found in the Appendix of the original article.

39 For studies of the gendered effects of Lean Production see Hadley, Karen. 1994. "Working Lean and Mean: A Gendered Experience of Restructuring in an Electronics Manufacturing Plant." Ph.D Thesis. Toronto; MacDonald, Cara. 1996. "En-Gendering Lean Production: Women Workers in the Ontario Independent Auto Parts Industry." MA Thesis. York University.

40 The percentage of women working as production workers was 12 percent of the entire sample. This represented 224 female direct production workers, including 109 women at Chrysler, 83 at GM, 14 at Ford, and 18 at CAMI.

41 On the enhanced role of learning see Adler, Paul S. 1992. "The Learning Bureaucracy: New United Motor Manufacturing Inc." *Research in Organizational Behaviour*, vol. 15, pp. 111–94.

CHAPTER 4

Flexible Work, Flexible Workers:

The Restructuring of Clerical Work in a Large Telecommunications Company

Bonnie Fox and Pamela Sugiman

TODAY, IN CONTEXT of strong global competition, deregulation of labour, and a proliferation of micro technologies, work is being restructured at a quickening pace.[1] In the words of David Harvey, we are in the midst of an era of "flexible accumulation," which "rests on flexibility with respect to 'labour processes,' 'labour markets,' products, and patterns of consumption. It is characterized by the emergence of ... above all, greatly intensified rates of 'commercial, technological and organizational innovation'" (emphases added).[2]

Rapidly changing technologies and "flexible" human resource management (HRM) strategies are arguably the most important elements of the restructuring of paid work. New technologies, after all, bear the potential to revolutionize work. Yet sociologists and organization theorists have long recognized that technology alone does not determine the nature of jobs. The reshaping of work through

technological change is often determined by the "authority of capital," not the "authority of technical know-how."[3] The content of jobs is a product of the way management organizes the labour process and deploys its workforce, rather than an objective (technical) necessity.[4] The dominant goal of human resource management is "flexibility." Employers have introduced flexibility in various forms. Most popular among flexibility strategies are the flexible organization of work (known as "flexible specialization" ["flex-spec"] or "functional flexibility") and employing labour in non-standard jobs ("numerical flexibility").

Research and debate about the nature and consequences of restructuring have burgeoned over the last couple of decades. Yet the literature is lacking in some important respects. One, much of the discussion has revolved exclusively around ideal-typical constructs such as Atkinson's model of the "flexible firm," which equates functional flexibility with "core" labour forces and numerical flexibility with "peripheral" labour forces.[5] Two, many writers contributing to the debate about the effects of flexible specialization have assumed that flex spec operates alone. In short, much of the scholarly writing is problematic in failing to carefully examine how various flexibility approaches have been implemented and played out in real work settings. Empirical accounts of restructuring, though relatively few, have highlighted the complexities of such workplaces. These studies suggest that real workplaces host a web of management strategies, are in a constant state of flux, and bear evidence of old organizational forms alongside the new.[6] Such studies prompt questions about what strategies different firms are actually using and when, for what kinds of work and workers; how functional and numerical flexibility interact (when they do); and their joint and separate effects on the workforce.

At a more general level, few contributors to the current restructuring debate have systematically examined management's own belief that workplace reorganization is based on rational, uniform, well-planned strategies.[7] An implicit assumption in much of the literature is that restructuring follows a clear, linear course and where it has unanticipated consequences, these are solely the outcome of resistance by labour.[8] Researchers thus need to further interrogate the rationality of management plans, highlight their ambiguity, and explore the effects of those plans with an eye to inconsistent and conflicting results.

Inquiries about management intentions have, to some extent, been eclipsed by questions about the outcomes of restructuring. The effects of flexible specialization, in particular, have generated considerable debate. Many researchers have asked whether the multi-skilling (or cross-training), job rotation and team organization that are often a part of flexible specialization reverse the job fragmentation, job simplification and erosion of workers' control which Taylorist management strategies entailed.[9] Much of this discussion too still needs to be grounded in empirical research.

Moreover, though questions about social relations among workers, and between labour and management, pervade the restructuring literature, the existing research is motivated primarily by inquiries about class, and largely overlooks gender and race relations. Given that class is unquestionably entangled with gender and race, a failure to understand the nexus of these sets of social relations will likely distort any analysis.

In this paper, we examine the process of restructuring as experienced by clerical workers in a Customer Payments Centre (CPC), the billing department of a major telecommunications company in Toronto, Canada. This department represents an interesting microcosm of larger trends in the economy. Directly following the introduction of advanced computer technology, management began to pursue both of the major types of "flexible" HRM strategies in the CPC: they organized workers into teams and flexibly specialized the labour process, and they hired increasing numbers of workers on a part-time or temporary basis.

This case study allows us to examine the restructuring process in its specifics. It reveals the nature of reorganization in a particular firm, workers' experiences of it, and its implications for worker-management relations and relations among employees themselves. It forces us to drop the assumption that flexible specialization and numerical flexibility are applied to different parts of the labour force, and prompts us to ask what happens when the two HRM strategies are used together, for the same workers.[10] More generally, it highlights the complexity and indeterminacy of management strategies—and the contradictory outcomes that sometimes follow from them. As well, our examination contributes to ongoing discussions about the feminization of clerical work. Although employees in the CPC perform work that may be described as typically "women's," significant numbers of men now fill the unit and work alongside women. We suggest that as jobs for both sexes increasingly take on the characteristics of "women's work" (that is, as they become bad jobs), gender divisions in the workplace may lessen somewhat, while class, racial, ethnic (and other) lines of demarcation may deepen.

The Literature

Several parallel bodies of literature examine restructuring, its impact on work, and workers' experiences of it. Studies of clerical work have been primarily concerned with the effects of computer technology. A much smaller body of research discusses the application of flexible human resource management (both numerical and functional) to women in clerical employment. Most discussions of flex-spec, however, have been based on studies of manufacturing jobs that are typically performed by men. We briefly review the major arguments and findings.

Studies of the introduction of microchip technology to clerical work indicate that the effects are neither simple nor obvious. While mainly concerned about predicting the job loss that can be expected from automation, research on the transformation of clerical work accompanying technological change has also

had much to say about how clerks experience the new office.[11] Some researchers argue that clerical work has been de-skilled as a result of office automation; others argue that the effects are mixed, with routine jobs undergoing greater fragmentation and simplification but other jobs necessitating greater skill.[12] Many writers claim that the new technology has intensified clerical work; some find increased monitoring of workers by management as a result of the new technology.[13] The effects of the new information technology vary by industry, size of office or firm, and management policies.[14] The only uniform finding is that health problems increase for clerical workers as a result of automation.[15]

The general conclusion of the most comprehensive reviews of this research is that technology itself has no necessary consequences for the contents of clerical work, its organization and thus workers' experiences. Researchers agree that technology cannot singlehandedly change the organization of work, and that management policies intervene to determine the way work is organized, and thus the effects of new technology.[16]

For manufacturing jobs, the focus of research on restructuring is on the effects of flexible work organization, or functional flexibility. A flex-spec labour process involves a cross-trained workforce, working in teams and rotating among jobs in a flattened job structure. Typically, it is accompanied by a goal of cooperation and flexible arrangements between labour and management, rather than adversarial relations based on strict contractual agreements.[17]

Where Taylorist management strategies have rationalized production by eliminating the need for workers to make decisions, a flex-spec organization attempts to eliminate "waste" by employing workers' knowledge of their jobs in the rationalization process.[18] Working in teams, employees are given responsibility for scheduling, planning the work, rotating workers among jobs, and meeting quotas. Increasing workers' responsibility, team organization diminishes the need for supervision—although it provides employees with no added authority.

Team work in manufacturing often occurs in the context of a "lean-production" model whereby stock is acquired "just-in-time," barely sufficient numbers of workers are hired, and thus buffers and cushions in the labour process are eliminated. The absence of "excess" labour under the "lean and mean" model means that employees must absorb the costs of production problems by extending their workday into mandatory overtime—becoming "accordion workers."[19] Additionally, management squeezes "wasted" time out of the production process by moving workers from job to job whenever there is "slack time." The cross-training of employees is aimed at reducing turnover time and eliminating down time rather than upgrading workers' skills.[20] Most writers argue that workers are simply acquiring a number of job-specific and company-specific skills for highly simplified jobs.

Meanwhile, weakened worker unity often accompanies a flex-spec labour process. Writers speculate that the organization of the workforce into teams may encourage competition among groups of workers insofar as they monitor each other's performance to ensure that no one "slacks off." As well, in many cases, management has eroded "internal labour markets," or job ladders, as it has flattened the occupational structure and even attacked entrenched seniority systems and other protections won by organized labour.

While the literature assumes that flexibility for women workers means part-time work, some studies show that women are also subject to flex-spec HRM.[21] Research on the insurance industry—a large employer of women—suggests that the white-collar work done by many women is being significantly reorganized. In tandem with computer technology, the reorganization of insurance work has meant not only degraded jobs for clerks doing data entry but also multi-task positions involving team work for women with good educational credentials.[22] The questions raised about flex-spec with respect to manufacturing jobs—requiring a close examination of the labour process and workers' experiences—have yet, however, to be pursued even with respect to the insurance industry.

Restructuring in the Customer Payments Centre

The Customer Payments Centre is located on an upper floor of a large, grey, nondescript building situated in a bleak industrial area just outside of Metropolitan Toronto. The Centre is staffed by approximately 200 clerical workers who process bill payments. Although these workers belong to a union, their collective power is extremely limited. Many members have long relinquished the belief that this union acts as the collective voice of workers, and some union stewards openly claim that one of their primary objectives is to ensure that workers do not file grievances against the company. The union, commonly referred to as "the Association," is affiliated with neither the provincially based Ontario Federation of Labour, nor the country's central labour body, the Canadian Labour Congress.

We interviewed ten groups of workers employed at this site. Each group consisted of four to five randomly selected individuals. In addition, we spoke with three supervisors and two representatives of mid/upper management. These interviews were supplemented by a review of selected union and company documents and observations of employees performing their work.

The clerical workforce in the CPC is divided into eight units, each of which is headed by a supervisor. Each supervisor, in turn, is accountable to a single manager who oversees the entire department. Staff in the various units of the CPC perform distinct but interrelated functions. These include processing "regular" residential customer payments made either by mail, pre-authorized cheque withdrawal, or through a bank; processing "irregular" mailed payments, including those by business clients; investigating and dealing with "problem" payments; and balancing the daily total payments. Altogether, CPC employees process between 100,000 and 120,000 transactions daily, in order to make a bank deposit by early afternoon. Work shifts begin as early as 6:00 am. and end at approximately 3:00 pm.

In recent years, the Centre has undergone tremendous technological and organizational change. Change is now a constant in this firm and it is occurring at an accelerated rate. For employees, its pace and intensity are alarming. The most notable recent transformation began in 1991, with the technological redesign of the workplace. In an effort to heighten efficiency and avoid impending mechanical problems, the company replaced highly outdated machinery with sophisticated new computerized equipment. Often referred to as "recognition technology," the newly introduced machines have the capacity to encode cheques and bills, read codes, match codes between cheques and bills, create microfilm and leave an audit trail for proof of deposit.[23] As well, personal computers were installed throughout the department, allowing workers access to central files containing customer information. The introduction of this new machinery was independent of any human resource management strategy; although some of the new technology facilitated the team organization that followed it, most did not.

Prior to these departmental changes, management began to seek greater flexibility in its clerical workforce on a company-wide basis. In 1990, upper-level management made a decision to hire workers on a temporary basis only. They also made a strong commitment to part-time employment. In the CPC, this meant that management was relying increasingly on temporary and part-time workers while introducing new technology and pressuring employees to work extra hours in order to adapt to the new machines and still meet pre-established work quotas.

In addition to numerical flexibility, approximately one year after the introduction of the new computer equipment the company adopted a philosophy known as Total Quality Management (TQM), with its goal of functional flexibility.[24] As a first step, management flattened the department's occupational structure, and compressed related pay scales. Higher-wage workers were transferred out of the CPC, leaving employees in only two (lower) wage bands. The majority of these workers occupy the lower of the two bands. Following this, supervisors introduced various employee incentive schemes, organized the workforce into teams, and began job rotation among team members. As well, in an effort to move away from its negative connotations, the firm abandoned the designation "clerical worker," replacing it with the now fashionable title of "associate." Furthermore, in teams, workers themselves took over many functions that were previously in the exclusive domain of management. For instance, team leaders became responsible for settling disputes among team members and scheduling team work.

Meanwhile over this period, there was a gradual transformation of the social composition of the workforce. Years ago, the CPC was informally known as the "blue-rinse floor" and the "hen house," as it was staffed largely by middle-aged women. The majority of these women were of British or European descent and they entered full-time employment after their children were grown. Coincident with the technological and organizational changes that transformed the CPC, many of these women "retired." Those who remain are in the units handling "irregular" mail and "problem" payments and checking the daily balance. Most of the current staff are young in comparison, ranging in age from their early twenties to early thirties. These newer employees are especially apparent in entry-level, temporary, and part-time jobs in the "regular" mail units.

Recently hired employees are also of diverse ethnic and racial origins. East Indians, West Indians, East Asians, South Asians, Italian Canadians, African Canadians and a number of other ethnic and racial groups are now represented in the CPC. Some of these workers are first-time immigrants to Canada. While such racial and ethnic diversity reflects the growing heterogeneity of the wider Toronto area, it is striking in this particular work site as such diversity is not characteristic of the workforce in the company's other locations.

As well, the sex composition of the Centre has shifted over the last several years. Clerical jobs in the CPC have traditionally been held by women, but increasing numbers of men have recently joined them. Young men are now scattered throughout the CPC and, in many cases, they work alongside women. In the regular residential mail units (where the least skilled jobs exist), 26 to 31 percent of employees are men. In the department where workers run the computer system and make daily balances, 44 percent of the workforce is male. While fewer men are located in other departments, their numerical representation is still not insignificant. Only one department in the CPC is filled exclusively by women. Here, workers are long-term employees of the company, and occupy the preferred permanent, full-time, better-paid jobs.

Costly New Technology

Beginning with the publication of Harry Braverman's *Labor and Monopoly Capital*, writers contributing to the labour-process literature (usually discussing scientific management) have tended to assume that management takes a carefully reasoned approach to the deployment of labour.[25] After all, given the high cost of capital investment, it is commonsensical to assume that employers attempt to utilize technological potential fully. In the CPC, however, use of the costly new technology, as well as the decision-making and implementation processes surrounding it, were haphazard and ill-conceived. Indeed because of misguided decision-making and poor planning on the part of management, the implementation period was one of chaos. Though a committee made up of supervisors from the various units in the department was officially responsible for the re-systematization, this committee was headed by a business graduate who was recruited from outside the firm. This outside consultant ignored many of the suggestions made by in-house supervisors. In turn, management introduced an insufficient number of machines, and employees were inadequately trained to operate the new equipment. Staff ended up doing their work largely by trial and error.

Furthermore, for almost a year after the new machines were introduced, everyone in the Centre, workers and supervisors alike, was putting in 11- to 13-hour days, and also working on Saturdays, in an effort to process payments in accordance with the usual production goals. Even part-time employees became "accordion workers." In fact, because part-time workers had put in excessively long hours, company policy eventually required management to convert many of them to full-time status. Management thereby lost the flexibility that these workers were meant to provide. The transition was so chaotic that for some time the department faced the prospect of having its work grind to a halt. It paid dearly to avoid that: it pressured employees to work overtime, at time-and-a-half or double their standard rate of pay.

In the end, payments were processed daily largely because of employees' own initiatives. With little guidance, workers taught themselves how to operate the new machines. Some workers viewed the firm's increased use of machinery as contradictory precisely because of the importance of worker ingenuity for doing the job well. Critical of the subordination of workers and the labour process to the authority of the machine, one woman stated that when one's work is totally dependent on a machine, "everything has to grind to a halt" when the machine breaks. She said, "before, so many hands would pick up the work and get it going, and now we're waiting for one machine to do it all." This worker continued, "hundreds of thousands of dollars [are spent]

for just maintenance of these machines. That money would pay for a lot of bodies who have eyes and can see and they don't break down completely." Paradoxically, a process aimed at removing some of the need for thinking on the part of workers relied, in the short term, on precisely this capacity. The job-specific knowledge possessed by long-term employees was especially important to the continuation of the labour process at a time when the firm was moving to temporary labour.

Not only was the company haphazard about introducing the technological change, ultimately it also failed to take the steps necessary to realize the productive potential of the new machines. According to a supervisor who was well versed in the technical details of the redesign, because employees were not properly trained, they did not utilize the equipment to its full potential. Yet management made no effort to rectify this. Indeed, it had not even collected the statistics necessary for an analysis of productivity before and after the conversion to new equipment.

Its chaotic introduction notwithstanding, the new machinery did enhance managerial control and intensify the labour process. With "state of the art" computer equipment, the company could more effectively enforce productivity quotas and monitor workers, especially those who performed highly routine tasks such as opening (regular) mail. On the mail-opening machines (on which workers check and sort documents), employees' names are automatically recorded, along with the number of documents they process and the speed at which the work is done. This method of surveillance had serious repercussions for employees because management adopted a harsh rate system at the same time that it introduced the new machines. When asked what happens if a worker does not meet the set rate, one (temporary) employee stated, "I was told if I didn't get to 600 [800 is the rate] by the third or fourth month [after starting], I wouldn't have a job." In the face of such threats, most workers attempted to work harder and faster in a race with the machine. Not surprisingly, many women and men described the CPC as "a very high-stress environment."

Though most employees recognized that the microchip technology facilitated greater managerial control and an intensification of the labour process, the extent to which it contributed to a further routinization and degradation of work depended largely on the specific nature of the job (including the degree of mechanization), and thus the unit in which people worked.[26] Jobs that had already been made routine with the old machinery were further degraded with the introduction of more advanced computer technology. Most regular mail processors, for example, likened their jobs after the re-systematization to those typically performed by the manual working class. In describing this work, a number of women and men used the terms "mindless," "no challenge," and "brain-dead boring." "You're a robot. [You] take [the bill] out, put it in," remarked one worker. A woman who had been with the firm for ten years commented, "I have never worked like in a factory before."

Alongside workers who processed regular payments, however, were those who handled the non-standard payments. While the same machinery was introduced in each unit, the mix of tasks that workers performed in non-standard mail necessitated that they continue to handle payments on a case-by-case basis, and decide themselves how best to proceed with each. Workers in these more challenging jobs believed that the new technology improved some aspects of their work. The computer created in many of these employees a feeling of greater control over the labour process, as it permitted easier access to information about customer accounts. Notably, it enabled them to solve problems for the customer directly, and this generated in some workers a feeling of personal effectiveness. "We can do it all ourselves, instead of sending problem payments to other units," explained one long-term employee. In short, the new technology reintegrated some jobs that previously had been fragmented. The technology in itself was not a predetermined, universalizing force.

Whatever their feelings about the impact of the new machinery on the exercise of skill and autonomy, employees uniformly believed that in combination with the rate system and the goal of same-day processing, the technology was highly detrimental to their health and well-being. While workers believed that the ergonomics of the new machines and recently purchased office furniture constituted some improvement over the old, most of them complained vociferously about experiencing more frequent and aggravating health problems than in the past. In part, this may have been because the department regularly violated official company policy that an employee should work on any one machine no longer than two consecutive hours.

Many workers suffered from repetitive-strain injuries such as tendinitis and carpal-tunnel syndrome and/or back and neck problems, eye strain, vision problems, chronic headaches, fatigue, nausea, and dizziness. Even those individuals who investigated problems with payments (generally a more varied task than routine mail processing) felt that their job had worsened with the re-systematization: scanning microfilm for errors is apparently harder on people's eyes than scanning paper. One woman described her experience: "We are processing different [kinds of] payments.... I have bifocal glasses ... I feel sick. I feel I cannot sit more than half an hour. I feel really dizzy and sick.... We have to look always a little down and it's too much pressure on your neck."

In spite of the number and severity of complaints, however, company officials claimed that health and safety were not matters of grave concern. One senior manager dismissively stated that such problems resulted from workers' own lack of knowledge about how best to use the chairs and machinery, for example. For the most part, management promoted a definition of "health and safety" that placed individual blame on workers, and exonerated the company itself from responsibility for the workers' problems. Not surprisingly, management's definition had little to do with the organization of work (the political economy of the workplace), and this view was not challenged by representatives of the employees' "Association." In summarizing the company's position on workers' health, a group of employees sarcastically reported that the corporation employs 41 physicians on staff, and recently held a flu-shot campaign. One employee said, "I took the St. John's Ambulance course. They [the firm] paid for it."

Working in Teams

Soon after the department acquired its new equipment and, in the process, increased its reliance on part-time and temporary workers, the company began to openly promote the managerial strategy known as Total Quality Management. In the CPC, TQM centred around the organization of workers into teams of varying sizes.[27] Team leaders established weekly work schedules and organized job rotation. Leaders were appointed by the supervisor of the unit. In theory, team leadership was to rotate among all members of the teams, but in practice some workers did not want to assume the position and others were never selected for it.

Central to the teams was a functionally flexible work organization. Workers were trained to do all of the jobs in their unit, as well as some jobs in other units within the department. They were then to rotate among the jobs in their unit, on a daily basis, according to the work schedule. Less frequently, they would perform jobs in other units as needed. Because workers typically moved laterally within a unit, between jobs of equivalent skill level, their tasks became more diversified (that is, they performed multiple tasks). Few employees upgraded their firm-specific skills; nor did they have an opportunity to acquire new skills that would be transferrable outside the firm.

Management encouraged competition among the teams in the regular mail units by measuring and publicizing team productivity every week. In addition, the company had established various employee award programmes to recognize contributions (by teams or individuals within teams) to objectives such as the team concept itself, heightened productivity, and "service excellence." Yet alongside such company practices stood management's rhetoric that all employees, regardless of team membership, should work cooperatively to meet the challenges of the highly competitive climate in which the company operated. This contradiction was one of many. TQM, as applied in this unit, made little sense to workers.

Another contradiction centred around job classifications, work content, and pay scales. Flex-spec was predicated on a flattened occupational structure and, consistent with this, the labour force had become fairly homogeneous with respect to pay. Nevertheless, jobs in the CPC varied considerably in content, and thus in skill requirements and levels of responsibility. Some of the work (most of it in the regular mails) was automated and monotonous, requiring virtually no thought; but in some of the other units (such as that in which the daily balance was made) the jobs demanded knowledge, skill and problem solving.

Variation in job requirements bore a rough correspondence to differences in the employee's terms of employment. The three standard mail units were composed of a mixture of permanent and temporary employees; many of the employees were part-time. The other units employed mostly permanent staff working on a full time basis; four of the five had only full-time employees. Despite the above-mentioned differences in employment status, skill, and level of responsibility, however, workers were all paid approximately the same wages, and all faced extremely limited prospects of upward mobility. Cognizant of this, workers from every category felt that they were being unjustly treated. The dearth of opportunities for mobility, and the absence of clear distinctions in pay and benefits from newer staff, especially angered senior employees working at jobs involving significant responsibility. In turn, more recently hired staff had higher levels of formal education than the more senior workers, and resumés at odds with their unchallenging jobs. Workers were frustrated on both counts.

Overall, workers' views of the team structure varied with their relationship to the company as well as the nature of their work. Long-term employees, many of whom strongly identified with the company and were performing jobs that both required extensive knowledge and

allowed autonomy and decision-making, generally held a positive view of team work (as they did of the new machinery). These workers did, however, resent being handed greater responsibility under the team organization. To the extent that supervisors had withdrawn from the actual work, the weight of the decisions employees made daily was greater than previously. According to a worker in non-standard mail, "It looks like you're just pushing paper but you're making decisions all the time, and informed decisions at that." In non-standard mail, the responsibility and limited discretionary power that workers held was, in fact, a source of stress. One employee explained that she worried excessively about decisions she had made during the day long after she left the workplace. She would think to herself, "'Oh, but this [payment] is a lot of money! What am I gonna do?' … You can't sleep all night 'cause you're afraid to come in the morning [for fear you handled the payment incorrectly]."

The majority of workers, many of whom were employed in the routine mail processing units, were highly critical of working in teams. The main complaint was about tensions arising among team members. One employee stated, "I don't think anybody's got a problem with the work. People have a problem with the people." A co-worker likewise remarked, "Before, you did your job and that was it; now you have to keep people happy." Yet another woman explained, "That's the biggest conflict up here—between people. It never was before."

What was most at issue was how quickly and competently co-workers performed their work. For many employees, who was and who was not "pulling their weight" on the team became an overriding concern. "Instead of one pair of eyes watching you, you've got more," said one woman. Another commented, "it's not management you have to worry about.... It's the people you work with." Thus, even workers who did not closely identify with company goals of heightened productivity and efficiency effectively patrolled one another.[28]

It is notable, though, that tensions among workers were not random. Some of the strongest conflicts and most bitter resentments in the Centre were between permanent (full-time and part-time) employees on the one hand, and temporary (part-time) workers on the other. While permanent employees were willing to cooperate and sometimes even make concessions in order to help the company prosper in a competitive market, they argued that temporary workers had no such identification with the company.[29] They believed that because of their relative indifference about the future of the company, temporary workers were neither responsible nor hardworking. According to one permanent worker, "we are aware that our company is going through a transition now. And this is another thing: we resent that they bring in all these temporary people who have no stake in the company."

The company did, however, drive temporary workers to sell themselves aggressively in order to remain in their jobs. And one way of doing this was to work at an extremely high rate, which meant avoiding handling any problematic payments, thus leaving them for more experienced workers. Temporary workers, therefore, had little inducement to work cooperatively in teams and indeed were motivated to outperform their co-workers. Accordingly, many of the workers felt that the team concept posed a fundamental contradiction: while employees were expected to work collectively, they were at the same time forced to promote themselves within the firm on an

individual basis. "How [then] do they expect the team spirit to carry?" asked one worker.

Tensions between temporary and permanent workers peaked several months prior to our interviews. The workers' own proposals for resolving such tensions underlines the seriousness of the division among these two categories of workers. Following the adoption of the new machinery in the regular mail unit, and prior to the introduction of teams, management removed the rates that set the standard for productivity. Shortly after the teams were established, several permanent employees made an astonishing move. They requested that management reinstall the old rate system. They took this extraordinary action because they believed that without the rates, the more recently hired temporary workers were avoiding the harder jobs and thus shifting the burden onto the shoulders of the (decreased number of) experienced permanent workers. Permanent employees felt that the new workers were simply not "pulling their weight." In their view, (former) close and careful supervision—notwithstanding its problems—meant that no one could avoid the harder work and everyone got credit for what they did.

What is clear here, then, is that functional flexibility and numerical flexibility (non-standard jobs) can, in practice, be incompatible with organizational strategies. Introducing flex-spec, or any other kind of team organization, into a workplace in which temporary employees are working alongside permanent employees is problematic. The different structural positions of the two categories of workers make for conflict between them. Of course, the resulting division within the workforce is favourable to management to the extent that it deflects anger based on class exploitation and directs it horizontally.

In this case, however, workers also displayed growing resentment toward supervisors for abdicating their "traditional" managerial role under the team organization. The withdrawal of supervisors from direct supervision was made possible by the mutual patrolling among workers. Employees noted, though, that under this arrangement conflict among workers in teams had, at times, escalated to such heights that they themselves had appealed to supervisors to intervene and mediate. In response to such requests, supervisors suggested that employees handle the problems on their own. One woman explained, "If there's a problem and you go to [your] manager, she'll turn around and say, 'You should deal with this on your team!'" A co-worker in the same unit added, "So, we've [workers] already killed each other. We can't agree on anything, and we come to you [the manager] and you still won't help us." Another worker complained, "Now everything's on us."

Furthermore, because supervisors no longer managed in direct view, workers wondered what they did, and the resulting resentment toward management was palpable. One woman exclaimed, "I can't figure out why they're called management!" Another worker expressed her belief that "management never does anything." According to even the general manager of the CPC, managers do not know the "work" of the department "at all." Yet in his view, management's withdrawal from direct supervision is a positive product of team organization—a more efficient use of managerial time and talent in that this redistribution of responsibilities permitted supervisors and managers to attend meetings and courses about market trends, company goals, policies, and methods of managing.

Most workers disagreed with this view.

Especially problematic in their eyes is that an absent management cannot adequately assess the performance of individual workers. In evaluating employees' performance, managers often relied on rates. But the rates used to measure productivity in the de-skilled mail processing jobs, for instance, fail to indicate quality, complexity, level of difficulty, and the like. Some employees thus compared current practices unfavourably with the previous system whereby supervision was much tighter. In their view, under the old system resting on much closer supervision, at least good work was noticed.

Workers were highly critical of their annual evaluations by management. The consensus was that only people who "blew their own horns" did well. Many employees also noted that supervisors' "favourites" were treated differently and evaluated more positively than others. Indeed, workers perceived favouritism to be the biggest problem in the department. Other employees claimed that management preferred to keep good workers in place because they were too valuable to lose; troublemakers were less useful and therefore were often promoted out of the unit. Management's distance from the labour process clearly generated distrust among the workers.

More directly contrary to management goals is that the tensions among workers on teams sometimes hampered productivity. After learning that productivity levels were down in her (regular) mail unit, one supervisor, with a nod from upper management, arbitrarily suspended job rotation and the team allocation of work for a week-long period. Employees in her unit were consequently forced to work in the same job, day after day. The result was a dramatic increase in productivity in this unit. Workers themselves had no say in determining this sudden shift in policy. Management's commitment to job rotation and team work was conditional upon workers' ability to meet established productivity/efficiency targets. When these work arrangements conflicted with the firm's bottom line goals, job rotation and team work were readily abandoned.

Team organization exacerbated other tensions among the workforce as well. Because team work enhanced the interdependence of workers, and replaced the formal rules and orders of supervisors with negotiations among co-workers, the stage was set for ethnic, racial and gender-based tensions. In fact, racial and ethnic strains were rife in the units processing the standard mail. That is, in the units featuring degraded work, team work promoted racial and ethnic tensions in addition to those between permanent and temporary workers, and the former tensions cross-cut the latter. In separate interviews, several women of colour reported that ethnic stereotyping and racial discrimination greatly affected their work lives, both structurally and experientially.[30] Many employees claimed that the workforce was divided hierarchically into ethnic cliques. Those at the bottom of the ladder felt marginalized and subordinated by both supervisors and co-workers, on the basis of ethnic and racial origin. A long-term employee commented, "I am the only Indian in my department. They are all Italian. They treat me like dirt. They are together. They cover each other and I am the only one in trouble all the time.... I don't understand what is going on."

In contrast to these racial and ethnic tensions, gender differences did not produce divisions. Some researchers have argued that restructuring in general, and flex-spec in particular, should reinforce and strengthen un-

equal gender relations, and even increase hostility between women and men—assuming that women and men are in different positions in a company.[31] Only a few writers have focused on how the current restructuring is creating more "women's jobs" for both women and men, and thus potentially eroding one source of conflict between the sexes.[32]

In the CPC, women and men reported that they got along very well, and liked working together. Our observations supported that assessment: women and men in the CPC seemed to interact easily and genially. Both women and men commented to us that the workday was made more pleasant by the presence of the other sex. Indeed, the undercurrent of sexuality sometimes present when women and men work together seemed to lighten the monotony of working in the units processing the regular mail. Ironically, then, the erosion of sexual segregation that may accompany restructuring can, in some cases, produce a reduction in gender tensions in the labour force.

Of course, there are overriding negative consequences. As we saw, in spite of variation in job content across the CPC, management views all jobs in the department in the same light—namely as "women's work"—and produced a flattened structure that reflected that view. This means that the men in these jobs are treated as women (that is, badly). A long-term, permanent male employee, who had helped install the present computer system and was responsible (along with one other employee and a technician from outside) for its operation, was classified in a lower band than that of most workers in the department. In order to move up, he was forced to file a union grievance. In spite of his sex, he had been treated like a female clerk.

Servicing the Customer

Exacerbating these new and deepening divisions within the workforce was a strong managerial emphasis on the individual merit and competitive drive of employees. While managers expressed an ideological commitment to the team concept, they clearly conveyed the message that the success of a worker depends on her or his independent ability to exceed the official job description. One recently upgraded woman said, "If you want to achieve, you have to push yourself. You have to initiate a lot of stuff." Another commented, "Just doing the work alone doesn't get you a promotion." The additional effort expected of workers, however, was only vaguely defined.

It was apparent, though, that the company was expanding all jobs to include a sales/personal service component. Management expected each and every worker directly to promote sales and increase the company's business, not only by providing efficient and informed telephone customer service but also by drawing on their personal talents and interpersonal skills in an attempt to make the customer feel valued and respected. According to one of many leaflets distributed by the company, employee "success" was measured in part by "[g]oing above and beyond the call of duty" in an effort to "delight the customer."

On the job daily, employees experienced this sales/service emphasis as an additional pressure. In the unit that was responsible for handling problem payments, workers attributed much of their daily stress to the company's unrelenting push to compete for new customers and "enhance customer loyalty." Functioning within a "service economy," most business clients themselves expected special treatment by the people who processed their payments. "You have more customers [now] who want kid-glove treatment," observed one worker.

To some extent, the relationship between customer and employee seemed to eclipse that which had formerly existed between supervisor and employee. Service workers have long been aware of the need to please a public clientele. In this new workplace scenario, however, the customer is a more direct participant in the monitoring and evaluation of workers.[33] For example, customer complaints were a key source of poor ratings in workers' annual reviews. Conversely, workers who could win new clients or keep important existing clientele by going "out of their way," "above and beyond" (for example, by meeting clients in the CPC lobby to review account statements or spending several hours on the telephone with one customer)—often on their own time and of their own initiative—were noticed and rewarded by management.

Some workers themselves expressed pride in their ability to display strong social skills on the job. Indeed, a number of women in the unit stated that their role in "helping the customer" allowed them to derive some meaning from otherwise alienating work. They did so by defining their job as a service to people rather than as routine paper processing. For offering this "service," furthermore, some women said they felt "appreciated" by customers. One employee remarked, "[s]ometimes, a customer is really nice and makes you feel happy for the whole day ... they'll ask your name, how's the weather ... I feel so good."

Without denying the importance of workers' own attempts to humanize their work and thereby dignify themselves, it is important to note that this emphasis on customer satisfaction also emerged as part of a refashioned, decentralized, managerial strategy of control—one that rests on shifting authority from the supervisor and employer to "the shoulders of non-managerial individuals."[34] Indeed, customers can be more effective disciplining agents than managers; in part, because the relationship between employees and their many anonymous clients does not, on the face of it, appear to be hierarchical and adversarial. Although servicing the customer was a source of strain, many workers felt obliged to process payments efficiently precisely because "the customer" was depending on them.

Along with enlisting the customer, management attributed the least popular and most brutal corporate decisions to the seemingly objective laws of the market.[35] Indeed, these two forces, the customer and the market, were often used in tandem. For example, top-management periodically relied on television monitors in the cafeteria to broadcast to workers the message that the company's survival depended on their being fiercely competitive. And they claimed that one way to maintain a competitive advantage was to offer outstanding customer service (especially to corporate clients). During these assemblies, managers delivered a punitive message, warning that jobs would be lost if workers did not make special efforts (and even concessions) in the interest of the firm's survival. One woman expressed the sentiments of many employees: "I'm doing my best for that customer. I'm conscious of it because that customer means my job." Another worker explained that company broadcasts often sound like "the axe is falling.... People are afraid to lose their jobs. They'll do what they need to do to keep their jobs." A co-worker added:

I wouldn't call it threats. They just tell you what the facts are.... If you want to help out by taking a reduced work week or whatever, then it's gonna make it easier ... look in the papers, how many companies are just laying off ... you're lucky that, at least, they give you a choice to help them.

In this refashioned workplace, even workers themselves were held accountable for the viability of their jobs.

This management approach, then, is one in which supervisors and managers are seemingly absent, yet retain strong (indirect) political control over the workforce. Management did not abdicate power; its power merely became diffused. Along with ensuring that workers regulate one another in team arrangements, management handed over some supervisory control to the customer, and accountability to the market. Management's retreat from the workplace, of course, was illusory. Workers never stopped feeling the "presence" of management. Paradoxically, it seems that as managers physically receded from the shop floor, they spent more time developing strategies of managing.

But because the power and logic of capital is unyielding, regardless of how well workers service the customer or concede to aid the health of the company, they will lose their jobs. Not satisfied with the organizational changes to date, as our interviews ended, company executives entered a new phase of restructuring—pursuing a philosophy they term "business transformation." According to the firm's spokespersons, the new business transformation means "looking at every single thing you do, backwards and forwards and upside down, and coming up with a way to do it faster, smarter." According to this philosophy, each unit in the firm must be accountable for its profitability. "If it's not successful, get rid of it," says one manager. As part of this plan, the company will "outsource" functions such as customer payments and close down the CPC.

Discussion and Conclusions

The case of the Customer Payments Centre throws into question the assumption that managerial strategies are always rationally planned, consistent, and effective—a view that managers themselves often reinforce in their promotion of TQM as a seamless method of managing. We observed irrationality, inconsistency, and contradictions in this unit of clerical workers. The employer was managing largely by trial and error. While company officials undoubtedly intended that the new computerized equipment would reduce their reliance on labour, the process of technological change in the CPC not only resulted in an unnecessarily high increase in labour costs (albeit temporarily), but also served to underline the ultimate dependence of management on workers' job-specific skills and initiative (again, at least in the initial period of adjustment). Meanwhile, the company introduced a management strategy that purported to humanize the workplace, championed a philosophy of worker involvement, and aimed to promote worker loyalty to the firm (TQM). Yet these organizational and ideological goals were advanced in the context of technological innovations that had already served, in part, to degrade and dehumanize the work. According to one worker, the philosophy of TQM makes little sense in the CPC because "it's [the unit] totally not people oriented; it's machine-oriented."

Adding to the contradictions, management heightened numerical flexibility, relying increasingly on part-time and temporary employees from whom loyalty could not be expected. The structural conditions of their employment made such a commitment unlikely. In turn, the insecurity that underlay part-timers' minimal commitment propelled them to protect their own interests. In so doing, they were poor candidates for working in teams. Clearly, in the case of the CPC, numerical flexibility and functional flexibility are at odds.

The indeterminacy of managerial methods, however, has not diminished the power of capital. In spite of these contradictory outcomes, the company continues to dominate the telecommunications market and boasts an exorbitantly high rate of profit. Furthermore, notwithstanding haphazard shifts in organizational policies, management has intensified its control of the workforce and the labour process. In the face of contradictory outcomes and unforeseen developments both within the organization and external to it, driven by their relentless pursuit of efficiency and profitability, employers have resorted to a "multiplicity of control strategies."[36] As sociologist Vicki Smith states, enlisting customers to regulate service workers and relying on workers in teams to monitor one another, [as well as promoting the idea of the objective necessity of the market] are "decentralized and subjective strategies that mesh with an occupational structure increasingly characterized by service and flexible manufacturing work."[37] They reflect the growing diffusion and open-endedness of managerial evaluation and control. These new strategies coexist with the old (for example, a harsh rate system, the routinization of many jobs, flattening the occupational structure).

The implications of this example of restructuring for worker-management relations generally, and worker resistance in particular, are not clear. New lines of division are being drawn in the CPC. While the feminization of women's and men's work has seemed to lessen both sex segregation and workplace conflicts between the sexes, there are growing tensions and rivalries among workers based on race and ethnicity, employment status (temporary, part-time or permanent, full-time), in intersection with seniority and skill level.

These new lines of demarcation, however, have not served to displace workers' anger toward management. Workers' consciousness of their exploitation by management has been heightened by a number of contradictions in their situation. Broad-banded jobs, with similar rates of pay and similarly poor promotion opportunities, host a labour force that is highly variable in terms of educational credentials, skills and knowledge of the department's labour process. Consequently, workers feel unjustly treated. Team organization, which removes management from direct supervision and precludes responsible evaluation of workers' performance, also induces clear resentment of management by employees. Given that the anger workers feel toward management is mediated by divisions among themselves, however, the form that worker resistance will assume is uncertain. Collective resistance will depend on the entry of another actor—a strong labour organization that must unify workers along fundamental bases. But insofar as workplace democratization has been illusory, workplace conflict is certain to persist, even if this particular work unit disappears.

Endnotes

We wish to thank the Metro Toronto Clerical Workers Labour Adjustment Committee, and especially Alice DeWolff, for allowing us the opportunity to do this case study for them. For helpful comments on an earlier draft of the paper, we thank Leah Vosko, Kate Bezanson, Tania DasGupta, Alice DeWolff, Mamina Gonick, Meg Luxton, David Rapaport, Ester Reiter, and Robert Storey.

1   Stanford, J. "Discipline, Insecurity and Productivity: The Economics Behind Labour Market 'Flexibility.'" In J. Pulkingham and G. Ternowetsky (eds.). 1996. *Remaking Canadian Social Policy*. Halifax: Fernwood Press, pp. 130–147.

2   Harvey, D. 1989. *The Condition of Postmodernity*. Oxford: Basil Blackwell, p. 147.

3   Pignon, D. and J. Querzola. 1978. "Dictatorship and Democracy in Production." In André Gorz (ed.). *The Division of Labour*. Sussex, England: Harvester Press, pp. 63–99.

4   Harman, H., R. Kraut and L. Tilly (eds.). 1987. *Computer Chips and Paper Clips,* Vol. 1. Washington, DC: Panel on Technology and Women's Employment, Commission on Behavioral and Social Sciences and Education. National Research Council, National Academy Press.

5   Atkinson, J. 1988. "Recent Changes in the International Labour Market Structure in the UK." In W. Buitelaar (ed.). *Technology and Work*. United Kingdom: Aldershot, pp. 133–149; see also Betcherman, G., K. McMullen, N. Leckie and C. Caron. 1994. *The Canadian Workplace in Transition*. Kingston: Queen's University, Industrial Relations Centre. In Canada, Betcherman et al. pose two "paths" for the new HRM models: (1) a "low-cost" path characterised by non-standard jobs, and (2) a "high-performance" path which features a skilled labour force, flexible work organization, commitment to training, employee involvement in decision-making, etc.

6 Russell, B. 1995. "The Subtle Labour Process and the Great Skill Debate: Evidence from a Potash Mine-Mill Operation." *Canadian Journal of Sociology* 20/3, pp. 359–386; Pignon and Querzola. "Dictatorship and Democracy..."

7 But see Garson, B. 1988. *The Electronic Sweatshop.* New York: Simon & Schuster; Proctor, S., M. Rowlinson, L. McArdle, J. Hassard and P. Forrester. 1994. "Flexibility, Politics and Strategy: in Defence of the Model of the Flexible Firm." *Work, Employment and Society* 8/2, pp. 221–242.

8 See Russell. "The Subtle Labour Process..."

9 Dohse, D., J. Ulrich and T. Malsch. 1985. "From 'Fordism' to 'Toyotism'? The Social Organization of the Labor Process in the Japanese Automobile Industry." *Politics and Society* 14/2, pp. 115–143; Hadley, K. 1994. "Working Lean and Mean: A Gendered Experience of Restructuring in an Electronics Manufacturing Plant." PhD Thesis: Ontario Institute for Studies in Education; Piore, M.J. 1986. "Perspectives on Labour Market Flexibility." *Industrial Relations* 25/2, pp. 183–201; Robertson, D., J. Rinehart, C. Huxley, and the CAW Research Group on CAMI. 1992. "Team Concept and Kaizen: Japanese Production Management in a Unionized Canadian Auto Plant." *Studies in Political Economy* 39, pp. 77–107; Reinhart, J., C. Huxley and D. Robertson. 1997. *Just Another Car Factory? Lean Production and Its Discontents.* Ithaca, New York: ILR Press; Russell, "The Subtle Labour Process..."; Shaiken, H., S. Herzenberg and S. Kuhn. 1986. "The Work Process Under More Flexible Production." *Industrial Relations* 25/2, pp. 167–182; Parker, M. and J. Slaughter. 1989. *Choosing Sides: Unions and the Team Concept.* Boston: South End Press; Tomaney, J. 1990. "The Reality of Workplace Flexibility." *Capital and Class* 40, pp. 29–55.

10 Atkinson. "Recent Changes..."

11 See Menzies, H. 1982. *Women and the Chip.* Montreal: The Institute for Research on Public Policy; Menzies, H. 1996. *Whose Brave New World?* Toronto: Between the Lines Press.

12 Applebaum, E. 1987. "Technology and the Redesign of Work in the Insurance Industry." In B.D. Wright, M.F. Ferree, G. Mellow, L. Lewis, M.D Samper, R. Asher and K. Claspell (eds.). *Women, Work and Technology.* Ann Arbor: University of Michigan Press, pp. 182–201; Baran B., and S. Teegarden. "Women's Labor in the Office of the Future: A Case Study of the Insurance Industry," 1987. In L. Beneria and C. Stimpson (eds.). *Women, Households and the Economy.* New Brunswick, New Jersey: Rutgers University Press, pp. 201–224; Crompton, R. and G. Jones. 1984. *White-Collar Proletariat .* London: Macmillan Press; Machung, A. 1984. "Word Processing: Forward for Business, Backward for Women." In K. Sacks and D. Remy (eds.). *My Troubles are Going to Have Trouble with Me.* New Brunswick, New Jersey: Rutgers University Press. pp. 124–139.

13 Feldberg, R. and E.N. Glenn. 1987. "Technology and the Transformation of Clerical Work." In R. Kraut (ed.). *Technology and the Transformation of While-Collar Work.* Hillsdale, New Jersey: Lawrence Erlbaum Associates. pp. 77–98; Lane, C. 1989. "New Technology and Clerical Work." In D. Gallic (ed.). *Employment in Britain.* Oxford: Basil Blackwell; Machung, "Word Processing..."

14 Carter, V. 1987. "Office Technology and Relations of Control in Clerical Work Organizations." In B.D. Wright et al (eds.). *Women, Work and Technology* Ann Arbor: University of Michigan Press. pp. 202–220; Hartmann, Kraut and Tilly. (eds.). *Computer Chips and Paper Clips.*

15 Hartmann, Kraut and Tilly (eds.). *Computer Chips and Paper Clips.*

16 Hartmann, Kraut and Tilly (eds.). *Computer Chips and Paper Clips;* Lane. "New Technology..."

17 Wells, D. 1993. "Are Strong Unions Compatible with the New Model of Human Resource Management?" *Relations industrielles* 48/1, pp. 56–83.

18 Dohse, Ulrich and Malsch. "From 'Fordism' to 'Toyotism'..."; Hadley. "Working Lean and Mean..."; Parker and Slaughter, *Choosing Sides*; Robertson, Rinehart, Huxley, and the CAW Research Group on CAMI. "Team Concept and Kaizen..."; Shaiken, Herzenberg and Kuhn. "The Work Process..."; Tomaney. "The Reality of Workplace Flexibility."

19 Hadley. "Working Lean and Mean..."

20 Hadley. "Working Lean and Mean..."; Tomaney, "The Reality of Workplace Flexibility..."

21 For a discussion of flexibility and part-time work, see Beechey, V. 1987. "Conceptualizing Part-Time Work." In V. Beechey (ed.). *Unequal Work.* London: Verso, pp. 149–169; Jenson, J. 1989. "The Talents of Women, the Skills of Men: Flexible Specialization and Women." In S. Wood (ed.). *The Transformation of Work?* London: Hutchinson; Walby, S. 1989. "Flexibility and the Changing Sexual Division of Labour." In S.Wood (ed.). *The Transformation of Work?* London: Hutchinson. Actually, numerical flexibility (non-standard work) is prob-

ably a more common management strategy than flexible specialization. See Atkinson, "Recent Changes…" Certainly non-standard work is on the rise in Canada. See Duffy, A. and N. Pupo. 1992. *Part-Time Paradox: Connecting Gender, Work and Family.* Toronto: McClelland & Stewart; Armstrong, P. "The Feminization of the Labour Force: Harmonizing Down in a Global Economy." 1996. In I. Bakker (ed.). *Rethinking Restructuring: Gender and Change in Canada.* Toronto: University of Toronto Press, pp. 29–54. In 1992, 30 percent of the Canadian labour force worked in non-standard jobs. See Betcherman, McMullen, Leckie, and Caron. *The Canadian Workplace In Transition.*

22 Applebaum. "Technology and the Redesign of Work…"; Baran and Teegarden. "Women's Labor…"

23 DeWolff, A. 1995. "Job Loss and Entry-Level Information Workers: Training and Adjustment Strategies for Clerical Workers in Metro Toronto." Toronto: Report of the Metro Toronto Clerical Workers Labour Adjustment Committee.

24 We asked several middle-level managers and two more senior managers about the decision-making process, especially the relationships between technological changes and organizational changes. None of the middle managers were able to offer an adequate explanation of the sequence or logic of decision-making in the company. The two upper-level managers suggested that decisions were made by one or two individuals only who seemed to have the power to implement whichever managerial philosophy was currently popular.

25 Braverman, H. 1974. *Labor and Monopoly Capital.* New York: Monthly Review Press.

26 See also Milkman, R.and C. Pullman. 1991. "Technological Change in an Auto Assembly Plant: The Impact on Workers, Tasks, and Skills." *Work and Occupations* 18/2), pp. 123–147; Zuboff, S. 1988. *In the Age of the Smart Machine: The Future of Work and Power.* New York: Basic Books.

27 In the regular mail processing units, each team consisted of 12 workers; in the irregular mail unit, seven people made up a team; and in the other units a team contained three or four workers.

28 See also Gottfried, H. and L. Graham. 1993. "Constructing Difference: The Making of Gendered Subcultures in a Japanese Automobile Plant." *Sociology* 27/4, pp. 611–628; Robertson, Rinehart, Huxley, and the CAW Research Group on CAMI. "Team Concept and Kaizen…"; Sinclair, A. 1992. "The Tyranny of a Team Ideology." *Organization Studies* 13/4, pp. 611–626.

29 Some of the workers we interviewed reported that they were banking their overtime hours rather than receiving financial compensation for overtime worked, in an effort to "help out the health of the company." In addition, for the same reason, a number of employees said that they had "voluntarily" agreed to take reduced work weeks, at a loss of pay.

30 This outcome was predicted by Hadley. "Working Lean and Mean…"

31 See Hacker, S. 1979. "Sex Stratification, Technology and Organizational Change: A Longitudinal Case Study of AT&T." *Social Problems* 26, pp. 539–557; Jenson. "The Talents of Women…"; Walby, "Flexibility and the Changing Sexual Division…"

32 See Armstrong. "The Feminization of the Labour Force…"; McDowell, L. 1991. "Life without Father and Ford: The New Gender Order of Post-Fordism." *Transactions of the Institute of British Geographers* 16. pp. 400–419.

33 See also Fuller, L. and V. Smith. 1991. "Consumers' Reports: Management by Customers in a Changing Economy." *Work, Employment, and Society* 5/1, pp. 1–16; Leidner, R. 1993. *Fast Food, Fast Talk. Service Work and the Routinization of Everyday Life.* Berkeley: University of California Press.

34 Smith, V. "Braverman's Legacy: The Labour Process Tradition at 20," *Work and Occupations* 21/4 (1994), p. 415.

35 See Pignon and Querzola. "Dictatorship and Democracy…" p. 75.

36 Smith, V. "Braverman's Legacy…" p. 414.

37 Smith, V. "Braverman's Legacy…" p. 415.

SECTION II: POST-FORDISM AT WORK

Critical Thinking Questions

Chapter 3: Listening to Workers: The Reorganization of Work in the Canadian Motor Vehicle Industry, Wayne Lewchuk and David Robertson

1. Discuss the differences and similarities between lean production and Fordist systems of work organization.

2. Should workers play a central role in decision-making in their workplace? Identify factors in the workplace that might either facilitate or impede greater worker participation in decision-making.

3. Should workers' perceptions of the benefits of, or problems with, the organization of their work be considered valid when one is conducting research on the transformation of the workplace?

Chapter 4: Flexible Work, Flexible Workers: The Restructuring of Clerical Work in a Large Telecommunications Company, Bonnie Fox and Pamela Sugiman

1. What links can be drawn between the technological redesign of the workplace and the implementation of new human resources management strategies?

2. Discuss how differences of gender, race, ethnicity, age and employment status affect relations among workers. Are these differences more likely to divide workers or can they serve as the basis for resistance to deteriorating working conditions?

3. Fox and Sugiman question the widely held assumption that workplace restructuring occurs as a result of rational and well-planned managerial strategies. If the authors' analysis is correct, how can we explain that workplaces continue to function?

Recommended Readings

Amin, Ash (ed.). 1994. *Post-Fordism: A Reader*. Oxford: Blackwell. A series of articles that introduce and engage with the debates about post-Fordism as both a new era in capitalism and a fundamental transformation in the methods of work organization.

Armstrong, Pat, Hugh Armstrong, Jacqueline Choinière, Eric Mykhalovskiy, and Jerry P. White. 1997. *Medical Alert: New Work Organizations in Health Care*. Toronto: Garamond Press. A critical assessment of the adoption of private-sector systems of work organization in public-sector workplaces. The book highlights the consequences of such systems for providers of health care and patients.

Elger, Tony and Chris Smith (eds.). 1994. *Global Japanization? The Transnational Transformation of the Labour Process*. London: Routledge. A collection of case studies that assess the influence of Japanese models of management and production on manufacturing in different parts of the Western world, and the consequences for workers.

Russell, Bob. 1999. *More with Less: Work Reorganization in the Canadian Mining Industry*. Toronto: University of Toronto Press. A detailed case study that analyzes the uneven implementation of new methods of work production in the mining industry in Canada, locating workplace changes in the context of economic restructuring and global processes.

Wood, Stephen (ed.). 1989. *The Transformation of Work? Skill, Flexibility and the Labour Process*. London: Unwin Hyman. A collection of original articles that focus on the fundamental transformation of work that began in the 1980s. This book makes an important contribution to theoretical developments on work in a changing world.

Related Websites

Canadian International Labour Network

http://www.ciln.mcmaster.ca/

The Canadian International Labour Network was a collaborative research venture housed at McMaster University. While the network stopped operating in 2002, links on the website provide access to research papers, the network's newsletter, labour-related data, labour legislation, and related networks and institutes.

Centre for Research on Work and Society

http://www.yorku.ca/crws/

The Centre for Research on Work and Society addresses contemporary issues facing labour in Canada. The Centre publishes *Just Labour: A Canadian Journal of Work and Society.*

Human Resources and Skills Development Canada's Labour Program

http://www.hrsdc.gc.ca/en/gateways/nav/top_nav/program/labour.shtml

The federal government's Labour Program focuses on work and labour issues. The website offers information on a variety of topics such as labour legislation, collective bargaining, labour education and training, and workplace equity.

Institute for Work and Health

http://www.iwh.on.ca/

The Institute is an independent, not-for-profit research organization that conducts and shares research on the health and safety of work and workplaces with workers, unions, employers, clinicians and policy-makers to promote, protect and improve the health of working people. The site includes a section on the Institute's publications.

National Website for Labour Jurisdiction Information Exchange

http://www.labour-info-travail.org/

This Canadian website provides links to departments or ministries of labour in each province and territory and at the federal level. It includes a library of information available in each jurisdiction on work-related topics such as labour relations, labour standards, women in employment, and workplace innovations.

Section III

Precariousness in the Labour Market

ANALYSES OF THE redesign of workplaces, which was the focus of the previous section of this book, have been taking place in tandem with empirical and theoretical enquiries into the changing nature of labour markets and employment relationships. Many scholars have argued that the advent of the post-industrial economy and the competitive requirements of the global order have been at the root of the significant rise in non-standard work arrangements that increasingly characterize industrialized countries. This trend signals an erosion of the postwar standard employment relationship that ensured stability and security for many workers, albeit mostly men in industrial and professional jobs. The articles in this section of the book take a closer look at specific examples of precariousness and feminization that underlie this shift in employment norms. Each article uses a different type of methodological approach, either quantitative or qualitative, to explore these processes in Canadian labour markets and workplaces. Both contributions highlight the patterns of inequality that accompany the transformation of employment relationships.

The contribution by Cynthia J. Cranford, Leah F. Vosko and Nancy Zukewich focuses on the changing forms of employment that define broader labour-market structures in Canada. The authors are particularly concerned with directing our attention to the gendered nature of precarious employment. They introduce the concept of the feminization of employment norms as a way of succinctly capturing the process whereby the standard employment relationship as a norm is being eroded and non-standard forms of employment that display characteristics of precarious employment typically associated with women and other marginalized groups are spreading. Cranford, Vosko and Zukewich use Statistics Canada data to examine the changing participation of women and men in four forms of wage work. Their findings highlight that between 1989 and 2001, full-time permanent employment decreased for both women and men, but women remain more likely than men to be employed in part-time and temporary wage work. In an attempt to further explore labour-market dynamics, Cranford, Vosko, and Zukewich develop a model that layers these distinct forms of employment with indicators of regulatory protection, control and wages. Their analysis points to a continuum of precariousness, with full-time permanent employees enjoying the lowest level of precariousness followed by full-time temporary and then part-time permanent employees. Part-time temporary employees are located at the furthest end of the continuum. The authors also reveal interesting gendered dimensions to this continuum, with inequalities surfacing between full-time permanent women and men, but with a convergence in precariousness emerging among part-time and temporary women and men. Cranford, Vosko, and Zukewich call for further research, both quantitative and qualitative, to develop a more in-depth understanding of the feminization of employment norms characterized by continuity as well as change in the social relations of gender.

In her article, Vivian Shalla examines a particular instance of the increasing feminization of employment and growing precariousness in the Canadian labour market. Her case study is an exploration of the contracting out, by Air Canada, of the work of its customer sales and service agents to travel agencies. She argues that contracting out was a strategy actively pursued to cut labour costs in order to allow Canada's major air carrier to remain competitive and prosper under airline-industry restructuring. Shalla demonstrates how the relatively invisible form of contracting out adopted by Air Canada has contributed to the degradation of the overall job of customer sales and service agents due to lost opportunities, increased job insecurity and further deskilling of their work. In her account of Air Canada's contracting-out practices, the author details how computer and telecommunications technologies are harnessed to spatially reorganize work and enhance labour flexibility. Shalla's analysis also reveals how the degradation of working conditions fosters more conflictual labour-management relations and contributes to the radicalization of workers. She discusses various defensive and proactive measures adopted by this group of white-collar workers and their union to halt the erosion of the standard employment relationship, thereby protecting their job security and the quality of their work. The author's case study illustrates the changing nature and conditions of women's white-collar, service-sector work in post-industrial society. In tracing how good jobs get turned into bad jobs, Shalla offers insights into the dynamics underlying growing inequality and polarization in industrialized societies. The author concludes with dire predictions for the employment of airline-industry workers given ongoing turbulence in air transportation.

CHAPTER 5

The Gender of Precarious Employment in Canada

Cynthia J. Cranford, Leah F. Vosko, and Nancy Zukewich

EVIDENCE OF THE decline of the standard employment relationship (SER) and its associated gender relations is escalating in Canada. The SER refers to a normative model of employment where the worker has one employer, works full-time, year-round on the employer's premises under his or her supervision, enjoys extensive statutory benefits and entitlements, and expects to be employed indefinitely (Muckenberger 1989; Schellenberg and Clark 1996; Vosko 1997). The SER became the statistical reality for (primarily white) men in Canada in the post-World War II era, yet forms of employment that fall outside this norm and that employ primarily women have grown since the late 1970s (Fudge and Vosko 2001a). Nevertheless, the SER remains the model upon which labour laws, legislation and policies are based, prompting a correlation between the growth in "non-standard" forms of employment and a rising precariousness that is highly gendered (Fudge and Vosko 2001b; Vallée 1999; Vosko 1997).

The aim of this article is to examine the links between gender, forms of employment and dimensions of precarious employment in the Canadian labour force.[1] Precarious employment is defined as forms of employment involving atypical employment contracts, limited social benefits and statutory entitlements, job insecurity, low job tenure, low earnings, poor working conditions and high risks of ill health. Thus, the term "precarious employment" places emphasis on the quality of employment. Gender is the process through which cultural meanings and inequalities in power, authority, rights and privileges come to be associated with sexual difference (Lerner 1997; Scott 1986). To speak of the "gendering" of a phenomenon is to focus attention on the process whereby sex differences become social inequalities. To argue that a phenomenon is gendered is to emphasize that gender shapes social relations in key institutions that organize society, such as the labour market, the state or the family (Acker 1992).

Few studies examine how dimensions of precariousness vary across forms of employment and fewer still focus on the gender of precarious employment. There is a common tendency to group together a broad range of employment forms and work arrangements, unified by their deviation from the SER, into a single category of "non-standard employment" (Carre et al. 2000; Economic Council of Canada 1990; Krahn 1991). However, there are important differences both between and within the forms of employment that fall outside the SER. For example, different regulatory challenges are posed by own-account self-employment, the triangular employment relationship characterizing wage work in the temporary-help industry and part-time permanent wage work (Duffy and Pupo 1992; Fudge, Tucker and Vosko 2003; Mayer 1996; Vosko 2000). With economic restructuring, there is also growing income polarization among full-time permanent paid employees (James, Grant and Cranford 2000; Luxton and Corman 2001). Finally, there are inequalities along lines of gender, "race" and ethnicity within both standard and non-standard forms of employment (Das Gupta 1996; Zeytinoğlu and Muteshi 1999).

The heterogeneity among forms of employment that fall outside the SER makes it necessary to question what have come to be normalized descriptive concepts—terms such as "non-standard employment." Scholars have begun to look within the category "non-standard employment" by distinguishing between person-level and job-level characteristics (Bourhis and Wils 2001), by focusing on the concentration of racialized groups in non-standard employment (Zeytinoğlu and Muteshi 1999) and by distinguishing between structural and social psychological dimensions

of changing employment relationships (Lowe, Schellenberg and Davidman 1999). However, few studies have examined how variations in dimensions of precariousness, both between and within forms of employment, are gendered.

In this article, we illustrate how precarious employment in the Canadian labour force reflects the feminization of employment norms. The feminization of employment norms denotes the erosion of the standard employment relationship as a norm and the spread of non-standard forms of employment that exhibit qualities of precarious employment associated with women (Vosko 2003). Although many scholars focus on the changing nature of work, profound continuities characterize the contemporary labour force; specifically, women, immigrants and people of colour continue to occupy the more precarious segments of the labour market (Arat-Koc 1997; Bakan and Stasiulus 1997). Analyses that fail to focus on the growth of precarious employment in relation to continuing gender inequalities may conceal important aspects of the contemporary labour market.

To advance this argument, the article proceeds in four parts. The first part reviews concepts used to describe and explain changing employment relationships and, in order to highlight the gender of precarious employment, offers the "feminization of employment norms" (Vosko 2003) as an alternative concept. The second part outlines the methodological approach. The third part of the article uses Statistics Canada data to examine the gender of precarious employment in the contemporary Canadian labour force by first examining the participation of women and men in mutually exclusive forms of employment and then layering four forms of wage work with other dimensions of precariousness, namely degree of regulatory protection, control and wages.[2] Gender differences along these dimensions both between and within forms of employment are of primary concern. The fourth part concludes by summarizing key findings and pointing to avenues for future research.

Conceptualizing Changing Employment Relationships

Non-Standard Employment

In the Canadian context, the growth of "non-standard employment" became a significant topic of discussion in the 1980s. The discussion intensified when the Economic Council of Canada pronounced that the growth of non-standard employment was outpacing the growth of full-time full-year jobs. In its study, *Good Jobs, Bad Jobs* (1990: 12), the Council reported that fully one-half of all new jobs created between 1980 and 1988 were "non-standard," which it defined simply as "those [jobs] that differ from the traditional model of the full-time job." In response to the Council's study, several government reports examined the growth of non-standard forms of employment and work arrangements (Advisory Group on Working Time 1994; Human Resources and Development Canada 1994).

Harvey Krahn produced the earliest study on the growth of non-standard employment in Canada. Krahn's (1991) broadest measure for non-standard employment was made up of four situations that differed from the norm of a full-time, full-year, permanent paid job: (1) part-time employment; (2) temporary employment, including employees with term or contract, seasonal, casual and all other forms of wage work with a predetermined end date; (3) own-account self-employment (i.e. self-employed persons with no paid employees); and

(4) multiple job holding. In a follow-up study, Krahn (1995) found that women remained more likely than men to have non-standard employment although as part-time and temporary employment grew, the proportion of men in these forms of employment also rose.

The employment situations comprising the broad definition of non-standard employment are not mutually exclusive, making it difficult to determine whether the more precarious types of employment are those that are growing (Vosko, Zukewich and Cranford 2003). Part-time employment includes paid employees and the self-employed (both own-account and employers), and the work of part-time employees can be of temporary or permanent duration. Furthermore, multiple job holding is more of an arrangement than a form of employment since all employed people can hold multiple jobs. There is thus a pressing need to move away from grouping together situations that are united primarily by their deviation from the standard employment relationship if we are to understand the extent of precarious employment in the labour force.

Precarious Employment

European statisticians and scholars have addressed the decline of the standard employment relationship and related concerns over underemployment, income insecurity and social exclusion, by elevating the notion of precarious employment (Silver 1992). The influential volume, *Precarious Jobs in Labour Market Regulation* (Rodgers and Rodgers 1989), reveals the central problem of focusing solely on forms of employment as a means of exploring employment change. To remedy this problem, Rodgers (1989: 3–5) identifies four dimensions central to establishing whether a job is precarious, each of which focuses on the quality of jobs. The first dimension is the degree of certainty of continuing employment; here, time horizons and risk of job loss are emphasized. Second, Rodgers introduces the notion of control over the labour process, linking this dimension to the presence or absence of a trade union and, hence, control over working conditions and pace of work. Rodgers' third dimension is the degree of regulatory protection through union representation or the law. Fourth, Rodgers suggests that income level is a critical element, noting that a given job may be secure in the sense that it is stable and long-term but precarious in that the wage may still be insufficient for the worker to maintain herself/himself as well as dependants.

The concept "precarious employment" takes us beyond the broad notion of non-standard employment. Nevertheless, much research on precarious employment overlooks gender. For example, the dimension of hours of employment must be included if we are to understand how precariousness is gendered (Vosko 2003).

The Feminization of Employment Norms

Recent feminist scholarship argues that changing employment relations are both shaped by and, in turn, shape enduring gender inequalities both inside and outside the labour market (Armstrong 1996; Bakker 1996; Fudge 1991; Spalter-Roth and Hartmann 1998; Jenson 1996; Vosko 2000). This process of continuity through change can be conceptualized as the feminization of employment norms, a concept that denotes the erosion of the standard employment relationship as a norm and the spread of non-standard forms of employment that exhibit qualities of precarious employment associated with women and other marginalized groups (Vosko 2003). Similar

processes have been described as the creation of more "women's work in the market" (Armstrong 1996: 30) and a new set of "gendered employment relationships" (Jenson 1996: 5).

In most Organization for Economic Cooperation and Development (OECD) countries, the post-World War II "gender order"—that is, the dominant set of gender relations operating in society (Connell 1987)—was shaped by the standard employment relationship (SER), yet empirically the SER and its associated gender order began to show signs of erosion in the early 1970s. The SER refers to a normative model of employment where a worker has one employer, works full-time, year-round on the employer's premises under his or her supervision, enjoys extensive statutory benefits and entitlements and expects to be employed indefinitely (Muckenberger 1989; Schellenberg and Clark 1996; Vosko 1997). The SER is based on what some characterize as a "patriarchal model" (Eichler 1997) and others conceive as a male breadwinner/female caregiver or "family wage" model (Fraser 1997). That is, the SER was designed to provide a wage sufficient for a man to support a wife and children. In Canada, in the immediate post-World War II period, the SER became the statistical reality for most (primarily white) men, while most women, as well as immigrants, migrants and racialized groups, were relegated to part-time, seasonal and other precarious forms of employment (Fudge and Vosko 2001a; also Bakan and Stasiulus 1997; Arat-Koc 1997). In the 1970s, fundamental cracks in the post-World War II gender order—related to macroeconomic instability in the global economy—began to appear and more employed people, including more men, lost their claim to the SER. At the same time, forms of employment falling outside this norm, such as contract, temporary and part-time employment, have grown.

The forms of employment that fall outside of the standard employment relationship have historically been, and continue to be, associated with women (Fudge and Vosko 2001a, 2001b; Spatler-Roth and Hartmann 1998). It is assumed their perceived roles in the daily and generational maintenance of people (i.e. social reproduction) lead women to freely choose part-time and temporary forms of employment and these assumptions justify women's concentration in less secure employment with lower wages and fewer benefits. A more complex interpretation of these patterns is that a set of gendered trade-offs contributes to the betterment of men's labour-market position and the entrenchment of precarious employment amongst women; recent research confirms that, among both employees and the self-employed, most men say they engage in part-time work in order to pursue their education but hardly any men trade off part-time work for caregiving, while many women say they engage in part-time work for reasons related to caregiving (Vosko 2002; also Armstrong 1996; Duffy and Pupo 1992; Women in Canada 2001). In short, feminist scholars argue that the over-representation of women in more precarious forms of employment is shaped by continuous gender inequalities in households resulting in women's greater responsibilities for unpaid domestic work compared to men.

Due to these processes of continuity and change, contemporary labour-market trends are best conceptualized as a feminization of employment norms, rather than as gender-less processes of casualization or erosion. Feminization is typically associated with only women's mass entry into the labour force or simply with the changing gender composition of jobs, but the "feminization of employment norms" refers to four facets of racialized and gendered labour-market trends: (1) high levels of formal labour force participation among women; (2) continuing industrial and occupational segregation; (3) income and occupational polarization both between and among women and men; (4) the gendering of jobs to resemble more precarious so-called "women's work"—that is, work associated with women and other marginalized groups.[3] Each of these facets of feminization increased in the 1990s in Canada (Vosko 2002).

This paper focuses in depth on the gendering of jobs and income polarization. Due to the shortcomings of existing surveys, we are unable to examine how intersections of "race" and gender contribute to the feminization of employment norms.[4] Also characterized as "harmonizing down" (Armstrong 1996), the gendering of jobs captures the fact that certain groups of men are experiencing downward pressure on wages and conditions of work much like those typically associated with "women's work," while many women continue to endure economic pressure (Vosko 2003). Similar processes have been conceptualized as the feminization of the labour process through the employment of undocumented immigrant women and men in restructuring industries (Cranford 1998). Indeed, empirical studies have shown that among men, it is primarily young men, racialized men and recent immigrant men who are experiencing this facet of the feminization of employment norms (Armstrong 1996; Cranford 1998; Vosko 2002). Income polarization is the result of occupational and income disparities between men and women, as well as among women and among men along the lines of "race," ethnicity, age and other social locations (Vosko 2000). Previous research has found growing income and occupational polarization among women by "race," ethnicity and immigrant status (Bakan and Stasiulus 1997; Das Gupta 1996; James, Grant and Cranford 2000; Vosko 2002).

Methodological Approach

There is a disjuncture between conceptual advances concerning changing employment relationships and methods suitable to measure these changes. Gendered processes and complex labour force trends are not easily detected with a single, quantitative method of analysis. At the same time, qualitative case studies are able to uncover complex processes but cannot depict broader patterns and trends. To remedy

this gap, the ensuing analysis proceeds in two steps.

First, in order to determine if the more precarious forms of employment are growing for women and men, we break down total employment into a typology of mutually exclusive forms. The typology, summarized in Figure 5.1, first differentiates employees from the self-employed. This distinction relates to an important dimension of precariousness—degree of regulatory protection (Fudge, Tucker and Vosko 2003).[5] Self-employed people are further distinguished by whether they are self-employed employers or own-account self-employed who have no employees. The own-account self-employed persons

Figure 5.1: Typology of Mutually Exclusive Employment Forms, Canada 2001*

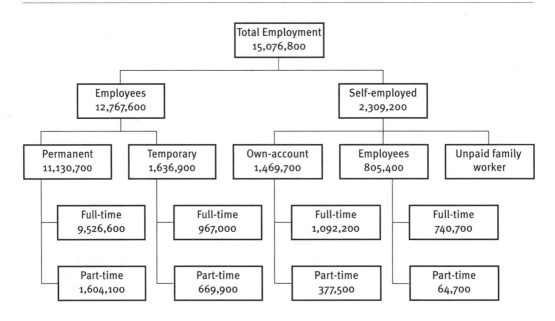

Source: Statistics Canada, Labour Force Survey 2001, Public Use Microdata File.
* Total Employment ages 15 and over

are arguably in a more precarious position than the self-employed who profit from others' labour. The analysis then addresses the degree of certainty of continuing work by categorizing employees by temporary or permanent status.[6] Temporary employees are less likely than permanent employees to have full access to collective bargaining and some aspects of employment standards legislation due to difficulties in establishing who is the employer for agency workers and due to short job tenure for other temporary workers (Vallée 1999; Vosko 2000). Finally, it is important to break down each employment form by part-time/full-time status[7] since this distinction is central to any analysis of the gender of precariousness. Eligibility for certain programs, such as Employment Insurance, is based on both hours and permanency (Vosko 2003). Together the white boxes represent what are conceptualized as the more precarious forms of employment.

The analysis consists of examining the growth in the mutually exclusive forms of employment, for women and men, using data from the General Social Survey (GSS) for the time periods 1989 and 1994 and the Labour Force Survey (LFS) for the time periods 1997 and 2001.[8] Unreliable estimates are suppressed.[9] We also calculate coefficients of variation in order to assess the degree of sampling variability.

In addition to those embedded in the form of employment itself, other dimensions of precariousness vary across forms of employment. Here we focus on the quality of four forms of wage work—full-time permanent, full-time temporary, part-time permanent and part-time temporary—by examining their relationship with three indicators of precariousness: firm size, union coverage and hourly wages. Firm

size less than 20[10] is a good indicator of the degree of regulatory protection among employees since labour law often does not apply in these firms and the pieces of legislation that do apply are ill-enforced or difficult to use (Fudge 1991). Union coverage[11] is a suitable indicator of precarious employment since unionized workers have a higher degree of control over the type of work they do and the pace and conditions under which they labour, more job security and a higher degree of regulatory protection written into collective agreements, compared to non-union workers (Rodgers 1989; Duffy and Pupo 1992). Hourly wage[12] is also a suitable indicator of precarious employment since it makes up an important part of income and is thus central to the ability to maintain an adequate standard of living.

The second stage of analysis focuses on employees at one point in time, 2001, and uses data from the Labour Force Survey (LFS).[13] It examines the percent of employees in each form of wage work who are employed in firms with less than 20 employees and who have union coverage, as well as their mean hourly wages. The analysis then focuses on gender differences in precarious employment within the four forms of wage work. In order to determine whether the gender observed differences are real or due to sampling error, we calculate t-tests of the differences between women and men of the same age within a given form of wage work.[14] We also calculate wage ratios relative to full-time permanent men, the form of employment still held by most men, both unionized and non-unionized. A large body of research illustrates that gender inequalities in the labour force are not only produced through direct discrimination resulting in unequal outcomes among women and men in similar locations in the economy, but also indirectly, for example through polarized occupational and income structures (Armstrong 1996; James, Grant and Cranford 2001; Vosko 2002; Women in Canada 2001). These relative wage ratios allow for an examination of differences between men and between women across forms of employment.

Both stages of the analysis—estimating the growth of non-standard forms of employment among women and men and assessing the quality of those forms of employment for women and men today—are necessary to empirically demonstrate the feminization of employment norms.

The Gender of Precarious Employment in Canada

The Growth of Precarious Forms of Employment

Examining mutually exclusive forms of employment brings insight into the relationship between non-standard forms of employment, growing precariousness and gender. Full-time permanent wage work is becoming less common, dropping from 67 percent of total employment in 1989 to 63 percent in 2001, although these employees still account for the majority of total employment (Table 5.1). The well-documented growth in self-employment in the 1990s (Hughes 1999) is largely due to growth in own-account self-employment, while self-employed employers declined during the same period. The number of people with temporary wage work rose steadily throughout the 1990s, fueled by the growth in full-time temporary wage work. The proportions of total employment with part-time temporary or part-time permanent wage work remained steady during this period (Table 5.1).

Examining these trends for women and men reveals both continuity and change in the

social relations of gender. While the absolute decline in full-time permanent wage work was slightly greater for men as compared to women, men were still more likely to have this form of wage work in 2001. Sixty-six percent of male total employment was full-time and permanent compared to 60 percent of female total employment (Table 5.1). Similarly, increases in full-time temporary wage work were observed for both women and men, yet the percent of women's total employment that was both part-time and temporary also increased significantly from 1989 to 2001. Furthermore, women were still twice as likely as men to be in part-time temporary employment in 2001. In contrast, the percent of women's employment that was both part-time and permanent declined. The percent of men's and women's employment that was own-account increased over the period, suggesting that both were engaging in more precarious types of self-employment (Table 5.1).

Continuity in gender inequality is further revealed when we examine the shares of women in the different forms of employment in the contemporary period (Figure 5.2). In 2001, the majority of those in forms of employment with inadequate regulatory protection were women. The widely documented concentration of women in part-time wage work (Duffy and Pupo 1992; Women in Canada, 2001) was still true of both employees and the self-employed by 2001. In 2001, women accounted for over six in ten of those with part-time temporary wage work and part-time self-employment (whether own-account or employers) and for nearly three-quarters of part-time permanent employees. In contrast, men accounted for the majority of those engaged in full-time employment, whether in temporary or permanent wage work or as own-account or self-employed

Table 5.1: Mutually Exclusive Employment Forms of Women and Men, Canada 1989–2001*

Form of Employment	Total Employment % of Total Employment				Employed Women % of Female Employment				Employed Men % of Male Employment			
	1989	1994	1997	2001	1989	1994	1997	2001	1989	1994	1997	2001
Employees												
Full-time Permanent	67	64	62	63	63	61	58	60	71	67	65	66
Full-time Temporary	4	5	6	6	3	4	5	6	4	5	6	7
Part-time Permanent	11	12	12	11	19	19	19	17	5	6	6	5
Part-time Temporary	3	3	4	4	4	3	5	6	2	2	3	3
Self-employed												
Own account	7	10	11	10	6	9	9	8	8	10	12	11
Full-time Own Account	5	7	8	7	3	5	5	5	7	8	10	10
Part-time Own Account	2	2	3	3	3	3	4	3	0.9^	1.2^	2	2
Employer	7	6	6	5	4	3	3	3	10	8	8	7
Full-time Employer	7	5	5	5	3	2	3	2	10	8	8	7
Part-time Employer	0.3^	0.4	0.5	0.4	0.6^	–	0.6	0.6	–	–	0.3	0.3
Total Employment (000s)	12,669.9	13,034.5	13,377.4	15,076.8	5,608.6	5,841.4	6,266.2	6,967.1	7,060.4	7,193.1	7,508.3	8,109.7

Source: Statistics Canada General Social Survey 1989 and 1994, Labour Force Survey 1997 and 2001, Public Use Microdata Files.

* Total employment ages 15 and over. Numbers rounded to the nearest thousand. LFS estimates include unpaid family workers.

– Indicates sample size too small to yield estimate.

^ Indicates high sampling variability (coefficient of variation between 16.6% and 33.3%). Estimates to be used with caution.

employers (Figure 5.2). The enduring concentration of women in all forms of part-time work suggests that profound continuities in gender inequality remain alongside the movement of more men into forms of employment where women labour.

Young men are engaged in precarious employment alongside women of all ages. In 2001, 60 percent of part-time permanent male employees were aged 15 to 24, compared to 29 percent of part-time permanent female employees. In contrast, only 31 percent of part-time permanent male employees were aged 25 to 54, compared to 61 percent of part-time permanent female employees. Similarly, 68 percent of part-time temporary male employees were aged 15 to 24, compared to 50 per-

cent of part-time temporary female employees; and only 23 percent of part-time temporary male employees were aged 25 to 54 compared to 43 percent of part-time temporary female employees.[15]

Similarly, increases in full-time temporary wage work were observed for both women and men, yet the percent of women's total employment that was both part-time and temporary also increased significantly from 1989 to 2001. Furthermore, women were still twice as likely to be in part-time temporary employment in 2001 when compared to men. In contrast, the percent of women's employment that was both part-time and permanent declined.

These findings illustrate the importance of conceptualizing labour-market trends as

---

Figure 5.2 Women's Share of Employment Forms, Canada 2001*

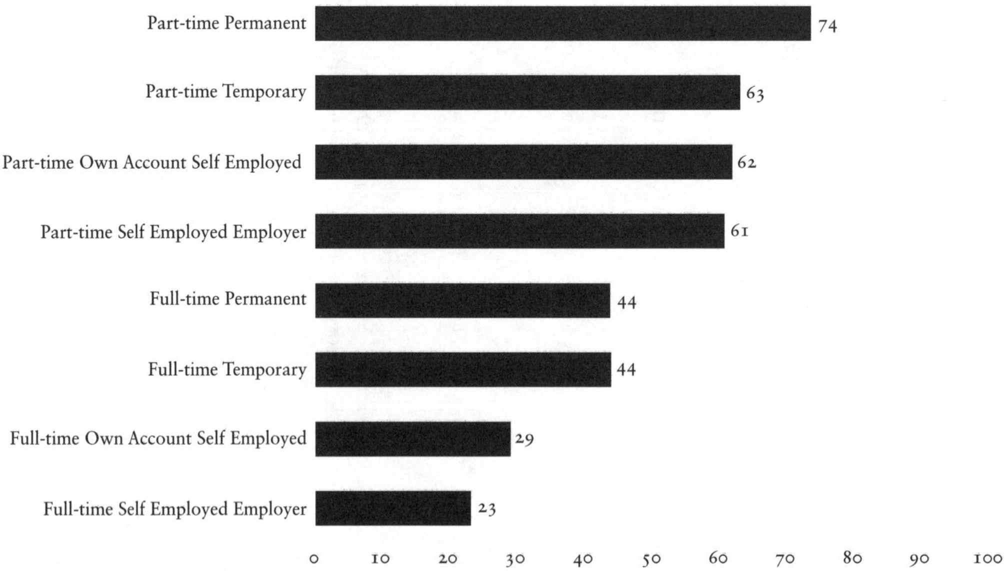

Source: Statistics Canada, Labour Force Survey 2001, Public Use Microdata Files.
* Total Employment ages 15 and over.

a feminization of employment norms. The growth of more precarious forms of employment affects both women and men, but has a greater impact upon women. Both women and men increased their participation in two forms—full-time temporary wage work and own-account self-employment—that are driving the growth of "non-standard employment." However, women also increased their participation in part-time temporary employment—a form of wage work that fits the least well with the standard employment relationship upon which labour and employment legislation are based. In addition, in 2001, precarious forms of employment were still more likely to employ women than men. By examining other dimensions of precarious employment, we can more fully understand how changing employment relationships contribute to insecurity in the Canadian labour force and how this process is gendered.

A Gendered Continuum of Precarious Wage Work

Layering forms of employment with the three additional indicators of precariousness, the typology gives way to a continuum of precarious wage work. Full-time permanent employees are the least precarious along multiple dimensions, but there are also important differences between the temporary and part-time employees. Precarious employment increases along the continuum in the following order: full-time permanent employees as the least precarious followed by full-time temporary, part-time permanent and part-time temporary employees as the most precarious (Table 5.2). Thus, full-time status defines precariousness more so than temporality. For example, only 17 percent of full-time permanent employees labour in firms with less than 20 employees, compared with over one in four employees in any of the other three forms of wage work. At the same time, full-time temporary employees are more likely to work in large firms, compared to employees in the two part-time forms. Thirty-four percent of full-time permanent employees are covered by a union contract, compared to 31 percent of full-time temporary employees. At the same time, part-time temporary employees are less likely to be covered by a union contract than part-time permanent employees, 21 percent compared to 27 percent. Finally, full-time

Table 5.2: A Continuum of Precarious Wage Work, Canada 2001*

Form of Wage Work	Total Employees	Firm Size Less than 20	Union Coverage	Hourly Wages	Hours per Week
	Estimate (000s)	% of Employees		Mean	
Full-time Permanent	9,526.6	17	34	$18.64	40
Full-time Temporary	967.0	26	31	$14.42	40
Part-time Permanent	1,604.1	28	27	$12.62	18
Part-time Temporary	669.9	29	21	$11.32	15
Total	12 767.6	20	32	$17.18	36

Source: Statistics Canada, Labour Force Survey 2001, Public Use Microdata Files.

* Employees ages 15 and over. Numbers rounded to the nearest thousand.

Table 5.3: Indicators of Precarious Wage Work for Women and Men, Canada 2001

Form of Wage Work	Age	EMPLOYEES Estimates (000's)		FIRM SIZE LESS THAN 20 Percent of Employees		COVERED BY UNION		HOURLY WAGES Mean		FEMALE/MALE Wage Ratio
		Men	Women	Men	Women	Men	Women	Men	Women	
Full-time Permanent	15–24	545.9	406.9	25	25	19	14*	11.94	10.63*	0.89
	25–54	4326.7	3405.5	15	18*	36	35*	21.12	17.23*	0.82
	55 +	502.7	338.8	16	20*	39	40	21.84	16.69*	0.76
	Total	5375.4	4151.2	16	19*	35	33*	20.26	16.54*	0.82
Full-time Temporary	15–24	165.9	131.9	32	27*	16	17	10.72	10.10*	0.94
	25–54	328.2	274.0	28	20*	37	38	17.39	14.69*	0.84
	55 +	44.5	22.4	35	—	—	—	17.52	14.38	0.82
	Total	538.6	428.3	30	22*	30	31*	15.34	13.26*	0.86
Part-time Permanent	15–24	249.3	340.6	23	25*	16	14*	8.26	8.19*	0.99
	25–54	129.3	724.9	27	30*	35	35	16.31	14.99*	0.92
	55 +	40.1	119.9	31	37*	—	29*	17.80	14.08*	0.79
	Total	418.8	1185.3	25	29*	23	28*	11.66	12.95*	1.11
Part-time Temporary	15–24	170.9	210.2	31	32	13	10*	8.51	8.18*	0.96
	25–54	57.1	178.7	30	24*	31	36*	15.98	14.8*	0.93
	55 +	23.0	30.1	31	—	—	—	16.36	15.65	—
	Total	250.9	419.0	31	28*	17	23*	10.93	11.55*	1.06
Total Employees		6583.7	6183.8	19	22*	33	31*	18.95	15.29*	0.81

Source: Statistics Canada, Labour Force Survey 2001, Public Use Microdata Files.

Δ Employees ages 15 and over. Numbers rounded to the nearest thousand.

*Women are statistically different from men of the same form and age group at the .05 level; wage ratios are reported only when significantly different.

^ Totals for part-time permanent and part-time temporary employees are misleading due to the different sex composition across the age groups. Most male part-time workers are 15–24, while large numbers of women part-time employees are 25–54. Since women aged 25–54 earn much more than men aged 15–24, the total wages of women are larger than the total wages of men despite the fact that men earn more in each age group.

– Indicates sample size too small to yield estimate

permanent employees earn on average over four dollars an hour more than full-time temporary employees do. Nevertheless, full-time temporary employees earn on average nearly two dollars an hour more than part-time permanent employees who, in turn, earn over a dollar an hour more than part-time temporary employees (Table 5.2.)

The continuum of precarious wage work is gendered in one way through the greater concentration of women in the most precarious forms of wage work. The analysis in the previous section illustrates that women are concentrated in part-time permanent and part-time temporary wage work and that their concentration in part-time temporary wage work grew in the 1990s. Combined with these findings, we can confirm that women are labouring in those forms of employment that are the most precarious on multiple dimensions. For example, part-time temporary employees were the most precarious in terms of firm size, union coverage and hourly wages, and 63 percent of these employees were women in 2001. In contrast, women made up only 44 percent of the least precarious employees—those with full-time permanent wage work (Figure 5.2).

Examining differences between women and men within the forms of wage work points to a second way the continuum of precarious wage work is gendered, one that reflects both continuity and change in gender relations. Among full-time permanent employees we find continuing gender inequalities (Table 5.3). In 2001, women in full-time permanent wage work were more likely than their male counterparts to labour for small employers, with the exception of youth (Table 5.3). These same women were less likely than their male counterparts to be covered by a union con-

tract, with the exception of those over age 55. Furthermore, women in full-time permanent wage work earned an average wage that is 82 percent of their male counterparts (Table 5.3). Their lower wage combined with fewer hours of work each week resulted in earnings of approximately $629 a week—$200 less than their male counterparts. Too often, commentators assume that full-time permanent jobs are "good jobs," while all other non-standard jobs are "bad jobs" (Economic Council of Canada 1990). In contrast, this analysis reveals that, along multiple dimensions, full-time permanent wage work is not as good for women as it is for men.[16]

Examining gender differences within the categories of temporary and part-time employees illustrates the gendering of jobs. Vosko (2003) theorizes the gendering of jobs as a process whereby certain groups of men are experiencing downward pressure on wages and conditions of work much like those typically associated with "women's work," while many women continue to endure economic pressure. These findings illustrate that this process is occurring among temporary and part-time employees primarily along the dimensions of regulatory protection and control (measured here as firm size and union coverage).

Among full-time temporary employees, men are more likely than their female counterparts to be employed by small firms, suggesting that they have less regulatory protection (Table 5.3). There is no statistically significant difference in union coverage between women and men temporary full-time employees, once age is controlled. Nevertheless, these men still earn a higher hourly wage than women, except those aged 55 and over. Importantly, the female/male wage gap is more pronounced

Table 5.4: Wage Precariousness Relative to Full-time Permanent Men, Canada 2001

| | | MEAN WAGE RATIOS RELATIVE TO FULL-TIME PERMANENT MEN | | | | | | Percent of Employees | |
| | | Total | | Union | | Non-Union | | | |
Form of Wage Work	Age	Men	Women	Men	Women	Men	Women	Men	Women
Full-time Permanent	15–24	1.00	0.89	1.00	0.95	1.00	0.89	8	7
	25–54	1.00	0.82	1.00	0.90	1.00	0.77	66	55
	55 +	1.00	0.76	1.00	0.83	1.00	0.71	8	5
	Total	1.00	0.82	1.00	0.90	1.00	0.77	82	67
Full-time Temporary	15–24	0.90	0.85	0.95	0.94	0.89	0.83	3	2
	25–54	0.82	0.70	0.94	0.80	0.75	0.63	5	4
	55 +	0.80	0.66	—	—	0.75	0.58	1	0
	Total	0.76	0.65	0.90	0.78	0.69	0.60	8	7
Part-time Permanent	15–24	0.71	0.69	0.68	0.72	0.70	0.69	4	6
	25–54	0.77	0.71	0.99	0.87	0.65	0.62	2	12
	55 +	0.81	0.64	0.87	0.79	0.81	0.59	1	2
	Total^	0.58	0.64	0.76	0.82	0.53	0.57	6	19
Part-time Temporary	15–24	0.71	0.69	0.73	0.78	0.72	0.69	3	3
	25–54	0.76	0.70	0.99	0.88	0.65	0.60	1	3
	55 +	0.75	0.72	—	—	0.73	0.64	0	0
	Total^	0.54	0.57	0.73	0.81	0.51	0.50	4	7

Source: Statistics Canada, Labour Force Survey 2001, Public Use Microdata Files.
Δ Employees ages 15 and over. Numbers rounded to the nearest thousand.
– Indicates sample size too small to yield estimate

among those aged 25 to 54 than among the youth (Table 5.3).

When examining gender differences among part-time employees (permanent and temporary) it is especially important to examine differences by age group. As discussed above, most women in part-time jobs were aged 25 to 54, while most men in part-time jobs were aged 15 to 24. Women aged 25 to 54 make much more than men aged 15 to 24, thus the age composition brings up the average wages of total women. The gender composition across age groups explains why the total wages for women were higher than they are for men although men earned higher wages in each age group.

Among part-time permanent employees, women across all age groups were more likely to work in small firms. They were more likely, as a group, to be covered by a union contract, but there was no statistically significant difference between women and men among those aged 25 to 54 (Table 5.3). This reflects, in part, the concentration of this cohort of women in the public sector where unionization rates are high (Armstrong 1996; Duffy and Pupo 1992). Nevertheless, women part-time permanent employees aged 25 to 54 earned an average wage just under 15 dollars an hour, compared to over 16 dollars an hour for their male counterparts. Young women and young men in this form of wage work earned significantly lower wages—slightly over eight dollars an hour.

The gendering of jobs is most evident when we examine gender differences among part-time temporary employees. Men in part-time temporary wage work were more likely than their female counterparts to be employed in small firms, except the young who, notably, made up most male employment in this form.

In turn, middle-aged women were more likely to be covered by a union contract than men in this form of wage work were, while the opposite was true among the youth. At first glance, women appear to be doing better than men in terms of wages. However, this advantage is explained by the age distribution. Within the oldest age group there is no statistically significant difference between women's and men's wages and there is little substantive gender difference between the young. However, among the 25 to 54 age group, women earned 93 percent of men's income (Table 5.3). These trends indicate a need to examine wages more closely.

Given that full-time permanent male employees are the least precarious, and most men are employed in this form of wage work, it is useful to compare women to this group of men in order to gain a more complete picture of the gender of precariousness in the labour force. Doing so reveals a second key facet of the feminization of employment norms—income polarization. These findings illustrate polarization in wages between full-time permanent male employees and both women and men in the other three forms of wage work. Most women in full-time temporary, part-time permanent and part-time temporary wage work are aged 25 to 54. On average, these women earn roughly 70 percent of the average wage received by full-time permanent men of the same age, reflecting gender polarization in wages across forms of wage work (Table 5.4). Unionization decreases this wage gap considerably but does not eliminate it. Most men in the more precarious forms of wage work are young. Among those aged 15 to 24, men in part-time permanent and part-time temporary wage work earn 69 percent and 71 percent, respectively, of full-time permanent men of the same age and this does not change significantly with unionization. Together these patterns illustrate wage polarization among men by form of employment alongside continuing gender inequality both within and between forms of wage work.

Alongside the gendering of jobs and wage polarization, it is also important to remember that only 15 percent of total male employment is full-time temporary, part-time permanent and part-time temporary wage work combined, compared to 29 percent of female employment (Table 5.1). This analysis of the quality of the four forms of wage work, together with the analysis of the spread of non-standard forms of employment, illustrate key aspects of the feminization of employment norms. The standard employment relationship is eroding as a norm and non-standard forms of employment that exhibit qualities of precarious employment associated with women and other marginalized groups are growing (Vosko 2003).

Conclusion

The gender order characterizing the post-World II War era is crumbling as the standard employment relationship (SER) is eroding as a norm. The contemporary period is characterized by complex trends because no new normative employment relationship and no new dominant gender order have yet emerged (Cossman and Fudge 2002; Vosko 2003). As a result, confining scholarly work to investigating the rise of non-standard employment not only masks enduring gender inequalities but also mystifies labour force trends.

The foregoing findings illustrate both a decline in the SER as a norm and enduring gender inequalities in line with the notion of

the feminization of employment norms. The feminization of employment norms denotes the erosion of the standard employment relationship as a norm and the spread of non-standard forms of employment that exhibit qualities of precarious employment associated with women and other marginalized groups (Vosko 2003). The empirical analysis demonstrates the growth of more precarious non-standard forms of employment and its gendered character. Both women and men have increased their participation in full-time temporary wage work and own-account self-employment, as these forms have grown, signalling growing precariousness among both women and men. Yet, women have also increased their participation in part-time temporary wage work, which is the most precarious form of wage work. Still, it is misleading to focus entirely on rates of change without also examining enduring continuities in women's concentration in precarious employment. Women are more likely than men to engage in part-time employment, whether in temporary or permanent wage work or in self-employment as either own-account workers or self-employed employers; and men still hold a greater share of full-time permanent wage work.

An understanding of the gender of precariousness is furthered by layering permanency and hours with additional dimensions of precarious employment among employees. Full-time permanent employees are the least likely to labour in small, non-union firms, suggesting higher levels of regulatory protection and control, and these employees earn higher wages than the other forms of wage work. However, there are also differences between temporary and part-time employees resulting in a continuum of precarious wage work. Precariousness increases in the following order: full-time permanent employees as the least precarious followed by full-time temporary, part-time permanent and part-time temporary employees as the most precarious.

Examining gender differences within and across forms of employment illustrates two key facets of the feminization of employment norms—the gendering of jobs and polarization in wages. Women in the least precarious form of employment continue to be more precarious than men. Full-time permanent male employees are more likely than their female counterparts to work in large, unionized firms and a significant female-to-male wage gap persists. This suggests that even those women in full-time permanent wage work have less regulatory protection, control and ability to support themselves and their dependents than do men. There is, therefore, a pressing need to break down the dominant concept "standard employment" and its association with a "good" job and to begin to ask: good for whom?

Alongside this pervasive gender inequality among employees with full-time permanent wage work, a convergence in precariousness at the bottom of the labour market is also underway. The gendering of jobs denotes the downgrading of employment to reflect the more precarious wages and working conditions historically reserved for women, so that certain groups of men are experiencing downward pressure on wages and conditions of work, while many women are enduring continued economic pressure (Vosko 2003). This study finds that, in the present period, the "gendering of jobs," is occurring along the dimensions of regulatory protection and control (measured here as firm size and union coverage), more so than in terms of income from wages. While men in temporary wage work (both full-time and part-time) are more likely than women to be employed in small firms, the opposite is true, in the permanent forms of wage work. Furthermore, among middle aged full-time temporary and part-time permanent employees, women and men are equally likely to be covered by a union contract. Despite this convergence in precariousness along these two indicators, women still earn significantly lower hourly wages compared to men within all forms of wage work.

When the wages of women and men in temporary and part-time forms of wage work are examined relative to the least precarious group (i.e., full-time permanent male employees), a picture of gendered polarization emerges. Both women and men in full-time temporary, part-time permanent and part-time temporary forms of wage work are doing more poorly than men in full-time permanent wage work. This indicates wage polarization among men by form of employment. However, gender inequality in wages is evident both between and within the forms of wage work.

Taken together, these findings on the gendering of jobs, wage polarization and the spread of precarious forms of employment illustrate the feminization of employment norms. The analysis reveals more gender parity within part-time permanent and part-time temporary wage work than within full-time permanent wage work; yet the former forms of employment fail to provide regulatory protection, control over work or an adequate wage for anyone. The growing, albeit still small, number of men in part-time and temporary wage work reflects growing inequality among men by form of employment. Nevertheless, 66 percent of men are employed in the least precarious form of employment—full-time permanent wage work. Furthermore, among men, it is primarily young men who are employed in temporary and part-time wage work, while women of all ages continue to be concentrated in these forms of employment. More women than men are located in segments of the labour force where multiple dimensions of precarious employment converge.

The continuing concentration of women in the most precarious forms of employment points to the need to examine more fully the relationship between precarious employment and activities related to social reproduction (i.e., the daily and generational maintenance of people). Qualitative research could also assist our understanding of how jobs are gendered by probing the meanings assigned by employers and workers to the work that women do. In order to explore fully the feminization of employment norms, future research must consider how precarious employment varies by other social locations, such as "race" and ethnicity, and key social contexts, such as occupation and industry.

Endnotes

1 This analysis is limited to precarious employment in the labour force and does not address issues of unemployment or entry into the labour force.

2 We use the term "wage work" to define employees who earn salaries as well as hourly wages. Statisticians use the term "paid work" for what we are here calling "wage work." We use the term wage work instead because, in feminist scholarship, paid work is more commonly contrasted to unpaid work and because the own-account self-employed are also paid (by their clients), but they are not paid wages.

3 For example, it is often asserted that migrant workers and other marginalized groups have access to forms of subsistence beyond the wage and this assertion is often used to justify paying them lower wages.

4 The LFS and the GSS collect excellent data on forms of employment that fall outside the SER but they do not collect adequate data on "race" or ethnicity. The LFS does not ask about visible minority or immigrant status. The GSS does ask about ethnic background. However, samples sizes for temporary workers in a given ethnic group are small. The census has larger sample sizes but does not ask questions about temporary work. The Survey of Labour and Income Dynamics (SLID) 2000 file will be available soon for public use, allowing researchers to examine temporary work among immigrants and racialized groups in the late 1990s.

5 For the most part, the self-employed are treated as entrepreneurs who do not require statutory protection; however, there is wide variation in coverage. See Fudge, Tucker and Vosko (2003) for an analysis of the coverage of independent contractors under common and civil law of employment, collective bargaining, employment standards, human rights, workers' compensation and social wage legislation across four Canadian jurisdictions. Due to this complexity and the scope of this article, here we only point to a few specific pieces of legislation.

6 Neither the LFS nor the GSS distinguish between temporary employees who work through an agency and other employees with a predetermined end date. These surveys do not ask questions about job permanency of self-employed workers.

7 Since 1997, the LFS has defined part-time workers as consisting of people (wage and salary workers and the self-employed) who usually work less than 30 hours per week at their main or only job. The 1989 and 1994 GSS estimates in this analysis have been revised to match the new definitions of part-time work in the LFS.

8 The LFS dates back to 1976 but the survey did not ask whether one was employed in a temporary job until 1997. The GSS collected this information as far back as 1989. However, the GSS was last conducted in 1994. The use of these two surveys does not significantly affect the results on change in various forms of employment over time because the variables that make up the form of employment-derived variable are measured in a similar way in the two surveys.

9 We followed Statistics Canada guidelines regarding either minimum estimate or minimum sample size cut-offs for each survey. The LFS recommends suppressing estimates smaller than 1,500. The GSS recommends

suppressing sample sizes that are less than 15, which corresponds to an estimate of roughly 30,000 when weighted.

10 The firm-size variable was recoded into a dichotomous variable: firm size less than 20/firm size 20 and over.

11 The union variable was recoded into a dichotomous variable that combined union members and those non-members who are covered by a union contract (collective agreement), compared to all those not covered by a union contract. We use union coverage, rather than union membership, because workers covered by a union contract generally have a more similar level of control and job security to union members than they do to non-union members.

12 In some cases, the standard deviations are high, indicating difference within a category. Standard deviations and median wages are available from the authors.

13 Most surveys do not collect data on indicators of precariousness for the self-employed, in part due the conception that all self-employed are entrepreneurs. An exception is the Survey of Self Employed (see Fudge, Tucker and Vosko 2003).

14 T-tests were run using a standardized weight. This does not account entirely for the sampling design of the LFS but the use of standardized weights is an accepted approximation. Without corrections for stratified samples, estimates of sampling error will be too great; thus, our estimates of statistically significant difference are conservative ones.

15 These figures are based on analysis of the 2001 LFS.

16 Human capital characteristics as well as gender-related wage biases also play a role in the persistent inequality between women and men in full-time permanent jobs.

References

Acker, J. 1992. "From Sex Roles to Gendered Institutions." *Contemporary Sociology,* Vol. 21, No. 5, 565.

Advisory Group on Working Time and the Distribution of Work. 1994. *Report of the Advisory Group on Working Time and the Distribution of Work.* Ottawa: Human Resources Development Canada.

Arat-Koc, S. 1997. "From 'Mothers of the Nation' to Migrant Workers." *Not One of the Family.* A. Bakan and D. Stasilus, eds. Toronto: University of Toronto Press, 53.

Armstrong, P. 1996. "The Feminization of the Labour Force: Harmonizing Down in a Global Economy." *Rethinking Restructuring: Gender and Change in Canada.* I. Bakker, ed. Toronto: University of Toronto Press, 29.

Bakan, A., and D. Stasiulus. 1997. "Making the Match: Domestic Placement Agencies and the Racialization of Women's Household Work." *Signs,* Vol. 20, No. 2, 303.

Bakker, I. 1996. "Introduction: The Gendered Foundations of Restructuring in Canada." *Rethinking Restructuring: Gender and Change in Canada.* I. Bakker, ed. Toronto: University of Toronto Press, 3.

Bourhis, A., and T. Wils. 2001. "L'éclatement de l'emploi traditionnel: les défis posés par la diversité des emplois typiques et atypiques." *Relations industrielles/Industrial Relations,* Vol. 56, No. 1, 66.

Carré, F., M. Ferber, G. Lonnie and S. Herzenberg. 2000. *Non-Standard Work Arrangements.* Madison, Wisc: Industrial Relations Research Association.

Connell, R. W. 1987. *Gender and Power: Society, the Person and Sexual Politics.* Stanford: Stanford University Press.

Cossman, B., and J. Fudge, eds. 2002. *Feminization, Privatization and the Law: The Challenge of Feminism.* Toronto: University of Toronto Press.

Cranford, C. 1998. "Gender and Citizenship in the Restructuring of Janitorial Work in Los Angeles." *Gender Issues,* Vol. 16, No. 4, 25.

Das Gupta, T. 1996. *Racism and Paid Work.* Toronto: Garamond Press.

Duffy, A., and N. Pupo. 1992. *Part-Time Paradox.* Toronto: McClelland and Stewart.

Economic Council of Canada. 1990. *Good Jobs, Bad Jobs: Employment in the Service Economy.* Ottawa: Ministry of Supply and Services.

Eichler, M. 1997. *Family Shifts, Policies and Gender Equality.* Don Mills, Ont.: Oxford University Press.

Fraser, N. 1997. *Justice Interruptus: Critical Reflections on the "Postsocialist" Condition.* London: Routledge.

Fudge, J. 1991. *Labour Law's Little Sister: The Employment Standards Act and the Feminization of Labour.* Ottawa: Canadian Centre for Policy Alternatives.

Fudge, J., and L. F. Vosko. 2001a. "Gender, Segmentation and the Standard Employment Relationship in Canadian Labour Law and Policy." *Economic and Industrial Democracy,* Vol. 22, No. 2, 271.

Fudge, J., and L. F. Vosko. 2001b. "By Whose Standards? Re-Regulating the Canadian Labour Market." *Economic and Industrial Democracy,* Vol. 22, No. 3, 327.

Fudge, J., E. Tucker and L. F. Vosko. 2003. "Employee or Independent Contractor? Charting the Legal Significance of the Distinction in Canada." *Canadian Labour and Employment Law Journal,* Vol. 10, No. 2, 193–230.

Hughes, K. 1999. "Gender and Self-Employment in Canada: Assessing Trends and Policy Implications." CPRN Study No. W/04. Changing Employment Relationships Series. Ottawa: Canadian Policy Research Networks.

Human Resources and Development Canada (HRDC). 1994. *Improving Social Security in Canada: A Discussion Paper.* Ottawa: Ministry of Supply and Services.

James, A., D. Grant and C. Cranford. 2000. "Moving Up but How Far? African American Women and Economic Restructuring in Los Angeles." *Sociological Perspectives,* Vol. 43, No. 3, 399.

Jenson, J. 1996. "Part-Time Employment and Women: A Range of Strategies." *Rethinking Restructuring: Gender and Change in Canada.* I. Bakker, ed. Toronto: University of Toronto Press, 92.

Krahn, H. 1991. "Non-Standard Work Arrangements." *Perspectives on Labour and Income,* Winter, 35.

Krahn, H. 1995. "Non-Standard Work on the Rise." *Perspectives on Labour and Income,* Winter, 35.

Lerner, G. 1997. *History Matters: Life and Thought.* New York: Oxford.

Lowe, G., G. Schellenberg and K. Davidman. 1999. "Rethinking Employment Relationships." CPRN Discussion Paper No. W/05. Changing Employment Relationships Series. Ottawa: Canadian Policy Research Networks.

Luxton, M., and J. Corman. 2001. *Getting By in Hard Times: Gendered Labour at Home and on the Job.* Toronto: University of Toronto Press.

Mayer, F. 1996. "Temps partiel et précarité." *Relations industrielles/Industrial Relations,* Vol. 51, No. 3, 524.

Muckenberger, U. 1989. "Non-standard Forms of Employment in the Federal Republic of Germany: The Role and Effectiveness of the State." *Precarious Employment in Labour Market Regulation: The Growth of Atypical Employment in Western Europe.* G. Rodgers and S. Rodgers, eds. Geneva: International Institute for Labour Studies, 227.

Rodgers, G., and J. Rodgers, eds. 1989. *Precarious Jobs in Labour Market Regulation: The Growth of Atypical Employment in Western Europe.* Geneva: International Institute for Labour Studies.

Rodgers, G. 1989. "Precarious Employment in Western Europe: The State of the Debate." *Precarious Jobs in Labour Market Regulation: The Growth of Atypical Employment in Western Europe.* G. Rodgers and J. Rodgers, eds. Geneva: International Institute for Labour Studies.

Schellenberg, G., and C. Clark. 1996. *Temporary Employment in Canada: Profiles, Patterns and Policy Considerations.* Ottawa: Canadian Council on Social Development.

Scott, J. 1986. "Gender: A Useful Category of Historical Analysis." *American Historical Review,* Vol. 93, 1053–1073.

Silver, H. 1992. "Social Exclusion and Social Solidarity: Three Paradigms." *International Labour Review,* Vol. 133, No. 5/6, 531.

Spalter-Roth, R., and H. Hartmann. 1998. "Gauging the Consequences for Gender Relations, Pay Equity and the Public Purse." *Contingent Work: Employment Relations in Transition.* K. Barker and K. Christensen, eds. Ithaca, N.Y.: Cornell University Press, 69.

Vallée, G. 1999. "Pluralité des statuts de travail et protection des droits de la personne: Quel rôle pour le droit du travail?" *Relations industrielles/Industrial Relations,* Vol. 54, No. 2, 277.

Vosko, L. F. 1997. "Legitimizing the Triangular Employment Relationship: Emerging International Labour Standards from a Comparative Perspective." *Comparative Labor Law and Policy Journal,* Vol. 19, Fall, 43.

Vosko, L. F. 2000. *Temporary Work: The Gendered Rise of a Precarious Employment Relationship.* Toronto: University of Toronto Press.

Vosko, L. F. 2002. *Rethinking Feminization: Gendered Precariousness in the Canadian Labour Market and the Crisis in Social Reproduction.* 18th Annual Robarts Lecture, York University, Toronto: Robarts Centre for Canadian Studies, York University, April 11.

Vosko, L. F. 2003. "Gender Differentiation and the Standard/Non-Standard Employment Distinction in Canada, 1945 to the Present." *Social Differentiation in Canada.* J. Danielle, ed. Toronto and Montreal: University of Toronto Press/University of Montreal Press, 25.

Vosko, L. F., N. Zukewich and C. Cranford. 2003. "Beyond Non-Standard Work: A New Typology of Employment." *Perspectives on Labour and Income.* Ottawa: Statistics Canada, Fall.

Women in Canada. 2001. *Work Chapter Updates.* Ottawa: Statistics Canada.

Zeytinoğlu, I. U., and J. K. Muteshi. 1999. "Gender, Race and Class Dimensions of Non-Standard Work." *Relations industrielles/Industrial Relations,* Vol. 55, No. 1, 133.

CHAPTER 6

Jettisoned by Design? The Truncated Employmen Relationship of Customer Sales and Service Age under Airline Restructuring[1]

Vivian Shalla

Introduction

OVER THE PAST two decades, we have witnessed an enormous growth in the body of literature on the various labour flexibility strategies adopted by employers to reduce workplace and labour-market rigidities and enhance firms' adaptability and survival prospects in the face of the economic vagaries of the late 20th century (Amadeo and Horton, 1997; Amin, 1994; Atkinson, 1985; Elger and Smith, 1994; Felstead and Jewson, 1999; Pollert, 1991a; Wood, 1989). Despite the impressive volume and variety of research on managerial approaches to the deployment of labour in a rapidly changing economy, there are nonetheless large gaps in our knowledge of the numerical flexibility strategies used in white-collar work and in our understanding of how these strategies are redesigning white-collar employment relationships. This is a serious shortcoming when one

considers the tremendous postwar growth in white-collar work, the recent transformations witnessed by white-collar workers and the centrality of white-collar work to what Glenday (1997) has referred to as the "knowledge/information/service economy." It means that our analyses and theories of paid work under contemporary capitalism are weakened. It also means that our knowledge and understanding of the changing nature of women's paid work and employment patterns are wanting, given their predominance in many white-collar jobs.

Through a case study of the contracting out to travel agencies of the work of Air Canada customer sales and service agents, this article[2] aims to expand our knowledge and refine our analysis of distancing strategies and of the process of employment relationship degradation in women's white-collar sales and service work.[3] Air Canada customer sales and service agents work at airport counters and in city sales and reservations offices across the country performing a variety of customer sales and service tasks.

Since the mid-1970s, Air Canada, like most air carriers worldwide, has pursued a strategy aimed at cutting labour costs, increasing overall labour flexibility and enhancing market share in its quest to survive and prosper in the face of economic turbulence and the massive restructuring of the airline industry characterized by deregulation, privatization, intense competition, concentration and globalization. In this context, Air Canada has been redesigning workplaces and redefining employment relationships. The contracting out of the work of its customer sales and service agents to travel agencies is an integral part of the company's search for greater labour flexibility and enhanced market share under economic and industry restructuring.

In this paper, I argue that the contracting out of customer sales and service agents' work to travel agencies is a specific form of work externalization or distancing that has contributed to the degradation of the employment relationship and thus to the degradation of the job of customer sales and service agents. Contracting out generated what I call a "truncated employment relationship" by shifting a large chunk of customer sales and service work to outside agencies. While many elements of the standard employment relationship have been maintained primarily because of worker resistance, the distancing process degraded the job category in terms of lost opportunities, increased job insecurity and a lower quality of work. Central to my analysis is an understanding of the way in which computer and telecommunications technologies are used to facilitate shifts in the location of work. I also show that the process of employment relationship degradation has fostered more conflictual labour-management relations and contributed to the radicalization of customer sales and service agents at Air Canada. In developing an analysis of the degradation of women's sales and service white-collar work, the article provides important insights into the larger process of growing inequality and polarization in industrialized societies, an issue that has been a long-standing concern of sociologists.

To elaborate these arguments, this article is divided into four sections. The first section presents a critical assessment of the flexibility literature, highlighting some of the gaps in our understanding of the distancing of white-collar work that impinge on our ability to construct stronger theories of work in the post-industrial economy. The second section consists of a detailed account and analysis of Air Canada's key actions and practices surrounding the contracting out of work. In the next section, I focus on the protracted struggle waged by workers and their union to resist, through defensive and proactive measures, managerial decisions and practices that erode the standard employment relationship. The concluding section discusses the truncated employment relationship of this group of white-collar service-sector workers and hints at rapidly emerging shapes of work-distancing that could have a significant impact on the employment relationship. I also reflect on how my study contributes to issues of relevance to sociological analysis in the areas of work and inequality.

Numerical Flexibility and Changing Employment Relationships

Numerical flexibility, also termed quantitative or employment flexibility, represents a key corporate approach to the deployment of labour that is redefining employment relationships and transforming labour markets as an integral part of a broader process of economic restructuring. Numerical flexibility refers to those strategies and practices that have been increasingly adopted by employers over the past few decades to contract the size of their permanent full-time core workforce and expand the use of non-direct and externalized labour, thereby turning labour into an even more easily manipulable quantity (Crompton et al., 1996; Felstead and Jewson, 1999; Gallie et al., 1998; Rubery and Wilkinson, 1994; Tarling, 1987). Data from Canada and other advanced industrial countries reveal that, since the mid-1970s, flexible work, a term used interchangeably with non-standard, atypical, contingent, precarious or marginal work, has grown systematically and has taken a wide array of forms (Casey et al., 1997; Cohany, 1996; Dex and McCulloch, 1997; Krahn, 1995; Polivka, 1996; Rodgers and Rodgers, 1989; Zeytinoğlu, 1999). Flexible work arrangements such as part-time work, seasonal and casual work, fixed term contracts, temporary work, self-employment, homework, telework and subcontracting have been on the rise and are seen as the future shape of employment for an increasing number of individuals.

Mounting statistical evidence on the changing trends and nature of employment practices and arrangements shows that the drive towards flexibility has resulted in an erosion of the standard employment relationship as the normative model of employment of the postwar era and thus in degraded employment relationships. While the data tell us much about the proliferation of different types of non-standard work and about the characteristics of those engaged in such work, we know much less about the actual processes behind the erosion of employment relationships through the flexibilization of work. The scholarly writing presents significant weaknesses because it fails to take a close look at how various flexibility practices have been applied in different workplaces. We thus lack detailed information about how standard secure jobs with good working conditions are turned into more contingent, insecure jobs with less favourable working conditions. Understanding these transformations requires taking into account managerial initiatives in redefining employment relationships as well as workers' actions in resisting the whittling away of the standard employment relationship, within the broader context of economic and structural change.

While some authors (Marginson, 1991; Pollert, 1988, 1991b) have been critical of the assumption of newness in the literature on employment flexibility, arguing that such strategies and practices have been historically used by employers to vary the amount of labour required, reduce dependency on full-time permanent workers and segment workers to deal with the problem of labour, what seems clear from the mounting evidence is that the pace of change and the extent to which employers are adopting flexible employment strategies and practices signal a heightened thrust towards numerical flexibility as an integral part of an economy in flux. Broad (2000) has claimed that we are witnessing a (re)casualization of labour as a key ingredient in the process of global restructuring directed at a renewal of capital accumulation. He joins a chorus of critical voices in arguing that flexibility approaches are being used to erode the terms and conditions under which standard workers are employed, thereby undermining the strength of organized labour and reasserting employers' control over labour processes and labour markets (Appay, 1998;

Burgess and Strachan, 1999; Dagg, 1997; Meulders, 2000; Peck, 1996; Vosko, 2000).

Studies have shown that the massive adoption of flexible employment practices has resulted in worsening employment conditions for many workers. When compared to full-time continuous standard employment, flexible non-standard employment has usually provided inferior working conditions in terms of wages and benefits, job security protection, promotional opportunities and unionization. Flexible employment practices and the transformation in labour markets that they engender thus have implications for the changing structure and patterns of inequality in society. Many have argued that the degradation of the employment conditions of an increasing number of workers underlies growing inequality and polarization in the labour market (Belous, 1989; Felstead and Jewson, 1999; O'Reilly and Fagan, 1998; Rosenberg and Lapidus, 1999). We need more in-depth knowledge, however, to better understand how employment relationship degradation engenders a redivision of labour, fosters shifts in occupations and reinforces dualism in the labour market.

Despite their greater labour force participation since the Second World War, or perhaps underlying this participation, women have been disproportionately engaged in flexible, non-standard, contingent work arrangements. Feminist scholars have put into question the assumed gender neutrality of numerically flexible strategies and practices that permeates much of the literature. Many point out that the standard postwar Fordist employment regime of full-time, permanent and secure work currently under attack has been more characteristic of men's (albeit not of all men's) paid work experience and that, because of their disadvantaged position in the labour

market and in the family, women have been, and continue to be, a preferred and available pool of labour for companies striving to boost numerical labour flexibility (Connelly and Macdonald, 1996; Duffy and Pupo, 1992; Rubery et al., 1996; Walby, 1989, 2000; Yeandle, 1999). However, as Armstrong (1996) has argued, with the feminization of employment in all sectors of the economy, whereby more of men's work takes on characteristics typical of women's work, numerical flexibility is increasingly colouring men's labour-market experience. This harmonizing down for some men under current economic restructuring has not led to the eradication of gender divisions and inequalities in the labour market. There is also mounting evidence that, with the expansion of flexible labour, inequalities among women are being exacerbated (Blossfeld and Hakim, 1997; Dex and McCulloch, 1995; Smith, 1993; Zeytinoğlu and Muteshi, 1999).

Because women have filled many of the white-collar jobs created over the course of the past several decades, the changing nature and conditions of white-collar employment relationships in the post-industrial economy are central to their experience of paid work and profoundly define their economic opportunities. Literature on distancing strategies in white-collar work has begun to give us a glimpse of the contours of women's role in such forms of flexible non-standard employment. In particular, studies on the temporary help industry (Casey, 1988; Gottfried, 1992, 1994; Rogers, 1995; Vosko, 2000), on self-employment (Crompton, 1993; Gauthier and Roy, 1997; Hughes, 1999; Jurik, 1998; Stanworth and Stanworth, 1995), and on home-working (Felstead and Jewson, 2000; Huws, 1984; Phizacklea and Wolkowitz, 1995), three important sites of women's white-collar work, have generated insights into the nature and extent of non-direct and externalized employment relationships. This research has been useful in identifying the characteristics of those engaged in these distanced employment relationships and in revealing the working conditions as well as gendered dimensions and inequalities arising from these particular labour-market contracts. It has also provided a critical analysis of how women in particular have become involved in specific types of externalized employment situations as a way to better balance their household and paid work responsibilities.

A major flaw plaguing the literature on distancing strategies in white-collar work is the lack of detailed attention paid to how new information and communications technologies are used to relocate and externalize such work and the impact of these changes on women's labour force work. An analysis of the use of technologies to facilitate shifts in where and when work can be performed is emerging from research on teleworking. Much of the literature has focused on documenting the extent, shape and potential of this form of distanced work as well as worker satisfaction with their working conditions and their perceptions of the new work reality (Devine et al., 1997; Jackson and van der Wielen, 1998; Huws et al., 1990; Provenzano, 1994; Templer, 1999; Thurman et al., 1990). Attention has also been paid to the gendered dynamics of teleworking and the construction of gendered identities of teleworkers (Armstrong, 1999; Mirchandani, 1999). Notwithstanding this important research, we know little about how new computer and telecommunications technologies are used to spatially reorganize and disperse white-collar service-sector work, modify and degrade employment relationships

and cause labour-market dislocations. The relative absence of focus on these processes is puzzling considering the explosion of not only academic, but also professional, government and popular literature on new high technologies; this literature celebrates the ability of such technologies to collapse and transcend space and time. The hype surrounding the immense capacity of new technologies has served to disguise particular applications and underlying power relationships in work and employment. A better understanding of the role of information technologies in redesigning employment relationships in white-collar jobs and in the service sector is also critical because of ongoing debates about the impact of new technologies on labour-market polarization in the post-industrial economy (Hughes and Lowe, 2000).

Searching for Flexibility: The Contracting Out of Work at Air Canada

In its quest to reduce costs and ensure profitability under airline industry restructuring and economic turbulence, Air Canada has adopted different employment practices and has fundamentally redesigned the labour process of customer sales and service agents. This article focuses on the contracting out of the work of customers sales and service agents to travel agencies, a key and highly successful strategy pursued by Air Canada to enhance labour flexibility and bolster its market position in the context of industry deregulation, cutthroat competition, concentration and globalization. The air carrier relied on several interconnected decisions and practices to contract out work; computer and telecommunications technologies were fundamental in facilitating this process. The externalization of work promoted a degradation of the employment relationship, thereby leaving workers with less job security, fewer opportunities and a diminished quality of work.

Distancing through Technology: Phase I

While Air Canada has always dealt with travel agencies and has depended on them to sell seats and provide services to its customers, it was only in the early 1970s that the company began to more fully integrate agencies into its marketing strategies to take advantage of the explosion in domestic, transborder and international air travel, and to retain and consolidate its position in a highly competitive environment.[4] Throughout the 1960s, the rise in Canada's population, economic expansion and the steady growth in real income stimulated demand for both leisure and business air travel. The introduction of faster, quieter and more comfortable aircraft during the 1960s made air travel quite attractive, especially when compared to other modes of transportation. The implementation of different types of fares, the expansion in the utilization of discounted promotional fares and the wider availability of economy-class service persuaded more people to fly. During the 1950s and 1960s, the federal government, which has regulatory authority over civil aviation, gradually removed some of the restrictions that controlled competition in the airline industry. Air Canada thus had to contend with intensifying competition from Canadian Pacific Air Lines Ltd. (CPAL) and charter carriers (especially Wardair Ltd.) on international and transborder routes, and from CPAL and regional carriers on domestic routes, all of whom were trying to take advantage of the boom in air travel.[5]

In response to these new trends, Air Canada turned to the travel agency industry as a prom-ising channel of distribution for its products. This marketing strategy effectively allowed for the work of customer sales and service agents to be more easily performed by outside companies. Travel agencies proliferated beginning in the 1960s when jet travel became widespread and a greater number of people chose to fly. Traditionally, the travel agency industry consisted of small independently run operations. Franchising expanded during the 1970s, a trend that was accompanied by a growing control of the air travel market by larger agencies. Furthermore, independent companies joined forces in consortiums and associations.[6] Travel agencies represented a broad channel of distribution because they were located in many large and small centres across the country and had access to a vast number of potential passengers. Travel agencies thus became significant players in air transportation.

Air Canada's ability to externalize customer sales and service agents' work was enhanced immensely with the implementation of ReserVec II, the company's automated central reservations system, which made use of advanced computer and telecommunications technologies. Introduced in the carrier's own offices in 1970, this comprehensive computerized reservations system, which fundamentally transformed the labour-intensive job of customer sales and service agents, ensured a faster and more convenient way of registering, storing, processing and retrieving data. In an attempt to exploit this new technology to enhance its competitive position and tap into growing and diversifying travel markets, Air Canada, following carriers in other countries, launched a project in 1972 to begin placing video display terminals (VDTs) in offices of major travel agencies.[7] This move provided travel agencies with direct on-line access to the carrier's central reservations system. It also marked the beginning of the off-premise programme, a company practice that greatly facilitated the partial externalization of the employment relationship by effectively contracting out the work of customer sales and service agents.

The contracting out of work to travel agencies intensified beginning in the mid-1970s when the airline industry entered a prolonged period of upheaval. The industry did not escape the vagaries of the economic crisis that began in the mid-1970s and the major economic swings since then have had an impact on air transportation. Ongoing deregulation in the airline industry in Canada and worldwide, which progressed slowly until the late 1970s, accelerated throughout the 1980s, bringing with it heightened competition on a global scale. An increase in the number of domestic, transborder and international routes and in flight frequencies, which put excessive capacity on the market, was an integral part of this new competitive environment. In the midst of this restructuring and in the context of a worldwide trend towards the partial or full privatization of government-owned air carriers, Air Canada was privatized in the late 1980s.[8] Throughout this period, the relaxation by governments of controls over tariffs resulted in a remarkable expansion of, and diversification in, fares and services which fundamentally altered the nature of air travel. Intense competition for market share gave rise to a complex variety of promotional fares. In addition, unprecedented fare discounting, which became a key marketing tool for air carriers, led to fierce price wars in Canada and abroad. This diversification in fares helped fill airplane seats that would otherwise have remained empty. Moreover, fundamental change in air travel brought with it a wider variety of tours, vacation pack-

ages, charter flights and other special services that were made available to customers as part of an effort to provide a complete product line that appealed to different segments of an ever-broadening travel market.

In this rapidly evolving environment, Air Canada forged ahead with its plans to fully integrate travel agencies into its promotion and distribution activities. Travel agencies were a prime selling force for air carriers and, in an effort to capture a larger share of the market, Air Canada undertook to supply travel agencies with the tools required to offer a more complete service to customers. The installation of VDTs in travel agencies initiated in the early 1970s continued apace. In 1977, the off-premise programme was expanded to include automated ticket printers, which had been introduced in company offices in 1974.[9] In 1986,[10] four years after they made their appearance in company locations, boarding-pass printers were also made available to travel agencies. This ReserVec II equipment was the outward and immediately visible manifestation of travel agencies' access to the centralized reservations system.

The automated reservations system and the myriad changes it has undergone represent a less visible, yet highly critical, dimension of the contracting-out process. Indeed, over the years, travel agencies benefitted from frequent enhancements to software programmes and from the abundance of information that was added to the central computer in the wake of rapid and massive restructuring in the airline industry. With the multiplication of travel products and special services, especially beginning in the late 1970s, the information stored in the computer was greatly expanded. In addition, as fares increased in variety and complexity under tariff deregulation, software programmes were continually developed to enhance automated pricing capabilities. ReserVec II grew tremendously in terms of flexibility and versatility to accommodate a number of passenger-handling functions and services. Much of the reference material needed to answer customers' queries and complete bookings was programmed into the computer. In most cases, the need to contact Air Canada customer sales and service agents to make reservations, provide other services, and obtain more specific information was significantly reduced or completely eliminated for agencies renting the ReserVec II technology. In the early 1980s, in order to assist travel agency staff, Air Canada established the automated agency support centre, a technical service desk for agencies linked to its centralized reservations system. Furthermore, software programs, such as management information systems and electronic mail service, were developed by Air Canada specifically for use by travel agencies. To compete with other carriers, Air Canada also improved commission plans, an incentive that made it more attractive for travel agencies to book seats on its flights.[11]

Distancing through Technology: Phase II

The globalization of the airline industry engendered fundamental changes that would have a major impact on the distribution of airline products and would further facilitate the externalization of the work of customer sales and service agents. With rapid deregulation of air transportation worldwide, which led to less restrictive air bilateral agreements between nations, carriers sought innovative strategies to ensure their position in the marketplace. Concentration resulting from acquisitions and mergers characterized the industry beginning in the mid-1980s. In Canada, with the unprecedented realignment in the owner-

ship structure of airline companies, by the late 1990s the industry was dominated by Air Canada and Canadian Airlines International Ltd. (CAIL).[12] In the face of the emergence of mega-carriers on the international scene, both Air Canada and CAIL sought to enhance their world presence by entering into commercial alliances with international carriers, a strategy that provided for mutual passenger exchange, improved connections and the extension of networks to a growing number of world destinations.[13]

Large computerized reservations systems, or what is known in the industry as global distribution systems, have emerged as a key tool in air carriers' struggle to remain competitive and ensure market domination. The redesign of the product distribution system strengthened the position of travel agencies within the travel industry and left airline workers worried about their future prospects. The ease with which the work of customer sales and service agents could be turned over to travel agencies was driven home in the early 1990s when Air Canada transferred travel agencies to Covia International Network's[14] sophisticated Apollo computerized reservations system. This transfer followed a partnership agreement reached in March 1989 between the Gemini Group Automated Distributions Systems Inc.[15] and Covia International Network.[16] The new Apollo computerized reservations system offered automated products more advanced than those included in ReserVec II as well as additional features that could significantly enhance travel agency capabilities and enable them to capture an even greater share of the air travel market. In the context of the globalization of travel automation, Covia International Network and Galileo[17] signed an agreement in early 1993 to merge their computerized reservations systems, thus creating a new company called Galileo International.[18] The enterprise meant the joining of forces of two of the industry's leading computerized reservations systems to create a huge global distribution network for travel products serving over 25,000 travel agencies worldwide. By 1999, this number had grown to approximately 40,000.[19]

The distribution of travel products through travel agencies subscribing to computerized reservations systems has obviously become an essential aspect of air carriers' marketing strategy. Beginning in the late-1980s, in an effort to expand their market share, airline companies have relied heavily on the ability of large external computerized reservations systems to secure travel agent subscribers and therefore build consumer loyalty. The global distribution networks have worked feverishly to develop new products and services and to market them to travel agencies. The predominance of global distribution networks with their focus on marketing to, and servicing the needs of, travel agencies represents a key aspect of the recent shift of customer sales and service agents' work to outside retailers.

Distancing and the Loss of Corporate Accounts

The introduction of computer and telecommunications technologies linking travel agencies to Air Canada's central reservations system and the more recent development of global distribution systems have been a major threat to the job security of customer sales and service agents because they make it extremely easy for travel agency personnel to perform the work of in-house agents. The growing presence and strength of the travel agency industry, concomitant with changes in the way corporations handle travel arrangements, has resulted in a significant shift in the provision of corporate air travel reservations and related services from air carriers to travel agencies. Indeed, over the years, many businesses chose to deal with travel agencies and some of Air Canada's corporate accounts switched to such agencies.[20] Moreover, during the economic crisis of the early 1980s, in-plant agencies began to take root as businesses eliminated their in-house travel services in an effort to cut costs. Such agencies, which are branches of existing travel agencies located entirely on the premises of companies, were established exclusively to service the travel needs of these commercial clients.[21] This new distribution channel provided travel agencies with exclusive access to several million dollars' worth of air travel reservations business.

By the mid-1980s, much of Air Canada's corporate business—which is a crucial market segment because these clients are the repeat, must-fly travellers who pay higher fares—was being handled by travel agencies,[22] with the exception of the lucrative federal government travel servicing contract. This account had been established by the then crown carrier in 1968 to fill the requirement for government travel. However, in 1986, in the midst of an increasing trend toward privatization, the federal government awarded the $120 million central travel service account to Marlin Travel Ltd., one of the country's largest travel agencies.[23] Air Canada customer sales and service agents thus lost another substantial amount of work. In 1991, the account was awarded to the Rider Travel Group, an agency that makes use of American Airlines' Sabre computer reservations system.[24] Air Canada did not bid on the contract. The federal government has since continued to award its travel account to the Rider Group.

Fostering Distancing through the Consolidation of Operations

Other initiatives undertaken by Air Canada also favoured the transfer of reservations, ticketing and other services to travel agencies. These company actions, which began slowly in the mid-1980s and accelerated in the late 1980s and early 1990s, were undertaken in the wake of the massive restructuring of the airline industry and swings in the economy. During this time, the company downsized its operations, reduced capacity or totally suspended services to many communities (which were sometimes taken over by partially or fully owned subsidiaries) and closed offices and entire bases. Hiring freezes, layoffs and general staff reductions also marked this period. Air Canada closed many of its city sales offices, mainly in communities it no longer directly served, leaving local travel agencies to handle customers seeking more personalized service. There are also indications that city sales offices in some cities were moved from prime locations to less accessible areas,[25] making it more convenient for customers to seek out travel agency offices, which are usually well located and easy to find.

In addition, Air Canada centralized its reservations services, a move that greatly reduced the number of company reservations offices. The trend towards closing regional reservations offices across Canada and shifting the work to bigger cities began in the early 1980s and accelerated dramatically throughout the mid- to late-1980s and early 1990s. These closures were part of major rounds of consolidations that saw the smaller but also some of the larger reservations offices disappear, leaving only four reservations centres in Toronto, Montreal, Vancouver and Winnipeg. This reorganization was made possible because of the availability of advanced call centralizing technology and lower telecommunications rates brought about by deregulation in the telecommunications sector. In 1996, Air Canada opened a reservations office in Saint John in the midst of the proliferation of call centres that were part of the province of New Brunswick's wider information-technology strategy for development.[26] Not only was the number of general reservations offices reduced, but other telephone reservations functions, including commercial and special accounts which had been handled by about fifteen offices in the early 1980s, were consolidated in the remaining centres.[27] Moreover, some of the specialized functions in those centres, such as tour desks, were eliminated and customer sales and service agents were instructed to refer clients to travel agencies or Air Canada city sales offices.[28]

As Air Canada downsized to fewer and fewer city sales and reservations offices to consolidate its operations and cut costs, the company's presence in many communities was reduced or eliminated. Consequently, in most towns and cities across Canada, air travellers seeking immediate and more personalized attention had little choice but to call upon local travel agencies to attend to their needs. In the wake of these changes, the employment security of customer sales and service agents was seriously threatened as jobs in both small and large communities disappeared.

Workers' Struggle against Employment Relationship Degradation at Air Canada

While Air Canada's actions and decisions surrounding the contracting out of work did result in a gradual erosion of the job security of customer sales and service agents, workers and their union actively resisted these assaults. The initial phase of the off-premise programme in the early 1970s marked the beginning of a protracted struggle between Air Canada and the Canadian Air Line Employees' Association (CALEA), the union representing customer sales and service agents, surrounding the contracting out of work to travel agencies. From the outset, the union voiced concerns that the off-premise programme would have an impact on the job security of CALEA members.[29] Job security was becoming a very important issue for customer sales and service agents. In the early 1970s, both the introduction of labour-saving technology and the modification of contract language that allowed the company to create more part-time positions had begun to raise fears of job loss. The implementation of the off-premise programme fuelled fears that job security would be further weakened. In this context, the contracting out of work was becoming a new and pivotal job security battleground.

In late 1975, the union filed a grievance, claiming that travel agencies' use of VDT equipment and their direct access to the ReserVec II data bank was in violation of article 2.03 of the collective agreement. Article 2.03, customer sales and service agents' job security clause negotiated in 1969, stipulated that "the Company will not permit any person not covered under this Agreement to do any tasks or duties covered under this Agreement, unless specifically provided for herein."[30] When the union submitted the matter to arbitration, it was confident of obtaining a favourable award because an arbitration decision in October 1975 had upheld its interpretation of the job security clause.

The grievance was awaiting an arbitration hearing when collective bargaining commenced in the summer of 1976. During contract talks, the company insisted that it needed to achieve some relief from article 2.03, which it considered the most restrictive article in the collective agreement, in order to continue to introduce VDTs in travel agencies without interference or further possible action on the part of the union.[31] The company argued that:

> The most important single objective of Air Canada's approach to these negotiations was to retain the Company's clear ability to market its product through travel agencies and similar enterprises. More than half of the Company's total sales revenue of $1 billion annually is generated by such enterprises. For Air Canada to remain economically viable, it was absolutely essential that it retain its right to do business with these companies.[32]

The union withdrew the arbitration and reluctantly agreed to a letter of understanding that allowed Air Canada to market its products through outside companies even though the latter's employees performed duties covered by the collective agreement.[33] The union's concession on this clause provided the company with tremendous flexibility to contract out work. It thus marked a decisive moment in the degradation of the employment relationship. Notwithstanding the weakening of the strong job protection language and despite its more limited resources, the union continued to challenge many management practices that it felt jeopardized customer sales and service agents' job security. The union fought back through the grievance process and during negotiations, but the strength of the employer represented a formidable obstacle. Air Canada was able to obtain relief during collective bargaining from the limitations imposed by contract language and by arbitration awards favourable to the union.

When negotiations began to renew the collective agreement expiring in the fall of 1984, Air Canada was adamant that significant improvements in productivity and efficiency were required in order for it to survive and prosper under newly deregulated skies in a global environment. Cost control, greater labour flexibility and enhanced productivity, which were focal points in discussions with all company employees, could be achieved through a relaxation of restrictions on those allowed to perform scope work, the elimination of restrictive scheduling and staffing practices (especially relating to part-time work), and major wage concessions.[34]

Job security was the single most important issue for customer sales and service agents,[35] especially given the looming threat of deregulation, impending massive technological change in the workplace and high unemployment. Concerned that it lacked the bargaining power, collective strength and resources required to protect members in the face of the fundamental reorganization in the industry and the worsening political and economic climate, the CALEA sought a merger with the powerful and progressive United Auto Workers (UAW)-Canada (which became the Canadian Auto Workers (CAW)-Canada in 1985 following a split from the international union)[36] and received support from this union during negotiations. The decision to merge with a union such as the CAW was quite significant and it was made possible largely because, by the mid-1980s, the CALEA had moved away from its identification as a white-collar association; it had grown into a stronger independent union and had become more progressive in its policies and militant in its actions.

After rejecting a final set of unacceptable company proposals that revolved around greater labour flexibility, customer sales and service agents, for the first time in their history, staged a full-scale strike against Air Canada in the spring of 1985. Workers and their union were determined to fight the company's concessionary demands because they feared that there would be a wholesale attack on jobs, working conditions and employment security similar to the American situation where, in the wake of deregulation in the late-1970s, air carriers had laid off thousands of workers and pushed unions into accepting wage cuts and freezes, two-tier pay scales, reduced benefits, increased working hours and less restrictive work rules. When the dust finally settled after a five-week strike, it was clear that the company had succeeded in obtaining enhanced labour flexibility through concessions that further weakened the job protection clause. The union withdrew two key grievances related to the contracting out of work.[37] It also accepted contract amendments whereby customer sales and service agents' tasks covered by the collective agreement, which were being carried out by non-company personnel as of September 25, 1984, could continue to be carried out by such workers.[38]

The agreement signed in 1985 worsened the job security of customer sales and service agents and made them vulnerable to further losses. Collective agreement language was watered down to the point where the company could contract out customer sales and service agents' work with relative ease. The union was subsequently more cautious in proceeding to arbitration on some grievances pertaining to travel agencies because the weakening of the job security clause, combined with the ambiguity of the contract language regarding what constituted the "marketing of the company's products," could lead to a far-reaching ruling that could seriously influence future arbitration cases dealing with the encroachment on customer sales and service agents' jobs by travel agencies.[39]

Innovative Job Security Enhancement Strategies

The union had always relied on the collective bargaining process and the grievance system to fight ongoing threats to members' job security. Despite its ability to win a strong job protection clause in the form of work jurisdiction in 1969, the union was unable to stop the company from contracting out the work of customer sales and service agents to travel agencies. In the context of the massive restructuring of the airline industry and workplace changes in the 1980s, the union recognized the need to develop innovative policies and programmes aimed at reversing the trend towards the weakening of job security resulting from the contracting out of work, the implementation of labour-saving technologies, greater use of part-time work, the consolidation of operations and massive layoffs. The union's initiatives revolved around the negotiation of a stronger technological change clause, innovative job expansion programmes and improved layoff and relocation provisions.

During collective bargaining in 1984–1985, the union managed to considerably strengthen the contract language on technological change that had been negotiated in 1966. The new clause,[40] which included a definition of technological change, a requirement of advance notice for such change and provisions for the establishment of a joint technological change committee, offered the union a better means to monitor the effects of technological innovations on members and address issues of concern. It also somewhat lessened the company's discretion in defining what was to be considered technological change. There were, however, limitations with the contract language. The union did not participate in setting the parameters of technological change and had no input in decisions on the nature of new technologies chosen. It was not consulted when plans for bringing in new technology were being made, but was informed only following major decisions. In addition, the definition of technological change did not cover modifications to work methods unrelated to machinery. Furthermore, the union was unsuccessful in obtaining guarantees that employees displaced by new technology would be retrained at the employer's expense.

Another main strategy adopted by the union to counter the erosion of job security consisted in promoting job expansion programmes. During the 1984–1985 contract talks, the union successfully negotiated a stronger job expansion clause. A 1978 letter of understanding on this matter, negotiated in order to mitigate the impact of concessions agreed to that year, was split into two distinct letters of understanding. These letters of understanding made both short-term and long-term positions outside the scope of the collective agreement available to customer sales and service agents.[41] Under these provisions, several agreements were reached to expand agents' tasks and duties, particularly in the areas of training, quality assurance, customer relations and external sales solicitation.[42] This not only resulted in improved job security, but provided more interesting and challenging work for a small number of agents. As a means of achieving a permanent expansion of the work performed by customer sales and service agents, the union attempted to bring these special assignments within the scope of the agreement on an exclusive basis through the creation of new job classifications.[43] While the union was unsuccessful in its efforts, it was nonetheless able to obtain, in 1986, a guaranteed minimum of 35 positions across the system under the letter of understanding covering long-term assignments.[44] This number was raised to 50 jobs following contract talks in 1988.[45] These guaranteed positions, though significant, were considerably fewer than that sought by the union.

To further secure jobs for customer sales and service agents and partly reverse the trend towards the transferring of bargaining unit work to travel agencies, especially in the wake of the loss of the government travel service contract, the union succeeded in negotiating the creation, in 1986, of a union travel service, thereby guaranteeing a unionized reservations facility for union travel arrangements.[46] Prior to the establishment of this new programme, the Canadian Labour Congress's 1984 convention had adopted a resolution tabled by the CALEA that encouraged all member unions to make reservations and purchase tickets through unionized travel outlets.[47] Given the lack of unionization of travel agency workers, this policy was aimed at directing business to those airline companies where workers were unionized. The union travel service met with some success. In a few larger cities a specialized union travel service work function was created, dedicated telephone lines were set up and customer sales and service agents were trained as sales representatives to solicit union business. Many unions were signed up as commercial accounts with some business being directed away from travel agencies and, as a result, a number of customer sales and service agent jobs were salvaged.[48]

The third major job security enhancement strategy pursued by the union consisted in negotiating stronger layoff and relocation provisions. Beginning in the mid-1980s, the union successfully bargained for improvements in this area in order to protect customer sales and service agents' employment and create more acceptable options in the event of staff reductions. The collective agreement signed following the strike in 1985 incorporated some of the most significant changes, and subsequent rounds of contract talks also led to stronger provisions. Notable amendments included increased advance notice of layoff, improved retention and accrual of seniority during layoff, greater ability for part-time and full-time workers to fill a vacancy in the other status in case of staff reductions, enhanced coverage of relocation expenses, increased severance pay, early retirement packages, and additional leaves of absence opportunities.[49] These initiatives resulted in reduced staff overages and fewer layoffs.

Although these various programmes and changes to the collective agreement served to protect the jobs of a number of customer sales and service agents and expanded the options for many others, they were not sufficient to counter the degrading effects of the massive transfer of work to travel agencies on the employment relationship. With the balance of power shifting heavily to employers, customer sales and service agents and their union have been in a very difficult position to resist these challenges.

The Truncation of the Employment Relationship: Discussion and Conclusions

Through a case study of the contracting out to travel agencies of the work of Air Canada customer sales and service agents under economic and airline industry restructuring, this article has provided important insights into four interconnected issues of relevance to sociological analysis in the areas of work and social inequality: the process of employment relationship degradation, the changing nature and conditions of women's white-collar service-sector work, the dynamics underlying growing inequality and polarization in society, and the role of technological change in the restructuring of work and employment.

By tracing how good jobs get turned into bad jobs, the article has portrayed employment relationship degradation as a process that has immediate and long-term consequences for workers. Air Canada's distancing strategy has contributed to the degradation of the employment relationship through slower growth in the number of in-house agents required to sell the carrier's products, an erosion of their job security, fewer opportunities and a further deskilling of their work.

Although the overall shift of customer sales and service agents' work to travel agencies had begun slowly, the trend accelerated throughout the 1970s, 1980s and 1990s. During the 1940s, the proportion of business secured from travel agencies was between 5 and 10 percent.[50] By 1977, more than half of the revenue Air Canada received from ticket sales was generated by travel agencies[51] and, by the late 1990s, over 80 percent of the business went through such channels. These statistics clearly signify that the volume of calls and the number of tickets that customer sales and service agents did not process because clients were being serviced by travel agencies were enormous. The growth of the customer sales and service agent job category was arrested

because such a heavy volume of business was handled by travel agencies. Notwithstanding other significant factors that played a role in eroding the job security of customer sales and service agents (such as ongoing workplace technological innovations, massive layoffs in the 1980s and 1990s, and an increase in part-time work) Air Canada's various actions and decisions to actively encourage and promote the use of travel agencies as a channel for the sale and distribution of its products and services greatly affected the job category. This form of work externalization is relatively invisible because the commercial relationship between air carriers and travel agencies does not follow the pattern of subcontracting or outsourcing typical in most other industries and sectors of the economy. Indeed, most such arrangements are based on the purchase of specified tangible physical goods, information products, services or a predetermined amount of time, whereas the contracting out of work to travel agencies involves the payment of a commission by air carriers to these agencies for the sale of an airplane seat. While this specific type of distancing tends to be less visible than others, its detrimental impact on workers is very real.

Customer sales and service agents not only experienced reduced job opportunities and the dilution of their job security because of Air Canada's heavy reliance on, and promotion of, travel agencies, but they also lived with the fear that these agencies could easily make their jobs redundant. During interviews, most customer sales and service agents who had been with Air Canada since the 1970s made reference to the tremendous growth in travel agencies over the years and spoke of their job security concerns. The following two quotes exemplify their frustrations and apprehensions:

Initially, when I first came in, we hardly knew what a travel agency was, there weren't that many. And gradually over the years, particularly in the late 1970s, they really got a big grip of the market and they were just opening up all over the place, mushroomed. And there was a bit of resentment in the rank and file because we felt that our jobs were being eroded by travel agencies and by Air Canada catering to the travel agencies. That's not changed. We still feel that way. We are still expected to do everything the travel agency wants us to do. When we come to Air Canada, we're told we want them to stay with Air Canada, they're generating a lot of business and we're there for them. And it's a dichotomy. You're really caught because you want to do your job. At the same time you're doing your job, you have a feeling, maybe I'm doing myself out of my job by doing my job so well.[52]

Travel agencies are another problem. They expect the world and Air Canada caters to them, and Air Canada is giving our jobs away to them. And they're used to getting catered to by Air Canada because agencies do 78 percent of Air Canada's ticketing right now and Air Canada would like them to do 100 percent. They bend over backwards, they contort all out of shape to give whatever the agencies want to them.... And the company is only too pleased to push as much business to travel agencies as they possibly can, and I wouldn't be surprised if sometime in the future, Air Canada bought a huge agency and staffed everybody at six bucks an hour and closed all reservations offices.[53]

While job loss and diminished opportunities represent the visible features of job insecurity, the changing nature of work, which remains deeply hidden in the abode of production, also heavily influenced the company's ability to render the job of in-house workers more insecure, thereby weakening the employment relationship. The ease with which Air Canada could contract out work underlines the deskilled nature of the customer sales and service agent job. While it is not possible in this article to provide a full analysis of the redesign of the labour process, it is important to note that an ongoing deskilling process, which was never direct and unmediated and was largely facilitated by advanced technologies and new forms of work organization, has characterized the work of customer sales and service agents over the past few decades.[54] What needs to be emphasized here is that the practice of parcelling out the work of customer sales and service agents reinforces deskilling. Indeed, with travel agencies having access to computerized reservations systems and being allowed to perform more customer sales and service tasks, the job of Air Canada agents has lost some of its interesting and challenging elements. Customer sales and service agents assigned to telephone sales are now found in one of the five call centres where the majority of workers spend much of their time on relatively routine tasks. Because the centralization of reservations operations has led to a reduction in the time agents spend waiting for calls, this reorganization has also brought about an intensification of work. In addition, because customers, especially business clients and people travelling extensively to a variety of destinations, increasingly deal with agencies, Air Canada employees are not handling the most interesting itineraries.

While customer sales and service agents have experienced a degraded employment relationship because of the inroads made by travel agencies, Air Canada has benefitted immensely from this growth and has been able to externalize some of the costs and risks of doing business. Contracting out represents a means to enhance labour flexibility when faced with competitive pressures and market uncertainties, two defining features of the airline industry throughout the past few decades. In an extensively deregulated and competitive market environment, air carriers have actively pursued commercial strategies to sell their main product, airplane seats, thereby ensuring market expansion. Because this product is perishable, air carriers depend heavily on distributors to help minimize wasted capacity and maximize profits. Relying on external travel agencies that have more direct access to an enormous potential passenger base to supply the constantly varying amount of labour required to help fill airplane seats has been highly effective for Air Canada.

By reducing the quantity of in-house labour required, the carrier has been able to cut down on the costs and minimize the risks associated with a permanent full-time workforce such as higher pay, better benefits, and worker development, training and control costs. The tasks of promoting air travel as well as selling tickets and other products to travellers and meeting some of their needs are highly labour intensive. The benefits associated with the externalization of these tasks should not be downplayed. One of the main advantages of this distancing strategy lies in the cost savings derived from the lower rates of pay and less generous benefits packages offered by non-unionized travel agencies when compared with those enjoyed by unionized customer sales and service agents.

For example, in 1996, travel agent salaries ranged from around $15,600 to $33,000, although these salaries could be supplemented by commissions paid by suppliers to the agencies.[55] Customer sales and service agents at Air Canada earned an entry level base salary of close to $18,000 and a maximum base salary of $39,000 after five years of service.[56] This amount does not include shift premiums, longevity pay and compensation for overtime and recall, benefits that are not generally available in travel agencies. In addition, customer sales and service agents have been able to secure a more generous benefits package, including longer guaranteed vacations, more statutory holidays, and better sick leave, parental leave and other leave provisions. Customer sales and service agents also enjoy greater job security and better working conditions through a host of collective agreement provisions. What seems clear is that a huge reduction in direct labour costs has been achieved by the air carrier through the contracting out of work to travel agencies.

The gradual externalization of a colossal amount of customer sales and service agents' work to travel agencies has led to a truncated employment relationship. Contracting out clearly weakened the standard employment relationship. However, many of the conditions associated with standard employment have been maintained largely because customer sales and service agents and their union fought to preserve these conditions in the face of a powerful employer demanding concessions. Air Canada's decisions and practices that threatened the standard employment relationship were systematically met with resistance by customer sales and service agents who feared that the contracting out of their work would result in a major attack on job security. While work externalization was not the only practice that fostered the overall degradation of work, it played a key role in the shift towards more conflictual labour-management relations and contributed to the radicalization of customer sales and service agents. The oppositional stance taken by these sales and service white-collar workers towards management stems from the material experience of subordination in the wage labour relationship and reflects increasing class polarization.

By carefully charting the consequences of work externalization, the study has provided important insights into the changing nature and shape of white-collar work, and particularly women's sales and service white-collar work in the post-industrial economy. The changing nature and direction of work under post-industrialism has become a central issue of contention in the sociology of work. My findings support the view that the trend towards flexible employment has negative repercussions on women's service-sector white-collar employment. The contracting out of work to travel agencies has played a significant role in restructuring the work of Air Canada customer sales and service agents. By undermining the job stability and opportunities of customer sales and service agents and hindering the growth of the job category itself while travel agency business grew,[57] the process of work externalization has contributed to an occupational shift and a further division within white-collar labour. The shift in the lines that divide labour has also meant worsening labour-market conditions for women. Better paid, secure and unionized jobs where women predominate are giving way to non-unionized jobs with lower pay and fewer benefits with less employment stability where women also predominate. The travel agency workforce,

like that of the customer sales and service group at Air Canada, is heavily dominated by women—close to 85 percent and close to 75 percent respectively. What is more, the job of customer sales and service agent at Air Canada has itself undergone a process of increasing feminization. Indeed, during the period from the early 1970s to the late 1990s that is covered in this article, the proportion of women customer sales and service agents grew from slightly over 60 percent in the early 1970s to approximately 70 percent in the early 1980s and, by the early 1990s, women represented 75 percent of agents. Clearly, the expansion and restructuring of white-collar service-sector employment, where women have found many of their good jobs as their labour force participation rose, have had contradictory effects on their employment opportunities.

Analyzing employment relationship degradation is therefore important, not only to trace the changing nature of white-collar employment, but also to better understand broader changes in the labour market and the dynamics underlying growing inequality and polarization in society. These issues have been central to sociological analysis and continue to merit attention not least because of the shifting employment base and new employment strategies adopted by corporations in the post-industrial economy. Through an investigation of deepening flexible employment practices, this article has provided insights into the relationship between the changing shape of paid employment and the process of polarization under post-industrialism. Many white-collar service-sector occupations, which are usually highly labour intensive, are currently undergoing fundamental transformations. Different forms of distancing practices, some of which may be quite unique to white-collar service-sector work, are being implemented in the context of these transformations and are contributing to a redefinition and destandardization of employment relationships throughout the economy. Given gender-based segmentation in the labour market, women and men will likely be differentially affected by these new employment trends, a situation that has significant consequences and long-term implications for divisions and inequalities in the labour market.

One final contribution of this article to sociological debates rests with questions surrounding the role of technological change in the transformation of work. The impacts of new information technologies on employment opportunities and on the nature of work have been hotly contested in the sociology of work. This case study has shown that the contracting out of customer sales and service agents' work to travel agencies was largely achieved through the implementation of computer and telecommunications technologies. By facilitating a shift in the location of work, the application of these new information technologies has helped to redefine the employment relationship, a change that has not been advantageous for this group of white-collar service-sector workers. The article thus challenges dominant assumptions of post-industrial theory that the information economy, with its promise of good work and enviable working conditions made possible by rapid technological innovations, is a haven for workers. It also highlights the link between the introduction of labour-saving technologies and the process of polarization.

The turbulence in the airline industry that has been raging for two decades has not yet run its course. Indeed, recent developments indicate that the bumpy ride is far from over, a situation that does not bode well for airline

workers. The takeover of CAIL by Air Canada in late 1999 means the merging of operations, including the integration of workforces. This reality, compounded by Air Canada's drive to increase labour flexibility and reduce costs in the context of intensified global competition and an economic downturn, will result in a further attack on the job security and working conditions of customer sales and service agents. In addition, global distribution systems will most likely become even bigger players in air travel and will exacerbate the trend towards contracting out. Finally, air carriers are moving towards the self-service concept, a change made possible by ongoing developments in computer and telecommunications technologies. The Internet, in particular, allows for a distancing strategy that relies on consumers to perform the unpaid work of booking their own flights. While travel agencies will be affected by consumers' ability to purchase their own tickets and will thus be compelled to restructure, they will nevertheless likely more fully integrate the Internet into their operations to take advantage of its potential and offer value-added service to clients. Customer sales and service agents at Air Canada may not be so lucky.

Current industry upheavals and the air carrier's search for new channels of distribution for its products will continue to impinge on the job security of customer sales and service agents and further undermine collective efforts to resist worsening conditions. The job expansion programmes and amendments to the collective agreement negotiated by the union, while significant, may not be sufficient to cushion Air Canada workers against industry restructuring that will foster ongoing employment relationship degradation. Transportation has been identified as part of the "dynamic services" of the post-industrial economy where workers are supposed to enjoy relatively favourable conditions. My study suggests, however, that we need to refocus our lens and take a close look at the actual degradation of work and employment that is all too often the reality faced by white-collar workers, many of them women, in the purportedly advantaged sectors of the post-industrial economy.

Endnotes

1 An earlier version of this paper was presented at the Annual Meeting of the Canadian Sociology and Anthropology Association, Edmonton, June 2000. This project was supported by a grant from the Social Sciences and Humanities Research Council of Canada. I am deeply indebted to the many CAW Local 2213 members, executive, district chairpersons and support staff, to representatives of the CAW-Canada Airline Division, and to Air Canada headquarters and local management who have generously given of their time and support to this research. I also wish to thank Wallace Clement, Ann Duffy and Bruce McFarlane for their helpful comments on previous drafts of this paper. The constructive suggestions of Nico Stehr and three anonymous *Canadian Journal of Sociology* reviewers are kindly appreciated.

2 This article draws on extensive archival material and in-depth interviews with workers, union representatives and company officials. It is part of a larger study that examines the degradation of the work process and the employment relationship, and the radicalization of white-collar workers through an investigation of the transformation of the work of customers sales and service agents at Air Canada. The analysis takes shape through an exploration of the effects of technological innovations on the organization of work, the complex question of skills/deskilling as a social process, the practice of monitoring workers with micro-electronic technologies, the contracting out of work made possible by information technologies, and the increase in non-standard and precarious work.

3 With the expansion of the service economy, white-collar work has grown tremendously to include a wide variety of occupations. This article focuses more specifically on sales and service occupations and not on professional, technical and managerial occupations. Sales and service occupations, along with clerical occupations, have often been termed pink-collar work because of the heavy concentration of women in such jobs.

4 Letter from J.C. Finlay, Assistant Director, Sales Management Planning, Air Canada, to J. Hayes, President, CALEA, March 5, 1970; Air Canada.1970. *Between Ourselves,* No. 343 (July), p. 10.

5 For a more complete historical overview of the changing structure of the airline industry, see Stevenson (1987).

6 Wykes, Jill. 1986. "The Business of Travel." *enRoute,* Vol. 14, No. 4 (April), pp. 42, 80–83, 86, 88, 92.

7 Air Canada. 1972. *Between Ourselves,* No. 362 (February), p. 9; CALEA and Air Canada, Minutes of a Union-Management Headquarters Meeting, Item M.205, March 1972.

8 International Civil Aviation Organization. 1989. *Annual Report of the Council*; Oum et al. 1990.

9 CALEA and Air Canada. 1977. Minutes of a Union-Management Headquarters Meeting, Item 234-K (April), Item 234-L (June).

10 Air Canada, *Horizons,* No. 699, December 15, 1986, p. 3.

11 Air Canada, *Horizons,* No. 622, June 15, 1983, p. 5, No. 635, January 17, 1984, pp. 1–2, No. 702, March 3, 1987, p. 1.

12 In early 1987, PWA Corp., parent company of Pacific Western Airlines Ltd. (PWA) (a former regional carrier), purchased 100 percent of Canadian Pacific Air Lines Ltd. (CPAL) and, in April of that year, the two carriers were integrated and continued business under the name Canadian Airlines International Ltd. (CAIL). In 1989, PWA Corp. acquired 100 percent of Wardair Inc.

13 Air Canada, *Annual Report,* 1985, p. 13, 1986, p. 21, 1987, p. 7, 1988, p. 7, 1989, p. 7, 1990, p. 8, 1991, pp. 8, 10, 1992, pp. 6, 9.

14 Covia, the second largest system in the United States, was half owned by United Airlines Inc. with five other carriers, USAir Inc., Alitalia, British Airways, KLM Royal Dutch Airlines and Swissair, owning the balance.

15 The Gemini Group was a joint venture created in the spring of 1987 between Air Canada and CAIL to merge their computerized reservations systems. When a partnership was struck in the early 1990s between PWA

Corp. (the parent company of CAIL) and AMR Corp. (the parent company of American Airlines Inc., the biggest airline in the United States), CAIL agreed to adopt the American carrier's Sabre computerized reservations system, the largest such system in the United States, and broke off links with the Gemini Group.

16 Air Canada, *Horizons,* No. 762, August 29, 1990, p. 5.

17 Galileo was controlled by nine European air carriers including Aer Lingus, Alitalia, Austrian Airlines, British Airways PLC, KLM Royal Dutch Airlines, Olympic Airways, Sabena, Swissair and TAP Air Portugal.

18 "Airline Reservations to Go Global on Galileo," *Financial Post,* February 3, 1993, p. 6.

19 Bob Mowat, "Galileo Re-Alignment Reinforces GDS's North American, Global Marketing Strategy," Baxter Travel Group, June 18, 1999.

20 Interviews 5, 17 and 30.

21 CALEA and Air Canada, Minutes of a Union-Management Headquarters Meeting, Item 429-C, April 1983.

22 Letter from R.J. Millette, Agency and Interline Director, Air Canada to a Passenger Agent, June 14, 1983.

23 CAW Local 2213 and Air Canada, Minutes of a Union-Management Headquarters Meeting, Item 267-H, June 1986, Item 267-J, December 1986, Item 267-L, May 1987, Item 267-M, September 1987.

24 CAW Local 2213 and Air Canada, Minutes of a Union-Management Headquarters Meeting, Item 267-X, November 1991.

25 CALEA, Minutes of a Union-Management District Meeting, Toronto, October 1983, December 1983; CAW Local 2213, Minutes of Negotiations between Air Canada and the CAW Local 2213, 1986; CAW Local 2213, Minutes of a Union-Management District Meeting, Montreal, April 13, 1989; CAW Local 2213 and Air Canada, Minutes of a Union-Management Headquarters Meeting, Item 403-P, August 1989, Item 478-D, February 1992.

26 Air Canada Press Release, "Official Opening of New Air Canada Call Centre Signals Better Service for Customers and More Airline Jobs," November 15, 1996.

27 Air Canada, *Horizons,* No. 678, January 23, 1991, p. 5.

28 Air Canada, Internal Correspondence, Toronto, May 26, 1989; Letter from C. Kryzaniwsky, President, CAW Local 2213, to Bargaining Committee Members, CAW Local 2213, July 7, 1989; CAW Local 2213, Minutes of a Union-Management District Meeting, Toronto, July 1989.

29 Letter from E.P. Galloway, Director, Central Region, CALEA, to K. Kerr, President, CALEA, January 3, 1972; CALEA and Air Canada, Minutes of a Union-Management Headquarters Meeting, Item M.205, March 1972, Item M.205A, May 1972.

30 Agreement between Air Canada and the CALEA, Contract No. 17, Effective: August 1, 1969–September 30, 1971, Article 2.03, p. 6.

31 Air Canada, Representation to the Anti-Inflation Board, January 10, 1977, pp. 10–11; Air Canada and CALEA, Joint Representation to the Anti-Inflation Board, n.d., p. 6.

32 Air Canada, Representation to the Anti-Inflation Board, October 1,1976, January 10, 1977, p. 10.

33 Agreement between Air Canada and the CALEA, Contract No. 20, Effective: October 1,1976–September 30, 1978, Letter of Understanding No. 7, p. 97.

34 CALEA, Minutes of Negotiations between the CALEA and Air Canada, July 12, 1984; Air Canada, "The Future is in Our Hands," Summation of Message from P. Jeanniot, President and Chief Executive Officer, Air Canada, circa August 1984; Air Canada, Field Management Update, CALEA Negotiations, October 31, 1984; Air Canada, Conciliation Brief, circa late 1984.

35 CALEA, President's Opening Remarks at the Commencement of Collective Bargaining with Air Canada, July 11, 1984; *CALEA, Negotiations Bulletin,* No.3, July 20, 1984, No.6, October 19, 1984.

36 The merger went into effect on July 1, 1985. The CALEA became known as the National Amalgamated Local Union of Airline Workers (local 2213).

37 Letter from the Labour Relations Department, CALEA, to Directors and District Chairpersons, CALEA, March 5, 1984; Letter from T. Saunders, President, CALEA, to District Chairpersons, CALEA, March 8, 1983; Air Canada, Level 2 Grievance Decision, May 30, 1983.

38 Agreement between Air Canada and the CALEA, Contract No. 23, Effective: September 26, 1984–September 21, 1986, Letter of Understanding No. 7, p. 91.

39 Interviews 30, 53 and 55.

40 Agreement between Air Canada and the CALEA, Contract No. 23, Effective: September 26, 1984–September 21, 1986, Article 18.07, pp. 65–66.

41 Agreement between Air Canada and the CALEA, Contract No. 23, Effective: September 26, 1984–September 21, 1986, Letter of Understanding No. 16, p. 108, Letter of Understanding No. 17, p. 110.

42 CAW Local 2213 and Air Canada, Minutes of a Union-Management Headquarters Meeting, Item 398-Y, July 1985, Item 398-AA, November 1985, Item 398-AB, February 1986, Item 398-AC, June 1986, Item 398-AG, May 1987, Item 398-AL, January 1990, Item 398-AM, August 1990, Item 398-AN, February 1991.

43 CAW Local 2213, Proposals for Negotiations between the CAW Local 2213 and Air Canada, 1986, 1988, 1990, 1992; CAW Local 2213, *Negotiations Bulletin,* July 24, 1986; CAW Local 2213, *Bargaining Backgrounder,* No. 2, 1990; CAW Local 2213, *Negotiations,* August 26, 1992.

44 Agreement between Air Canada and the CAW Local 2213, Contract No. 24, Effective: September 22, 1986–September 18, 1988, L16.02.01, p. 122.

45 Agreement between Air Canada and the CAW Local 2213, Contract No. 25, Effective: September 19, 1988–September 30, 1990, L16.02.01, p. 110.

46 CAW Local 2213, Proposals for Negotiations between the CAW Local 2213 and Air Canada, 1986.

47 CALEA, *Skyways,* May/June 1984, p. 6.

48 Letter from Z. Clark, Vice-President, Passenger Sales and Service—Canada, Air Canada, to all General Managers—Canada, Air Canada, June 4, 1987; Letter from C. Kryzaniwsky, President, CAW Local 2213, to District Chairpersons, Unit 1 Air Canada, CAW Local 2213, June 8, 1987; CAW Local 2213 and Air Canada, Minutes of a Union-Management Headquarters Meeting, Item 460-C, September 1987.

49 Various articles and letters of understanding: Agreement between Air Canada and the CALEA, Contract No. 23, Effective: September 26, 1984–September 21, 1986; Agreement between Air Canada and the CAW Local 2213, Contract No. 24, Effective: September 22, 1986–September 18, 1988; Agreement between Air Canada and the CAW Local 2213, Contract No. 25, Effective: September 19, 1988–September 30, 1990; Agreement between Air Canada and the CAW Local 2213, Contract No. 26, Effective: October 1, 1990–September 30, 1992; Agreement between Air Canada and the CAW Local 2213, Contract No. 27, Effective: October 1, 1993–September 30, 1996.

50 TCA, Monthly Report to the Board of Directors, January 1942, No. 52, March 3, 1942, p. 6.

51 Air Canada, Rationale Underlying the Air Canada–CALEA Collective Agreement, January 10, 1977, Exhibit 1, p. 10.

52 Interview 23.

53 Interview 15.

54 A full analysis of the deskilling of customer sales and service agents' work and of the role played by technological change in this deskilling is one of the main objects of a larger study I am currently completing on work in the airline industry.

55 Canadian Tourism Research Institute. *Future Skill Requirements in the Retail Travel Industry: Final Report.* Ottawa: Canadian Tourism Human Resource Council, Fall 1997, p. 10.

56 Agreement between Air Canada and CAW Local 2213, Contract No. 27, Effective: October 1, 1993–September 30, 1996, Article 5.04, p. 6.

57 Canadian Tourism Research Institute, *Future Skill Requirements in the Retail Travel Industry: Final Report,* Ottawa: Canadian Tourism Human Resource Council, Fall 1997, p. 6.

References

Amadeo, Edward J. and Susan Horton (eds.). 1997. *Labour Productivity and Flexibility.* New York: St. Martin's Press.

Amin, Ash (ed.). 1994. *Post-Fordism: A Reader.* Oxford: Blackwell.

Appay, Beatrice. 1998. "Economic Concentration and the Externalization of Labour." *Economic and Industrial Democracy* 19(1): 161–184.

Armstrong, Pat. 1996. "The Feminization of the Labour Force: Harmonizing Down in a Global Economy." pp. 29–54. In Isabella Bakker (ed.). *Rethinking Restructuring: Gender and Change in Canada.* Toronto: University of Toronto Press.

Armstrong, Nicola José de Freitas. 1999. "Flexible Work in the Virtual Workplace: Discourses and Implications of Teleworking." pp. 43–61. In Alan Felstead and Nick Jewson (eds.). *Global Trends in Flexible Labour.* London: Macmillan.

Atkinson, John. 1985. *Flexibility, Uncertainty and Manpower Management. IMS Report No. 89.* Brighton: University of Sussex.

Belous, Richard S. 1989. *The Contingent Economy: The Growth of the Temporary, Part-Time and Subcontracted Workforce.* Washington, D.C.: National Planning Association.

Blossfeld, Hans-Peter and Catherine Hakim (eds.). 1997. *Between Equalization and Marginalization: Women Working Part-Time in Europe and the United States of America.* Oxford: Oxford University Press.

Broad, Dave. 2000. *Hollow Work, Hollow Society? Globalization and the Casual Labour Problem in Canada.* Halifax: Fernwood.

Burgess, John and Glenda Strachan. 1999. "The Expansion in Non-Standard Employment in Australia and the Extension of Employers' Control," pp. 121–140 in Alan Felstead and Nick Jewson (eds.). *Global Trends in Flexible Labour.* London: Macmillan.

Casey, Bernard, Hilary Metcalf and Neil Millward. 1997. *Employers' Use of Flexible Labour.* London: PSI.

Casey, Bernard. 1988. "The Extent and Nature of Temporary Employment in Britain." *Cambridge Journal of Economics* 12: 487–509.

Cohany, Sharon R. 1996. "Workers in Alternative Employment Arrangements." *Monthly Labor Review* 119(10): 31–45

Connelly, Patricia and Martha MacDonald. 1996. "The Labour Market, the State, and the Reorganizing of Work: Policy Impacts," pp. 82–91. In Isabella Bakker (ed.). *Rethinking Restructuring: Gender and Change in Canada.* Toronto: University of Toronto Press.

Crompton, Rosemary, Duncan Gallie and Kate Purcell (eds.). 1996. *Changing Forms of Employment Organisations, Skills and Gender.* London: Routledge.

Crompton, Susan. 1993. "The Renaissance in Self-Employment." *Perspectives on Labour and Income* 5(2): 22–32.

Dagg, Alexandra. 1997. "Worker Representation and Protection in the 'New Economy,'" pp. 75–118. In *Collective Reflection on the Changing Workplace: Report of the Advisory Committee on the Changing Workplace.* Ottawa: Public Works and Government Services Canada.

Devine, Kay Stratton, Laurel Taylor and Kathy Haryett. 1997. "The Impact of Teleworking on Canadian Employment," pp. 97–116. In Ann Duffy, Daniel Glenday and Norene Pupo (eds.). *Good Jobs, Bad Jobs, No Jobs: The Transformation of Work in the 21st Century.* Toronto: Harcourt Brace.

Dex, Shirley and Andrew McCulloch. 1997. *Flexible Employment: The Future of Britain's Jobs.* London: Macmillan.

_____. 1995. *Flexible Employment in Britain: A Statistical Analysis.* Manchester: Equal Opportunities Commission.

Duffy, Ann and Norene Pupo. 1992. *Part-time Paradox: Connecting Gender, Work and Family.* Toronto: McClelland and Stewart.

Elger, Tony and Chris Smith (eds.). 1994. *Global Japanization? The Transnational Transformation of the Labour Process.* London: Routledge.

Felstead, Alan and Nick Jewson (eds.). 1999. *Global Trends in Flexible Labour.* London: Macmillan.

Felstead, Alan and Nick Jewson. 1999. *In Work, At Home: Towards an Understanding of Homeworking.* London: Routledge.

Gallie, Duncan, Michael White, Yuan Cheng and Mark Tomlinson. 1998. *Restructuring the Employment Relationship.* Oxford: Clarendon Press.

Gauthier, James and Richard Roy. 1997. *Diverging Trends in Self-Employment in Canada*, Research Paper R-97-13E. Ottawa: Human Resources Development Canada.

Glenday, Daniel. 1997. "Lost Horizons, Leisure Shock: Good Jobs, Bad Jobs, Uncertain Future," pp. 8–34. In Ann Duffy, Daniel Glenday and Norene Pupo, *Good Jobs, Bad Jobs, No Jobs: The Transformation of Work in the 21st Century.* Toronto: Harcourt Brace.

Gottfried, Heidi. 1994. "Learning the Score: The Duality of Control and Everyday Resistance in the Temporary-Help Service Industry," pp. 102–127. In John M. Jermier, David Knights and Walter R. Nord (eds.). *Resistance and Power in Organizations.* London: Routledge.

Gottfried, Heidi. 1992. "In the Margins: Flexibility as a Mode of Regulation in the Temporary Help Service Industry," *Work, Employment and Society* 6(3): 443–460.

Hughes, Karen D. 1999. *Gender and Self-Employment in Canada: Assessing Trends and Policy Implications.* Ottawa: Canadian Policy Research Networks.

Hughes, Karen D. and Graham S. Lowe. 2000. "Surveying the 'Post-Industrial' Landscape: Information

Technologies and Labour Market Polarization in Canada." *Canadian Review of Sociology and Anthropology* 37(1): 29–53.

Huws, Ursula. 1984. *The New Homeworkers: New Technology and the Changing Location of White-Collar Work.* London: Low Pay Unit.

Huws, Ursula, Werner B. Korte and Simon Robinson. 1990. *Telework: Towards the Elusive Office.* Toronto: John Wiley and Sons.

Jackson, Paul J. and Jos M. van der Wielen (eds.). 1998. *Teleworking: International Perspectives.* London: Routledge.

Jurik, Nancy C. 1998. "Getting Away and Getting By: The Experiences of Self-Employed Homeworkers." Work and Occupations 25(1): 7–35.

Krahn, Harvey. 1995. "Non-Standard Work on the Rise." Perspectives on Labour and Income 7(4): 35–42.

Marginson, Paul. 1991. "Change and Continuity in the Employment Structure of Large Companies." pp. 32–45. In Anna Pollert (ed.). *Farewell to Flexibility?* Oxford: Blackwell.

Meulders, Daniele. 2000. "European Policies Promoting More Flexible Labour Forces," pp. 251–263. In Jane Jenson, Jacqueline Laufer and Margaret Maruani (eds.). *The Gendering of Inequalities: Women, Men and Work.* Aldershot: Ashgate.

Mirchandani, Kiran. 1999. "Legitimizing Work: Telework and the Gendered Reification of the Work-Nonwork Dichotomy." *Canadian Review of Sociology and Anthropology* 36(1): 87–107.

O'Reilly, Jacqueline and Colette Fagan (eds.). 1998. *Part-Time Prospects: An International Comparison of Part-Time Work in Europe, North America and the Pacific Rim.* London: Routledge.

Oum, Tae Hoon, W.T. Stanbury and Michael W. Tretheway. 1990. *Airline Deregulation in Canada and its Economic Effects*, Working Paper #90-TRA-013. Vancouver: University of British Columbia.

Peck, Jamie. 1996. *Work-Place: The Social Regulation of Labor Markets.* New York: Guilford Press.

Phizacklea, Annie and Carol Wolkowitz. 1995. *Homeworking Women: Gender, Racism and Class at Work.* London: Sage.

Polivka, Anne E. 1996. "A Profile of Contingent Workers." *Monthly Labor Review* 119(10): 10–21.

Pollert, Anna (ed.). 1991a. *Farewell to Flexibility?* Oxford: Blackwell.

Pollert, Anna. 1991b. "The Orthodoxy of Flexibility." pp. 3–31. In Anna Pollert (ed.), *Farewell to Flexibility?* Oxford: Blackwell.

____.1988. "Dismantling Flexibility." *Capital and Class* 34: 42–75.

Provenzano, Liza A. 1994. "Telecommuting: A Trend Towards the Hoffice?" *Current Issues Series*. Kingston: Industrial Relations Centre, Queen's University.

Rodgers, Gerry and Janine Rodgers (eds.). 1989. *Precarious Jobs in Labour Market Regulation: The Growth of Atypical Employment in Western Europe.* Geneva: International Institute for Labour Studies.

Rogers, Jackie Krasas. 1995. "Just a Temp: Experience and Structure of Alienation in Temporary Clerical Employment." *Work and Occupations* 22(2): 137–166.

Rosenberg, Sam and June Lapidus. 1999. "Contingent and Non-Standard Work in the United States: Towards a More Poorly Compensated, Insecure Workforce," pp. 62–83 in Alan Felstead and Nick Jewson (eds.). *Global Trends in Flexible Labour.* London: Macmillan.

Rubery, Jill and Frank Wilkinson (eds.). 1994. *Employer Strategy and the Labour Market.* New York: Oxford University Press.

Rubery, Jill, J. M. Smith and C. Fagan. 1996. *Trends and Prospects for Women's Employment in the European Union in the 1990s.* Brussels: European Commission, Equal Opportunities and Family Policy Unit.

Smith, Vicki. 1993. "Flexibility in Work and Employment: The Impact on Women," pp. 195–216. In Samuel B. Bacharach (ed.). *Research in the Sociology of Organizations*, Vol. 11. Greenwich, Connecticut: JAI Press.

Stanworth, Celia and John Stanworth. 1995. "The Self-Employed without Employees—Autonomous or Atypical?" *Industrial Relations Journal* 26(3): 221–229.

Stevenson, Garth. 1987. *The Politics of Canada's Airlines: From Diefenbaker to Mulroney.* Toronto: University of Toronto Press.

Tarling, Roger (ed.) 1987. *Flexibility in Labour Markets.* New York: Academic Press.

Templer, Andrew, Marjorie Armstrong-Stassen, Kay Devine and Norm Solomon. 1999. "Telework and Teleworkers," pp. 77–95. In Isik Urla Zeytinoğlu (ed.). *Changing Work Relationships in Industrialized Economies.* Amsterdam: John Benjamins.

Thurman, Joseph E., Vittorio Di Martino, Michele Jankanish and Linda Wirth. 1990. "Telework: An Overview." *Conditions of Work Digest* 9(1). Geneva: International Labour Organization.

Vosko, Leah F. 2000. *Temporary Work: The Gendered Rise of a Precarious Employment Relationship*. Toronto: University of Toronto Press.

Walby, Sylvia. 2000. "Re-Signifying the Worker: Gender and Flexibility," pp. 81–91. In Jane Jenson, Jacqueline Laufer and Margaret Maruani (eds.). *The Gendering of Inequalities: Women, Men and Work*. Aldershot: Ashgate.

____. 1989. "Flexibility and the Changing Sexual Division of Labour," pp. 127–140. In Stephen Wood (ed.). *The Transformation of Work? Skill, Flexibility and the Labour Process*. London: Unwin Hyman.

Wood, Stephen (ed.). 1989. *The Transformation of Work? Skill, Flexibility and the Labour Process*. London: Unwin Hyman.

Yeandle, Sue. 1999. "Gender Contracts, Welfare Systems and Non-Standard Working: Diversity and Change in Denmark, France, Germany, Italy and the UK," pp. 141–165. In Alan Felstead and Nick Jewson (eds.). *Global Trends in Flexible Labour*. London: Macmillan.

Zeytinoğlu, Isik Urla and Jacinta Khasiala Muteshi. 1999. "Changing Work Relationships: Enacting Gender, Race/Ethnicity and Economic Class," pp. 1–17. In Isik Urla Zeytinoğlu (ed.). *Changing Work Relationships in Industrialized Economies*. Amsterdam: John Benjamins.

Zeytinoğlu, Isik Urla (ed.). 1999. *Changing Work Relationships in Industrialized Economies*. Amsterdam: John Benjamins.

Archival Sources

Air Canada Records, National Archives of Canada, Ottawa.

Canadian Air Line Employees' Association Records, National Archives of Canada, Ottawa.

CAW-Canada Records, Local 2213, National Office, Toronto.

CAW-Canada Records, Airline Division, Toronto.

SECTION III: PRECARIOUSNESS IN THE LABOUR MARKET

Critical Thinking Questions

Chapter 5: The Gender of Precarious Employment in Canada, Cynthia J. Cranford, Leah F. Vosko, and Nancy Zukewich

1. Discuss the ways in which dimensions of precariousness vary across forms of employment.

2. Do the decline of the standard employment relationship and the feminization of employment norms lead to greater equality or inequality between women and men in the labour market?

3. What are some of the potential long-term consequences for the Canadian economy of the trend toward precariousness in the labour market?

Chapter 6: Jettisoned by Design? The Truncated Employment Relationship of Customer Sales and Service Agents under Airline Restructuring, Vivian Shalla

1. Discuss how computer and telecommunications technologies can be used in various ways to facilitate the contracting out of work in the service sector. Are new technologies at the heart of the spatial reorganization of work or are other factors more important in explaining this reorganization?

2. Can the actions of workers and their unions play a significant role in protecting job security in the workplace? Should job security be a predominant concern for workers in the post-industrial economy?

3. How does a detailed study of one particular group of workers help us better understand broader transformations in the Canadian workplace and labour market?

Recommended Readings

Armstrong, Pat. 1996. "The Feminization of the Labour Force: Harmonizing Down in a Global Economy," pp. 29–54 in Isabella Bakker (ed.). *Rethinking Restructuring: Gender and Change in Canada*. Toronto: University of Toronto Press. A statistical analysis of labour-force trends in Canada during the early 1990s (a period of rapid economic restructuring), which highlights the gendered nature of the downward spiral in the labour market.

Broad, Dave. 2000. *Hollow Work, Hollow Society? Globalization and the Casual Labour Problem in Canada*. Halifax: Fernwood. A study of the re-casualization of work in Canada as an integral aspect of economic globalization and neo-liberalism. The book also focuses on the consequent deepening polarization in society and discusses alternative societal models.

Felstead, Alan and Nick Jewson (eds.). 1999. *Global Trends in Flexible Labour*. London: Macmillan. A collection of original articles that examine employment trends and new work arrangements in different countries, with a focus on developing stronger conceptual insights into the flexibilization of employment.

O'Reilly, Jacqueline and Colette Fagan (eds.). 1998. *Part-Time Prospects: An International Comparison of Part-Time Work in Europe, North America and the Pacific Rim*. New York: Routledge. A compilation of readings that offer a cross-national comparison of the common and divergent patterns in the utilization of part-time employment. The articles also assess the debates surrounding the gendered nature of part-time work.

Shalla, Vivian. 2004. "Time Warped: The Flexibilization and Maximization of Flight Attendant Working Time." *Canadian Review of Sociology and Anthropology*, Vol. 41, No. 3, pp. 334–368. A case study of the impact of economic restructuring and globalization on the nature of working time in the airline industry, with a focus on how new working-time regimes are degrading the employment relationship of service workers.

Vosko, Leah F. (2000) *Temporary Work: The Gendered Rise of a Precarious Employment Relationship*. Toronto: University of Toronto Press. A detailed examination of the historical development and contemporary nature of temporary employment that illustrates the changing forms of employment and their gendered underpinnings.

Related Websites

Canadian Employment Research Forum

http://www.cerf.mcmaster.ca

The Canadian Employment Research Forum is a non-profit corporation that promotes the development of policy-related empirical research, and provides a forum for representatives from governments, universities, business, labour, and other communities to discuss and debate issues related to employment in Canada.

Canadian Policy Research Networks

http://www.cprn.org/en/network.cfm?network=4

The Canadian Policy Research Network is a think tank made up of several networks that deal with a variety of social and economic issues. Its Work Network explores labour market and workplace change and the evolving interface between learning and work.

Gender and Work Database

http://www.genderwork.ca/

The gender and work database is an online tool for researchers interested in topics pertaining to women and work. It contains a wide range of information on the labour market, the domestic sphere, and trade unions.

World Bank Labor Markets Group

http://web.worldbank.org/WBSITE/EXTERNAL/TOPICS/EXTSOCIALPROTECTION/EX-TLM/0,,contentMDK:20223806~menuPK:584842~pagePK:148956~piPK:216618~theSitePK:390615,00.html

The World Bank Labor Markets Group consists of specialists working on key issues for client countries. It provides research and analysis, training courses and seminars.

Section IV

Working in the Free-Trade Zones of the North and South

A GROWING AND influential body of research has pointed to the impact of neo-liberal economic policies on the development paths of Third World countries. These development strategies, often referred to as structural adjustment policies, have usually relied on the establishment of production facilities in free-trade zones. These geographically delimited areas are set up to attract foreign investors who benefit from significant government incentives and rely extensively on an available, low-wage and compliant workforce. Such strategies, while arguably of a different nature, have also been adopted by governments in underdeveloped regions of First World nations in the hopes of fuelling sustainable growth in the local economy. In order to illustrate the similarities and differences between these development strategies, one article in this section of the book focuses on the production of goods in the economic South and the other article concentrates on the production of services in the economic North. Both analyze the consequences for workers and working conditions of these development strategies and shine a light on the processes that shape and reshape local and global divisions of labour.

Naomi Klein's article, taken from her book *No Logo: Taking Aim at the Brand Bullies*, provides a vivid account of working conditions in free-trade zones, and examines the broader global structures that foster the spread of these zones. She argues that since the 1980s, a growing number of multinationals have been divesting themselves of directly producing the items that carry their name, focusing their resources instead on developing, promoting, and managing their brand name. According to Klein, this shift in priorities of mega-corporations is changing the face of global employment. The author discusses corporations' practice of closing their own factories and outsourcing production, mostly to offshore contractors who set up factories in the burgeoning free-trade, or export-processing, zones of Third World countries that have been hanging their hopes on these zones as an economic development strategy. Klein takes a closer look at the employment and life conditions of workers in the Cavite export-processing zone in the Philippines where various types of consumer goods are produced mostly for large corporations and strictly for the export market. She documents the difficult, unhealthy and abusive conditions that workers, mostly young women, must endure to earn less than subsistence wages. Through a discussion of the efforts and modest successes of organizations set up to support workers' constitutional rights to organize unions and fight for better working conditions, Klein offers hope that workers' lives in the free-trade zones could improve, even if only modestly, although she remains skeptical about these zones as a viable development strategy for Third World countries.

Ruth Buchanan's article also examines the impact of processes of globalization and development strategies on work and workers in specific localities. Her focus, however, is not on product manufacturing in Third World countries, but on the provision of telephone services in New Brunswick, Canada. Her central argument is that the strategies and responses of three sets of actors—governments, firms, and workers—to the uncertainties of globalization all played a key role in facilitating the development of, and giving shape to, the call centre industry in New Brunswick during the 1990s. Buchanan traces the initiatives undertaken by the provincial government in its efforts to: a) attract firms specializing in the provision of telephone services to ensure the creation of much-needed employment and boost a sagging economy; and, b) produce a local labour force that was attractive to these firms. She also demonstrates that multinational firms made strategic decisions to create call centres in New Brunswick based on the province's development of a telecommunications infrastructure, its extension of various incentives and, most importantly, on their belief that an educated and flexible labour force was readily available. Key to Buchanan's analysis of the dynamic process of restructuring, however, is the importance she places on the responses of local workers and the public to the provincial government's and multinational firms' attempts to mould a hard-working, loyal, and compliant labour force, and on their strategies to deal with the demanding conditions of routinized, yet fairly decent-paying, teleservice jobs. Buchanan concludes that globalization and global restructuring will continue to be made and remade at the local level because of particular local histories and cultures that play an important role in mediating broader social structures and processes.

CHAPTER 7

The Discarded Factory:

Degraded Production in the Age of the Superbrand

Naomi Klein

Our strategic plan in North America is to focus intensely on brand management, marketing and product design as a means to meet the casual clothing wants and needs of consumers. Shifting a significant portion of our manufacturing from the U.S. and Canadian markets to contractors throughout the world will give the company greater flexibility to allocate resources and capital to its brands. These steps are crucial if we are to remain competitive.

–JOHN ERMATINGER, *president of Levi Strauss Americas division, explains the company's decision to shut down twenty-two plants and lay off 13,000 North American workers between November 1997 and February 1999*

MANY BRAND-NAME multinationals, as we have seen, are in the process of transcending the need to identify with their earthbound products. They dream instead about their brands' deep inner meanings—the way they capture the spirit of individuality, athleticism, wilderness or community. In this context of strut over stuff, marketing departments charged with the managing of brand identities have begun to see their work as something that occurs not in conjunction with factory production but in direct competition with it. "Products are made in the factory," says Walter Landor, president of the Landor branding agency, "but brands are made in the mind."[1] Peter Schweitzer, president of the advertising giant J. Walter Thompson, reiterates the same thought: "The difference between products and brands is fundamental. A product is something that is made in a factory; a brand is something that is bought by a customer."[2] Savvy ad agencies have all moved away from the idea that they are flogging a product made by someone else, and have come to think of themselves instead as brand factories, hammering out what is of true value: the idea, the lifestyle, the attitude. Brand builders are the new primary producers in our so-called knowledge economy.

This novel idea has done more than bring us cutting-edge ad campaigns, ecclesiastic superstores and Utopian corporate campuses. It is changing the very face of global employment. After establishing the "soul" of their corporations, the superbrand companies have gone on to rid themselves of their cumbersome bodies, and there is nothing that seems more cumbersome, more loathsomely corporeal, than the factories that produce their products. The reason for this shift is simple: building a superbrand is an extraordinarily costly project, needing constant managing, tending and re-plenishing. Most of all, superbrands need lots of space on which to stamp their logos. For a business to be cost-effective, however, there is a finite amount of money it can spend on all of its expenses—materials, manufacturing, over-head *and* branding—before retail prices on its products shoot up too high. After the multi-million-dollar sponsorships have been signed, and the cool hunters and marketing mavens have received their checks, there may not be all that much money left over. So it becomes, as always, a matter of priorities; but those priorities are changing. As Hector Liang, former chairman of United Biscuits, has explained: "Machines wear out. Cars rust. People die. But what lives on are the brands."[3]

According to this logic, corporations should not expend their finite resources on factories that will demand physical upkeep, on ma-chines that will corrode or on employees who will certainly age and die. Instead, they should concentrate those resources in the virtual brick and mortar used to build their brands; that is, on sponsorships, packaging, expansion and advertising. They should also spend them on synergies: on buying up distribution and retail channels to get their brands to the people.

This slow but decisive shift in corporate pri-orities has left yesterday's nonvirtual produc-ers—the factory workers and craftspeople—in a precarious position. The lavish spending in the 1990s on marketing, mergers and brand extensions has been matched by a never-be-fore-seen resistance to investing in production facilities and labour. Companies that were tra-ditionally satisfied with a 100 percent markup between the cost of factory production and the retail price have been scouring the globe for factories that can make their products so inexpensively that the markup is closer to 400 percent.[4] And as a 1997 United Nations (UN) report notes, even in countries where wages were already low, labour costs are get-ting a shrinking slice of corporate budgets. "In four developing countries out of five, the share of wages in manufacturing value-added today is considerably below what it was in the 1970s and early 1980s."[5] The timing of these trends reflects not only branding's status as the perceived economic cure-all, but also a corresponding devaluation of the production process and of producers in general. Brand-ing, in other words, has been hogging all the "value-added."

When the actual manufacturing process is so devalued, it stands to reason that the people doing the work of production are likely to be treated like detritus—the stuff left behind. The idea has a certain symmetry: ever since mass production created the need for branding in the first place, its role has slowly been expanding in importance until, more than a century and a half after the Industrial Revolution, it occurred to these companies that maybe branding could replace production entirely. As tennis pro Andre Agassi said in a 1992 Canon camera commercial, "Image is everything."

Agassi may have been pitching for Canon at the time but he is first and foremost a member of Team Nike, the company that pioneered the business philosophy of no-limits spending on branding, coupled with a near-total divestment of the contract workers that make its shoes in tucked-away factories. As Phil Knight has said, "There is no value in making things any more. The value is added by careful research, by innovation and by marketing."[6] For Phil Knight, production is not the building block of his branded empire, but is instead a tedious, marginal chore.

Which is why many companies now bypass production completely. Instead of making the products themselves, in their own factories, they "source" them, much as corporations in the natural-resource industries source uranium, copper or logs. They close existing factories, shifting to contracted-out, mostly offshore, manufacturing. And as the old jobs fly offshore, something else is flying away with them: the old-fashioned idea that a manufacturer is responsible for its own workforce. Disney spokesman Ken Green gave an indication of the depth of this shift when he became publicly frustrated that his company was being taken to task for the desperate conditions in a Haitian factory that produces Disney clothes. "We don't employ anyone in Haiti," he said, referring to the fact that the factory is owned by a contractor. "With the newsprint you use, do you have any idea of the labour conditions involved to produce it?" Green demanded of Cathy Majtenyi of the *Catholic Register*.[7]

From El Paso to Beijing, San Francisco to Jakarta, Munich to Tijuana, the global brands are sloughing the responsibility of production onto their contractors; they just tell them to make the damn thing, and make it cheap, so there's lots of money left over for branding. Make it *really* cheap.

Exporting the Nike Model

Nike, which began as an import/export scheme of made-in-Japan running shoes and does not own any of its factories, has become a prototype for the product-free brand. Inspired by the swoosh's staggering success, many more traditionally run companies ("vertically integrated," as the phrase goes) are busy imitating Nike's model, not only copying the company's marketing approach, as we saw in "No Space," but also its on-the-cheap outsourced production structure. In the mid-nineties, for instance, the Vans running-shoe company pulled up stakes in the old-fashioned realm of manufacturing and converted to the Nike way. In a prospectus for an initial public stock offering, the company lays out how it "recently repositioned itself from a domestic manufacturer to a market-driven company" by sponsoring hundreds of athletes as well as high-profile extreme sporting events such as the Vans Warped Tour. The company's "expenditure of significant funds to create consumer demand" was financed by closing an existing factory in California and contracting production in South Korea to "third party manufacturers."[8]

Adidas followed a similar trajectory, turning over its operation in 1993 to Robert Louis-Dreyfus, formerly a chief executive at advertising giant Saatchi & Saatchi. Announcing that he wanted to capture the heart of the "global teenager," Louis-Dreyfus promptly shut down the company-owned factories in Germany, and moved to contracting-out in Asia.[9] Freed from the chains of production, the company had newfound time and money to create a Nike-style brand image. "We closed down everything," Adidas spokesperson Peter Csanadi says proudly. "We only kept one small factory which is our global technology centre and makes about 1 percent of total output."[10]

Though they don't draw the headlines they once did, more factory closures are announced in North America and Europe each week—45,000 U.S. apparel workers lost their jobs in 1997 alone.[11] That sector's job-flight patterns have been equally dramatic around the globe. Though plant closures themselves have barely slowed down since the darkest days of the late-eighties/early-nineties recession, there has been a marked shift in the reason given for these "reorganizations." Mass layoffs were previously presented as an unfortunate necessity, tied to disappointing company performance. Today they are simply savvy shifts in corporate strategy, a "strategic redirection," to use the Vans term. More and more, these layoffs are announced in conjunction with pledges to increase revenue through advertising spending, with executives vowing to refocus on the needs of their brands, as opposed to the needs of their workers.

Consider the case of Sara Lee Corp., an old-style conglomerate that encompasses not only its frozen-food namesake but also such "unintegrated" brands as Hanes underwear, Wonderbra, Coach leather goods, Champion sports apparel, Kiwi shoe polish and Ball Park Franks. Despite the fact that Sara Lee enjoyed solid growth, healthy profits, good stock return and no debt, by the mid-nineties Wall Street had become disenchanted with the company and was undervaluing its stock. Its profits had risen 10 percent in the 1996–97 fiscal year, hitting $1 billion, but Wall Street, as we have seen, is guided by spiritual goals as well as economic ones.[12] And Sara Lee, driven by the corporeal

stuff of real-world products, as opposed to the sleek ideas of brand identity, was simply out of economic fashion. "Lumpy-object purveyors," as Tom Peters might say.[13]

To correct the situation, in September 1997 the company announced a $1.6 billion restructuring plan to get out of the "stuff" business by purging its manufacturing base. Thirteen of its factories, beginning with yarn and textile plants, would be sold to contractors who would become Sara Lee's suppliers. The company would be able to dip into the money saved to double its ad spending. "It's passé for us to be as vertically integrated as we were," explained Sara Lee CEO John H. Bryan.[14] Wall Street and the business press loved the new marketing-driven Sara Lee, rewarding the company with a 15 percent jump in stock price and flattering profiles of its bold and imaginative CEO. "Bryan's shift away from manufacturing to focus on brand marketing recognizes that the future belongs to companies—like Coca-Cola Co.—that own little but sell much," enthused one article in *Business Week*.[15] Even more telling was the analogy chosen by *Crain's Chicago Business*: "Sara Lee's goal is to become more like Oregon-based Nike Inc., which outsources its manufacturing and focuses primarily on product development and brand management."[16]

In November 1997, Levi Strauss announced a similarly motivated shake-up. Company revenue had dropped between 1996 and 1997, from $7.1 billion to $6.8 billion. But a four percent dip hardly seems to explain the company's decision to shut eleven plants. The closures resulted in 6,395 workers being laid off, one-third of its already downsized North American workforce. In this process, the company shut down three of its four factories in El Paso, Texas, a city where Levi's was the single largest private employer. Still unsatisfied with the results, the following year Levi's announced another round of closures in Europe and North America. Eleven more of its North American factories would be shut down and the total toll of laid-off workers' rose to 16,310 in only two years.[17]

John Ermatinger, president of Levi's Americas division, had a familiar explanation. "Our strategic plan in North America is to focus intensely on brand management, marketing and product design as a means to meet the casual clothing wants and needs of consumers," he said.[18] Levi's chairman, Robert Haas, who on the same day received an award from the UN for making life better for his employees, told *The Wall Street Journal* that the closures reflected not just "overcapacity" but also "our own desire to refocus marketing, to inject more quality and distinctiveness into the brand."[19] In 1997, this quality and distinctiveness came in the form of a particularly funky international ad campaign rumored to have cost $90 million, Levi's most expensive campaign ever, and more than the company spent advertising the brand in all of 1996.

"This Is Not a Job-Flight Story"

In explaining the plant closures as a decision to turn Levi's into "a marketing company," Robert Haas was careful to tell the press that the jobs that were eliminated were not "leaving," they were just sort of evaporating. "This is not a job-flight story," he said after the first round of layoffs. The statement is technically true. Seeing Levi's as a job-flight story would miss the more fundamental—and more damaging—shift that the closures represent. As far as the company is concerned, those 16,310 jobs are off the payrolls for good, replaced,

according to Ermatinger, by "contractors throughout the world." Those contractors will perform the same tasks as the old Levi's-owned factories—but the workers inside will never be employed by Levi Strauss.

For some companies a plant closure is still a straightforward decision to move the same facility to a cheaper locale. But for others—particularly those with strong brand identities like Levi Strauss and Hanes—layoffs are only the most visible manifestation of a much more fundamental shift: one that is less about where to produce than how. Unlike factories that hop from one place to another, these factories will never rematerialize. Midflight, they morph into something else entirely: "orders" to be placed with a contractor, who may well turn over those orders to as many as ten subcontractors, who—particularly in the garment sector—may in turn pass a portion of the subcontracts on to a network of home workers who will complete the jobs in basements and living rooms. Sure enough, only five months after the first round of plant closures was announced, Levi's made another public statement: it would resume manufacturing in China. The company had pulled out of China in 1993, citing concerns about human-rights violations. Now it has returned, not to build its own factories, but to place orders with three contractors that the company vows to closely monitor for violations of labour law.[20]

This shift in attitude toward production is so profound that where a previous era of consumer goods corporations displayed their logos on the facades of their factories, many of today's brand-based multinationals now maintain that the location of their production operations is a "trade secret," to be guarded at all costs. When asked by human-rights groups in April 1999 to disclose the names and addresses of its contract factories, Peggy Carter, a vice president at Champion clothing, replied: "We have no interest in our competition learning where we are located and taking advantage of what has taken us years to build."[21]

Increasingly, brand-name multinationals— Levi's, Nike, Champion, Wal-Mart, Reebok, the Gap, IBM and General Motors—insist that they are just like any one of us: bargain hunters in search of the best deal in the global mall. They are very picky customers, with specific instructions about made-to-order design, materials, delivery dates and, most important, the need for rock-bottom prices. But what they are *not* interested in is the burdensome logistics of how those prices fall so low; building factories, buying machinery and budgeting for labour have all been lobbed squarely into somebody else's court.

And the real job-flight story is that a growing number of the most high-profile and profitable corporations in the world are fleeing the jobs business altogether.

The Unbearable Lightness of Cavite: Inside the Free-Trade Zones

Despite the conceptual brilliance of the "brands, not products" strategy, production has a pesky way of never quite being transcended entirely: *somebody* has to get down and dirty and make the products the global brands will hang their meaning on. And that's where the free-trade zones come in. In Indonesia, China, Mexico, Vietnam, the Philippines and elsewhere, export processing zones (as these areas are also called) are emerging as leading producers of garments, toys, shoes, electronics, machinery, even cars.

If Nike Town and the other superstores are the glittering new gateways to the branded dreamworlds, then the Cavite Export Process-

ing Zone, located ninety miles south of Manila in the town of Rosario, is the branding broom closet. After a month visiting similar industrial areas in Indonesia, I arrived in Rosario in early September 1997, at the tail end of monsoon season and the beginning of the Asian economic storm. I'd come to spend a week in Cavite because it is the largest free-trade zone in the Philippines, a 682-acre walled-in industrial area housing 207 factories that produce goods strictly for the export market. Rosario's population of 60,000 all seemed to be on the move; the town's busy, sweltering streets were packed with army jeeps converted into minibuses and with motorcycle taxis with precarious sidecars, its sidewalks lined with stalls selling fried rice, Coke and soap. Most of this commercial activity serves the 50,000 workers who rush through Rosario on their way to and from work in the zone, whose gated entrance is located smack in the middle of town.

Inside the gates, factory workers assemble the finished products of our branded world: Nike running shoes, Gap pajamas, IBM computer screens, Old Navy jeans. But despite the presence of such illustrious multinationals, Cavite—and the exploding number of export processing zones like it throughout the developing world—could well be the only places left on earth where the superbrands actually keep a low profile. Indeed, they are positively self-effacing. Their names and logos aren't splashed on the facades of the factories in the industrial zone. And here, competing labels aren't segregated each in its own superstore; they are often produced side by side in the same factories, glued by the very same workers, stitched and soldered on the very same machines. It was in Cavite that I finally found a piece of unswooshed space, and I found it, oddly enough, in a Nike shoe factory.

I was only permitted one visit inside the zone's gates to interview officials—individual factories, I was told, are off limits to anyone but potential importers or exporters. But a few days later, with the help of an 18-year-old worker who had been laid off from his job in an electronics factory, I managed to sneak back to get the unofficial tour. In the rows of virtually identical giant shed-like structures, one factory stood out: the name on the white rectangular building said "Philips," but through its surrounding fence I could see mountains of Nike shoes piled high. It seems that in Cavite, production has been banished to our age's most worthless status: its factories are unbrandable, unswooshworthy; producers are the industrial untouchables. Is this what Phil Knight meant, I wondered, when he said his company wasn't about the sneakers?

Manufacturing is concentrated and isolated inside the zone as if it were toxic waste: pure, 100 percent production at low, low prices. Cavite, like the rest of the zones that compete with it, presents itself as the buy-in-bulk Price Club for multinationals on the lookout for bargains—grab a really big shopping cart. Inside, it's obvious that the row of factories, each with its own gate and guard, has been carefully planned to squeeze the maximum amount of production out of this swath of land. Windowless workshops made of cheap plastic and aluminum siding are crammed in next to each other, only feet apart. Racks of time cards bake in the sun, making sure the maximum amount of work is extracted from each worker, the maximum number of working hours extracted from each day. The streets in the zone are eerily empty, and open doors—the ventilation system for most factories—reveal lines of young women hunched in silence over clamoring machines.

In other parts of the world, workers live inside the economic zones, but not in Cavite: this is a place of pure work. All the bustle and color of Rosario abruptly stops at the gates, where workers must show their ID cards to armed guards in order to get inside. Visitors are rarely permitted in the zone and little or no internal commerce takes place on its orderly streets, not even candy and drink vending. Buses and taxicabs must drop their speed and silence their horns when they get into the zone—a marked change from the boisterous streets of Rosario. If all of this makes Cavite feel as if it's in a different country, that's because, in a way, it is. The zone is a tax-free economy, sealed off from the local government of both town and province—a miniature military state inside a democracy.

As a concept, free-trade zones are as old as commerce itself, and were all the more relevant in ancient times when the transportation of goods required multiple holdovers and rest stops. Pre-Roman Empire city-states, including Tyre, Carthage and Utica, encouraged trade by declaring themselves "free cities," where goods in transit could be stored without tax, and merchants would be protected from harm. These tax-free areas developed further economic significance during colonial times, when entire cities—including Hong Kong, Singapore and Gibraltar—were designated as "free ports" from which the loot of colonialism could be safely shipped back to England, Europe or America with low import tariffs.[22] Today, the globe is dotted with variations on these tax-free pockets, from duty-free shops in airports and the free banking zones of the Cayman Islands to bonded warehouses and ports where goods in transit are held, sorted and packaged.

Though it has plenty in common with these other tax havens, the export processing zone is really in a class of its own. Less holding tank than sovereign territory, the Export Processing Zone (EPZ) is an area where goods don't just pass through but are actually manufactured, an area, furthermore, where there are no import and export duties, and often no income or property taxes either. The idea that EPZs could help Third World economies first gained currency in 1964 when the United Nations Economic and Social Council adopted a resolution endorsing the zones as a means of promoting trade with developing nations. The idea didn't really get off the ground, however, until the early eighties, when India introduced a five-year tax break for companies manufacturing in its low-wage zones.

Since then, the free-trade-zone industry has exploded. There are 52 economic zones in the Philippines alone, employing 459,000 people—that's up from only 23,000 zone workers in 1986 and 229,000 as recently as 1994. The largest zone economy is China, where by conservative estimates there are 18 million people in 124 export processing zones.[23] In total, the International Labour Organization says that there are at least 850 EPZs in the world, but that number is likely much closer to 1,000, spread through 70 countries and employing roughly 27 million workers.[24] The World Trade Organization estimates that between $200 and $250 billion worth of trade flows through the zones.[25] The number of individual factories housed inside these industrial parks is also expanding. In fact, the free-trade factories along the U.S.–Mexico border—in Spanish, *maquiladoras* (from *maquillar,* "to make up, or assemble")—are probably the only structures that proliferate as quickly as Wal-Mart outlets: there were 789 maquiladoras in 1985. In 1995, there were 2,747. By 1997, there were 3,508 employing about 900,000 workers.[26]

Regardless of where the EPZs are located, the workers' stories have a certain mesmerizing sameness: the workday is long—14 hours in Sri Lanka, 12 hours in Indonesia, 16 in Southern China, 12 in the Philippines. The vast majority of the workers are women, always young, always working for contractors or subcontractors from Korea, Taiwan or Hong Kong. The contractors are usually filling orders for companies based in the U.S., Britain, Japan, Germany or Canada. The management is military-style, the supervisors often abusive, the wages below subsistence and the work low-skill and tedious. As an economic model, today's export processing zones have more in common with fast-food franchises than sustainable developments, so removed are they from the countries that host them. These pockets of pure industry hide behind a cloak of transience: the contracts come and go with little notice; the workers are predominantly migrants, far from home and with little connection to the city or province where zones are located; the work itself is short-term, often not renewed.

As I walk along the blank streets of Cavite, I can feel the threatening impermanence, the underlying instability of the zone. The shed-like factories are connected so tenuously to the surrounding country, to the adjacent town, to the very earth they are perched upon, that it feels as if the jobs that flew here from the North could fly away again just as quickly. The factories are cheaply constructed and tossed together on land that is rented, not owned. When I climb up the water tower on the edge of the zone and look down at the hundreds of factories, it seems as if the whole cardboard complex could lift up and blow away, like Dorothy's house in *The Wizard of Oz.* No wonder the EPZ factories in Guatemala are called "swallows."

Fear pervades the zones. The governments are afraid of losing their foreign factories; the factories are afraid of losing their brand-name buyers; and the workers are afraid of losing their unstable jobs. These are factories built not on land but on air.

"It Should Have Been a Different Rosario"

The air the export processing zones are built upon is the promise of industrialization. The theory behind EPZs is that they will attract foreign investors, who, if all goes well, will decide to stay in the country, and the zones' segregated assembly lines will turn into lasting development: technology transfers and domestic industries. To lure the swallows into this clever trap, the governments of poor countries offer tax breaks, lax regulations and the services of a military willing and able to crush labour unrest. To sweeten the pot further, they put their own people on the auction block, falling over each other to offer up the lowest minimum wage, allowing workers to be paid less than the real cost of living.

In Cavite, the economic zone is designed as a fantasyland for foreign investors. Golf courses, executive clubs and private schools have been built on the outskirts of Rosario to ease the discomforts of Third World life. Rent for factories is dirt cheap: 11 pesos per square foot—less than a cent. For the first five years of their stay, corporations are treated to an all-expenses-paid "tax holiday" during which they pay no income tax and no property tax. It's a good deal, no doubt, but it's nothing compared to Sri Lanka, where EPZ investors stay for ten years before having to pay any tax.[27]

The phrase "tax holiday" is oddly fitting. For the investors, free-trade zones are a sort of corporate Club Med, where the hotel pays for everything and the guests live free, and where integration with the local culture and economy is kept to a bare minimum. As one International Labour Organization report puts it, the EPZ "is to the inexperienced foreign investor what the package holiday is to the cautious tourist." Zero-risk globalization. Companies just ship in the pieces of cloth or computer parts—free of import tax—and the cheap, non-union workforce assembles it for them. Then the finished garments or electronics are shipped back out, with no export tax.

The rationale goes something like this: *of course* companies must pay taxes and strictly abide by national laws, but just in this one case, on this one specific piece of land, for just a little while, an exception will be made—for the cause of future prosperity. The EPZs, therefore, exist within a kind of legal and economic set of brackets, apart from the rest of their countries—the Cavite zone, for example, is under the sole jurisdiction of the Philippines' federal Department of Trade and Industry; the local police and municipal government have no right even to cross the threshold. The layers of blockades serve a dual purpose: to keep the hordes away from the costly goods being manufactured inside the zone, but also, and perhaps more important, to shield the country from what is going on inside the zone.

Because such sweet deals have been laid out to entice the swallows, the barriers around the zone serve to reinforce the idea that what is happening inside is only temporary, or is not really happening at all. This collective denial is particularly important in Communist countries where zones house the most Wild West forms of capitalism this side of Moscow: this is *definitely* not really happening, *certainly* not here where the government in power maintains that capital is the devil and workers reign supreme.

In her book *Losing Control?*, Saskia Sassen writes that the zones are a part of a process of carving up nations so that "an actual piece of land becomes denationalized...."[28] Never mind that the boundaries of these only-temporary, not-really-happening, denationalized spaces keep expanding to engulf more and more of their actual nations. Twenty-seven million people worldwide are now living and working in brackets, and the brackets, instead of being slowly removed, just keep getting wider.

It is one of the zones' many cruel ironies that every incentive the governments throw in to attract the multinationals only reinforces the sense that the companies are economic tourists rather than long-term investors. It's a classic vicious cycle: in an attempt to alleviate poverty, the governments offer more and more incentives; but then the EPZs must be cordoned off like leper colonies, and the more they are cordoned off, the more the factories appear to exist in a world entirely separate from the host country, and outside the zone the poverty only grows more desperate. In Cavite, the zone is a kind of futuristic industrial suburbia where everything is ordered; the workers are uniformed, the grass manicured, the factories regimented. There are cute signs all around the grounds instructing workers to "Keep Our Zone Clean" and "Promote Peace and Progress of the Philippines." But walk out of the gate and the bubble bursts. Aside from the swarms of workers at the start and end of shifts, you'd never know that the town of Rosario is home to more than two hundred factories. The roads are a mess, running water is scarce and garbage is overflowing.

Many of the workers live in shantytowns on the outskirts of town and in neighboring villages. Others, particularly the youngest workers, live in the dormitories, a hodgepodge of concrete bunkers separated from the zone enclave by only a thick wall. The structure is actually a converted farm, and some rooms, the workers tell me, are really pigpens with roofs slapped on them.

The Philippines' experience of "industrialization in brackets" is by no means unique. The current mania for the EPZ model is based on the successes of the so-called Asian Tiger economies, in particular the economies of South Korea and Taiwan. When only a few countries had the zones, including South Korea and Taiwan, wages rose steadily, technology transfers occurred and taxes were gradually introduced. But as critics of EPZs are quick to point out, the global economy has become much more competitive since those countries made the transition from low-wage industries to higher-skill ones. Today, with 70 countries competing for the export-processing-zone dollar, the incentives to lure investors are increasing and the wages and standards are being held hostage to the threat of departure. The upshot is that entire countries are being turned into industrial slums and low-wage labor ghettos, with no end in sight. As Cuban president Fidel Castro thundered to the assembled world leaders at the World Trade Organization's 50th-birthday celebration in May 1998, "What are we going to live on? ... What industrial production will be left for us? Only low-tech, labour-intensive and highly contaminating ones? Do they perhaps want to turn a large part of the Third World into a huge free trade zone full of assembly plants which don't even pay taxes?"[29]

As bad as the situation is in Cavite, it doesn't begin to compare with Sri Lanka, where extended tax holidays mean that towns can't even provide public transportation for EPZ workers. The roads they walk to and from the factories are dark and dangerous, since there is no money for streetlights. Dormitory rooms are so overcrowded that they have white lines painted on the floor to mark where each worker sleeps—they "look like car parks," as one journalist observed.[30]

Jose Ricafrente has the dubious honor of being mayor of Rosario. I met with him in his small office, while a lineup of needy people waited outside. A once-modest fishing village, his town today has the highest per capita investment in all of the Philippines—thanks to the Cavite zone—but it lacks even the basic resources to clean up the mess that the factories create in the community. Rosario has all the problems of industrialization—pollution, an exploding population of migrant workers, increased crime, rivers of sewage—without any of the benefits. The federal government estimates that only 30 of the zone's 207 factories pay any taxes at all, but everybody else questions even that low figure. The mayor says that many companies are granted extensions of their tax holiday, or they close and reopen under another name, then take the free ride all over again. "They fold up before the tax holiday expires, then they incorporate to another company, just to avoid payment of taxes. They don't pay anything to the government, so we're in a dilemma right now," Ricafrente told me. A small man with a deep and powerful voice, Ricafrente is loved by his constituents for the outspoken positions he took on human rights and democracy during Ferdinand Marcos's brutal rule. But the day I met him, the mayor seemed exhausted, worn down by his powerlessness to affect the situation in his own backyard.[31] "We cannot even provide the basic services that our people expect from us," he said, with a sort of matter-of-fact rage. "We need water, we need roads, we need medical services, education. They expect us to deliver all of them at the same time, expecting that we've got money from taxes from the places inside the zone."

The mayor is convinced that there will always be a country—whether Vietnam, China, Sri Lanka or Mexico—that is willing to bid lower. And in the process, towns like Rosario will have sold out their people, compromised their education system and polluted their natural resources. "It should be a symbiotic relationship," Ricafrente says of foreign investment. "They derive income from us, so the government should also derive income from them.... It should have been a different Rosario."

Working in Brackets

So, if it's clear by now that the factories don't bring in taxes or create local infrastructures, and that the goods produced are all exported, why do countries like the Philippines still bend over backward to lure them inside their borders? The official reason is a trickle-down theory: these zones are job-creation programs and the income the workers earn will eventually fuel sustainable growth in the local economy.

The problem with this theory is that the zone wages are so low that workers spend most of their pay on shared dorm rooms and transportation; the rest goes to noodles and fried rice from vendors lined up outside the gate. Zone workers certainly cannot dream of affording the consumer goods they produce. These low wages are partly a result of the fierce competition for factories coming from other developing countries. But, above all, the government is extremely reluctant to enforce its own labour laws for fear of scaring away the swallows. So labour rights are under such severe assault inside the zones that there is little chance of workers earning enough to adequately feed themselves, let alone stimulate the local economy.

The Philippine government denies this, of course. It says that the zones are subject to the same labour standards as the rest of Philippine society: workers must be paid the minimum wage, receive social security benefits, have some measure of job security, be dismissed only with just cause and be paid extra for overtime, and they have the right to form independent trade unions. But in reality, the government views working conditions in the export factories as a matter of foreign trade policy, not a labour-rights issue. And since the government attracted the foreign investors with promises of a cheap and docile workforce, it intends to deliver. For this reason, labour department officials turn a blind eye to violations in the zone or even facilitate them.

Many of the zone factories are run according to iron-fist rules that systematically break Philippine labour law. Some employers, for instance, keep bathrooms padlocked except during two fifteen-minute breaks, during which time all the workers have to sign in and out so management can keep track of their nonproductive time. Seamstresses at a factory sewing garments for the Gap, Guess and Old Navy told me that they sometimes have to resort to urinating in plastic bags under their machines. There are rules against talking, and at the Ju Young electronics factory, a rule against smiling. One factory shames those who disobey by posting a list of "The Most Talkative Workers."

Factories regularly cheat on their workers' social security payments and gather illegal "donations" from workers for everything from cleaning materials to factory Christmas parties.

At a factory that makes IBM computer screens, the "bonus" for working hours of overtime isn't a higher hourly wage but doughnuts and a pen. Some owners expect workers to pull weeds from the ground on their way into the factory; others must clean the floors and the washrooms after their shifts end. Ventilation is poor and protective gear scarce.

Then there is the matter of wages. In the Cavite zone, the minimum wage is regarded more as a loose guideline than as a rigid law. If $6 a day is too onerous, investors can apply to the government for a waiver on that too. So while some zone workers earn the minimum wage, most—thanks to the waivers—earn less.[32]

Not Low Enough: Squeezing Wages in China

Part of the reason the threat of factory flight is so tangible in Cavite is that compared with China, Filipino wages are very high. In fact, everyone's wages are high compared with China. But what is truly remarkable about that is that the most egregious wage cheating goes on inside China itself.

Labour groups agree that a living wage for an assembly-line worker in China would be approximately US87 cents an hour. In the United States and Germany, where multinationals have closed down hundreds of domestic textile factories to move to zone production, garment workers are paid an average of US$10 and $18.50 an hour, respectively.[33] Yet even with these massive savings in labour costs, those who manufacture for the most prominent and richest brands in the world are still refusing to pay workers in China the 87 cents that would cover their cost of living, stave off illness and even allow them to send a little money home to their families. A 1998 study of brand-name manufacturing in the Chinese special economic zones found that Wal-Mart, Ralph Lauren, Ann Taylor, Esprit, Liz Claiborne, Kmart, Nike, Adidas, J.C. Penney and the Limited were only paying a fraction of that miserable 87 cents—some were paying as little as 13 cents an hour.

The only way to understand how rich and supposedly law-abiding multinational corporations could regress to 19th-century levels of exploitation (and get caught repeatedly) is through the mechanics of subcontracting itself: at every layer of contracting, subcontracting and homework, the manufacturers bid against each other to drive down the price, and at every level the contractor and subcontractor exact their small profit. At the end of this bid-down, contract-out chain is the worker—often three or four times removed from the company that placed the original order—with a paycheck that has been trimmed at every turn. "When the multinationals squeeze the subcontractors, the subcontractors squeeze the workers," explains a 1997 report on Nike's and Reebok's Chinese shoe factories.[34]

"No Union, No Strike"

A large sign is posted at a central intersection in the Cavite Export Processing Zone: "DO NOT LISTEN TO AGITATORS AND TROUBLE MAKERS." The words are in English, painted in bright red capital letters and everyone knows what they mean. Although trade unions are technically legal in the Philippines, there is a widely understood—if unwritten—"no union, no strike" policy inside the zones. As the sign suggests, workers who do attempt to organize unions in their factories are viewed as troublemakers, and often face threats and intimidation.

One of the reasons I went to Cavite is that I had heard this zone was a hotbed of "trouble-making," thanks to a newly formed organization called the Workers' Assistance Center. Attached to Rosario's Catholic church only a few blocks from the zone's entrance, the center is trying to break through the wall of fear that surrounds free-trade zones in the Philippines. Slowly, they have been collecting information about working conditions inside the zone. Nida Barcenas, one of the organizers at the center, told me, "At first, I used to have to follow workers home and beg them to talk to me. They were so scared—their families said I was a troublemaker." But after the center had been up and running for a year, the zone workers flocked there after their shifts—to hang out, eat dinner and attend seminars. I had heard about the center back in Toronto, told by several international labour experts that the research and organizing on free-trade zones coming out of this little bare-bones operation is among the most advanced being done anywhere in Asia.

The Workers' Assistance Center, known as WAC, was founded to support the factory workers' constitutional right to fight for better conditions—zone or no zone. Zernan Toledo is the center's most intense and radical organizer, and though he is only 25 and looks like a college student, he runs the center's affairs with all the discipline of a revolutionary cell. "Outside the zone, workers are free to organize a union, but inside they cannot stage pickets or have demonstrations," Toledo told me in my two-hour "orientation session" at the center. "Group discussions in the factories are prohibited and we cannot enter the zone," he said, pointing to a diagram of the zone layout hanging on the wall.[35] This catch-22 exists throughout the quasi-private zones. As the International Confederation of Free Trade Unions report puts it: "The workers are effectively living in 'lawless' territory where to defend their rights and interests they are constantly forced to take 'illegal' action themselves."[36]

In the Philippines, the zone's culture of incentives and exceptions, which was intended to be phased out as the foreign companies joined the national economy, has had the opposite effect. Not only have new swallows landed, but unionized factories already in the country have shut themselves down and reopened inside the Cavite Export Processing Zone in order to take advantage of all the incentives. For instance, Marks & Spencer goods used to be manufactured in a unionized factory north of Manila. "It only took ten trucks to bring Marks & Spencer to Cavite," a labour organizer in the area told me. "The union was eliminated."

Cavite is by no means exceptional in this regard. Union organizing is a source of great fear throughout the zones, where a successful drive can have dire consequences for both organizers and workers. That was the lesson learned in December 1998, when the American shirtmaker Phillips-Van Heusen closed down the only unionized export apparel factory in all of Guatemala, laying off 500 workers. The Camisas Modernas plant was unionized in 1997, after a long and bitter organizing drive and significant pressure placed on the company by U.S. human-rights groups. With the union, wages went up from US$56 a week to $71 and the previously squalid factory was cleaned up. Jay Mazur, president of the Union of Needletrades, Industrial and Textile Employees (UNITE)—America's largest apparel union—called the contract "a beacon of hope for more than 80,000 maquiladora workers in Guatemala."[37] When the factory closed, however, the beacon of hope turned into a flash-

ing red danger signal, reinforcing the familiar warning: no union, no strike.

Patriotism and national duty are bound up in the exploitation of the export zones, with young people—mostly women—sent off to sweatshop factories the way a previous generation of young men were sent off to war. No questioning of authority is expected or permitted. In some Central American and Asian EPZs, strikes are officially illegal; in Sri Lanka, it is illegal to do anything at all that might jeopardize the country's export earnings, including publishing and distributing critical material.[38] In 1993, a Sri Lankan zone worker by the name of Ranjith Mudiyanselage was killed for appearing to challenge this policy. After complaining about a faulty machine that had sliced off a co-worker's finger, Mudiyanselage was abducted on his way out of an inquiry into the incident. His body was found beaten and burning on a pile of old tires outside a local church. The man's legal adviser, who had accompanied him to the inquiry, was murdered in the same way.[39]

Despite the constant threat of retaliation, the Workers' Assistance Center has made some modest attempts to organize unions inside the Cavite zone factories, with varying degrees of success. For instance, when a drive was undertaken at the All Asia garment factory, the organizers came up against a very challenging obstacle: worker exhaustion. The biggest complaint among the All Asia seamstresses who stitch clothes for Ellen Tracy and Sassoon is forced overtime. Regular shifts last from 7 a.m. to 10 p.m., but on a few nights a week employees must work "late"—until 2 a.m. During peak periods, it is not uncommon to work two 2 a.m. shifts in a row, leaving many women only a couple of hours of sleep before they have to start their commute back to the factory. But that also means most All Asia workers spend their precious thirty-minute breaks at the factory napping, not talking about unions. "I have a hard time talking with the workers because the workers are always very sleepy," a mother of four tells me, explaining why she has had no luck in her attempts to bring a union to the All Asia factory. She has been with the company for four years and still lacks basic job security and health insurance.

Work in the zone is characterized by this brutal combination of tremendous intensity and nonexistent job security. Everyone works six or seven days a week, and when a big order is due to be shipped out, employees work until it is done. Most workers want some overtime hours because they need the money, but the overnight shifts are widely considered a burden. Refusing to stay, however, is not an option. For instance, according to the official rule book of the Philips factory (a contractor that has filled orders for both Nike and Reebok), "Refusal to render overtime work when so required" is an offense "punishable with dismissal." The same is true at all the factories I encountered, and there are many reports of workers asking to leave early—before 2 a.m., for instance—and being told not to return to work the next day.

Overtime horror stories pour out of the export processing zones, regardless of location: in China, there are documented cases of three-day shifts, when workers are forced to sleep under their machines. Contractors often face heavy financial penalties if they fail to deliver on time, no matter how unreasonable the deadline. In Honduras, when filling out a particularly large order on a tight deadline, factory managers have been reported injecting workers with amphetamines to keep them going on 48-hour marathons.[40]

What Happened to Carmelita ...

In Cavite, you can't talk about overtime without the conversation turning to Carmelita Alonzo, who died, according to her co-workers, "of overwork." Alonzo, I was told again and again—by groups of workers gathered at the Workers' Assistance Center and by individual workers in one-on-one interviews—was a seamstress at the V.T. Fashions factory, stitching clothes for the Gap and Liz Claiborne, among many other labels. All of the workers I spoke with urgently wanted me to know how this tragedy happened so that I could explain it to "the people in Canada who buy these products." Carmelita Alonzo's death occurred following a long stretch of overnight shifts during a particularly heavy peak season. "There were a lot of products for ship-out and no one was allowed to go home," recalls Josie, whose denim factory is owned by the same firm as Carmelita's, and who also faced large orders at that time. "In February, the line leader had overnights almost every night for one week." Not only had Alonzo been working those shifts, but she had a two-hour commute to get back to her family. Suffering from pneumonia—a common illness in factories that are suffocatingly hot during the day but fill with condensation at night—she asked her manager for time off to recover. She was denied. Alonzo was eventually admitted to hospital, where she died on March 8, 1997—International Women's Day.

I asked a group of workers gathered late one evening around the long table at the center how they felt about what happened to Carmelita. The answers were confused at first. "Feel? But Carmelita is us." But then Salvador, a sweet-faced twenty-two-year-old from a toy factory, said something that made all of his co-workers nod in vigorous agreement. "Carmelita died because of working overtime. It is possible to happen to any one of us," he explained, the words oddly incongruous with his pale blue *Beverly Hills 90210* T-shirt.

Much of the overtime stress could be alleviated if the factories would just hire more workers and create two shorter shifts. But why should they? The government official appointed to oversee the zone isn't interested in taking on the factory owners and managers about the overtime violations. Raymondo Nagrampa, the zone administrator, acknowledged that it would certainly be better if the factories hired more people for fewer hours, but, he told me, "I think I will leave that. I think this is more of a management decision."

For their part, the factory owners are in no rush to expand the size of their workforce, because after a big order is filled there could be a dry spell and they don't want to be stuck with more employees than work. Since following Philippine labour law is "a management decision," most decide that it is more convenient for management to have one pool of workers who are simply forced to work more hours when there is more work and fewer when there is less of it. And this is the flip side of the overtime equation: when a factory is experiencing a lull in orders or a shipment of supplies has been delayed, workers are sent home without pay, sometimes for a week at a time. The group of workers gathered around the table at the Workers' Assistance Center burst out laughing when I asked them about job security or a guaranteed number of working hours. "No work, no pay!" the young men and women exclaim in unison.

The "no work, no pay" rule applies to all workers, contract or "regular." Contracts, when they exist, last only five months or less,

after which time workers have to "recontract." Many of the factory workers in Cavite are actually hired through an employment agency, inside the zone walls, that collects their checks and takes a cut—a temp agency for factory workers, in other words, and one more level in the multiple-level system that lives off their labour. Management uses a variety of tricks in the different zones to keep employees from achieving permanent status and collecting the accompanying rights and benefits. In the Central American maquiladoras, it is a common practice for factories to fire workers at the end of the year and rehire them a few weeks later so that they don't have to grant them permanent status; in the Thai zones, the same practice is known as "hire and fire."[41] In China, many workers in the zones have no contracts at all, which leaves them without any rights or recourse whatsoever.[42]

It is in this casual new relationship to factory employment that the EPZ system breaks down completely. In principle, the zones are an ingenious mechanism for global wealth redistribution. Yes, they lure jobs from the North, but few fair-minded observers would deny the proposition that as industrialized nations shift to higher-tech economies, it is only a matter of global justice that the jobs upon which our middle classes were built should be shared with countries still enslaved by poverty. The problem is that the workers in Cavite, and in zones throughout Asia and Latin America, are not inheriting "our" jobs at all. Gerard Greenfield, former research director of the Asian Monitoring and Resource Centre in Hong Kong, says, "One of the myths of relocation is that those jobs that seemed to be transferred from the so-called North to the South are perceived as similar jobs to what was already being done before." They are not. Just as company-owned manufacturing turned—somewhere over the Pacific Ocean—into "orders" to be placed with third-party contractors, so did full-time employment undergo a mid-flight transformation into "contracts." "The biggest challenge to those in Asia," says Greenfield, "is that the new employment created by Western and Asian multinationals investing in Asia is temporary and short-term employment."[43]

In fact, zone workers in many parts of Asia, the Caribbean and Central America have more in common with office-temp workers in North America and Europe than they do with factory workers in those Northern countries. What is happening in the EPZs is a radical alteration in the very nature of factory work. That was the conclusion of a 1996 study conducted by the International Labour Organization, which stated that the dramatic relocation of production in the garment and shoe industries "has been accompanied by a parallel shift of production from the formal to the informal sector in many countries, with generally negative consequences on wage levels and conditions of work." Employment in these sectors, the study went on, has shifted from "full-time in-plant jobs to part-time and temporary jobs and, especially in clothing and footwear, increasing resort to homework and small shops."[44]

Indeed, this is not simply a job-flight story.

A Floating Workforce

On my last night in Cavite, I met a group of six teenage girls in the workers' dormitories who shared a six-by-eight-foot concrete room: four slept on the makeshift bunk bed (two to a bed), the other two on mats spread on the floor. The girls who made Aztek, Apple and IBM CD-ROM drives shared the top bunk; the ones who sewed Gap clothing, the bottom. All

were the children of farmers, away from their families for the first time.

Their jam-packed shoebox of a home had the air of an apocalyptic slumber party—part prison cell, part *Sixteen Candles*. It may have been a converted pigsty, but these were sixteen-year-old girls, and like teenage girls the world over they had covered the gray, stained walls with pictures: of fluffy animals, Filipino action-movie stars, and glossy magazine ads of women modeling lacy bras and underwear. After a little while, serious talk of working conditions erupted into fits of giggles and hiding under bedcovers. It seems that my questions reminded two of the girls of a crush they had on a labour organizer who had recently given a seminar at the Workers' Assistance Center on the risks of infertility from working with hazardous chemicals.

Were they worried about infertility?

"Oh, yes. Very worried now."

All through the Asian zones, the roads are lined with teenage girls in blue shirts, holding hands with their friends and carrying umbrellas to shield them from the sun. They look like students coming home from school. In Cavite, as elsewhere, the vast majority of workers are unmarried women between the ages of 17 and 25. Like the girls in the dorms, roughly 80 percent of the workers have migrated from other provinces of the Philippines to work in the factories—a mere five percent are native to the town of Rosario. Like the swallow factories, they too are only tenuously connected to this place.

Raymondo Nagrampa, the zone administrator, says migrants are recruited for the zone to compensate for something innate in "the Cavite character," something that makes local people unfit to work in the factories situated near their homes. "I don't mean any offense to the Cavite personality," he explained, in his spacious air-conditioned office. "But from what I gather, this particular character is not suited for the factory life—they'd rather go into something quickly. They do not have the patience to be right there in the factory line." Nagrampa attributes this to the fact that Rosario is so close to Manila "and so we can say that the Cavitenians are not running scared with regard to getting some income for their daily subsistence.…

"But in the case of those from the provinces, from the lower areas, they are not exposed to the big-city lifestyle. They feel more comfortable just working in the factory line, for, after all, this is a marked improvement from the farm work that they've been accustomed to, where they were exposed to the sun. To them, for the lowly province rural worker, working inside an enclosed factory is better off than being outside."

I asked dozens of zone workers—all of them migrants from rural areas—about what Raymondo Nagrampa had said. Every one of them responded with outrage.

"It's not human!" exclaimed Rosalie, a teenager whose job is installing the "backlights" in IBM computer screens. "Our rights are being trampled and Mr. Nagrampa says that because he has not experienced working in a factory and the conditions inside."

Salvador, in his 90210 T-shirt, was beside himself: "Mr. Nagrampa earns a lot of money and he has an air-conditioned room and his own car, so of course he would say that we prefer this work—it is beneficial to him, but not to us.… Working on the farm is difficult, yes, but there we have our family and friends and instead of always eating dried fish, we have fresh food to eat."

His words clearly struck a chord with a homesick Rosalie: "I want to be together with my family in the province," she said quietly, looking even younger than her nineteen years. "It's better there because when I get sick, my parents are there, but here there is no one to take care of me."

Many other rural workers told me that they would have stayed home if they could, but the choice was made for them: most of their families had lost their farms, displaced by golf courses, botched land-reform laws and more export processing zones. Others said that the only reason they came to Cavite was that when the zone recruiters came to their villages, they promised that workers would earn enough in the factories to send money home to their impoverished families. The same inducement had been offered to other girls their age, they told me, to go to Manila to work in the sex trade.

Several more young women wanted to tell me about those promises, too. The problem, they said, is that no matter how long they work in the zone, there is never more than a few pesos left over to send home. "If we had land we would just stay there to cultivate the land for our needs," Raquel, a teenage girl from one of the garment factories, told me. "But we are landless, so we have no choice but to work in the economic zone even though it is very hard and the situation here is very unfair. The recruiters said we would get a high income, but in my experience, instead of sending my parents money, I cannot maintain even my own expenses."

So the workers in Cavite have lost on all counts: they are penniless *and* homeless. It's a potent combination. In the dormitories, sleep deprivation, malnutrition and homesickness mingle to create an atmosphere of deep disorientation. "We are alien in the factories. We are also alien in the boarding-house because we all come from faraway provinces," Liza, an electronics worker, told me. "We are strangers here."

Cecille Tuico, one of the organizers at the Workers' Assistance Center, was listening in on the conversation. After the workers left to make their way through Rosario's dark streets and back to the dormitories, she pointed out that the alienation the workers so poignantly describe is precisely what the employers look for when they seek out migrants instead of locals to work in the zone. With the same muted, matter-of-fact anger I have come to recognize in so many Filipino human-rights activists, Tuico said that the factory managers prefer young women who are far from home and have not finished high school, because "they are scared and uneducated about their rights."

The Zones' other Product: A New Kind of Factory Worker

Their naiveté and insecurity undoubtedly make discipline easier for factory managers, but younger workers are preferred for other reasons, too. Women are often fired from their zone jobs in their mid-twenties, told by supervisors that they are "too old," and that their fingers are no longer sufficiently nimble. This practice is a highly effective way of minimizing the number of mothers on the company payroll.

In Cavite, the workers tell me stories about pregnant women forced to work until 2 a.m., even after pleading with the supervisor; of women who work in the ironing section giving birth to babies with burns on their skin; of women who mold the plastic for cordless phones giving birth to stillborn infants. The

evidence I hear in Cavite is anecdotal, told to me quietly and urgently by women with the same terrified expression I saw when conversation turned to Carmelita Alonzo. Some of the stories are certainly apocryphal—fear-fueled zone legends—but the abuse of pregnant women in export processing zones is also well documented and the problem reaches far beyond Cavite.

Because most zone employers want to avoid paying benefits, assigning workers to a predictable schedule or offering any job security, motherhood has become the scourge of these pink-collar zones. A study by Human Rights Watch that has become the basis for a grievance under the North American Free Trade Agreement (NAFTA) side agreement on labour found that women applying for jobs in the Mexican maquiladoras routinely had to undergo pregnancy tests. The study, which implicates such investors in the zones as Zenith, Panasonic, General Electric, General Motors and Fruit of the Loom, found that "pregnant women are denied hiring. Moreover, maquiladora employers sometimes mistreat and discharge pregnant employees."[45] The researchers uncovered mistreatment designed to encourage workers to resign: pregnant women were required to work the night shift, or to take on exceptionally long hours of unpaid overtime and physically strenuous tasks. They were also refused time off work to go to the doctor, a practice that has led to on-the-job miscarriages. "In this way," the study reports, "a pregnant worker is forced to choose between having a healthy, full-term pregnancy and keeping her job."[46]

Other methods of sidestepping the costs and responsibilities of employing workers with children are reported on a more haphazard basis throughout the zones. In Honduras and El Salvador the garbage dumps in the zones are littered with empty packets of contraceptive pills that are reportedly passed out on the factory floor. In the Honduran zones there have been reports of management forcing workers to have abortions. At some Mexican maquiladoras, women are required to prove they are menstruating through such humiliating practices as monthly sanitary-pad checks. Employees are kept on 28-day contracts—the length of the average menstrual cycle—making it easy, as soon as a pregnancy comes to light, for the worker to be dismissed.[47] In a Sri Lankan zone, one worker was reported to be so terrified of losing her job after giving birth that she drowned her newborn baby in a toilet.[48]

The widespread assault on women's reproductive freedoms in the zones is the most brutal expression of the failure on the part of many consumer-goods corporations to live up to their traditional role as mass employers. Today's "new deal" with workers is a non-deal; one-time manufacturers, turned marketing mavens, are so resolutely intent on evading any and all commitments that they are creating a workforce of childless women, a system of footloose factories employing footloose workers. In a letter to Human Rights Watch explaining why it discriminated against pregnant women in the maquiladoras, General-Motors stated plainly that it "will not hire female job applicants found to be pregnant" in an effort to avoid "substantial financial liabilities imposed by the Mexican social security system."[49] Since the critical report was published, GM has changed the policy. It remains, however, a stark contrast to the days when the company made it a banner policy that the adult men working in its auto plants should earn enough not only to support a family of

four but to drive them around in a GM car or truck. General Motors has cut about 82,000 jobs in the U.S. since 1991 and expects to cut another 40,000 by the year 2003, moving production to the maquiladoras and their clones around the globe.[50] A far cry from those days when it proudly proclaimed, "What's good for General Motors is good for the country."

Migrant Factories

Within this reengineered system, the workers aren't the only ones on a day pass. The swallow factories that employ them have been built to maximize flexibility: to follow the tax breaks and incentives, to bend with the currency devaluations and benefit by the strict rule of dictators. In North America and Europe, job flight is a threat with which workers have become all too familiar. A study commissioned by the NAFTA labor commission found that in the United States, between 1993 and 1995, "employers threatened to close the plant in 50 percent of all union certification elections…. Specific, unambiguous threats ranged from attaching shipping labels to equipment throughout the plant with a Mexican address, to posting maps of North America with an arrow pointing from the current plant site to Mexico." The study found that the employers followed through on the threats, shutting down all or part of newly unionized plants, in 15 percent of these cases—triple the closing rate of the pre-NAFTA 1980s.[51] In China, Indonesia, India and the Philippines the threat of plant closure and job flight is even more powerful. Since the industries are quick to flee escalating wages, environmental regulation and taxes, factories are made to be mobile. Some of these swallow factories may well be on their third or even fourth flight, and as the history of subcontracting makes clear, they touch down more lightly at each new stop.

When the flying multinationals first landed in Taiwan, Korea and Japan, many of their factories were owned and operated by local contractors. In Pusan, South Korea, for instance—known during the eighties as "the sneaker capital of the world"—Korean entrepreneurs ran factories for Reebok, L.A. Gear and Nike. But when, in the late eighties, Korean workers began to rebel against their dollar-a-day wages and formed trade unions to fight for better conditions, the swallows once again took flight. Between 1987 and 1992, 30,000 factory jobs were lost in Korea's export processing zones, and in less than three years one-third of the shoe jobs had disappeared. The story is much the same in Taiwan. The migration patterns have been clearly documented with Reebok's manufacturers. In 1985, Reebok produced almost all its sneakers in South Korea and Taiwan and none in Indonesia and China. By 1995, nearly all those factories had flown out of Korea and Taiwan and 60 percent of Reebok's contracts had landed in Indonesia and China.[52]

But on this new leg of the journey, the factories were not owned by local Indonesian and Chinese contractors. Instead they were owned and run by the same Korean and Taiwanese companies that ran them before the move. When the multinationals pulled their orders from Korea and Taiwan, their contractors followed, closing up shop in their home countries and building the new factories in countries where labour was still cheap: China, Indonesia, Thailand and the Philippines. One of these contractors—the largest single supplier for Reebok, Adidas and Nike—is a Taiwanese-owned company called Yue Yuen. Yue Yuen has closed most of its factories in its homeland

of Taiwan and chased the low wages to China, where it employs 54,000 people in a single factory complex. For Chi Neng Tsai, one of the company's owners, it simply makes good business sense to go where the workers are hungry: "Thirty years ago, when Taiwan was hungry, we also were more productive," he says.[53]

Taiwanese and Korean bosses are uniquely positioned to exploit this hunger: they can tell workers from personal experience what happens when unions come in and wages go up. And maintaining contractors who have had the rug pulled out from under them once before is a stroke of management genius on the part of the Western multinationals. What better way to keep costs down than to make yesterday's casualties today's wardens?

It is a system that doesn't do much for the sense of stability in Cavite, or for the Philippine economy in general, which is already unusually vulnerable to global forces, since the majority of its companies are owned by foreign investors. As Filipino economist Antonio Tujan told me, "The contractors have displaced the Filipino middleman."[54] In fact, Tujan, the director of a Manila-based think tank highly critical of Philippine economic policy, corrects me when I refer to the buildings I saw inside the Cavite Export Processing Zone as "factories." They aren't factories, he says, "they are labour warehouses."

He explains that since all the materials are imported, nothing is actually manufactured in the factories, only assembled. (The components are manufactured in yet another country, where the workers are more highly skilled, though still cheaper than U.S. or European workers.) It's true, now that Tujan mentions it, that when I climbed up the water tower and looked down on the zone, part of what contributed to the unbearable lightness of Cavite was that apart from one incinerator, there were no smokestacks. That's a bonus for the air quality in Rosario but odd for an industrial park of Cavite's size. Neither was there any local rhyme or reason to what was being produced. When I walked the zone's freshly paved streets, I was surprised by the variety of manufacturing going on. Like most people, I had thought that Asian export zones were mostly filled with garment and electronics producers, but not Cavite: a factory making car seats sat next to one making sneakers, across the way from a factory with dozens of aluminum speedboats piled up by its gate. On another street, the open doors of a factory revealed racks of dresses and jackets, right next to the plant where Salvador made novelty key chains and other small toys. "You see?" says Antonio Tujan. "We have a country whose industry is so deformed, so unbelievably mishmash, that it cannot exist by itself. It's all a myth, you know. They talk about industrialization in the context of globalization, but it's all a myth."

No wonder the promise of industrialization in Cavite feels more like a threat. The place is a development mirage.

The Shoppers Take Flight

The fear that the flighty multinationals will once again pull their orders and migrate to more favorable conditions underlies everything that takes place in the zones. It makes for an odd dissonance: despite the fact that they have no local physical holdings—they don't own the buildings, land or equipment—brands like Nike, the Gap and IBM are omnipresent, invisibly pulling all the strings. They are so powerful as buyers that the hands-on involvement owning the factories would entail has come to look, from their perspective, like needless

micromanagement. And because the actual owners and factory managers are completely dependent on their large contracts to make the machines run, workers are left in a uniquely weak bargaining position: you can't sit down and bargain with an order form. So even the classic Marxist division between workers and owners doesn't quite work in the zone, since the brand-name multinationals have divested the "means of production," to use Marx's phrase, unwilling to encumber themselves with the responsibilities of actually owning and managing the factories, and employing a labour force.

If anything, the multinationals have more power over production by not owning the factories. Like most committed shoppers, they see no need to concern themselves with how their bargains were produced—they simply pounce on them, keeping the suppliers on their toes by taking bids from slews of other contractors. One contractor, Young Il Kim of Guatemala, whose Sam Lucas factory produces clothing for Wal-Mart and J.C. Penney, says of his big-brand clients, "They're interested in a high-quality garment, fast delivery, and cheap sewing charges—and that's all."[55] In this cutthroat context, each contractor swears he could deliver the goods cheaper if the brands would only start producing in Africa, Vietnam or Bangladesh, or if they would shift to homeworkers.

More blatantly, the power of the brands may occasionally be invoked to affect public policy in the countries where export zones are located. Companies or their emissaries may make public statements about how a raise in the legal minimum wage could price a certain Asian country "out of the market," as Nike's and Reebok's contractors have been quick to tell the Indonesian government whenever strikes get out of hand.[56] Calling a strike at a Nike factory "intolerable," Anton Supit, chairman of the Indonesian Footwear Association, which represents contractors for Nike, Reebok and Adidas, called on the Indonesian military to intervene. "If the authorities don't handle strikes, especially ones leading to violence and brutality, we will lose our foreign buyers. The government's income from exports will decrease and unemployment will worsen."[57] The corporate shoppers may also help draft international trade agreements to reduce quotas and tariffs, or even lobby a government directly to loosen regulations. In describing the conditions under which Nike decided to begin "sourcing" its shoes in China, for instance, company vice president David Chang explained that "one of the first things we told the Chinese was that their prices had to be more competitive with our other Far East sources because the cost of doing business in China was so enormous.... The hope is for a 20 percent price advantage over Korea."[58] After all, what price-conscious consumer doesn't comparison shop? And if a shift to a more "competitive" country causes mass layoffs somewhere else in the world, that is somebody else's blood on somebody else's hands. As Levi's CEO Robert Haas said, "This is not a job-flight story."

Multinational corporations have vehemently defended themselves against the accusation that they are orchestrating a "race to the bottom" by claiming that their presence has helped to raise the standard of living in underdeveloped countries. As Nike CEO Phil Knight said in 1996, "For the past 25 years, Nike has provided good jobs, improved labour practices and raised standards of living wherever we operate."[59] Confronted with the starvation wages in Haiti, a Disney spokesperson told *The Globe and Mail,* "It's a process all developing countries go through, like Japan and Korea, who were at this stage decades ago."[60] And there is no shortage of economists to spin the mounting revelations of corporate abuse, claiming that sweatshops are not a sign of eroded rights but a signal that prosperity is just around the corner. "My concern," said famed Harvard economist Jeffrey D. Sachs, "is not that there are too many sweatshops but that there are too few ... those are precisely the jobs that were the stepping stones for Singapore and Hong Kong and those are the jobs that have to come to Africa to get them out of back-breaking rural poverty."[61] Sachs's colleague Paul Krugman concurred, arguing that in the developing world the choice is not between bad jobs and good jobs but between bad jobs and no jobs. "The overwhelming mainstream view among economists is that the growth of this kind of employment is tremendous good news for the world's poor."[62]

The no-pain-no-gain defense of sweatshops, however, took a severe beating when the currencies of those very countries supposedly benefiting most from this development model began crashing like cheap plates. First in Mexico, then Thailand, South Korea, the Philippines and Indonesia, workers were, and in many cases still are, bringing home minimum-wage paychecks worth less than when the "economic miracle" first came to bless their nations years ago. Nike's public-relations director, Vada Manager, used to claim that "the job opportunities that we have provided to women and men in developing economies like Vietnam and Indonesia have provided a bridge of opportunity for these individuals to have a much better quality of life,"[63] but by the winter of 1998, nobody knew better than Nike that that bridge had collapsed. With currency devaluation and soaring inflation, real wages in Nike's Indonesian factories fell by 45 percent in 1998.[64] In July of that year, Indonesian president BJ. Habibie urged his 200 million citizens to do their part to conserve the country's dwindling rice supply by fasting for two days out of each week, from dawn until dusk. Development built on starvation wages, far from kick-starting a steady improvement in conditions, has proved to be a case of one step forward, three steps back. And by early 1998 there were no more shining Asian Tigers to point to, and those corporations and economists that had mounted such a singular defense of sweatshops had had their arguments entirely discredited.

The fear of flying has been looming large in Cavite of late. The currency began its downward spiral a few weeks before I arrived, and since then conditions have only worsened. By early 1999, the price of basic commodities like cooking oil, sugar, chicken and soap had increased by as much as 36 percent from the year before. Paychecks that barely made ends meet now no longer accomplish even that. Workers who had begun to find the courage to stand up to management are now living not only under the threat of mass layoffs and factory flight but with the reality. In 1998, 3,072 businesses in the Philippines either closed down or scaled back operation—a 166 percent increase over the year before.[65] For its part, Nike has laid off

268 workers at the Philips factory, where I had seen, through the surrounding fence, the shoes lying in great piles. A few months later, in February 1999, Nike pulled out of two other Philippine factories as well, these ones located in the nearby Bataan export zone; 1,505 workers were affected by the closures.[66] But Phil Knight didn't have to do the dirty work himself—he just cut the orders and left the rest to the contractors. Like the factories themselves, these job losses went unswooshed.

The transience woven into the fabric of free-trade zones is an extreme manifestation of the corporate divestment of the world of work, which is taking place at all levels of industry. Cavite may be capitalism's dream vacation, but casualization is a game that can be played at home, and contracting out, as *Business Week* reporter Aaron Bernstein has written, is trickling up. "While outsourcing started in manufacturing in the early 1980s, it has expanded through virtually every industry as companies rush to shed staff in everything from human resources to computer systems."[67] The same impetus that lies behind the brands-versus-products and contracts-versus-jobs conflict is fueling the move to temp, part-time, freelance and homework in North America and Europe.

This is not a job-flight story. It is a flight-from-jobs story.

Endnotes

1 Landor Web site.
2 Schweitzer, Peter. "People Buy Products Not Brands." J. Walter Thompson White Papers series, undated.
3 "Big Brand Firms Know the Name Is Everything." *Irish Times,* 27 February 1998.
4 Ortega. *In Sam We Trust,* 342.
5 "Trade and Development Report, 1997." United Nations Conference on Trade and Economic Development.
6 Katz. *Just Do It,* 204.
7 Majtenyi, Cathy. 1996. "Were Disney Dogs Treated Better Than Workers?" *Catholic Register,* 23–30 December, 9.
8 "Extreme Spreadsheet Dude." *Baffler* no. 9, 79; and *Wall Street Journal,* 16 April 1998 (on-line).
9 Gilardi, John. 1995. "Adidas Share Offer Set to Win Gold Medal." Reuters, 26 October.
10 *Globe and Mail,* 26 September 1997.

11 Kernaghan, Charles. 1998. "Behind the Label: 'Made in China,'" prepared for the National Labor Committee, March.

12 *Los Angeles Times,* 16 September 1997, D5. Furthermore, Sara Lee's investors had been getting a solid return on their investment but the stock "had gained 25 per cent over the prior 12 months, lagging the 35 per cent increase of the benchmark Standard & Poor's 500-stock index."

13 Peters, *The Circle of Innovation,* 16.

14 Leonhardt, David. 1998. "Sara Lee: Playing with the Recipe." *Business Week,* 27 April, 114.

15 Ibid.

16 Waters, Jennifer. 1997. "After Euphoria, Can Sara Lee Be Like Nike?" *Crain's Chicago Business,* 22 September, 3.

17 Munk, Nina. 1999. "How Levi's Trashed a Great American Brand." *Fortune,* 12 April, 83.

18 "Levi Strauss & Co. to Close 11 of Its North American Plants." Business Wire. 22 February 1999, B1.

19 *Wall Street Journal,* 4 November 1997, B1.

20 Ramey, Joanna. 1998. "Levi's Will Resume Production in China After 5-Year Absence." *Women's Wear Daily,* 9 April, 1.

21 "Anti-Sweatshop Activists Score in Campaign Targeting Athletic Retailers." *Boston Globe,* 18 April 1999.

22 Thoman, Richard S. 1956. *Free Ports and Foreign Trade Zones.* Cambridge: Cornell Maritime Press.

23 These are International Labor Organization figures as of May 1998 but in "Behind the Label: 'Made in China,'" by Charles Kernaghan, March 1998, the figures on China's zone are much higher. Kernaghan estimates that there are 30 million inside the zones, and that there are 400—as opposed to 124—special economic zones inside China.

24 The International Labor Organization's Special Action Program on Export Processing Zones. Source: Auret Van Heerden.

25 This estimate was provided by Michael Finger at the World Trade Organization in a personal correspondence. No official figures are available.

26 Figures for 1985 and 1995 provided by the WTO. Figures for 1997 supplied by the Maquila Solidarity Network/Labor Behind the Label Coalition, Toronto.

27 *World Accounting Report.* July 1992.

28 Sassen, Saskia. 1996. *Losing Control? Sovereignty in an Age of Globalization.* New York: Columbia University Press. 8–9.

29 "Castro Dampens WTO Party." *Globe and Mail,* 20 May 1998.

30 Cottingham, Martin. 1993. "Cut to the Bone." *New Statesman & Society,* 12 March, 12.

31 Personal interview, 2 September 1997.

32 The Workers' Assistance Center, Rosario.

33 "Globalization Changes the Face of Textile, Clothing and Footwear Industries." International Labor Organization press release, 28 October 1996.

34 "Working Conditions in Sports Shoe Factories in China Making Shoes for Nike and Reebok," by Asia Monitor Resource Centre and Hong Kong Christian Industrial Committee, September 1997.

35 Personal interview, 1 September 1997.

36 "Behind the Wire: Anti-Union Repression in the Export Processing Zones," a report by the International Confederation of Free Trade Unions.

37 Greenhouse, Steven. 1999. *New York Times.* 29 February.

38 Goldenberg, Suzanne. 1997. "Colombo Stitch-Up." *Guardian,* 7 November.

39 Cottingham. "Cut to the Bone." 12.

40 Goldenberg. "Colombo Stitch-Up."

41 "The Globe-Trotting Sports Shoe" by Peter Madden and Bethan Books, published by Christian Aid.

42 Kernaghan. "Behind the Label: 'Made in China.'"

43 From a panel discussion at "International Relocation" conference held in Brussels on 19–20 September 1996.

44 "Globalization Changes the Face of Textile…" ILO.

45 "Submission Concerning Pregnancy-Based Discrimination in Mexico's Maquiladora Sector to the United States National Administrative Office," submitted by Human Rights Watch Women's Rights Project, Human Rights Watch/Americas, International Labor Rights Fund, and Asociacion National de Abogados Democraticos, 15 May 1997.

46 "No Guarantees: Sex Discrimination in Mexico's Maquiladora Sector," Human Rights Watch Women's Rights Project, August 1996.

47 Eggertson, Laura. 1997. "Abuse Part of Jobs at Mexican Firms." *Globe and Mail,* 14 October.

48 Cottingham. "Cut to the Bone."

49 "General Motors Corporation's Response to June 28, 1996 Letter from Human Rights Watch." The statement was attached to a letter dated 14 August 1996 signed by Gregory E. Lau, Executive Director, Worldwide Executive Compensation and Corporate Governance.

50 *Wall Street Journal,* 21 November 1997 (on-line).

51 Bronfenbrenner, Kate. 1997. "We'll Close! Plant Closings, Plant-Closing Threats, Unions Organizing and NAFTA." *Multinational Monitor,* 18, no. 3, March.

52 Fischer, David. "Global Hopscotch." *U.S. News and World Report,* 5 June 1995.

53 Sander, Henny. 1996. "Sprinting to the Forefront." *Far Eastern Economic Review,* 1 August, 50.

54 Personal interview, 3 September 1997.

55 Ortega. *In Sam We Trust,* 250.

56 "South Korea Will Leave Indonesia if Strikes Continue," *Straits Times* (Singapore), 30 April 1997, 18. The article reported that Reebok's Indonesian executive Scott Thomas had met with South Korean officials, saying that if the worker strikes continued in Indonesia, the company might relocate again, saying Reebok "could place its orders easily with other countries if the situation persisted."

57 *Jakarta Post,* 30 April 1997.

58 "Nike in China" (abridged), Harvard Business School, 9-390-092, 12 August 1993.

59 "Nike Joins President Clinton's Fair Labor Coalition," PR NewsWire, 2 August 1996.

60 Reed, Christopher. 1997. "Sweatshop Jobs Don't Put Food On Table." *Globe and Mail,* 9 May.

61 Myerson, Allen R. 1997. "In Principle, a Case for More 'Sweatshops.'" *New York Times,* 22 June, 4–5.

62 Ibid.

63 "Labour-Women Say Nike Supports Women in Ads, But Not in Factories," Inter Press Service, 29 October 1997.

64 "Raising Wages a Penny an Hour," National Labor Committee press release, 29 March 1999. Wages fell from 27 cents an hour to 15 cents an hour, even after Nike announced a six percent raise.

65 "High Unemployment, Higher Prices and Lower Wages," Ibon press release, 15 March 1999.

66 "Two Shoe Firms Close RP Shops," *Philippine Daily Enquirer,* 22 February 1999. The two factories were P.K. Export, which laid off 300 workers in 1998 and employed another 767 when the closure was announced, and Lotus Footwear, which employed 438 workers when it filed a notice of factory closure.

67 Bernstein, Aaron. "Outsourced—And Out of Luck." *Business Week,* 17 July 1995, 60–61.

CHAPTER 8

1-800 New Brunswick:

Economic Development Strategies, Firm Restructuring, and the Local Production of "Global" Services

Ruth Buchanan

IN NEW BRUNSWICK, a small, underdeveloped and relatively isolated province on the Atlantic Coast of Canada, the tides of global economic transformation can be seen from a distance. At least, this is what I believed when, as a young academic interested in globalization, I relocated to Fredericton in 1993. I assumed this because globalization scholars at the time tended to be located in and focus their attention on major urban centres. Their arguments suggested that if the virtual networks that made up the global economy could be described as located in any place, it had to be a global city. The nearest one could actually get to globalization from Fredericton, I imagined, would be Boston, or better, New York. Although those cities were not far away geographically, within the hierarchy of the global economic order, it seemed as if they couldn't get any farther.

However, I soon came to understand what this chapter intends to illustrate: that pro-cesses of globalization are also taking place in New Brunswick, albeit in forms quite distinct from that of the global centre. I wasn't in the province very long before I noticed a number of recognizable themes emerging in local economic news: the implications of new telecommunications technologies, restructuring and reorganizations by firms, and the shifting roles of local, provincial and federal governments. In particular, between 1991 and 1996, a convergence of strategies being pursued by government, firms, and workers created an attractive environment within the province for the location of call centre operations.[1] Call centres are centralized offices where large numbers of employees perform most of their work over the telephone. The call centre industry encompasses both inbound telephone services via 1-800 numbers provided by a wide range of firms (from courier companies to airlines, hospitality industries and financial institutions) as well as outbound telephone services like telemarketing, survey research and fundraising. Firms reorganizing to reduce costs are increasingly turning to the creation of call centres through which a diverse range of functions can be centralized, at some distance from both customers and head office, for more cost-efficient delivery. New Brunswick early on realized that it could market itself as a cheap, productive location for these types of operations. Between 1991 and 1997, the teleservices sector accounted for a significant proportion of job creation in the province, providing approximately 6,000 new jobs in a province of less than three quarters of a million people. The provincial government played an essential role in both initiating and encouraging the sector's growth, actively soliciting firms and offering incentives to those that chose to relocate. The implementation of the call centre development strategy happened to correspond with a second wave of consolidation and restructuring of call centre operations by many firms, which contributed to the province's success in attracting nearly 40 such centres by 1997.

As I began to realize that the intersecting dynamics at work in New Brunswick were also linked to what I had understood as globalization, yet operated according to a distinct logic of their own out on the periphery, it was necessary to revisit my assumptions about current processes of economic transformation. Globalization is not a single process that radiates outward or downward from an integrated core; rather globalization(s) can be seen as an amalgamation of processes that draw on the particularities of local history and the agency of local workers and communities as much as larger forces of economic integration or transformation. Globalization(s) occur through a multiplicity of interactions and institutions that are necessarily localized, in

spaces that have their own histories, needs and instrumentalities.[2] This chapter is an effort to illuminate the complex ways in which global processes are interpreted and transformed by institutions and actors operating within more circumscribed scales of influence; or put simply, how the global is (re)made in the local.

From this perspective, the New Brunswick call centre story can be understood as an important piece of the globalization puzzle, in which transformation and growth within the services sector are crucial. While at one time the economic role of services was seen as secondary to the role played by production in economic activity, services are now understood as central to current processes of spatial and institutional restructuring. In particular, attention has been paid to the increasing significance of intermediate activities such as the provision of legal, marketing, financial and management expertise to businesses (producer services). Both the rapid expansion of producer services and their consolidation as the economic core of major cities have been identified as key factors in the spatial and institutional reorderings currently underway (Sassen 1991; Castells 1996). Yet, the emergence of global cities is only one piece of a two-fold process. Intensified polarization of economic activity is producing both agglomeration and decentralization. While uneven development is not a new feature of capitalist forms of social organization, both the sheer intensity and the geographic and institutional forms characterizing current restructuring point toward a need to understand decentralization as much as agglomeration.

While much useful empirical work has been done recently on the growth of producer services in core areas, this focus fails to answer questions about how the new dynamics of uneven development may have also transformed the processes through which workers and communities on the periphery are positioned in relation to these emerging centres. Nor does it examine sufficiently the ways that firms participate in these changes, through both spatial restructuring and the internal reorganization of work processes. This chapter begins where this existing research leaves off.

Through the presentation of a case study of the New Brunswick call centre industry, it will be possible in this chapter to examine the intersection of forces that are producing current restructuring, and to highlight the interaction between three separate sets of actors: multinational firms, regional government, and the individuals who make up local labour markets. First, as I've already suggested, by selecting a case study far from global centres and in the context of the production of routine consumer marketing and services, I will examine the interlinked spatial and organizational dimensions of restructuring by firms.

Second, it is important to observe that the new economy has ushered in not only this "new geography of centrality and marginality" but also a new set of institutional relationships and instrumentalities through which this geography is produced, and these relationships restructured (Sassen 1996). One of the most important of these is the state, albeit often a regional state. Much initial research on the state in conditions of globalization lent itself most readily to propositions that states are losing their role in the regulation of economic activity, both domestic and transnational. Recently, another current aspect of research has emerged which has focussed on the region as an essential level of coordination of economic activity in the context of late 20th century capitalism (Storper 1997). One can find many examples of regional and local governments which have used regulatory and marketing initiatives to expand their role in economic development, often far away from global cities or national capitals (Sabel 1996). This study adds to the evidence that the state is not simply being "hollowed out," but that governments frequently play an important role in the current economic transformation through their interaction with restructuring firms. Hence, this chapter also examines the changing institutional role of the state, and the state as an instrument of restructuring, through the example of the provincial government of New Brunswick during the leadership of former Premier Frank McKenna.

Third, while the coexistence of these simultaneous tendencies of agglomeration and decentralization is structured by the relationship between two evolving institutional frameworks—the state and the firm—it is not determined by them. In order to fully explain the trajectory of restructuring in any particular locality, it is necessary to examine not only transformations in the organization of firms, and in the regulatory apparatus of the regional state, but also the responses of local actors in adapting to and/or resisting the changes brought about in their communities through these larger processes. In the New Brunswick example, the attitudes of workers and the public toward the jobs created by the call centres also played a significant role in the largely successful unfolding of the call centre strategy, a role which was well understood by both the firms and the provincial government. Initially, the availability of capable potential employees was a significant factor in bringing firms to the province, while low turnover rates and high productivity of New Brunswickers employed as call centre workers helped to make many of the new centres successful by firm standards.

However, low wages and difficult working conditions at some call centres created significant pressures for the employees, straining their coping skills, their sense of fairness and propriety and leading them to become more publicly demanding. Both the government and the firms took seriously the ongoing need for compliant labour from the start, and continued to work at constructing a public image of the call centres as providing valued and respectable work. It was the interaction between these localized struggles of workers, restructuring strategies of firms, and economic development efforts of government that collectively functioned to produce and reproduce the call centre industry in New Brunswick. This is the process, the global being made and remade in the local, that this chapter seeks to examine.

The Local Production of 1-800 Services: Restructuring Firms, Reorganizing Work

The spatial reorganization of firms that underpinned the rapid growth of the number of call centres in New Brunswick over the past six years is called "back officing" in industry circles. Certain lower skilled jobs such as telemarketing, teleservice, data entry, rate or credit checking are separated from the rest of a firm's operations and relocated to a suburban or offshore location where labour, rents and other costs are generally lower. By relocating to sites where suitable employees are cheap and plentiful, and there are few other employment options, the productivity returns for firms can be quite significant.[3] However, the gains produced by relocating production are usually limited; firms seeking further cost savings must eventually either increase the productivity of their workforce by other means, or relocate production further offshore in search of even cheaper

labour (Appelbaum 1993). Recent studies of corporate reorganization and labour identify two approaches to increasing productivity in the context of the current volatile economy (Economic Council of Canada 1990; Duffy, Glenday and Pupo 1997). These correspond to two ideal types: the sweatshop and the flexible firm. Firms which choose the low road of the sweatshop depend on a steady supply of ready labour, investing as little as possible in their employees, who tend to burn out and turn over at a high rate. At the other end of the spectrum, firms seeking to "flexibilize" may invest heavily in their labour force, rely on internal labour markets and depend on being rewarded with greater loyalty, commitment and productivity from employees. For employees, this can either mean increasing demands for more work with negligible wage increases or further opportunities for training, skills utilization and autonomy within the labour process.

While these ideal types capture many important features of the structural dynamics of current restructuring, the dichotomy they present is not always neatly reflected in particular cases. This is because the current process of economic transformation, of which the New Brunswick story is one example, is also a product of ongoing conflicts and accommodations among locally situated social actors. Therefore, this chapter examines the differences among the ways that firms have approached the reorganization of their operations to incorporate telephone services provided from New Brunswick for their Canadian, or in some cases, North American customers, and explores some of the implications of these different routes on the relationships among the firm, its employees and customers. The choice of low or high road does not appear, in this context, as distinct or predetermined as theorists have presumed. Several firms have, while locating telephone service operations in a site where labour is relatively cheap and there are few strong local regulatory disincentives, avoided the classic "low road" approach. Rather, they may emphasize the quality of calls as well as—or even more than—quantity in evaluating worker productivity; they may invest more in training and compensating workers; they may use teams to motivate employees to work together, and they may encourage promotion within the firm.

The spatial restructuring, driven by the search for the ideal combination of cheap and productive labour, that brings firms to New Brunswick often takes place at the same time as, and is connected to, changes in the ways in which firms utilize information technologies and how they organize work. Call centres locating in the province share basic forms of organization, information technologies and geographically oriented restructuring strategies, although there are a few significant differences among them. The companies relocate only their telephone operations to the province, leaving higher paid employees in creative, managerial, and marketing functions in other locations. Physical separation from the rest of the operations can lead to increasing skills polarization and literal disappearance of the segregated workers from career paths within the firm (Belt, Richardson and Webster 1999; Shalla 1997). It also permits the implementation of significantly different expectations in terms of shift work, productivity quotas, salaries, and seniority from a firm's employment practices in other locations. Many of the firms locating centres in New Brunswick are consolidating operations formerly carried out in a number of sites into one "national" centre. Most of the centres in the province make or re-

ceive calls throughout Canada. Some provide support or backup to centres located in the United States as well.

The provision of services by telephone has been rapidly expanding over the past decade. With the establishment of sophisticated networked databases, firms that provide reservation services, for example, can provide detailed "local" information about a specific hotel, such as how far it is from a corner store, a gym or a park.[4] That this information can be provided despite the despatialized nature of the linkage between the telephone service representative and the customer is an important aspect of quality service. In addition to the hospitality sector, airlines, banks, courier companies, and office equipment suppliers have all recently expanded or consolidated call centres in New Brunswick. The service centres make it possible for the firms to claim that they are improving access to their services by offering the 1-800 number through extended hours (in some cases 24-hour service). At the same time it reduces both labour costs and overhead through locating a large group of (usually) new employees under one roof. In some cases, it has the added advantage of enabling the reduction or elimination of unionized locations elsewhere. While some of the larger firms which have opened centres in New Brunswick have offered employees the opportunity to transfer to the new centre, most of the employees who currently work in the centres are New Brunswickers.

Most of the call centres require their employees to adhere to carefully worded scripts. While some of these scripts are necessary to comply with regulatory standards, as in the sale of insurance, much of the scripting is intended to bring employees into conformity with a company-dictated standard of good service. Just as the computer database inadequately replaces local knowledge, the scripts that many of the telephone workers are required to adhere to (for both inbound and outbound calls) are a poor substitute for the interpersonal engagement of the face-to-face encounter. Yet, if employees seek to deviate from the scripts to improve the effectiveness of the call, they can be disciplined. The highly monitored nature of the call centre environment, which one worker described as "Big Brotherish," makes deviation without detection difficult. However, there are often significant incentives to amend the scripts, particularly in a telephone sales environment where performance bonuses can make up a large proportion of employee income. Sometimes supervisory staff collude with this process. In one American-owned telemarketing firm it was widely recognized that the scripts sent by the American head office were highly ineffective for selling to a Canadian public much less used to "hard-sell" techniques. Changes were made in the New Brunswick office for the use of the local callers. When head office called in from its location in the southern United States to remotely monitor calls at the New Brunswick office, local management warned employees so that they could return to the original scripts.[5]

Interviews with call centre employees reinforced the suggestion that productivity requirements and working conditions in New Brunswick compared unfavourably with those in other parts of the country. An employee with one firm that had another call centre in London, Ontario said, "People sort of know that the rules are quite different in London— they don't know in a big way, but they don't work overnight shifts. They, you know, I think they've got more clout in London."[6]

A similar observation was made by a local union representative who had transferred from Ontario to a newly opened call centre.[7] Based on information that he had gained from his many years of experience with the company, and from reviewing logs at other call centres after his election to the union position, he was convinced that the company was selectively trying to establish higher productivity quotas at the new New Brunswick location so that it would then be able to phase out centres in other locations by claiming that they were not performing as well.

In a mail-out survey I conducted in the summer of 1996, firms were asked to indicate a number of factors influencing their decision to select New Brunswick as a site for their consolidation or relocation. The one factor selected by almost all the firms was the telecommunications infrastructure in the province, which, through interviews, I came to understand as including both the technology offered by New Brunswick Telephone Company (NB Tel) and the support services it provided for call centre operations. The availability of a bilingual workforce and government incentives were next, followed by wage rates and the educational accomplishments of the workforce. Notably, the two factors which set New Brunswick apart from other sites in the view of these firms are both outcomes of the distinct local history of the province. While each of these histories can be elaborated upon in much more detail, I can only briefly indicate their particularities here.

In the 1970s, NB Tel made a series of decisions about infrastructure development which turned out to be crucial in giving them a head start on developments in the 1990s. The decisions were determined by two things: the lack of a single large urban centre in the province and the fact that one of the two multinational companies operating out of the province, owned by the McCain family, was located in the hamlet of Florenceville, in a relatively remote northwest area of the province. Instead of introducing more advanced services only in one or two large urban centres, as most other telephone companies were doing at the time, NB Tel had strong incentives to make its most advanced digital network ubiquitous throughout the province from the start. Thus, as more advanced uses of telephones became widespread through telematics, New Brunswick found itself already equipped with a fully digital network.[8]

Similarly, the labour force in New Brunswick has been shaped by a long history of economic disadvantage and high unemployment, recently buttressed by the decline of formerly key sectors such as the fisheries, mining and shipbuilding. A significant proportion of the income level of New Brunswickers had traditionally been made up through social programmes, funded by federal transfer payments. By the early 1990s, reform of both the nationally regulated unemployment scheme and the provincially governed welfare benefits had introduced strict new eligibility requirements and reduced benefits. At the outset, the call centre job creation strategy was envisioned by the provincial government as tied to its efforts to move welfare recipients off the roles and into paid employment.[9] This initiative quickly dropped from public view when it became clear that there was an abundance of educated New Brunswickers not on welfare in line for the new jobs. Many of them were young people, university or college students or recent graduates who might otherwise have had to leave the province to look for work. Most of this generation of workers did not look favourably upon unions[10] and didn't have pre-conditioned expectations about what

a workplace would provide to them. In this way, they were ideal employees for companies coming to New Brunswick looking for higher productivity, a lot of flexibility (many of the centres have demanding shift schedules) and fewer demands from their workforce.

The firms that reorganized to place centralized calling operations in New Brunswick were at the same time reorganizing space within the workplaces themselves. Generally, the call centre environment tends to resemble Bentham's Panopticon.[11] Employees in call centres work in public isolation: in a large room filled with cubicles, grouped in islands or rows, each equipped with headsets and computers. One of the larger call centres I visited resembled a large aeroplane hanger with hundreds of diminutive cubicles arranged in clusters throughout the wide open space. Very little personalization of workspaces is permitted. While each individual is tethered to his or her own workspace by the headset, supervisors can monitor the calls of any worker at any time without their knowledge. In addition, for each employee, at the end of the day, a computer printout can be produced which provides an exact statistical breakdown of that caller's daily output.

Through the combination of random in-person monitoring and constant on-line monitoring, individual employees' performance is rendered highly visible to management, as well as to other employees (Clement 1992; Belt, Richardson and Webster 1999). Both inbound and outbound centres often use large visual displays to publicize performance levels and goals. In inbound centres, electronic displays may show the number of calls (or minutes per call) in the queue at any given time; outbound centres may display sales figures for various "teams." It is important that calls neither wait too long in the queue, nor that callers have to make repeat calls to solve one problem. However, what most call centres do not explicitly acknowledge is that these goals are in conflict, and as the section below on the role of call centre workers will examine, call centres are organized so that it falls to individual employees to develop strategies for successfully negotiating the contradiction between providing good service to each customer and meeting productivity quotas for dealing with high volumes of calls.

Many call centres have recently adopted what they call a "team" approach, although the impact of teams on the organization of work is often quite insignificant. In outbound centres, productivity is generally measured quantitatively on the basis of sales figures, or by a combination of percentage of successful sales and "talk time" (the length of each call). Teams are used either to keep track of employees selling particular campaigns, which are usually associated with particular incentive structures dictated by the client, or within a particularly large campaign, they may be used for in-house motivational purposes, with charts and displays showing the relative performance.

Within firms operating large in-house customer service bureaus the impact of the transition to a "team-oriented" workplace can be more substantial, yet as an employee interviewed at one very large firm observed, the implementation of a "team-oriented" approach can be done in a way that significantly increases workloads without reorganizing work. By reorganizing workers into teams, her company had saved cost by eliminating a higher paid level of supervisory positions, while transferring those responsibilities onto the interviewee, who was an already overworked and less-well-paid team leader. However, employees interviewed at other firms reported that they welcomed the additional responsibil-

ities that came with membership in a "team" since they offered chances for collaboration, creativity or problem solving, were perceived as routes to career advancement or simply as a break from the monotony of the phones. The difference seemed to lie in whether the firm organized employee time in such a way that additional work responsibilities attached to team work were recognized and accounted for in the context of the employee's workday. Those firms most wedded to the Panopticon model of supervision appeared least able to make this shift. This often-touted "high road" to flexibility seems to require a much more decentralized workplace, with greater autonomy and less supervisory scrutiny of individual employees than is common among call centres.

"If You Have the Work, We Have the Force": Inventing a Local Economic Development Strategy[12]

Call centres are made possible by telematics, the combination of telecommunications and software technologies that can coordinate, through the predictive dialling of outbound or switching of inbound calls, the simultaneous connection of a telephone call and the display of account information to a service representative. Although this technology is not particularly new, its dissemination to places like New Brunswick has facilitated the corporate reorganizations that are bringing the call centres there as well. However, back-officing is both a fickle and footloose type of investment. Most firms rent their premises and bring in computers and other equipment purchased elsewhere. The government of New Brunswick had to work to distinguish itself from the plethora of other possible generic locations for this type of work and establish the province as an attractive "site" for call centre operations.

There were a number of factors that made this an attractive initiative for the government of Premier Frank McKenna early in its mandate. Firstly, the McKenna government took initiatives to reform welfare and other social programmes along fiscally conservative lines in the early 1990s, for example by developing workfare programmes (in some cases mandatory) and strengthening enforcement against welfare fraud, to reduce disincentives to work. To make those initiatives politically palatable, however, it was necessary to also produce a serious job creation initiative. At the outset, call centres were discussed in the context of welfare reform, and a programme was conceived, and briefly implemented, which put welfare recipients to work on the phones.[13] This programme didn't last very long as it soon became clear that there were many more qualified people, not on welfare, who would line up for these jobs. Although government officials were always careful to point out that the call centres were only a small part of a more comprehensive job creation strategy for the province, at least in terms of numbers of jobs created, the call centre strategy eventually grew to become the cornerstone of the provincial government's job creation efforts.[14]

At first, the strategy was to establish that it was possible to compete with most other places in North America on purely economic logic. Wages and rents were low, payroll taxes non-existent and workers' compensation very affordable in the province compared to other locations. In addition, the way in which the New Brunswick Telephone Company was organized made it possible to lease the phones and switching technologies that firms required at relatively low rates (compared to the costs of purchasing this type of equipment elsewhere). While NB Tel is in the private sector, both government sources and those interviewed at NB Tel referred to the working relationship between the two entities as a "close" one. While the precise extent to which NB Tel, a private company, and the provincial government collaborated on the call centre strategy is not clear, it is significant that the original impetus for the strategy came from a government employee who had recently relocated from NB Tel.[15] While the government appeared to take the lead in initiating a firm's move to the province through marketing, providing cost/benefit analyses, and financial incentives, the service provided by NB Tel was identified by most firms as a major factor in the decision to relocate.

In addition to providing a favourable cost comparison to firms considering relocation, the province also offered forgivable loans to offset costs to firms associated with start-up and training of new employees. In the first five years of the programme, the province paid out more than 28 million dollars to call centres.[16] According to Premier McKenna, this amount was necessary in order to compete with similar offers from other jurisdictions.[17] The amounts of the loans were public information, but the basis on which they were calculated was not.[18] A very general estimate based on the relationship between the size of the operation and the "loan" would place the amounts at approximately $10,000 per job. Most of the grants were contingent on the creation by a firm of a specified number of full-time equivalent positions over a period of three years. Failure to do this could result in a loan being called, although this had not occurred as of May, 1997. Firms were reluctant to comment on the role played by the loans in encouraging their relocation to New Brunswick rather than another province, although they appear to have had some influence. Finally, in terms of more formal, statutory changes, while the province did eliminate the provincial sales tax on 1-800 numbers, it appears to have passed no other legislation specifically to attract call centres.[19] While economic factors such as local labour and real estate costs, the technological services and support offered by NB Tel, and the payment of financial incentives go some way in explaining the relocation of a few firms to New Brunswick, they do not tell the whole story.

In order to adequately explain the rapid emergence of a market for call centres in New Brunswick, one needs to integrate an analysis of shifts and initiatives at the level of discourse with these economic realities. While few would argue that ideas and images circulating in the mainstream media have had both a powerful constraining and enabling influence on public perceptions about the economy, and on policy makers, the work of the imagination is not frequently singled out as a driving force in the transformation of either economic relations or regulatory institutions.[20] Yet, I would argue that the strategic marketing of New Brunswick as a site for call centre operations involved the constructive work of the imagination along two intersecting dimensions: first, in realizing New Brunswick's aspirations to become a desired location for call centres, and secondly, in constituting a willing, committed and docile labour force to work at those centres. In order to transform external perception of itself into an attractive site for this type of investment, the province commissioned studies, placed advertisements, sent representatives to telemarketing conferences, arranged private meetings between the Premier and corporate heads and offered significant sums to firms choosing to relocate. Throughout, it held out the existence

of a large, willing, well-educated, bilingual workforce as one of the key factors in attracting firms. The success of the strategy depended in large measure upon the truth of that claim.

At the same time as it was seeking out the call centres, the province also had to market at another level, promoting the centres to New Brunswickers as a good place to work. The call centres were tied to a wider set of policies intended to promote information technology and computer literacy within the province. People were promised that the call centres would be their "on-ramp to the information highway." They were touted by the Premier as "high-skill, high wage, pollution free jobs."[21] At least in part, through actively disseminating its vision of a potential teleservice and telemarketing industry both within the province and outside of it, the government was able to bring one into being, even though the reality may have failed to match the rhetoric in many cases.[22]

This two-level process—marketing a distinctive local labour force while actively engaged in constituting it—was most vividly illustrated by a particular teleservice industry event which I attended in Moncton, NB in 1996. I found myself seated in a ballroom overflowing with people first thing in the morning. The crowd was mixed, men and women, some in business dress, some casual, and they ranged widely in age. The event had been advertised as a teleservice industry job fair, one of the first of its kind in North America. What made it unique was the fact that no actual jobs were involved. None of the firms which attended the fair said that they were using it to fill immediate employment requirements.[23] The primary purpose of the job fair, put on by a group called the "Teleservice Labour Force Development Committee" which appeared to be tied to the Greater Moncton Economic Development

Committee, was to generate a database of "potential call centre employees" for the local Chamber of Commerce.

Each of the several hundred people who attended one of the three "information sessions" during the day was asked to fill out a form listing his or her name, age, and qualifications, including language skills. The data were then entered on to a list which would primarily be used to assure companies considering locating in the province that there continued to be a large pool of eager, well-educated and bilingual people in Moncton waiting for the chance to work at a call centre. The job fair followed a period in which the press had reported that the incredible Moncton success story had tapped out the local labour market, and that companies were choosing to locate in competing locations, including most obviously neighbouring Charlottetown, PEI, rather than take their chance on Moncton's dwindling labour force.

As the crowded ballroom and conversations with call centre managers in Moncton attested, the reports of the labour pool's demise was premature at best. Few, if any, of the call centres found it necessary to advertise for employees. Most received at least 10 unsolicited applications for every position they needed to fill and continued to receive a regular flow of enquiries on an ongoing basis, whether or not they were hiring. Many preferred to conduct their hiring through local temporary services agencies, by employing a regular percentage of their staff (sometimes as much as 50 percent) through the agency, and hiring as permanent employees a select few after they had worked at the firm full-time for several months or even a year.

In the ballroom, there was a screening of a 10-minute promotional video intended to market Moncton to potential call centre employers. It emphasized the high degree of education, training and specialization of the "new talent" located in the area, the low cost of doing business in the region, including reduced operating expenses and cost of living savings. The technological and service advantages offered by NB Tel were also praised. After the video, human resources managers from several of Moncton's largest call centres (some of whom had been featured giving "testimonials" in the video) gave presentations which emphasized the rewarding nature of customer service work and the opportunities presented by working in a dynamic, information-technology driven industry. They identified the qualities that a good customer service representative should have as communication skills, willingness to work flexible shifts, a people-oriented personality, and the ability to work in a team environment. Later, the general qualifications for employment at call centres were laid out by a representative of the local business association. These were identified as a high school diploma and basic keyboarding skills. Bilingualism and some customer service experience were also considered helpful, and could be indicated on the form.

The "Job Fair" revealed that the work of representing call centre jobs as highly desirable, career-oriented opportunities was not only done by the provincial government; municipal governments, local Chambers of Commerce, the industry association and the firms themselves have all been actively involved in the ongoing construction of a certain image of call centre work. In addition to participating in these types of events, the firms reinforce the idea of this work as "professional" through such things as the enforcement of fairly formal dress codes, despite the fact that employees are never seen by customers.[24] Many of the larger companies spend a significant proportion of the two to three week training period educating employees in the firm's "philosophy" and policies. Employees (even those working through temporary agencies) were given opportunities to compete for prizes that were usually corporate merchandise of one type or another. Opportunities to advance within the firm are held out as the "carrot" to new employees; one interviewee reported that she had been interviewed by a woman who had started with the firm as a teleservice representative, and told her that she had been promoted six times. The clear message the employees are to receive, despite firm organizational strategies which appear to indicate the contrary, is that they too will be promoted and that teleservice is merely the first step in a career with the company.[25]

The successful "professionalization" of call centre work within New Brunswick is in sharp contrast to the situation elsewhere, as revealed by the views of call centre employees interviewed in Toronto and Winnipeg.[26] Particularly in Toronto, they referred to the work as a marginal, temporary stop-gap until something better came along. In New Brunswick, while the jobs tend to occupy the same marginalized place in a firm's organizational structures, most employees I spoke with, apart from several university students, approached the job as a permanent position. Several younger call centre employees reported that they had picked teleservice as their chosen career. The seriousness with which New Brunswick call centre employees approach their jobs is bolstered by the fact that most of those who work at the centres have at least some post-secondary education, including some with two-year degrees from newly minted community college courses

in teleservice. Some have paid $1,400 for a 35-week course offered by a private firm that boasts of placing 90 percent of its graduates directly into local teleservice jobs. While these courses may serve only a limited training function even for inbound call centre employment, where most workers are hired with no previous experience and are on the job after about two weeks of training, they do provide another avenue through which prospective workers can be socialized and funneled into these positions. It would appear that the most important function of employee training, in-house, in community colleges or in private firms, is to encourage new employees to see themselves and the work as serious and important; to give workers a sense of themselves as professionalized participants in the larger corporate world, the boundaries of which extend well beyond the province of New Brunswick.[27]

Life on the Line: Accommodation and Resistance in Call Centre Work

I have suggested that New Brunswickers' attitudes and actions in responding to the influx of call centre work are also an important aspect of how the global search for productive labour unfolded itself in this part of the Maritimes. Companies who located to New Brunswick found the workers initially to be eager, determined and uncomplaining.[28] The interviews I conducted with employees generally supported this view. Many were very pleased to have obtained what they considered to be a good job in a call centre. Even when they expressed concerns in confidential interviews with this researcher, they were often qualified in their criticisms of their employers. One woman who does shift work for a firm that provides financial services expressed concerns about the ease with which a company might exploit the reasonableness of its employees:

I love my job. Like, what are you going to say. But mostly people are happy. But I guess I think companies owe—I think people are going more than halfway. The employees are good people, you know, they don't want the sun and the earth. There are just some things that would be fairer. They wouldn't say that I don't think. So, I have been sitting on the fence watching, but people are pretty happy—I think the potential is there to abuse the situation.

In her own workplace, she is one of a significant number of part-time employees who never know from week to week how many hours or what shifts they will be asked to work. Employees are routinely sent home partway through a shift if a centre is slow, even though many of them commute quite significant distances. Similar workplace practices were the impetus for the unionization of a telefundraising centre in Toronto in 1996, yet unionization was not an alternative publicly embraced by the call centre employees I spoke with in New Brunswick.[29]

Among some workers, reluctance to complain might stem as much from a fear of reprisal as a general attitude of acceptance. Most call centres that were not unionized made no secret of their hostility toward the possibility. Although many might agree that unionization could improve conditions, one employee observed, "They're so afraid of that word because immediately they think they are going to lose their job if they talk union at all."[30] Although job security was identified as an important issue by New Brunswickers, only those few who have gained permanent employee status at one

of the three unionized centres reported that they felt that their jobs were secure.[31]

Although it is clear that New Brunswickers were happy for the influx of jobs and reluctant to do anything that might jeopardize them, few anticipated what coping with the day-to-day demands of the work would require. Service jobs which involve almost constant interactions with customers require very well developed interpersonal communication skills, yet these skills are rarely recognized as such. In addition to the written scripts discussed in an earlier section, the performance of these jobs requires employees to enact "emotional scripts" which reflect gendered social expectations. Arlie Hochschild, in her influential study of flight attendants, identified the performative, gendered, and largely invisible work done by service workers as "emotional labour" (Hochschild 1983; Wharton 1993). Emotional labour is a useful term because it brings into focus one of the least visible ways in which women's social roles in the private sphere are both extrapolated into workplace expectations and personalized, so that they become part of job requirements, yet not identified as "skills" (Hall 1993; Jenson 1989; Poynton 1993). While approximately 80 percent of call centre workers in New Brunswick are women, everyone who works in a call centre has to develop ways of managing the "feminized" emotional and interpersonal demands the jobs placed upon them (Belt, Richardson and Webster 1999; Duffy and Pupo 1992; Jenson 1989; 1996).

Telephone work may be more challenging than other types of service work because of the "narrow bandwidth" of the method of communication. Call centre workers must have the ability to immediately communicate a friendly, helpful and professional demeanor in a few spoken words. The work involved in projecting friendliness over the phone appears to be quite similar to that described in studies of waitresses and flight attendants, where a key component of the job is the ability to continue to smile regardless of how you feel or how others treat you. One call centre employee said that they were told to smile while they were speaking to customers on the phone because it would make them sound friendlier. She said that she believed that it did work, and if she was having trouble with a particular caller, would silently ask herself whether she was smiling.[32] Not only must workers be able to sound friendly on the phone, they must continue to be friendly as unhappy or upset customers complain and criticize, enacting the script of the deferential "servant" over the phone. Although it might seem less likely, there also seems to be a component of scripted flirtation in call centre work just as there is in waitressing. One young woman who was the top salesperson in a telemarketing centre, when asked to share the secret of her success, admitted that she used a different tone of voice if the caller was a man. Her sales pitch for men was higher, more singsong, and definitely more flirtatious, while her pitch for women was lower, firm, and businesslike. The two-tone approach had also worked to dramatically improve the sales of one of her female friends at work who had formerly been having trouble making quota.[33] Although the call centre jobs are attractive to potential employees because they are perceived as office jobs and because they pay better than minimum wage, many workers find that the demands of the jobs raise their stress levels beyond what they are prepared to accept. In comparing her own work experiences, one interviewee ranked telemarketing below waitressing because of

the stress level, despite the better pay. She no longer worked as a telemarketer, but had gone to the media to publicize working conditions among telemarketers in her city. "I would rather stay on my feet for eight hours a day and work waitress work than sit there for four hours and be stressed out the way I would be stressed out." In describing the job stresses, many workers refer to the confined nature of the work, the repetition, the monotony. One woman, who had worked for a couple of years at call centres while going to school, explained why she could not imagine herself returning to phone work as follows:

> I'm burnt out on phones. The thought of tethering myself to another desk, to be stuck there for eight hours, only being able to move within a ten-foot radius, for eight hours, doing the same thing every 90 seconds.... I don't think I could do it anymore. I just don't have the patience to handle it.[34]

Keeping the customer happy is as important a part of the telephone worker's job as the teller's, the waitress's or the retail salesperson's. However, it can be much more difficult, particularly where someone has been on hold for 10 or 15 minutes. Teleworkers refer to angry callers as "irates." How well one deals with "irates" can be a key component in performance evaluations as well as in an individual's ability to cope with the work over the longer term. Employees seem to vary significantly in how effective they are at managing "irates," as well as in the extent to which the calls "get to them." Those workers who could establish a degree of emotional distance between themselves and the caller appeared to be the least likely to experience the jobs as overwhelmingly stressful. Since evaluations are generally based on talk time as well as quality or outcome (usually "conversions," meaning sales), it is important for callers to "get control" of a call and deal with the problem in as short a time as possible, while still leaving the customer with the impression that they are important. One interview subject shared a handout distributed to employees at her workplace that provided tips on how to reduce talk time by getting control of a conversation and keeping it, which included asking specific questions and politely but firmly refocusing callers attention back to the matter at hand if they had a tendency to stray.

Not all call centre workers were happy to rely on the employers' scripts and tips for dealing with customers or potential customers. Some identified with the people they were calling and were reluctant to pressure them into a purchase or a reservation. One woman who worked selling insurance for an outbound telemarketing firm said that she told management when they put her on a "campaign" that she felt was not a good deal, that she would not work as hard to sell that particular product. She was a top performer elsewhere, and had good relationships with her superiors, so she felt that she could do this without putting her job in jeopardy.[35] Others simply managed the dilemma by resisting silently, refusing to cross certain self-imposed lines to make a sale, even if it meant that they would have poor performance records. Over time, this might mean that they would earn significantly less money, or even lose their jobs. In larger urban centres like Toronto, many telemarketing employees simply move on to another firm.

While the outbound centres relied almost exclusively on quantitative performance indicators, in the inbound call centre environment there could be a significant amount of variation between firms. In the effort to implement a more customer-service oriented form of work organization, some have chosen to base all, or a significant component, of their employee evaluations on the results of (qualitative) customer satisfaction surveys rather than on numbers of calls serviced in a given period or other (readily available) quantitative measures. Employees subjected to exclusively quantitative measures of productivity had a harder time understanding or learning how to improve their performance. They are often less motivated to do so, because they perceive that the standards are unfair or arbitrary,[36] and would be more likely to engage in acts of resistance, including work slow down, using up sick days, or subversion of the monitoring system.

Rather than being empowered by their workday access to the information highway as they might have imagined, call centre workers more often find themselves disempowered, and even dehumanized by it. One call centre employee described her relationship to the technology in terms of Heidegger's notion of the "standing reserve," that is, "things that are not even regarded as objects, because their only important quality has become their readiness for use" (Heidegger 1977). As she put it, "you are standing waiting until that call comes in to use you to make money. And you are simply another part of that machine."[37] Increasing the amount of authority a worker is given to solve customer problems seems likely to increase both their level of job satisfaction and reduce their inclination to subvert the system, while those who can't do anything for irate customers except transfer them to a supervisor may, out of frustration, be less inclined to try to learn ways to deal with upset callers. More autonomy allows the worker room to accommodate her own goals and aspirations, her sense of herself as a professional worker, to the demands and stresses of the work. On the other hand, the limited autonomy and highly quantitative productivity indicators in most call centres tend to undermine the "professionalization" approach that had been so successful in bringing employees to the centres in the first place. Despite this apparent contradiction, most firms studied in New Brunswick (with a few exceptions)[38] continued to prefer hierarchical forms of work organization and high levels of employee monitoring and control to the risk of granting more autonomy and flexibility to employees, despite the likelihood that employees would be better able to utilize the skills they have, and be more productive and more satisfied at work.

While New Brunswickers seem less willing to take their chances on finding another position that might be marginally better than teleworkers elsewhere, there are more alternatives for experienced teleworkers as the number of firms located in the province's three small urban centres increases. It may be that the hyper-mobile telemarketing culture of Toronto will yet be replicated in New Brunswick in the future. However, for the time being, the major ways in which employees accommodate themselves to call centre work in New Brunswick is through the notion of "professionalization" that I discussed above. In marked contrast to other urban centres, where telework (especially telemarketing) is held in such low regard that workers are embarrassed to reveal what they do for a living, having a call centre job in New Brunswick is still a very desirable thing. This may stem from the contrast between inbound and outbound centres. A greater proportion of centres that have located in the province are inbound, and tend to pay better wages, hire full-

time employees and offer benefits and some limited opportunities for advancement. These are the types of jobs that New Brunswickers imagine when they think of call centres, and in the current economic climate and low cost of living in the province, they can be described as "good jobs." While many call centres in the province don't offer these "good jobs," even those working at other centres imagine that they will have an opportunity to move up from one to the other.

However, the call centre story in New Brunswick is young yet. While many of those I interviewed there said that they imagined themselves working at the call centre for a long time, none had actually been doing the work for more than three years. Even those with "good jobs," after a couple of years, appear to start having difficulties with the work. One woman whom I interviewed in April of 1997 told me that she was on the edge of quitting her job, although it paid $14 an hour, because of the "constant negatives" that make up her working day. Six months later, when I spoke with her again, she was still working at the same job, but still on the edge of leaving. She had been a frequent user of sick days and often went home early when she was having a difficult time with the work. She said that the "money was a trap" that kept her in the job despite the growing signs of stress that she was observing in her own life. After being refused a period of unpaid leave, she was seriously considering taking a stress leave, even though she feared what her family and friends will think about a 23-year-old who can't "handle it."[39]

Even though the approach of most New Brunswickers to surviving call centre work appears to incline towards more accommodation than explicit resistance, there may be a point at which this tendency will shift. The work appears to become more difficult for people over time, and employers' expectations and demands will likely increase in the future. Either way, more pressures on employees will likely result in more people finding their coping skills stretched to the maximum. The qualities of New Brunswickers that make them such an attractive local labour force, their serious attitudes towards the work, the eagerness to perform well, the low turnover rates, and reluctance to unionize may gradually shift as New Brunswickers learn that the call centre jobs are not all that they were promised to be.

Conclusion

The first two sections of this chapter examined the role of strategic decisions on the part of the provincial government and restructuring firms which have converged in the emergence of a growing local specialization in the provision of telephone services in New Brunswick. I argued that the emergence of this market was created through the initiative of the provincial government in both constituting, through external marketing efforts, the province as a "desirable site" for call centre operations and simultaneously producing, by internally promoting the call centre jobs, a local labour force which was attractive to firms. Firm relocation decisions, in my assessment, were driven in large measure by their belief in the existence of this labour force. I then went on to suggest, in the third section, that the role of the workers themselves also had to be taken into account. While the provincial government and the firms were the participants in the initial negotiations that led to the arrival of call centres in the province in order to understand the unfolding dynamic of call centre restructuring, one must see it as the product of ongoing negotiations between firms

and their workers, conditioned by the social and political climate of the province.

I have only begun to tell this story here. Further research needs to be conducted on the emerging tactics of employees as they adapt to the conditions of work in the call centres. There is some evidence of increasing rates of turnover at call centres in the province which present the most stressful working conditions. I've suggested that people may not be able to perform at a high level in these types of repetitive and monotonous jobs over extended periods of time. The use of stress and sick leave in those workplaces that have such benefits may also increase as employees begin to feel more secure in their jobs. Over time, the strategies and responses of workers will play an increasingly important role in the evolution of the "call centre" market here. This role will be particularly important given the findings of this chapter regarding the double-edged nature of the story surrounding the emergence of the call centre phenomenon. While the valorization of the call centre work as "professional" has brought workers into the labour force and imbued them with new levels of optimism and aspirations about their future, many will end up being disappointed by their inability to advance or the limited skills they acquire in the job. On the other hand, while firms are currently pleased with the high levels of productivity their new workforces are displaying, it may only be a matter of time before employees, encouraged by their ability to move between centres, begin to make greater demands in terms of wages, working conditions or shifts. At this stage, in trying to assess the impact of call centres on the province of New Brunswick, it is difficult to come up with either a wholehearted critique or endorsement. The eventual outcome of developments here, like other sites where global processes meet local actors, will depend on a longer trajectory of locally based struggles and accommodations.

Thus, while the changes in New Brunswick are clearly driven by familiar structural global processes, such as the centralization of high-profit activities and decentralization of routine functions by firms and the increasing segmentation and flexibilization of labour, this chapter aims to illustrate how local histories and cultures also play an important role in the process of change currently "taking place" there. In this way, this account of call centres in New Brunswick leavens hegemonic accounts of globalization with the particularities of local history and the agency of workers and communities struggling to retain or recapture opportunity, security and even prosperity on the current shifting economic terrain. It illustrates the uneasy accommodation in a particular locality of a number of strands of the current transformation, the implications of new telecommunications technologies, firm level restructuring, the changing role of government at all levels and the accommodations and resistances of the local labour force, without ascribing to any of them a determining role. Rather, the story is the amalgam of tactical responses to the uncertain conditions of globalization simultaneously pursued by governments, firms, and workers.

Endnotes

1 This chapter draws on interviews and field work conducted for a larger case study of the emergence of the New Brunswick call centre industry over the past several years. A mail survey of companies which had relocated to the province was conducted between May and July of 1996, and site visits to eight call centres were made during that time. In addition, semi-structured interviews with 10 call centre managers and 30 employees were conducted between May 1996 and July 1997. Several follow-up interviews were also conducted in December of 1997. The research was supported by the Canadian Institute for Advanced Research in the fall semester of 1996. The Law Foundation of New Brunswick and the University of British Columbia Hampton Fund also provided assistance.

2 Jane Jenson suggested this helpful wording to me.

3 A recent half-page advertisement placed in the *Globe and Mail* by the Government of New Brunswick cites a Deloitte and Touche Nacore 1995 Benchmarking Study, "It is not uncommon to achieve labour cost savings of more than 20 percent and real estate cost savings of more than 33 percent by back-officing."

4 One interview participant suggested, however, that the databases are only as reliable as the franchisees. Much information on the database that she worked with (for a centre that supported a number of hotel chains) was inaccurate, out of date or incomplete.

5 I will discuss further the ways in which individual employees adapt to both the monitored and scripted nature of their jobs in a subsequent section.

6 Personal interview with call centre worker, Fredericton, NB, July, 1996.

7 Personal interview with union representative, St. John, NB, June 12, 1997.

8 Personal interview with Brian Freeman, Acting Director, Information Highway Secretariat, Department of Economic Development and Tourism, May 16,1997.

9 New Brunswick was one of the first Canadian jurisdictions to introduce a mandatory workfare programme. Freeman, Alan. 1993 "New Brunswick Hits the Books After Years of Hard Knocks." *The Globe and Mail,* January 16.

10 Some referred to the experience of their parents; others had followed media coverage of a few recent, bitter and unsuccessful strikes. The two-year strike of refinery workers at the Irving plant in St. John, ending in 1996, was notable both for its length and the outcome for the workers, all of whom were replaced.

11 I owe this useful analogy to Zuboff (1988).

12 The slogan is borrowed from a half-page advertisement placed by the province of New Brunswick in *The Globe and Mail* (national edition) in January, 1998.

13 Students from NB Works, the workfare programme, and the NB Community College were invited to the opening of the United Parcel Service Centre in Fredericton. The Premier was reported as having said to them, "I want you to know that all the hard work that you have made to upgrade your skills is going to give you a chance at a job. I want you to go back to your classes and tell others that there is hope out there." "Thank Yous All Around as NB Lands UPS Jobs," *Telegraph Journal,* January 12, 1995.

14 By 1999, call centres employed approximately 9,000 people in the province, according to the Department of Economic Development and Tourism, personal communication, October 20, 1999.

15 Personal interview with Brian Freeman, Department of Economic Development and Tourism, May 14, 1997. Freeman joined the Department of Economic Development and Tourism in 1989, at the same time as Kevin Bulmer, whom he credits with the suggestion that the province might have an economic development "driver" in the telecom sector. He advised that Bulmer had come to government from NB Tel.

16 Meagher, David, "$28 Million Aid to Call Centres," *The [Fredericton] Daily Gleaner,* May 1, 1996.

17 "We have never really been able to compete with the other provinces in terms of money because we have never had as much. So, usually we try to put as much on the table ... enough on the table so we will not be thrown out of that game and that the rest of our competitive advantage will allow us to win. But, most of the competitors, we could beat ... jurisdictions with more money." Interview with Frank McKenna, December 29, 1997.

18 Brian Freeman advised that there was no specific programme in place for loans (i.e., number of dollars per job created) but that the loans were part of an individualized process of negotiation with a firm considering relocation.

19 A search of revisions to provincial statutes and regulations in the areas of employment standards, labour, occupational health and safety and taxation between 1990–1995 conducted by a University of New Brunswick (UNB) law student working as a research assistant on this project in the summer of 1996 revealed no other significant changes that would benefit call centre operations.

20 The idea of the imagination as functioning in this constructive way, as work rather than play, comes from Appadurai (1996:31): "The image, the imagined, the imaginary—these are all terms that direct us to something critical and new in global cultural processes: the imagination as a social practice ... the imagination has become an organized field of social practices, a form of work (in the sense of both labour and culturally organized practice), and a form of negotiation between sites of agency (individuals) and globally defined fields of possibility."

21 "Premier Challenged on Job Creation," *The Daily Gleaner,* August 2, 1995.

22 In an interview with CBC Radio May 27,1997, Premier Frank McKenna acknowledged the difference in wages and working conditions among the call centres; in particular, the contrast between inbound and outbound centres, and commented that the province was focussing its efforts on "moving up the food chain" in its efforts to attract more investment in inbound centres, and particularly, technical support bureaus which would require a more highly skilled workforce. He later confirmed this observation, and added that it was necessary to provide work for people of "all skill sets," so the fact that call centres presented a range in remuneration levels and working conditions didn't seem to him to present a problem. Personal interview, December 29, 1997.

23 Two call centre employees whom I interviewed subsequently (December 1997) reported that they had been hired six and nine months after attending the "Job Fair" (one was in Moncton, the other attended a similar event in St. John, NB). In both cases, the employee was contacted for an interview by a temporary agency which provided employees to one of the larger centres in their respective cities. Both hope that they will eventually be hired on by the firm. Personal interviews, December 1997.

24 One 20-year-old man showed me a dress code protocol which precluded him from wearing his earring to work, despite the fact that he worked a graveyard shift, along with only two other employees, two nights a week.

25 The significance of the collective construction of a "professionalized" attitude towards low-skilled work is developed in a very interesting study by Leslie Salinger (1997) which contrasts the attitudes towards work of two very different immigrant Latina domestic worker cooperatives. In one of these cooperatives, both the value of the work done by the women and their perceptions of themselves as workers were effectively transformed through a dynamic of professionalization which characterized the groups operations.

26 Personal interviews were conducted with 40 call centre employees in Toronto and Winnipeg in June and July, 1998 as part of a Status of Women Canada report (Buchanan and Koch-Schulte 2000). For a preliminary discussion of the comparative views of teleworkers on the nature of their jobs, see Buchanan (forthcoming 2000).

27 Incidentally, an instructor at a community college course designed for call centre work advised that basic North American geography was one of the subjects that their course included, and added that she had been quite amazed at the lack of basic geographic knowledge displayed by some of her students.

28 An employee at an outbound centre in St. John reported, "They cannot believe the quality here in Canada and they are amazed at the quality of people here at this call centre. Our accuracy rate is fantastic, just phenomenal compared to the other ones. They rate us against the other call centres and we're number one and we've only been in business here for six months. We're beating call centres that have been in business two and three years." Personal interview with a female call centre worker, June 13, 1996, St. John.

29 I spoke with five employees and former employees of the unionized Toronto centre in October 1996. Several specifically identified the practice of sending slow-performing callers home early as the key factor in mobilizing workers to organize, although many other workplace practices were also unacceptable. When asked how she was able to convince her fellow telefundraisers to sign union cards, one organizer claimed she relied on skills she had acquired raising money for charities at the company. "We're telemarketers, right? We were using telemarketing techniques to sign people up! What better people. It got to the point where there were so many people we were signing up that we had almost like a script.... We used good selling techniques, so we would explain the situation to people, tell them how urgent it was, make them feel as if they were involved in something special, that's another technique. Tell them this is the first telemarketing centre in Canada to have an organizing drive." Personal interview, November 18, 1996. Shortly after the unionization drive, the company opened a second (non-union) centre in New Brunswick, which was closed in the spring of 1998.

30 Personal interview with call centre worker, St. John, June 13, 1996.

31 Incidentally, this meant that gaining access to employees for interviews was quite difficult. For example, the union representative at one workplace who was assisting me in contacting workers for a confidential offsite meeting had difficulty finding individuals who were not afraid they might lose their jobs. In the end, only four workers (out of a workforce of several hundred) attended the confidential meeting in a private home, three of whom were union representatives.

32 Personal interview with call centre worker, April 1997.

33 Personal interview with 28-year-old woman, April 16, 1997. Another young woman interviewed in Toronto, July 1998 reported that she was particularly successful in sales to men, due to the effects of her low husky voice. In fact, her boss at the telemarketing centre where she worked had told her she "should do phone sex." She quit one week later.

34 Interview with 22-year-old woman, St. John, December 23, 1997.

35 Personal interview with telemarketing worker, St. John, November 4, 1996.

36 For example, all of the performance evaluations in one fundraising centre studied were based on the amount of money brought in during a shift. This was despite significant variations in returns produced by the lists of phone numbers forwarded to individual callers by the predictive dialler, over which the callers had no control. Similarly, in the service bureaus, the use of quantitative indicators to measure productivity, such as the measurement of time a caller spent on "not ready" (not available for new inbound calls), could be frustrating for employees. Quantitative indicators excluded time spent after a call resolving a customer's problem.

37 Interview with call centre employee, Toronto, Ontario, November 18, 1996.

38 For example, one firm as part of a more general management restructuring, had expanded the authority of front-line customer service representatives to issue cash refunds or rewards to unhappy customers to $200 without the need for authorization from a supervisor. Previously, a refund for the same amount would have had to have been authorized by several levels of management. The same firm claimed to be increasingly relying on customer satisfaction surveys to evaluate productivity of their employees, although quantitative measures were also available to them. Interview with Human Resources Manager, Moncton, November 22, 1996.

39 Personal interview with call centre worker, December 1997.

References

Appadurai, Arjun. 1996. *Modernity at Large: Cultural Dimensions of Globalization.* Minneapolis: University of Minnesota.

Appelbaum, Eileen. 1993. "New Technology and Work Organization: The Role of Gender Relations." In Belinda Probert and Bruce W. Wilson (eds.). *Pink Collar Blues: Work Gender and Technology.* Carlton, Vic: Melbourne University Press.

Belt, Vicki, Ranald Richardson and Juliet Webster. 1999. "Smiling Down the Phone: Women's Work in Telephone Call Centers." unpublished.

Buchanan, Ruth (forthcoming). "Life on the Line: Survival Strategies of Teleworkers in Canada," in Frank Munger (ed.), *Low Wage Ghetto: Work, Hope and Poverty at the Margins of the New World Order,* London: Sage.

Buchanan, Ruth and Sarah Koch-Schulte (2000). *Gender on the Line: Technology, Restructuring and the Reorganization of Work in the Call Center Industry.* Policy Research Series, Ottawa: Status of Women Canada.

Clement, Andrew. 1992. "Electronic Workplace Surveillance: Sweatshops and Fishbowls." *The Canadian Journal of Information Science,* 17 (4): 18–45.

Castells, Manuel. 1996. *The Rise of the Network Society,* Cambridge: Blackwell.

Duffy, Ann, Daniel Glenday and Norene Pupo (eds.). 1997. *Good Jobs, Bad Jobs, No Jobs: The Transformation of Work in the 21st Century.* Toronto: Harcourt Brace and Company Canada.

Duffy, Anne and Norene Pupo. 1992. *Part-Time Paradox: Connecting Gender, Work and Family.* Toronto: McClelland and Stewart.

Economic Council of Canada. 1990. *Good Jobs, Bad Jobs: Employment in the Service Industry.* Ottawa: Ministry of Supply and Services.

Heidegger, Martin. 1977. *The Question Concerning Technology and other Essays.* New York: Harper and Row.

Hall, Elaine J. 1993. "Smiling, Deferring and Flirting: Doing Gender by Giving 'Good Service.'" *Work and Occupations,* 20 (4): 452–471.

Hochschild, Arlie Russell. 1983. *The Managed Heart: Commercialization of Human Feeling.* Berkeley: University of California Press.

Jenson, Jane. 1989. "The Talents of Women, the Skills of Men: Flexible Specialization and Women." In *The Transformation of Work?: Skill, Flexibility and the Labour Process.* Stephen Wood (ed.). London: Unwin Hyman.

_____. 1996. "Part-Time Employment and Women: A Range of Strategies." In Isabella Bakker (ed.). *Rethinking Restructuring: Gender and Change in Canada.* Toronto: University of Toronto Press.

Meagher, David. 1996. "$28 Million in Aid to Call Centres." *The [Fredericton] Daily Gleaner,* 1 May.

Poynton, Cate. 1993. "Naming Women's Workplace Skills: Linguistics and Power." In Belinda Probert and Bruce W. Wilson (eds.). *Pink Collar Blues: Work, Gender and Technology.* Carlton, Vic: Melbourne University Press.

"Premier Challenged on Job Creation." 1995. *The Daily Gleaner,* August 2.

Sabel, Charles. 1996. "Bootstrapping Reform: Rebuilding Firms, the Welfare State and Unions." *Politics and Society,* 23 (1): 5–48.

Salinger, Leslie. 1997. "A Maid by Any Other Name: The Transformation of 'Dirty Work' by Central American Immigrants." In Lamphere, Ragone and Zavella (eds.). *Situated Lives: Gender and Culture in Everyday Life.* New York: Routledge: 271–291.

Sassen, Saskia. 1991. *The Global City: New York, London, Tokyo.* Princeton NJ: Princeton University Press.

_____. 1996. *Losing Control?: Sovereignty in an Age of Globalization.* New York: Columbia University Press.

_____. 1997. *Informalization as a Systemic Trend in Advanced Market Economies* (unpublished).

Shalla, Vivian. 1997. "Technology and the Deskilling of Work: The Case of Passenger Agents at Air Canada." In Duffy, Ann, Daniel Glenday and Norene Pupo (eds.). *Good Jobs, Bad Jobs, No Jobs: The Transformation of Work in the 21st Century.* Toronto: Harcourt Brace and Company Canada.

Storper, Michael. 1997. *The Regional World: Territorial Development in a Global Economy.* New York: Guilford Press.

Wharton, A. 1993. "The Affective Consequences of Service Work: Managing Emotions on the Job." *Work and Occupations,* 20 (2): 205–232.

Zuboff, Shoshana. 1988. *In the Age of the Smart Machine: The Future of Work and Power.* New York: Basic Books.

SECTION IV: WORKING IN THE FREE-TRADE ZONES OF THE

Critical Thinking Questions

Chapter 7: The Discarded Factory: Degraded Production in the Age of the Superbrand, Naomi Klein

1. Compare the working conditions in the Cavite free-trade zone to those of jobs you have held. Why have workers in free-trade zones not been able to insist that existing employment standards be upheld?

2. Discuss the gendered nature of work in free-trade zones. Has the establishment of free-trade zones created the basis for transforming gender relations at work and in the home?

3. What links can be drawn between work and working conditions in export-processing factories in developing countries and consumer practices in advanced industrialized countries?

Chapter 8: 1-800 New Brunswick: Economic Development Strategies, Firm Restructuring, and the Local Production of "Global" Services, Ruth Buchanan

1. Discuss the similarities and differences between development strategies of underdeveloped regions of the First World and those of Third World countries. Are there similarities in the consequences of these strategies for workers in First and Third worlds?

2. Do call centres provide workers with opportunities to develop transferable skills? What does the example of call centres tell us about skills that are often overlooked in the workplace?

3. How does Buchanan's article help link the processes of restructuring in local economies to the larger processes of globalization? Could Buchanan's research strategy and analysis be used to study processes of change in other communities across Canada?

Recommended Readings

Caspersz, Donella. 1998. "Globalization and Labour: A Case Study of EPZ Workers in Malaysia." *Economic and Industrial Democracy*, Vol. 19, No. 2, pp. 253–286. A case study that analyzes the interplay among class, gender, ethnicity, and nationalism to explain the creation of a labour force for export-processing zones in Malaysia.

Cravey, Altha J. 1998. *Women and Work in Mexico's Maquiladoras*. New York: Rowman and Littlefield. An exploration of how the reorientation of Mexico's development strategy is based on a new gender division of labour in workplaces and households, and how the growth of export-processing zones has been key to the creation of a global female industrial labour force.

Pearson, Ruth. 1998. "'Nimble Fingers' Revisited: Reflections on Women and Third World Industrialisation in the Late Twentieth Century." In Cecile Jackson and Ruth Pearson (eds.), *Feminist Visions of Development: Gender Analysis and Policy*. New York: Routledge, pp. 171–188. A discussion of research findings on Third World women factory workers that serves as the basis for a critical assessment of explanations of women's incorporation into the labour force.

Richardson, Ranald and Vicki Belt. 2001. "Saved by the Bell? Call Centres and Economic Development in Less Favoured Regions." *Economic and Industrial Democracy*, Vol. 22, No. 1, 2001, pp. 67–98. An article that looks at the conditions that foster the growth of call centres as an economic development strategy for less favoured regions in the United Kingdom.

Sussman, Gerald and John A. Lent (eds.). 1998. *Global Productions: Labor in the Making of the "Information Society."* Cresskill, New Jersey: Hampton Press. A collection of essays that explore the nature of communication and information work around the world. The essays seek to develop a better understanding of the global integration of production and the new international division of labour, overlapping processes that are shaped through corporations' use of modern telecommunications and electronic information networks.

Related Websites

Coalition for Justice in the Maquiladoras

http://www.coalitionforjustice.net/

The Coalition for Justice in the Maquiladoras is a tri-national, multi-sectoral coalition of religious, labour, environmental, community and women's groups in Mexico, the United States and Canada. The website contains information, in the form of alerts, about practices of various corporations operating in the maquiladoras that the coalition monitors.

Maquila Solidarity Network

http://www.maquilasolidarity.org/

The Maquila Solidarity Network is a labour and women's rights advocacy organization that promotes solidarity with grassroots groups in Mexico, Central America, and Asia working to improve conditions in maquiladora factories and export-processing zones. The site includes a resource centre that contains a list of publications.

European Network of Excellence in Human Language Technologies

http://www.elsnet.org/ccorglist_c.html#Canada

The European Network of Excellence in Human Language Technologies is an organization supported by the European Commission. The site contains factual information on call centres in different countries including those located in Canada.

John F. Henning Center for International Relations

http://henningcenter.berkeley.edu/projects/exportzones.html

The Henning Center is a project of the University of California at Berkeley Labor Center that promotes the study of labour in the global economy. The site includes information on a project to develop leadership training and resource materials for workers in export-processing zones, as well as information on developments since 2001 at the Kukdong apparel factory, a specific manufacturing plant in Mexico's maquiladora.

Worker Rights Consortium

http://www.workersrights.org/about.asp

The Worker Rights Consortium is a non-profit organization created by college and university administrations, students and labour rights experts. It assists in the enforcement of manufacturing Codes of Conduct adopted by colleges and universities to ensure that factories producing clothing and other goods bearing college and university names respect the basic rights of workers. The site contains a large "press releases" page and numerous reports on the assessment of factories located in different countries.

Section V

Unfree Labour: Migrant Workers and Citizenship

A GROWING BODY of literature in the social sciences has been preoccupied with analyzing various dimensions of international labour migration flows. In an increasingly globalized world, national borders seem to disappear as workers migrate in search of employment and a better life for themselves and their families. A large majority of migrants originate from the poorest regions of the world. The insertion of migrants into advanced capitalist societies has therefore been seen as problematic because they lack the economic and political power to guarantee for themselves basic human rights enjoyed by citizens of the receiving countries. The two articles in this section of the book focus on how migrant workers from Third World countries who come to Canada through the two main programs created to fill labour shortages are constructed as partial, lesser, or non-citizens and are denied basic rights of citizenship. They also highlight the racialized and gendered hierarchical relations and divisions that give shape to citizenship rights. Both articles emphasize that the conditions of admittance of migrant workers create a pool of unfree labour that is open to exploitation and to abuse by employers and the broader community.

In their contribution, Donna Baines and Nandita Sharma use the case of the growing number of people categorized as non-immigrant migrant workers in Canada to argue that citizenship is a mechanism used by nation-states to selectively distribute resources and privileges, thereby creating lesser, or non-citizens who are legally and ideologically denied full participation and protections. Through an analysis of the Non-Immigrant Employment Authorization Program, they demonstrate that in the context of fluid global labour markets, the legal and social category of citizen is used to help maintain a pool of highly exploitable workers who can be described as modern-day indentured labourers. The authors highlight how these migrant workers' temporary status and the assumption that they should not have the right to remain in Canada as permanent residents are key factors that lead to their greater vulnerability and social exclusion. Baines and Sharma are critical of traditional and outdated liberal and social democratic notions of citizenship because they fail to adequately meet the needs of today's highly mobile labour force. They propose that more relevant understandings of citizenship be developed that would end the restrictions on the movement of individuals, families, and communities and that would affirm people's entitlement to remain where they are living, or the right to not be displaced, as well as people's self-determined option to migrate, or the right to move within and across borders. Baines and Sharma conclude that such entitlements would be in line with capital's ability to move around the world with few legal restrictions, and would create a more level playing field for workers from less affluent countries and regions.

Daiva K. Stasiulis and Abigail B. Bakan also examine issues of migrant labour and citizenship, but their focus is on the growing migration of Third World women to Canada through the foreign domestic worker policy to take up positions as nannies, maids, and caregivers in private households. They analyze how global structural realities, such as uneven development, extreme poverty, and structural adjustment policies, create conditions that compel women from Third World countries to seek employment and citizenship on virtually any terms in richer First World countries. The authors also look at how First World countries, such as Canada, are both able and willing to exploit this growing supply of cheap labour in order to resolve social and economic problems within their own territorial boundaries. Stasiulis and Bakan argue that even though Canada's foreign domestic worker policy is often regarded as less abusive than policies in other countries that strive to develop this labour pool, it is nonetheless typical in its construction of the non-citizenship rights of foreign domestic workers. The authors analyze the processes whereby migrant domestic workers find themselves excluded from many basic citizenship rights that Canadians take for granted, such as the choice of employer and domicile, while their employers enjoy full citizenship rights. Stasiulis and Bakan contend that even though better-off First World citizen-women experience some alleviation from their female oppression, the generalized condition of women's oppression is being perpetuated rather than eradicated through programs and policies such as the in-home employment of migrant domestic workers. They conclude with a call for a critical assessment of structural adjustment policies nationally and internationally to address the global problem of labour exploitation.

CHAPTER 9

Migrant Workers as Non-Citizens:

The Case against Citizenship as a Social Policy Concept

Donna Baines and Nandita Sharma

Introduction

FACILITATING THE MOVEMENT of individuals and communities from second-class citizenship to full, participatory citizenship has been a preferred social justice strategy for many on the Left. Indeed, within the Canadian social policy and community development literature, the debate over how to re-energize concepts such as citizenship has raged hotly since the mid-1980s.[1] Citizenship is not, however, an unproblematic or wholly inclusive concept. Numerous authors have argued that concepts like citizenship are highly homogenizing and belie the differences in power and resources that criss-cross imagined communities of common interest.[2]

Throughout the history of citizen-making, statuses such as second-class citizen and non-citizen have coexisted continuously alongside the status of full citizen.[3] Our experience in

mobilizing this concept in activism, education and policy development has led us to question whether citizenship can function at the level of theory, policy, or practice without non-citizens and second-class citizens, or whether these marginalizations are an essential part of how citizenship works in the world. While an exact "one-to-one" correspondence between theory and practice rarely occurs in the nitty-gritty world of social activism and social change, the concepts we use in social policy development and social activism are intensely political practices and merit careful review lest we inadvertently legitimize and extend injustice and inequality. As Catrina Brown (2000) cautions regarding the use of purportedly liberatory concepts in social change projects, what we think we're doing isn't always what we are doing.[4]

We argue that rather than expanding social rights and entitlements for all people living in

Canada, citizenship has been and is completely tied up in notions of gender, nationhood, colonialism, neocolonialism and a binary opposition of the Self-citizen/Other-non-citizen. In the context of globalization and the increased movement of people and capital across borders, citizenship continues to be used to define who is entitled to rights and protections and who is excluded. In the larger community of Canada, nationhood and citizenship have been strategies that marginalize, exploit, and ensure the continuity of differently entitled and empowered groups.[5] Using the case of the growing number of people categorized as "non-immigrant" migrant workers in Canada, we argue that, in the context of fluid global labour markets, part of the function of the present legal and social category of citizen is to maintain a pool of highly exploitable and socially excluded workers. These workers are not merely marginalized individuals viewed by some sectors of society as second-class citizens. These workers are both legally and ideologically classified as non-citizens operating within larger society as modern-day indentured labourers. Indeed, migrant workers can be seen as the quintessential non-citizens in Canada since both their forced temporary status and the common-sense notion that they should not have the right to stay as permanent residents ensures their vulnerability in all aspects of life in Canada.

Since 1973, over four million temporary employment authorizations have been issued by the Canadian government through the Non-Immigrant Employment Authorization Program (NIEAP). Contrary to some assertions, the NIEAP cannot be dismissed as a benign program used mainly to bring people to Canada for purposes that are truly transitory, such as being members of sports teams, visiting university lecturers or entertainers.[6] While it is true that not all people recruited by the NIEAP can be considered as indentured workers and that the NIEAP works to bring in employees for both professional and non-professional occupations,[7] it is just as true that for the majority of the years under study, facilitating the entry of unfree labour is the main accomplishment of this program. After omitting all those who enter through the NIEAP for such purposes, as we have done for this paper, the number of people living and working in Canada as migrant workers—those who work within unfree employment relations—constitutes the majority of those admitted through this program.

People working as migrant workers can be found living in the same neighborhoods, housing projects, cities, towns and farms that have been the target of numerous community development and social policy strategies. They are also employed in a wide variety of occupations and participate in the churches, mosques, temples, voluntary societies and social groupings that comprise civil society. In short, these non-citizen-Others are very much part of Canadian society and are unlikely to be identified by neighbours or friends as unfree or people less deserving of rights and respect, although ideologically and by law they are rendered as permanently non-rights-bearing non-citizens.

Building on the illustration of migrant workers, we argue that we need new understandings of social rights and mass mobilization strategies that meet the needs of today's highly mobile labour force better than the traditional liberal and social democratic notions of citizenship. While right-of-centre politics promote their own version of citizenship as a series of obligations (including the necessity of participating in paid work regardless of the level of pay, conditions of work or amount and intensity of unpaid labour required within the home), these strategies are definitely not those we seek. Rather, new understandings of citizenship must recognize communities' and individuals' entitlement to stay where they are living (that is, to not be displaced), as well as everyone's self-determined option to move (that is, to immigrate).[8] It is necessary that we connect the collective and individual entitlement to stay or to move, for one without the other would not end the crisis in international migration that over 150 million people face every year. Moreover, the recognition of the inter-relatedness of communities and individuals also must be connected within social justice strategies in order to recognize that hierarchies of power are criss-crossed by race, gender, class, ability, sexual orientation, and positioning within particular regions, all of which result in unequal access to the resources needed to make major changes in one's life.[9]

Simply having the legally recognized right to move, for example, would reproduce the current situation whereby an ever-increasing number of people cross international borders but are positioned as inferiorized and therefore highly vulnerable persons in nationalized labour markets. Indeed, the political Right is increasingly offering the following as a strategy for improving competitiveness within labour markets: changing nothing in regards to the conditions causing the massive migration and nothing to eliminate the highly differentiated categorizations of permanent versus temporary or even illegal status within Canada, while calling for greater labour mobility.[10] Yet any strategy for freeing up the cross-border movements of people that does not at the same time eliminate the reasons for such movements as well as state-sanctioned distinctions

between people working and living within any given nationalized territory will fail to improve the situation of those doing the moving and continue to serve as a mechanism of exclusion, protectionism, and the advancement of certain groups of people at the expense of many.

While underdeveloped in the North American literature, concepts that challenge the hegemony of national citizenship are hotly debated in other parts of the world. For example, global citizenship,[11] supranational citizenship,[12] and global consciousness[13] are topics of lively debate in Europe and the South.[14] Moreover, social movements, such as the Sans-Papiers efforts to demand justice for (im)migrants in France and no borders networks which argue against immigration controls are well developed within many of the European Union-member states and show signs of influencing corresponding movements throughout the world.[15] Many of these concepts reflect the growing need to develop policy concepts and strategies that simultaneously reflect a global sense of collective belonging and entitlement, as well as local autonomy and self-sufficiency within the context of inter-related individuals and communities who are positioned unequally vis-à-vis access to and use of power and resources.

Citizenship: Tracing the Racialized and Gendered Content

The left-of-centre literature on citizenship falls into three loose groupings: that which maintains that social citizenship is universalistic[16] and the most desirable form of citizenship, that which critiques the gendered and racialized aspects of this concept and its operation in social policy,[17] and that seen in the new literature emerging on either global citizenship and/or supranational social entitlements.[18]

The concept of social citizenship is closely associated with the development of the post-war welfare state in England and Northern Europe following the end of the Second World War. North American and British sources generally recognize T.H. Marshall as the architect of this concept.[19] T.H. Marshall's use of social and other forms of citizenship were not gender- or racially neutral and did not apply to all individuals in an equal and universalistic manner. Rather, as we examine below, the concept of citizenship contained gendered and racialized assumptions embedded in the policies and relations of the emerging welfare states of England and North America (the same was true in Europe but this discussion is too lengthy for this article). Despite the lively debate that has occurred within feminist and anti-racist literature, most of the debate on social rights and citizenship continues to operate as if these concepts have been largely liberatory and provided, or could potentially provide, equal benefit to all.[20]

In his famous speech at Cambridge in 1950, T.H. Marshall publicly promoted his idea that there have been three evolutionary stages of citizenship: civil, political and social. Marshall saw each stage as a decisive advance in humanism and social equality. While he acknowledged that the first stage, civic citizenship, was a mechanism to free labour from its ties to the land in the 18th century, thus making it available for the rapidly expanding free market in nation-states, he also saw and lauded the establishment of civil rights such as liberty of the person, freedom of speech, thought, and faith, the right to own property, the right to conclude contracts, and the right to some level of justice.[21] As Fraser and Gordon note,[22] Marshall, in a highly inaccurate reading of 18th-century civil rights, fails to qualify that these rights were

not available to the majority of people.[23] In fact it was not until the last quarter of the 19th century that unfree employment relationships were rendered illegal for even the white, male citizens of England.[24] Slavery for Indigenous, Black and Asian peoples was in widespread existence during the period Marshall discusses and many civil rights were not formally extended to those who had previously been enslaved until more than two centuries later.[25]

Women were also excluded from most of these rights.[26] For example, married white women did not have the right to own property until almost two hundred years later, with the property-owning rights of unmarried women and women of colour expanding unevenly across nations and regions over the subsequent several decades. It is not possible, therefore, to argue that civic citizenship represents a distinct historical moment or period; rather, it represents the beginning of a lengthy gendered and racialized struggle.[27]

Marshall's second stage, political citizenship, is similarly historically imprecise. He argues that the 19th century was the era of political citizenship in which the right to elect and be elected was extended to the population of Britain. Initially, only white male property owners were given the right to vote and run for public office. Gradually the right to elect and be elected was provided to white men owning increasingly smaller and less significant property until it was eventually extended to all white men. Women and men of colour were not included in these rights until much later and, in some cases, only after extensive struggle[28] with women of colour's entitlement to these rights expanding unevenly over an even more lengthy period of time.

The third and highest stage of Marshall's schema is the 20th-century welfare-state recognition of social citizenship, or "the right to a modicum of economic welfare and security, the right to share in full social heritage, to live the life of a civilized being according to the standards prevailing in society."[29] Numerous authors note that social citizenship as pioneered by Marshall and Beveridge[30] was, and in certain cases still is, integrally based on heterosexual women and men occupying very separate spheres in society and maintaining distinct relationships to dependency and independence.[31] As the quote below reveals, social citizenship explicitly incorporates the notion of a breadwinning male as the complement to a financially dependent, homemaking woman within the framework of nation-building strategies:

> The great majority of married women must be regarded as occupied in work which is vital, though unpaid, without which their husbands could not do their paid work and without which the nation could not continue.[32]

Similarly, Leonard Marsh, one of the major architects of Canada's postwar welfare system, argued that the social security system applied to a woman primarily in her capacity as a housewife.[33] Both Beveridge and Marsh argued that women need not make claims on the welfare state as individuals; rather, they should make claims through the wage and insurances of their men.

Commenting on the gendered aspect of Canadian citizenship, Donna Baines notes that the sexist content of the exclusions inscribed in social citizenship have shaped and restricted the claims that women and other groups have made on the state.[34] Family Allowance, for example, a programme thought to embody Canadian social citizenship and universality, was intricately connected to the reproduction of appropriate gender roles, gendered workforces, unpaid labour in the home and maternalism or policies and discourses that "exalted women's capacity to mother, and applied to society as a whole the values attached to that role: care, nurturance and morality."[35] Baines argues that Family Allowance provided Canadian women with minimal state financial support for the job of mothering children while the many other forms of work performed by women, such as elder care, cleaning, sewing, cooking, provisioning, and emotional support, remained unrecognized and unpaid. Family Allowance provided mothers with a small sum of money, which was never sufficient to keep a single-parent family out of poverty. It was sufficient, however, to reward and assist families who had access to a male breadwinner's income.[36] Anna Pratt calls this the familialization of society wherein the two-parent heterosexual family with a male breadwinner and a financially dependent, stay-at-home mother was encouraged through state policy.[37] Likewise, Mimi Abramovitz terms this same process the family ethic in which men are expected to be part of the paid labour force regardless of wages or working conditions and women are expected to work unpaid in the home regardless of safety or financial security.[38]

Baines also argues that income redistribution programmes based on a percentage of wages, such as Unemployment Insurance/ Employment Insurance, reproduce women's marginal position in the paid workforce and subtly remind women that their main job is that of unpaid home worker or mother-citizen rather than as a full citizen actively engaged in all parts of social and economic life.[39] Similarly, state programmes of social assistance in

Canada historically have provided assistance to various categories of worthy, stay-at-home women and their children (initially assistance was provided only to widows, then gradually to other categories of decreasingly worthy women such as wives of disabled soldiers, women who had been deserted by husbands and, much later, divorced women and single parents) thus reproducing exploited and marginalized roles for women as mothers, workers, and citizens. [40]

Feminist, anti-racist literature such as Fiona Williams's (1989) further establishes that social citizenship made explicit use of national boundaries and identities to further determine to whom citizenship rights would be extended, as well as who would be excluded inside those national boundaries. Williams traces how immigration was used at various points in England's postwar history to expand the national labour force, while citizenship was continually evoked to justify why these workers and their families did not have the same social and political rights as non-immigrant workers. [41] Similarly, authors such as Nira Yuval-Davis[42] have used terms such as "the multi-layered citizen" or "differentiated citizenship"[43] in an attempt to show that citizenship is not a universalistic phenomenon. Citizenship is experienced very differently by women, people of colour and those marginalized by state policies, region and location. In a special edition of *Feminist Review* devoted to citizenship, Nira Yuval-Davis[44] argues that liberal understandings of citizenship are based on notions of gender-neutral, racially neutral and regionally homogenized individuals who are strangers to each other,[45] rather than differently empowered, positioned and interrelated individuals and communities. Yuval-Davis notes that a more complete conceptualization

of citizenship must analyze people's membership across sub-, cross-, and supranational collectivities as well as within states. In the same edition of *Feminist Review,* Ruth Lister (1997) asserts that citizenship can continue to be a useful theoretical and political tool through a reconstruction of the public-private dichotomy that simultaneously embraces an international agenda; in other words, issues that have been designated as women's private work or private concerns in the home must be politicized on an international level and made central to social justice strategies. Lister also argues that the politics of difference can be reconciled with the universalistic intentions of citizenship through this same process of reconstructing the private and the public.[46] Uma Narayan likewise argues for a feminist reconstruction in which citizenship would serve largely as a reminder that we are not isolated individuals but participants in a shared national life, and that we all have a stake in the decency and humaneness of our policies and public arrangements.[47]

The literature on migrant workers also contains important discussions of how a vulnerable labour force is maintained at a national and intra-national level. Daiva Stasiulus and Abigail Bakan, for example, reconceptualize citizenship as an ideological construct that is negotiated between differently empowered individuals and the state. This negotiation is criss-crossed with relations of class, race, and gender which are best understood within the broader international context of globalized markets and hierarchies among states. Stasiulus and Bakan note that citizenship and non-citizenship are "usually mediated and socially constructed to work as oppositional by the border-control mechanisms, laws and discourse of nation-states."[48] In a separate article, Stasiulus argues that as economic and social conditions worsen in First World countries, citizenship, immigration and refugee policies have been used increasingly to construct Third World peoples as ethnic/racial cultural threats and to restrict their access to First World citizenship. Noting that current immigration policies in First World countries conflict with international conventions on human and refugee rights, Stasiulus argues that those struggling to establish policies that recognize "deterritorialized" and transborder human rights must address the worldwide decline of liberal democracies that has occurred concomitantly with the rise of economic globalization.[49] Yasmeen Abu-Laban[50] also critiques the role that formal citizenship in Western industrialized countries has played in relation to migration. Calling for deterritorialized or global forms of belonging, rights and participation rather than nation-state-based citizenship, Abu-Laban suggests ways that differences such as gender, race, ethnicity and class need not reproduce inequality and injustice through the administration of citizenship controls and policies. Sunera Thobani[51] argues that historic and contemporary nation-building in Canada involves the construction of citizens as white, while people of colour are simultaneously constructed as non-Citizen/Others; indeed she notes that one category is unthinkable without the other. Thobani shows how the Reviews of Social Security and Immigration Policy constructed immigrant women, understood as women of colour, as non-citizen/Others who must be legally prevented from gaining citizenship even while they make their labour available to the Canadian labour market. Moreover, these non-rights-bearing citizens must be understood to be a threat to the Canadian nation through their reproduction of future generations of outsiders who may lay

claim to Canadian citizenship because of their place of birth.[52]

Lesser and Non-Citizens: A Project of the Canadian State

Similar to the material discussed above, this article argues that the existence of non- or lesser citizens is central to the operation of the citizenship concept in Canada. The hierarchies of belonging organized through the global system of nation-states have worked to naturalize the subordinate status of migrant workers through the operation and general acceptance of two related notions: that it is legitimate for states to discriminate against foreigners, and that only citizens have any entitlement to make claims against the state. As these notions are not peripheral but form the core of any political theory and practice of nation-states, the mobilization of these hegemonic notions has allowed the Canadian state to introduce, legitimize and expand the category of migrant worker. References to notions of citizenship are the present-day vehicle through which the racialization, gendering and classing of lived experiences in Canada occurs. As Nandita Sharma puts it:

> The very construction and reproduction of the category "Canadian citizen" ... activates the category of "non-citizen." As such, the notion of "citizenship" is not a philosophical absolute but the mark of a particular kind of relationship that people have with one another.[53]

The colonial experience of Indigenous peoples demonstrates that Canadian nation-building and the construction of the Canadian citizenship involves "Othering" populations that exist beyond the borders of Canada, as well as populations that exist within the space occupied by Canada. Merely expanding the groups of people recognized and belonging in Canada is insufficient to remedy this problem. This is because the operation of citizenship in Canada is inextricably joined to notions of Canadian-ness. Sharma shows that, historically, state practices in Canada have continuously re-organized the non-citizen status of various Othered populations in Canada through legislative changes to immigration policies and policies governing those classified as "Indians."[54] Historically, ideas of Canadian-ness and citizenship emerged with the colonization of Aboriginal societies and lands by France and Britain.[55] The later transference of France's colonial territory to the British Crown, and the subsequent establishment of the Canadian nation-state as a dominion of Britain in 1867 continued these processes. As a result of the colonization processes and their part in the ongoing projects of capitalism, a hierarchy of Canadian citizen-ness has been established. This hierarchy places those seen as descendants of the British and French nations in a dominant position over Aboriginal people and various Others. Throughout Canadian history, state policymakers have perpetuated Canadian identity as European or, in other words, as white.[56] Many authors have noted that the more recent policy on multiculturalism has not significantly altered this racialized signifying process (Bannerji, 2000; Ng, 1995). Himani Bannerji has persuasively argued that practices of multiculturalism in Canada have actually worked to reorganize the white identity of Canadian-ness.[57]

From the beginning, Canadian state laws on citizenship and immigration have helped to organize a hierarchical ordering of insiders and outsiders living and working within Canadian society. This ordering has been/is decidedly racialized as well as gendered.[58] Indeed, restrictions on entry based on national origin were established almost simultaneously with the creation of the Dominion of Canada in 1867.[59] People from various European colonies or former colonies in Asia, Africa, Latin America and the Caribbean—all constructed as falling outside the scope of Western civilization—were denied equal entry to, and hence citizenship in, Canada. At times some groups, like people from China, were completely excluded (1923–1947). Or, as is the current practice, desperate groups of people are placed in detention centres after gaining entrance to Canada through means deemed to be illegal by the state.[60]

Notions of Canadian-ness have also been connected to the racialized gendering of class in Canada. Those recognized as Canadians are seen as entitled to certain things ("good" jobs, political power, resources distributed by the state, capital, and so forth) that Others are not. This special entitlement has been justified and naturalized through a harkening back to the imagined community of the Canadian nation.[61] This community with its social programs is held responsible for only those fully considered its members—not Others who are either undeserving or should rely on their own people. The Self and Other of Canadian-ness can be seen as having been directly transposed onto the categories of citizen/non-citizen.

To summarize, Canada has come to exist in relation to the colonization of Indigenous peoples and their lands, the privileging of white settlers and the subordination of people immigrating from the colonized South. The ongoing theft of Indigenous wealth has, in part, positioned Canada as a First-World state within the system of global capitalism. To this day, whether one is accorded citizenship or non-citizenship in Canada depends very much upon the global inequalities organized by this system.

The notion of citizenship is the glue that holds the nation-state together in a seemingly natural community authorized to exclude Others. The coherence of the nation-state system relies greatly upon the sovereignty story.[62] This story is based on the notion that there exists within nation-states a coincidence of identity, territory and authority.[63] This story helps to naturalize the heterogeneous Canadian community and conceal how it is criss-crossed with race, class, and gender hierarchies, including privileged access to entry to Canada, job mobility within the country, jobs themselves, social programs, political participation and so forth.

Migrant Workers

The political problems that saturate the concept of citizenship are not just historical in nature. Present-day examples also exist. The case of migrant workers is one of the most poignant examples of people living and working in Canada whose basis for invisibility and exploitation within the country is the legal category and concept of citizenship. Migrant workers are a large group of people who, as a condition of entering, residing and working in Canada, are required to work as modern-day indentured workers. People so categorized enter this country through a combination of laws and regulations loosely collected under the Non-Immigrant Employment Authorization Program (NIEAP) introduced on 1 January 1973.[64]

A person entering Canada under the NIEAP is required to "work at a specific job for a spe-

cific period of time for a specific employer."[65] Migrant workers cannot change any of their conditions of entry or employment without receiving written permission from an immigration officer. If s/he leaves the stipulated employer or changes occupations without the approval of the government, for instance, s/he is subject to deportation. Under the regulations of the NIEAP, workers cannot stay in Canada beyond the length of time stated on their temporary employment authorization form. They are, however, able to renew their foreign worker visa if the employer agrees. Even for those who are able to successfully do so, however, a migrant worker's status in Canada is permanently temporary because people classified as migrant workers cannot apply for permanent residency (or landed status).[66] People are brought in to work and are expelled only to be replaced by others. In this sense, the NIEAP operates as a "revolving door of exploitation."[67]

Since they are not permitted to stay in Canada other than to work for a pre-specified employer, migrant workers do not have the civic citizenship rights of freedom of labour-market or geographical mobility. The imposition of unfree employment relationships work to deny them the ability to qualify for and access a wide array of social programs and services associated with the social citizenship entitlements of the Northern welfare-states. Formal political citizenship or the right to elect and run for election is also denied to people with this immigration and employment designation. Who are the people who enter through the NIEAP and what kind of work do they do in Canada?

Non-professional employment organized through the NIEAP consistently accounts for about three-quarters of all jobs filled by migrant workers in Canada. In 1973, the top three occupational groupings employing migrant workers were service (17.2 percent), farming (13.3 percent) and fabricating, assembly and repair (11.4 percent). Together these three occupations accounted for approximately 42 percent of all jobs filled through the NIEAP that year. [68] Ten years later in 1983, service (29 percent), farming (9.5 percent), and fabricating, assembly and repair (13.2 percent) accounted for about 52 percent of all migrant workers' occupations.[69] In 1993, the number of migrant workers had again risen, this time by over 65,000, to reach 153,988.[70] Again, service industry (11.3 percent) and the farming sector (14.1 percent) were in the top three of all occupational groupings.[71] Fabricating, assembly and repair remained in the top five of all occupations employing unfree contract workers.

The number of professionals admitted through the NIEAP has also remained constant throughout the period under study. In 1973, 23 percent of all workers admitted under temporary visas were within the professional category.[72] Twenty years later, the proportion of professionals remained consistent at 24 percent. Even though professional and relatively high-cost workers do not face the same degree of exploitation and subordination as low-cost labour, most of these workers are not the high-flyers touted as the future global worker. Managers and administrators account for only a small minority of people entering as professionals.[73]

The vast majority of people admitted under temporary employment authorizations within the professional category, like their non-professional counterparts, are unfree. They do not have the ability to choose whom to work for and where to work. Much of the pressure to impose conditions of unfreedom upon their labour power comes from professional associations, like those governing doctors.[74] These groups have successfully lobbied the state for a monopoly position in regards to assignment and a right to exercise closure.[75]

For instance, instead of admitting licensed physicians as permanent residents and allowing them entry to professional organizations, the Canadian state annually admits well over 300 physicians to the country under temporary employment visas where they are used to meet needs in "under serviced areas and in certain short supply specialties."[76] Instead of seeing the shortages of physicians in specific geographical or specialty related areas as quantitative, these shortages are arguably qualitative, for they coincide with the least desirable jobs and the least desirable locations in which Canadian or physicians with citizenship or permanent resident status prefer not to practice.[77] The low preference rate of these positions is due to the fact that they generally offer lower pay and lesser chance for career enhancement.[78]

While it is clear that both low-cost and high-cost labour power is being imported as an unfree labour force, there are important gender differentiations between those who fill such occupations. In 1991, the last year in which statistics are collected for employment authorizations issued by occupation and sex, we see that women are over-represented in the service (89 percent) and clerical (65 percent) occupations. Men are strongly over-represented in the natural sciences, engineering and mathematics (89 percent), managerial (83 percent) and fabricating and repair (93 percent).[79] Overall, men are highly over-represented within professional occupations while women are concentrated and over-represented in service, particularly the personal service occupations such as domestic work.[80] This is not atypical of the distribution of women and men within the Canadian labour market at large. Thus, it seems that the NIEAP reflects and further entrenches the gendered division of labour already in operation in Canada.

Likewise, the NIEAP reorganizes the racialized character of the Canadian labour market. For instance, of all people entering as professionals through the NIEAP in 1973, 89 percent were from the economically advanced countries (EACs) of the Global North.[81] This is especially true in the case of managing and administration jobs, which are disproportionately held by people from the EACs: 90 percent in 1973. This fact has remained consistent throughout the operation of this program. In 1993, 78 percent of all professionals were from the EACs while 91 percent of all managers and administrators were from these countries. Given the branch-plant nature of the Canadian economy and its domination by capital headquartered in the USA, it is not surprising that many of these professionals come from the USA. In 1973, for instance, they made up almost 60 percent of all professionals entering the country.[82]

Workers from the less economically advanced countries (LEACs) of the Global South, on the other hand, largely find themselves within subordinate occupational categories. Approximately 90 percent of workers from the LEACs are employed in non-professional occupations.[83] Thus, it appears that the NIEAP essentially mirrors both the gendered and racialized labour market already in existence in Canada. Indeed, the top three occupations in that year—service, farming, and fabricating assembly and repair—mainly employed people coming from the LEACs.[84]

Within certain of the lowest-paying occupations with documented poor working conditions, people from the LEACs, particularly women, predominate. For instance, by 1987 in the occupation of domestic worker, 95 percent of whom are women, over 80 percent were recruited from the LEACs.[85] Indeed, this proportion has progressively increased since 1973.[86] These trends fit the worldwide pattern of migration from the LEACs to the EACs where, because of the historical cheapening of the labour power of people from the LEACs, particularly that of women, it is more cost-effective to employ these workers.[87]

With the introduction of the NIEAP, there has been a substantial repositioning of the status (permanent resident versus temporary migrant worker, or immigrant and non-immigrant) of people recruited to work in Canada. As Table 9.1, shows, in 1973, 57 percent of all people classified as workers entering Canada came with permanent resident status. By 1993, of the total number of workers admitted to Canada in 1993, only 30 percent received this status while 70 percent came in as migrant workers on temporary employment authorizations (or foreign work visas).

Through the implementation of the NIEAP, the Canadian government has successfully shifted its immigration policy away from a policy of permanent (im)migrant settlement towards an increasing reliance upon unfree, migrant labour. Indeed, soon after the NIEAP was introduced, most people migrating to Canada to work were entering as unfree migrant workers. In every year since 1975 (with the exception of 1978 and 1979), the number of non-immigrant migrant workers far exceeded the number of workers given permanent residency. Since that time, anywhere from 57 to 78 percent of all workers entering Canada have done so under the unfree conditions imposed by their temporary employment authorizations.

Table 9.1: Total Number of (Im)migrant Workers in the Canadian Labour Market by Calendar Year: Permanent Residents "Destined" to the Labour Market and Temporary Visa Workers, 1973 to 1993

Year	Destined (Immigrant Workers)[88]	Visa ("Non-Immigrant" Workers)[89]	Total (All (Im)migrant Workers)[90]
1973	92,228 (57%)	69,901 (43%)	162,129 (100%)
1974	106,083 (60)	71,773 (40)	177,856 (100)
1975	81,189 (51)	77,149 (49)	158,338 (100)
1976	61,461 (47)	69,368 (53)	130,829 (100)
1977	47,625 (41)	67,130 (59)	114,755 (100)
1978	34,762 (71)	14,459 (29)	49,221 (100)
1979	47,949 (60)	31,996 (40)	79,945 (100)
1980	63,479 (39)	98,681 (61)	162,160 (100)
1981	56,676 (37)	96,750 (63)	153,426 (100)
1982	55,023 (35)	101,509 (65)	156,532 (100)
1983	36,540 (29)	87,700 (71)	124,240 (100)
1984	37,468 (25)	113,297 (75)	150,765 (100)
1985	36,949 (22)	134,167 (78)	171,116 (100)
1986	63,479 (30)	150,467 (70)	213,946 (100)
1987	56,676 (26)	157,492 (74)	214,168 (100)
1988	73,134 (27)	194,454 (73)	267,588 (100)
1989	94,412 (36)	169,004 (64)	263,416 (100)
1990	109,840 (38)	176,377 (62)	286,217 (100)
1991	127,870 (40)	191,392 (60)	319,262 (100)
1992	137,360 (43)	178,280 (57)	315,640 (100)
1993	65,130 (30)	153,988 (70)	219,118 (100)

Source: Employment and Immigration Canada, 1980; 1981; 1982; 1983; 1984; 1985; 1986; 1987; 1988; 1989; 1990; 1991; 1992; 1993; Citizenship and Immigration Canada, 1995; INTERCEDE, 1993, 1994.

In some years, the number of migrant workers has exceeded the total number of landed immigrants in Canada (i.e., all those destined workers plus family class plus refugees plus entrepreneurs). This occurred most recently in 1988 when 161,929 landed immigrants entered the country while 194,454 workers entered through the NIEAP. It occurred most dramatically in 1986 when over 50,000 more unfree migrant workers were admitted than the total number arriving as landed immigrants.

In reviewing the benefits that result from unfree employment relationships with migrant workers, we see that the outcome is decidedly in favour of both the state and employers within the receiving countries. In personal interviews conducted with officers at Citizenship and Immigration Canada (CIC), it was repeatedly stated that the NIEAP is an employer-driven program.[91] The program allows employers to request migrant workers according to their short- or long-term needs and permits state officials to apply restrictions to such workers while timing their arrival to best suit current labour-market conditions.[92]

Thus, through the use of the NIEAP, not

only is the Canadian state able to control the timing of labour migration, it is also in the position to determine the conditions of entry for those it classifies as migrant workers. Through the use of the NIEAP the state has, to a great extent, controlled the scale, structure and course of labour migration into Canada and has contributed to the creation of a highly flexible (that is: precarious) labour force.[93] In other words, the Canadian government, through the regulations of the NIEAP, has produced a category of people in Canada that we have come to know as migrant workers.

What allows migrant workers to be used as a cheap and largely unprotected form of labour power are not any inherent qualities of the people themselves, but state regulations that make this group of people powerless. Essentially, because they have been categorized as permanent non-citizens, people entering Canada as migrant workers do not have many of the *de facto* or *dejure* civic, social or political rights associated with Canadian citizenship. For example, migrant workers in Canada often work within occupations that are not generally covered by minimum wage or other labour protections, such as farm work or personal domestic labour.[94] Further, migrant workers cannot expect to be covered by employment insurance, welfare, pensions, workplace safety insurance or Medicare, as these are reserved only for those classified as citizens or permanent residents.[95]

The clear discrimination faced by workers admitted under the NIEAP in regards to social programs is further compounded by the fact that they pay fees and taxes to the government for services that they may be legally denied. Indeed, to enter Canada under the unfree conditions imposed by temporary employment authorizations, workers are charged a non-refundable "processing fee." In 1993, this fee was $100 (CDN). In 1993, the state received over $15 million from the 153,988 workers admitted under this program. Furthermore, in the years between 1973 and 1981, migrant domestic workers alone paid over $11 million into social program funds but were not eligible to make claim on these funds because of their non-immigrant, visitor status.[96]

Aside from the labour-market and geographical limitations placed upon them, another method of controlling or limiting the resistance of migrant workers is to deter them from unionizing. In some cases there is a formal denial of such a right, as in the case of farm workers in Ontario where the government enacted legislation to retroactively exempt farm workers from the Agricultural Labour Relations Act.[97] Overall, the reality that this workforce is constituted as temporary and rotated in and out of the country also hinders efforts to form collectives. In some cases, workers are prevented from forming associations by more simple or personal control mechanisms.[98] In other cases, as for migrant domestic workers who are forced to live in the residence of their employer, their ability to organize and ultimately strike is severely constrained by the fact that their workplace is also their place of residence.[99]

The construction of the NIEAP with its creation of migrant workers in Canada, then, has been useful to both employers seeking a more competitive workforce as well as the state in its process of implementing neo-liberal policies. It is argued that, in this way, the NIEAP has allowed the state to have the maximal benefit of importing labour from all over the world without having to finance the overhead costs of labour reproduction.[100] Thus, the NIEAP allows certain costs of labour-force renewal to be externalized to another state, and saves the Canadian state a considerable sum of money.[101] In this sense, we can see that citizenship has indeed acted as a tool available to employers and the Canadian state in their re-organizing efforts.

Implications for Social Policy and Social Justice Work

Earlier in this article we asked whether citizenship can function without non-citizens and second-class citizens, or whether the existence of internal and external non-citizens is an essential part of how citizenship operates in a world of national states. The argument above illustrates how Canadian-ness and Canadian citizenship are used to create non-citizens who are legally and ideologically denied full participation and protections. As noted earlier, the creation of non- or lesser citizens is naturalized through the operation and general acceptance of two related notions: that it is legitimate for states to discriminate against foreigners, and that only citizens have any entitlement to make claims against the state or to receive its protection. These protections and the possibility for participation are provided to those legally and socially constituted as full Canadian citizens as a matter of course. Citizenship, then, is a mechanism for distributing resources and privileges that are denied to many. While it is beyond the scope of this article, we would also argue that citizenship resources and privilege are apportioned in unequal ways, even for those accorded citizenship status. Here we are referring, in particular, to the status of second-class citizen that continues to be accorded to all those who do not meet the heterosexual, white, middle-income, able-bodied, male standards inscribed in various ways in the concepts of political, civic, and social citizenship since

the notions first emerged in the 18th century.[102] As Yuval-Davis (1997) and others note, women, people of colour, and many other internal populations are positioned by policy, cultural practices and ideology as not deserving full citizenship rights.[103]

In Canada, these populations also include diverse Indigenous people, so-called homeless people, people with mental illnesses and disabilities, and so forth. Hence, responses to the injustices promoted by and through citizenship discourses and real, existing policy must address the ways that these groups have been distanced from power, resources, and affirming identities within the so-called larger community of Canada.

The contradictory entitlements and marginalizations of citizenship have been intensified in recent years by the processes known as globalization. These processes have been shown to be devastating for most people around the world.[104] The renewed attention paid to global processes, however, may also provide the opportunity to understand the global context of the standards of living, social programmes and national citizenship that many in the North take for granted. As this discussion has shown, the existing dichotomy of citizen/Self, and non-citizen or lesser citizen/Other operates in hierarchical and exclusionary ways, in significant part because of how national states contain notions of citizenship and are able to dictate differential conditions for life for variously categorized groups living and working within the territory of the nation and the state.[105]

Restrictions on the autonomous movement of people and distinctions amongst those within nationalized states exist to protect and preserve those who benefit from the richer economies and societies of the North. At the same time, other state policies continue to facilitate the ongoing transfer of wealth from the South to the North, thereby contributing to the uprooting of people and the current crisis of international migration. Restrictions on mobility also act as a smokescreen, concealing the colonial relations and domination of Indigenous populations that work to exploit the riches of dispossessed people in Northern countries. Through practices of colonialism and imperialism, and the re-structured forms of neocolonialism and neoimperialism, national states in the North have been able to usurp much of the wealth from the South to finance Northern development projects.[106]

Earlier we noted that the social-policy and community-development literature has been involved in a lively debate on how or whether to rebuild notions of social citizenship. This debate generally centres on what role social citizenship and its concomitant policies and programmes should play within the new restructured and globalizing economies of the North. The evidence presented in this article shows that social citizenship has always contained notions of inequality and operated comfortably alongside concepts of citizenship within immigration policy that explicitly developed the possibility for people to live and work in Canada without full social or any other type of citizenship rights. In relation to social policy development, our recommendation is that citizenship be abandoned as a rallying cry for increasing social justice. This concept has proven itself to be corrupt throughout its existence and it has been thoroughly taken over by the Right to mean narrow national privileges in return for full participation in paid work and the market. Instead citizenship needs to be replaced by a whole new set of concepts and initiatives. In the area of immigration, refugee and border policies, our investigation into the

operation of the concept of citizenship leads us to conclude that those pursuing agendas of social justice must demand an end to restrictions on human mobility and distinctions amongst people within nationalized states. It is the restriction on mobility and its concomitant restrictions on who will live and work as full citizens within the privileged Northern nations that gives a category such as migrant worker any basis for existence.

Capital can already move around the world with few restrictions and, increasingly, capitalists have been granted national treatment rights through trade agreements, thereby eliminating distinctions amongst investors (i.e., under Articles 301, 1102, 1202, 1405, 1703 of the North American Free Trade Agreement).[107] Providing labour the same entitlement to move where opportunities exist—without discriminatory treatment upon their arrival—undermines the benefits capital can expect to receive when moving to low wage regions. It also provides leverage to those trying to improve or retain local wages and living conditions as it removes the state-mandated vulnerability imposed upon those deemed to be illegal or migrant workers.

Instead of restrictions on the movement of individuals, families and communities, policies are required that affirm each person's entitlement to stay where they are living (that is, to not be displaced), and each person's self-determined entitlement to leave (that is, to move within and across borders). While there is reason to object to the unregulated global movement of capital, the removal of restrictions on movement of people across and within borders as well as the recognition of their right to remain where they are should be advanced by progressive forces as these promote a more level playing field for workers from less affluent countries and regions. People need not stay in areas of the world that have been made oppressive, dangerous or intolerable, although they may return to these areas at future times should conditions change. In addition, the North will no longer be able to protect its wealth by simply shutting out the less advantaged and profiting from wars fought far away. While individuals from wealthy regions may take advantage of the free movement of labour to improve their own already promising life prospects, the removal of restrictions on the movement of labour will provide humanitarian options to millions presently seeking to leave war-torn and impoverished regions. Likewise, the recognition of everyone's right to stay means that people need not fear deportation or state-enforced separation of families and communities. This strategy needs to be accompanied by practices devoted to ending processes that displace people, such as unfair trade, production practices that benefit the North at the expense of the South, wars and profiting from wars, a lack of global aid during natural disasters and crop failures and so forth. A global sense of collective and connected belonging and entitlement that simultaneously incorporates local autonomy and self-sufficiency is needed to address the ongoing operation of North-South exploitation and marginalization of those rendered Others.

There are, therefore, two important policy measures that need to be implemented concomitant to open borders. The first is a concerted effort to raise standards of living, wages and quality of life in economically depressed areas of the world. The regional equalization policies of the European Union (EU) provide a limited example of this type of policy.[108] Lower wage regions within the EU can access funds to develop economic infrastructure, thereby raising wages and standards of living which provides incentives for labour to remain in the region rather than moving to higher-waged countries. The goal of this type of policy is to remove the existence of low-wage economies and hence, their obvious benefits for investors and businesses.

In other words, with wages equalized across large regions, entrepreneurs and corporations must base their investment decisions on factors other than the low-wage advantage. Free movement of labour would also erode the power of capital to maintain reserve armies of unemployed as the jobless would have the real option of moving to more vibrant economic areas or remaining in areas undergoing infrastructure development and the promise of a better future. The development of infrastructure and its concomitant expansion in local employment can provide the basis for improved environmental and social protections as communities feel they can reject corporate demands for lower taxes and standards of all types. Policy development must also focus on strengthening labour standards and social programmes across the board in the currently affluent countries in order to ensure that Third World enclaves are not recreated for immigrant workers entering the economies of the North.[109]

As mentioned earlier, while these concepts may be new to North Americans, supranational social and economic policies have been the centerpiece of debate for government and non-government circles in many other parts of the world. Notions such as supranational citizenship, while often an improvement on nation-based citizenship concepts, still contain a top-down, state-imposed operation of community, policy development and power that assume a race, class and gender equality that simply does not exist at this point. Collectivity and belonging must instead be based on a grassroots sense of building community through the recognition and support of the struggles and goals of differently empowered, local and global communities of interest. Stasiulis argues that those promoting post-national rights will have to combat the illiberal tendencies of "actually existing liberal democracies" which have seen a worldwide expansion along with the expansion of the global capitalist economy.[110] Given the worldwide expansion of illiberal democracies, it is exceedingly difficult to advance the types of policy programmes we have discussed above despite the fact that the right to move and the right to remain have been included in Article 13 of the Universal Declaration of Human Rights since 1948.[111] Again as Stasiulis notes, the immigration, refugee and border laws of nation-states tend to stand in direct conflict with United Nation (UN) rights and show no sign of ceding authority to or increasing the credibility of these international declarations.[112] Given the limited scope for action and reform available at this point, our intellectual and political task is also somewhat minimalist. As activists, intellectuals and community members we need to focus on new ways to define membership and membership criteria for local and extra-local community that do not reproduce hierarchical concepts of who "belongs" and who does not. Our goal must be to avoid self-interested exclusions, parochialism and the existence of legally constituted, unequal groups of people within larger society. To this end, social policy and social justice projects need to understand belonging not as national citizenship but rather as a worldwide, or as the Zapatista's argue, a "transcontinental" perspective of solidarity and openness coupled with support for local participation, democracy, and self-sufficiency.

Endnotes

1 Glenn Drover, "Redefining Social Citizenship in a Global Era," *Social Work and Globalization. Special Issue: Canadian Social Work Review* 17 (2000), pp. 29–49; James Midgley, "Globalization, Capitalism and Social Welfare: A Social Development Perspective," *Social Work and Globalization Special Issue: Canadian Social Work Review* 17 (2000), pp. 13–28; R. Scott Evans and Derouin, Jodey Michael, "New Winds are Blowing: Current Trends in Public Support for the Canadian Welfare State," *Canadian Review of Social Policy* 45–46 (Spring-Fall 2000), pp. 219–228; Judy Rebick, "Democratizing the Welfare State," *Canadian Review of Social Policy* 45–46 (Spring-Fall 2000), pp. 5–18; Peter Leonard, *Postmodern Welfare: Reconstructing an Emancipatory Project* (London: Sage Publications, 1997); Donna Baines, McGrath, Susan, and Moffat, Ken, *The Social Security Review: A Project in Discipline* (University of Toronto: Faculty of Social Work, 1999, unpublished manuscript); Gary Teeple, *Globalization and the Decline of Social Reform* (Toronto: Garamond Press, 1995); Patricia Evans, "Ontario's Welfare Policy and Single Mothers: Restructuring the Debate," in Janine Brodie, (ed.), *Women in Canadian Public Policy* (Toronto: Harcourt Brace and Company, 1994); Allan Moscovitch, "From the Conservative Ill-Fare State to a Renewed Welfare State," *Canadian Review of Social Policy* 32 (Winter 1993), pp. 1–12; Ernie Lightman, "Conditionality and Social Assistance: Market Values and the Work Ethic," in Graham Riches and Ternowetski, Gordon, (eds.), *Unemployment and Welfare. Social Policy and the Work of Social Work* (Toronto: Garamond Press, 1990), pp. 91–105.

2 Yasmeen Abu-Laban, "Reconstructing an Inclusive Citizenship for a New Millennium: Globalization, Migration and Difference," *International Politics* 37 (December 2000), pp. 509–526; Yasmeen Abu-Laban, "Keeping 'em Out: Gender, Race, and Class Biases in Canadian Immigration Policy," in V. Strong-Boag, S. Grace, A. Eisenberg and Anderson, J. (eds.), *Painting the Maple: Essays on Race, Gender, and the Construction of Canada* (UBC Press: Vancouver, 1998), pp. 69–82; Fiona Williams, "Reflections on the Intersections

of Social Relations in the New Political Economy," *Studies in Political Economy* 55 (1998), pp. 173–190; Veronica Strong-Boag, Grace S., Eisenberg A. and Anderson J., "Introduction" to *Painting the Maple...*; Leonard, *Postmodern Welfare...*; Ruth Lister, "Citizenship; Towards a Feminist Synthesis," *Feminist Review* 57 (Autumn 1997), pp. 28–48; Uma Narayan, "Towards a Feminist Vision of Citizenship: Rethinking the Implications of Rights, Political Participation and Nationality," in Mary Shanley and Uma Narayan (eds.), *Reconstructing Political Theory: Feminist Perspectives* (University Park, Pennsylvania: Pennsylvania University Press, 1997), pp. 48–67; Daiva Stasiulis, "International Migration Rights, and the Decline of 'Actually Existing Liberal Democracy,'" *New Community* 23/2 (1997), pp. 197–241; Daiva Stasiulis and Bakan, Abigail B., "Negotiating Citizenship: The Case of Foreign Domestic Workers in Canada," *Feminist Review* 57 (Autumn 1997), pp. 112–139; Nira Yuval-Davis, "Women, Citizenship and Difference," *Feminist Review* 57 (Autumn 1997), pp. 4–27; Nira Yuval-Davis, "The Citizenship Debate: Women, Ethnic Processes and the State," *Feminist Review* 39 (1991), pp. 58–68; Nandita Sharma, "Birds of Prey and Birds of Passage: The Movement Capital and Migration of Labour," *Labour, Capital and Society* 30/1 (Spring 1997), pp. 8–38; Donna Baines, "Rebel Without a Claim: Women's Changing Basis to Claim on the State," *Canadian Social Work Review* 13/2 (1996), pp. 187–204; Roxana Ng, "Multiculturalism as Ideology: A Textual Analysis," in Marie Campbell and Ann Manicom (eds.), *Knowledge, Experience and Ruling Relations, Studies in the Social Organization of Knowledge* (Toronto: University of Toronto Press, 1995), pp. 35–49; Roxana Ng, "Sexism, Racism, Canadian Nationalism," in Himani Bannerji (ed.), *Returning the Gaze: Essays on Racism, Feminism and Politics* (Toronto: Sister Vision Press, 1993), pp. 182–196; Roxana Ng, *The Politics of Community Services: Immigrant Women, Class and the State* (Toronto: Garamond Press, 1988); Etienne Balibar, "Es Gibt Keinen Staat in Europa: Racism and Politics in Europe Today," *New Left Review* 186 (March/April 1991), pp. 18–20.

3   Abu-Laban, "Reconstructing an Inclusive..."; Abu-Laban, "Keeping 'Em Out..."; Sunera Thobani, "Nationalizing Canadians: Bordering Immigration Women in the Late Twentieth Century," *Canadian Journal of Women and the Law* 12/2 (2000), pp. 279–312; Lister, "Citizenship..."; Narayan, "Towards a Feminist Vision..."; Stasiulis and Bakan, "Negotiating Citizenship..."; Baines, "Rebel Without a Claim..."; Ng, "Multiculturalism as Ideology..."; Ng, "Sexism, Racism..."; Ng, *The Politics of Community Services...*; Nancy Fraser and Gordon, Linda, "Contract Versus Charity. Why There is No Social Citizenship in the United States," *Socialist Review* 3 (1992), pp. 45–67.

4   Catrina Brown, "Postmodernism and Feminist Practice," unpublished paper presented at the Joint Conference of the International Federation of Social Workers and the International Association of Schools of Social Work (Montreal, Canada: 2000).

5   Nandita Sharma, "Maintaining the Master-Servant Relationship: Canadian Immigration," *Kinesis* (May 2000); Thobani, "Nationalizing Canadians..."; Abu-Laban, "Keeping 'Em Out..."; Narayan, "Towards a Feminist Vision..."; Stasiulis, "International Migration Rights..."; Stasiulis and Bakan, "Negotiating Citizenship..."; Ng, "Multiculturalism as Ideology..."; Ng, *The Politics of Community Services...*

6   Monica Boyd contends that Canada's Non-Immigrant Employment Authorization Program cannot be called a "guest worker" program because of the large number of workers entering the country in professional occupations. She argues that the conceptualization of any labour recruitment program as a "guest" worker program should be reserved for programs that permanently recruit workers for low-skilled jobs that are situated amongst the lowest paying (Monica Boyd, "Temporary Workers in Canada: A Multifaceted Program," *International Migration Review* 20/4 (1986), pp. 938–939). Boyd bases these arguments on the operation of "guest" worker programs in western Europe. However, she makes assumptions about these programs that are sometimes incorrect. She assumes that such programs are solely designed to recruit labour for low-skilled jobs; however, many people who work under the auspices of these programs are employed in high-skilled jobs. For example, Corrigan has shown that, as in Canada, guest workers in western Europe are employed in a variety of jobs, including skilled jobs in the advanced technological sectors, such as automobile manufacturing (Philip Corrigan, "Feudal Relics or Capitalist Monuments? Notes on the Sociology of Unfree Labour," in *Sociology* 11/3 (1977), p. 445). Likewise, Connell has shown that systems of forced rotational employment can encompass a wide variety of occupations and are highly subject to domestic economic needs and concerns. As such, it is not the occupation being filled which defines conditions of non-freedom but the lack of mobility rights imposed upon "guest" workers (John Connell, "Far Beyond the Gulf: The Implications of Warfare for Asian Labour Migration," *Australian Geographer* 23/1 (1993), pp. 44–50).

7   For the purposes of this paper, two categories have been constructed from the broad occupational groupings

of workers entering under the NIEAP. Those in the professional category include managerial; administrative; natural sciences, engineering and mathematics; social sciences and related; religion, and teaching. Non-professional categories include: medicine and health; clerical; sales; service; farming, horticultural and animal-husbandry; fishing, hunting, trapping; forestry and logging; mining and quarrying including gas and oil; processing; machining; fabricating, assembling and repairing; construction; transport equipment operating; material handling; and other crafts and equipment operating.

8 We are avoiding the use of the term "rights" due to its contemporary usage by neo-liberals to mean the obligations and responsibilities to the market and private family assumed by individuals in return for minimal governance and interference from governments.

9 See Lister, *Citizenship…*; Narayn, "Towards a Feminist Vision…"; Nira Yuval-Davis, *Gender and Nation* (London: Sage, 1997).

10 "South Africa's Migrant Workers: A Ticket to Prosperity," *The Economist* (2 September 2000).

11 Richard Falk, "The Making of Global Citizenship," in S. van Steenbergen (ed.), *The Condition of Citizenship* (London: Sage Publications, 1994), pp. 129–149.

12 Williams, "Reflections on the Intersections…."

13 Roland Robertson, *Globalization* (London: Sage Publications, 2000).

14 See also Abu-Laban, "Reconstructing an Inclusive…"; James Ife, "Localized Needs and a Globalized Economy: Bridging the Gap with Social Work Practice," *Social Work and Globalization Special Issue: Canadian Social Work Review* 17 (2000), pp. 50–64; Drover, "Redefining Social Citizenship"; A. Hoogvelt, *Globalization and the Post-Colonial World: The New Political Economy of Development* (London: Macmillan, 1997); Nira Yuval-Davis, "The Multilayered Citizen," *International Feminist Journal of Politics* 1/1 (June 1999); Yuval-Davis, *Gender and Nation;* Nira Yuval-Davis, "The Citizenship Debate: Women, Ethnic Processes and the State," *Feminist Review* 39, pp. 58–68.

15 Etienne Balibar, "'Es Gibt Keinen Staat'"; Teresa Hayter, *Open Borders: The Case Against Immigration Controls* (London: Pluto Press, 2000).

16 T.H. Marshall, *Citizenship and Social Class* (London: Pluto Press, 1950); Dietrich Rueschemeyer, "Welfare States and Democratic Citizenship," in E. Broadbent (ed.), *Democratic Equality. What Went Wrong?* (Toronto: University of Toronto Press, 2001), pp. 79–95; Moscovitch, "From the Conservative Ill-Fare State…"

17 Abu-Laban, "Reconstructing an Inclusive…"; Abu-Laban, "Keeping 'em Out…"; Thobani, "Nationalizing Canadians…"; Williams, "Reflections on the Intersections…"; Strong-Boag *et al,* "Introduction" to *Painting the Maple…;* Leonard, *Postmodern Welfare…;* Lister, *Citizenship…;* Narayan, "Towards a Feminist Vision…"; Stasiulis, "International Migration Rights…"; Stasiulis and Bakan, "Negotiating Citizenship…"; Yuval-Davis, *Gender and Nation;* Yuval-Davis, "The Citizenship Debate…"; Sharma, "'Race,' Class and Gender and the Making of 'Difference': The Social Organization of 'Migrant Workers' in Canada," *Atlantis: A Women's Studies Journal Special Issue: "Whose Canada Is It? Immigrant Women, Women of Colour, Citizenship and Multiculturalism"* 24/2 (Winter 2000); Baines, "Rebel Without a Claim…"; Fraser and Gordon, "Contract Versus Charity… "

18 For example, Hayter, *Open Borders;* Balibar, "Es Gibt Keinen Staat…"; Williams, "Reflections on the Intersections…"

19 Marshall, *Citizenship and Social Class.*

20 Ian Angus, "Subsistence as a Social Right: A Political Ideal for Socialism?" *Studies in Political Economy* 65 (Summer 2001), pp. 117–136; Dietrich Rueschemeyer, "Welfare States and Democratic Citizenship" (2001); Patrick Kearans, "Need and Welfare: 'Thin' and 'Thick' Approaches," in Andrew Johnson, McBride F., and Smith, Patrick J. (eds.), *Continuities and Discontinuities: The Political Economy of Social Welfare and Labour Market Policy in Canada* (Toronto: University of Toronto Press, 1994), pp. 44–61; Leon Muszynski, "Defending the Welfare State and Labour Market Policy," in Andrew Johnson et al. (eds.), *Continuities and Discontinuities* (1994), pp. 306–326; Allan Moscovitch, "From the Conservative Ill-Fare State…"; Ernie Lightman, "Conditionality and Social Assistance…"

21 Marshall, *Citizenship and Social Class.*

22 Fraser and Gordon, "Contract Versus Charity…."

23 Marshall's assumption that free wage labour was a universal experience during the 18th century in England is also found in the work of Karl Marx. Marx, writing at a time when the trade in Asian peoples as "coolie (indentured) labour" was growing, viewed the development of free wage labour as a defining feature of

capitalist social relations. He maintained that capital was able to "arise only when the owner of the means of production and subsistence finds the free worker available, on the market, as the seller of his [sic] own labour-power" (1977), p. 274. Sharma ("Race, Class and Gender…") argues that both Marshall and Marx are able to make such assumptions by dismissing the lived experiences that non-white workers had of capitalism, especially in the white settler colonies.

24 Robert J. Steinfeld, *The Invention of Free Labor: The Employment Relation in English and American Law and Culture, 1350–1870* (University of North Carolina: Chapel Hill and London, 1991), pp. 115, 160.

25 Fraser and Gordon, "Contract Versus Charity…"

26 Lister, "Citizenship…"; Baines, "Rebel Without a Claim…"; Fraser and Gordon, "Contract Versus Charity…"; Narayan, "Towards a Feminist Vision…."

27 Baines, "Rebel Without a Claim…"

28 Abu-Laban, "Reconstructing an Inclusive…"; Fraser and Gordon, "Contract Versus Charity…"

29 Marshall, *Citizenship and Social Class,* p. 8.

30 Sir William Beveridge, *Social Insurance and Allied Services* (New York: Macmillan, 1942).

31 Fraser and Gordon, "Contract Versus Charity…"; Anna Pratt, "'So Long As There Are Homes'—The Easy Abandonment of Family Allowances in Canada: A Search for Explanations," unpublished thesis (Toronto: University of Toronto Centre of Criminology, 1994); Fiona Williams, *Social Policy: A Critical Introduction* (London: Polity Press, 1989); Mimi Abramovitz *Regulating the Lives of Women* (Boston: Southend Press, 1988).

32 Beveridge, *Social Insurance…*, p. 49.

33 Cited in Ann Porter, "Women and Income Security in the Post-War Period: The Case of Unemployment Insurance 1945–1962," *Labour/Le Travail* (Spring 1993), p. 114.

34 Baines, "Rebel Without a Claim…"

35 Seth Koven and Michel, Sonya (eds.), *Mothers of a New World. Maternalist Politics and the Origins of Welfare States* (London: Routledge, 1993), p. 4.

36 Baines, "Rebel Without a Claim…"

37 Pratt, "So Long As There Are Homes…"

38 Abramovitz, *Regulating the Lives…*

39 Baines, "Rebel Without a Claim…"

40 For a full discussion, see Little (1994).

41 Williams, *Social Policy.*

42 Yuval-Davis, "The Multilayered Citizen…"

43 Iris Young, *Justice and the Politics of Difference* (Princeton: Princeton University, 1990).

44 Yuval-Davis, "Women, Citizenship and Difference… "

45 Maurice Roche, *Rethinking Citizenship* (Cambridge: Polity Press, 1992).

46 Lister, "Citizenship…"

47 Narayan, "Towards a Feminist Vision…" p. 65.

48 Stasiulis and Bakan, "Negotiating Citizenship…" p. 118.

49 Stasiulis, "International Migration Rights… ."

50 Abu-Laban, "Reconstructing an Inclusive…"

51 Thobani, "Nationalizing Canadians…," p. 283.

52 *Ibid.*

53 Sharma, "Race, Class and Gender…," p. 5.

54 Sharma, "Race, Class and Gender…"; see also Frances Abele and Stasiulis, Daiva, "Canada as a White Settler Colony: What about Indigenous and Immigrants?" in Wallace Clement and Williams, Glen (eds.), *The New Canadian Political Economy* (Montreal, Kingston: McGill-Queen's University Press, 1989).

55 See also Abu-Laban, "Reconstructing an Inclusive…"

56 Ng, "Multiculturalism as Ideology…"

57 Himani Bannerji, *Dark Side of the Nation…*; Ng, "Multiculturalism as Ideology…"

58 Abu-Laban (2000). Also, see Judith Ramirez, "Domestic Workers Organize!" *Canadian Woman Studies 412* (Winter 1982) or Stasiulis and Bakan, "Negotiating Citizenship…" for a fuller discussion of the operation of gender and class within the category of migrant worker.

59 Restrictions existed in Canada's immigration legislation beginning in the 1880s, first targeting the Chinese

and later all potential immigrants of colour. A White Canada policy was codified in the Immigration Act of 1910, amended by the Act of 1919 and included in subsequent order-in-council and legislation as well as the 1952 Immigration Act (Hawkins, 1991), p. 16. Discrimination was liberalized in the 1960s with the operation of a points system. However, the opening-up of immigration policy in the 1960s did not eliminate discrimination as racialized, gendered and class inequality continued to structure who got in and under what conditions. While the points system, lauded as an objective form of admitting new immigrants, did do away with the racist construction of desirables/undesirables by eliminating the "most-preferred-country" clause, it nonetheless transferred the racialized and gendered meanings of Canadian-ness to other categories, such as skills, education, the ability to speak one of the two official Canadian languages and "adaptability." Also, as Vic Satzewich (1989) rightly notes, "post-1962 migration did not ... take place in an ideological climate denuded of the negative evaluations of certain races." Victor Satzewich, "Racism and Canadian Immigration Policy: The Government's View of Caribbean Migration, 1962–1966," *Canadian Ethnic Studies* 21/1 (1989), pp. 77–97.

60 See Sharma, "Maintaining the Master-Servant Relationship..."

61 Benedict Anderson, *Imagined Communities* (London: Verso, 1991).

62 Sharma, "Maintaining the Master-Servant Relationship..."

63 Jan Jindy Pettman, "Transcending National Identity: The Global Political Economy of Gender and Class." Paper presented at the International Studies Association Conference, Toronto (March 1997).

64 The NIEAP, while not the first immigration program designed to recruit people to work as indentured, migrant workers in Canada, helped to consolidate and expand pre-existing programs (see Sharma, 1995 and 2000, for a detailed discussion of the workings of the NIEAP).

65 Citizenship and Immigration Canada, *Hiring Foreign Workers: Facts for Canadian Employers* (Ottawa: Ministry of Supply and Services, 1994), p. 1.

66 Migrant workers working as domestics enter Canada under a specific policy called the Live-in Caregiver Program. This policy permits domestic workers who satisfy stringent criteria over a two-year period to apply for landed immigrant (or permanent resident) status. It is important to note that this is the only group of migrant workers who are accorded these rights. Scholars and activists speculate that these rights were granted due to a severe shortage of domestic labour in concert with extensive organizing and public pressure on the government (see Abigail Bakan and Stasiulis, Daiva, "Structural Adjustment, Citizenship," 1996).

67 For a more complete discussion of the concept "revolving door of exploitation," see Judith Ramirez, "Domestic Workers Organize!..."

68 Citizenship and Immigration Canada, Unpublished material from the Electronic Information Management Office (Hull, Quebec, 1995).

69 *Ibid.*

70 Citizenship and Immigration Canada, *Hiring Foreign Workers,* 1994b.

71 Citizenship and Immigration Canada, Electronic Information Management Office...

72 *Ibid.*

73 Managers and administrators usually account for less than 25 percent of all professionals entering Canada under temporary employment authorizations (CIC, 1995).

74 Bolaria, B. Singh, "From Immigrant Settlers to Migrant Transients: Foreign Professionals in Canada," in Vic Satzewich (ed.), *Deconstructing a Nation: Immigration, Multiculturalism and Racism in '90s Canada* (Fernwood Publishing: Halifax, 1992).

75 Sacks has defined closure as the process by which professions "regulate market conditions in their favour, in the face of actual or potential competition from the outside."

76 Joint Working Group, Federal/Provincial Advisory Committee on Health/Human Resources and National Committee on Physical Manpower. *Report of the Joint Working Group on Graduates of Foreign Medical Schools* (Health and Welfare Canada: Ottawa, 1982), p. ii.

77 S.S. Mick, "The Foreign Medical Graduates," *Scientific American* 232/2 (1975), pp. 14–21.; T.K. Ishi, "The Political Economy of International Migration: Indian Physicians to the United States," *South Asian Bulletin* 2/1 (1982), pp. 3958.

78 Bolaria, "From Immigrant Settlers...," p. 224.

79 Employment and Immigration Canada, *1991 Immigration Statistics* (Ottawa: Ministry of Supply and Services, 1992).

80 *Ibid.*

81 While much more work needs to be done to examine the complex re-racialization of some as "white" and others as "non-white," it can be argued that as in the past, the process of racialization is related to a person's or group's positioning within labour markets (see Backhouse, 2000). Moreover, while one cannot always read how people will be racialized within Canada from their stated countries of citizenship, it is safe to assume that most people recruited as migrant workers from national states within the Global South are racialized as "non-whites" within Canada.

82 Citizenship and Immigration Canada. Electronic Information Management Office...

83 *Ibid.*

84 *Ibid.*

85 Cynthia D. Cornish, "Unfree Wage Labour, Women and the State: Employment Visas and Foreign Domestic Workers in Canada," MA Thesis. University of Victoria (1992), pp. 92–93.

86 Sedef Arat-Koc, "Immigration Policies, Migrant Domestic Workers and the Definition of Citizenship in Canada," in Victor Satzewich, (ed.), *Deconstructing a Nation: Immigration, Multiculturalism and Racism in '90s Canada* (Halifax: Fernwood, 1992); Cornish, Unfree Wage Labour....

87 Sharma, "Birds of Prey..."

88 "Destined" refers to the number of people admitted to Canada as permanent residents who have indicated that they intend to enter the labour market. This category includes people admitted under all classes of immigrants (family, refugees, self-employed, retired, assisted relative and independent). These people have the right to choose their occupation, their employer and their location of residence. In other words, they are able to work as free wageworkers within Canada. This category excludes entrepreneurs, who were added to this category in 1978, and investors, who were included in 1988.

89 "Visa" refers to the number of people admitted to Canada for periods less than or over one year and working in Canada during the calendar year recorded. The total of visa workers includes workers entering through the NIEAP plus the Foreign Domestic Movement Program (1982–1991) and the Live-in Caregiver Program (1992–1993). For the years 1989–1993, the category "backlog clearance," given to refugees granted temporary employment authorizations while waiting for their status to be determined, is also excluded.

90 This category includes all those entering the country under the above "destined" and "visa" categories

91 Sharma, "Maintaining the Master-Servant Relationship..."

92 Employers are matched with employees by overseas agencies set up to recruit workers in their country of last residence (Dias, 1994, p. 140). If this fails, employers are told that visa officers at Canadian government offices abroad can help them recruit temporary visa workers (CIC, 1994a). The role of these offices is to provide employers with advertising, interviewing facilities and advice on local laws and immigration processing times (CIC, 1994a). Employers who require a large number of workers are able to arrange for blocks of labour through bilateral agreements between the governments of Canada and other nations.

93 The use of the term "flexible" in regards to contracted, migrant workers highlights that labour-market flexibilities for employers usually translate into "rigidities" for the workers. For instance, unfree migrant workers are unable to make certain decisions available to workers who are seen by employers as less "flexible."

94 Workers employed under temporary work visas are caught in a double bind since on the one hand they are bound by employment agreements witnessed and enforced by the federal immigration department, but on the other hand they are not protected by the terms of such an agreement because labour legislation is under provincial jurisdiction. Labour law and therefore workers' rights differ significantly from province to province, with Ontario now having the least protections for farm workers and British Columbia providing the most comprehensive protections and benefits. In the BC case these protections and benefits are likely to be repealed with the election of the anti-labour government of Gordon Campbell in 2001.

95 It is important to note that with immigration laws that require sponsors of family members to be financially responsible for each person sponsored for a period of up to 10 years, sponsors are legally responsible for returning any social service assistance monies that those they sponsored may collect. This renders many of those who enter Canada through the Family Class, a disproportionate number of whom are women and children, dependent upon their sponsors, thereby rendering them more vulnerable to both labour-market and relationship abuses (Abu-Laban, "Keeping 'Em Out!...").

96 Arat-Koc, "Immigration Policies..."

97 Carole Pearson, "Farm Workers in Canada," *Our Times* 20/6 (2002), p. 26.

98 The fear of deportation if the employer is displeased in any way is also a control mechanism shaping migrant workers' militancy and should not be underestimated, particularly given the conditions that force many of these workers to migrate in search of employment abroad in the first place. For example, Wall has found that many migrant farm workers, in their attempt to secure future employment in Canada, do not organize because of fear of retaliation by the employer upon whom they pin their hopes for future work in the country (Ellen Wall, "Personal Labour Relations and Ethnicity in Ontario Agriculture," in Satzewich (ed.), *Deconstructing a Nation*, p. 269.

99 Bridget Anderson, *Doing the Dirty Work? The Global Politics of Domestic Labour* (London: Zed Books, 2000).

100 B. Singh Bolaria, "From Immigrant Settlers to Migrant Transients: Foreign Professionals in Canada," in Satzewich, *Deconstructing a Nation*, p. 212.

101 Burawoy, M. *Manufacturing Consent. Changes in the Labor Process under Monopoly Capitalism* (Chicago: University of Chicago Press, 1979).

102. Lister, "Citizenship..."; Baines, "Rebel without a Claim..."; Fraser and Gordon, "Contract Versus Charity..."

103 Yuval-Davis, *Gender and Nation...*

104 Jim Torczyner, "Globalization, Inequality and Peace Building: What Social Work Can Do," *Social Work and Globalization: Special Issue: Canadian Social Work Review* 17 (2000), pp. 123–148; A. Bendana, Powerlines. *U.S. Domination in the New Global Order* (New York: Olive Branch Press, 1996); G. Epstein, J. Graham and J. Nembhard, (eds), *Creating a New World Economy* (Philadelphia: Temple University Press, 1993).

105 Internally marginalized populations such as Indigenous people and poor people are constructed as Other and hence, share a certain common ground with non-citizen Others.

106 As Vandana Shiva notes: "According to the United Nations Development Program, while $50 billion flows annually from the North to the South in terms of aid, the South loses $500 billion every year in interest payments on debts and from the loss of fair prices for commodities due to unequal terms of trade." Vandana Shiva, *Biopiracy: The Plunder of Nature and Knowledge* (Between the Lines: Toronto, 1997).

107 See John Dillon, "Trade Talks are Key to the New World Order," in *Pro-Canada Dossier* 30 (March-April 1991).

108 See Williams, "Reflections on the Intersections...," among others, for a discussion of some of the raced, classed and gendered problems associated with supranational citizenship in the EU.

109 See Ng, "Restructuring Gender, Race, and Class Relations..."

110 Stasiulis, "International Migration Rights..."

111 Article 13 of the Universal Declaration of Human Rights states that "Everyone has the right to freedom of movement and residence within the borders of each State. Everyone has the right to leave any country, including his own, and to return to his country."

112 Stasiulis, "International Migration Rights..."

CHAPTER 10

Underdevelopment, Structural Adjustment, and Gendered Migration from the West Indies and the Philippines[1]

Daiva K. Stasiulis and Abigail B. Bakan

AMONG CRITICS OF neo-liberal globalization policies, the recognition that structural adjustment programmes operate to the detriment of the majority of the residents of underdeveloped countries is widespread. The literature in this vein is extensive, documenting the alarming growth in unemployment, underemployment, consumer prices and disparities in wealth, and the nosedive taken in incomes, basic government services and the status of women and children.[2] In this chapter, we examine one aspect of the detrimental effects of structural adjustment programmes—the increasing pressure felt by women of Third World origin to emigrate abroad and take up positions as nannies, maids and caregivers in First World households.

A brief summary can identify the parameters of the conditions underlying and shaping this migration process. Within developing countries, dislocated rural labour is inadequately absorbed in the factories of the export processing zones. The World Bank and the International Monetary Fund (IMF) have insisted that in return for the service of debts, Third World governments pursue policies which induce their citizens to seek jobs and money elsewhere.[3] Foreign currency earnings are important means of procuring foreign exchange for labour-sending states.[4] Changes associated with structural adjustment have had a considerable impact on migratory flows, especially, though not exclusively, from less developed to more developed states. The governments of developed, or economically advanced, countries, in turn, have accepted the cheap and exploitable labour of these migrants, for both political and economic reasons.

The acceptance of migrants from the South, however, has occurred within strict terms. Third World migrants filled labour shortages during periods of expansion from the 1950s to 1970s, at times despite considerable opposition and anti-immigrant hostility from some sections of the more established populations of these countries. Even during periods of recession, however, which have become increasingly frequent since the mid-1970s, migrants and immigrants of colour have been recruited to fill occupations spurned for their degraded conditions by workers with other employment options.[5] In addition, labour-receiving states are increasingly recruiting temporary rather than permanent forms of migration to augment the flexibility of their labour markets and facilitate the process of migrant return during periods of retrenchment.

The global implications of structural adjustment have also influenced recent debates on the politics of citizenship. First World countries, drawing upon long historical practices of racial/ethnic exclusion, and since the mid-1970s experiencing growing deficits, have increased the policing of Third World migrants' access to the rights normally associated with First World citizenship. Referring to Europe, Balibar[6] points out how complex the mapping of citizenship and citizenship rights has become. Some "fundamental social rights" have been extended to "guest workers" and their families both through "national law, and even Community law," yet national laws in most advanced societies are decidedly discriminatory against non-nationals. In First World states, citizenship, and access to rights traditionally associated with citizenship, are withheld even to long-term residents and their second-generation children of races and/or ethnicities viewed as alien, inassimilable and undesirable. While this is not a new phenomenon, since the return in the mid-1970s of an era of long-term economic crisis and instability, and especially since the post-September 11, 2001 "security" regimes, nationalist policies have reversed an earlier postwar trend of a relative relaxation of border controls.[7]

The implications of these recent shifts in global labour allocation and the politics of citizenship are also gendered. Despite considerable debate regarding the relative merits of the preferential employment or exploitation of women workers in global export processing zones, there is growing recognition that, on balance, structural adjustment policies have increased the burden of women's oppression in Third World states.[8] Diane Elson, for example, has identified the dependence of structural adjustment polices upon the increased provision of women's unpaid labour as a means to compensate for a decline in the level and quality of services, devaluation in local currency and the rise in prices of consumer goods. Women's increased and unpaid work operates as a shock absorber to promote the apparent "efficiency" of market-oriented mechanisms.[9]

One major growth area of First World employment for impoverished Third World women that has resulted from this global pattern is domestic service, in particular the provision of childcare or nanny service, and increasingly elder care in the private homes of First World families. Despite the contraction in access to legal migration channels for poor Third World citizens to First World countries, available evidence suggests that employment demands for migrant women as domestic workers in Europe and North America are either remaining the same or increasing. The sheer volume of Third World migrants seeking domestic service jobs in First World countries, as well as in newly industrializing countries, have rendered contemporary domestic work "an international business with political implications."[10] The industry has been further augmented by the involvement of governments of both employers and domestic workers, the IMF, and a host of intermediaries such as recruiting and placement agencies. The increased "supply" of women to work in this occupation has coincided with a socially and economically constructed "demand" for in-home care, particularly the provision of childcare, in the core zones of the global system.

The demand side of the equation has also resulted from changes in the contemporary world system. The increased participation rate of married women with children in the waged workforce that began after the Second World War has tended to continue over the years of long-term global crisis. Provision for childcare in most advanced capitalist states, however, has not kept up with the increased demand. The prohibitive costs of public childcare ensure that there is an economic incentive to opt for live-in care rather than childcare organized in the public sphere.[11] The unabated demand for live-in childcare is a consequence of cuts in the provision of state regulated and/or subsidized childcare.

The following discussion focuses on the impact of poverty and under-development in producing an increasingly large pool of women workers in search of First World citizenship rights. The migration of Third World women to Canada through the foreign domestic worker policy (currently the Live-In Caregiver Programme (LCP)) is taken as a clear instance of the link between the global debt crisis and international migration of Third World women. Our argument is twofold. First, we argue that structural forces, that is, generalized conditions of global unevenness exacerbated and amplified by imperialist structures and policies, tend to create conditions which force female citizens of poor states to seek citizenship on virtually any terms in richer states. Second, we maintain that First World states, such as Canada, are both able and willing to exploit this increased supply in order to advance their own policies of structural adjustment. The example of domestic worker policy illustrates how policies damaging to the interests of women in general, such as the cutting or elimination of public childcare, is rendered palatable, and even beneficial, to women of selectively high income and status within the boundaries defined by First World citizenship.

Central to this argument is the claim that the Canadian example is, in its general contours, typical of state policy internationally in the construction of the non-citizenship rights of foreign domestic workers. Such a claim could be contested insofar as Canada's foreign domestic worker policy is often regarded as the least abusive among the many countries across the globe employing foreign domestic workers. For example, in January 1988, the Aquino government in the Philippines responded to public protest of the abuse of overseas domestic workers by announcing a blanket ban on Filipina domestic workers going abroad. Within a few months of the announced ban, Canada was exempted from the Philippine government's restriction on the grounds that the domestic workers employed there were not subject to objectionable conditions.[12] Similarly, in Bridget Anderson's impressive comparative analysis of the conditions of domestic workers on an international scale, Canada's LCP is described as a policy that goes "a long way to regulating the situation"[13] of abusive conditions for domestic workers.

The argument presented here takes exception to this pride of place for Canada's domestic worker policy. We contend that the LCP appears as a favourable policy only because the conditions of domestic workers on a world scale are so universally oppressive. Yet the measure of abuse considered to be "acceptable" for domestic workers is itself subject to specialized criteria. These criteria are a feature of several factors: the generally degraded status of women's work in the home, the absence of comprehensive public support for childcare, the denial of citizenship rights to immigrant labour, racist assumptions about women of colour and the social construction of class divisions among women that are brought into focus with the private employment of domestic workers. Thus, we argue that Canada's foreign domestic policy is more typical than atypical on an international scale, and therefore offers lessons that have relevance well beyond Canadian borders.

Poverty, Underdevelopment, and Migrant women

The process of recruitment of migrant women workers to perform paid domestic labour in developed capitalist states is structurally linked to the uneven process of international economic development, international migration patterns and regulations, as well as racially and ethnically specific ideologies. Despite the end of formal colonial dependence, the legacy of imperialism has combined with modern conditions of indebtedness to generate large pools of Third World migrant labour. Female migrant labour in most Third World states fills the demand in the domestic care industry of economically advanced states. Kathy McAfee summarizes succinctly a view now commonly identified in the critical literature:

> The historic policies and practices of First World countries, and the international organisations these countries dominate, have served to exacerbate the conditions of poverty from which migrant women hope to escape. Structural adjustment policies, readily advocated by the International Monetary Fund (IMF) and the World Bank in particular, entail government cuts in social service budgets and public-sector employment, economic controls which favour the export of commodities over local market expansion, and tax incentives to transnational corporations. Adjustment programmes are designed to ensure that indebted countries earn more foreign exchange and that the money they earn is used to repay their loans and to promote private investment. But the actual effect of structural adjustment is to deepen the dependency, poverty and debt.... Structural adjustment programmes are tailor-made by the World Bank, the United States Agency for International Development (USAID), and other creditors for each country, but have a common thrust: to transfer more funds from impoverished debtor nations into the coffers of the Northern governments, commercial banks and multilateral lending agencies to which they are officially indebted. [14]

Extreme economic and political crises have arisen in Third World countries directly as a result of decades of the burden of international debt. One result of escalating poverty, income inequality and unemployment is increased pressure to migrate in search of employment. Migration often occurs first from rural to urban areas and to export processing zones, but much of it is directed to newly industrializing countries and developed economies of the North. While pressures to migrate from poor sending countries have increased, opportunities for legal immigration are directly tied to occupational demand in the receiving countries. Moreover, the gendered and racialized ghettoization of the labour markets of prospective countries of destination limits, conditions and moulds the character of prospective migration. Those who wish to migrate can do so legally only if they can prove that they are specifically suited to meet the employment profiles in demand: enter the female Third World immigrant domestic.

Before turning to the specific case of foreign domestic workers in Canada, and the conditions in the primary Third World source regions of the Caribbean and the Philippines from which they originate, a brief consideration of the more general place of paid domestic labour within conditions of modern capitalism is in order.

Domestic Service and Third World Migrant Women

Domestic service in the home long pre-dated contemporary capitalist global relations. In fact, pre-capitalist economies were largely based on the provision of family labour.[15] With the emergence of modern capitalism came a contraction in family size, and a reduction in the amount of labour performed in the private home relative to that performed in socialized industrial and service production units. Changes in this direction have been particularly rapid and pronounced since the large-scale participation of married women in the paid workforce, characteristic of the most advanced sections of the global economy. As Mary Romero summarizes:

> The transformation of homemaking activity from production to consumption became more complete and led to new developments for homemakers after World War II.... Both working- and middle-class

women's entrance into the workforce contributed to the general upward trend of women's employment in the twentieth century.... [However,] [t]he double-day syndrome originated from the social expectation that employed women would fulfill their families' needs through daily activity in the workforce and in the home.[16]

As new employment opportunities for women workers have developed, those able to gain alternative employment to paid domestic work have continually elected to do so. In advanced Western countries in Europe and North America, women moved out of private domestic service and into the growing industries and services in ever increasing numbers. A situation of chronic labour shortage came to characterize domestic service under conditions of modern capitalism. The so-called "servant problem" emerged as the number of women willing to work as the private servants of other women declined. By the 1950s, even the anthropologist Margaret Mead offered suggestions on "how to survive" without a maid.[17]

Commercial enterprises also took advantage of the market opportunities that became available. As economic boom conditions continued in the 1950s and 1960s, household appliances were advertised in North America as a means of automating housework and technologically "solving" the "servant problem." The single most demanding arena of private household labour, however—the provision of childcare, particularly for children of pre-school age—is resistant to automation. Under conditions of a chronic labour shortage, classical economics would predict an increase in wages and an improvement in the quality of working conditions as a means to attract and retain labourers. Domestic labour, however, has proven to be remarkably "immune to the regulatory infection"[18] of the market.

Generated by conditions of chronic poverty in the Third World, the large supply of workers who are collectively highly motivated to achieve secure employment for themselves and their families has been used to offset pressures for improvements in the conditions of domestic care. The existence of this labour pool has thus mitigated against the operation of a pure market model of supply and demand with reference to domestic labour. The denial of citizenship rights to immigrant workers and the racialized image of the Third World domestic worker, who is considered uniquely and "naturally" suited to serve the needs of First World women and their families, has tended to ensure that what one author has called "the despised calling" has become identified with the labour of women of colour.[19]

These restrictive conditions have ensured that domestic service in the context of global restructuring has taken on contradictory dimensions. At the same time as being the most spurned occupation for those who are entitled to the right of labour mobility, it is one of the most coveted for those with no other employment or migratory options. In the United States, for example, the notion of "housekeeping for the Green Card,"[20] is paralleled in the Canadian context by the practice of "doing domestic to get landed."[21] Moreover, racial and gendered barriers to labour mobility also restrict the alternative employment options for domestic workers, even once formal citizenship is obtained. Palmer points out, for example, that in the United States, Black southern women who had migrated north in the 1930s to work as domestics, found that unlike earlier

generations of Euro-American immigrants, alternative sources of employment were not made available to them, even years after arrival in Northern cities.[22] In Canada, Brand notes that at least until the Second World War, "at least 80 per cent of Black women in Canadian cities worked in domestic service. Industrialisation did not have the overwhelming impact on Black women wage earners that it did on white women."[23]

Migration and paid domestic service are thus elements of a global process of linkages, in which gendered and racialized ideologies play a central part. The particular legislative restrictions and conditions governing foreign domestic labour vary from country to country. Nonetheless, there is clearly an overall pattern in which domestic labour is subject to greater and more exceptional levels of restriction relative to other forms of employment. In countries where labour rights in general are minimal, foreign domestic workers will be subject to the greatest level of oppression and abuse, when measured on an international scale; where labour rights in general are relatively greater, as in the Canadian context, the conditions of foreign domestic workers may indeed be relatively less abusive compared with those of domestics in other countries. The conditions for domestic workers are, however, in all countries, at a level considered unacceptable for virtually every other occupation within the norms of nation-specific labour force conditions.[24]

Canada's Foreign Domestic Worker Policy

It is in comparison with the experiences of domestics in countries such as Saudi Arabia, Bahrain and Hong Kong that Canada's foreign domestic worker policy appears to offer some protection and security for the employees involved. The argument presented here departs from this view of the Canadian policy. Rather than preventing or ameliorating the threat of abuse of workers, Canada's LCP actually only serves to institutionalize such a threat. Moreover, the LCP has been structured by various federal governments over decades with the full knowledge of a highly vulnerable pool of foreign worker applicants, upon whom exceptionally restrictive conditions are imposed.

In Canada, the federal legislation governing the recruitment of in-home domestic care, the LCP, was formulated to facilitate and regulate the recruitment of migrant workers. To be eligible by Canadian law to hire a domestic worker through the LCP, the prospective employing family must indicate ability to provide a room in the family home, for which rent would be deducted from wages earned, and to meet a minimum combined annual income.[25] The policy itself is constructed as a "special," separate piece of immigration legislation, applying only to those foreign workers seeking work in Canada as live-in domestics as a temporary means to obtain permanent immigration status. This fact alone indicates the unique conditions to which foreign domestic workers are subject, separated out from the normal pool of immigrant applicants to Canada. This distinct immigration policy, administered at the federal level, also exempts foreign domestic workers from the generalized regulation of labour legislation, which is administered provincially. The employment standards for domestic workers vary from province to province. Moreover where foreign domestic workers are covered by specific provincial labour legislation, this has tended to be the result of domestic advocacy movements organizing to ensure coverage, not the largesse of any particular provincial government.[26]

From the mid-1950s, when legislation was enacted specifically to recruit Caribbean women workers to Canada as live-in domestics, to the present policy enacted in 1992, the federal government has insisted upon maintaining a distinct and exceptional institutional mechanism to govern the migration and work lives of foreign domestic workers. Another notable characteristic of the foreign domestic legislation is that there has been a secular trend towards increasing restrictions on the rights of the workers themselves, despite public lobbying and documented studies calling for equalizing the rights of foreign domestics with those of other workers.[27]

With the 1973 introduction by the Canadian federal government of the Temporary Employment Authorization Programme, for example, domestic workers received short-term work permits rather than the previous scheme's provision of permanent resident status upon arrival. These women were permitted to stay in Canada conditionally upon the performance of domestic work for a designated employer, thus transforming "domestic workers into … disposable migrant labourers, not unlike European 'guest workers.'"[28] During the 1970s, the citizenship rights of foreign, and especially Caribbean, domestics thus deteriorated further. While many European domestics continued to enter Canada as landed immigrants, Caribbean domestics increasingly entered on temporary employment visas, which gave maximum control to the state and employers over the conditions of work and residence of women-of-colour domestics.[29] Migrant domestics were compelled to endure restrictions in freedoms generally considered unacceptable under liberal democracies, and rejected by other workers, including those performing the same type of work outside private households.[30]

The Canadian government's programme of recruiting foreign domestic workers under temporary work permits effectively created an indentured or captive labour force. Moreover, this was a source of cheap labour: the costs of original production (nurturance, education, etc.) had been borne elsewhere, and workers were often reluctant to quit regardless of how exploited or intolerable their work and living situations. The motivation for administering foreign domestics through the temporary employment visa system, with no recourse to the previous option of applying for landed immigrant status from within Canada, was clearly stated by the government in 1976: the aim was to impede the turnover of foreign workers out of compulsory live-in domestic service.[31]

In 1981, a revised policy, entitled the Foreign Domestic Movement (FDM), was introduced which further institutionalized this objective. Under this programme, a foreign domestic worker was eligible to apply for landed immigrant status after two years of live-in service with a designated employer. Employers could only be changed with the approval of a federal immigration officer. If the worker successfully achieved landed status, all of the restrictions associated with the FDM ceased to apply, providing access to all formal citizenship rights open to permanent residents.

The right to apply for permanent status after two years of residence from inside Canada was heralded as a victory by domestic worker advocates, and it was indeed a concession to the demands of domestic workers themselves. Nevertheless, the 1981 policy included a number of regulations that continued the pattern of exceptional, and discriminatory, treatment for foreign domestic workers. It institutionalized the potential for employer abuse, including the threat of deportation while the worker remained effectively imprisoned by temporary-residence, and compulsory live-in, status. If after three assessments the domestic worker had not been accepted for permanent resident status, by law she would be required to return to her country of origin. The alternative would be to remain illegally in Canada and to work in the shadow economy.

Other criteria, such as the requirements of educational upgrading to prove "self-sufficiency" as a condition of achieving landed immigrant status, were also imposed on those who entered Canada through the FDM. Domestic workers and their advocates challenged these restrictions and criticized the use of criteria not applied to assess the suitability for landing of any other group of immigrants whose occupations, like those of domestic workers, were in high demand in Canada. Notwithstanding these protests, the government's policy remained in place for a decade. Only when the government came under a legal challenge was the policy altered. The government's failure to withstand a 1990 legal challenge to the FDM policy was pivotal in prompting the raising of formal qualifications for entry into Canada of foreign domestic applicants.[32]

Once again, the specific reforms to the policy in 1992 did not decrease the considerable restrictions imposed on the rights of foreign domestic workers. Under the 1992 LCP guidelines, the upgrading requirements were eliminated in assessments for landed status for foreign domestics, who were now called "caregivers." To offset this apparent liberalization in the policy, however, eligibility criteria for entry into Canada by migrant caregivers became more restrictive. In other words, the exceptional criteria for eligibility for permanent residential status under the FDM were simply front-loaded to the point of application for admission into the LCP.

Criteria for entry into the LCP originally called for the equivalent of a Canadian grade 12 education, plus six months of full-time formal training in a field or occupation related to the caregiver job sought in Canada. Within months of the programme's inception, the latter training requirement was amended to allow for experience in lieu of training. Once again, however, this amendment resulted from the public outcry from domestic workers and worried potential employers.[33] The official reasons given by the Immigration Department for upgrading the admissions criteria for foreign domestics were, first, the perceived need to upgrade the quality of childcare, and second, to facilitate the entry into the larger labour market of those domestics who had attained landed status. According to the federal government, without adequate educational backgrounds, domestic workers who had obtained permanent resident status after completing the required two years of live-in service continue to find employment in only the most poorly remunerated jobs.

The two most repressive aspects of the Foreign Domestic Movement were retained under the LCP. This in spite of the government's attempt to sell the new programme through the rhetoric of "reform" resulting from "widespread consultation."[34] These features are (i) the temporary migrant or "visitor" status; and (ii) the compulsory live-in requirement for foreign domestic workers. Accordingly, it is recognized that this "program is unique"[35] as it applies specific restrictions on the rights

of foreign domestic workers that are relevant to no other category of workers, regardless of their immigration status. The two restrictions of compulsory living-in with the employer, and the temporary immigration status of the labourer, go hand-in-hand. According to the governmental reviews that led to the formulation of the LCP, Canada's shortage of waged domestic labour exists only within the live-in market. Were it not for this labour shortage, foreign labour would not be in demand.

While the most repressive features of earlier domestic worker policy were retained, a change was introduced in regard to the legal status of the programme. It became a regulatory programme, rather than one established by policy.[36] Several scholars had pointed out the tenuousness and ambiguous legal status of the FDM and previous domestic worker policies which had existed in a series of revised policy decisions,[37] and a "myriad of little rules ... applied to monitor and control" foreign domestics.[38] While the impact of the FDM had been extremely coercive and punitive of the behaviour of foreign domestics, the rules and regulations of the FDM programme had no legal authority, forming part of the Immigration Manual only rather than part of the Immigration Act and the Immigration Regulations.[39] Despite original hopes on the part of some advocates that such a change in the legal status might benefit domestic workers seeking permanent residence, the evidence points to a continuation of harassment and bureaucratic challenges.

The features of compulsory living-in and enforced temporary residence are those most commonly identified to produce abusive and unsafe working conditions. These features also have been consistently opposed by leading domestic workers' rights advocates in Canada.[40] Studies of paid domestic service in the United

States have repeatedly identified the single most effective change in domestic labour leading to improved working conditions as the move away from live-in to live-out service.[41] The continued imposition of the combined compulsory live-in requirement and temporary residential status is therefore notable for its exceptional treatment of an identifiable group of women workers, usually of Third World origin, recruited for the sole purpose of private domestic service. Effectively, the Canadian government's insistence on retaining these restrictive measures as a pre-condition for eligibility, "established a class of people good enough to do their dirty work, but not good enough to be permanent residents."[42]

While the percentage of entrants into the LCP from the Philippines has remained high (between 61 and 75 percent of total entrants in the 1990s), the overall numbers of domestics entering under the LCP have been drastically reduced. Thus, the number of entrants into the LCP in 1997 (1606) was less than one-fifth of the number of entrants in 1991 (8,630), the last year of the FDM, and only 15 percent of the 1990 figure (10,739).[43] The precipitous drop in numbers of migrants entering through the LCP reflects a choking off of an important source for legal entry into Canada, and of the prospect for acquisition of Canadian residence and citizenship for Third World women.

The difficulties in gaining access in Canada to positions as a foreign domestic have forced many female migrant workers to work in undocumented statuses, for example, entering as visitors, asylum seekers or refugees or students, and remaining to work illegally. Although there are no accurate figures regarding undocumented foreign women working as private household workers, anecdotal sources suggest that the numbers are large and growing. The results of the questionnaire survey in our study of 50 domestic workers in Toronto conducted in 1994 and 1995 suggest that for national origin/regional groups facing barriers to legal entry as domestic workers, entry as visitors and unlawful work in a shadow economy are already well-established practices.[44] Workers' undocumented status further increases the power of employers within personal domestic service. Employers may utilize the threat of the employee's conviction under Canadian law or deportation to enforce arbitrary demands. They are particularly apt to do so in a context where the Canadian government is under no obligation to offer labour protection to undocumented workers.

Canada's foreign domestic worker policy thus shares in common with the policies of other countries the imposition of exceptionally harsh restrictions, considered unacceptable for workers in other industries, or for those, such as legal citizens, who have the option of seeking alternative sources of employment. In studies on domestic labour internationally, the terms used to describe situations normally considered to be illegal, archaic and barbaric include "precapitalist" and "premodern," with analogies made to "slavery."[45] Canada's institutionalization of compulsory live-in status, combined with the threat of denial of permanent residence, amounts to a condition of indentured labour. The fact that the condition of indenture is temporary does not in any way mitigate the susceptibility of the employee to abuse. The temporary condition is a standard feature of indenture, and is rendered effective in regulating domestic workers precisely because it holds the promise of increased citizenship rights at the end of the two-year term. In other words, the stick would not be effective without the promise of a carrot.

There is extensive documentation of conditions of abuse commonly experienced by foreign domestic workers in Canada. Since such abuse takes place within the confines of a private home, however, enforcement and regulation of procedures to correct such abuses are both rare and extremely difficult. The overriding threat of deportation to conditions of poverty and chronic unemployment in the Third World ensures a structural pattern of intimidation, where the citizen-employer and the non-citizen employee do not face each other on equal terms. Since the 1950s, Canada has drawn upon two major Third World source regions as recruitment areas for foreign domestic workers where the threat of deportation is sufficiently harsh that even the most oppressive employment options within Canada seem to offer a more secure alternative. It is to the conditions in these regions that we now turn our discussion.

Conditions in the Caribbean and Philippines Fostering Female Migration

The conditions of underdevelopment within the English Caribbean and the Philippines are central to the historic role of these regions as the major Third World source areas for the recruitment of foreign domestics in Canada. How Canadian domestic worker policy has been constructed to take advantage of these conditions, and has adapted its regulations accordingly, is critical to situating Canada's foreign domestic policy in the context of global restructuring.

The English Caribbean region as a whole incorporates a wide variety of nations and is influenced by a complexity of economic, social and political factors. In general, however, until the 19th century internal migration was negligible and external migration involved only a fraction of the population. Those who did migrate were usually of middle- or upper-class background, hoping to advance their prospects by obtaining permanent residence in Europe or North America.[46]

During the 1960s and 1970s, this pattern started to change, with large numbers of residents from the Commonwealth Caribbean seeking migration abroad. Most of the major studies of Caribbean migration for this period maintain that the increase was not necessarily a response to unemployment, but of increased opportunities elsewhere for well-educated, relatively high-status professionals.[47] This is not to suggest that unemployment did not exist. On the contrary, the British West Indies has seen chronic rates of unemployment ranging between 20 and 30 percent of the workforce. Instead, it was the effect of restrictive immigration laws in some of the most favoured destination countries that ensured only the most skilled workers were permitted to enter.[48]

The period of the 1960s and 1970s saw an increase in emigration outlets for Caribbean workers at the same time as political independence was negotiated with the British imperial state.[49] Newly independent Caribbean governments hoped to offset chronic unemployment and secure sources of foreign currency in the form of remittances by encouraging migration abroad. Studies of trends in West Indian out-migration indicate that there have been two major post-Second World War waves, one from 1955–61, with destinations mainly to the United Kingdom; and a second from 1979–85, matching the previous wave in terms of both volume and rate of departure, but destined primarily to North America. By 1980, it was estimated that 20 to 30 percent of the Caribbean region's total population was residing outside the region, largely in Europe and North America.[50] This diaspora was not evenly experienced among the island nations of the Caribbean. By 1973, Jamaica, the largest of the British Caribbean nations with a population of about two million, registered more than half a million citizens living off the island.[51] Remittances have therefore developed into a critical component for family survival in the region. Estimates of the value of remittances to the British West Indies are difficult to verify, given the variations among the islands and poor statistical records. One study provides a 1978 estimate of US$23 billion, roughly equivalent to 10 percent of the region's merchandise exports; a 1982 study suggests that remittances were the principal source of hard currency in several of the small islands in the region.[52] Though there is only "fragmentary evidence," over long historic trends, available data indicates that "remittance flows are significant."[53] Remittances from Latin America and the Caribbean taken as an aggregate indicate a significant increase in family dependence on overseas remittances, particularly since 1990.[54] Jamaica has seen the level of remittances exceed 10 percent of the country's gross domestic product (GDP).[55] In many rural districts in Jamaica, remittances have surpassed farm income as the main source of revenue.[56]

Evidence suggests that the early years of this emigration wave favoured the exodus of male workers. This coincided with the internal migration of female workers from the rural areas into the cities, particularly to work as domestic servants for private homes and in the burgeoning tourist and hotel industries.[57] This pattern reinforced another: the historically large proportion of households headed by sole-support mothers. According to Momsen, though the proportion of female household heads varies greatly across the region, in general "[w]omen have had to accept responsibility for the financial support of their children since emancipation because of both male migration and male economic marginality."[58] In 1970, the Commonwealth Caribbean recorded 35 percent of all households headed by women; a 1986 study confirmed this figure, finding a ratio of one in three households to be under female headship.[59] This factor, and the decline of agriculture as a source of profitable employment, compelled women to seek new sectors of work.[60] Domestic labour in Canada was one such avenue.

Prior to 1962, Canada had an explicitly racist governmental policy restricting West Indian immigration to Canada. According to the 1958 Director of the Immigration Branch of the Department of Citizenship:

> [I]t is not by accident that coloured British subjects other than negligible numbers from the United Kingdom are excluded from Canada.... They do not assimilate readily and pretty much vegetate to a low standard of living. Despite what has been said to the contrary, many cannot adapt themselves to our climatic conditions.[61]

In 1955, this policy was amended to permit a limited number of West Indian women workers to enter Canada on condition that they remain in domestic service with a contractually designated employer for one year; after this time they were permitted to obtain other employment. This policy, like those that were to follow, was distinctly discriminatory. Unlike domestic workers from Europe, the West Indian workers received no government assistance in the cost of passage. Moreover, although permanent resident status was obtained upon arrival, Caribbean domestics were subject to special conditions of compulsory live-in domestic labour and the threat of deportation. Such restrictions did not apply to domestics from European source countries.[62]

Between 1973 and 1981, West Indian women workers were admitted as domestic workers on temporary employment visas. Others entered as skilled workers, particularly in nursing when there were periodic labour shortages, or as sponsored relatives. The numbers as a whole, however, were relatively small and since that period have been declining relative to other source countries. Canada's labour policy favoured female over male West Indian migrants. In 1967, the ratio was 43 males to 57 females; by 1980 the ratio had narrowed slightly but remained skewed, with 46 males to 54 females. By 1987, the ratio had stabilized at approximately 45 males to 54 females.[63] Regardless of the ratio, however, total numbers of West Indian migrants declined. Between 1973 and 1978, of all those who obtained landed immigrant status in Canada, those from all Caribbean source countries totalled only 10 percent; by 1980, that figure was six percent.[64] Conversely, one of the most rapidly increasing alternative source regions of immigration to Canada overall, as well as in the migration of foreign domestics, was the Philippines.

In the year from July 1975 to June 1976, 44.8 percent of all entrants to Canada on temporary employment visas assigned to in-home domestic work were from the Caribbean, and only 0.3 percent were from all countries in Asia; by 1990, only 5 percent of entrants on the Foreign Domestic Movement programme were from the Caribbean, while over 58 percent were from the Philippines.[65] Canada, however, is only one destination country for Filipino migrants. While Filipino workers are scattered in almost all regions of the world, the vast majority of Filipino migrant household workers abroad work in Asia (particularly Hong Kong and Singapore) and the Gulf Region (Saudi Arabia, United Arab Emirates). Between 1982 and 1990, the total number of Filipino processed contract workers had almost doubled.[66] Throughout the 1990s, the numbers of migrants deployed abroad continued to climb, increasing from 660,122 in 1996 to 841,628 in 2000.[67] Only immigration that passes through official channels, however, is counted in reported statistics. According to the International Labour Organization, among Asian women in general, the 1990s have also witnessed considerable increases in illegal migration, when workers are considered to be the most vulnerable to abuse.[68] This trend is known to be widespread in the Philippines. Even if we only consider the official statistics for labour migration, however, by 1995 the estimated size of the total Filipino workforce abroad, comprising both temporary contract migrants and those who have settled permanently abroad, was about 4.2 million.[69]

The period since the 1980s has also witnessed an increasing proportional exodus of female migrant labour. By the end of the 1980s, women comprised between 40 and 50 per cent of all Filipino migrants.[70] The proportion of female Filipino migrants has increased rapidly as their share has grown from 61 percent in 1998 to 70 percent in 2000.[71] This has in part been a response to high levels of demand for nurses, office workers, domestic workers and other types of service worker, as well as entertainers, sex trade workers and mail order brides in Asia, the Middle East, Europe and North America.[72] By 1991, domestic workers comprised the majority of

Filipino women workers registered with the central government's Philippine Overseas Employment Administration (POEA).[73] By the mid-1990s, domestic workers counted for nearly 45 percent of the overall number of newly hired overseas female contract workers registered with the Philippines government.[74]

The unprecedented rise of Filipino emigration reflects both the growing internationalization of labour markets and the persistence of underdevelopment in the Philippine economy.[75] Development in the Philippines has been hampered by colonization by the Spanish, and since the turn of the century, by colonial and neo-colonial policies of the United States. A pervasive legacy of the Philippine neo-colonial status vis-à-vis the United States has been the latter's right to maintain over 20 bases and military installations in the country. The withdrawal of the US military in 1992, though a symbolic recognition of greater Philippine autonomy, proved only a token concession. The Philippines's development problems were exacerbated in the 1990s not least through a significant reduction in American aid.[76]

A number of structural factors linked to underdevelopment have triggered the large volume of labour flows from the country. These include the increasing scarcity of land, urban growth without sufficient expansion in urban employment to meet the supply of dislocated and landless agricultural workers, massive overseas indebtedness and the general poor performance of a predominantly foreign-owned economy.[77] The Philippines achieved formal independence from the United States in 1946. Prior to this, the semi-feudal landlord-tenant system was heavily promoted by the ruling elite at the expense of the free-holding sectors of the peasantry.[78] Critical development problems in the Philippines are,

however, not only economic; they have been exacerbated by political instability. Between 1972 and 1981, Philippines President, Ferdinand Marcos, sought to suppress civil unrest in the form of peasant, worker and student militancy, through the imposition of martial law.[79] Marcos's economic policies provided an open invitation for foreign investors to control any area of the economy through "service contracts" entered into with Filipino citizens and domestic corporations.[80]

In 1984, following the assassination of Senator Benigno Aquino, leader of the opposition to the Marcos regime, some 86,000 workers were laid off by various corporations. More than 50 percent of families were living below the officially defined poverty threshold. The removal of Marcos and the installation of the Aquino government in 1986 through a popularly supported military revolt, while increasing popular hope for change, did not in fact lead to further economic development. The government of Aquino, and since 1992, those of Ramos, Estrada and Macapagal-Arroyo, have not significantly alleviated the economic distress felt by almost all Filipinos. The only exception is an elite section of Philippine society, fully committed to intensifying domestic and international links to free market policies. Official unemployment in the Philippines is among the highest in the Asia Pacific region, at 10.5 percent in 2001, with an additional official rate of underemployment at 17.5 percent.[81] Out-migration has become a structural feature of the Philippine capitalism. The export of labour offsets domestic unemployment rates. In addition, remittances support the domestic economy and help to service the government's huge foreign debt. According to the POEA, the government agency tasked to oversee the systematic export of labour:

[A]bout US$2.17 billion was generated by the government on remittance of migrant workers from 1982–85 alone. Under Aquino, US$5.98 billion were remitted through legal banking channels from 1986–91. Under Ramos, a total of US$16.68 billion was generated from remittances of migrant workers in a period of 4 years (1992–95).... For the year 2000, total remittances recorded by the [Central Bank of the Philippines] is US$6.05.[82]

Key to understanding the unstable nature of the Philippine economy is the debt crisis and the impact of structural adjustment policies. The effects of the chronic debt crisis is summed up by Pomeroy: "A relentless chaining of the Filipino people into a helpless debt situation constituted part of the coldly planned process of reorganizing and reorienting the Philippine economy to suit the needs and operations of U.S. big corporations."[83] The Philippine experience with IMF-World Bank lending policies began in 1958, and has resulted in enormous and escalating international financial debt, amounting to $28.6 billion by 1986; by 1999 the official debt figure had risen to $52.2 billion. Augmenting the size of international debt for the non-oil-producing country were the 1973–74 and 1979–80 increases in world prices of oil, which plunged the trade balance of the Philippines into ever-steeper deficit.[84] The significance of these remittances to servicing the foreign debt are illustrated by the fact that "87% (US$5.9 billion) of the US$6.79 billion remittances in 1999 went to debt servicing ... [Moreover,] given the fact that as of June 2000 Philippine debt ... reached US$52.2 billion, labor export is likely to continue to be tied to the politics of foreign debt...."[85]

US-dictated demands by the World Bank for "structural adjustment" of the Philippine economy included several policies: a devaluation of the peso, import liberalization, export-oriented development, wage restraints, no-strike measures, cuts in social services and further concessions for foreign investors.[86] Export-oriented development led to land conversions that displaced peasants from their livelihood, and thus contributed to unemployment in the rural areas.[87] According to Ludmilla Kwitko, "[U]nofficial figures suggest that combined under and unemployment run as high as 40–50%."[88]

Women have suffered disproportionately from job loss in the Philippines's service industries, and through the retrenchments and shutdowns in manufacturing that have formed part of the structural adjustment process. The bulk of private-sector service workers in the Philippines are found in retail trading, and are composed of street vendors, hawkers and operators of five-and-dime stores, beauty parlours and repair shops. These enterprises, based on minimal capital and technology, offer little potential for improving productivity and reflect unstable wage relations or ownership of only the most minor means of production.[89] However, women workers are often favoured as employees in the large export processing zones. Even these conditions, however, where there is employment but also extreme exploitation, have not produced any generalized decline in emigration.[90] CALABARZON, one of the largest export processing zones and a model of future Philippine development, is a case in point. CALABARZON is a massive industrial development complex named after the five provinces which intersect in the 16,229 square kilometre zone with a population of 8.3 million—Cavite, Laguna, Batangas, Rizal and Quezon. Billed in the region's promotional literature as "CALABARZON—Where doing business is a pleasure," the investment haven is described as "[t]he most dynamic region in the country," one which "also enjoys social and political stability."[91] The CALABARZON project is a 20-year model project in the government's Medium-Term Philippine Development Plan. Under the official development assistance package from Japan, US$3,126 billion was expected for the first five years. Of 441 factories operating in the CALABARZON industrial area, 195 of them employ predominantly women workers. The plants are mostly assembly-type factories—in electronics, automobile assembly, garments and textiles, food and beverages and ceramics. According to one study:

> Some companies have a policy of hiring only young, single women. Applicants are required to undergo pregnancy tests, even if they are single. There is no consideration for the conditions of pregnant workers nor for mothers with young children—pregnant workers also work the night shift, and those whose children are sick are forced to resign.[92]

Thus in spite of high and rising levels of education, working women in the Philippines continue to experience gender discrimination and stereotyping at all levels of the occupational structure.[93] The consistent decline in the value of the peso that has accompanied structural adjustment has made it difficult for Filipinas to meet the daily basic needs of their families as real incomes have decreased while prices of goods and services have increased.

Since 1974, with the formulation of the Philippine Labour Code,[94] the Philippines government has vigorously pursued overseas

employment as a means of alleviating chronic unemployment and balance of payments problems.[95] Individuals and households have also pursued overseas employment as a means of survival, and of improving economic opportunities for Filipino families.[96] A 1988 household income and expenditures survey revealed that 15.5 percent of families in the Philippines receive income from abroad contributing about 30 percent of their total incomes.[97] By 1998, one-third of the Filipino population, or approximately 20 million people, were estimated to be directly supported through remittances of overseas workers, a majority of whom are women.[98] One common family strategy is to subsidize the higher education of one family member who is then sent abroad to earn wages that are comparatively much higher than potential earnings in the Philippines. However, the structural pressures towards overseas migration are demonstrably greater than individual family strategies. As Mitter summarizes:

> By 1979, the Philippine government was earning $1 billion from foreign remittances, nearly 15 percent of its total export earnings. Recruitment and the sending of remittances were not left to the personal choice of the workers either…. In 1983, to increase the amount of currency coming back to the Philippines, the government passed a decree which compelled a large number of Filipino workers abroad to remit between 50 and 80 percent of their wages. The penalty for non-compliance would be refusal to renew or extend passports, non-renewal of employment contracts, and in cases of subsequent violations, repatriation to the Philippines.[99]

Filipino migrant workers tend to have higher-than-average education. According to a 1980 study, over 50 percent of Filipino migrant workers surveyed had completed some college education, in comparison with only 12.5 percent of the Philippine labour force.[100] In the context of a 40 percent unemployment rate among nurses in the Philippines, nursing degrees are deliberately acquired as passports to work abroad, and thereby increase family living standards. What is calculated less frequently than the economic impact of overseas employment, both for the individual migrant worker and for the Philippine economy, are the dire social consequences of long-term separation of family members entailed in contract migration, as well as widespread abuse and exploitation of migrant workers abroad.[101]

Implications for Citizenship

Poverty and underdevelopment, exacerbated by structural adjustment policies that serve the interests of foreign commercial banks and corporations, are responsible for producing the pool of migrant female labour available to work as maids and nannies abroad. Nonetheless, foreign domestic worker policies of states such as Canada, and the gatekeeping mechanisms that serve to enforce such policies, fashion the specific terms and conditions of access for Third World migrant women into developed states as a means of escaping such extreme poverty. Regulation of citizenship rights is thus central to the process that compels—to put the case crudely—poor women from Third World countries to work as domestic employees for rich women and families in First World countries.

A common analytical expression used to explain the increasing role of poor women in the international migration matrix is the trend towards "the feminisation of (im)migrant labour." This phrase summarizes the increasing proportion of female migrant labour relative to male. This gendered transition is fairly recent, but it has taken place in some countries at a very rapid rate. The Philippines is particularly notable. Since the mid-1980s, the migration trend has tended to shift from one consisting largely of single males, or male workers with dependent family members, to one in which women are now, at 60 to 70 percent of the total migrant population, far exceeding men.

However, the phrase "feminisation of (im)migrant labour" risks distorting the actual implications of this trend. Rather than seeing increasing opportunities for migrant women workers relative to male workers, in fact tightening controls on poor, Third World immigrant labour, both male and female, have created a decline in opportunities. It is in the most oppressive employment niches that women have tended to be "favoured" as migrant workers. Secure industrial opportunities for male immigrant workers have tended to decrease. Women workers with no other source of employment at home or abroad are forced to accept highly exploited working conditions where sex stereotyping and abuse are virtually endemic. Domestic and personal service labour, which in the receiving countries is overwhelmingly stereotyped as female labour, has grown proportionally as an international employment outlet for Philippine and other Asian migrant women as the gender ratio has shifted.[102] Moreover, in receiving nations, including Canada, Europe and the more developed nations of Asia such as Hong Kong and Singapore, foreign domestic workers are overwhelmingly employed in households where they are under the managerial direction of other, wealthy, women. As Heyzer and Wee note, an "ironic consequence of these class implications is that the employment of a foreign domestic worker has become a status symbol of the newly prosperous in the richer countries."[103] Class issues regarding immigration patterns, and the presence or absence of immigrants' rights, reinforce gender-based discrimination in specific and selected ways, which the term "feminization" tends to falsely universalize and obfuscate.

An alternative approach, suggested here, includes a consideration of rights constituted and denied through citizenship policies of nation-states. While migrant domestic workers lack many basic citizenship rights, including the choice of employer and domicile, their employers, in contrast, generally enjoy full citizenship rights. For citizen-women with economic and social means, the in-home employment of migrant domestic workers provides an outlet to partially alleviate the conditions of their female oppression. However, this happens on an individual basis, paid for on the market, leaving the systemic conditions of women's oppression intact and in some ways reinforced.

Despite individual relief of the burdens of private home care, the generalized condition of women's oppression is perpetuated. Rather than female employer and employee experiencing a commonality of oppression based on gender, the result is a division of interests, where class, racial and citizenship distinctions become paramount.

The international circulation of Third World female domestics is but one of several major flows in contemporary global migration. The systematic reproduction of foreign domestic workers is legally separate from, and structurally subordinate to, "normal" immigration flows internationally. Despite Canada's less abusive foreign domestic worker policy relative to those of some other countries, Canada is inextricably linked to this global pattern, both benefiting from and contributing to the structural exploitation of Third World women. This global pattern of structural exploitation suggests the need for a critique of contemporary policies of structural adjustment in both national and global state contexts.

Endnotes

1   This chapter draws upon Abigail B. Bakan and Daiva Stasiulis, "Structural Adjustment, Citizenship, and Foreign Domestic Labour: The Canadian Case," in Isabella Bakker, ed., *Rethinking Restructuring: Gender and Change in Canada* (University of Toronto Press, 1996). We are grateful to Anne-Marie Murnaghan for her valuable research assistance.

2   See e.g., Kevin Danaher, ed., *Democratizing the Global Economy* (Philadelphia: Common Courage Press, 2001); Michel Chussodovksy, *The Globalization of Poverty: Impacts of IMF and World Bank Reforms* (New Jersey: Zed Books, 1999); Susan George, *The Debt Boomerang: How Third World Debt Hurts Us All* (Boulder: Westview Press, 1992); Kathryn Ward, ed., *Women Workers and Global Restructuring* (Ithaca: Cornell University Press, 1990); Paul Harrison, *Inside the Third World* (Harmondsworth: Penguin Books, 1993), especially 448–85; Paula Sparr, ed., *Mortgaging Women's Lives* (London: Zed Books, 1994).

3   For background on the theoretical and empirical context to this phenomenon, see e.g., Parreñas, *Servants of Globalization;* Saskia Sassen-Koob, "Labour Migrations and the New International Division of Labour," in June Nash and Maria Patricia Fernandez-Kelly, eds, *Women, Men and the International Division of Labour* (Albany: State University of New York Press, 1983), 175–204.

4   See Nigel Harris, *The New Untouchables: Immigration and the New World Worker* (Harmondsworth: Penguin Books, 1995), 60.

5   See George, *The Debt Boomerang,* 110–35.

6 Etienne Balibar, "*Es Gibt Keinen Staat in Europa:* Racism and Politics in Europe Today," *New Left Review* (March/April 1991), 186:18.

7 11 September 2001 is the date when the US World Trade Centre in New York City and the Pentagon building in Washington DC were the targets of extensive terrorist attacks. The full implications of this historic event go beyond the scope of this study. However, it should be noted that in virtually every major receiving country in the world, racialized criteria in the selection and rights of immigrants were increased and given greater official license. On the historical context, see Robin Cohen, *The New Helots: Migrants and the International Division of Labor* (Vermont: Gower Publishing Co., 1987).

8 See e.g., Brigitte Young, "The 'Mistress' and the 'Maid' in the Globalized Economy," in Leo Panitch and Colin Leys, eds, *Socialist Register, 2001: Working Classes, Global Realities* (London: Merlin Press, 2001); Sylvia Chant, *Women and Survival in Mexican Cities: Perspectives on Gender, Labor Markets and Low-income Households* (New York: Manchester University Press, 1991); L. Lim, "Women's Work in Export Factories: the Politics of a Cause," in I. Tinker, ed., *Persistent Inequalities* (New York: Oxford University Press, 1990).

9 Diane Elson, "Male Bias in Macro-economics: The Case of Structural Adjustment," in Diane Elson, ed., *Male Bias in the Development Process* (New York: Manchester University Press, 1991). On the specific implications of gender to the international division of labour and the global process of capital accumulation, see Ward, ed., *Global Restructuring;* Swasti Mitter, *Common Fate, Common Bond: Women in the Global Economy* (London: Pluto Press, 1986); Thanh-Dam Truong, *Sex, Money and Morality: Prostitution and Tourism in South-East Asia* (London: Zed Books, 1990) and Vickers, *Women and the World Economic Crisis.*

10 Enloe, *Bananas, Beaches and Bases, 177.*

11 Canada, the focus of this study, is a case in point. While costs and quality of care vary considerably, and there are no national standards by which to measure cost per service, "the typical cost of a regulated child care space for a three-year-old is between $4000 and $6000 per year (even higher in Ontario).... [P]arents ... in 1988 were found to be spending about 8 per cent of the family's pre-tax income, or nearly 18 per cent of the mother's pre-tax income on child care costs." "Introduction" to *Our Children's Future: Child Care Policy in Canada,* eds, Gordon Cleveland and Michael Krashinsky (Toronto: University of Toronto Press, 2001), 9.

12 Ludmilla Kwitko, "Filipina Domestic Workers and the New International Division of Labour," Paper presented at the Asia in the 1990s: Making and Meeting a New World Conference (Queen's University, Kingston, 1993), 1, 21.

13 Bridget Anderson, *Britain's Secret Slaves: An Investigation into the Plight of Overseas Domestic Workers* (United Kingdom: Anti-Slavery International and Kalayaan, 1993).

14 Kathy McAfee, *Storm Signals: Structural Adjustment and Development Alternatives in the Caribbean* (London: Zed Books and Oxfam America, 1991), 7.

15 On the relationship between the changes in production and the role of domestic service in the family with the emergence of western capitalist societies, see e.g., Rhonda Rapoport and Robert Rapoport, "Work and Family in Contemporary Society," in John N. Edwards, ed., *The Family and Change* (New York: Knopf, 1969): 385–408; L.A. Tilly and J.W. Scott, *Women, Work and Family* (New York: Holt, Rinehart and Winston, 1978) and Mary Romero, *Maid in the USA* (New York: Routledge, 1992), 47–70.

16 Romero, *Maid in the USA,* 64–5.

17 Linda Martin and Kelly Segrave, *The Servant Problem: Domestic Workers in North America* (Jefferson NC: McFarland, 1985), 69.

18 This phrase, taken from a somewhat different context, belongs to Phyllis Palmer. See "Housewife and Household Worker: Employer-Employee Relationships in the Home, 1928–1941," in Carol Groneman and Mary Beth Norton, eds, *'To Toil the Livelong Day': America's Women at Work 1780–1980* (Ithaca: Cornell University Press, 1987), 180.

19 Elizabeth Clark-Lewis, "This Work had an End...," in Carol Groneman and Mary Beth Norton, eds, *"To Toil the Livelong Day": America's Women at Work 1780–1980* (Ithaca: Cornell University Press, 1987), 197.

20 See Shellee Colen, "'Housekeeping' for the Green Card: West Indian Household Workers, the State and Stratified Reproduction in New York," in Roger Sanjek and Shellee Colen, eds, *At Work in Homes: Household Workers in World Perspective* (Washington DC: American Ethnological Society Monograph Series, 1990), 93.

21 Audrey Macklin, "Foreign Domestic Worker: Surrogate Housewife or Mail Order Servant?," *McGill Law Journal,* 37: 3 (1992).

22 Phyllis Palmer, *Domesticity and Dirt: Housewives and Domestic Servants in the United States, 1920–1945* (Philadelphia: Temple University Press, 1989), 67 ff.

23 Dionne Brand, *No Burden to Carry: Narratives of Black Working Women in Ontario 1920s–1950s* (Toronto: Women's Press, 1991), 15.

24 For a consideration of the domestic workers industry internationally, see Noeleen Heyzer, Geertje Lycklama a Nijeholt and Nedra Weerakoon, eds, *The Trade in Domestic Workers; Causes, Mechanisms and Consequences of International Migration* (Kuala Lampur and London: Asian and Pacific Development Centre and Zed Books, 1994) and Parreñas, *Servants of Globalization.*

25 As of April 1992, that minimum in Ontario was $65,000 per year, about $20,000 above the national combined average annual family income. See Estanislao Oziewicz, "Nanny Policy Called Necessary Protection," *The Globe and Mail* (29 April 1992). However, in 2000, the average gross annual income in Canada for a family employing a live-in domestic worker on the LCP has been estimated to be $100,000. Louise Langevin and Marie-Claire Belleau, *Trafficking in Women in Canada,* 22.

26 The regulations regarding foreign domestic workers' hours of work, overtime pay, minimum wage laws and the right to organize in trade unions vary between the provinces. Ontario had the earliest and widest range of protective legislation for domestic workers, followed by Quebec and BC. Not coincidentally, these are also the provinces where the largest and most effective domestic rights' organizing has taken place.

27 This pattern is analysed in more detail in Abigail B. Bakan and Daiva Stasiulis, "Foreign Domestic Worker Policy in Canada and the Social Boundaries of Modern Citizenship," *Science and Society,* 58: 1 (Spring 1994), 7–33. See also Patricia Daenzer, *Regulating Class Privilege: Immigrant Servants in Canada 1940s–1990s* (Toronto: Canadian Scholars' Press, 1993) and Langevin and Belleau, *Trafficking in Women in Canada.*

28 Macklin, "Foreign Domestic Worker," 691.

29 Overall, in 1974, four times as many domestics arrived in Canada on employment visas than as immigrants (Daenzer, *Regulating Class Privilege,* 92).

30 In making the distinction between private domestic service jobs and service jobs performed in restaurants, hotels, hospitals, etc., we do not want to suggest that we are glorifying the latter. Indeed, as Evelyn Nakano Glenn, points out, like domestic service, low-level service jobs offer poor wages, few or limited benefits, low rates of unionization, and in general "subject workers to arbitrary supervision" ("From Servitude to Service Work: Historical Continuities in the Racial Division of Paid Reproductive Labor," *Signs: Journal of Women in Culture and Society,* 18: 1 (1992), 22–3). Nevertheless, service workers "appreciate not being personally subordinate to an employer and not having to do 'their' dirty work on 'their' property'" (23). Further while "[r]elations with supervisors and clients are hierarchical, ... they are embedded in an impersonal structure governed by more explicit contractual obligations and limits" (23).

31 See Daenzer, *Regulating Class Privilege,* 87–108.

32 The "Pinto case," heard by the Federal Court Trial Division, involved the appeal of a prospective Ontario employer (Pinto) of a woman from Delhi, India. The domestic worker had been refused entry into Canada under the FDM by a Canadian visa officer. (See the Federal Court of Canada, Nov. 27, 1990.) The reason given for the refusal was that the woman had insufficient experience under the policy guideline calling for one year of previous "relevant experience." The applicant's claim was based on the prospective employee's experience as a single mother and as a school teacher with 16 years of practice.

33 Margaret Young, "Canada's Immigration Programme: Background Paper" (Ottawa: Minister of Supply and Services, 1994), 20–1.

34 It should be noted that the issue of what constitutes government "consultation" with concerned constituencies regarding this policy is a subject of considerable debate. In a letter dated 3 March 1992, Glenda P. Simms, Ph.D., then President of the Canadian Advisory Council on the Status of Women (CACSW), wrote to Bernard Valcourt, the Minister of Employment and Immigration responsible for the FDM review process. She stated that she was "most disappointed" that a senior governmental official meeting with the CACSW "for the most part could not provide adequate information on your consultation review process. The group was advised that employers' letters to the Minister and employment agencies' complaints about domestic workers had been the basis for the department's consultation" (Glenda Simms, 3 March 1992). Valcourt's response to this was that "Those consulted include domestic worker advocacy groups, other federal government departments, provincial government officials, national and municipal day care associations, employer and employment agency representatives, academics and other concerned individuals.... In making the changes, we have aimed for a balance between the needs of domestic workers and employers" (Bernard Valcourt, 26 August 1992).

35 Young, "Canada's Immigration Program," 20.

36 In the Operations Memorandum for the LCP, one of the key points of change is stated to be the "legislative basis" of the new programme "to ensure that participants possess certain qualifications pertaining to their education, training and language skills before their application for an employment authorisation can be considered." "Operations Memorandum" (Draft), LCP, Employment and Immigration Canada, 23 April 1992, 2.

37 Patricia M. Daenzer, "Ideology and the Formation of Migration Policy: The Case of Immigrant Domestic Workers, 1940–1990," Ph.D. dissertation (Department of Social Work, University of Toronto, 1991), 208; Macklin, "Foreign Domestic Worker," 740; Barbara Jackman, "Admission of Foreign Domestic Workers," (on file with authors), 1, 4.

38 Jackman, "Admission of Foreign Domestic Workers," 3–4.

39 Unlike the *Immigration Act* and the *Immigration Regulations, 1978,* which are publicly promulgated, formal, legal instruments, the *Immigration Manual* consists of "informal instructions addressed to bureaucrats charged with administering immigration policy…. The Preface to the Manual makes [explicit] that: 'Where conflict or inconsistency exists between these guidelines (including related Operations Memoranda) and the provisions of the *Immigration Act,* Regulations and related legislation, the latter must take precedence.'" See Macklin, "Foreign Domestic Worker," 698–9.

40 See e.g., Sedef Arat-Koc and Fely Villasin, *Caregivers Break the Silence* (Toronto: Intercede, 2001); Punam Khosa, *Review of the Situation of Women in Canada* (Toronto: National Action Committee on the Status of Women, July 1993), 16–17 and Fely Villasin, "Domestic Workers' Struggle for Equal Rights in Canada," in Mary Ruby Palma-Bertran and Aurora Javate de Dios, eds, *Filipino Women Overseas Contract Workers: At What Cost?* (Manila: Goodwill Trading Co., 1992), 77–80.

41 Romero, *Maid in the USA,* 139–62, provides a valuable summary of these studies and an analysis of their findings and theoretical conclusions.

42 Martin and Segrave, *The Servant Problem,* 121.

43 Data collected from the Department of Citizenship and Immigration.

44 Specifically, our survey indicated that 14 of 25 West Indian domestic workers entered Canada as visitors and one claimed asylum as a refugee; only 10 entered through either the FDM or LCP. In contrast, 23 of 25 Filipinas entered Canada on the FDM or LCP while only two entered as visitors. These results are further discussed in Chapter 4, and in Daiva Stasiulis and Abigail B. Bakan, "Negotiating Citizenship: The Case of Foreign Domestic Workers in Canada," *Feminist Review,* No. 57 (Autumn 1997), 112–39.

45 See Judith Ann Warner and Helen K. Henderson, "Latina Women Immigrants' Waged Domestic Labour: Effects of Immigration Reform on the Link Between Private Households and the International Labour Force" (American Sociological Association, paper, 1990) cited in Romero, *Maid in the USA,* 190–1, n. 29; Evelyn Nakano Glenn, *Issei, Nisei, War Bride: Three Generations of Japanese American Women in Domestic Service* (Philadelphia: Temple University Press, 1986); Anderson, *Britain's Secret Slaves.*

46 Following British conquest in the mid-17th century, the Caribbean was exploited as a region rich in land and capital-generating plantation agricultural conditions. In contrast, it was an area short in the supply of labour, particularly following the near-genocide suffered by the indigenous Amerindian population. After the early failure of a movement favouring white European indentured labour, the African slave trade soared and fuelled the profits of the colonial planters, primarily through the export of sugar and related products. With emancipation in 1838, an extensive peasantry developed as freed slaves turned to private land cultivation and resisted field labour in protest at the legacy of slavery. Women played a central role in agricultural marketing, first during the plantation period for the sale of slave-grown produce, and then after emancipation. While other employment options have opened for women, this tradition has continued until the present time. See Eric Williams, *Capitalism and Slavery* (Chapel Hill: University of North Carolina Press, 1944), which remains, despite volumes of contemporary debate, the best single concise historical source on this period for the Caribbean region. See also Janet Henshall Momsen, "Gender Roles in Caribbean Agricultural Labour," in Malcolm Cross and Gad Hueman, eds, *Labour in the Caribbean* (London: Macmillan Caribbean, 1988), 141–58; and Janet Henshall Momsen, ed., *Women and Change in the Caribbean* (London: James Currey, 1993); Lil Despradel, "Internal Migration of Rural Women in the Caribbean and its Effects on Their Status," in UNESCO, *Women on the Move: Contemporary Changes in Family and Society* (1984), 93–109, and Abigail B. Bakan, *Ideology and Class Conflict in Jamaica: The Politics of Rebellion* (Montreal: McGill-Queen's University Press, 1990), 18–67.

47 See e.g., C. Peach, *West Indian Migration to Britain: A Social Geography* (London: Oxford University Press, 1968).

48 See e.g., Vic Satzewich, "Racism and Canadian Immigration Policy: The Government's View of Caribbean Migration, 1962–66," *Canadian Ethnic Studies*, XXI: 1 (1989), 77–97.

49 For an insightful account of this process, focusing on the Jamaican experience, see Trevor Munroe, *The Politics of Constitutional Decolonization, 1944–62* (Jamaica: Institute of Social and Economic Research, 1972).

50 Dennis Conway, "Migration and Urbanisation Policies: Immediate Needs for the 21ˢᵗ Century," *Caribbean Affairs*, 3: 4 (October–December 1990), 73–4

51 European Economic Commission (1973) as cited in Lil Despradel, "Internal Migration of Rural Women in the Caribbean," 97.

52 The first figure is drawn from Gurushi Swamy, "International Migrant Workers' Remittances: Issues and Prospects," *World Bank Working Papers,* no. 481 (Washington DC: World Bank, 1981); the second is from Hymie Rubenstein, "The Impact of Remittances in the Rural English Speaking Caribbean," in William F. Stinner, Klaus de Albuquerque and Roy S. Bryce-Laporte, eds, *Return Migration and Remittances: Developing a Caribbean Perspective,* RILES Occasional Paper, no. 3 (Washington DC: Research Institute and Ethnic Studies, 1982). For a discussion of remittances to the region in general, and a review of the literature, see, Wilbert O. Bascom, "Remittance Inflows and Economic Development in Selected Anglophone Caribbean Countries," in Sergio Diaz-Briquets and Sidney Weintraub, eds, *Migration, Remittances and Small Business Development: Mexico and Caribbean Basin Countries* (Boulder: Westview Press, 1991), 71–99.

53 Conway, "Migration and Urbanisation Policies," 75.

54 A study by Multilateral Investment Fund, created in 1993, estimated that remittances to the Latin American and Caribbean region are expanding at an overall annual rate of 7–10 percent. Stephen Fidler, "Middle East, Latin American and Caribbean: New Migrants Spur Growth in Remittances," *Financial Times,* 17 May 2001 <http://www.jubilee2000uk.org/finance/latin_america_migrants_growth_remittances.htm>.

55 Remittances in 2000 were at 11.7 percent of gross domestic product. Stephen Fidler, "Middle East, Latin American and Caribbean."

56 See Orlando Patterson, "Reflections on the Caribbean Diaspora and its Policy Implications," in K. Hall and D. Benn, eds, *Contending with Destiny: The Caribbean in the 21st Century* (Kingston: Ian Randle), 500–10 and Anthony Weis, "On a Precipice: Globalization and Small Farmers in Eastern Jamaica," Doctoral dissertation (Queen's University, Kingston, Ontario, 2003).

57 Despradel, "Internal Migration of Rural Women in the Caribbean," 101; Housewives Association of Trinidad and Tobago, *Report on Employment Status of Household Workers in Trinidad* (Port of Spain: HATT, March 1975).

58 Janet Henshall Momsen, "Gender Roles in Caribbean Agricultural Labour," in Malcolm Cross and Gad Hueman, eds, *Labour in the Caribbean* (London: Macmillan Caribbean, 1988), 147.

59 Momsen, "Gender Roles in Caribbean Agricultural Labour," 147 and Dorian Powell, "Caribbean Women and their Response to Familial Experiences," *Social and Economic Studies,* 35: 2 (1986), 83–127.

60 By 1970, women's paid participation rate in the Caribbean labour force overall had been superseded by work in the expanding service sector, largely fuelled by tourism and the hotel industry. See Peggy Antrobus, "Employment of Women Workers in the Caribbean," in Pat Ellis, ed., *Women of the Carribean* (New Jersey: Zed Books, 1986) and Lorna Gordon, "Women in Caribbean Agriculture," in Pat Ellis, ed., *Women of the Caribbean* (New Jersey: Zed Books, 1986), 31–2, and 35–40; Peggy Antrobus, "Gender Issues in Caribbean Development," in Stanley Lalta and Marie Freckleton, eds, *Caribbean Economic Development: The First Generation* (Kingston, Ja.: Ian Randle Publishers, 1993), 68–77; Joycelin Massiah, ed., "Women in the Caribbean," *Social and Economic Studies,* Special Number, Part One (vol. 35, no. 2, June 1986) and Part Two (vol. 35, no. 3, September 1986); Helen I. Safa and Peggy Antrobus, "Women and the Economic Crisis in the Caribbean," in Lourdes Beneria and Shelley Feldman, eds, *Unequal Burden: Economic Crises, Persistent Poverty, and Women's Work* (Boulder: Westview Press, 1992), 49–82 and Pat Ellis, ed., *Women of the Caribbean* (London: Zed Press, 1986).

61 Cited in Satzewich, "Racism and Canadian Immigration Policy," 77.

62 The policy was implemented on a limited quota basis, with 100 Caribbean women admitted in the first year, and subsequent increases up to 280 per year. The plan was explicitly enacted, and then extended into the 1960s, to assuage the demands of Caribbean governments. For its part, the Canadian government expressed explicit concern that upon achieving permanent status, sponsored relatives from the Caribbean would enter Canada and alter the racial complexion of Canadian society. However, Canada's economic interests in the

English Caribbean, ranking third in the world after the United States and Britain, compelled concern that some accommodation to the region's political leaders on the immigration front were in order. See Satzewich, "Racism and Canadian Immigration Policy," and Daenzer, *Regulating Class Privilege,* on the rise and fall of the West Indian Domestic Scheme; see also Agnes Calliste, "Canada's Immigration Policy and Domestics from the Caribbean: The Second Domestic Scheme," in Jesse Vorst et al, eds, *Race, Class, Gender: Bonds and Barriers* (Toronto: Garamond Press, 1991) and Frances Henry, "The West Indian Domestic Scheme in Canada," *Social and Economic Studies* 17: 1 (1968). On Canada's historic economic interests in the region, see Brian Douglas Tennyson, ed., *Canadian-Caribbean Relations: Aspects of a Relationship* (Sydney, Nova Scotia: Centre for International Studies, 1990); Robert Chodos, *The Caribbean Connection* (Toronto: James Lorimer, 1977) and Abigail B. Bakan, David Cox and Colin Leys, eds, *Imperial Power and Regional Response: The Caribbean Basin Initiative* (Wilfrid Laurier University Press, 1993).

63 See Wolseley W. Anderson, *Caribbean Immigrants: A Socio-Demographic Profile* (Toronto: Canadian Scholars' Press, 1993), 73 ff.

64 The largest single source country was Jamaica, followed by Guyana, Haiti and Trinidad. Anthony Richmond for Statistics Canada, *Current Demographic Analysis: Caribbean Immigrants* (Ottawa: Minister of Supply and Services, 1989), 3.

65 After 1973 and prior to 1981, live-in domestic workers arrived on temporary employment visas with no special provision for the attainment of permanent resident status. Sheila McLeod Arnopoulous, *Problems of Immigrant Women in the Canadian Labour Force* (Ottawa: Canadian Advisory Council on the Status of Women, January 1979): 61; "Statistical Profiles" (November 1990); Task Force on Immigration Practices and Procedures, *Domestic Workers on Employment Authorizations* (Government of Canada, Office of the Minister of Employment and Immigration, April 1981), 48–50 and "Foreign Domestic Workers in Canada— Where Do They Come From? How Has That Changed Over Time?," *The Moment* 2, vol. 5 (1991), 5. See also Strategic Planning and Research Directorate, Employment and Immigration Canada, "Statistical Profiles," n.d. Table 2, 3.

66 In 1982, the number of processed contract workers from the Philippines was 314,284, compared with 598,769 in 1990. Moreover, the number of processed Filipino contract workers increased twenty-fold over a 16-year period, from just over 36,000 in 1975 to almost 700,000 in 1991. See Benjamin V. Carino, "Migrant Workers from the Philippines," in G. Batistella and A. Paganoni, eds, *Philippine Labour Migration: Impact and Policy* (Quezon City: Scalabrini Migration Center, 1992), 7, 6.

67 See Graziano Battistella, "Data on International Migration from the Philippines," *Asian and Pacific Migration Journal,* 4: 4 (1995), 589–99; Ramon Bultron, "Recruitment Costs, State Exaction and Government Fees," Paper delivered at the International Migrant Conference on Labor-Export and Forced Migration Amidst Globalization, Manila, 4–8 November 2001, 2.

68 International Labour Organization, Press Release, "Female Asian Migrants: A Growing But Increasingly Vulnerable Workforce," 5 February 1996, <webinfo@ilo.org>.

69 Philippine National Statistics Office, reported in Ligaya L. McGovern, "The Export of Labor and the Politics of Foreign Debt (The Case of Overseas Filipino Domestic Workers)," Paper presented at the International Migrant Conference on Labor Export and Forced Migration Amidst Globalization, Manila, 4–8 November 2001, 2.

70 Ludmilla Kwitko, "Filipina Domestic Workers and the New International Division of Labour," 2; Vickers, *Women and the World Economic Crisis,* 90.

71 Antonio Tujan Jr, "Labor Export and Forced Migration under Globalization," Paper presented at the International Migrant Conference on Labor-Export and Forced Migration Amidst Globalization, Manila, Philippines, 4–8 November 2001, 3.

72 Carino, "Migrant Workers from the Philippines," 13.

73 Mary Ruby Palma-Beltran, "Filipina Women Domestic Workers Overseas: Profile and Implications for Policy," *Asian Migrant,* 4: 2 (April–June 1991), 3–13.

74 Battistella, "Data on International Migration from the Philippines," 590.

75 The emergence of massive overseas employment of Filipinos coincided with the opening of the Middle East labour market. Maruja M.B. Asis, "The Overseas Employment Programme Policy," in G. Batistella and A. Paganoni, eds, *Philippine Labour Migration: Impact and Policy* (Quezon City: Scalabrini Migration Center, 1992), 69.

76 Ludmilla Kwitko, "Filipina Domestic Workers and the New International Division of Labour," 8; see also Emmanuel S. de Dios and Joel Rocamora, eds, *Of Bonds and Bondage: A Reader on Philippine Debt* (Manila: Transnational Institute, Philippine Centre for Policy Studies and Freedom of Debt Coalition, 1992).

77 It is beyond the scope of this discussion to account for why the Philippines, unlike South Korea and Taiwan, with whom it shares many characteristics, did not become a Newly Industrialized Country. Angeles's account, however, is persuasive, suggesting that the role of the state, burdened by the presence of a strong landlord class, has served to block the enactment of progressive land reform and the emergence of a strong indigenous entrepreneurial class.See Leonora Angeles, "Why the Philippines Did Not Become a Newly Industrializing Country," *Kasarinlan,* 7, 2 and 3 (1991/92), 91.

78 Kwitko, "Filipina Domestic Workers," 8.

79 Carino, "Migrant Workers from the Philippines," 18.

80 William J. Pomeroy, *The Philippines: Colonialism, Collaboration, and Resistance!* (New York: International Publishers, 1992), 235–6.

81 Ray Brooks, "Why is Unemployment High in the Philippines?," IMF Working Paper (International Monetary Fund, Asia Pacific Department, 2002), <http://www.imf.org/external/pubs/ft/wp/2002/wp0223.pdf> (4 March 2002).

82 Bultron, "Recruitment Costs, State Exaction and Government Fees," 4.

83 Pomeroy, *The Philippines,* 239.

84 Pomeroy, *The Philippines,* 238.

85 Episcopal Commission for the Pastoral Care of Migrant and Itinerant People, Reported in Ligaya L. McGovern, "The Export of Labour and the Politics of Foreign Debt," 5.

86 Vickers, *Women and the World Economic Crisis,* 89; Pomeroy, *The Philippines,* McGovern, "The Export of Labour and the Politics of Foreign Debt," 4.

87 McGovern, "The Export of Labour and the Politics of Foreign Debt," 4.

88 Kwitko, "Filipina Domestic Workers," 9.

89 Ka Crispin Beltran, "Message to the International Migrant Conference," Address delivered to the International Migrant Conference on Labor-Export and Forced Migration Amidst Globalization, Manila, 4–8 November 2001, 3.

90 Interviews with the authors and CALABARZON community organizers or women workers, 3 June 1995.

91 "CALABARZON—Where Doing Business is a Pleasure," promotional flyer, Philippines, n.d., 3.

92 Center for Women's Resources, *Economic Growth in 1994—At Whose Expense: Facts and Figures for Filipino Women on the 1994 Philippine Economy and Politics,* February 1995, 23.

93 Kwitko, "Filipina Domestic Workers," 90.

94 The signing into law of the May 1974 Philippines Labour Code "signalled earnest government involvement with overseas employment." The Code provided for the creation of the Overseas Employment Development Board (OEDB) to undertake a systematic programme for the overseas employment of land-based workers, banned direct hiring and made mandatory remittance of overseas workers' earnings. While the 1974 Code was intended to block participation of the private sector in recruitment and placement, these tasks proved too onerous for the government to handle. Thus, in 1978, the government relegated to the private sector control over recruitment and placement of Filipino workers. Asis, "Overseas Employment Program Policy" (1992), 71–2.

95 Economists acknowledge the substantial contribution of overseas migrants' remittances in offsetting the oil bill and improving the balance of payments, especially during the mid-1980s, a period marked by massive foreign exchange problems and foreign capital flight. However, they differ in their assessments of the impact of migration on economic development in the Philippines. The most persuasive accounts conclude that overseas employment is only palliative in character, and that more lasting solutions to the country's critical development problems must address deeper structural factors. For further discussion of the impact of overseas employment on development in the Philippines, see Manolo I. Abella, "International Migration and Development," in Batistella and Paganoni (1992); Noel Vasquez, "Economic and Social Impact of Labour Migration," in Batistella and Paganoni (1992), 39–67; Graziano Battistella, "Migration Opportunity or Loss?" in Batistella and Paganoni, eds, Philippine Labour Migration: Impact and Policy (Quezon City: Scalabrini Migration Center, 1992), 113–34; and Carino, "Migrant Workers from the Philippines," 19.

96 Ruby Palma-Beltran, "Filipina Women Domestic Workers Overseas," 46. These figures are considered to

be conservative, as they do not incorporate those who depart as tourists and are therefore not registered as official overseas workers. Macklin, "Foreign Domestic Worker," 695.

97 Manolo I. Abella, "International Migration and Development," 30.

98 Adelle Blackett, "Making Domestic Work Visible: The Case for Specific Regulation," (Geneva: ILO, Labour Law and Labour Relations Branch, 1998), 4, n. 15.

99 Mitter, *Common Fate, Common Bond,* 37.

100 Carino, "Migrant Workers from the Philippines," 13–14.

101 See Parreñas, *Servants of Globalization* and Vasquez, "Economic and Social Impact of Labour Migration," 60–62 for a discussion of the impact of overseas migration on migrants' families and communities.

102 Regarding the Philippines, Battistella notes that "[f]emale migration is concentrated on practically three sectors: domestic work, entertainment and health, which make up 82 per cent of the annual deployment of newly hired contract workers." Battistella, "Data on International Migration" (1995), 590.

103 Noeleen Heyzer and Vivienne Wee, "Domestic Workers in Transient Overseas Employment: Who Benefits, Who Profits," in N. Heyzer, G. Lycklama a Nijeholt and N. Weerakoon, eds, *The Trade in Domestic Worker: Causes, Mechanisms and Consequences of International Migration* (London: Zed Books, 1992).

SECTION V: UNFREE LABOUR: MIGRANT WORKERS AND CITIZENSHIP

Critical Thinking Questions

Chapter 9: Migrant Workers as Non-Citizens: The Case against Citizenship as a Social Policy Concept, Donna Baines and Nandita Sharma

1. Discuss how today's mobile global labour force raises issues about traditional notions of citizenship in advanced industrialized countries.

2. What changes could be made to the Non-Immigrant Employment Authorization Program (NIEAP) to improve the employment rights and working conditions of migrant workers?

3. Could a reworked concept of citizenship, as proposed by Baines and Sharma, help eradicate racialized and gendered inequalities in Canadian society?

Chapter 10: Underdevelopment, Structural Adjustment, and Gendered Migration from the West Indies and the Philippines, Daiva K. Stasiulis and Abigail B. Bakan

1. How do gendered and racialized ideologies shape the Canadian foreign domestic worker policy?

2. Would ending the compulsory live-in aspect of the foreign domestic worker policy modify the citizenship rights of women migrant domestic workers?

3. Does the foreign domestic worker policy have an impact on the household gender division of labour in Canada? What has been the impact of the policy on structural inequalities among women?

Recommended Readings

Barrón, Antonieta. 1999. "Mexican Women on the Move: Migrant Workers in Mexico and Canada." In Deborah Barndt (ed.), *Women Working the NAFTA Food Chain: Women, Food and Globalization*. Toronto: Second Story Press, pp. 114–126. An article that shows how the agricultural labour markets in Canada and Mexico are interconnected, and how deregulation following the North American Free Trade Agreement has shaped the composition of the labour force in both countries.

Basok, Tanya. 2002. *Tortillas and Tomatoes: Transmigrant Mexican Harvesters in Canada*. Montreal and Kingston: McGill-Queen's University Press. A detailed examination of the insertion of foreign migrant agricultural workers into the Canadian labour market through the Seasonal Agricultural Worker Program, and a conceptual exploration of how these workers are structurally shaped as unfree labour.

Parreñas, Rhacel Salazar. 2001. *Servants of Globalization: Women, Migration, and Domestic Work*. Stanford: Stanford University Press. A comparative study of Filipina migrant domestic workers in Rome and Los Angeles that explores the links between the supply of labour in a Third World country and the demand for labour in two advanced industrialized countries. The book makes a major contribution to the analysis of the international division of reproductive labour.

Schecter, Tanya. 1998. *Race, Class, Women and the State: The Case of Domestic Labour in Canada*. Montreal: Black Rose Books. An examination of the role of the Canadian state in the development of policies that have kept migrant domestic workers of colour in a relationship of subordination, as well as of the role played by Canadian women in influencing government policy pertaining to domestic workers.

Stasiulis, Daiva K. and Abigail B. Bakan. 2003. *Negotiating Citizenship: Migrant Women in Canada and the Global System*. New York: Palgrave Macmillan. An in-depth analysis of how, within the broader context of neo-liberalism and globalization, migrant Third World women workers of colour from the West Indies and the Philippines have endeavoured to negotiate rights of citizenship.

Related Websites

December 18

http://www.december18.net/web/general/start.php?lang=EN

December 18 is an online network that focuses on issues facing migrant workers such as globalization, refugees, trafficking of human beings and international development issues. The electronic bulletin "Migrant.News" provides information about international migration, treatment of migrants, and protection of migrants' human rights. The site also includes other publications on migration.

International Migration Branch of the International Labour Organization

http://www.ilo.org/public/english/protection/migrant/

The International Migration Branch (MIGRANT) assists countries in policy formulation, and in establishing or strengthening legislation, administrative measures, structures, and practices for effective management of labour migration. The site includes information on the different programs, policy documents and other resources of the Branch.

Justicia for Migrant Workers

http://www.justicia4migrantworkers.org/

Justicia for Migrant Workers is a non-profit collective that promotes the rights of seasonal Caribbean and Mexican migrant workers who participate in the Canadian federal government's Seasonal Agricultural Workers Program (SAWP). It conducts research on migrant agricultural labour in North America and lobbies government to change policies of the SAWP.

Migrants Rights International

http://www.migrantwatch.org/index.html

Migrants Rights International is a non-governmental organization and federation of migrant organizations and non-governmental organizations promoting the human rights of migrants. The site includes a resource page that provides links to the organization's bulletin and other publications.

North-South Institute

http://www.nsi-ins.ca

The North-South Institute is a non-profit organization that provides research and analysis on foreign policy issues in three areas: finance, debt, and development assistance; trade, labour, and migration; and governance, civil society, and conflict prevention.

Section VI

Neo-Liberalism and the Dismantling of the Welfare State

MANY HAVE ARGUED that the Keynesian welfare state, the compromise among capital, labour, and the state, was one of the most significant developments of the postwar era. The economic and social reforms of this era, which have been the basis of social citizenship, provided workers and their families with a basic standard of living as well as with the ability to attain a certain level of personal development and fulfillment, and to participate more fully in society. The two articles in this section of the book are representative of the growing body of international scholarship that has investigated the neo-liberal attack of the past three decades on the Keynesian welfare state. Both articles acknowledge the significance of global structural factors and market forces in reconfiguring the nature and role of nation-states. However, through an analysis of the Canadian case, they lay bare the role of national factors and political choices in reshaping the state and in redefining dominant values around entitlement and obligation.

Stephen McBride's article, taken from his book *Paradigm Shift: Globalization and the Canadian State*, traces the shift in economic and political thought that began in Canada in the mid-1970s following the demise of the long postwar economic boom. He is critical of claims that the move from a Keynesian paradigm to a neo-liberal paradigm is the result of global developments and argues instead that national factors, and particularly decisions by governments of both liberal and conservative stripes, are key to explaining this transition. McBride's analysis demonstrates that proponents of neo-liberalism have tended to blame fiscal crises during the 1970s and 1980s on the policies and programs of the Keynesian welfare state because they were seen to interfere with the free operation of national and global markets that promote competitive behaviour and discourage dependency among the population. The author shows that the attack on the legitimacy of the Keynesian welfare state and the adoption of a neo-liberal agenda have resulted in a significant retrenchment of the Canadian state. He examines measures that have been introduced to reduce the role and influence of the state. Among the more significant measures have been a redirection of fiscal and monetary policy, cutbacks in government employment, greater privatization and deregulation, and a fundamental redirection in social, health, and labour-market policies. McBride's analysis of state retrenchment highlights how the paradigm shift of the past few decades has left Canadian workers and citizens more vulnerable to market forces, and therefore more insecure. He concludes by reasserting that nation-states, rather than global factors, are the authors of social policy directions.

Jane Pulkingham and Gordon Ternowetsky also explore the demise of the Canadian welfare state. They argue that the neo-liberal restructuring and cutbacks that began in earnest in the mid-1980s under the Conservative government of Brian Mulroney and became deeply entrenched in the 1990s under the Liberal government of Jean Chrétien led to the dismantling of employment policies, universality of social programs, and safety net provisions, three features that were the backbone of the centrist, evolutionary post-World War II Canadian welfare state. Firstly, Pulkingham and Ternowetsky demonstrate that the federal government's postwar policies underpinning its commitment to full, or at least high, employment have been abandoned in favour of active labour-market policies that both modify the threshold of what is considered an acceptable level of high employment, and decrease entitlement and coverage for the unemployed. Secondly, through an examination of changes to services and income transfers that had come to constitute the welfare state, the authors trace the gradual undermining of the principle of universality and its replacement with targeting measures. The final section of the article examines how the introduction of the Canada Health and Social Transfer, a major policy initiative in the mid-1990s, ushered in an era of drastic curtailments of the safety-net provisions that had provided a minimum of protection for the poorest and most vulnerable, many of whom are children. Pulkingham and Ternowetsky argue that these major policy initiatives represent a relinquishing by the federal government of its historical role of financing, developing and maintaining national programs and standards. They conclude that the process of state retrenchment signals an unequivocal shift to a minimalist, decentralized state that abandons responsibility for the collective well-being of its citizenry.

CHAPTER 11

Domestic Neo-Liberalism

Stephen McBride

As long as Keynesian ideas held sway, most people concerned about public policy saw the active involvement of government in achieving goals (such as full employment) as a legitimate function. Although the practice of Keynesianism was less enthusiastic in Canada than in some other countries and, certainly, proved to be imperfect (Campbell 1987), the framework was encouraged by an international economic regime that tended to support national economic management. Everywhere there were strong domestic pressures for more interventionist states to provide economic stability and social security—political goods that differentiated the postwar state from its predecessor before the war.

By the mid-1970s the long postwar economic boom that, in reality, had its shares of ups and downs was widely recognized as being over. A more difficult economic environment was at hand. Two international oil crises drove inflation higher, though in political debates rising prices were often attributed to domestic causes. Prime among the domestic reasons advanced to explain inflation were increased wages stemming from the power of labour under a full-employment regime. The popular interpretation of inflationary pressures became "too much money chasing too few goods"—an explanation that overlooked the possibility that wages were simply chasing externally induced inflation. From this point of view, wage controls became the remedy for inflation.

Some commentators argued that a decline in profits had occurred (Gonick 1987:341–42; Heap 1982:81). Others predicted capital flight—that multinational corporations would shift their manufacturing investments to the newly industrializing centres of the Third World, where cheap pools of labour could be readily found. The deregulation of the international monetary system with the termination of Bretton Woods also led to instability. A process of deindustrialization, "a widespread, systematic disinvestment in the nation's basic productive capacity" (Bluestone and Harrison 1982:6), became apparent in the recession of the 1980s. Whole sectors of the industrial heartlands of North America were dubbed "rustbelts." In Canada, employment in goods-producing industries fell from 34.8 percent of the labour force in 1951 to 26.7 percent in 1981, a pattern replicated in most other Organization for Economic Cooperation and Development (OECD) nations (Economic Council of Canada 1984:157, Table 11-5). Accompanying these painful adjustments was a rapid technological change as corporations strove to modernize, cut labour costs and restore profitability.

Unemployment in OECD countries steadily rose from about three percent of the labour force in the 1950s and 1960s to much higher levels in the 1970s and 1980s (see McBride 1992). Official unemployment figures in Canada peaked in 1983 at almost 12 percent. Economic assumptions concerning a trade-off between unemployment and inflation proved invalid as the two indicators rose in tandem. Inflation rates climbed steadily during the 1970s, reaching double-digit figures and easing only after 1982 (see, for example, Ruggeri 1987: 297, Table 3). A new phenomenon, "stagflation," the coexistence of economic recession and high inflation, made its appearance in public discourse.

The sense of crisis occasioned by these developments provided an opportunity for long-standing critics of the Keynesian revolution in economic thought to emerge from obscurity. The economics profession, undergoing what amounted to a paradigm shift, returned to a version of neo-classical orthodoxy of the kind that Keynes and like-minded economists had overturned, with the help of the Great Depression, two generations earlier. The revived ideas found powerful backers, mostly in a business sector concerned about increasing state intervention in the economy. This coalition of neo-classical economists and corporate interests pushed right and centre political parties to a decisive break with Keynesianism. The left, as represented by social-democratic parties, was not long in following (see, for example, McBride 1996).

The shift of paradigms between 1975 and 1984 was far from smooth, and other options certainly seemed to be available throughout the period. One example was the Science Council of Canada's advocacy of interventionist nationalism. Generally, however, these years also saw an incremental retrenchment of public programs, efforts to minimize the public's expectations of government, and advocacy of a reduced role for the state in the economy and social affairs

The fiscal crisis generated by budget deficits contributed to the questioning of the legitimacy of the Keynesian welfare state. A more balanced assessment might have led to the conclusion that major problems of public debt occurred after the abandonment of Keynesianism and the adoption of neo-liberalism. Implementation of that alternative paradigm, with its arsenal of high interest rates that cured inflation by driving the economy into recession, led to government revenue shortfalls on the one hand and growing expenditures on the other.

Nonetheless, it was the social welfare state that came to be seen as a creator of economic distortions. While never as generous in its contributions as opponents suggested, the welfare state did to some degree modify market outcomes.[1] As the Macdonald Commission Report put it, the welfare state is "an embodiment of concepts of sharing which subordinates market results ... to citizenship concerns and community values" (Canada 1985, vol. 1:45).The welfare state was not all bad news from the perspective of capital. Its defenders argued that social welfare provisions allowed for the creation of a much more secure, healthy and educated labour force: "A comprehensive system of income security may therefore help improve productivity, transform bad jobs into good ones, and hence boost economic growth" (Esping-Andersen 1983:32). Or, as Bob Russell (2000:41) put it in describing New Labour in Britain and its Canadian imitators' view of the matter: "The welfare state is optimally an adjunct to capitalist economic development, not an alternative to market-based failure." Still, the ability of the welfare state to decommodify a portion of the potential labour force did enhance the bargaining power of labour, and under conditions in which a fundamental reorientation of economic strategy was on the agenda, social welfare policy became a target. Increasingly critics depicted the welfare state as "a destabilizing influence that has indeed given rise to a new set of economic problems" (Russell 1991:489).

The Globalization Hypothesis

Globalization sometimes features as an explanation of the changes that began to occur in the 1970s and have intensified since then. Sometimes the argument depends on the interaction of economic globalization with other factors such as "societal pluralization" (Rice and Prince 2000: ch.1)—defined as the phenomenon of growing diversity within societies. For others, economic and technological factors formed the centrepiece of globalization's influence. Economic forces, and actors such as multinational corporations, were said to have outgrown national boundaries, with the economic basis of national autonomy eroding. Thus, "Keynesian fiscal and monetary policy is rendered largely ineffective in open global financial markets" (Simeon 1991: 47–48, 49). Or, as Thomas Courchene argues, "This situation poses major concerns for national welfare states since they were ... geared to national production machines" (quoted in Simeon and Janigan 1991: 39). Academic interpretations are matched by business organizations' oft-expressed view that state efforts to regulate economic activity not only are ineffective but also act as a barrier to the economic success of the private sector.

Ramesh Mishra (1999:15) summarizes the full globalization hypothesis as containing three elements: the greater openness of economies has eroded national autonomy, which has been supplanted by supranational authority; capital mobility has curtailed the state's policy options; and the only option for national governments is to move to a residual welfare state—a policy of "competitive austerity."

Mishra (1999:24) concludes: "There seems to be no compelling logic of globalization that requires the downsizing of government, retrenchment of social programmes and substantial deregulation of labour markets. Such measures are being pursued by English speaking countries but amount to little more than old neo-liberal domestic policies now rationalized and legitimized in the name of globalization."[2]

The neo-liberal agenda was one response to the perceptions in the 1970s and 1980s of economic crisis, some of which originated in the international economy. But much of its early emphasis was domestic and concentrated on clearing the domestic obstacles to international liberalization. In this sense globalization is as much or more of a consequence of neo-liberalism at the national level than the reverse. Neo-liberalism has involved political action aimed at reducing or removing impediments to the operation of market forces, including global market forces. Various justifications, economic and moral, have been advanced for placing markets in this privileged position. An economic argument, for instance, is that markets enhance competitiveness in a global economy and that international competition has beneficial effects on efficiency in the domestic economy. A "moral" argument is that people removed from the discipline of the labour market lose independence and become undesirably dependent on social programs.

The chief impediment to the free operation of markets is the state, and a number of measures have been advanced to reduce its role. Among these are fiscal policy, government employment, privatization, social policy, labour-market policy and health policy.[3]

Fiscal and Monetary Policy

The main neo-liberal themes—that government is too large, deficits unacceptable, the tax system in need of reform, and spending priorities are in need of revision—entered public discourse before the election of the Mulroney government in 1984. But with that event they moved from the status of ideas that might reluctantly be endorsed, out of crisis-driven necessity, to the centre of policy discussions (see Wilson 1984).They have remained at the centre despite a 1993 election in which the successful Liberal campaign promised a different approach. In practice, the Liberal govern-

ment of Jean Chrétien adopted the neo-liberal fiscal agenda much more vigorously than did its predecessor.

The government justified expenditure restraint by declaring the need to balance the budget. Governments were ideologically committed to the *means* of expenditure restraint (cutting state expenditures) rather than the *end* of a balanced budget (which could also have been achieved by tax increases). This approach was taken up because reduced expenditures typically meant a smaller role for the state, especially in the crucial economic and social areas.[4] The government's primary focus, both rhetorically and in reality, was on the expenditure side of the ledger. According to the *Budget Plan 1995* the ratio of expenditure reductions to tax revenue increases was projected to increase from 4.4:1 in 1995–96 to 8.3:1 in 1997–98. Early signs of this imbalance in successive governments' treatment of expenditures and revenues led some observers to depict the deficit as a "Trojan horse" for a somewhat different agenda: reduction of the state's role (Doern, Maslove and Prince 1988:28).

Although expenditures, including those on personnel, bore the brunt of neo-liberal policies, considerable evidence suggests that deficits and rising public debt had little to do with profligate expenditures by government. Rather, these phenomena were the product of foregone tax revenues, high interest rates, and recessions that were partly due to the implementation of neo-liberal economic policies. Rather than originating in the Keynesian era, these problems flourished *after* the monetarist economic theories favoured by neo-liberal politicians took root.[5]

A number of writers have drawn attention to the scope and impact of the loopholes, tax breaks, and tax expenditures that led to the shortfall in revenues after 1975 (Maslove 1981; McQuaig 1987; Ternowetsky 1987; Wolfe 1985). Apart from this revenue shortfall, the main cause of increased deficits was high real interest rates resulting from monetary policy (Chorney 1988; McQuaig 1995). A Statistics Canada project—the Mimoto study—attributed 50 percent of the increased deficit incurred between 1975–76 and 1988–89 to revenue shortfalls relative to GDP, 44 percent to an increase in debt charges relative to gross domestic product (GDP), and only six percent to higher program spending relative to GDP (McIlveen and Mimoto 1990; see also Klein 1996).

Indeed, from negative or low positive rates in the 1970s, real interest rates climbed under the impetus of monetarist policies to average around six percent in the 1980s, peaking at nine percent in 1990. Even in the "low interest rate era" of the late 1990s they remained in the four to six percent range (Statistics Canada, cat. no. 11-010, 62-001). High real interest rates perform a classic function of redistributing wealth in that they protect and even expand the value of money—a result that particularly benefits creditors and the affluent, to the detriment of debtors and the less affluent. High interest rates contributed to economic slowdown and recession in both 1981–82 and 1990–93 (McQuaig 1995: ch. 3; Krehm 1993).

Thus many of the problems associated with fiscal policy, such as the deficit, which provided the pretext for implementing neo-liberal, expenditure-cutting and state-reducing policies, had their origins in neo-liberal political choices made in the monetary policy area.

Table 11.1: Federal Budgetary Expenditures as a Percentage of GDP

	Total Expenditures (%)	Prog. Expenditures (%)	Public Debt (%)
1980–81	20.1	16.7	3.4
1981–82	21.1	16.9	4.2
1982–83	23.6	19.2	4.5
1983–84	23.6	19.2	4.4
1984–85	24.4	19.4	5.0
1985–86	23.3	17.7	5.2
1986–87	23.0	17.6	5.2
1987–88	22.5	17.3	5.2
1988–89	21.7	16.3	5.4
1989–90	21.7	15.8	5.9
1990–91	22.3	16.0	6.3
1991–92	22.9	16.9	6.0
1992–93	23.1	17.5	5.6
1993–94	21.8	16.6	5.2
1994–95	20.9	15.5	5.5
1995–96	19.7	13.9	5.8
1996–97	18.0	12.6	5.4
1997–98	17.1	12.4	4.7
1998–99	17.1	12.4	4.6

Source: Public Accounts (various years); Budget Papers.

After 1984 there was a slight reduction in federal expenditures (as a percentage of GDP) until the recession of the early 1990s. The size of the federal state was still greater in the early 1990s than it had been in the early 1980s, indicting the gradualism and limited impact of neo-liberalism; but the total expenditures understate the impact of neo-liberal policies (see Table 11.1). If program expenditures are considered in isolation from debt-servicing costs, the impact is more striking. In the recession of the early 1980s, spending on programs climbed to 19.4 percent of GDP. In the 1990s recession this item accounted for a peak of 17.5 percent of GDP before falling dramatically to 12.4 percent by the end of the decade—the lowest level for decades.

Government Employment

Another indicator of the shrinking state is the number of people employed by it (see Table 11.2.)

The reduction in government employment has been concentrated at the federal and crown corporation (government business enterprises) levels, which is where the state's role in the economy and society has been most reduced. Employment at the provincial/territorial level has declined less, and at the municipal level it even increased in the 1990–99 period. To some extent, however, the statistics covering the entire decade understate employment impacts at those two levels, because provincial/territorial employment in 1992 reached a high for the decade (from which it had declined seven percent by 1999), and municipal employment peaked in 1994 (after which it had declined by almost two percent by 1999). Total government employment declined by five percent over the decade, but by seven percent after its 1992 peak.

But the impact of downsizing was most dramatic at the levels of federal and government business enterprises. The decline in employment in the federal government in

Table 11.2: State Employment 1990–99

Year	Federal Govt.*	Prov.,Terr. Govts.	Local Govt.	Total Govt.	Govt. Business Enterprises	Total Public Sector
1990	406,336	1,387,076	869,170	2,662,582	364,773	3,027,355
1991	415,387	1,401,733	888,733	2,705,853	350,927	3,056,779
1992	411,278	1,409,252	904,250	2,724,780	338,454	3,063,235
1993	404,734	1,397,171	909,991	2,711,896	325,581	3,037,477
1994	394,106	1,375,802	909,161	2,679,069	323,622	3,002,690
1995	371,053	1,370,443	907,405	2,648,900	308,935	2,957,835
1996	356,099	1,335,090	907,147	2,598,335	272,828	2,871,163
1997	337,713	1,315,126	891,483	2,544,322	258,426	2,802,748
1998	330,981	1,314,617	891,560	2,537,188	260,903	2,798,061
1999	330,003	1,312,806	893,709	2,536,519	262,451	2,798,970
% change (1990-99)	-19	-5.5	+3	-5	-28	-7.5

* Federal government employment figures include military personnel.

Source: Statistics Canada, Cansim various.

particular—19 percent—illustrates the shrinking impact of the central government.

Privatization and Deregulation

In seeking to roll back the boundaries of the state, neo-liberals in Canada, like elsewhere, have targeted Crown corporations and state regulatory activity (Laux 1991:289–91). Some analysts argue that the attack has been less rapid and extensive in Canada than elsewhere, perhaps because of the initially small size of the public sector (Bank of Canada 1997:28). To some extent Canadian neo-liberals were impeded because in this case their doctrines ran counter to a well-established national tradition of public enterprise (Hardin 1989; Smith 1990:40). Reliance on public enterprise is an historically important Canadian cultural characteristic (Hardin 1989:104; Stanbury 1988:120).The public enterprise tradition, which predates Confederation, was the product of necessity in that the state undertook works considered to be beyond the capacity of the private sector and for much of the country's history encountered little ideological resistance in doing so (Taylor: 1991:97–100).

Despite this long tradition, in recent decades governments have privatized an impressive range of Crown corporations in what can only be described as a sustained attack (see Tables 11.3 and 11.4).

Indeed, much of the employment decline in the government business enterprises sector in the 1980s was the result of privatization, although other factors (efficiency drives, for example) have also had an effect on employment (see Table 11.5). Again, federal privatization has been in the vanguard of this decline. Possibly because there is so little left at the federal level, the big initiatives in the future are expected to come through provincial privatizations, especially of utilities. In addition to the cases of outright privatization, other forms of partial or creeping privatization are prominent in both federal and provincial jurisdictions. Apart from the Canada Communication Group, formerly the Queen's Printer, most of the federal government's plans for privatization after the mid-1990s involved commercialization and joint public-private-sector ventures in areas such as weather services, food inspection, space technology and defence supply (Finance Canada 1995).

Commercializing the Public Sector

Beginning in the 1990s the federal government started to contract out service delivery to private firms (Bank of Canada 1997; McFettridge 1997)—the upkeep of national parks in 1997, and the earlier system of franchising Canada Post outlets, for example. An increased use of contractors came in some core areas of federal jurisdiction, such as employment insurance—with an especially huge increase in contracting out after the new generation of labour-market development agreements came into effect in the late 1990s (interview, public-sector union official, April 1998). The switch included work that was formerly central to the employment service, such as counselling and assessment of clients, and the contractors performed little or no monitoring or quality control over the work. The next stage of contracting out was to be that of "non-decision functions of Employment Insurance" benefits (HRDC 1997), which would include the receipt and review of applications, handling routine enquiries, verification of records of employment, and issuing cheques. In the space of a decade, one union official argued, the ethos of Human Resources

Table 11.3: Largest Privatizations of Federal Crown Corporations

Name	Sector	Year	Sale Proceeds $m
CNR	Transport	1995	2,079
Petro-Canada	Oil and gas	1991	1,747
NavCanada	Transport	1996	1,500
Air Canada	Transport	1988	474
Teleglobe	Telecommunications	1987	441
Canadian Development Corporation	Financial	1987	365
Nordion International	Manufacturing	1991	161
Telesat	Telecommunications	1992	155
de Havilland	Manufacturing	1986	155
Canadair	Manufacturing	1986	141
TOTAL		1986–96	7,218

Source: Bank of Canada 1997: 30–31.

Table 11.4: Largest Privatizations of Provincial and Municipal Crown Corporations

Name	Sector	Year	Sale Proceeds $m
Alberta Government Telephones	Telecommunications	1990	1,735
Manitoba Telephone Systems	Telecommunications	1996	860
Cameco	Mining	1991	855
Nova Scotia Power Corporation	Electricity Generation	1992	816
Alberta Energy Company	Oil and gas	1975	560
Syncrude	Oil and gas	1993	502
Edmonton Telephones	Telecommunications	1995	468
Potash Corp. of Saskatchewan	Mining	1989	388
Suncor	Oil and gas	1992	299
Vencap Equities Alberta	Financial	1995	174
TOTAL		1975–96	6,657

Source: Bank of Canada 1997: 30–31.

Table 11.5: Government Business Enterprises Employment: Selected Years

	Federal	Provincial/Territorial	Total Government Business Enterprise Employment
1981	225,115	170,910	439,231
1985	215,044	157,869	420,091
1990	154,327	159,876	364,773
1995	135,763	126,371	308,935
2000	89,534	124,176	260,966
% change			
1981–2000	-60	-27	-40.5

Source: Cansim D466042, D466397, D466490 (1 Aug. 2000).

Development had altered from that of helping people find work and improving economic conditions through developing the expertise of working Canadians, to a simple routine of cost-saving and processing individuals so that they would remain on the books for as short a period as possible.

This increased use of contracting out of services achieves two neo-liberal goals. Although the state continues to provide funds, it transfers the delivery of services and the profit-making opportunities associated with that function to the private sector. This move, among other things, enables a competitive market to insinuate itself within the state structure (Shields and Evans 1998:77).

Some provincial governments introduced competitive bidding for services such as highway maintenance and computer support. Municipal garbage collection and snow removal have also been contracted out. The usual rationale for such measures is to increase efficiency and achieve cost-savings. The Canadian Union of Public Employees (CUPE 2000) has documented the growth of partial privatization in a number of areas, including health and education, and links the measures to deteriorating services without, in most cases, compensatory gains in efficiency.

Social Policy

The establishment of the Canadian version of a Keynesian welfare state was largely complete by 1971. Almost immediately the edifice came under attack. Some programs, such as unemployment insurance, were reduced in generosity during the 1970s (McBride 1992: ch. 6), but, for the most part, the main features of the welfare state remained in place when the neo-liberal Mulroney Conservatives took office in 1984.

The precise impact of the Mulroney government on existing programs was a matter of debate in the 1980s and early 1990s. The prevailing view was that change was incremental and consisted of erosion rather than outright dismantling (Banting 1987:213). In retrospect it appears that incrementalism and "stealth" over a protracted period produced fundamental change. The very means of implementing changes in social programs indicated a cautious approach on the part of Canadian neo-liberals. Common techniques included transforming universal into selective programs, tightening eligibility requirements, and imposition of ceilings on program costs—or, alternatively, attempting to make programs self-financing or subject to "clawbacks" over a certain benefit level (Houle 1990). Stephen Phillips (2000:5–6) notes that in 1979 universal programs paid out 43 percent of income security benefits, and by 1993, 0 percent. Benefits paid in social insurance programs increased; but the most dramatic increase, from 14.2 percent of total income security benefits to 43 percent, came in selective or targetted programs (see also MacDonald 1999).

Economic initiatives such as the free-trade agreement also played a part, perhaps, in permitting neo-liberal social policy to be introduced "through the back door" (Mishra 1990:99; Hurtig 1991: ch. 22). But caution was deemed necessary because of continued public support for social programs. The Liberal Party's election campaign in 1993 seemed to recognize the deep-rooted attachment of Canadians to social programs and widespread fears about those programs being under threat (Liberal Party 1993). Again, however, once the Liberals were in office, their implementation of neo-liberal prescriptions proved more energetic even than that of the preceding government.

The 1995 federal budget marked a fundamental shift in the role of the federal state in Canada. This was the point at which erosion of social programs ended and demolition began. Prior to the budget one prominent journalist commented: "All manner of rhetoric will be used to mask Ottawa's decline: 'reinventing government,' 'flexible federalism,' 'modernizing Canada'.... The essence of the matter, however, is this: the shrinking of the federal government, attempted by the Conservatives under the guise of fiscal restraint and constitutional reform, will now be accelerated by the Liberals through non-constitutional means" (Jeffrey Simpson, *Globe and Mail* 27 Jan. 1995). Others defined the budget as an "epiphany in fiscal federalism and national social policy" (Prince 1999:176) or as the end of an era: "It is now clear that the Minister of Reconstruction's White Paper on Employment and Income of 1945 can be regarded as one bookend on a particular period in Canadian history, and Paul Martin's February [1995] budget as the other" (Kroeger 1996:21).

The case for 1995 as the termination point of the Keynesian welfare state rests on the primacy of deficit reduction over maintenance of the social safety net. The determination to reduce the deficit through spending reductions in the social policy area quickly resulted in declining federal transfers to provinces and a fundamental redesign of the unemployment benefit system. The reduced federal commitment to social programs was accomplished not only by eroding transfer payments but also by diminished federal conditions attached to the funds transferred. The major change occurred in 1996 with the introduction of the Canada Health and Social Transfer (CHST).

From 1977 to 1996 the federal government had provided funding in two social policy areas—post-secondary education and health care—under a financial arrangement known as Established Programs Financing (EPF). Funding for social assistance and welfare was transferred under the Canada Assistance Plan (CAP). EPF, introduced in 1977, replaced earlier cost-sharing arrangements that had split health and post-secondary education costs on a 50-50 basis. The new formula was a block funding arrangement in which the federal contribution was partly cash and partly tax points transferred to the provinces. Its effect was to decentralize funds and therefore political power over these policy areas. It represented a substantial, and historical, devolution of power from the federal to the provincial governments (Taylor 1987:435).

Under EPF, increases in the federal contribution were tied to the growth of gross national product (GNP) and population rather than, as previously, to increased real costs. Under the "six and five" anti-inflation program, the government limited EPF payments for post-secondary education. It imposed further ceilings on EPF in 1986, 1990–91, and 1991–92; and the 1991 budget extended the freeze until 1994–95, after which it was to revert to the constraint of GNP growth minus three percent (Canadian Council on Social Development 1990; Wilson 1991:70–71). The Canadian Council on Social Development (1990:2) analyzed the effect of these measures:

Since the money raised by the tax points continues to grow—it is not limited—all reductions in the growth of the block fund come out of the federal cash transfers. This means that the cash portion of federal block funding shrinks over time.... Federal cash to the provinces for medicare and higher education will shrink ... to zero by about

2004 under Bill C-69.... Less and less federal money for medicare and colleges and universities puts the financial burden of these programs squarely on the shoulders of the provinces, and he who pays the piper calls the tune. The federal government's ability to influence national standards or guidelines will diminish.

In 1996 the EPF and the Canada Assistance Plan (CAP), which had also been subject to ceilings during the 1990s, were rolled into the Canada Health and Social Transfer, a single block funding scheme. The CHST removed most remaining federal conditions attached to the transfers. No matching expenditures were required of provinces, as had been the case, for example, under CAP. The new scheme eliminated the other conditions attached to CAP, with the exception of a prohibition on residency requirements. The CHST contained no conditions as far as post-secondary education was concerned, and federal enforcement mechanisms were either diminished or less

direct than formerly. Moreover, "welfare," traditionally less well regarded in public opinion than either education or health, came into the same funding pool, which placed it at a competitive disadvantage (MacDonald 1999:77).

Funding reductions under the CHST added to those that had occurred under the earlier funding mechanisms (see Table 11.6). Social policy advocates regarded the erosion of the cash component of the transfer, which fell by 33 percent between 1993 and 1998, as the key indicator. As cash transfers went down, the argument ran, so too did Ottawa's ability to insist on national standards. The federal agenda in this area was certainly driven by the Finance Department, and fiscal motives enjoyed priority. However, as Ken Battle and Sherri Torjman (1996:64) also point out, the government approach also fitted into a constitutional agenda of decentralization: "Ottawa is seeking ways of 'renewing' itself and its relationship with the provinces—especially in light of the Quebec referendum which threatens to break up the country. The Canada Health and Social

Table 11.6: Canada Health and Social Transfer (CHST) (in $Billions)

	Cash	Tax Transfers	Total
CAP/EPF*			
1993–94	18.8	10.2	29
1994–95	18.7	10.7	29.4
1995–96	18.5	11.4	29.9
CHST**			
1996–97	14.7	12.2	26.9
1997–98	12.5	13.3	25.8
1998–99	12.5	14.2	26.7
1999–2000	14.5	14.9	29.4
2000–01***	15.5	15.3	30.8

* CAP = Canada Assistance Plan, EPF = Established Program Financing
** CHST = Canada Health and Social Transfer
*** projection

Source: <http://www.fin.gc.ca/budget00/bp/bpch6_1e.htm#health>.

Transfer has high symbolic value in that it represents a move by the federal government to retreat from provincial territory." The abrogation of the federal capacity to sustain national standards thus had a rationale beyond that of fiscal restraint.

With the return of budget surpluses in the later 1990s, and the approach of another election, the federal government made moves to restore some of the funding cuts and repair some of the damage inflicted on social programs. Michael J. Prince terms this the "reparation agenda," but notes that it stopped well short of restoring programs to their original levels of financial support. Moreover, reflecting on the period 1980 to 2000 he identifies a "general trend" of "cuts to programs, and challenges to their legitimacy as well as that of their clients.... Some federal social programs are relatively intact and untouched by retrenchment and dismantling, but many programs have been altered in fundamental ways" (Prince 1999:189). This assessment can serve as a general verdict on the fate of social programs under neo-liberal hegemony. Indeed, some analysts have depicted the fiscal surplus, which was to finance the restoration agenda, as having been largely disbursed to tax cuts and debt repayment, with only a very small proportion truly representing new spending on programs (Stanford 2000). In addition, efforts to decentralize and privatize delivery continued (Russell 2000).

The government's approach to social policy had predictable results including the growth of various types of inequality (Yalnizyan 1998:127). For example, focusing on market incomes (wages, salaries, self-employment and investment income) of families with children under 18, Armine Yalnizyan notes that in 1973

the top 10 percent of such families earned an average income 21 times higher than those at the bottom. By 1996, "still near the peak of the business cycle in [the 1990s], and so presumably a 'good' time for reducing disparities—the top 10% made 314 times as much as the families in the bottom 10%" (Yalnizyan 1998:45). She explains this astonishing statistic by noting that almost three-quarters of low-income families still did not have any work, and hence market income, while in 1973 almost two-thirds of low-income families had at least some work. Until the mid-1990s, Yalnizyan argues, government intervention—programs, taxation, income transfers—tended to stabilize after-tax income, notwithstanding the severe increase in market-income inequality. But, she notes, recent changes in the tax and transfer systems were about to change that situation dramatically.

Support for this view comes from recent Statistics Canada data. A study of family income finds that after tax-income in 1998 had risen and now exceeded, by 1.7 percent, average after-tax income in the pre-recession peak year of 1989. In itself this speaks volumes about the impact of neo-liberal policies on incomes. Most pertinent is the observation that income inequality increased during the second half of the 1990s. The study notes that in the early part of the decade, "Taxes and transfers held the ratio of highest-to-lowest after-tax incomes at just under five to one. During the second half of the 1990s, as transfers declined, the ratio widened from about 4.8 to one in 1994 to 5.4 to one in 1998" (Statistics Canada, *The Daily* 12 June 2000:4). A Vanier Institute (2001) study attributes the slight increase in family incomes in the late 1990s almost entirely to an increase in the number of hours worked rather than to increased hourly wages. Average incomes for unattached individuals, who made up one-third of all households in Canada, were down by 2.6 percent over the decade from 1989, with much of the decline being concentrated among young adults. For families, 60 percent experienced an after-tax real income decline in the 1990s. The poorest 20 percent of families (average income in 1998—$17,662) had the biggest decline—5.2 percent; the richest 20 percent (average income in 1998—$96,175) experienced a 6.6 percent increase (Vanier Institute 2001:7–8).

While economic and income growth picked up in the late 1990s, the overall picture remained inferior to the postwar Keynesian years. Growth in real disposable income per capita was 1.3 percent in the 1980s and 0.1 percent in the 1990s (though 2.3 percent in the 1997–June 2000 period). This finding compares to figures of 2.2 percent for the 1950s, 3.0 percent for the 1960s, and 4.2 percent for the 1970s (Maxwell 2001: 6).

Behind these income statistics is a job market that delivers a deteriorating stock of jobs. Mike Burke and John Shields (1999) term this the "hour glass" job market, in which significant groups of the population are excluded from employment opportunities, and considerable polarization exists—not just in incomes, but in security of employment and vulnerability to the economic cycle—among those who do manage to find employment.

Health

From time to time studies identify ways in which globalization, or more correctly international agreements such as the North American Free Trade Agreement (NAFTA), is having an impact on the Canadian health-care system. Such effects include creeping privatization, primarily through the contracting out of services (CCPA *Monitor* July/ August 1995:5), and Bill C-22, which anticipated NAFTA provisions on intellectual property rights (Fuller 1996:18). Under Bill C-22 patent protection for name brand drugs was originally extended from four to ten years. In 1993 the protection was extended to 20 years. The result has been rapidly escalating pharmaceutical costs. Some provincial health plans reduced coverage in order to contain costs (CCPA Monitor March 1995:9). There is also what Burke (2000:180–81) terms the discourse of efficiency, which is linked in business rhetoric to globalization. When applied to the health-care sector this discourse promotes markets, decentralization and individualism.

Although international conditioning frameworks do have a demonstrable effect, domestic sources, notably the dominance of the neo-liberal paradigm, have been responsible for most of the changes. As with social policy and services generally, it may be that the full effect of the international influences lies in the future.

Earlier funding changes, such as the 1977

Table 11.7: Income Inequality in the 1990s				
	MARKET INCOME		AFTER-TAX AND TRANSFERS	
	Top 20%	Bottom 20%	Top 20%	Bottom 20%
1989	41.9	3.8	37.0	7.6
1998	45.2	3.1	38.8	7.1

Source: Statistics Canada, *The Daily*, 12 June, 2000

change to block funding in the form of Established Programs Financing (EPF), with minimal conditions attached, had the predictable effect of increasing provincial variations in medical coverage and billing practices. In 1984 the federal government responded by passing the Canada Health Act (CHA), which reaffirmed the conditions stipulated in the 1967 Medical Care Act—universal coverage, accessibility, portability, comprehensiveness and public administration—and provided that federal funds would be withheld, on a dollar for dollar basis, for every dollar of extra billing or hospital user fees that provinces permitted. Reflecting on the experience since 1984, Susan Silver (1996:77) comments that the "'stick' of the CHA has been effective as long as the federal government has the political will and the financial means to enforce it."

The Mulroney Conservative government was constrained from making substantial changes to medicare by the Liberal decision to pass a new Canada Health Act just before the 1984 election and by the immense popularity of the program (Weller 1996:130). The Conservatives were forced to vote for the Liberal measure or face the prospect of it becoming the main issue in the election. Having voted for it, they were bound by its provisions as long as medicare itself retained its public support. This same constraint also applied to the Liberal successor, though perhaps to a diminishing extent.

Although rhetorically committed to the principles of the Canada Health Act, the Chrétien government undermined the federal government's ability to sustain national standards in the health field. The declining cash portion of federal transfers for health care purposes (see Table 11.5) reduced the federal capacity to oppose user fees, private health clinics, the delisting of covered services, and the variety of other means by which the market is being allowed to creep into a system previously based on quite different principles.

The decline in the public portion of the total health bill (from a normal level of 75 or 76 percent to 69.8 percent in 1997) could be used as an indicator of "passive privatization," characterized as "a generalized retreat of the state from the provision of health care services and an enlargement of the health space occupied by the private sector" (Burke 2000:182). As Burke (183–85) notes, such indicators are but part of an ongoing and intense commodification of the health system. In a careful analysis of the determinants of the increased private share of health-care costs in Canada, Livio Di Matteo (2000) concludes that the decline in real per capita health transfers from the federal government has eroded the public share in public health expenditures, a factor combined with the effects of changes in the distribution of income. In particular, "Those in the top 20 percent of the income distribution appear to have a preference for greater private health expenditures," Di Matteo (2000:108) points out, referring to the group that under the neo-liberal paradigm has done rather well in terms of income share.

The retention of a cash component to CHST transfers, announced in the 1996 budget, did appear to ensure continued federal authority. Questions continued to be posed, however, about whether the federal government retained the political will to perform this function.

One leading health policy analyst concluded that the Liberal Party's political will was being exercised in an entirely different direction:

The Liberals have done an about face…. A government elected on the plank of preserving medicare is governing in a manner that will undermine and then destroy it. The end result for the Canadian health care system will be its eventual return to the private, profit-making market. That will inevitability lead to precisely what the Liberal Party itself said it would in the 1993 election campaign, namely a two-tiered, inequitable system—one that will be far more expensive and less efficient than the current one, and yet will suffer from most of the same problems. (Weller 1996:143)

Even though the Liberals reached an agreement with the provinces to transfer an additional $23.5 billion over five years for health care, concerns about the nature of their commitment to a public health-care system remained. Reports of the new federal-provincial health deal emphasized that the money came with few strings attached *(Globe and Mail* 12 Sept. 2000). Given the recent Alberta legislation, Bill 11, which extended private, for-profit health care and may have also exposed Canada's hospital sector to the provisions of NAFTA and the General Agreement on Trade in Services (GATS) (see Evans et al. 2000), this is a remarkable omission.

(Un)Employment Insurance and Labour-Market Policy

Reduced spending on social support has been accompanied by an increased emphasis on "active" measures that would enable individuals to enter or re-enter the labour market rather than remain dependent on social assistance. As social policy's star waned, that of labour-market policy waxed, at least rhetorically. That area en-

tered the process of being transferred from the federal to provincial level, and there it is likely to function, using policies such as workfare (Rehnby and McBride 1997), chiefly as a social control adjunct to residual social programs.

The evolution of Canadian labour-market policy falls into four broad periods. First came a period of rather limited activity, lasting until the mid-1960s. Next was a period of increased state intervention, in which programs multiplied, which lasted through the late 1980s. From the late 1980s to the mid-1990s, an attempt was made to create neo-corporatist training institutions in the name of achieving a high-skills, high-value-added competitive economy. That period has largely been succeeded by the current approach of labour-market deregulation and devolution.

Throughout the earlier periods the active components of labour-market policy were underpinned by a relatively generous system of unemployment insurance (UI)—one that was often criticized for its generosity and passivity.[6] In 1996 the federal government announced its withdrawal from the training sphere and began a radical restructuring of the renamed employment insurance (EI) system along with the transfer of responsibility for active employment measures to the provinces.

That transfer consisted of a variety of programs funded through the Employment Insurance account. The clientele who could access them was for the first time extended to include people not currently drawing benefits from the unemployment insurance account. Such measures would include wage subsidies, temporary income supplements, support for self-employment initiatives, partnerships for job creation and, where provinces requested, skills loans and grants. Provinces that assumed responsibility for delivery of active measures could also opt to take over the delivery of labour-market services—screening, counselling, placement—from the federal government. The federal government was to withdraw from labour-market training over a three-year period, or sooner if provinces wanted. It would no longer be involved in purchase of training, funding apprenticeships, co-op education, workplace-based training or project-based training (HRDC 1996a, 1996b).

Some $2 billion would be available for active measures directed to claimants and some former claimants of unemployment insurance. If EI coverage rates had remained constant, the pool of clients to be served by the devolved programs would expand. Given an actual decline in coverage, however, the pool would shrink, though without providing any great fiscal advantage to the provinces. Those individuals not covered by EI would require provincial social assistance, and a declining pool might stimulate future reductions in federal funding.

Three types of active measures were to be transferred to the provinces immediately: targetted wage subsidies, to aid employers in hiring, and thus providing on-the-job experience; self-employment assistance to help individuals start their own businesses; and job-creation partnerships with provinces, the private sector and communities. Two other programs were to be pre-tested: targetted earnings—wage top-ups to encourage the unemployed to accept low-paid jobs; and skills loans and grants, which would be implemented only with the consent of a province. Under this program funds would be made available so that individuals could choose the form of training best suited to them. This approach rests on the observation, disputed by some provincial

officials (interview, B.C. official, March 1998) that better results, defined as end-of-program employment, are obtained when people share in the costs of the training they receive (HRDC 1996c:17–18).

Despite the asymmetrical arrangements that are emerging as a result of devolution to the provinces, some common neo-liberal principles run through the new labour-market development agreements. For example, they typically contain language committing the governments to reduce dependency on public assistance, and they elicit a commitment, on the part of those who do receive assistance under employment benefits and support measures, to take primary responsibility for identifying their own employment needs and locating services necessary to meet those needs. This approach includes, if appropriate, sharing the cost of such assistance (see, for example, the Canada-British Columbia Agreement on Labour Market Development 3.1.h).

Indeed, the "results"-based orientation of the Employment Insurance Act consists precisely of these targets and, measured by these standards, achieved early success. Reporting to the minister on the first year of experience with the new act, the Canada Employment Insurance Commission showed that income benefits had declined by 8.4 percent, the number of initial claimants had dropped by 14.5 percent, and there had been an increase in the number of clients receiving short-term interventions such as information and counselling, and a decrease in those receiving longer-term interventions such as training. As a result, "average costs per participant in Employment Benefits and Support measures declined from $7300 to $3900," or by 46.6 percent (HRDC 1998:ii–iii).

The federal authorities retained a limited range of labour-market policy responsibilities—

employment insurance benefits, provision of a national system of labour-market information and exchange, support for interprovincial sectoral development and developing responses to national economic crises, and jurisdiction over a one-time Transitional Jobs Fund (HRDC 1996b: 1). But these reforms completed a long-term trend to ending federal Consolidated Revenue funding for employment measures. Any future federal money for these purposes will come from the employment insurance account. On current evidence, many of the services that remain will be contracted out.[7]

The federal government also restructured the unemployment insurance system (HRDC 1995). The program had already ceased to be generous by international standards. The 1996 changes to the system (see HRDC 1996b) included calculating qualification periods in terms of hours worked rather than weeks worked. The department claimed that this would be more equitable for part-time workers and women workers in particular, and that it reflected the labour-market reality of increasing part-time work. Other changes reduced the benefit replacement rate for repeat claimants and introduced a supplement for low-income family claimants, increased the clawback of benefits from high-income earners and reduced premiums and maximum insurable earnings.

Coverage declined sharply. A Canadian Labour Congress (1999) study based on Statistics Canada data shows that in 1997 the percentage of unemployed workers covered by UI was less than half of what it had been in 1989—36 percent as compared to 74 percent. Women, whose coverage had declined from 70 percent in 1987 to 31 percent in 1997,[8] and young people—55 percent to 15 percent—were particularly hard hit (see Table 11.8).

The primary reason for declining coverage seems to be that the number of weekly hours required to qualify jumped from 15 to 35, with an immediate impact on part-time workers. Women were overrepresented among this group. Young people were also hurt by the change in regulations. In their case an additional factor was the tripling of the total hours required to qualify for benefits, from 300 to 910 hours for new entrants.

A government study (Applied Research Branch, Strategic Policy, HRDC 1998) estimates the decline in the beneficiaries to unemployed ratio at almost 50 percent in the 1989–97 period (83 percent to 42 percent). The report attributes just under half of the decline to policy and program changes. The rest is due to labour-market changes such as increased long-term unemployment. The effects were to increase the number of "exhaustees," produce more unemployed people who lacked previous work experience, and increase the number of people who were "self-employed."

In addition to the coverage issue, benefits are of shorter duration and the benefit rate has fallen steadily from 66.6 percent to 55 percent

Table 11.8: Percentage of Unemployed Receiving Unemployment Benefits

	1989	1990	1991	1992	1993	1994	1995	1996	1997	% change
Men	77	77	72	63	59	52	47	44	39	-49
Women	70	69	63	58	52	47	40	37	31	-55
All	74	73	68	61	56	50	44	41	36	-55

Source: Canadian Labour Congress 1999.

(under the new system repeat claimants can receive as little as 52 percent).The changes not only continue a long-standing process of dismantling the 1971 employment insurance system[9] but also further reduce the individual security formerly provided by the system.

In fitting with the "reparation agenda," in September 2000 the Liberal government announced the reversal of several of its 1996 reforms to the unemployment insurance system. These included removal of penalties for seasonal workers with repeat claims and an extension of the limit at which benefits are clawed back to $48,000 from $39,000 *(Globe and Mail* 29 Sept. 2000).

Made in Canada

Retrenchment of the state has been a chief characteristic of national politics over the last two decades. While the global context—and the rhetoric surrounding the need to be competitive and efficient in a global economy—may have had some bearing on the direction of policy, the available evidence indicates that the causation has been domestic. This tendency may be due to the dominance of neo-liberal policy prescriptions and/or the increased strength of business relative to labour, as power resource theory might suggest.[10] In either event it is not necessary to look beyond national borders for an explanation. Significantly, as the federal deficit came under control and a surplus emerged, speculation grew about how the government might make use of the "fiscal dividend." With an election in the offing there were signs that federal purse strings were loosening—which only seems to confirm that social policy has been driven by domestic rather than global factors.

Endnotes

1 But only to some degree; Leo Panitch has referred to welfare's redistributive effects as "socialism in one class" (cited in Leys 1980:52), because the transfers are largely "from younger, employed workers, to retired, unemployed workers, workers' widows and one-parent families."

2 For a somewhat sceptical view of the claims of "strong" versions of globalization theory, see Evans, McBride and Shields 2000.

3 For a fuller, though still incomplete account of neo-liberal policy measures, see McBride and Shields 1997, and the contributions to Burke, Mooers and Shields 2000.

4 As Gamble (1988) points out in his analysis of Thatcherism, the neo-liberal state was far from uniformly weak.

5 For an overview of monetarism, see McBride 1992: ch. 3.

6 For a review and rebuttal of literature suggesting that the unemployment insurance system acted as a disincentive to work and hence raised the unemployment rate, see Jackson 1995:3–9; see also McBride 1992: ch. 6.

7 Since, at the time of the Charlottetown Accord, the federal authorities contemplated transferring unemployment insurance to the provinces (interview, former HR/DC official, July 1996), it is possible that further devolution will occur. Indeed, the posture of HRDC with respect to contracting out of functions would seem well suited to preparing the ground for this eventuality. Such a trajectory has been made more likely by the major shift towards radical decentralization of federalism favoured by Ontario, traditionally an upholder of a strong role for Ottawa. An Ontario position paper on the constitution called for unemployment insurance to be run jointly by the federal and provincial governments or by the provinces alone *(Globe and Mail* 16 Aug. 1996).

8 The Canadian Labour Congress's (CLC) figures refer only to women on lay-off and do not include those on maternity leave.

9   See McBride 1992: ch. 6 for details of earlier rounds of restrictions.
10 For a test and partial confirmation of power resource theory in the social policy area, see S. Phillips 1999.

References

Applied Research Branch, Strategic Policy, Human Resources Development Canada. 1998. *An Analysis of Employ-ment Insurance Benefit Coverage*. Ottawa: HRDC.

Bank of Canada. 1997. *Review*. Ottawa (Summer).

Banting, Keith. 1987. *The Welfare State and Canadian Federalism*. 2nd edition. Montreal: McGill-Queen's University Press.

Battle, Ken and Sherri Torjman. 1996. "Desperately Seeking Substance: A Commentary on the Social Security Review." In Jane Pulkingham and Gordon Ternowetsky (eds.). 1996. *Remaking Canadian Social Policy: Social Security in the late 1990s*. Halifax: Fernwood.

Bluestone, Barry and Bennett Harrison. 1982. *The Deindustrialization of America*. New York: Basic Books.

Burke, Mike. 2000. "Efficiency and the Erosion of Health Care in Canada." In Mike Burke, Colin Mooers and John Shields (eds.). *Restructuring and Resistance: Canadian Public Policy in an Age of Global Capitalism*. Halifax: Fernwood.

Burke, Mike, Colin Mooers and John Shields (eds.). 2000. *Restructuring and Resistance: Canadian Public Policy in an Age of Global Capitalism*. Halifax: Fernwood.

Burke, Mike and John Shields. 1999. *The Job-Poor Recovery: Social Cohesion and the Canadian Labour Market*. Toronto: Ryerson Social Reporting Network.

Campbell, Robert M. 1987. *Grand Illusions: The Politics of the Keynesian Experience in Canada, 1945–75*. Peterborough, Ontario: Broadview.

Canada. 1985. *Report : Royal Commission on the Economic Union and Development Prospects for Canada*. 3 vols. Ottawa: Minister of Supply and Services.

Canadian Council on Social Development (CCSD). 1990. *Canada's Social Programs Are in Trouble*. Ottawa.

Canadian Labour Congress (CLC). 1999. *Left Out in the Cold: The End of UI for Canadian Workers*. Ottawa.

Canadian Union of Public Employees (CUPE). 2000. *Who's Pushing Privatization*. Ottawa.

Chorney, Harold. 1988. *Sound Finance and Other Delusions: Deficit and Debt Management in the Age of Neo-Liberal Economics*. Montreal: Concordia University.

Di Matteo, Livio. 2000. "The Determinants of the Public-Private Mix in Canadian Health Care Expenditures, 1975–1996." *Health Policy* 52.

Doern, G. Bruce, Allan M. Maslove and Michael J. Prince. 1988. *Public Budgeting in Canada: Politics, Economics and Management*. Ottawa: Carleton University Press.

Economic Council of Canada. 1984. *Western Transition*. Ottawa: Minister of Supply and Services.

Esping-Andersen, Gosta. 1983. "After the Welfare State." *Public Welfare* (Winter).

Evans, B. Mitchell, Stephen McBride and John Shields. 2000. "Globalization and the Challenge to Canadian Democracy: National Governance under Threat." In Mike Burke, Colin Mooers and John Shields (eds.). 2000. *Restructuring and Resistance: Canadian Public Policy in an Age of Global Capitalism*. Halifax: Fernwood.

Evans, Robert G., Morris L. Baber, Steven Lewis, Michael Rachlis and Greg L. Stoddart. 2000. *Private Highway, One-way Street: The Deklein and Fall of Canadian Medicare*. Vancouver: UBC Centre for Health Services and Policy Research.

Finance Canada. 1995. *Budget 1995*. Fact Sheets 9. Ottawa.

Fuller, Colleen. 1996. "Doctoring to NAFTA." *Canadian Forum* (June).

Gamble, Andrew. 1988. *The Free Economy and the Strong State*. London: Macmillan.

Gonick, Cy. 1987. *The Great Economic Debate*. Toronto: Lorimer.

Hardin, H. 1989. *The Privatization Putsch*. Halifax: Institute for Research on Public Policy.

Heap, Shaun Hargreaves. 1980/81. "World Profitability Crisis in the 1970s: Some Empirical Evidence." *Capital and Class* 12.

Houle, François. 1990. "Economic Renewal and Social Policy." In Alain-G. Gagnon and James P. Bickerton (eds.). 1990. *Canadian Politics: An Introduction to the Discipline*. Peterborough, Ontario: Broadview.

Human Resources Development Canada (HRDC). 1995. *News Release*. Ottawa, 1 December.

_____. 1996a. *News Release; Government of Canada Offers Provinces and Territories Responsibility for Active Employment Measures*. Ottawa (30 May).

_____. 1996b. *Getting Canadians Back to Work*. Ottawa (30 May).

_____. 1996c. *Employment Insurance: A Guide to Employment Insurance*. Ottawa.

_____. 1997. "Delivery of Non-Decisional Activities; Agreements with Third Parties." Draft document, mineo. Ottawa.

_____. 1998. *1997 Employment Insurance: Monitoring and Assessment Report*. Ottawa.

Hurtig, Mel. 1991. *The Betrayal of Canada*. Toronto: Stoddart.

Jackson, Andrew. 1995. *The Liberals' Labour Strategy (and its consequences for workers)*. Ottawa: Canadian Centre for Policy Alternatives.

Klein, Seth. 1996. "Good Sense Versus Common Sense: Canada's Debt Debate and Competing Hegemonic Projects." M.A. thesis, Department of Political Science, Simon Fraser University, Vancouver.

Krehm, William. 1993. *A Power Unto Itself: The Bank of Canada*. Toronto: Stoddart.

Kroeger, Arthur. 1996. "Changing Course: The Federal Government's Program Review of 1994–95." In Amelita Armit and Jacques Bourgault (eds.). *Hard Choices or No Choices: Assessing Program Review*. Toronto: Institute of Public Administration of Canada.

Laux, Jeanne Kirk. 1991. "Shaping or Serving Markets? Public Ownership after Privatization." In Daniel Drache and Meric S. Gertler (eds.). *The New Era of Global Competition: State Policy and Market Power*. Montreal and Kingston: McGill-Queen's University Press.

Leys, Colin. 1980. "Neo-Conservatism and the Organic Crisis in Britain." *Studies in Political Economy: A Socialist Review* 4 (Autumn).

Liberal Party. 1993. *Creating Opportunity: The Liberal Plan for Canada*. Ottawa.

MacDonald, Martha. 1999. "Restructuring, Gender and Social Security Reform in Canada." *Journal of Canadian Studies* (Summer).

Maslove, Allan M. 1981. "Tax Expenditures, Tax Credits and Equity." In Bruce G. Doern (ed.) *How Ottawa Spends Your Tax Dollars: Federal Priorities 1981*. Toronto: Lorimer.

Maxwell, Judith. 2001. *Towards a Common Citizenship: Canada's Social and Economic Choices*. Ottawa: Canadian Policy Research Networks.

McBride, Stephen. 1992. *Not Working: State, Unemployment, and Neo-Conservatism in Canada*. Toronto: University of Toronto Press.

_____. 1996. "The Continuing Crisis of Social Democracy: Ontario's Social Contract in Perspective." *Studies in Political Economy* 50 (Summer).

McBride, Stephen and John Shields. 1997. *Dismantling a Nation*. 2nd ed. Halifax: Fernwood.

McFettridge, D.G. 1997. *The Economics of Privatization*. Montreal: C.D. Howe Institute.

McIlveen, Murray and Hideo Mimoto. 1990. "The Federal Government Deficit, 1975–76 to 1988–89." Mimeo. Ottawa. Statistics Canada.

McQuaig, Linda. 1987. *Behind Closed Doors: How the Rich Won Control of Canada's Tax System*. Markham, Ontario: Viking.

_____. 1995. *Shooting the Hippo: Death by Deficit and Other Canadian Myths*. Toronto: Viking.

Mishra, Ramesh. 1990. *The Welfare State in Capitalist Society: Policies of Retrenchment and Maintenance in Europe, North America and Australia*. Toronto: University of Toronto Press.

_____. 1999. "After Globalization: Social Policy in an Open Economy." *Canadian Review of Social Policy* 43.

Phillips, Stephen. 2000. "The Demise of Universality: The Politics of Federal Income Security in Canada, 1978–1993." Paper presented at the annual meeting of the British Columbia Political Studies Association, Victoria (May).

Prince, Michael J. 1999. "From Health and Welfare to Stealth and Farewell: Federal Social Policy, 1980–2000." In Leslie A. Pal (ed.) *How Canada Spends 1999–2000*. Toronto: Oxford University Press.

Rehnby, Nadene and Stephen McBride. 1997. *Help Wanted: Economic Security for Youth*. Ottawa: Canadian Centre for Policy Alternatives.

Rice, James J. And Michael J. Prince. 2000. *Changing Politics of Canadian Social Policy*. Toronto: University of Toronto Press.

Ruggeri, G.C. 1987. *The Canadian Economy: Problems and Policies*. 3rd ed. Toronto: Gage Publishing Company.

Russell, Bob. 1991. "The Welfare State and the Politics of Constraint." In B. Singh Bolaria (ed.). *Social Issues and Contradictions in Canadian Society.* Toronto: Harcourt Brace.

_____. 2000. "From the Workhouse to Workfare: The Welfare State and Shifting Policy Terrains." In Mike Burke, Colin Mooers and John Shields (eds.). 2000. *Restructuring and Resistance: Canadian Public Policy in an Age of Global Capitalism.* Halifax: Fernwood.

Shields, John and B. Mitchell Evans. 1998. *Shrinking the State.* Halifax: Fernwood.

Silver, Susan. 1996. "The Struggle for National Standards: Lessons from the Federal Role in Health Care." In Jane Pulkingham and Gordon Ternowetsky (eds.). *Remaking Canadian Social Policy: Social Security in the Late 1990s.* Halifax: Fernwood.

Simeon, Richard. 1991. "Globalization and the Canadian Nation-State." In Bruce G. Doern and Bryne B. Purchase (eds.). *Canada at Risk? Canadian Public Policy in the 1990s.* Toronto: C.D. Howe Institute.

Simeon, Richard and Mary Janigan (eds.). 1991. *Toolkits and Building Blocks: Constructing a New Canada.* Toronto: C.D. Howe Institute.

Smith, Janet. 1990. "Canada's Privatisation Programme." In J.J. Richardson (ed.). *Privatisation and Deregulation in Canada and Britain.* Aldershot, England: Dartmouth.

Stanbury, William. 1988. "Privatization and the Mulroney Government, 1984–1988." In Andrew B. Gollner and Daniel Salée (eds.). *Canada under Mulroney: An End-of-Term Report.* Montreal: Véhicule Press.

Stanford, Jim. 2000. "The Facts Ma'am. Just the Facts: Assessing the Liberals' Allocation of the Fiscal Dividend." *Behind the Numbers* 3, 2 (November).

Taylor, D. Wayne. 1991. *Business and Government Relations: Partners in the 1990s.* Toronto: Gage.

Taylor, Malcolm. 1987. "The Canadian Health Care System After Medicare." In David Coburn, Carl D'Arcy, Peter New and George Torrance (eds.). *Health and Canadian Society: Sociological Perspectives.* 2nd ed. Markham, Ontario; Fitzhenry and Whiteside.

Ternowetsky, Gordon W. 1987. "Controlling the Deficit and a Private Sector Led Recovery: Contemporary Themes of the Welfare State." In Jacqueline Ismael (ed.). *The Canadian Welfare State: Evolution and Transition.* Edmonton: University of Alberta Press.

Vanier Institute of the Family. 2001. *The Current State of Canadian Family Finances—2000 Report.* Ottawa.

Weller, Geoffrey R. 1996. "Strengthening Society I: Health Care." In Andrew F. Johnson and Andrew Stritch (eds.). *Canadian Public Policy: Globalization and Political Parties.* Toronto: Copp Clark.

Wilson, Michael H. 1984. *Economic and Fiscal Statement.* Ottawa: Department of Finance.

_____. 1991. *The Budget.* Ottawa: Department of Finance.

Wolfe, David A. 1985. "The Politics of the Deficit." In Bruce G. Doern (research coordinator). *The Politics of Economic Policy* Vol. 40 Royal Commission on the Economic Union and Development Prospects for Canada. Toronto: University of Toronto Press.

Yalnizyan, Armine. 1998. *The Growing Gap: A Report on Growing Inequality between the Rich and the Poor in Canada.* Toronto: Centre for Social Justice.

CHAPTER 12

Neo-Liberalism and Retrenchment:

Employment, Universality, Safety-Net Provisions, and a Collapsing Canadian Welfare State.[1]

Jane Pulkingham and Gordon Ternowetsky

Introduction

THE COMMITMENT TO full employment and the provision of universal services constitutes the "first line of defence" for maintaining national, minimum standards (Esping-Andersen 1990; Mishra 1990: 18–20, 26). The second line is safety-net provisions for protecting the living standards of the poor and most vulnerable. In commenting on the impact of social policy retrenchments of the Canadian welfare state during the 1980s, Mishra (1990: 79) concludes that, "in the absence of external or internal shock ... social developments are likely to remain centrist and evolutionary." He recognizes that the dismantling of unemployment policies, universality and safety-net provisions have "weakened" the welfare state. In his view, however, these have been piecemeal and the welfare state, after the neo-liberal assault of the 1980s, remains intact.

This assessment of the Canadian welfare state was made several years ago. Today, however, the validity of this position is questionable. In the areas of employment and unemployment policies, universality and safety-net provisions, the retrenchments initiated by Prime Minister Mulroney, and later consolidated by Prime Minister Chrétien, may well have resulted in a collapse of these pivotal features of the centrist, evolutionary post-World War II welfare state. This essay examines the question: How far down the road of neo-liberal reconstruction has the Canadian welfare state gone? This is done by reviewing key changes in the Canadian welfare state that have taken place over the last decade and a half. The analysis suggests that during the 1980s and 1990s the first line of defence, full or high employment, has been abandoned, and universality of income transfers has been replaced by selective and targetted programs. In terms of safety-net provisions, the second line of defence, the new Canada Health and Social Transfer (CHST), has fundamentally altered the welfare state in this country. It entrenches a decentralized welfare state and ushers in an era of declining and uneven citizenship rights, disintegrating safety-net provisions and increased insecurity for the most vulnerable groups, such as women, children, the poor and the unemployed.

Employment and Unemployment

In many analyses, including Mishra's, full employment is depicted as a pillar of the post-World War II welfare state in most Western capitalist societies. A number of qualifications need to be made in order to clarify the meaning of full employment in the history of the Canadian welfare state. First, full employment was never pursued in Canada, although there was a policy of high (or near-full) employment. Second, the principle of full employment operated essentially for core-sector, male workers only. Women were defined primarily as dependents, not workers, and were excluded from the definition of full employment.

During the 1980s and 1990s, anti-inflationary employment policies further redefined the meaning of full or high employment. In the 1980s, full employment translated into an official unemployment level of 6.5 percent (Minister of Supply and Services 1985). In the 1990s, the equivalent unemployment rate is eight percent (Department of Finance 1994: 20). In today's economy, this means that "full employment" is predicated on the existence of 1.2 million unemployed. But even this level of full employment has not been achieved. Between October 1990 and October 1997, for example, the official monthly unemployment rate exceeded nine percent for 84 months in

a row. When discouraged workers—those who drop out of the labour force because they believe no job is available—are added to these official figures, the real rate of unemployment is above 13 percent, or more than two million unemployed people (CCPA 1997: 1, 5).

The policy response to unemployment in the 1990s reflects the prevalence of a neo-liberal social policy ideology. This ideology entails a preoccupation with market conditions; "active" labour-market and employment policies and a retreat from the principle of full, or near-full, employment; Unemployment Insurance and welfare reform. These reforms reinforce the neo-liberal fixation with reducing public expenditures, program costs and government deficits and debt, and more importantly, buttress the centrality of the wage-labour obligation and point to the emergence of a gender-neutral worker-citizen model (Pulkingham 1998; Scott 1996; Brodie 1995; Fraser and Gordon 1994). With this model, the basis for women's claims on the state is inverted—now they are positioned as workers first and male dependents second.

In the case of Unemployment Insurance (UI), reform 1990s-style rests on a rejection of the notion that an intensification of non-standard employment should be met with extended coverage and expanded protection. This stands in sharp contrast to the view prevailing in the early 1970s when UI last underwent significant amendment. At that time changes led to increased coverage and entitlement. Under the Mulroney government, a new phase of UI reform was introduced in 1989–90 (through Bill C-21). Although the trend toward reduced generosity began in the mid- to late-1970s (Green and Riddell 1993: S108; Forget et al. 1986), unlike previous reforms in this phase there has been an aggressive pursuit of the goal of producing savings (more precisely, containing rising public expenditures and reducing the federal deficit), and "active" rather than "passive" income support.

Privatization of UI is one of the most significant changes introduced with Bill C-21 in the early 1990s. Here the government converted UI financing from a tripartite (employee, employer, government) arrangement, to one financed by employees and employers only. This represents a clear shift from public, collective responsibility to individual responsibility. Failure to consider the privatization of UI may mean a serious underestimation of the impact of neo-liberal retrenchments on the welfare state (Mullaly 1993). Primarily under the Chrétien Liberal government, a further range of restrictive changes has been implemented, including benefit rate reductions, the imposition of more strict claimant reporting and entrance requirements, disqualifying leavers ("voluntary" or through "misconduct") and reductions in the duration of claims (entitlement rules) (Employment and Immigration Canada 1994). These changes, introduced piecemeal over a number of years, culminated in the implementation of a new Employment Insurance (El) system—Bill C-12, July 1996—which replaced the Unemployment Insurance Act and the National Training Act.

The new EI system represents an intensification of efforts already begun in this privatization phase. In particular, there are two key issues—entitlement and coverage—that need to be considered. Although UI began as a limited and restricted program, since its inception coverage expanded gradually and now stands at 93 percent of the labour force (HRDC 1996: Part A, Section 2: 6). EI will increase this to 97 percent through the inclusion of all part-time workers. But increased coverage is distinct

from entitlement. Increased coverage is meaningless unless the corollary, entitlement, is also enhanced. While EI will increase coverage, it also imposes more restrictive qualifying rules and eligibility requirements, and therefore curtails entitlement. This will accelerate the precipitous decline in the ratio of beneficiaries to unemployed persons, which has already dropped from 87 percent in 1990 (Canadian Labour Congress 1995: 2) to 46 percent in January 1996 (Hargrove 1996: A17). More recent data show that by November 1996, after the implementation of El, the percentage of unemployed receiving benefits had dropped to 35.1 percent (Statistics Canada 1997).

Despite recognition of the increasing precariousness of stable, full-time employment (HRDC 1994), UI reform, culminating in the new EI system, is a central component of the government's strategy to facilitate a business agenda through labour-market deregulation, reduced wage demands, increased economic insecurity and the discipline of labour (Stanford 1996: 137–138, 144). The net effect is the dismantling of a major component of the first line of defence for maintaining minimum standards in periods of high unemployment.

Universal Social Programs

The principle of universality, reflected in a range of services such as primary and secondary education, health care, public pensions and (formerly) taxable cash benefits for families with children (Family Allowance), "constitutes perhaps the core element of the post-war welfare state" (Mishra 1990: 23). In this era of neo-liberal policy-making, however, it is much maligned and beleaguered.

The neo-liberal critique of universal programs is that they are an inefficient use of resources in two ways. First, because benefits go to rich and poor alike, they are not adequately targetted to those most in need of assistance. Second, at a time when governments are wrestling to pay down deficits and debts, universal programs are unaffordable. Instead, it is argued that the allocation of scarce public resources should be selective, targetted through income and means-testing, so that only those who truly are the most needy receive assistance rather than money being "wasted" on those who are not.

The process of undermining universality began with the Conservatives, under Mulroney. Over the course of two successive terms in office, the Conservatives made four attempts to break with the principle of universality. Although the first attempt in 1984 was unsuccessful, at least in the immediate term, the effect of subsequent forays was more than symbolic (Mishra 1990; Department of Finance 1984). In the second try in 1985 the government proposed the partial de-indexation of the Family Allowance and Old Age Security, and was successful in accomplishing this with the former. Thus began the era of "social policy by stealth" (Battle and Torjman 1996) where payments increase only by the amount that inflation exceeds three percent (partial de-indexation). This results in a gradual but inevitable deterioration in the value of benefits.

In 1989, the federal government proceeded with its third and more serious attack—imposition of a clawback and partial indexation of the income threshold above which the clawback is applied on the Family Allowances of higher-income families. A similar clawback also was imposed on Old Age Security for higher-income individuals (Hess 1992).[2] Through the benefit clawback, the government directly undermined the principle of universality by introducing an income-contingent component. In addition, the partial indexation both of the income threshold above which the clawback is applied and of increases in the benefit ensured that the proportion of people eligible for full benefits and the value of these benefits would decline steadily over time.

Despite these developments, some have argued that in the 1980s the Conservatives retreated politically from enacting major changes to universal social programs. Attempts to alter them are variously described as a "fizzle" and a "half-hearted attempt to break with the centrist consensus in Canada over social protection" (Mishra 1990: 75). This view is not unanimous. Others (Mullaly 1993; McBride and Shields 1993; Pulkingham and Ternowetsky 1996) argue that welfare state retrenchment under the Mulroney government is more consequential, reflected in a significant erosion of the principle of universality through the clawback of Family Allowance and Old Age Security and in other policies, in particular the privatization of Unemployment Insurance.

Perhaps one can equivocate about the impact of neo-liberalism in Canada in the 1980s, but the outcome of the 1990s is unequivocal. The fourth offensive against universality came in 1992 with the abandonment of Family Allowance and introduction of the Child Tax Benefit. With this action, the government made absolutely clear its rejection of the principle of universality and the direction in which previous amendments to Family Allowance (and arguably Old Age Security) were headed.

One of the main reasons given for implementing the Child Tax Benefit was to better target low-income families with children—a long-standing principle of neo-liberalism (Canada 1992; Phipps 1993). Family Allowances, the Refundable Child Tax Credit and the Non-Refundable Child Tax Credit were combined into a single Child Tax Benefit. It is important to note that not only was there no new money in this package, but also that parents on welfare (the poorest of the poor) and Unemployment Insurance recipients received exactly the same under the Child Tax Benefit as they did under the previous system.[3] As detailed below, only working parents were eligible for additional benefits from the Child Tax Benefit.

Moreover, the Child Tax Benefit was partially de-indexed in that the income levels at which it was paid are adjusted only when inflation exceeds three percent. Between 1992, when the Child Tax Benefit was first announced, and the 1998 Federal Budget, inflation remained under three percent. As a result, many poor families with nominal increases in income "are being pushed above the income threshold for receiving the Child Tax Benefit" (CCSD 1996a: 2). By not indexing this child benefit to inflation, the federal government cut out families in need and saved some $150 million a year in Child Tax Benefit payments—a clear example of social policy by stealth that disadvantages those for whom the targetted Child Tax Benefit is purportedly designed.

While Child Tax Benefit improvements in this targetted system were to go only to working poor families, not all of the working poor benefited (NCW 1992). This preferential treatment stems from the principle of "less eligibility," another tenet of neo-liberalism that suggests some poor are deserving while others are undeserving. This principle is embodied in the earned income supplement (later renamed the Working Income Supplement), a major new initiative of the Child Tax Benefit when it was first introduced in 1992 by the Conservative government (Canada 1992).

Targetted to the working poor, the Working Income Supplement was not available to families with children where a parent was not in the paid labour force, whether or not they received EI or social assistance. A study of financial work incentives provided to welfare mothers suggests that the Working Income Supplement was based on the premise that people on welfare do not want to work, and that incentives are needed to prod them into taking work (Low 1996: 191; see also Phipps 1993).

In the 1996 Federal Budget, the principle underlying the Working Income Supplement was entrenched by the Liberals, with proposed increases from $500 to $750 in 1997 and $1000 in 1998 (Department of Supply and Services 1996). While it is important to assist low-income employed families with children, the Working Income Supplement was also a "disciplinary" mechanism (McBride and Shields 1993: 34), as it disenfranchised non-employed families with children. This disenfranchisement took place at a time when it was increasingly difficult to find paid employment. Not only is it inappropriate to tie child benefits to a work test, but given the persistence of high unemployment, the Working Income Supplement disregarded the structural circumstances confronting individuals and families with children who are in receipt of EI or social assistance.

The Working Income Supplement also entrenched a low-wage strategy. It did this in a number of ways. In the first place it was part of a broader welfare strategy aimed at reducing income assistance benefits while increasing the requirement to work. In addition, because of these policies, low wages became more attractive even if remuneration levels were unable to meet basic needs. In this context the Working Income Supplement acted as a low-wage subsidy, making low-wage jobs more tolerable, enlarging the pool of people willing to take up low-wage jobs, and thereby intensifying a downward pressure on wages.

The Working Income Supplement was also a gendered policy. It penalized many of the working poor, particularly women, who work part-time and receive low or minimum wages. This occurred as the Working Income Supplement began to kick in at an annual wage of $3,750. After $10,000, the full amount of the supplement was paid, up to a threshold of $20,921. With high unemployment and the spread of low-wage, part-time work, income thresholds of $3,750 and $10,000 were too high in that they excluded workers earning less. For example, in 1992, when this supplement was first announced, the minimum wage for full-time, full-year work hovered around the $10,000 level in most provinces (Clark 1995: 3). This means that part-time workers, many of whom are women with children, were excluded from receiving the full value of the Working Income Supplement. The Working Income Supplement not only abandoned the poor who received EI or social assistance, but it also kept out the poorest of the working poor. In this respect, the Child Tax Benefit failed in its purported intent to better target families with children who are in greatest need.

The new Canada Child Tax Benefit/National Child Benefit introduced in the 1997–98 Federal Budget (Canada 1997a, 1997b) and clarified in the joint federal/provincial paper *The National Child Benefit* (Federal and Provincial/Territorial Governments 1997) will further reinforce the distinction between the "worthy" or "deserving" poor and those that are "undeserving." The Canada Child Tax Benefit (CCTB) will be introduced in two stages:

Stage One begins in July 1997 and the second stage in July 1998. This new system of child benefits maintains many of the problematic features of the CTB. In Stage One enriched entitlements continue only for poor parents that are in the workforce. This is a fundamental flaw. It continues the practice whereby benefits that are earmarked for poor children are made contingent upon the workforce participation of parents. In practice, this means that more than 60 percent of Canada's poor children will gain nothing from this new program (Valpy 1997).

In Stage Two, the basic Canada Child Tax Benefit and the modified Working Income Supplement are combined into a single federal government payment. But income source rather than work status of parents becomes the yardstick for determining whether families will benefit financially. In this stage the federal government will permit provinces and territories to deduct a sum equivalent to the enriched Working Income Supplement component of the Canada Child Tax Benefit from income assistance payments made to families. The key phrase in the budget document (one that would have been agreed to earlier in consultations with provincial social service ministers) is that "families on social assistance would receive no less overall" than they currently obtained through provincial and territorial welfare payments (Canada 1997a: 6). What this means is that these families will probably gain nothing from the new Canada Child Tax Benefit/National Child Benefit. This is the case as, unlike for families with equivalent net income from employment, part of the value of the federal Canada Child Tax Benefit/National Child Benefit will be deducted from families whose income derives from welfare. The income of these families will remain pegged at the different income assistance rates that are current in the provinces and territories (these are far below accepted standards of income adequacy).

Another key phrase is that "enriched federal benefits will enable provinces and territories to redirect" extra social assistance funds to "other programs targeted at improving work incentives and supporting children in low-income families" (Canada 1997a: 6; Canada 1997b: 19). Two points regarding these services are warranted. One is that they will be funded through the savings that accrue to the provinces and territories by deducting the enriched component of the federal Canada Child Tax Benefit/National Child Benefit from poor families with children whose source of income is income assistance. A second point is that many of these services envisioned by the federal, provincial and territorial governments were previously mandated legally through the Canada Assistance Plan (CAP). With the CHST, these mandated services are lost. Now it appears that these services and benefits will be financed, in part, through the money earmarked for children in poverty. It is clear, however, that most of this money will be used for low-income working families. The current documentation on the Canada Child Tax Benefit/National Child Benefit says very little about services and benefits for families and children whose main source of income is public assistance (Canada 1997a: 6; Federal and Provincial/Territorial Governments 1997). In effect, CAP provisions that disallowed workfare as a condition for receipt of assistance and services are now being replaced by a system of services based on a work test.

Changes to Old Age Security announced in the 1995 federal budget signaled a further

narrowing of the form of citizenship-based entitlement to income support for the elderly. In the first instance, beginning July 1996, the government changed the operation of the clawback such that eligibility for benefits is now contingent on the previous year's declared income. This means that the clawback is imposed before rather than after paying out the full benefit. Such a policy is informed by the dubious assumption that income amounts are continuous from year to year. What it may mean, however, is that for some the benefit is not available when it is most needed.

In the second instance, the government announced that Old Age Security, the Guaranteed Income Supplement, the age credit and the pension income credit would be abolished and replaced in 2001 with a new (family) income-tested Senior's Benefit. Heralded as the "most significant policy initiative on elderly benefits in the past thirty years" (Prince 1996: 218), the proposed benefit contained several features which signified a marked departure from the principles of Old Age Security operating since 1952. These include the complete disappearance of horizontal equity in an elderly benefit system premised on the value that all seniors regardless of their income have a right to income support as seniors; the adoption of an explicitly selective approach focusing on vertical equity, thus reducing the program's constituency for near-seniors and future generations of seniors; and the use of family rather than individual income as the basis for income testing, which serves to disentitle those (predominantly women) with low individual incomes when they are in a relationship with a middle- to high-income earning partner.

In the face of concerted public pressure, the government recently (July 1998) announced it would not implement the Senior's Benefit. Its rationale is that, for the moment, cuts to this program are no longer necessary or defensible as the government has paid down the deficit and is running annual surpluses. However, considered in the light of the historical changes to Old Age Security and child benefits documented in this paper, it is likely that this retreat is only temporary.

Despite their lack of popularity among politicians and governments, universal programs are a vital and effective means of supporting children and families. In mapping a way forward, beyond the neo-liberal agenda, we need to relearn the value of universality. In part, this entails recognizing the failure of targeted programs, such as the Child Tax Benefit, to alleviate poverty (see Phipps 1993; Esping-Andersen 1990; McDaniel 1993). For example, one study of child and family benefits under different welfare regimes draws a number of relevant conclusions (Phipps 1993). Income support programs that are targeted to those most in need (to achieve the minimal goal of poverty alleviation) are comparatively ineffective as an anti-poverty strategy. Evidence pointing to considerably lower rates of poverty among families with children in European, especially Scandinavian, countries suggests that pursuit of the "'social democratic' goal of reducing over-all income inequality" is far more effective than the "'liberal' goal of poverty reduction" (Phipps 1993: 40). Key to the social-democratic model are universal programs and means/income-tested programs that provide benefits to the majority of the population—as opposed to means/income-tested programs that target benefits only to the extremely needy (Phipps 1993: 31). In both instances, not only is there less stigma associated with benefit take-up (and therefore greater utilization of programs), but also programs are much less vulnerable to erosion and elimination because the basis of support is widespread. Finally, the fact is that all universal benefits are conditional (though not income-contingent) and target specific groups of beneficiaries. In this way, universal programs are an effective way to target benefits.

Social Safety-Net Provisions

As illustrated above, the first line of defence has been cast aside in Canada. During the 1980s and 1990s full employment was gradually redefined as eight percent unemployment. Universal programs, such as the Family Allowance, were replaced by the income-tested and targeted Child Tax Benefit and later by the Canada Child Tax Benefit/ National Child Benefit. The universality of Old Age Security was also eliminated with the tax clawbacks that began in 1989. The Chrétien government's planned Senior's Benefit, which is family income-tested and targetted to those with low income (Department of Finance 1996a), represented the end of universal entitlements for seniors, although for the moment the government has retreated from this policy initiative.

How about safety-net provisions, the second line of defence geared to provide minimum income and services to the poor and most economically disadvantaged? In this regard the introduction of the CHST, which replaces CAP, is a fundamental weakening of Canada's social safety net.

The impact of the CHST can best be understood by looking at the kind of coverage that is lost with the elimination of CAP. Overall, the termination of CAP represents the end of federal legislation that specifically earmarks safety-net provisions for the poor and vulnerable. Under CAP approximately two-thirds of federal transfers went to "welfare assistance" and the remainder to "welfare services." The former involves cost-shared public (welfare) assistance dollars, and the latter cost-shared services that include subsidized daycare to help poor parents enter the workforce, rehabilitative services, counselling and child welfare. The limitations of CAP notwithstanding, its demise in 1996 represents the end of legally mandated services designed to "help lessen, remove or prevent the causes and effect of poverty, child neglect and dependence on public assistance" (Canada 1985:1). A major piece of Canadian legislation, geared to prevent, rehabilitate and alleviate the poverty of the most unprotected, has been cast aside.

In contrast with CAP, the CHST's ability to protect those dependent on the safety net is deficient. The CHST is a reduced block fund that combines CAP transfers with those that previously were designated for education and health under the umbrella of established program financing. In its first two years—1996–97 and 1997–98—total CHST transfers will be some $7 billion less than they would have been had the education, health and CAP transfers remained separate, and at their 1995–96 funding levels (Department of Finance 1995). So there is now less money to deal with health, education and safety-net demands that show no signs of subsiding.

Moreover, as a block fund, the CHST does not designate where final expenditures need to be made (i.e., for education, health or welfare, or any of these). These decisions are made by the provinces and territories. What the federal government has set up is a situation where dollars that were traditionally spent on the

safety net are now in direct competition with the spending needs of health and education. If we compare the political clout of the health and education sectors with that of social assistance, there are grounds for assuming that welfare dollars will be further squeezed as the competition for scarce resources heats up (CCSD 1996b: 2).

Under CAP, provinces had a financial mechanism for responding to growing need as one-half of their additional allocations could be recouped through the 50-50 federal/provincial cost-sharing mechanism of CAP.[4] The CHST, in contrast, is not only a reduced fund, but the level of dollars transferred is fixed, and provinces, in both good and bad economic times, need to make do with their fixed annual allotment. What this ensures is that, in periods of economic decline, there will be fewer federal dollars and therefore less money in total to respond to the growing need for income and related safety-net supports.

Similarly, national minimum standards are now abandoned. Under CAP, safety-net expenditures were shared by the federal government only if the provinces and territories complied with certain conditions. These included providing assistance to all people judged in need; ensuring benefits' levels meet basic needs; not imposing a work requirement as a condition of assistance; setting up an appeal procedure for individuals to challenge welfare decisions; and guaranteeing that residency would not be a requirement of assistance (NCW 1995; CCSD 1996b: 1). Under the CHST only the last condition remains but, as witnessed in British Columbia (see below), ways were sought to circumvent even this and impose a residency requirement as a condition of assistance. When the CHST was first announced, these kinds of setbacks were foreshadowed, and it was predicted that the elimination of the right to assistance "opens the way for jurisdictions to provide little or no assistance to those in need" (CCSD 1996b: 2).

Not only are national standards gone, but also, as an instrument of social policy, the CHST constitutes the legislative framework for the devolution of most federal safety-net powers to the provinces. It is the backdrop for a decentralized welfare state, where the role of the federal government in terms of setting and enforcing national standards, services and priorities is clearly curtailed (Pawley 1996). CAP provided the legislation and "fiscal carrots" to induce provinces to develop and mount "services for child protection ... family counseling, rape crisis centres, shelters for women and subsidized day care" (CCSD 1996c: 5). Over time, depending on the circumstances and political whim of different provinces, these services can now easily disappear. They are no longer mandated by legislation or directly supported by cost-shared transfers. The same scenario is applicable to welfare assistance as there is no longer a compulsion to provide assistance to those in need. In 1994, some 3.1 million Canadians received social assistance. Another 1.1 million received help through CAP-funded services. Out of these the largest group of recipients were women and children (NCW 1995: 4, 5). Women, as employees and service users/recipients/clients, will suffer a disproportionate impact by these changes. In particular, low-income women will fare worse because they are most likely to rely on social assistance and the many social services that were previously CAP-funded, such as daycare subsidies, home care, women's shelters, rape crisis centres and legal aid. As levels of basic protection continue to decline, we can anticipate that those formerly receiving basic assistance from the state

will turn, in increasing numbers, to food banks and other non-government agencies for support. A more privatized, residual, neo-liberal welfare state seems inevitable as communities, charitable organizations, families and women take on responsibilities formerly assumed by the state (Bach and Rioux 1996). Recent research undertaken by the National Anti-Poverty Organization (NAPO) (1996, 1997), the National Council of Welfare (1997) and others (Pulkingham and Ternowetsky 1998) provide firm evidence of this assertion. These studies demonstrate that declining social assistance benefit levels, along with administrative changes that disentitle people from state support, have led to a growing reliance on charities such as food banks and to a devolution of state responsibilities to the informal sector of friends, families and communities.

The CHST is funded both through tax points,[5] transferred from the federal government to the provinces, and a cash transfer. The size of the cash component is declining and is predicted to disappear around 2006 (Battle and Torjman 1996). The concern of the social policy community is that, as the cash component declines, so does Ottawa's ability to enforce adherence to the one remaining residency requirement of the CHST (CCSD 1996c).[6] In the February 1996 federal budget, a new five-year cash floor of $11.1 billion for CHST funding was put in place (Department of Finance 1996b). This new cash floor gives Ottawa the leverage for some provincial compliance, at least until 2003–04. However, by the time this cash floor takes effect (1999–2000), the cash transfers lost to the provinces since the start of the CHST will reach $16.6 billion (Department of Finance 1996c). The size of this reduction, in conjunction with the elimination of all but the residency requirement, "will likely translate into widespread cuts to programs and supports directed at the most vulnerable Canadians" (Birchall 1996: 1). The safety net has been thrown wide open and Ottawa, in part by its effort to download its financial obligations, is surrendering its role and power to sustain a national system of safety-net provisions. The funding levels and limited conditions of the CHST have already set in motion a range of disparate measures of last resort that differ from province to province.

The impact of neo-liberalism on safety-net provisions is evident in British Columbia's new initiative, B.C. Benefits. Announced in early 1996, it is designed to ensure support goes to "people truly in need" (Province of British Columbia 1996a: 2), a clear neo-liberal perspective on the proper role of welfare. The view that the security provided by provincial income assistance is a work disincentive that keeps people from actively seeking employment is also a long-standing, neo-liberal critique of the welfare state (McBride and Shields 1993: 19). B.C. Benefits operationalizes these concerns by reducing benefit levels for a number of recipients and by denying benefits to those not willing to participate in "active" workfare and learnfare programs. To further this policy, the B.C. government has recently abandoned the "unemployable" category, in part paving the way for further legitimizing a work test as a prerequisite for social assistance. While it is too early to judge how this will unfold, there are substantial savings for the province embodied in this strategy. At the time B.C. Benefits was introduced, the B.C. Minister of Human Resources denied that the elimination of the "unemployable" category was a cost-saving measure. However, he also admitted that the "government has no choice but to restructure the welfare system because

of the massive cutbacks in [federal] transfer payments" resulting from the implementation of the CHST (Sarti 1997: A1).

Until recently, the B.C. government also disallowed benefits to claimants who could not prove three months' residence in the province. While this has been reversed, the point is that under CAP this would not have been possible. However, under the vague requirements of the CHST (Remus 1996), the maneuverability of the provinces has increased and it seems that there is now room to circumvent the residency requirement.

Another form of disentitlement occurs under B.C. Benefits administrative changes for income assistance. With B.C. Benefits, the unemployed who have quit or been fired from a job are automatically disentitled from assistance. This can be reversed only at the discretion of the minister. Previously, under GAIN (Guaranteed Annual Income for those in Need), those who quit or were fired from a job were eligible for basic assistance, although they could be disentitled at the discretion of the minister. This intersects with changes to Unemployment Insurance introduced in 1993 by which those who "voluntarily" quit or were fired from a job are disqualified from UI benefits. In B.C. this means that those who have quit or been fired from a job are now ineligible for both EI and social assistance. This is a further narrowing of citizenship rights that were previously guaranteed under CAP. Instead, what we are witnessing is the widespread emergence of policies that disentitle people from the right to benefits previously provided by the state.

Across-the-board reductions for employable recipients, the granting of support only if employables participate in workfare and learnfare programs, and the elimination of the unemployable category all point to an erosion of the safety net. One result of these changes is the reduction in the adequacy of benefits. The Social Planning and Research Council of B.C. argues that the lower income assistance rates that followed the introduction of B.C. Benefits represent a form of "legislated poverty" (SPARC of BC 1997). This SPARC study compares B.C. Benefits' shelter and support allowances with daily living costs. If one receives the maximum B.C. Benefit there is still a substantial shortfall in the income required to meet the costs of daily living. A single adult has approximately 48 percent of what is needed, a single parent with one child receives around 64 percent, and B.C. Benefits for two adults with two children represent 55 percent of the income SPARC reports is required to meet daily costs. It is indeed not surprising that people are turning to charitable, non-government agencies and food banks for help, as current levels of assistance are too low. As the SPARC study concludes, "a major contributing factor in the increased demand for food banks" is the inadequacy of B.C. Benefits income assistance levels (SPARC of BC 1997: iv).

Savings from the above changes in rates and eligibility are being used to increase training and workfare opportunities and to fund the new Family Bonus that provides up to $103 per child (Province of British Columbia 1996b). Ostensibly, the Family Bonus is geared to help families with children. In reality, it is only available to parents who are in the paid labour force. Families with children on social assistance but not members in the paid labour force gain nothing from the Family Bonus. While they do receive it, the entire value is deducted from the support component of the monthly social assistance entitlement. This differential treatment of the working poor and unemployed families on social assistance

revives the old distinction between the "deserving" and "undeserving" poor, a notion of neo-liberalism that finds expression in the reduction of safety-net provisions for welfare families.

Conclusion

This chapter looked at the question: How far down the neo-liberal road of welfare state reconstruction have we gone? The above discussion shows that, in the key policy areas of employment, universal social programs and safety-net provisions, the Canadian welfare state has all but collapsed. While there is some controversy about whether the Canadian welfare state has been "demolished" or simply eroded, in part this is a dubious debate. Clearly the Canadian welfare state still exists. It has, however, changed in form and coverage. Until the 1980s, the post-World War II welfare state in Canada was increasingly centrist, with programs and coverage that evolved incrementally. Today, these centrist and evolutionary features of the Canadian welfare state have changed. During the 1980s and the 1990s, the federal government has abandoned its role in key areas of financing, development and maintenance of national programs and standards. Motivated in part by its effort to off-load fiscal responsibility, it has reduced protection for the unemployed in times of high and increasing unemployment, eliminated universal entitlements and dismantled legislation that once guaranteed minimum safety-net provisions across the nation. This is concrete evidence that the post-World War II centrist and evolutionary welfare state is being abandoned.

What these developments imply is that, in the face of growing economic insecurity, the state will continue to assume less and less responsibility for the collective well-being of its citizenry. In the areas of employment, universal and safety-net measures, the residual welfare state is being reduced to a role of last resort. But even in this context, benefit levels and entitlements are so low, unpredictable and in some cases no longer available, that basic needs must increasingly be met by charitable organizations, the family and a weakened non-government sector. The dismantling of the welfare state begun in the 1980s and further consolidated in the 1990s points to a future of an increasingly minimalist welfare state that will do little to reverse the widespread economic vulnerability of the people who live and work in this country.

Endnotes

1   This is a modified version of our chapter "The Changing Context of Child and Family Policies" in Pulkingham and Ternowetsky (eds.), *Child and Family Policies: Struggles, Strategies and Options* (1997).

2   The "clawback" is a complex mechanism by which the federal government taxes back benefits paid to higher-income families and pensioners (in the case of Old Age Security). Families and individuals with incomes above specified thresholds are required to return a portion or all of the benefits they received in the previous year.

3   Under this new system of child benefits, the equivalent to married credit and the child-care deduction remain intact, although the value of the child-care deduction was increased by the Conservatives when the plan was first introduced and again later by the Liberals. The child-care deduction is a regressive tax measure. It reduces the tax paid for middle- and upper-income earners, but provides no benefit to poor families with children that do not pay tax. In the same way, the equivalent to married credit in a lone-parent family treats the oldest child as a spouse and provides a tax credit equal to the spousal deduction. Once again, this only assists lone parents who earn enough money to pay taxes.

4   In 1990, this 50-50 formula changed for the richest three provinces, Ontario, Alberta and British Columbia. After 1990, a cap on annual CAP transfers was set at five percent increases for these provinces. This had the effect of substantially reducing the federal share of welfare expenditures made by these provinces (NCW 1995: 7).

5   Tax point transfers are "a reduction of federal tax rates allowing provinces to raise additional revenues without increasing the overall tax burden" (Department of Finance 1996b: 1).

6   There is a similar concern that enforcement of the standards of the Canada Health Act will be compromised.

References

Bach, M. and M. Rioux. 1996. "Social Policy. Devolution and Disability: Back to Notions of the Worthy Poor." In Jane Pulkingham and Gordon Ternowetsky (eds.). *Remaking Canadian Social Policy: Social Security in the late 1990s.* Halifax: Fernwood Publishing.

Battle, Ken and Sherri Torjman. 1996. "Desperately Seeking Substance: A Commentary on the Social Security Review." In Jane Pulkingham and Gordon Ternowetsky (eds.). *Remaking Canadian Social Policy: Social Security in the late 1990s.* Halifax: Fernwood Publishing.

Birchall, C. 1996. "Open Letter to Paul Martin re: Budget 1996." Ottawa. Canadian Council on Social Development.

Brodie, Janine. 1995. *Politics on the Margins: Restructuring and the Canadian Women's Movement.* Halifax: Fernwood Publishing.

Canada. 1997a. *Towards a National Child Benefit System.* Ottawa: Department of Finance.

____. 1997b. *Working Together Towards A National Child Benefit.* Ottawa: Department of Finance.

____. 1992. *The Child Benefit. A White Paper on Canada's New Integrated Child Tax Benefit.* Ottawa: Minister of Supply and Services.

____. 1985. *Notes on Welfare Services Under the Canada Assistance Plan.* Ottawa: Minister of National Health and Welfare.

Canadian Council on Social Development (CCSD). 1996a. "Children and the 1996 Federal Budget: Backgrounder." Ottawa: Canadian Council on Social Development.

_____. 1996b. "Maintaining a National Safety Net: Recommendations on the Canada Health and Social Transfer." Position Statement. Ottawa: Canadian Council on Social Development.

_____. 1996c. *Social Policy Beyond the Budget*. Ottawa: Canadian Council on Social Development.

Canadian Labour Congress (CLC). 1995. "Federal Budget 1995: Canadian Labour Congress Analysis." Unpublished Brief. Ottawa: Canadian Labour Congress.

Clark, C. 1995. "Work and Welfare: Looking at Both Sides of the Equation." *Perception* 19 (1).

Department of Finance. Canada. 1996a. "Government Proposes New Seniors Benefit." News Release. Ottawa: Department of Finance.

_____. 1996b. "Canada Health and Social Transfer: Backgrounder." Ottawa: Department of Finance.

_____. 1996c. *Canada Health and Social Transfer: New Five Year Funding Arrangement*. Ottawa: Department of Finance.

_____. 1995. *Budget Speech*. Ottawa: Minister of Supply and Services.

_____. 1994. *Agenda: Jobs and Growth. A New Framework for Economic Policy*. Ottawa: Department of Finance.

_____. 1984. *A New Direction for Canada: An Agenda for Economic Renewal*. Ottawa: Minister of Supply and Services.

Department of Supply and Services. 1996. *The 1996 Federal Budget*. Ottawa: Supply and Services.

Employment and Immigration Canada. 1994. *Unemployment Insurance Accounts: Forecasts from 1996 to 1998*. Ottawa: Employment and Immigration Canada.

Esping-Andersen, Gosta. 1990. *The Three Worlds of Welfare Capitalism*. Princeton: Princeton University Press.

Federal and Provincial/Territorial Governments. 1997. *The National Child Benefit*. Online: http:/www.intergov. gc.ca./docs/intergov/ncb/ncbpamp_e.htm

Forget, C. et al. 1986. *Commission of Inquiry on Unemployment Insurance*. Ottawa: Minister of Supply and Services.

Fraser, Nancy and Linda Gordon. 1994. "A Genealogy of Dependency: Tracing a Keyword of the U.S. Welfare State." *Signs* 19 (21).

Green, D.A. and C.W. Riddell. 1993. "The Economic Effects of Unemployment Insurance in Canada: An Empirical Analysis of UI Disentitlement." *Journal of Labor Economics* 11 (1/2).

Hargrove, B. 1996. "Whose Unemployment-Insurance Surplus is it Anyway?" *Globe and Mail*, March 18, A17.

Hess, M. 1992. *The Canadian Fact Book on Income Security Programs*. Ottawa: Canadian Council on Social Development.

Human Resources Development Canada (HRDC). 1996. *Employment Insurance: Impacts of Reform*. Submission to the House of Commons Standing Committee on Human Resources Development, January 23. Ottawa.

_____. 1994. *Agenda: Jobs and Growth: Improving Social Securrity in Canada*. Ottawa: Supply and Services.

Low, William. 1996. "Wide of the Mark: Using 'Targeting' and Work Incentives to Direct Social Assistance to Single Parents." In Jane Pulkingham and Gordon Ternowetsky (eds.). *Remaking Canadian Social Policy: Social Security in the late 1990s*. Halifax: Fernwood Publishing.

McBride, Stephen and John Shields. 1993. *Dismantling a Nation: Canada and the New World Order* (First Edition). Halifax: Fernwood Publishing.

McDaniel, S.A. 1993. "Where the Contradictions Meet: Women and Family Security in Canada in the 1990s." In D. Ross et al. (eds.) *Family Security in Insecure Times: National Forum on Family Security*. Ottawa: Canadian Council on Social Development.

Minister of Supply and Services. 1985. *Report of the Royal Commission on the Economic Union and Development Prospects for Canada. Volume 2*. Ottawa: Minister of Supply and Services.

Mishra, Ramesh. 1990. *The Welfare State in Capitalist Society: Policies of Retrenchment and Maintenance in Europe, North America and Australia*. Toronto: University of Toronto Press.

Mullaly, R. 1993. *Structural Social Work: Ideology, Theory and Practice*. Toronto: McClelland and Stewart.

National Anti-Poverty Organization (NAPO). 1997. "Monitoring the Impacts on Social Assistance Recipients of Welfare Cuts and Changes: An Update–March 21, 1997." Ottawa: National Anti-Poverty Organization.

_____. 1996. "Monitoring the Impacts on Social Assistance Recipients of Welfare Cuts and Change: October 17, 1996." Ottawa: National Anti-Poverty Organization.

National Council of Welfare (NCW). 1997. *Another Look at Welfare Reform: A Report by the National Council of*

Welfare. Ottawa: Minister of Public Works and Government Services Canada.

____. 1995. *The Budget and Block Funding*. Ottawa: Minister of Supply and Services.

____. 1992. *The 1992 Budget and Child Benefits*. Ottawa: Minister of Supply and Services.

Pawley, H. 1996. "Devolution Favoured by BCNI Would Wreck Canada." *CCPA Monitor* 3 (5).

Phipps, S.A. 1993. "International Perspectives on Income Support for Families with Children." Paper presented at Canadian Employment Research Forum Workshop on Income Support. Ottawa, Ontario. September.

Prince, M. 1996. "Historical Analysis of Public Pension Schemes in Canada." In L. Newman, M. Prince and J. Cutts (eds.). *Reforming the Public Pension System in Canada: Retrospect and Prospect*. Victoria Papers in Public Policy No. 1 Victoria: Centre for Public Sector Studies.

Province of British Columbia. 1996a. *BC Benefits: The Initiative*. Victoria: Ministry of Social Services.

____. 1996b. "Government Replaces Welfare for Youth with Job Search Assistance." News Release. Victoria: Office of the Premier.

Pulkingham, Jane. 1998. "Remaking the Social Divisions of Welfare: Gender, 'Dependency' and U.I. Reform." *Studies in Political Economy* 56.

Pulkingham, Jane and Gordon Ternowetsky. 1998. "A State of the Art Review of Income Security Reform in Canada." *International Development Research Centre Working Series Paper #4*. Ottawa: IDRC.

Pulkingham, Jane and Gordon Ternowetsky. 1997. "The New Canada Child Tax Benefit: Discriminating between the 'Deserving' and 'Undeserving' among Poor Families with Children." In Jane Pulkingham and Gordon Ternowetsky (eds.). *Child and Family Policies: Struggles, Strategies and Options*. Halifax: Fernwood Publishing.

Pulkingham, Jane and Gordon Ternowetsky. 1996. "The Changing Landscape of Social Policy and the Canadian Welfare State." In Jane Pulkingham and Gordon Ternowetsky (eds.). *Remaking Canadian Social Policy: Social Security in the late 1990s*. Halifax: Fernwood Publishing.

Remus, C. 1996. "Unraveling the Ties that Bind: The Decentralization of National Social Programs." *Briarpatch* 25 (9).

Sarti, R. 1997. "17,000 facing cutback in welfare cheques under new regulations." *Vancouver Sun*, April 2, B1, B4.

Scott, K. 1996. "The Dilemma of Liberal Citizenship: Women and Social Assistance Reform in the 1990s." *Studies in Political Economy* 50 (Summer).

Social Planning and Research Council of BC (SPARC of BC). 1997. *Widening the Gap: A Comparison between the Daily Living Costs and Income Assistance Rates (BC Benefits) in British Columbia*. Vancouver: Social Planning and Research Council of BC.

Stanford, Jim. 1996. "Discipline, Insecurity and Productivity: The Economics behind Labour Market 'Flexibility.'" In Jane Pulkingham and Gordon Ternowetsky (eds.). *Remaking Canadian Social Policy: Social Security in the Late 1990s*. Halifax: Fernwood Publishing.

Statistics Canada. 1997. "Regular Beneficiaries without Earnings and Unemployed." *Unemployment Insurance Monthly Statistics*. Ottawa: Statistics Canada Labour Division.

Valpy, M. 1997. "A Down Payment, But Where Does it Lead?" *Globe and Mail*, February 20, A21.

SECTION VI: NEO-LIBERALISM AND THE DISMANTLING OF THE WELFARE STATE

Critical Thinking Questions

Chapter 11: Domestic Neo-Liberalism, Stephen McBride

1. Why does McBride refer to the transformation of the Canadian state over the past two decades as a "paradigm" shift?

2. What are the consequences for Canadian workers of some of the measures adopted by the federal and provincial governments under neo-liberalism? Should the state act as an impediment to the free operation of markets?

3. What links can be drawn between globalization and the transition to a neo-liberal state in Canada?

Chapter 12: Neo-Liberalism and Retrenchment: Employment, Universality, Safety-Net Provisions, and a Collapsing Canadian Welfare State, Jane Pulkingham and Gordon Ternowetsky

1. How has state retrenchment exacerbated insecurity for vulnerable groups in Canadian society? Does the state have a responsibility to protect vulnerable groups in society?

2. Has the fundamental redesign of Canada's two main social programs, the Canada Assistance Plan and Unemployment Insurance, changed workers' relationship to the labour market?

3. Are universal or targetted social programs best suited to promote equality and foster social cohesion? Under what conditions are citizens of a country more likely to support one strategy over the other?

Recommended Readings

Bashevkin, Sylvia. 2002. *Welfare Hot Buttons: Women, Work, and Social Policy Reform.* Toronto: University of Toronto Press. A comparative assessment of social policy reforms in Canada, the United Kingdom and the United States, three countries that have adopted some variant of Third-Way politics. The author carefully considers the impact of these changes on women's position in these three Western industrialized countries.

Broad, David and Wayne Antony (eds.). 1999. *Citizens or Consumers? Social Policy in a Market Society.* Halifax: Fernwood Publishing. A compilation of original articles that document the weakening of postwar social citizenship and its replacement with a form of citizenship geared towards the capitalist market.

Burke, Mike, Colin Mooers and John Shields (eds.). 2000. *Restructuring and Resistance: Canadian Public Policy in an Age of Global Capitalism.* Halifax: Fernwood Publishing. A collection of articles that take a close look at the major policy areas in Canada that have been deeply affected by the shift from the Keynesian welfare state to the neo-liberal regime. The contributors also pay attention to strategies of resistance that have taken shape in the wake of the new policy regime.

Kingfisher, Catherine (ed.). 2002. *Western Welfare in Decline: Globalization and Women's Poverty.* Philadelphia: University of Pennsylvania Press. A series of articles that investigate the situation of poor single mothers in five Western industrialized countries that have implemented welfare reform under neo-liberal oriented governments.

Prince, Michael J. 1999. "From Health and Welfare to Stealth and Farewell: Federal Social Policy, 1980–2000." In Leslie A. Pal (ed.) *How Ottawa Spends 1999–2000—Shape Shifting: Canadian Governance Towards the 21st Century.* Toronto: Oxford University Press, pp. 151–196. An article that traces the fundamental changes in Canadian federal social policy over a 20-year period that marks the demise of the welfare state. The article identifies four major phases of change that, while distinct, all rely on the politics of stealth to dismantle social programs.

Pulkingham, Jane and Gordon Ternowetsky (eds.). 1996. *Remaking Canadian Social Policy: Social Security in the Late 1990s.* Halifax: Fernwood Publishing. A collection of articles that explore the economic, political and ideological factors that led to the federal Liberal government's Social Security Review in the mid-1990s.

Related Websites

Campaign 2000

http://www.campaign2000.ca/

Campaign 2000 is a cross-Canada public education movement that publishes research on indicators of child poverty and develops public education resources. It puts out an annual national Report Card on Child Poverty in Canada, and prepares discussion papers on public policies pertaining to child poverty.

Canadian Centre for Policy Alternatives

http://www.policyalternatives.ca/

The Canadian Centre for Policy Alternatives is a progressive independent research institute concerned with issues of social and economic justice. It has produced numerous studies on issues related to neo-liberalism and the welfare state such as welfare-to-work, income inequality, social housing, child poverty, and health.

Centre for Social Justice

http://www.socialjustice.org/

The Centre for Social Justice is an advocacy organization that seeks to strengthen the struggle for social justice. The Centre conducts research, education and advocacy in a bid to narrow the gap in income, wealth and power, and enhance peace and human security.

Centre for the Study of Living Standards

http://www.csls.ca/

The Centre for the Study of Living Standards is a Canadian organization that conducts research on trends in living standards. The Centre has developed an index of economic well-being and conducts research in the area of productivity. It also publishes the *International Productivity Monitor*.

Institute for Research on Public Policy

http://www.irpp.org/

The Institute for Research on Public Policy is an independent think tank that conducts research on a wide range of policy issues such as economic performance, social progress, and democratic governance.

National Anti-Poverty Organization

http://www.napo-onap.ca/en/index.html

The National Anti-Poverty Organization is a non-profit organization that works for the eradication of poverty in Canada. Through research and other activities, it addresses issues such as social assistance, unemployment, social housing, federal budget priorities, human rights, minimum wages, and youth poverty.

Section VII

Education, Training, and Skills in a Knowledge-Based Economy

THE NOTION THAT we have entered a knowledge-based economy where jobs increasingly require a highly trained and highly skilled workforce is one of the most widespread beliefs about work and employment in advanced capitalist societies. Another commonplace belief is that the underperformance of economies, along with unemployment and poverty, are the result of a skills shortage and a skills–jobs mismatch that can be rectified by educational institutions changing the basic skills that are taught and by workers being willing to engage in lifelong learning. While keenly aware of the importance of education, training and advanced skills, the authors of the two articles in this section of the book take a critical look at these widespread beliefs through an examination of the Canadian situation. They unearth some of the fundamental contradictions of these widely held assumptions and raise concerns about the potentially long-term detrimental impacts of what many have called the new learning culture, especially in light of the market's inability to deliver the promised high-skilled, high-paying, and satisfying jobs for the majority of workers and job-seekers.

In his article, David Livingstone focuses on the complex interconnections between training and employment. He reports on research conducted in Toronto in 1994 that sought to understand the work experiences, learning activities and attitudes of university graduates and high school dropouts who were living in what he calls the credential gap. This gap refers to discrepancies between the formal educational attainments of job-holders and the attainments required by employers. Livingstone is interested in uncovering how people living in the credential gap struggle to maintain a level of security under difficult economic circumstances, as well as their perceptions of both the credential gap and job entitlements. Livingstone's analysis of the job–education gap is brought to life by extensive quotations from in-depth interviews, a research method that allows for the realities and thoughts of research participants to be expressed in their own words. His findings reveal that both underemployed university graduates and underqualified high school dropouts were critical of the lack of match between formal educational credentials and the demands of the jobs they performed, and of the unchallenging nature of these jobs. He also uncovered that those living on both sides of the credential gap hung their hopes on further education or retraining as a way of finding or holding on to a job, and that both groups were actively engaged in the pursuit of more education to achieve economic security. Finally, Livingstone reports that while most of the underqualified and underemployed respondents had a sense of entitlement to a better job, they nonetheless saw themselves as active agents in mediating the constraints and institutional forces that structure their job opportunities.

In an article taken from his book *Retooling the Mind Factory: Education in a Lean State*, Alan Sears also examines the links among education, skills, and employment, but his focus is on education reform under neo-liberalism. He challenges the widely held assumption that the education system needs to be better adapted to the changing nature of work and especially to the dramatic shift in skill requirements that tends to be driven by new information and computer technologies. Sears's argument is that education reform is primarily a response to the disciplinary requirements of new methods of work organization, such as lean production, that rest on an erosion of the expectations of citizenship built into the postwar public education system. He uses the case of education reform under the Conservative government in Ontario during the 1990s to illustrate how the state embraced the neo-liberal business agenda and undertook to retool the school system to produce more compliant workers ready to take their place in a transformed labour market. Sears takes a closer look at the new focus on testing, measurement, and classification, the revival of streaming, and the shift to vocationalism. He questions how these initiatives will enhance the generic skills required for the knowledge economy that is assumed to be taking hold in Canada. The author concludes with a discussion of how the development of a lean and instrumental ethos reorients education towards the market and buttresses neo-liberal free market structures and ideology. For Sears, education reform has more to do with encouraging a cultural shift than with imparting specific skill sets.

CHAPTER 13

Living in the Credential Gap:

Responses to Underemployment and Underqualification

David W. Livingstone

I've been doing joe-jobs for years. I've been laid off from part-time jobs that nobody wanted five years ago. For this I spent years in university. None of my friends have real jobs and that includes people with business and law degrees who went through school convinced there would be gold at the end of the rainbow. My parents didn't raise me to believe, nor did I ever think, that I would end up on a jobless scrap heap. But it's a possibility I find myself thinking about more and more these days.

(M. ERFANI, *as cited in Ferguson*)

Introduction

THIS CHAPTER FOCUSES on the experiences and perceptions of people living in the credential gap. The credential gap refers to discrepancies between the formal educational attainments of current job holders and the attainments now required by employers to enter such jobs. The gap has two sides. The underemployed are job incumbents who have substantially more schooling than their employers require for job entry. The underqualified are job incumbents who have substantially less schooling than their employers now require for such jobs; typically, their underqualification has been created by credential inflation since they took the job. The underemployed have at least one credential higher than their job currently requires; the underqualified have at least one credential less than their job now requires. Unemployed people will also be considered here as either underemployed or underqualified in terms of the discrepancy between their schooling and the educational requirements of their last job.

The reality for many people, and especially those on both sides of this credential gap, is that now, as in the dirty thirties, there are simply not enough jobs of any sort to go around. There is a general surplus of labour in almost all skill categories in Canada (Sharpe, 1993). The question here is how people in these credential categories are struggling to find security in the present difficult conditions. The basic claim of the chapter is that further education has become a pervasive means of coping with job insecurity on both sides of the credential gap. Primary interest is devoted to paid work experiences, the role of further learning in practical coping strategies and future plans, and general perceptions of the relationship between education and employment. I begin with a review of the relevant research literature on the credential gap and the further-education practices of people in the gap. Then I present findings from in-depth interviews, conducted in Metro Toronto in the spring of 1994, with underemployed recent university graduates and underqualified school dropouts.

Tracing the Credential Gap

In any market economy, the sweep of change is continual. Interfirm competition, technological innovation, and negotiations between employers and employees over working conditions and benefits all lead to incessant shifts in the number and type of jobs available. Population growth cycles, modified household needs, and new legislative regulations also frequently serve to alter the supply of labour. At the same time, popular demand for general education and specialized training increases as people seek more knowledge, different skills, and added credentials in order to live and work in such a changing society. So there are always "mismatches" between employers' aggregate demand and requirements for employees on the one hand, and the aggregate supply and qualifications of job seekers on the other. In protracted economic slumps such as the dirty

thirties and the period since the 1970s, these mismatches are much more evident. The most common features have been heightened levels of unemployment and of people needing social assistance. But with the cumulative expansion of formal schooling, a distinctive feature of the current slump has been the large supply of highly educated and credentialled people who cannot find commensurate jobs.

The two most widely recognized post-World War II changes in patterns of paid employment in Canada have been the sectoral shift from resource extraction manufacturing to services, and the growing participation of women in the workforce. These trends have continued during the current economic slump. By the end of the 1980s, the service sector's share of total employment had increased to over 70 percent, while the proportion of the adult female population in the workforce had jumped to about 60 percent (Economic Council of Canada, 1991). Coincident with these trends and computerization has been a decline in the proportion of jobs requiring basic literacy and numeracy skills, and an increasing reliance on educational credentials and specific vocational preparation rather than general practical competence for entry into relatively secure, well-paid, full-time jobs. One of the most extensive recent Canadian studies concludes that, between 1971 and 1986, employment shifted towards white-collar service occupations that required relatively high levels of education and training, that the changing industrial structure had mixed effects on overall skill levels, and that the shift to services did not reduce the concentration of women in relatively low-skilled jobs (Economic Council of Canada, p. 109). To put it more bluntly, the educational and training requirements of the occupational structure seem to be increasing generally, but "good jobs" and "bad jobs" are becoming more polarized, and women still tend to be relegated to insecure, poorly paid, part-time jobs within the expanding service sector.

There continues to be heated dispute among scholars as to whether the skills actually needed to perform most jobs are increasing or declining.[1] But there is little doubt that the entry requirements for bottom-end jobs have recently increased. Estimates of the recent extent of aggregate change in educational requirements for job entry in Ontario are provided by self-reports in the biennial Ontario Institute for Studies in Education (OISE) Survey of Educational Issues (Livingstone, 1992; Livingstone, Hart, & Davie, 1993). The major change over the past decade has been an increase in the proportion of jobs requiring a high school diploma (nearly doubling from 24 percent to 45 percent), while jobs requiring less than a diploma have experienced a comparable decrease. The proportion of the workforce requiring postsecondary credentials remained fairly stable at about a third over this period (see also Economic Council of Canada, 1991, p. 105; Lowe, 1992, pp. 66–67).

The average number of years of schooling completed by Canadians in the labour force has increased steadily since World War II. The Canadian labour force is among the most highly schooled in the world, rivalled only by that in the United States (OECD, 1989, 1993). Since the current economic slump began (in the early 1970s), the proportion of the labour force with only elementary schooling has dropped from over 20 percent to less than 10 percent, while the share with a university degree has risen from under 10 percent to over 15 percent (Sharpe, 1990, pp. 21–81; Statistics Canada, 1993). More detailed estimates of recent changes in the formal educational attainments of the Ontario labour force suggest that, between 1982 and 1992, the proportion with less than a high school diploma dropped from 40 percent to 25 percent, while the proportions with high school diplomas, college certificates, and university degrees all increased.

So both job entry requirements and formal educational attainments are both increasing significantly. But how are they related? Two things are clear. First, in spite of greater aggregate educational attainments, there is a trend towards increasing structural unemployment; that is, an enduring deficit of jobs for job seekers beyond the small number of people moving between jobs at any given time. While unemployment rates continue to fluctuate with the business cycle, there has been a long-term upward trend since the early 1950s, and there is little prospect that unemployment rates will fall much below 10 percent in the current "jobless recovery" (Kumar, Arrowsmith, & Coates, 1991). Second, those with little formal schooling are increasingly being relegated to chronic unemployment and social assistance. The relative level and duration of unemployment of those with only elementary schooling who have remained in the workforce have increased substantially since the 1970s (Betcherman, 1991, pp. 112–116).

A certain amount of mismatch between educational attainments and job entry requirements is generally regarded as normal in a market economy. Young job entrants often compete for positions for which they are overqualified, in the expectation that they will be able to climb career ladders to more suitable jobs. Older workers can retain jobs for which the formal entry requirements have increased, on the basis of their experience and seniority. Employers are often flexible about educational requirements, using them in conjunction with other specific or intuitive criteria, but tend to avoid hiring highly overqualified applicants (Bills, 1992, pp. 79–92; Roizen & Jepson, 1985).

Education–job mismatches first emerged as a public issue in North America in the late 1960s, when the rapid increase in educational attainments of the baby boom generation encouraged employers to inflate credential requirements for low-skill jobs, and when growing numbers of postsecondary graduates were unable to obtain the levels of jobs that they expected.[2] As the economic slump set in during the 1970s and postsecondary enrolment continued to expand, the "overeducation" or "underemployment" of highly qualified labour force entrants was widely heralded (Freeman, 1976). In the 1980s, with the widespread diffusion of computers in the workplace, "undereducation" or "underqualification" of functionally illiterate workers and students in general became a more central public issue (see Kozol, 1985; Rose, 1989). During the present decade, the declared objective of further development of all human resources in the context of "global competition" appears to have superseded "mismatches" as the central public issue in education–workplace relations (see Marshall & Tucker, 1992; Wirth, 1992). But credential mismatches at least as large as those of the 1970s still persist within the employed workforce.

According to self-reports in the most recent national survey (Lowe, 1992, pp. 58–59), in 1989 nearly a third of employed Canadians with university degrees had jobs that did not require a degree, over 40 percent of those with college certificates had jobs that required less formal schooling, and about a third of the workers with high school diplomas also had jobs that did not require them. Conversely, about a third of the workers with either high school diplomas or less formal schooling held jobs for which employers now require higher educational credentials. For example, to push a broom in a steel mill now requires a grade 12 diploma. The most careful recent U.S. estimates indicate that, during the 1980s, about one-third of college graduates took jobs that did not require degrees, while the continued absence of good adult literacy programs has left millions of Americans increasingly underqualified (Hecker, 1992, pp. 3–12).

Estimates of recent trends in the matching of attainments and requirements within the employed Ontario labour force indicate that, over the past decade, the general pattern of the credential gap has been very stable (Livingstone et al., 1993). A small majority of workers have continued to hold jobs in which the current entry requirements match their own formal schooling. The remainder have been almost equally distributed between the two mismatched statuses, about 20 percent underemployed, and about 20 percent underqualified. The only notable change has been that the proportion of employees without high school diplomas who are underqualified for their jobs doubled during the decade, from a quarter to half, which may suggest mounting pressure on such workers to upgrade their formal education. In addition, women consistently tended to be somewhat more underemployed than men, reflecting their continuing relegation to job ghettos in spite of increased education; visible minorities have been more underemployed than white people, reflecting continued systemic discrimination in hiring practices.[3] While both the 1989 Canadian survey and the Ontario time series document that younger postsecondary graduates are more likely to be underemployed, there is no clear evidence that this status has increased overall within the employed labour force during the past decade. Credential inflation has apparently held underemployment at bay.

Attitudinal Effects of the Credential Gap

In more subjective terms, both the 1989 national survey and the Ontario time series have found that employees with more formal schooling are generally much more likely to feel that their jobs are closely related to their education (Krahn, 1992, pp. 110–111; Livingstone, Hart, & Davie, 1987; Livingstone, Hart, & Davie, 1995). But it is also true that those who have jobs with lower requirements are more likely to feel overqualified, including only about 10 percent of those who have jobs with university requirements, but over 30 percent of those with less than high school requirements (Lowe, 1992, pp. 58–59). However, perhaps even more pertinent, the vast majority of workers think that the skill requirements of both their own jobs and jobs in general have increased in recent times. They also perceive that there is a surplus of qualified applicants for jobs at virtually all skill levels, but increasingly believe that—in spite of these surpluses—obtaining a postsecondary education is ever more vital to getting along in this society, and to qualifying for a future job (Livingstone et al., 1987; Lowe 1992, pp. 89–107). Thus, although there are large numbers of employed people and growing numbers of unemployed people living in the credential gap, individual faith in the power of more formal education as a key response to this problem also appears to be growing.

Some of the early research on education–job mismatches focused on the sentiments of the underemployed, based on the commonly expressed presumption that highly educated

youth would become disenchanted with established institutions because of society's failure to provide jobs commensurate with their educational achievements (O'Toole, 1975a, 1975b). Although highly educated unemployed people and the extremely underemployed occasionally have expressed critical political views, the vast majority of the underemployed have been largely indistinguishable from the general population in their political consciousness and behaviour to date. Most of the relevant research has been conducted in the United States (see, e.g., Burris, B., 1983; Burris, V., 1983; Derber, 1978; Jolin, 1987; Rachel, 1987; Smith, 1986). The few relevant Canadian studies have found very limited radicalizing effects associated with either youth unemployment or underemployment (see, e.g., Baer & Lambert, 1982, pp. 173–195; Tanner, Lowe, & Krahn, 1984, pp. 27–29). Several U.S. and Canadian studies have pointed out the centrality of job-entitlement beliefs in young people's economic and political worldviews. But as the most extensive Canadian study (conducted in the mid-1980s) concluded with regard to the political views of highly educated youths, their sense of job entitlement was more pragmatic than radical. Rather than searching for radical solutions, most of these underemployed youths still saw job creation as the solution to the unemployment crisis (Krahn, Hartnagel, & Tanner, 1986, p. 17).

Some suggestion of more recent tendencies in job-entitlement beliefs is provided by the OISE surveys (Livingstone et al., 1993, 1995). Since the mid-1980s, nearly half of the Ontario labour force has consistently rejected the proposition that educational attainment entitles one to a better job, while only about a third has felt thus entitled. The underqualified predictably hold lower entitlement beliefs, but the underemployed also express quite mixed views on this issue. Thus, only weak job-entitlement sentiments may now exist in the overall Ontario workforce. Younger workers do express higher entitlement beliefs, especially extremely underemployed workers. But regardless of feelings of entitlement, the majority of Ontario workers of all ages and educational statuses have also agreed in these surveys with the view that it is their own fault if they have not obtained a good job. To the extent that such surveys can detect personal sentiments, the tendency to self-blame among the underemployed does not appear to have diminished as the job shortage has persisted.

The Quest for Further Education

If most people tend to blame themselves for the failure to get a decent job, and continue to believe that more advanced education is needed to get along and to find a better job, then participation in further education would likely increase during an economic slump. This seems to have been the case in Canada recently. National surveys indicate that general participation rates in institutionally provided adult education programs have increased from about 4 percent in 1960 to 20 percent in 1983 and 27 percent in 1991 (see Devereux, 1984, p. 4; Nobert & McDowell, 1994, pp. 40–49; Selman & Dampier, 1991, p. 80). According to the 1989 national survey, over a quarter of employed Canadians had plans to begin an educational program during the next five years. The underemployed were at least as likely as other employees to plan further education, in the belief that they needed to obtain even more education to compete effectively for a better job (Lowe, 1992, pp. 58–59).[4]

A more detailed analysis of recent participation patterns in Ontario adult education programs is presented in Table 13.1. Between 1986 and 1992, participation rates of the total adult population almost doubled from 20 percent to 36 percent, while those in the active labour force increased their participation from 24 percent to 39 percent. Significant increases were found in all age groups and at all levels of formal educational attainment, especially among younger adults and high school dropouts. Young employed high school dropouts tripled their participation rates. The increased participation of both underemployed and underqualified workers in general was relatively slight and inconsistent compared with the larger continual gains among matched workers and the dramatic increases among the unemployed. But the participation of young underemployed postsecondary graduates also more than doubled. There is no sign in these voluntary participation rates of any growing disenchantment with the extrinsic value of education to enhance job chances among either the underemployed or any other discernible social group (see Livingstone, 1992). However, adult participation rates may have tapered off more recently as programs have been cut back and costs have escalated (Livingstone et al., 1995).

In this context, the gap between the growing corporate rhetoric about the vital importance of human resource development and the limited actual support among Canadian and U.S. employers for training programs becomes more intelligible. North American employers appear to be underinvesting in employee-training programs relative to most other Organization for Economic Cooperation and Development (OECD) countries.[5] But there is little short-term incentive for employers to invest in training when skill surpluses abound and both current and prospective employees are already making extraordinary efforts to get further education to qualify for better jobs (Osberg, 1993, pp. 39–40).

The most immediate consequence of this combination of popular demand and employer reluctance is the greater growth of general certification and general-interest courses than of substantial job-training programs, as has been the case in Ontario adult education programs since the mid-1980s (Livingstone et al., 1993, pp. 26–27). In the long term, this trend portends a labour force that is even more highly educated relative to general job entry require-

ments, but with less relevant skills to do specific jobs. In any event, with or without much employer support of substantial job-linked training programs, more and more people will likely continue to seek further education wherever they can find it.

In fact, at least during the current economic slump, many people have been pursuing further education to a much greater extent than the equating of education with institution-centred programs would suggest. A now extensive line of empirical research, initiated by my colleague Allen Tough, documents that most adults have been involved in deliberate, self-directed learning projects beyond school and training pro-

Table 13.1: Annual Participation Rate in Adult Education Programs by Age, Educational Attainment, and Education–Job Match, Ontario Labour Force, 1986-92

Have taken a further education course in past year	1986 (%)	1988 (%)	1990 (%)	1992 (%)
Total adult population	20	24	31	36
Total labour force	24	29	34	39
Age				
18–29	28	37	41	53
30–49	25	30	35	39
50+	17	19	20	25
Educational attainment				
Elementary only	7	17	20	21
High school incomplete	13	19	24	35
High school diploma	29	30	33	37
Community college certificate	33	40	45	47
University degree	38	42	45	47
Education–job match				
Underemployed	24	34	37	33
Matched	27	31	38	43
Underqualified	28	26	32	33
Unemployed	10	25	29	50
Total N	1011	1032	1000	1070

Source: *Public Attitudes Towards Education in Ontario, 1986: Sixth OISE Survey*, by D. W. Livingstone, D. Hart, & L. E. Davie, 1987, Toronto: OISE Press.

grams, including several major learning projects each year involving hundreds of hours.[6] A substantial amount of self-directed learning is now occurring among people in virtually all walks of life. In particular, the little prior research on the learning practices of economically disadvantaged adults with low formal education suggests that the vast majority do a significant amount of self-directed learning. For example, the most thorough research to date with undereducated rural adults in the United States has found that they engaged in an average of four major learning projects per year at an average of over 400 hours (Leean & Sisco, 1981; Sisco, 1983). Studies of economically disadvantaged urban adults, high school dropouts, functional illiterates, and the unemployed have all found similar patterns.[7] As Tough rightly concludes, the differences found in the amount of self-directed learning within any group have been much larger than the differences between groups constituted in terms of gender, age, income, class, and even country.[8]

There are no known prior studies of the self-directed learning activities of underemployed postsecondary graduates, but the research cited above regarding their participation in organized further education suggests that they are no less keen on voluntary learning activities than most other folks. Whether or not people in general have become more involved in self-directed learning in the current economic slump is a question yet to be addressed by a field of empirical research whose life span basically corresponds with this slump. The remainder of this chapter is concerned with looking more closely at the work experiences, learning activities, and attitudes of some currently underemployed and underqualified adults.

Living in the Credential Gap

In the spring of 1994, my research team conducted semi-structured interviews with both underqualified and underemployed adults in the Greater Toronto Area. The interview covered the respondent's general social background, educational and employment histories, current learning activities, and attitudes concerning relations between learning and work in this society. The 10 underqualified interviewees were volunteers from adult basic education upgrading classes. The 10 underemployed interviewees responded to an advertisement posted in a university job-placement centre. Summary profiles appear in Table 13.2. The underqualified were all school dropouts and were mainly middle-aged people who had been recently laid off. The underemployed were all university graduates and were mainly young people employed in relatively low-skill jobs. While no claim to representativeness can be made, the composition of both groups was in keeping with the recent general trends discussed previously.[9] The findings presented here deal with (1) personal experience of the gap between educational attainments and job requirements, (2) current learning activities, (3) future education and job plans, (4) perceptions of the general extent of education–jobs matching, (5) job-entitlement beliefs, and (6) personal views on closing the education–jobs gap.

Experiencing the Credential Gap

Interviewees who had experienced the underqualification side of the credential gap often stressed the importance of on-the-job learning for their prior jobs, while typically denying the need for formal educational credentials

Table 13.2: Interviewee Profiles*

Underqualified (U/Q)		Underemployed (U/E)	
1	early 30s, male, unemployed factory worker, grade 10	1	mid-30s, male, coat checker, BA
2	mid-50s, male, unemployed welder, grade 7	2	early 20s, female, unemployed, BA
3	late 50s, female, unemployed hospital cleaning worker, no formal schooling	3	late 30s, female, community worker, LLB
4	late 40s, male, unemployed kitchen worker, grade 11	4	mid-20s, female, waitress, BA
5	early 40s, female, unemployed factory worker, grade 4	5	mid-20s, male, part-time cook, MA
6	early 50s, male, unemployed factory worker, grade 9	6	mid-40s, male, unemployed, MA
7	late 30s, male unemployed store clerk, grade 9	7	mid-30s, male, unemployed, LLB
8	mid-30s, male, unemployed plasterer, grade 6	8	early 20s, female, part-time clerical assistant, MA
9	early 30s, female, part-time nurses' aid, grade 9	9	mid-20s, female, telemarketer, BEd
10	early 30s, female, temporary electrical assembly, grade 11	10	mid-20s, female, part-time admitting clerk, BA

* The interview extracts cited in the text are identified by these terms; e.g., (U/Q4) refers to the underqualified kitchen worker.

and sometimes denigrating the relevance of advanced schooling for this work:

> It was a dirty job. You had to work hard and learn as you go. You didn't really need a diploma, just know how to read and be agreeable and hard working.... I used a bit of knowledge that I learned in school shop courses, but really learned a lot from my workmates. (U/Q1)

> I didn't need grade 9 to work on the line. I've got eyes, ears, strong hands—that's how

I learn. It was there in front of you—you either picked it up or you got your butt kicked until you learned it! Some of these people with a BA are as brainless as a cockroach, sorry to say. Without a book, they're practically useless. (U/Q6)

The one job entry requirement that was widely recognized was literacy:

> I was hired on the basis of experience. Now the job requires grade 12. I tried to hide my illiteracy. When it came to doing memos in

front of people, I needed to go to the office to look for a dictionary. But I was good at my job. I worked hard on correspondence courses to be able to do the writing. Instead of just laying us off, they should have sent us to learn computer skills. Instead, they hired young people, and after a few months everyone with a background like us was laid off. (U/Q3)

The underemployed university graduates were just as dismissive of the formal educational requirements of their jobs, but also tended to belittle the practical training involved and to stress the need for the personal qualities they did possess, such as patience to be able to tolerate work they found demeaning:

[Coat checking] does involve being able to be efficient.... You need the ability to keep a cool head. But pretty much any trained chimpanzee could do it. (U/E1)

The only qualifications [to be a telemarketer] are that you have to be fluent in English and have some knowledge of computers. Grade 9 would be plenty. The most important thing is to be able to be patient and polite. I haven't been able to use any of my education in this job. (U/E9).

The overall impression left by these interviews was that both the underemployed and the underqualified found formal educational credentials to be only superficially related to the jobs they had performed. Most importantly, neither the underemployed nor the underqualified found their jobs to be mentally very demanding. Virtually every interview conveyed a sense of wasted potential, of knowledge and talents that were impossible to use in the jobs

these people had been able to obtain. This sentiment was just as strong among the high school dropouts as among the university graduates. As one of the factory workers put it, "You never had to use your mind in that plant" (U/Q5).

Current Learning Activities

Both groups of respondents were asked an updated and abbreviated version of Allen Tough's Interview Schedule for Studying Some Basic Characteristics of Learning Projects.[10] Detailed comparisons of the learning practices of the two groups may not be very helpful because the underqualified were all enrolled full time in adult basic academic upgrading programs that dominated their learning time, while a few of the underemployed had graduated from university degree programs within the past year, and their time estimates referred only to the period since completing the degree. However, comparisons with prior research are at least suggestive.

The underqualified group had undertaken an average of six major learning projects over the past year totalling around 2,100 hours, of which about 20 percent were self-directed. The most comparable prior study, conducted at the beginning of the 1970's with full-time male students in a Metro Toronto academic upgrading program (students who were nominated by their instructors as having an "average" involvement in learning) found the average time on learning projects to be about 1,280 hours, of which only 8 percent were self-directed.[11] These scant data indicate that underqualified working people involved in upgrading programs devote much more time to major learning projects than the established 500-hour average of the adult population in general, and at least suggest that both the total time devoted to learning activities and the proportion of self-directed learning time may have increased among the underqualified during the past generation. Indeed, in spite of their upgrading program requirements, the underqualified people in our study were spending about 450 hours per year on self-directed learning projects.

As previously mentioned, there is no comparable prior study of the learning activities of the underemployed. The underemployed group in our study undertook an average of nine major learning projects over the past year totalling almost 1,400 hours, of which about 90 percent were self-directed. These results suggest that underemployed university graduates also devote much more time to learning activities than the established population average, and that the vast majority of their projects are self-directed. Some of the underemployed expressed disinterest in further institution-centred education because of the frustration of not finding a training-related job. As one interviewee put it, "I'm sort of sick of being educated. What more do I have to do?" (U/E7). But aside from two respondents who indicated they were still exhausted from the rigours involved in having recently finished postgraduate degree programs (U/E8 and 9), these underemployed university graduates were generally spending far more time on self-directed learning activities than most people.

These findings might also be taken as suggesting that underqualified high school dropouts have less predisposition or capacity to engage in self-directed learning activities than underemployed university graduates do. But this inference would ignore some important factors. The most obvious one is the constraint of full-time enrolment in the academic upgrading program on other, optional learning projects; university students, including a few interviewees prior to their recent graduation, also spend much lower proportions of their learning time on self-directed projects. Perhaps more importantly, self-directed learning is probably underestimated, especially among working-class people, because of a tendency to deny a major learning component in some manual activities,[12] just as many professional- and managerial-class people find it difficult to recognize important manual components in their work. For example, one of our respondents, who would be classified as functionally illiterate by most standards, resisted the notion that any of her activities beyond the upgrading program could constitute a learning project. But she also added that "I like meeting people and learning about things, and I do a lot of sports and practical things like crocheting. But it's all old stuff, not real learning" (U/Q5). Finally and most fundamentally, the entire tradition of research on self-directed learning projects is based on a conceptual model of an individually realized intentional learning process. Particularly in many working-class households and communities, a significant amount of important learning occurs without planning, in collective learning processes.[13] Such learning is beyond the scope of conventional measures of learning activities, again serving to underestimate the scale of working-class learning.

The current study is subject to the same limitations in this regard as prior research. However, at least our results are consistent with and shed a little further light on the recent large-scale survey findings that underqualified high school dropouts are increasingly participating in further education, and that underemployed young people also continue to be actively involved in further learning.

Future Education and Job Plans

The interviewees' responses to questions about their future plans and aspirations concerning education and jobs provide further insights into the persistent belief on both sides of the credential gap about the power of education to improve future life chances.

Among the underqualified, there was a virtually unanimous and certain equation between further educational credentials and a better job:

I'd like to do an advanced credit course and take a skill. I've got to get some education. I don't know exactly what now, but I have to see if I can get a better job. Want to learn more about my hobbies too. I hope I'll be able to get a job if I get some school in— looks like a lot of people hope so! (U/Q1)

I'm discouraged because I didn't pass the math test to get in to the program I wanted. It takes so long to go through all the upgrading courses, and I'm afraid I'll be too old to find a job. But education is so very important. I don't mind going to school the rest of my life because I enjoy learning.... I want to get enough training to open my own food business—and get a high school diploma with math when I retire. (U/Q3)

I'd love to get my grade 11, that's my dream .... I'd really like to be an auto mechanic, but I'm not able to get it—don't have enough skills in my head, too little education. Education is still my dream. I feel I've been deprived of something. If I had the education, I wouldn't be here today. Education gives you power.... I'm not a smart person, but I'm not a stupid person. (U/Q5)

For the underemployed, the equation between more education and better jobs is far less certain. But the apparent necessity to respond to this uncertainty by pursuing yet more formal education also remains largely unquestioned:

I don't have anything I would call a plan at this point.... If I am to remain in the field that I am in, I need to learn a lot more about computers, accounting, and other things specific to the field, basically improving my qualifications. In today's economy, the employer expects you to have it when you walk in the door. But, to be honest, I've no idea what I want to do with the rest of my life. (U/E1)

I think I will be going back for my doctorate, it seems, the way jobs are.... I'd like to be a professor or open a small business. I'm pretty sure I can get these jobs. It will take a while, but I need more education. It's just one last hurdle! (U/E5)

If a student loan comes through, I'm going to broadcasting school. And I've got to get computer training.... [After completing several degrees,] I should have an answer, but I just want a job. There's a huge gap between the dream and most of this stuff. It's so far away for me. (U/E6)

So, in spite of their common experience of a superficial connection between their formal educational attainments and the requirements of their current or recent jobs, both underqualified school dropouts and underemployed university graduates continued to act as if and believe that more education is the personal solution to living in the credential gap.

General Perceptions of the Credential Gap

As previously noted, general population surveys have found that most people believe there is an oversupply of qualified people at all job levels. But how does the overall relationship between education and jobs look as viewed from opposite sides of the credential gap?

Underqualified interviewees were most likely to see underqualification for jobs as the prevalent condition:

A lot of people need more education. There's been a basic breakdown. We need more education and qualified learning skills. (U/Q5)

Lots of people need more training, especially older employees to keep up. Some training just creates human robots for everything. But every day they're coming out with new things. (U/Q6)

But there was also a widespread perception that the supply of highly qualified job seekers exceeds the available jobs:

Many people have more qualifications than the jobs need. There just aren't enough jobs. We have to take what's there for survival. (U/Q2)

There's definitely more education and fewer jobs—that's the situation right now …. There are people who have master's degrees working at the local Burger King. (U/Q9)

Among the underemployed interviewees, there was virtual unanimity that an oversupply of educated people is the prevalent condition. Most respondents tended to view this oversupply and overqualification in terms of a screening device:

There are guys with advanced degrees who are parking attendants at Ontario Hydro. I guess the logic is "Gee, look at the labour market. If we can get people with more education to fill these jobs, why not?" (U/E6)

I tend to feel that people are overqualified and educational credentials are simply used as a screening mechanism. And I doubt that there are many really underqualified in this situation of low employment (U/E7)

However, some underemployed respondents saw this situation as the unavoidable consequence of the growing democratic demand for education:

Things in general may average themselves out, but in my situation I see lots of people who have too much education for what they are doing. Half of the telemarketers here have university degrees. But you can't stop people from taking education. (U/E9)

There was no discernible tendency among these interviewees to deny the existence of the credential gap. Those on opposite sides of the gap were likely to focus on and generalize from their respective conditions of underqualification or underemployment. But many school dropouts were almost as sceptical about any general condition of underqualification as they were about artificially high formal requirements for their prior jobs, while very few of the underemployed even considered the notion of having too little education for available jobs. However selectively perceived, the credential gap was very real in the respondents' minds.

Job-Entitlement Beliefs

In the previously cited large-scale surveys (Livingstone et al., 1987, 1995; Lowe, 1992), underqualified school dropouts have been most likely to deny their entitlement to a better job, while young underemployed postsecondary graduates have been most likely to assert such a right. The tendency to self-blame for failure to obtain a better job has been found to be widespread among both the underqualified and the underemployed. The present study allows a more nuanced assessment of these entitlement beliefs within both groups.

For the unemployed school dropouts intent on upgrading their skills, there was little inclination to deny their right to a better job, but plenty of reasons for not being able to get one:

Everybody deserves a better job, but it requires more qualifications. I don't blame nobody. You can't sit down and feel sorry for yourself. Just get up and do the right thing. You have to keep working. (U/Q9)

If you're trained, you should be able to have a decent job. But people aren't hiring. I've looked for a long time in a lot of places. You really get tired of it.... I can tell you right now there's a lot of people I see around, and I can guarantee you they won't be going far in life.... Now it's too late for many, and the economy is terrible now. (U/Ql)

Some of the underqualified expressed more fatalistic views about job entitlement:

If you're lucky, you will get a better job. It's a tough economic situation, and I don't have adequate training or education yet.

But, anyways, it depends on one's luck. (U/Q10)

If I get more education, I may deserve a better job, but I don't deserve it with what I've got now. My parents didn't give me enough education. They made me leave school and go out and work. (U/Q5)

The underemployed respondents also generally asserted their entitlement to a better job, mainly on the basis of having met what they perceived to be their side of the education-job bargain. But their rationales for failure were often complex:

Sure, I deserve better than this. But society also deserves better out of me.... I've made lots of mistakes, and nobody owes me anything. But there are many larger forces, like institutionalized forms of discrimination, that are major obstacles. (U/E6)

Why shouldn't we have a good job if we go through the system and qualify to do it! I have more to offer. I'm not being challenged. I think I could really do something else.... But I probably made the wrong [educational] choices. I didn't pick a concrete option that would make me employable.... But equal access to education is not a reality. I think it's determined where you're going to get to by who you are, and what you look like, and what your parents did or didn't do. (U/E10)

I deserve better because I did everything they said. I got my degree, I can speak both languages, I'm learning computers. I mean, I have more basic knowledge than most people. I can do any job that someone tells me. I've never failed at anything before, it's frustrating!... I can't blame myself because, again, I think I did everything I was told to. I guess I blame the university system and the government for telling you that this is what you need. Maybe I'm just crude, but you don't go to school just to improve yourself, you go to get a job! (U/E2)

But a few underemployed graduates did reject any job-entitlement rights—on the classic liberal ground of individual responsibility:

I deserve any opportunity that I can create for myself, that I work for. Am I qualified for a better job? Yes, I am. Deserve a job, that's another issue altogether.... I truly believe most of what happens to an individual is up to an individual, especially in cases like mine, where I've had lots of advantages.... Basically, you get what you pay for, and if you haven't paid for it, you don't get it. And whether that payment takes the form of training, or motivation, or drive, or any of those other things, it's still a form of payment to get what you want. I mean we are in a capitalist, consumerist society. (U/El)

In general, the sense of entitlement to a better job was widely held among both underqualified and underemployed interviewees. Conversely, the tendency to blame oneself for the failure to get a better job seemed to be weak in both groups. People on both sides of the credential gap fingered bad economic conditions, shortsighted government policies, irrelevant educational programs, and other institutional forces. But they typically saw themselves as active agents—at least of their own present and future educational choices—in the context of such constraints.

Closing the Gap

The interviewees were also asked about their suggestions for overcoming the education–jobs gap in the foreseeable future. The following extracts are intended to convey a sense of the diversity of ideas generated.

Most of the underqualified school dropouts proposed more extensive and relevant job training to respond to employers' escalating requirements. Nearly all saw more education in some form as pivotal to closing the gap, whether the educational initiative comes from individuals, educational institutions, or governments:

The focus should be on changing education and getting people interested in getting advanced skills. It's an employer's market. People need a lot more training. Government should have more training programs out there and not pick and choose who takes the programs. (U/Q1)

Educational institutions should ask what companies need and adapt their programs accordingly. Students are being misled, and postsecondary graduates are not well prepared for jobs. But things will get better. (U/Q8)

Government should cut taxes so business will come back and there will be more work available. So many people are going back to school to upgrade right now, I'm worried there won't be enough good jobs. Computers are taking over a lot of things.

But education is the key. Without it, people don't get anywhere. (U/Q4)

But some of the underqualified thought that the popular demand for more—and more useful—education may in turn force some democratizing workplace reforms, which might help to narrow the gap by creating more decent jobs:

The system is screwed up. I don't expect much change. The rich want to stay rich, so you can't expect they're going to give up so easy. But people are staying longer in school, and more people are going back. Maybe employees will be more able to have more say in workplace changes. (U/Q9)

We need to look into workplace changes more. Slow down computerization and save manual labour jobs…. Get some serious leaders who are for the people. Everything comes back to the solidarity of working people. Let people interact, with the less qualified learning from the overqualified. (U/Q7)

Most of the underemployed university graduates seemed to be reconciling themselves to the prospect that many of their generation may never obtain the fulfilling jobs they had dreamt about while completing their degrees. But there was no hint that giving up further career-related educational aspirations would be a reasonable response to chronic underemployment:

There's always going to be a gap. Somebody's going to be on the cutting edge, and it'll be up to the rest of the people to catch up. How many people are good enough to

get to the very top? The rest are going to be going into subsidiary positions where they will be overqualified. I'm sure it's worse now than it's ever been…. But no education is a waste. (U/E1)

For the underemployed like me, there's nowhere to go in the job, and the employer can't create a new position. There certainly should be better vocational counselling in the schools. But where do you start to change the workplace? I have no idea…. If I didn't have two degrees, I still wouldn't be happy in this job. But you can't stop people from learning more. (U/E9)

Some of the underemployed did express the hope that interactive educational and workplace reforms will lead to a more human-centred system. But even among those who are most critical of capitalism's economic imperatives, the persistence of education–job gaps was generally taken as inevitable:

We need a society which puts human beings first, not money. The education system needs to be more geared to practicalities. Whatever you learn you should be able to apply to your job. Learning on the job should also be recognized as learning experience by educational institutions. It works both ways. There should be an ongoing process of on-the-job and in-school learning. But education–job gaps are bound to happen, because the economy is changing and types of qualifications don't match, because institutions of learning have different timetables and don't react so fast to the market…. There needs to be more coordinated planning among governments, schools/colleges, and business. But businesses are not taking that initiative at all.... The people who control things need a massive dose of education to bring them down to the human level as opposed to a preoccupation with money. (U/E3)

Many of the underqualified and underemployed interviewees were receptive to a variety of possible workplace reforms that we asked them about, including job-enrichment initiatives, a shorter normal workweek, work-sharing, increasing men's share of housework, and employee ownership and control of businesses. But most of them continued to express considerable scepticism about realizing changes substantial enough to have any real impact on narrowing the gap between education and jobs during their lifetimes.

Conclusion

It is clear that most people now see an upgrading trend in the entry requirements for jobs, as well as a surplus of qualified job applicants at most levels. It is also fairly clear that one of the most common responses to finding or retaining a decent job is to seek more education and training. This mind-set is as common among underemployed university graduates as it is among underqualified school dropouts. These people have a deep-seated recognition of the arbitrariness of the formal educational credentials required for the jobs they have had. They understand, more intimately than those living within the comfort of job requirements matched to their educational attainments, that employers are upping the ante for job entry and that the link between entry requirements and educational attainments is being loosened in an "employer's market." Those living in the credential gap give no serious indication

of giving up on the faith that more education should get them a better job. Indeed, their current situation seems to have provoked in many at least a quiet sense of desperation that they must continue to get more and still more education, training, or knowledge in order to achieve any economic security. These sentiments resonated through most of our interviews. They were most movingly expressed by a laid-off factory worker and an unemployed recent university graduate:

> After upgrading, I'm going to an adult high school to get some training credits—unless I score a job, and then training's kaput. I don't think that will happen. I've looked for any kind of a job—not hiring, too much experience, not enough experience, just hired somebody else, et cetera. It gets very depressing. I'm trying hard. (U/Q1)

> My life is spiralling out of control. A while ago I just started crying—I don't have a job and I'm crying. So I've got to [hesitates] sort of centre myself.... I'm just floundering, and I don't even know what I'm doing—walking into walls. And that's probably why I want to go back to school.... Then at the placement centre, I finally went nuts and demanded some postings. One was a receptionist at a driving school, but you had to speak Cantonese. I just went home and started crying again. I just give up. I went, "Forget this, this is garbage." And that's just the worst feeling. I never give up. For my whole life, I've had to fight to become what I want. Then, when I graduated, they told me I was either too good or I didn't have two years' experience or some computer language. And now it's not French anymore, it's Cantonese [laughs]. And I'm going,

"Oh, I give up." But then, maybe we have to start learning other languages, stop being so ethnocentric and North American, think about the future and the outside world. I don't know. It's kind of bleak. (U/E2)

The conviction of these underemployed and underqualified people that our current economic system can produce the jobs to which they feel entitled has been shaken severely. But in the absence of any economic alternative that seems plausible, most of those living on both sides of the credential gap are actively engaged in trying to revise rather than reject this conviction. As in the dirty thirties, the waste of human potential is immense and gut-wrenching. Now as then, the economic polarization between the haves and the have-nots has increased greatly. The difference is that the pursuit and promise of further education are now playing a much larger role than make-work programs in preoccupying the swelling number of the outcasts and misfits of the labour market.

Acknowledgement

This chapter is a revised version of a paper presented at the annual meeting of the Canadian Sociology and Anthropology Association, University of Calgary, June 1994. I would like to thank all the interviewees. I also gratefully acknowledge the interviewing assistance of Chi-hung Chen, Henry Chow, Mike Hersh, Patrice Milewski, Najja Modibo, Peter Sawchuk, and especially Megan Terepocki; the general assistance of Pramila Aggrawal, Kathryn Church, Kari Dehli, Doug Hart, Ted Harvey, Harvey Krahn, Barbara Marchant, Kristine Pearson, Wally Seccombe, Jennifer Stephen, Allen Tough, and Marilyn Venn Norman; and the comments of the editors and several anonymous reviewers.

Endnotes

1   For critical reviews of the relevant literature (including the "upgrading thesis" associated most closely with Daniel Bell's postindustrial-society views, and the "deskilling thesis" mainly linked to Harry Braverman's analysis of capitalist degradation and routinization of wage labour), see Livingstone (1987); Spenner (1985); and Wood (1989).

2   The most influential early critical study of these mismatches was probably Berg (1970), followed by Collins (1979).

3   Both gender and ethnic differences in the credential gap are dealt with in detail in Livingstone (1996).

4   The 1986 Ontario survey found that over 50 percent of the adult population planned to take further-education courses at some point and that postsecondary graduates were more than three times as likely as those with only elementary schooling to indicate such plans; see Livingstone et al. (1993, pp. 6–7).

5   Economic Council of Canada (1991, pp. 111–136); Betcherman (1992, pp. 25–33); and Sharpe (1990, pp. 21–31). For a revealing case study of the substantive limits of many job-retraining programs, see Dunk and Nelson (1992).

6   As Tough (1978, p. 252, 1979) summarized the central findings from an array of these studies in the 1970s, the typical learner conducts five distinct learning projects per year in distinct areas of knowledge and skill, and spends about 100 hours on each of these learning efforts. This body of research has been prone to various conceptual and methodological criticisms, including sampling bias in favour of urban, middle-class, English-speaking North Americans; a focus on individualistic learning processes; interview formats that may predispose some respondents to gratuitous responses; and arbitrary operationalization of what counts as a learning project. For a recent critical overview of the relevant literature, see Candy (1993).

7   For studies on voluntary learning activities of economically disadvantaged urban adults, see Booth (1976)

and Serre (1978, pp. 16–20); on younger and older school dropouts, see Armstrong (1971), Brookfield (1982, pp. 48–53), and Virgin and McCatty (1976); on functional illiterates, see Eberle and Robinson (1980), Kratz (1980, pp. 134–137), and Peters, Johnson, and Lazzara (1981); and on unemployed learners, see Johnson, Levine, and Rosenthal (1977).

8 Personal communication from Allen Tough, April 26, 1994.

9 These are selective samples that, given the difficulties of identifying the populations of underemployed and underqualified people, were chosen primarily on criteria of accessibility. They exclude the most extreme cases of both underqualification and underemployment. The underqualified interviewees all had sufficient material resource support, motivation, and basic education to qualify for upgrading programs. The underemployed interviewees were all fairly recent graduates actively seeking better employment through the placement centre. There are substantial numbers of people living in more difficult conditions of chronic underqualification and underemployment. Our further research attempts to address this limitation through interviews with clients of food banks, and with the first representative sample survey of both underemployed and underqualified workers drawn from the 1994 OISE Survey of Educational Issues. See Livingstone (1996).

10 Copies of this interview schedule and listings of more recent related research reports are available from Allen Tough, Department of Adult Education, OISE. Aside from minor modifications of the thematic probes (e.g., the addition of "learning computers"), the main difference from Tough's original format is that—because of time constraints in administering the interview schedule—we have asked respondents to give us time estimates for a typical week during the past 12 months rather than more detailed project-by-project estimates.

11 Armstrong (1971, p. 34). Armstrong's study was focused on matched comparisons of the learning activities of 20 "high learners" and 20 others whose involvement in learning appeared to be average. These subgroups from a population of 330 adult students were determined by the combination of instructors' nominations and a threshold of 300 hours devoted to noncredit learning projects (according to an early version of Tough's interview schedule). Thus, in comparison with our group, Armstrong's sample of "average learners" is foreshortened at both ends: The instructors presumptively excluded low-level learners, and Armstrong selected high-level learners. Nevertheless, his study provides the only roughly comparable data in Toronto or Canada.

12 A classic ethnographic study of this tendency traces the presumptive denial of mental aspects of manual labour among working-class lads who rejected an academic school culture and headed for manual jobs. See Willis (1977).

13 For provocative discussions, see Foley (1987) as well as, more generally, Scott (1990) and Zolberg (1972, pp. 183–207).

References

Armstrong, D. 1971. "Adult Learners of Low Educational Attainment: The Self-Concepts, Backgrounds, and Educative Behavior of Average and High-Learning Adults of Low Educational Attainment." Unpublished doctoral dissertation, University of Toronto.

Baer, D., & Lambert, R. 1982. "Education and Support for Dominant Ideology." *Canadian Review of Sociology and Anthropology,* 19 (2), 173–195.

Berg, I. 1970. *Education and jobs: The great training robbery.* New York: Praeger.

Betcherman, G. 1992. "Are Canadian Firms Underinvesting in Training?" *Canadian Business Economics, I* (1), 25–33.

Bills, D. 1992. "The Mutability of Educational Credentials as Hiring Criteria: How Employers Evaluate Atypically Highly Credentialed Job Candidates." *Work and Occupations,* (February), 19(1), 79–95.

Booth, N. 1979. "Information Resource Utilization and the Learning Efforts of Low-Income Urban Adults." (Doctoral dissertation, University of Maryland). *Dissertation Abstracts International,* 40, 3048.

Brookfield, S. 1982. "Successful Independent Learning of Adults of Low Educational Attainment in Britain: A Parallel Educational Universe." Paper presented at the 23rd annual Adult Educational Research Conference, University of Nebraska, Lincoln. (April).

Burris, B. 1983. "The Human Effects of Underemployment." *Social Problems,* 31(1), 96–110. (October).

Burris, V. 1983. "The Social and Political Consequences of Overeducation." *American Sociological Review, 48,* 454–467. (August).

Candy, P. 1993. *Self-Direction for Lifelong Learning: A Comprehensive Guide to Theory and Practice*. San Francisco: Jossey-Boss.

Collins, R. 1979. *The Credential Society*. New York: Academic Press.

Derber, C. 1978. "Unemployment and the Entitled Worker: Job-Entitlement and Radical Political Attitudes among the Youthful Unemployed." *Social Problems*, 26 (1), 26–37. (October).

Devereux, M. 1984. *One in Every Five: A Survey of Adult Education in Canada*. Ottawa: Supply and Services.

Dunk, T., and R. Nelson. 1992. *Release, Retrain, Readjust: The Three R's of the New Economic Reality in Resource Hinterlands*. Paper presented at the annual meeting of the Canadian Sociology and Anthropology Association, University of Prince Edward Island, Charlottetown, PEI. (June).

Eberle, A., and S. Robinson. 1980. *The Adult Illiterate Speaks Out*. Washington, DC: National Institute of Education.

Economic Council of Canada. 1991. *Employment in the Service Economy*. Ottawa: Economic Council of Canada.

Ferguson, J. 1994. "Biologist, 28, Fears her Dreams are Lost." *Toronto Star*, p. D5. (March 27).

Foley, G. 1987. "Adult Education for the Long Haul." Paper presented at the 27th national conference of the Australian Association of Adult Education, Sydney. (September).

Freeman, R. 1976. *The Overeducated American*. New York: Academic Press.

Hecker, D. 1992. "Reconciling Conflicting Data on Jobs for College Graduates." *Monthly Labour Review*, 3–12. (July).

Johnson, V., H. Levine and E. Rosenthal. 1977. "Learning Projects of Unemployed Adults in New Jersey." Unpublished paper, Educational Advancement Project, Rutgers Labor Education Center, New Brunswick, NJ.

Jolin, M. 1987. "The Occupational 'Mismatching' Problem Re-examined: 'Overeducation,' Financial Satisfaction, and Community Participation in Rhode Island." Unpublished doctoral dissertation, Brown University.

Kozol, J. 1985. *Illiterate America*. Garden City, NY: Anchor Press-Doubleday.

Krahn, H. 1992. *Quality of Work in the Service Sector*. Ottawa: Statistics Canada.

Kratz, R. 1980. "Implications of Self-Directed Learning for Functionally Illiterate Adults." Paper presented at the 21st annual Adult Education Research Conference, Vancouver. (May).

Kumar, P., D. Arrowsmith, & M. Coates. 1991. *Canadian Labour Relations: An Information Manual*. Kingston: IRC Press, Queen's University.

Leean, C., and B. Sisco. 1981. *Learning Projects and Self-Planned Learning Efforts among Undereducated Adults in Tural Vermont*. Washington, DC: National Institute of Education.

Livingstone, D. W. 1987. "Job Skills and Schooling." *Canadian Journal of Education*, 12 (1), 1–30.

Livingstone, D. W. 1992. "Lifelong Learning and Chronic Underemployment: Exploring the Contradiction." In P. Anisef and P. Axelrod (eds.). *Transitions: Schooling and Employment in Canadian Society* (pp. 113–125). Toronto: Thompson Educational Publishing.

Livingstone, D. W. 1996. *The Education–Jobs gap: Underemployment or Economic Democracy*. Boulder, CQ Westview Press.

Livingstone, D. W., D. Hart, and L. E. Davie. 1987. *Public Attitudes Towards Education in Ontario, 1986: Sixth OISE survey*. Toronto: OISE Press.

Livingstone, D. W., D. Hart, and L.E. Davie. 1993. *Public Attitudes Towards Education in Ontario, 1992: Ninth OISE survey*. Toronto: OISE Press.

Livingstone, D. W., D. Hart, and L. E. Davie. 1995. *Public Attitudes Towards Education in Ontario, 1994: Tenth OISE survey*. Toronto: OISE Press.

Lowe, G. 1992. *Human Resource Challenges of Education, Computers and Retirement*. Ottawa: Statistics Canada.

Lowe, G., H. Krahn, T. Hartnagel, and J. Tanner. 1986. "Class, Labour Market and Educational Influences on Young People's Explanations of Unemployment." Paper presented at the 11th World Congress of Sociology, New Delhi. (August 19).

Marshall, R., and M. Tucker. 1992. *Thinking for a Living: Education and the Wealth of Nations*. New York: Basic Books.

Robert, L. and R. McDowell. 1994. "Adult Education and Training." In *Profile of Post-Secondary Education in Canada: 1993 Edition*. Ottawa: Education Support Branch, Human Resources Development Canada.

Organization for Economic Co-operation and Development. 1989. *Educational Attainment and the Labour Force Employment Outlook*. Paris: Author.

Organization for Economic Co-operation and Development. 1993. *Education at a Glance—OECD Indicators*.

Paris: Author.

Osberg, L. 1993. "Social Policy and Macro Policy in a Federal State." *Canadian Business Economics,* 2(1), 36–45.

O'Toole, J. 1975a. "The Reserve Army of the Underemployed: I — The World of Work." *Change, 7,* 26–33, 63. (May).

OToole, J. 1975b. "The Reserve Army of the Underemployed: II — The Role of Education." *Change,* 26–33, 60–62.

Peters, J. M., M. Johnson, and P.Lazzara. 1981. "Adult Problem Solving and Learning." Paper presented at the 62nd annual conference of the American Educational Research Association, Los Angeles. (April).

Rachel, L. 1987. "Assessing the Extent and the Political Implications of Underemployment among College Graduates." Unpublished doctoral dissertation, University of Colorado, Boulder.

Roizen, J., and M. Jepson. 1985. *Degrees for Jobs: Employer Expectations of Higher Education.* Guildford, Eng.: SRHE & NFER-Nelson.

Rose, M. 1989. *Lives on the Boundary.* New York: Penguin.

Scott, J. C. 1990. *Domination and the Arts of Resistance: Hidden Transcripts.* New Haven, CT: Yale University Press.

Selman, G., and P. Dampier. 1991. *The Foundations of Adult Education in Canada.* Toronto: Thompson Educational Publishing.

Serre, F. 1978. "The Importance of Learning Alone: A Study of Self-Planned Learning Projects." *Adult Learning,* 3(2).

Sharpe, A. 1990. "Training the Workforce: A Challenge Facing Canada in the 90s." *Perspectives on Labour and Income* (pp. 21–30). (Winter).

Sharpe, A. 1993. "The Rise of Unemployment in Ontario." Paper presented at the conference Unemployment: What Is to Be Done? Laurentian University, Sudbury, ON. (March).

Sisco, B. 1983. "The Undereducated: Myth or Reality?" *Lifelong Learning: The Adult Years,* 6 (8), 14–15, 24. (April).

Smith, H. 1986. "Overeducation and Underemployment: An Agnostic View." *Sociology of Education,* 59, 85–99. (April).

Spenner, K. 1985. The Upgrading and Downgrading of Occupations: Issues, Evidence, and Implications for Education. *Review of Educational Research,* 55 (2), 125–154.

Statistics Canada. 1993. *The Labour Force.* Ottawa: Author.

Tanner, J., G. Lowe and H. Krahn. 1984. "Youth Unemployment and Moral Panics." *Perception,* 7 (5), 101–117.

Tough, A. 1978. "Major Learning Efforts: Recent Research and Future Directions." *Adult Education [U.S.],* 28 (4), 250–263.

Tough, A. 1979. *The Adult's Learning Projects: A Fresh Approach to Theory and Practice in Adult Learning* (2nd ed.). Toronto: OISE Press.

Virgin, A. E., and C. McCatty. 1976. *High School Dropouts: Characteristics of Their Post-School Learning and Their Perceptions of Why They Left.* Report to North York Board of Education.

Willis, P. 1977. *Learning to Labour: How Working Class Kids Get Working Class Jobs.* Farnborough, Eng.: Saxon House.

Wirth, A. 1992. *Education and Work for the Year 2000: Choices We Face.* San Francisco: Jossey-Boss.

Wood, S. 1989. "The Transformation of Work?" In S. Wood (ed). *The Transformation of Work?* (pp. 1–43). London: Unwin Hyman.

Zolberg, A. 1972. Moments of Madness. *Politics and Society,* 2 (2).

CHAPTER 14

Education for an Information Age?

Alan Sears

THE HARRIS GOVERNMENT in Ontario presented education reform as a practical necessity. This was expressed in compressed form in the 1999 Budget Speech when Finance Minister Ernie Eves addressed education concerns in very practical terms. "Increased accountability, a stronger link between schools and the job market, and better career planning for students will continue to improve our education system" (Eves 1999:19). The shift to a post-liberal mode of education is portrayed as the sensible response to a rapidly changing occupational structure, driven particularly by the spread of information technology. In this chapter, I argue that education reform is not propelled by a dramatic shift in skills required in the labour market, although it is tied to the disciplinary requirements of systems of lean production.

Skills for the Information Age?

The case for education reform is grounded in claims about the changing labour market. One of the stated aims of the educational

system is to prepare people for the world of employment. The labour market is changing in important ways and so it must follow that the educational system should also change. The Ontario Ministry of Education makes the case that people will need more education to find a place in this changing labour market. "As the restructuring of Ontario's economy continues, it is expected that demand for both full-time and part-time study will increase, as people of all ages pursue learning to acquire knowledge and skills to remain competitive in the workplace" (Ontario Ministry of Education and Training (OMET) 1996b:51). Yet technological change in capitalist society has not usually been associated with a generalized increase in skill requirements. Indeed, Harry Braverman (1974) argued that there has been a tendency towards *deskilling* as labour processes have changed through the 20th century. At the same time, formal educational requirements have increased. This chapter will examine the contradictory relationship between skills and education.

There is an obvious basis for the widely held

assumption that workers would need more education in the contemporary world. New information technologies seem to demand new levels of skill while new management strategies emphasize flexibility and "continuous improvement" methods that supposedly tap workers' creativity. Livingstone describes this assumption that increased skills should be required as the "prevailing myth of 'post-industrial' work" (Livingstone 1996:79).

Claims about a skills shortage are based specifically on the immediate shortfall in the supply of trained workers for high technology jobs. Premier Harris made this point very strongly at an address to a conference on the future of Ontario Universities sponsored by the Council of Ontario Universities and the Bank of Nova Scotia. "Who in the university system will decide to reduce enrolments or close programs when there are few jobs available in a profession, like certain professional or PhD programs? For example, do we need 10 PhD programs in geography, or six in sociology? Who is responsible for opening or expanding programs where there are significant shortages, like computer science and software engineering?" (Harris 1997:7).[1]

Industry-based organizations in the high-technology sector have certainly claimed that there is a skills shortage in the area. A Canadian Advanced Technology Association (CATA) member survey from 1997 estimated that there were 20,000 vacant information technology jobs in Canada at that point and the Software Human Resources Council estimated that there would be as many as 50,000 vacant information technology jobs by the year 2000 (OMET 1998a). Yet a paper by David Stager (1999) for the Applied Research Branch of Human Resources Development Canada argues, "The conclusion at this time in the debate about an IT [information technology] shortage, seems to be the Scottish verdict, 'Not proven.'" He points out that there is no really solid basis for projecting labour supply and demand in the information technology field, but as far as it is possible to project, "there should not be an emerging problem of shortage over the next five to seven years—which is a very long time in a sector where technology is changing quickly"(Stager 1999:47). Claims for a shortage of information technology specialists in the United States have been "clouded by a lack of unambiguous data" (47). These have been based largely on employer surveys that might reflect employers' wishes to see a greater supply of skilled labour in the sector to give them more control over the hiring process. "There is no doubt that employers prefer to have a large queue of applicants so that they have more scope to select those with specialized skills and even personalities to suit the firm's needs" (49).

The case for a labour shortage in information technology is open to debate. Even if there is a shortage in that sector, it seems excessive to retool the whole education system in response to a localized and temporary demand for just one category of workers. We need, then, to turn to the overall question of skill requirements in a changing labour market. Lean production is bringing into play new technologies and methods of work organization. The optimistic account of lean production presents it as a method for increasing worker autonomy and skill in the labour process. The classical statement of this is the comment by Womack, Jones and Roos that "by the end of the next century we expect that lean assembly plants will be populated almost entirely by highly skilled problem solvers" (Womack, Jones and Roos 1990:102).

Skills and Lean Production

Studies on the changing world of work and lean production do not conclude that we are seeing a dramatic increase in autonomy and skill requirements. The optimistic story that lean production represents a sharp departure from the standardization and monitoring associated with Taylorist mass production methods does not hold up. Lean production builds on the central Taylorist techniques of breaking jobs down into elemental tasks, organizing work around a sequence of specified tasks to be carried out as management instructs, and tight management control over the process as a whole (Parker and Slaughter 1994:75). It is in many ways a streamlined version of mass production that reduces buffers, increases stress and attempts to deploy workers' knowledge to intensify work (Moody 1997:85; Parker and Slaughter 1994:80–84).

Workers tend to develop their own knowledge of work processes, learning to do things better to gain some control over the pace of work or to gain break time. Lean production attempts to harvest this knowledge and use it to speed up the processes (Garrahan and Stewart 1992:76). Workers at the CAMI plant in Ingersoll, for example, realized over time that the suggestions they were submitting to management were actually being used to reduce staffing and speed up work intolerably (Rinehart, Huxley and Robertson 1997). Moody wrote that the outcome of lean production "is not worker empowerment or autonomy: it is highly standardized work timed down to the last breath" (Moody 1997:88).

There is a good argument, then, that the changes that we are seeing in the workplace are not in any simple sense about upping the level of skill. Lean production fits in with the general tendency, described in Braverman's influential work, *Labor and Monopoly Capital,* towards the degradation of work since the early 20th century through the implementation of Taylorist scientific management methods. Braverman (1974:90–121) argues that Taylor's approach to scientific management was premised on detailed management control over the way work was executed. This was crucial if management were to control the labour process. The *conception* of the task should be separated as completely as possible from its *execution.* Workers would therefore be responsible for executing specified tasks with a minimum of discretion. Braverman traced the implementation of these principles through a variety of occupations, including clerical and service jobs as well as industrial work.

We are, therefore, not seeing a general trend towards increased skill and autonomy in Braverman's sense of combining conception and execution. Braverman himself disputed the claim that new levels of science and technology at work are associated with skills upgrading. Rather, there is often a polarization of skill, with a greater divergence between a small layer of highly trained specialists and the mass of workers (Braverman 1974: 425–26).

New Kinds of Problem-Solving?

Even if we are not seeing a trend towards upgrading, that does not necessarily mean that there is no change in the skill requirements for jobs. Tony Elger (1982:45) argues in his critique of Braverman that mass production throughout the 20th century has not produced a homogenous deskilled labour force, but rather a complex and differentiated occupational structure requiring diverse skills and abilities. Different skills may be required as labour processes are transformed, even if this change does not mark an "upgrading" in Braverman's sense of the word.

John Holmes (1997) argues that skill requirements in the pulp industry have changed as part of the process of restructuring. There is a new emphasis on interpersonal skills (associated with teamwork) and on particular problem-solving skills (which he labels as "intellective," following Zuboff [1988]). "Workers need to make sense of data by using inferential reasoning and systemic thinking rather than by responding to physical cues (the sight, feel, smell or even taste of pulp finish or paper), which in the past made the worker a skilled papermaker" (Holmes 1997:10). The labour process has shifted so that the monitoring of the production process is mediated by machines rather than done in a direct hands-on fashion. This is a change in skills rather than "upgrading." Indeed, the occupational position of paper machine operators who had been crucial in older labour processes has been downgraded through technological change and work reorganization (21).

Zuboff (1988:75) argued that the spread of computer technologies has been associated with new requirements for "intellective skills"; that is, problem-solving capacities that draw on analytical skills, reasoning and a capacity for abstraction. It is difficult to ascertain just how universally true this is. Mishel and Teixiera (1991:22–24) state that there is very little basis for firm generalizations about these changes in skill requirements at a society-wide level, but they do identify some general trends from scholarly literature, journalism and statements from business leaders. Overall, the requirement for a basic level of literacy and numeracy is widespread in the job market. Employers find it more difficult to deploy or

retrain workers without these skills. This is an important consideration and there has been a curious lack of focus on mass literacy issues in debates about deskilling (Wood 1982:19).

Furthermore, there are new skill requirements among those innovative firms that are implementing "best practice" methods of work organization: "In these firms, jobs are being restructured so that workers are expected to independently solve technical problems that come up in the course of their work, to learn new tasks on a fairly regular basis, and to interact extensively with fellow workers, frequently as part of a 'team'" (Mishel and Teixiera 1991:23). The most important new requirements in these firms are "for the social and 'higher-order' skills upon which problem-solving, adaptability and team work are based" (52). These leading-edge practices are not the norm, however. Competitive pressure might push more firms in this direction, but there are many other restructuring options that do not rely on worker problem-solving or teamwork in these ways. Rather than being a model for widespread work restructuring, these "best practices" might be primarily responses to particular challenges relevant only to limited sections of the labour market. Longer-term studies seem to indicate that the rate of change in skill requirements has generally been declining rather than increasing since the 1960s (23–24, 17–18).

It is possible that restructuring has led to an increase in the need for intellective skills in the workplace, although it is difficult to know with certainty the extent of these requirements. Further, the need for intellective skills in the workplace does not explain the contemporary round of educational restructuring. Intellective skills, such as communications and problem-solving abilities, are already at the core of secondary and post-secondary curricula, particularly in the academic, liberal arts and general education streams, and it is quite possible that the increased need for these skills contributed to the near doubling of post-secondary enrolments from 1971 to 1991.[2] This might also help explain the advantage that people with post-secondary education currently have in the labour market. A Statistics Canada (1995:1) study showed that individuals with post-secondary education were less likely to be unemployed than those without:

> In June 1992, the unemployment rate for less-educated young people (20- to 29-year-olds without a post-secondary degree, diploma or certificate) was nearly 17%. Among 1990 post-secondary graduates, only trade/vocational graduates experienced a higher rate (20%). All other categories of 1990 graduates had lower unemployment rates in June 1992. Graduates who fared better were those who earned career/technical (10%), bachelor's (11%), master's (8%) or doctorate (6%) degrees. (Statistics Canada 1995:1)

It is quite conceivable that one of the factors contributing to the increase in educational requirements for many jobs is the need for generic skills (broad conceptual abilities and communication skills without occupationally specific content). These generic skills are already developed in humanities and social sciences programs (Organization for Economic Cooperation and Development (OECD) 1993:25), and the Vision 2000 (1990:9) report on community colleges in Ontario argued that they should move more to the core of the college curriculum. At the secondary level, these skills would be most strongly associated with the academic stream.

The requirement for more generic skills might help explain a longer-term trend for increased educational requirements in the workforce dating back to before the education reforms were implemented. This is debatable, however, as it is quite possible that we are mainly seeing credential inflation in a tight labour market and an increasing stigmatization of people with a low level of formal education (Hoddinott and Overton 1996:210–14). In either case, the requirement for particular skills does not explain the direction of educational restructuring. Indeed, the restructuring has a heavy vocationalist emphasis that seems to emphasize more specific occupational preparation rather than generic skills. Mike Harris, for example, seemed to be arguing against an emphasis on generic skills when he said, "We seem to be graduating more people who are great thinkers, but they know nothing about math or science or engineering or the skill sets that are really needed (Mackie 2000:A7)."

Standards Not Skills

Certainly, there is a claim that the current restructuring in Ontario is about developing generic skills in students. An Ontario government public discussion document argues that there is currently a problem with the skills students have upon graduation. "There are … more young people who arrive at the next stage of their careers—university, college, or the search for a first job—without the skills and knowledge required for success…. Some high school graduates do not have high enough literacy and math skills to function effectively in the workplace" (OMET 1996a:3–4).

The solution to the challenge of skills development, according to the Ontario government, is quite simply to raise standards. "All students should have a high-quality curriculum with demanding standards" (OMET 1996a:6). The conception of "demanding standards" in OMET materials is twofold: increased compulsion and more measurement. The policy changes in Ontario suggest that education reformers strongly dispute the ways skills have been taught in the recent past. Education reformers believe students have been given too much choice and insufficient opportunity to fail. In general terms, the education reform agenda has focused on increasing the compulsion in the teaching of skills. At the most obvious level, this has meant increasing the number of required courses. In Ontario, the number of compulsory courses required for a secondary school degree will be increased from 16 to 18 out of 30. This increase is attributed to a need for skills development, reflecting a "public desire for an increased emphasis on math, language and science, and preparation for responsible citizenship" (OMET 1998b:1).

More important than an overt increase in pedagogical compulsion is the emphasis on the construction of standards in terms of measurement. Standards are defined in a discussion document on the secondary school curriculum as "statements of required results whose meaning is made very clear by Performance Indicators" (OMET 1996c:5). This emphasis on standards is related specifically to generic skills. As the Ministry of Education business plan states, "The Ministry will finalize provincial standards, so that students will have a solid foundation in the areas of language and mathematics" (Ontario 1996:77).

The assertion here is that more detailed measurement, combined with increased opportunity to fail, will increase the students' skill foundation. The curriculum is thus being reshaped around standardized testing. There

are many problems with this kind of testing, which tends to focus classroom learning on test preparation and imposes limits on the curriculum. There is also a great deal of debate about whether the broad skills required in the workforce are those that will be measured in the tests. The problem is that breaking down skills into measurable units for province-wide tests severely limits what can be measured. Meaghan and Cassis argue that these tests measure the ability to "recall facts, define words, perform routine operations rather than higher learning skills such as analyzing, synthesizing, forming hypotheses and exploring alternative ways of solving problems" (Meaghan and Cassis 1995:46).

There is an even more fundamental issue about measurement here. Rather than ensuring that more people actually acquire these skills, the goal of educational restructuring seems to be to identify those who have learned them and those who have not. Programs that actually promote the "threshold level" literacy skills that might be required in the changing labour market are actually being cut in Ontario. The most important example of this is the slashing of adult education programs since the Harris government was elected. The government changed the funding model for adult education in 1996, reducing expenditure per student by over 50 percent (Battagello 1996: A3, Lewington 1998:A8). The new funding formula introduced the next year forced local boards to make even deeper cuts to adult education. In Toronto, angry protesters took over the meeting room as trustees voted to cut adult education programs serving 4,000 students (Sheppard 1998:A1). But this is not simply an Ontario phenomenon. Hoddinott and Overton (1996) illustrate the ways that the privatization of adult education, and the increased pathologization of people who are not literate, have eroded basic skills development through Newfoundland's literacy campaign which began in 1988 and peaked in the early 1990s.

Programs that teach literacy skills to adults are being cut while the measurement of these skills in the schools is being increased. The problem of teaching literacy is reduced to the question of "standards" in the Harris education reform agenda: if you test it, they will come. The challenge of teaching those students who have trouble meeting these standards is not really discussed—the emphasis is on measurement and classification.

New report cards in Ontario are part of this shift to measurement. The standardized report cards were introduced first at the elementary school level (Education Improvement Commission 1997:2). At the secondary school level, failure in the standardized Grade 10 literacy course is to be indicated on the transcript and will prevent graduation (OMET 1998b:3). Transcripts will also show all attempts at a course rather than just the successful one as had previously been the practice, ensuring that failure leaves its mark. "This reform will give students an incentive to excel the first time they take a course" (OMET 1996a:10).

Streaming and Labour-Market Polarization

The renewed emphasis on streaming is consistent with this focus on measurement and classification of students. Streaming is returning to Grade 9, although in such a way as to permit shifting between streams the following year. Overall, the secondary system will stream students towards universities, colleges or no post-secondary education,[3] and a new teacher-advisor system will help direct students towards appropriate streaming choices beginning in Grade 7 (OMET 1998b:1–2). The more standardized testing and reporting procedures are sure to provide some of the basis for streaming.

It is difficult to see how this emphasis on measurement and streaming will equip more students with the generic skills (basic literacy, numeracy, reasoning and problem-solving) that might be required in the workforce. Rather, the aim seems to be to differentiate education on the basis of students' prior acquisition of these skills.[4] Those who have trouble with these skills will be streamed towards no post-secondary education and a very dismal future on the margins of the labour market.[5] Of course, more education in itself would not resolve the problem of labour-market polarization that is built into the lean system.

This emphasis on the differentiation of students contradicts the universalistic pretensions of public education as a basis for citizenship. I argued above that the educational optimism of the broad welfare state was connected to an emphasis on the development of particular forms of subjectivity through schooling. The more "child-centred" approaches represented an attempt to keep more students in school by limiting the opportunities to fail out of the system. There was a confidence that simply keeping people in that space would contribute to the development of citizens with a basic cultural formation.

Educational restructuring marks an important shift away from that emphasis on citizenship associated with the liberal education model. Lean production requires a downward polarization of parts of the working class as part of the "management by stress" strategy that drives workers through insecurity.[6] The school system prepares students for that differentiation, trying to prevent the elevated humanistic expectations that might accompany citizenship.

Measuring and streaming students are associated with the new vocationalist approach to education. The new vocationalism centres on the acquisition of specific skills that are allegedly relevant in the job market, skills that are developed through the establishment of measurable performance goals in the training process (Jackson 1992:78). It also represents a behaviourist attack on traditional pedagogical approaches (Avis 1991:118–19). This vocationalism has very little to do with developing the kinds of generic literacy, numeracy or reasoning skills described above. It is concerned more with measurement than with teaching. This approach serves to shift the horizons of possibility for individual students by developing a measure of their performance so that their occupational expectations might fit the labour market they face. It is about new differentiated forms of subjectivity and discipline required for an increasingly polarized society. This means shattering any universalistic expectations that the welfare state educational system might have generated.

The Economic Council of Canada (1992) report, "A Lot to Learn," argued for a new attention to vocational education at the secondary level. It argues that too many students have shifted out of vocational programs that are not highly regarded (17–18), and identifies a problem of expectations. "Partly the problem is one of misplaced expectations: most parents, and the students themselves, aspire to the prestigious positions via university or college—often with little comprehension of what this actually entails" (17–18).

The report does not mention that in the real labour market it is not only "prestigious positions" that require post-secondary education. The job prospects for people with only secondary education are becoming increasingly limited. It is quite possible that the "academic bias" the report identifies (Economic Council of Canada (ECC) 1992:25, 53) is actually a rational response by students and parents to the changes in the labour market that increasingly marginalize those without post-secondary education in a situation of chronic youth unemployment. Many of the vocational programs in secondary schools are terminal streams that offer credentials for which there is little demand.

The overall problem facing young people entering the labour market seems to be a lack of employment prospects. Morissette, Myles and Picot cite evidence that there is an abundant supply of labour across Canada for the foreseeable future. In this view, young workers entering the labour force face a "demand deficit" rather than a "skills deficit": "there is simply not enough demand for their labour irrespective of skills levels" (Morissette, Myles and Picot 1995:43).

This "demand deficit" has an impact on all young people, although it affects most sharply those without post-secondary education. In the present context a relatively educated workforce is in fact underemployed. Livingstone (1996:76–77) writes that this underemployment takes many forms. Some people are unemployed, while others who aspire to full-time work find themselves in part-time or temporary jobs. The skills and knowledge of those who are employed full-time are often under-used, their formal credentials might exceed requirements and many feel overqualified for their jobs. The response of business leaders and governments has been "to reform the educational system and encourage people to seek more and better training." (Livingstone 1996:77–78).

The Ideology of Training

The emphasis on training was particularly prominent in the late 1980s and early 1990s. Dunk, McBride and Nelson (1996:3–4) discuss ways in which the training ideology read the structural problem of chronic unemployment as an issue of labour-force preparation. The blame was thus divided between individuals, who were not taking responsibility for retooling themselves to meet the needs of a changing economy, and the educational system that was not keeping up. This focus provided a politically palatable argument for cutting social programs. "Indeed, the ideology of training may serve as the perfect rationale for stripping the income security programs and diverting funds towards retraining activities. The income security programs are viewed as 'passive' and dependency-inducing; retraining is 'active' and leads to independence" (Dunk, McBride and Nelson 1996:3). The training emphasis largely disappeared by the mid-1990s. The idea of a skills deficit is still useful in the educational field to support restructuring: "What's more, our world has changed, but our schools have not kept up. We have unemployed high school graduates and a shortage of technically skilled workers" (OMET 1996a:4).

Overall, however, there is far less focus on training ideology. This signals the exhaustion of what Jessop (1991:98) describes as the "neo-statist" social democratic response to capitalist restructuring, which emphasized the use of state resources to improve labour-force preparation. This training orientation has a long history in social democratic policy. It was certainly prominent in British Labour Party policy in the 1960s (Centre for Contemporary Cultural Studies (CCCS) 1981:143–45). Education and training figured prominently in the political vocabularies of the both the Liberal and New Democractic Party (NDP) Ontario governments that preceded the Harris Conservatives. This focus on training for high skills represented a strategy for a new form of social citizenship in the context of the emergence of lean production through capitalist restructuring. The high-skills strategy was centrally nationalist, suggesting that the economic future of the nation lay in the skills of the population (Avis 1996b:74).

The shift away from training is not simply a result of the 1995 change of government in Ontario. Even before the NDP government was defeated, the process of educational restructuring and attacks on public-sector workers was already well underway (Martell 1995). The material and ideological lines of the lean state project sharpened dramatically throughout the 1990s and governments of every political stripe have largely accepted the new parameters. This has included a recognition that there is no national "high skills, high pay" route to prosperity in the contemporary context (see Avis 1996a:114). It is also associated with an ideological shift that has legitimized "welfare-bashing" and enabled governments to skip the training ideology and pass directly to welfare and education "reform."

David Livingstone (1996, 1999) argues that we need to reverse our perspective on the gap between education and jobs. We face a shortage of good jobs rather than a shortage of skills. An increasing number of employed people have more preparation than their jobs require, while many prepared people are unemployed or underemployed. This "education–jobs gap" has been disguised by credential inflation and employer concerns about skills shortages. The real problem we are seeing is the waste of the knowledge and abilities of workers who are underemployed or unemployed (Livingstone 1999:96).

It seems quite possible that the "education–jobs gap" is not a temporary conjunctural problem for young people, but the longer-term product of labour-market restructuring. Morissette, Myles and Picot (1995:41–43) argue that young people might be pioneers in a new labour market. They are more likely to be employed in newer industries, workplaces where new technologies have been introduced, and in places where labour contracts have been substantially reworked. It is quite possible that the employment conditions of the young today will spread through the labour market as the position of older, more protected, workers is eroded through restructuring or attrition.

Educational restructuring aims to prepare young people for their place in this new labour market. This is not centrally a matter of augmenting skills but rather of diminishing expectations. The story about education during the broad welfare state period was that good jobs awaited those who made their way through the system. That no longer fits with experience, and the next section examines the ways in which expectations are to be remade to fit with new realities.

Lean Discipline

The core of state education has been from the outset the development of particular forms of discipline. Citizenship has been the most important of those disciplinary forms since the public education system was developed in the 19th century. The focus on citizenship-formation has been so successful over time that it is now largely incorporated into the taken-for-granted world view of the population.

Educational restructuring involves a major reorientation of the system away from the discipline of welfare state citizenship. The process of capitalist restructuring has generated new disciplinary requirements for a lean world. The endless drive for intensification of work requires new forms of motivation to push people to try to meet ever-rising standards of productivity. A study comparing different ways of organizing work in the Canadian automobile parts sector found that workers in lean production plants were more likely than those in traditional "Fordist" workplaces to say that the workload was too heavy, that it was increasing, and that they would be unlikely to be able to maintain the pace until the age of sixty (Lewchuk and Robertson 1997:74–77). Domestic labour, unpaid work in the household such as cooking, cleaning and caring, has also intensified; the restructuring of health care and social programs increases the work required to care for household members, family or friends.

The welfare state educational system was not preparing students for this lean world of relentless intensification in all aspects of life. Citizenship generated too many expectations, whether ethical or material. The lean world requires the erosion of the expectations of citizenship to create an atmosphere of "management by stress," not only in the workplace, but in society as a whole (see Parker and Slaughter 1994). "Management by stress" in its educational form is one of the pillars of the new discipline.

Management by stress is necessary, but not sufficient, for the disciplinary reorientation associated with lean production. Garrahan and Stewart (1992:115–17, 138) argue that management by stress was combined with a new participatory ethos in the Nissan plant they studied in Britain. Teamwork played an important role in the development of that participatory ethos, which they describe as "self-subordination." "Teamwork depends precisely upon self-subordination for it shifts the locus of control onto individuals who perceive themselves as guardians of quality and flexibility" (Garrahan and Stewart 1992:94).

Restructuring education involves a move from citizenship towards lean discipline, combining increased stress with new forms of self-subordination. The stress level is upped by new performance standards, harsher consequences for failure to perform and an increasingly competitive atmosphere resulting from a harsh youth labour market combined with the focus on standards. At the same time, self-subordination is cultivated through the development of a hardened work ethos, new forms of individual responsibility, efforts to increase identification with corporate goals, the promotion of consumerism and consumer-empowerment strategies that include participatory elements.

The Vocationalist Ethos

One of the central claims of educational restructuring has been that it will make education more "relevant." Students in Ontario, whatever their destination after high school, "must be focused on relevant learning" (OMET 1996c:3). The secondary school curriculum should be "rigorous, relevant and results-oriented" (Ontario 1996:77). Ontario schools began to focus excessively on citizenship to the detriment of work skills in the 1960s, "being more concerned with 'civilizing' the young than with giving them the tools they need to become productive and independent" (OMET 1996a:4).

Relevance is defined particularly in terms of preparation for employment. The Economic Council of Canada argued that many "judge the quality of the educational system by its success in preparing students for the labour market" (1992:4). A central problem in the secondary schools is "a woeful lack of pragmatic technical and vocational programmes to prepare young people for the world of work" (47). The Canadian Chamber of Commerce Task Force on Education and Training (TFET) echoes these concerns (1989:39), which also suggested that more practical preparation for the workforce was required.

This focus on "relevance" in terms of labour-market preparation was central to the educational restructuring undertaken by Britain's Thatcher government. The "new vocationalism" was a central theme in Thatcherite education-reform efforts by the middle of the 1980s (Johnson 1991:56). It combined specific concerns about the content of education with particular pedagogical approaches—the content was to become more job training-oriented, while the pedagogy was to shift in a behaviourist direction (Avis 1991:118–19).

The vocationalist focus is not centrally oriented on skills education, despite some of the rhetoric that surrounds it. Rather, it is about the development of new subjectivities more closely attuned to the requirements of the labour market (see Avis 1996a:108). This is about skill if we accept that the "skill" employers demand most is "a willingness to organize one's life according to the demands made by employers and to form an element in a mobile, flexible and malleable workforce" (CCCS 1981:145).

In education the vocationalist direction places a great emphasis on work habits, measurement and identification with the goals of employers. The aim is to form students who fit into the labour market as it exists, rather than challenge its limits. At the core of this vocationalism is an assumption that students and capitalists share a common interest in the preparation of potential workers for whatever their place might be in the labour market, glossing over real conflicts (Avis 1996a:108). Students are taught to define their life goals in terms of the requirements of employers, rather than in terms of their own needs.

The business community quite strongly identifies a "skills" shortage at the level of labour discipline. This is clear in the survey of small businesses conducted by the Canadian Federation of Independent Business (CFIB) (1996) about employment issues. Respondents were asked to comment on the qualities they looked for in young employees. "The four most important are in fact character qualities, which have little to do with education levels. In their young workers, employers look for discipline, reliability, adaptability and the will to stay at the job. Basic education and good communication skills are other important factors. Technical or computer skills and a degree or diploma, while important in demonstrating raw skills, are not seen as the best indicators for measuring the quality of potential new young employees" (CFIB 1996:27).

More than 45 percent of those surveyed reported that they had trouble finding qualified people to hire (CFIB 1996:28). Most (68 percent) of those who reported this trouble identified a lack of potential employees with particular skills in their locality. The report discusses the sectors in which these shortages are most reported (manufacturing, transportation and communication sectors), but does not elaborate on which specific skills are in short supply.[7] A smaller number of employers (13 percent) identified specific problems with basic language and numbers skills (29). At the same time, almost half of those reporting difficulties finding qualified employees also identified problems with labour discipline:

A disturbingly high 45 per cent also said that worker indifference and poor work attitudes were at least partially responsible for the problem. These concerns are related to the fact that many small businesses have to compete with social assistance payments for workers. In other cases, business owners believe that workers' wage expectations are too high for the type of job performed. (CFIB 1996:29)

This construction of the problem of labour discipline maps together indifference, bad work habits, overly high wage expectations and a "weakness" for social programs. The emphasis on labour discipline issues in the CFIB report corresponds with the findings of a survey of United States employers that reported that only five percent saw educational or skill requirements as increasing, while 80 percent described their primary concern as the work habits and social comportment of potential employees (Commission on the Skills of the American Workforce 1990, cited in Mishel and Teixeira 1991:24).

The Canadian Chamber of Commerce Task Force on Education and Training (TFET 1989) discussed a number of employer concerns about the preparation of young people for the labour market: the lack of certain basic skills (reading, writing and analytical and interpersonal skills); underdeveloped work habits; a lack of knowledge of the labour market and employment opportunities; an undue emphasis on academic as opposed to vocational courses;

obsolete approaches and equipment in vocational education; and an insufficient emphasis on overcoming the stereotypes that, for example, discourage women from pursuing math and the sciences.

The new vocationalism represents an attempt to reorient the educational system to address these and similar complaints from business. The professed aim is a closer integration of the school system with the labour market, to develop students who are better prepared for the world of work. Before examining the ways in which this is to be achieved, we must examine the claim about attuning education to the needs of the labour market.

Skills Planning in a "Free" Market

The very nature of the capitalist "free" labour makes specific job training on the basis of a detailed planning process both impossible and undesirable from the perspective of employers. The employment demand and occupational structure of capitalist societies changes constantly, albeit at a highly uneven and unpredictable pace. A paper on skills shortages published by the Applied Research Branch of Human Resources Development Canada puts this clearly. "Economic theory suggests that skills shortages and surpluses are expected to be a permanent feature of decentralized labour markets" (Roy, Henson and Lavoie 1996:58). Further, the emphasis on continuous improvement and constant change built into lean production methods makes skills-planning particularly difficult at the present time (see Avis 1996b:75–76).

Even if it were possible to predict the occupational needs for a decade hence, it would not suit employers to have an exact match between supply and demand. While employers prefer to avoid labour shortages, they often benefit from situations of oversupply that weaken unions, drive down wages and allow for greater management control over the process of hiring and firing. There is therefore a long history of employer ambivalence about vocationalism in education. Employers have often seen vocational schooling that focuses too directly on narrow training as an intrusion into the free labour market and the workplace (Davies 1986:43–44). Capitalists do not necessarily want employees who know how to do the job "right" because that would interfere with management's prerogative to tell them precisely how to do it. Nor do they want graduates to feel entitled to a particular kind of job.

It is not necessarily obvious, then, that neo-liberal governments should be pushing for state intrusion into the job training realm at a time when a rapidly changing occupational structure makes the identification of future needs virtually impossible. The need for "flexibility" (to use a term that is popular with management) in conditions of rapid change would seem to constitute a strong argument for general rather than vocational education: "In light of considerable uncertainty about future requirements for specific skills and the increased importance of workplace-centered learning, there is growing consensus that the educational system should place greater emphasis on the transmission of fundamental skills" (Wolfe 1989:14). But the new vocationalism in education is not really about fine-tuning the school system to particular occupational configurations and job-specific competencies. Instead, it represents a new approach to preparing students' subjectivities for the changing worlds of work, including both paid and domestic labour.

Liberal education employed a relatively

indirect approach to preparing students for work, subordinating it to a larger process of moral formation. The goal of liberal education was to cultivate citizens, raising the cultural level of the presumably vulgar masses as a precondition to their full participation in society as citizens. This required a complex balance between the proscription of "indigenous" cultural forms among workers and oppressed peoples and the creation of new cultural spaces that provided for inclusion conditional on the internalization of particular habits and values. The complex balance has always been a terrain of class struggle.

The cultural apparatus of citizenship prepared people for the world of work in various ways. At the core of the liberal educational system is the acceptance of authority, although in complex ways that combine punishment, deference to "expertise" and self-regulation. Time-discipline is deeply internalized to the point of naturalization. The individual who emerges at the end of the process of liberal education is self-active and self-regulating, accepting in "normal times" the horizons of possibility imposed by existing social relations. Of course, this acceptance is often partial and contradictory.

Undermining the Culture of Citizenship

The problem is that capital is seeking to shift those horizons of possibility in the effort to form a lean world. This means undermining the culture of citizenship. Lloyd and Thomas (1998) argue that one of the central aspects of the cultivation of citizenship was the creation of a pedagogical space that combined the formal equality of students with authority relations based on the act of attending to the teacher.[8] The teacher role combines surveillance and punishment with exposition based on presumed expertise and disinterest. Education thus plays a key role in creating the space for the formation of an "imagined community" oriented around the capitalist state:[9] "What is practically required to effect this ideal is the moral formation of the citizen by an increasingly specialized cultural, not technical, pedagogy that occupies a separate space in its own right—a space that is steadily delineated by the state for society" (Lloyd and Thomas 1998:146).

The looser connection between liberal education and the world of work is actually central to the formation of citizens. The creation of a more abstract realm in the classroom allows for the creation of a supposedly neutral space in which the real inequalities, conflicts and interests of everyday life can be (formally) put aside. "In effect, education is the process which draws the subject from immediacy and particularism, from a class perspective, to a general perspective through which he can be united, not only with middle class reformers, but with the nation as a whole, as citizens" (Lloyd and Thomas 1998:132).

The construction of a supposedly neutral space of culture is conceived as the place of true humanity, in which the person who is fragmented by the complex divisions of labour in contemporary society is put back together again (Hunter 1990:163–67; Lloyd and Thomas 1998:117). All of this is founded on the constitution of economics, politics and culture as separate spheres of existence in capitalist society (Lloyd and Thomas 1998:80). The space of culture is thus neutralized by leaving aside politics and economics, and rising above them into the moral domain of true humanity.

In short, liberal education relies heavily on the appearance of neutrality in the preparation of individuals for their place in capitalist society. It does not demean students by treating them as mere economic units (see the Hall-Dennis report, PCAOESO 1968:27). Nor does it insult them by preaching a specific political creed. Rather, it elevates people, turning vulgar children into worthy citizens. Of course, this process is not nearly so innocent of politics and economics as it pretends. Through liberal education, students are taught (objectively) that the limits of capitalist society are the natural and eternal boundaries of human possibility. Thus their personal horizons of possibility are caught up within the existing world of the labour market, the family form and organized or commercialized leisure.

The new vocationalism represents a willingness on the part of education reformers to dispense with this appearance of neutrality. The lean world has less room for the aesthetic realm of culture and its pretensions of disinterest. Politics and culture are to be bluntly subordinated to economics as social life is reoriented sharply towards the market. Education must prepare students for their place in the market: as sellers of their capacity to work and as consumers of goods and services that include commodified culture. Note that the state is not written out of this account, despite any neo-liberal protestations about free markets. The state must actively pursue the project of placing people in the market, proscribing alternatives and prescribing appropriate codes of behaviour.

There are serious risks in this strategy. The high ground of "disinterest" is being abandoned. This shift has already contributed to an important wave of resistance by teachers, students, trustees and parents. It is quite conceivable that a more "interested" form of education will give rise to new forms of contestation. But capitalists and state policy-makers are clearly willing to take risks to reshape society in ways they see as more advantageous.

Developing a Market Orientation

The new vocationalism serves to orient education to the market. There is a constituency for this market-defined conception of relevance. Students facing a dismal labour market are likely to be somewhat sympathetic to the idea that education should provide them with competitive advantages. Parents may have some sympathy for the direction of these reforms as they seek out opportunities for their children to succeed. Corrigan put it quite starkly: "Put in its extreme form, a further commodification of education will only work because, for a significant section of parents, their children represent commodities through which they realize themselves" (Corrigan 1988:30). Further, the intensive commodification of everyday life in capitalist society and the entry of large portions of the working class into consumer society have paved the way for an ideology of the market that emphasizes diversity, choice and self-realization rather than cruelty, dislocation and the chronic inability to match resources to needs. The meaning of the market is different in a society where shopping is a major leisure activity.

Vocationalism is a central means by which education is being reoriented towards the market. The goal of lean schooling is to teach students how to realize themselves through the market, both by marketing themselves and meeting their needs through the market. In the language of OMET (1996d:6), students are to "develop enterprising skills and attitudes such as self-reliance, network-building, informed risk taking and flexibility." This means that school life must be redefined in terms of an increased emphasis on work rather than socialization of the "whole person," a raised level of competition to meet standards and not fail, an individualization of responsibility, and a remodelling of pedagogical relationships to cast students as developing entrepreneurs and consumers rather than budding citizens.

The new vocationalism, then, is part of the orientation towards the market. It represents an attempt to retool schools to fit in with "post-Fordist economic culture" (Arnold 1996:234). This moves what has been described in the British context as "enterprise culture" to the heart of the educational system (see Deem 1994:30). Students are to commodify themselves, to develop the competencies and habits that will suit the needs of the ultimate consumer, their employer (see Jackson 1987:355). This involves a sharp turn towards a utilitarian education in which work discipline and required skills become the supreme achievement. The "neutral" orientation of education towards meeting the needs of employers thinly veils an ideological alignment of schooling with pro-business politics (see Tasker and Packham 1994:154).

The shift towards a new vocationalism can be found at all levels in the Ontario educational system. One of the important ways that it is being accomplished at the Grade 1–9 levels is through a focus on "outcomes-based" curriculum, which was reflected in the 1995 Common Curriculum and has been intensified by the subsequent Harris reforms.[10] The focus is on the measurement of observable results so that the "content, learning activities, and learning resources are means for achieving outcomes, not ends in themselves" (Wideman 1995:4). Nancy Jackson (1987:356–58) argues that outcomes-based learning has its roots in Taylorist scientific management and focuses on the development of those competencies that

employers define as desirable. Outcomes-based learning is the pedagogical foundation for the utilitarian education represented by the new vocationalism.

The new vocationalism imposes elements of a work orientation onto schooling from a very early age. Beginning in Grade 1 students are to compile a portfolio that reflects their "progress in the areas of learner, interpersonal and career development" (OMET 1996d:12). This portfolio is to include evidence of their achievements, documentation of extracurricular activities and personal reflections. By Grade 7 it is to include an annual education plan with identified goals; by Grade 9 or 10 it is to include "the student's tentative post-secondary destination" (OMET 1996d:12). The portfolio is both an "objective" source of information for career planning and the beginnings of an orientation towards self-marketing.

This portfolio is an important part of the policy to "teach career awareness early and throughout the students' education" (OMET 1996d:2). Even in the Grade 1–6 curriculum students are expected to "make connections with the world of work" (OMET 1996d:5). In Grades 7–9 students will begin "to consider choices among real alternatives that will affect their lives and careers"; by Grades 10–12 they are to "target career options" (OMET 1996d:6). Of course, this is a lean world where the best laid plans may go awry and so students should learn to "make choices without losing the flexibility to respond to changing circumstances" (OMET 1996d:6).

A similar emphasis on career planning was a feature of educational restructuring in Thatcher's Britain. Phil Hodkinson (1996) argued that the career-planning strategies that were promoted there had little to do with the ways young people actually navigate through the job market. The assumption underlying "career planning" is that young people should use technically rational decision-making in their "choice" of a career. The career planning model assumes the young person should dispassionately assess her or his own capacities, thoroughly examine the actual possibilities available in the job market (now and in the future) and then make a rational choice. "Such a technical view of decision-making assumes that the process is fundamentally unproblematic, beyond the engineering difficulty of improving information and guidance" (Hodkinson 1996:124).

Hodkinson (1996:125–27) found that this technically rational approach to career planning did not fit with the actual experiences of young people finding their way into paid employment. They used a more complex process that brought together their actual contacts in the work world; their own aspirations and tastes; the aspirations others (for example, parents) had for them; and their work-related experiences, which could reinforce or erode their desire for a particular direction.

Career planning is difficult at any time in a capitalist economy, let alone in a period of rapid restructuring. The problem of "transition from school to work" has much more to do with chronic youth unemployment than with the job-search skills of young people. It is difficult to imagine that a career-planning approach that does not engage with the real world that students inhabit is going to have a huge impact on their actual job-market experiences.

However, the orientation of education around a rationalized conception of career planning does have important ideological implications. It places the responsibility for success or failure in the job market on the shoulders of individual students. It hides the

real obstacles to procuring "satisfactory employment" (a contradictory term at the best of times). The "career planning" model ignores the very real constraints and opportunities that young people face as a result of their location in relations of structured inequality (Hodkinson 1996:121).

Career planning places a labour-market orientation at the centre of the educational experience so that students are prepared to sell themselves. Education is then oriented to the needs of employers, who are the ultimate consumers of students' capacity to work (see Dickson 1991:110). It then opens the door to new "partners" from the business community who can help orient students to the "real world" of what employers want in a workforce (see OMET 1996d:7).

The career planning orientation also imparts a "lean ethos" to students, teaching them that education (and other aspects of life) should be approached instrumentally as a means to the only end that counts: the world of work. The 40 hours of forced "volunteer" work in the community similarly contributes to imparting the "lean ethos." Being a productive citizen means working for free as well as being paid as we all pitch in together to fill the void left by cuts to social programs. The compulsory community service is to be paired with an increased emphasis on cooperative education and work placements to offer students "real-life experience" (OMET 1998). "Real life" in a lean world means work, generally under supervision.

At the post-secondary level, it is arguable that this lean ethos underlies much of the shift away from the liberal arts currently in place in universities. It seems highly unlikely that it is actually a question of skills. Above, I argued that insofar as there is a real shift in skill requirements, it is actually about an increased need for "intellective" skills. It would seem that a liberal arts education would fit the bill. Yet the liberal arts seem to be going out of fashion as educational restructuring continues. The problem with the liberal arts seems to be that they are not "practical" enough (see OECD 1993:28–30) but there is every reason to believe that a liberal education contributes to the development of "intellective" skills. The concern seems to be less practicality as such (that is, the applicability of learned skills to the world of work) than it is instrumentality (the idea that every aspect of schooling should be assessed only in terms of its apparent utility in the world of work). This instrumentality is concerned with the assertion of utility in the workplace rather than the development of the skills actually required. It is rather like a competitive swimmer who refuses to lift weights and only wants to prepare for a race by doing something useful: swimming.

We are seeing an important shift towards a more instrumental ethos in education. The University of Phoenix, with its business-oriented curriculum, part-time teaching faculty and heavy use of information technologies, is in many ways the model for a lean post-secondary institution (or enterprise) that has dispensed with many of the practices of older liberal arts institutions. This university is now being recognized in Canada (British Columbia and Ontario) as part of the new opening towards privatized post-secondary education. An article in *New Yorker* magazine described discussion in classes at the University of Phoenix: "[i]n this class and the others I attended the students were engaged and the discussion was spirited. What was a little hard to get used to, though, was the lack of intellectual, as opposed to professional, curiosity. Ideas had value only insofar as they could be put to use—if they could *do* something for you" (Traub 1997:121).

This lack of "intellectual curiosity" may actually be a deficit when it comes to learning generic skills. I would argue that the instrumental approach to education has little to do with skills and a great deal to do with attitudes. The lean ethos does not fit comfortably with the rather open-ended and contemplative tradition of the liberal arts.

Endnotes

1 There are two versions of this speech issued from Premier Harris' office, one of which omits the specific reference to sociology and geography.

2 The near doubling of enrolments is discussed in Goodall (1994:41). See also Canadian Educational Statistics Council (1996:115) discussing the dramatic increase in university participation rates from 1977–78 until 1992–93. The proportion of 18–24 year olds attending university jumped from 11 percent in 1985 to 19.5 percent in 1993.

3 For an excellent critique of the class bias in streaming, see Curtis, Livingstone and Smaller (1992).

4 The idea that measurement was in large part aimed at identifying abilities rather than teaching them drew on an early discussion of Thatcherite education reforms which suggested that the "back to basics" approach was aimed at "revealing natural differences in ability" and achieving "competitive differentiation" (CCCS 1981:251).

5 This is not to argue that generic skills cannot be learned in more vocationally grounded ways. Indeed, in many ways the aim of education should be to bring together our physical and intellectual work on the world and to move between concrete practices and more abstract generalizations. The separation of academic and vocational training limits these possibilities.

6 Parker and Slaughter (1994) discuss management by stress at the level of the firm. I would argue that the same conception can be applied more broadly at the level of society as a whole.

7 The report also notes that "businesses in the services sector are less likely than those in the goods producing sectors to report shortages, even though service sector employment tends to be faster growing" (CFIB 1996:28).

8 Hunter (1988:59–61) discussed this space in terms of the formation of a disciplinary regime through a process of sympathetic surveillance by the teacher in the classroom and the playground.

9 The term "imagined community" derives from Anderson (1983:16).

10 The Common Curriculum began as a project of the Liberal Peterson government and was completed towards the end of the Rae NDP government (Wideman 1995:2–3). It is an important reminder that educational restructuring was well underway before the Harris Tories were elected.

References

Anderson, Benedict. 1983. *Imagined Communities: Reflections on the Origin and Spread of Nationalism*. London: Verso.

Arnold, Michael. 1996. "The Hi-Tech, Post-Fordist School." *Interchange*, 273, 274: 225–50.

Avis, James.1996a. "The Enemy Within: Quality and Managerialism in Education." In James Avis, Martin Bloomer, Geoff Esland, Denis Glesson and Phil Hodkinson (eds). *Knowledge and Nationhood: Education, Politics and Work* (London: Cassell), pp. 105–20.

____. 1996b. "The Myth of the Post-Fordist Society." In James Avis, Martin Bloomer, Geoff Esland, Denis Glesson and Phil Hodkinson. *Knowledge and Nationhood: Education, Politics and Work* (London: Cassell), pp. 71–83.

____. 1991. "The Strange Fate of Progressive Education." In Education Group II, Department of Cultural Studies. *Education Limited* (London: Unwin Hyman), pp. 31–86, 114–39.

Battagelo, Dave. 1996. "Adult Ed Business Program Facing Axe." *Windsor Star*, 10 May, A3.

Braverman, Harry. 1974. *Labor and Monopoly Capital*. New York: Monthly Review Press.

Canadian Chamber of Commerce Task Force on Education and Training (TFET). 1989. *Putting Business into Training: A Guide to Investing in People*. Ottawa: Canadian Chamber of Commerce.

Canadian Education Statistics Council. 1996. *A Statistical Portrait of Education at the University Level in Canada*. Ottawa: Statistics Canada.

Canadian Federation of Independent Business (CFIB). 1996. *On Hire Ground*. Toronto: CFIB.

Centre for Contemporary Cultural Studies (CCCS). 1981. *Unpopular Education: Schooling and Democracy in England Since 1944*. London: Hutchison.

Corrigan, Paul. 1988. "Gerbil: The Education Reform Bill." *Capital and Class*, 35, pp. 29–33.

Curtis, Bruce, D.W. Livingstone and Harry Smaller. 1992. *Stacking the Deck: The Streaming of Working-Class Kids in Ontario Schools*. Toronto: OS/OS.

Davies, Bernard. 1986. *Threatening Youth: Towards a National Youth Policy*. Milton Keynes: Open University Press.

Deem, Rosemary. 1994. "Free Marketeers or Good Citizens? Education Policy and Lay Participation in the Administration of Schools." *British Journal of Education Studies*, 421, pp. 23–37.

Dickson, Harley D. 1991. "The Three 'D's' of Vocational Training: Deskilling, Disempowerment and Devaluation." In T. Wotherspoon (ed.). *Hitting the Books: The Politics of Educational Retrenchment* (Toronto: Garamond Press), pp. 101–18.

Dunk, Thomas, Stephen McBride and Randle W. Nelson. 1996. "Introduction." In T. Dunk, S. McBride and R.W. Nelson (eds.). *The Training Trap: Ideology, Training and the Labour Market. Socialist Studies, Volume 11*. Winnipeg/Halifax: Society for Socialist Studies/Fernwood, pp. 1–12.

Economic Council of Canada (ECC). 1992. *A Lot to Learn: Education and Training in Canada*. Ottawa: Minister of Supply and Services.

Education Improvement Commission. 1997. *The Road Ahead: A Report on Learning, Class Size and Staffing*. Toronto: Education Improvement Commission.

Elger, Tony. 1982. "Braverman, Capital Accumulation and Deskilling." In Stephen Wood (ed.), *The Degradation of Work?* London: Hutchison, pp. 23–53.

Eves, Ernie. 1999. *1999 Ontario Budget, Budget Speech: Foundations for Prosperity*. Toronto: Queen's Printer.

Garrahan, Philip and Paul Stewart. 1992. *The Nissan Enigma: Flexibility and Work in a Local Economy*. London: Mansell.

Goodall, Alan. 1994. "Two Decades of Change: College Postsecondary Enrolment 1971–1991," *Education Quarterly Review*, pp. 41–56.

Harris, Mike. 1997. "Notes for remarks by The Honourable Mike Harris, MPP, Premier of Ontario, Council of Ontario Universities Summit," Toronto: Office of the Premier.

Hoddinott, Susan and Jim Overton. 1996. "Dismantling Public Provision of Adult Basic Education: The Anti-Literacy Politics of Newfoundland's Literacy Campaign." In Thomas Dunk, Stephen McBride and Randle W. Nelson (eds.). *The Training Trap: Ideology, Training and the Labour Market. Socialist Studies, Volume 11*. Winnipeg/Halifax: Society for Socialist Studies/Fernwood.

Hodkinson, Phil. 1996. "Careership: The Individual, Choices and Markets in the Transition into Work." In James Avis, Martin Bloomer, Geoff Esland, Denis Glesson and Phil Hodkinson. *Knowledge and Nationhood: Education, Politics and Work*. London: Cassell, pp. 121–39.

Holmes, John. 1997. "In Search of Competitive Efficiency: Labour Process Flex in Canadian Newsprint Mills," *Canadian Geographer*, 411, pp. 7–25.

Hunter, Ian. 1990. "Personality as Vocation: The Political Rationality of the Humanities," *Economy and Society*, 194, pp. 153–92.

____. 1988. *Culture and Government: The Emergence of Literary Education*. London: Macmillan.

Jackson, Nancy. 1992. "Training Needs: An Objective Science?" In Nancy Jackson (ed.). *Training for What? Labour Perspectives on Skill Training*. Toronto: Our Schools/Our Selves Foundation.

____. 1987. "Skill Training in Transition: Implications for Women." In J. Gaskell and A. McLaren (eds.), *Women and Education: A Canadian Perspective*. Calgary: Detselig.

Jessop, Bob. 1991. "The Welfare State in Transition from Fordism to Post-Fordism." In Bob Jessop, Hans Kastendick, Klaus Neilsen, and Ove K. Pedersen (eds.). *The Politics of Flexibility: Restructuring State and Industry in Britain, Germany, and Scandinavia*. Aldershot: Edward Elgar, pp. 82–105.

Johnson, Richard. 1991. "A New Road to Serfdom? A Critical History of the 1988 Act." In Education Group II, Department of Cultural Studies, *Education Limited*. London: Unwin Hyman, pp. 31–86.

Lewchuk, Wayne and David Robertson. 1997. "Working Conditions Under Lean Production: A Worker-Based Benchmarking Study." In Paul Stewart (ed.). *Beyond Japanese Management: The End of Modern Times?* London: Frank Cass, pp. 60–81.

Lewington, Jennifer. 1998. "Going to Bat for Adult Education." *The Globe and Mail*, 12 March, p. A8.

Livingstone, David W. 1999. *The Education–Jobs Gap: Underemployment or Economic Democracy*. Toronto: Garamond Press.

____. 1996. "Wasted Education and Withered Work: Reversing the 'Postindustrial' Education-Jobs Optic." In Thomas Dunk, Stephen McBride and Randle W. Nelson (eds.). *The Training Trap: Ideology, Training and the Labour Market. Socialist Studies, Volume 11*. Winnipeg/ Halifax: Society for Socialist Studies/Fernwood.

Lloyd, David and Paul Thomas. 1998. *Culture and the State*. London: Routledge.

Mackie, Richard. 2000. "Ontario Colleges Get More Cash to Cope with Growing Enrolment." *The Globe and Mail*. 22 February, A7.

Martell, George. 1995. *A New Education Politics: Bob Rae's Legacy and the Response of the OSSTF*. Toronto: James Lorimer and Our School/Our Selves.

Meaghan, Diane and François Cassis. 1995. "Quality Education and Other Myths." *Our Schools/Our Selves*, 71, pp. 37–53.

Mishel, Lawrence and Ruy A. Teixiera. 1991. *The Myth of the Coming Labor Shortage: Jobs, Skills and Incomes of America's Workforce 2000*. Washington: Economic Policy Institute.

Moody, Kim. 1997. *Workers in a Lean World*. London: Verso.

Morissette, René, John Myles and Garnett Picot. 1995. "Earnings Polarization in Canada, 1969–1991." In Keith G. Banting and Charles M. Beach (eds.). *Labour Market Polarization and Social Policy Reform*. Kingston: School of Policy Studies, Queen's University, pp. 23–50.

Ontario, Government of. 1996. *Doing Better for Less: Introducing Ontario's Business Plans*. Toronto: Government of Ontario.

Ontario Ministry of Education and Training (OMET). 1998a. "Backgrounder: Access to Opportunities." Toronto: Ministry of Education and Training. 29 May.

____. 1998b. "Backgrounder: Highlights of the New High School Program." Toronto: Ministry of Education and Training.

____. 1996a. "Excellence in Education: High School Reform." Toronto: Ministry of Education and Training.

____. 1996b. "Excellence, Accessibility, Responsibility: Report of the Advisory Panel on Future Direction for Postsecondary Education." Toronto: Ministry of Education and Training.

____ 1996c. "Curriculum for Ontario Secondary Schools." Toronto: Ministry of Education and Training.

____. 1996d. "Choices into Action: Guidance and Career Education Policy, Grades 1 to 12." Toronto: Ministry of Education and Training. Detailed Discussion Document.

Organisation for Economic Cooperation and Development (OECD). 1993. *Higher Education and Employment: The Case of Humanities and Social Sciences.* Paris: OECD.

Parker, Mike and Jane Slaughter. 1994. *Working Smart: A Union Guide to Participation Programs and Reengineering.* Detroit: Labor Notes.

Provincial Committee on Aims and Objectives of Education in the Schools of Ontario (PCAOESO). 1968. *Report.* Toronto: Ontario Department of Education (Hall-Dennis).

Rinehart, James, Christopher Huxley and David Robertson. 1997. *Just Another Car Factory? Lean Production and Its Discontents.* Ithaca, New York: ILR Press.

Roy, Richard, Harold Henson and Claude Lavoie. 1996. "A Primer on Skill Shortages in Canada." Ottawa: Applied Research Branch, Strategic Policy, Human Resources Development Canada. R-96-8E.

Sheppard, Michelle. 1998. "Trustees Vote to Cut Adult Education." *Toronto Star*, 16 April, A1.

Stager, David. 1999. "Labour Market Trends and Projections for Systems Analysts and Computer Programmers in Canada." Ottawa: Applied Research Branch, Strategic Policy, Human Resources Development Canada. R-99-4E.

Statistics Canada. 1995. "The Daily." 19 September.

Tasker, Mary and David Packham. 1994. "Changing Cultures? Government Intervention in Higher Education 1987–93." *British Journal of Education Studies*, 422, pp. 150–62.

Traub, James. 1997. "Drive-Thru U.: Higher Education for People Who Mean Business." *The New Yorker*, 20 & 27 (October), pp. 114–23.

Vision 2000. 1990. *Vision 2000: Quality and Opportunity: A Summary.* Toronto: Ontario Council of Regents.

Wideman, Ron. 1995. "The Common Curriculum: Policies and Outcomes, Grades 1–9." *Orbit*, 261, pp. 2–5.

Wolfe, David. 1989. "New Technology and Education: A Challenge for the Colleges." In Vision 2000 Study Team 2 (eds.). *Vision 2000: Colleges and the Changing Economy* Toronto: Ontario Council of Regents.

Womack, J.P., Daniel T. Jones and Daniel Roos. 1990. *The Machine that Changed the World.* New York: Harper Collins.

Wood, Stephen.1982. "Introduction." In Stephen Wood (ed.). *The Degradation of Work?* London: Hutchison, pp. 11–23.

Zuboff, Shoshana. 1988. *In the Age of the Smart Machine: The Future of Work and Power.* New York: Basic Books.

SECTION VII: EDUCATION, TRAINING, AND SKILLS IN A KNOWLEDGE-BASED ECONOMY

Critical Thinking Questions

Chapter 13: Living in the Credential Gap: Responses to Underemployment and Underqualification, David W. Livingstone

1. Taking into account Livingstone's findings, what is the likelihood that you will be living in the credential gap during your first 10 years in the labour market following your graduation from university? Could this experience shake your faith that the pursuit of higher education is a guaranteed route to financial security and personal fulfillment?

2. Would it be more appropriate to make changes to the education system or to the labour market to ensure that Canadian workers are able to develop their full potential?

3. What are the long-term consequences for the Canadian economy of a growth in the number of underemployed and overqualified workers?

Chapter 14: Education for an Information Age?, Alan Sears

1. Discuss Sears's argument that the new standards and measurement systems introduced in Ontario high schools during the 1990s were implemented to meet the requirements of the neo-liberal business agenda.

2. Should the public education system in your province respond to the changing needs of the global economy or should it be built around a liberal education that encourages the development of generic skills?

3. Do the reforms to the education system discussed by Sears conceal or make more transparent the hierarchies and inequalities of a class-based society?

Recommended Readings

Cohen, Marjorie Griffin (ed.). 2003. *Training the Excluded for Work: Access and Equity for Women, Immigrants, First Nations, Youth and People with Low Income.* Vancouver: UBC Press. A series of articles that demonstrate how government policies surrounding training programs have resulted in a heavy reliance on private and market-based training schemes, a shift in direction that has undermined equity instead of addressing social inequalities.

Livingstone, David W. and Peter H. Sawchuk. 2004. *Hidden Knowledge: Organized Labour in the Information Age.* Aurora: Garamond Press. These detailed case studies of the learning opportunities and practices of workers in various Canadian work settings challenge dominant theories of learning and skills, and question some of the widely held assumptions about the knowledge-based economy.

Marquardt, Richard. 1998. *Enter at Your Own Risk: Canadian Youth and the Labour Market.* Toronto: Between the Lines. An examination of the complex and difficult transitions between school and the labour market that Canadian youths face in the turbulent economy of late 20th-century capitalism.

Sears, Alan. 2003. *Retooling the Mind Factory: Education in a Lean State.* Aurora: Garamond Press. An exploration of the reform of the Ontario school system, a key policy initiative of the neo-liberal "Common Sense Revolution" of the 1990s that was founded on a glorification of the free market and a rejection of non-market alternatives. The book focuses on economic, political, ideological and cultural dimensions of education reform.

Turk, James L. (ed.) 2000. *The Corporate Campus: Commercialization and the Dangers to Canada's Colleges and Universities.* Toronto: James Lorimer and Company. A collection of articles that scrutinize recent transformations in post-secondary education in Canada. The articles show that these changes are moving institutions of higher learning away from a focus on the public interest and remodelling them according to corporate interests.

Related Websites

Centre for the Study of Education and Work

www.oise.utoronto.ca/csew/

The Centre for the Study of Education and Work focuses on learning and work issues. The Centre develops research and teaching programs and promotes policy initiatives connected to both the paid and unpaid workplace.

InFocus Programme on Skills, Knowledge, and Employability (IFP/SKILLS)

www.ilo.org/public/english/employment/skills

Through advocacy activities, knowledge development and services, this program of the International Labour Office promotes the improvement of training policies and programs worldwide, with special emphasis on training strategies that support the integration of groups that are disadvantaged in the labour market. The "Publications and Working Papers" page under the "Information Resources" section of the site includes documents on various topics, such as lifelong learning and skills training for youth.

National Literacy Program

www.hrsdc.gc.ca/en/gateways/nav/top_nav/program/nls.shtml

The federal government's National Literacy Program works to promote literacy as an essential component of a learning society and to make Canada's social, economic and political life more accessible to people with weak literacy skills. The site contains information on national and international literacy surveys, and on other relevant topics.

School to Work Transitions

http://www.arts.ualberta.ca/transition/index.htm

The site includes publications based on results from longitudinal studies of the school-to-work transition of Alberta youth undertaken by researchers at the University of Alberta. It also includes data analyses currently underway, and plans for future follow-up surveys.

Work and Learning Network for Research and Policy

http://www.wln.ualberta.ca/

The Work and Learning Network is a community of individuals and organizations engaged in research related to work and learning. The Network has a Western Canadian focus and is interested in issues pertaining to diversity, equity and workplace reform.

Work and Lifelong Learning Research Network

http://www.wallnetwork.ca/index.html

The Work and Lifelong Learning Research Network is a project of the Centre for the Study of Education and Work at York University. The network seeks to bring visibility to current learning and work issues and trends.

Section VIII

The Labour Movement in Transition

THE POSTWAR PERIOD of economic growth and the institutionalization and attenuation of class conflict through the establishment of a legalistic industrial relations system provided the labour movement with more security and a certain degree of power to fight for the improvement of working conditions at the level of the workplace, and to contribute to the establishment of progressive social and employment policies at the broader societal level. The dramatic weakening in the economic and political influence of unions over the past three decades represents one of the most significant developments in the world of work. The two articles in this section of the book take a close look at the demise of the Canadian labour movement and the consequent whittling down of workers' rights and freedoms in the wake of the consolidation of neo-liberalism on a global scale. Also of concern is the potential for the labour movement to link with other progressive movements and participate in larger political projects to create better futures for workers and their families, especially in light of the fundamental challenges faced by unions.

The article by Leo Panitch and Donald Swartz is taken from the most recent edition of their book *From Consent to Coercion* in which they argue that the past three decades have witnessed a continual and coercive assault on trade union rights and freedoms in Canada as federal and provincial governments of every political stripe have embraced the neo-liberal business agenda. They focus on the deepening of this coercive regime by successive federal Liberal governments and by provincial governments across Canada throughout the 1990s and into the first few years of the new millennium. The authors demonstrate that the federal Liberal government's promises to reverse the regressive labour legislation and other anti-labour actions by its Conservative predecessor never materialized. Instead, they discuss in detail how the Liberal government led a sustained attack on workers' freedoms. Panitch and Swartz then examine measures adopted by provincial governments across the country that have resulted in the suppression of workers' rights. They not only discuss the deleterious effects on workers' rights of the adoption of the

Common Sense Revolution in Ontario by the Conservative government, but also pay attention to the policies adopted by New Democratic provincial governments that have contributed to the coercive regime. In the final section of the article, the authors take a closer look at more recent Supreme Court rulings in cases pertaining to workers' freedom of association, and find that the higher court has been inclined to protect only certain trade union rights and only in a limited manner. Panitch and Swartz's overall analysis highlights that developments in the legislation governing industrial relations in Canada over the past 15 years have resulted in a gradual suppression of those elements of liberal democracy that specifically pertain to workers' rights and freedoms.

The contribution by Sam Gindin and Jim Stanford focuses on the potential for the Canadian labour movement to act as a leading agent for fundamental social transformation in the current context of neo-liberal restructuring. The authors point to the main difficulties and challenges confronting the labour movement as it came to grips with the erosion of the postwar institutionalization of industrial relations and the end of the period of rapid economic growth beginning in the mid-1970s. They discuss efforts by the labour movement to make gains in the workplace, and to ensure its own viability as a progressive movement. They focus on issues such as organizing the unorganized, mobilizing the organized, developing a progressive bargaining agenda, pursuing internal democracy and accountability, rebuilding labour's political voice, and linking with other struggles. Gindin and Stanford identify three developing political projects on Canada's left with which the labour movement must engage in order to build its transformative capacities: the growth of protest movements in civil society (for example, the anti-globalization campaign); concerted efforts to rebuild social democracy; and attempts to revive a socialist left. While Gindin and Stanford recognize that labour has been greatly weakened and continues to be on the defensive following more than two decades of neo-liberalism, they are nonetheless optimistic that the labour movement can play a central role in rekindling an anti-capitalist and transformative movement.

CHAPTER 15

Neo-Liberalism, Labour, and the Canadian State

Leo Panitch and Donald Swartz

Under the law of the land, workers have the right to strike and we have to respect the law of this land.
— PRIME MINISTER JEAN CHRÉTIEN[1]

It is ridiculous to suggest that a so-called emergency piece of legislation should last for an eternity.
— PAUL ANSTEY, Halifax PSAC negotiating team member[2]

The 1990s will probably go down as the most stressful decade for public-sector industrial relations since the inception 25 years earlier of collective bargaining for public sector workers.
— GENE SWIMMER[3]

THE EXTENSION OF a global neo-liberal order, defined in terms of free capital flows, the ascendancy of financial capital, and the spread of commodification into every aspect of social life, led to even greater pressures on organized labour through the 1990s. In the private sector, the turn to lean production methods to meet the growing demands of competitiveness in the global economy dramatically altered the relationship that workers had both to their jobs and to each other.[4] The lean workplace, contracting out and part-time work combined to produce a flexible workforce beset by job insecurity at the very time governments considerably reduced the eligibility for and fund-ing of unemployment insurance and social assistance. Consequently, many workers were forced to accept part-time employment for low pay, while others were required to work more overtime to maintain the same levels of income or to simply keep their jobs.[5] For public-sector workers, these same pressures coincided with an increased downsizing trend by federal and provincial governments. This trend partly reflected a new free market ideology centred on the notion that the state's role in the economy leads to inefficiency and waste, and partly old-fashioned business pressures to reduce the size of fiscal deficits.[6] But it was also a reflection of the state's embrace of neo-liberalism itself, as the operations of government were altered to reflect the logic of the marketplace and to engage the private sector as never before in the direct provision of public services.

Wage settlements through the 1990s ran considerably lower than in the 1980s in both the public and private sectors. It was only through increased hours of work that real wages, which had stagnated over the 1980s, rose somewhat in the 1990s. The difficulty in securing workers' consent to this economic trajectory ensured that federal and provincial governments would continue their assault on trade union freedoms into the 21st century, as suggested in Table 15.1, which summarizes the incidence of back-to-work legislation since 1950.

Clearly, the government resorted to back-to-work legislation more frequently during the 1990s than the 1980s, despite the fact that a wage freeze that took away the bargaining rights of its own employees was in effect until 1997. Many provincial governments also had "6 and 5" type wage freezes in place during much of the decade, making back-to-work legislation redundant. Yet there were still 16 instances of back-to-work legislation in the provinces in the 1990s, and as the wage freezes finally expired at the end of the decade, the use of back-to-work laws by provincial governments reached unprecedented heights.

This chapter begins with an examination of the record of the federal government since the election of the Liberals in 1993. Despite Jean Chrétien's declaration of respect for workers' right to strike, his government not only failed to cancel the 1991 freeze on public employees' wages and hence on collective bargaining imposed by the Tories, but also extended it for two additional years. Within a mere six months of being elected, the federal Liberals resorted to back-to-work legislation to end a legal strike by Vancouver dock workers. We then turn to developments in the provinces, beginning in Ontario with the Common Sense Revolution of the Mike Harris Conservative government that replaced the New Democratic

Table 15.1: Back-to-Work Measures 1950–2002

	Federal	Provincial	Total	Annual Average
1950–1954	1	0	1	0.2
1955–1959	1	1	2	0.4
1960–1964	2	1	3	0.6
1965–1969	2	8	10	2.0
1970–1974	4	12	16	3.4
1975–1979	6	19	25	5.0
1980–1984	1	21	22	4.4
1985–1989	5	22	27	5.4
1990–1994	5	7	12	2.4
1995–1999	4	9	13	2.6
2000–2002	0	16	16	5.3

SOURCES: Compiled from data supplied by Federal-Provincial Relations Branch, Labour Canada; and Canada, Human Resources Development Canada *Labour Program* (annual) 1993–4 to 2001–2. Figures include both legislation and Orders-in-Council.

Party (NDP) in 1995, and ending in British Columbia, where Gordon Campbell's Liberals defeated the NDP government in 2001 and have followed the same stark neo-liberal agenda. Particular attention is given to the records of the NDP governments in the West, where they not only failed to undo many of the repressive measures of their predecessors, but also, as in the case of the NDP in Ontario, made their own contributions to the era of coercion. The chapter concludes with an analysis of the recent Supreme Court rulings in cases pertaining to workers' freedom of association. We show that the court has come to recognize that trade union rights merited some protection, but only insofar as the workers in question were a vulnerable group. Protection did not extend to the rights to bargain or to strike.

The Federal Government in the Chrétien Era

The 1993 general election was a disaster for the Progressive Conservative Party. Popular anger with the Tories ran deep among Canadians, and Brian Mulroney's departure could not save the party from being reduced to two seats in the House of Commons. Against the backdrop of the recession of the early 1990s, new Conservative leader Kim Campbell's assertion that the unemployment rate would not be reduced until the end of the 20th century looked either callous or an abject admission of helplessness. Given also the unpopularity of the NDP in Ontario and the regional politics of both the Reform Party and the Bloc Québécois, it is not surprising that the Liberals won a majority government (albeit with only 41 percent of the popular vote).

The Liberals' campaign document, dubbed the Red Book, had outlined a vision of Canada that was very different from the previous nine years of Tory rule. The party promised to renegotiate the impending North American Free Trade Agreement (NAFTA) to include effective protections for labour and the environment, to scrap the GST, and to abandon the previous government's misguided monetary policies. The Red Book included a commitment to protect social programs, and perhaps more importantly, to take an active role in job creation.[7] Liberal politicians promised to treat public-sector employees with more respect than had the Mulroney government, with Chrétien in particular affirming his party's commitment to free collective bargaining. In fact, he had explicitly declared his opposition to the 1991 legislated wage freeze in a letter to the Professional Institute of the Public Service.[8]

In the event, the Liberals did not take long to stray from their election platform, and to fully embrace, indeed even expand upon, the neo-liberal project inaugurated by the Conservatives. NAFTA was ratified almost immediately, with no substantive changes to the deal. And with only a slight push from the international bond-rating agencies, Finance Minister Paul Martin was allowed to place the deficit issue at the top of the government's agenda.[9] His first budget contained measures that prolonged the 1991 wage freeze for federal public-sector workers (which had been due to end in 1995) for two additional years by extending the life of contracts until 1997, thus unilaterally foreclosing on collective bargaining in the federal public sector. The removal of certain loopholes that under the Tories had permitted some annual increments to be paid to 80,000 employees during the earlier freeze was particularly odious, because its impact was felt the most by the lowest paid workers.[10] Fiscal restraint was accompanied, under the rubric of the New Public Management philosophy, by policies for downsizing, contracting out, and inserting private-sector management techniques into public-sector organizations. By 1998 the Chrétien government had actually gone farther in its pursuit of a neo-liberal downsizing of the state than the Tories, providing well over 50,000 federal employees with "pink slips and running shoes."[11]

No less than three pieces of back-to-work legislation within its first two years in office signalled that the government was not inclined to tolerate any resistance from the unions. The tone was set when 3,500 workers at the Port of Vancouver, having been without a contract for over a year, went on strike in the last week of January 1994. By February 1, the federal government had already appointed a mediator, and back-to-work legislation was tabled on February 8. With all-party support, the bill passed in one day. A year later, 500 foremen at the ports (represented by the International Longshoremen's and Warehousemen's Union) who had been working without a new contract since January 1992 finally struck on March 13, 1995. The federal government again stepped in two days later with back-to-work legislation. This time, there was a more active response from the opposition parties, notably the Bloc Québécois (BQ), which not only argued that the coercive intervention was premature, but also called for a law to ban scabs, to no avail. There is no little irony in the fact that a party dedicated to Quebec sovereignty led the defence of the right to strike on the west coast of Canada.

The West Coast Ports Operations Act 1995 was passed at the mid-point of another strike that would also be ended through the use of legislation. The act revealed how such coercion can produce divisions among unions, while reinforcing unity among the capitalist classes. When the Brotherhood of Maintenance of

Ways Employees in Northern Ontario and southern British Columbia launched successive one-day strikes at CP Rail on March 8 and 9, management responded by locking the workers out, and suspending all pay and benefits. The union knew full well that its decision to extend the strike nationally was bound to provoke back-to-work legislation. The old railway unions had grown so used to this strategy (the first such measure was used in the railways in 1950) that they saw it as inevitable. But the Canadian Auto Workers (CAW), which as a result of recent mergers now represented 4,500 shopcraft workers at CP, felt calling a national strike immediately would therefore be, as Buzz Hargrove put it, "playing into the company's hands." He wanted to use other measures "to force the company back to the bargaining table," while giving shippers time to find alternate means of transportation for their goods.[12] As the Brotherhood went ahead and extended the strike, the CAW tried to find ways of keeping its members on the job, but rank-and-file CAW members, once confronted with a picket line, refused to cross.[13] The rift between the unions would last for the duration of the strike, and grew more dramatic as the dispute spilled over to CN and to VIA, directly involving 10,000 more CAW members. The strike threatened to spill over further to Ford and General Motors due to the lack of parts the plants needed for just-in-time production.[14]

The rail companies were initially divided on the issue of a legislated end to the dispute. But the government soon made clear its intentions not only to go ahead with legislation but also to impose a settlement that leaned towards the employer position on the key issue of job and income security.[15] Major organizations of Canadian capitalists chimed in to lend their support, including the Canadian Industrial Transportation League, with 400 member companies, the Canadian Manufacturers' Association, and individual corporations like GM, Ford, and various mining companies.[16] In contrast to this unity within capital, the tensions between the various railway unions over the issue of strategy highlighted the intense problems with fragmented bargaining under a regime that includes recourse to ad hoc measures to end strikes. This strike also highlighted the weakness of the federal NDP in the 1990s in voicing opposition to the assault on trade union freedoms. Only a single NDP MP, Bill Blaikie, joined the BQ in scuttling attempts by the government to fast-track the legislation. Bloc Leader Lucien Bouchard, who himself had helped the Mulroney Tories pass back-to-work legislation in 1989, now called the Liberals "trigger-happy."[17] Legislation ending the strike was passed on March 26, 1995, supported by the NDP after certain demands for impartiality in arbitration were met. The BQ, however, continued to oppose the legislation right to the end, claiming that the NDP's support for it demonstrated its drift to the political right.

Given the history of struggle for—and against—the right to strike over the previous two decades, it was perhaps inevitable that postal workers would be drawn into a confrontation with the Chrétien government. When, during negotiations, Canada Post announced plans to cut 4,000 jobs, Canadian Union of Postal Workers (CUPW) president Darrell Tingley saw the plan as an attempt to force a strike in order to push the government to use back-to-work legislation. The Alliance of Manufacturers and Exporters, for their part, jumped in to call for the permanent removal of the right to strike for postal workers since they performed an "essential service."[18] Lack of progress in negotiations led the union

to walk on November 20, 1997, one day after the corporation laid off 15,000 workers.

Initially, the Prime Minister seemed to promise not to intervene, going so far as to say (and thereby blithely ignoring the record of Liberal governments in which he served) that "Under the law of the land, workers have the right to strike and we have to respect the law of this land."[19] Mediation started on November 24, but Canada Post was in no mood to compromise, encouraged by inflammatory statements by Alfonso Gagliano, the Public Works Minister, which explicitly contradicted the Prime Minister's initial statement.[20] Gagliano, who was responsible for Canada Post, was later to leave office under a cloud of corruption allegations. By the end of the month, the government introduced back-to-work legislation. It imposed a settlement with a wage increase less than that already agreed to by Canada Post, and included a clause referring to the need of Canada Post to remain competitive. Several opposition members refused to give the bill unanimous consent, and even the Reform Party called the imposed settlement "mean spirited." The NDP, as part of is objection, demanded that the clause dealing with competitiveness be removed for it to give consent to fast-track the bill.[21] The government accordingly removed the clause, but retained reference to Canada Post's need to improve productivity, reach financial stability, and operate efficiently. The imposed wage settlement remained in the final legislation.[22]

The decade reached a climax in a strike by Public Service Alliance of Canada's (PSAC) blue-collar workers in 1999. Because of the Mulroney government's 1991 wage freeze and its three-year extension by the Chrétien government, PSAC members had only received one raise in a nine-year period, with the government's offer only one per cent in each of two years. Shortly after rotating strikes began in mid-January 1999, Treasury Board, in a classic example of recourse to what we have called permanent exceptionalism, suggested that the union was violating the 1991 *Wages and Compensation Act* that had been used to end the last PSAC strike. This assertion sparked a member of the Halifax PSAC negotiating team to remark: "It is ridiculous to suggest that a so-called emergency piece of legislation should last for an eternity."[23] The strategy of rotating strikes continued for several weeks as PSAC sought to avoid calling a full strike, which it believed would lead to back-to-work-legislation. On March 10, PSAC organized a demonstration in Ottawa, bringing in 500 support pickets from Montreal. They were met by a phalanx of riot police with German shepherds, clubs, and pepper spray, foreshadowing the intolerance of the democratic right to protest that was soon to be seen at anti-poverty and anti-globalization demonstrations.[24]

With the looming possibility of disruptions to the delivery of tax returns and grain shipments, the government on March 22 introduced back-to-work legislation (Bill C-76). The bill opportunistically included provisions that would allow the government to order an end to a strike of prison guards represented by PSAC that had not even started yet.[25] With the sword at its neck, the union settled in the early hours of March 24, and won some minor concessions from the settlement provided for in the bill. The government still went ahead with the bill, just in case PSAC members did not ratify the deal. This showed the government's "arrogance" and "hypocrisy," according to Daryl Bean, PSAC's president: "It's offensive to the extreme that a government would proceed with the legislation after a tentative agreement has been reached."[26]

Hypocrisy was indeed a badge that the Liberal government seemed to wear proudly as it reneged on its promises to pursue a better working relationship with government employees. Provincial governments, if they needed any encouragement, could point to the Chrétien government's actions in extending the era of coercion to the 21st century.

Ontario's Common Sense Counter-Revolution

Bob Rae's NDP government had alienated its own supporters when it defined Ontario's fiscal problems in terms of union resistance to public-sector expenditure cuts. The most tragic legacy of this alienation was that it paved the way for the NDP's collapse in the June 1995 election, and for the success of the stark, right-wing discourse of Mike Harris's Common Sense Revolution. The Harris government promised to cut welfare payments, end employment equity, balance the budget, cut taxes, reduce the size of the public-sector labour force, and change labour law via explicitly business-friendly, anti-union measures. And, unlike Rae's NDP and Chrétien's Liberal governments, Harris's Conservatives kept their promises. They infamously started by immediately cutting welfare benefits by 21.6 percent, followed up quickly by Bill 7, the *Labour Relations and Employment Statute Law Amendment Act, 1995.* Bill 7 repealed the progressive sections of the NDP's Bill 40, and replaced it with a model of industrial relations that was dedicated to undermine trade unionism under the guise of promoting "flexibility, productivity and employee involvement in the workplace."[27]

Bill 7 passed without public consultations despite opposition not only from the unions but even from some sectors of capital and the police.[28] The act repealed the ban on scabs, put limits on when unions could call strike votes (no sooner than 30 days prior to the termination of a contract), and set up a system of union certification that required a vote in all cases and made decertification votes easier to call.[29] It also removed successor rights for public-sector unions, because, as Management Board chair, Dave Johnson, put it, "We felt to go down the road to privatization, we needed total flexibility."[30] By the end of the *annus horribilis* of 1995, the Conservatives had also repealed the law that allowed for farm labourers to unionize, ended the Employment Equity program introduced under the NDP, and introduced the notorious *Savings and Restructuring Act* (Bill 26). The latter was an omnibus bill that involved drastic cuts to public expenditures, including cutting 13,000 public-sector workers' jobs, sweeping new powers that allowed Queen's Park to unilaterally restructure municipalities and hospitals, and special requirements that arbitrators respect government concerns in adjudicating disputes with firefighters, police, health workers, and others who did not have the legal right to strike.[31]

The first sign that the Common Sense Revolution was not so common—that it would require considerable coercion to implement—came on the day of the Tories' first Throne Speech, when riot police were let loose on demonstrators on the steps of Queen's Park.[32] This conflict only helped to inspire additional resistance, which soon took shape in an imaginative series of one-day strikes in cities across Ontario, organized by the Ontario Federation of Labour in conjunction with networks of social justice groups. The Days of Action, as they were known, captured widespread national and international attention. Beginning in London on December 11, 1995, the protests continued in Hamilton on February 23 and 24,

1996 (where more than 100,000 marched), in Waterloo on April 19, and in Peterborough on June 24. The strategy reached its apex on October 24 and 25, 1996, when some 200,000 people took over the streets of Toronto, shutting down Bay Street, the Stock Exchange, public transit, and a great many businesses and government offices.[33]

At this point in time, it seemed like the strategy had a great deal of potential. As Sam Gindin argued, its importance lay in that it "went beyond legislative politics and focused on where the real power in our society lies: the banks and private corporations ... went beyond waiting for the next election, and set out to mobilize public support to defend our social rights and, through this, to build a social movement."[34] Yet the movement broke down, in no small part due to divisions over strategy. Most of the private-sector unions, and especially the Steelworkers, wanted to link the strategy to electoral politics by providing the NDP with a platform at the demonstration. The networks of social justice organizations that involved as many as 300 groups in Toronto and were supported by the CAW and most of the public-sector unions, wanted to clearly stress the extra-parliamentary aspect of the movement. Some elements on this side even looked forward to building towards a general strike.[35] The debilitating division over both means and ends led to a five-month delay before the next Day of Action in Sudbury on March 21–22, 1997, which the local labour council failed to endorse, although many unions did contribute funds and organizers.[36] Several smaller protests were organized over the following months, but all of the energy and enthusiasm created through the earlier successes in Hamilton and Toronto had, by then, withered away.

In the event, the Harris government continued its counter-revolution in a manner that targetted union rights in particular. On May 14, 1998 the government moved to prohibit from unionizing people on social assistance who had been forced into "workfare" programs, on the grounds that workfare participants were volunteers.[37] While calling this the *Prevention of Unionization Act* was a rare moment of linguistic honesty, the *Economic Development and Workplace Democracy Act* (Bill 31), introduced on June 4, 1998 was another exercise in Orwellian Newspeak. Along with further barriers to certification and easier rules for decertification, the act empowered the government to ban strikes at certain large industrial construction sites, in the name of boosting investor confidence. Moreover, the act eliminated automatic certification rights when the Labour Board found that an employer had used intimidation to sway workers away from unionization drives.[38] Then, following the Harris government's re-election in June 1999, Bill 139, the *Labour Relations Amendment Act, 2000*, was passed, which made it mandatory for employers in unionized workplaces to post procedures for decertification, provided for a one-year cooling off period, and fast-tracked applications to decertify a new union.[39] These changes to the *Ontario Labour Relations Act* (OLRA) were coupled with changes to the *Employment Standards Act* (ESA), which enabled employers to require employees to work up to 60 hours per week without receiving overtime, if the average workweek over a four-week period did not exceed 44 hours.[40] The changes particularly affected the most vulnerable sections of the working class who had no union protection against their employers.

This disdain for trade union rights was mirrored in the government's dealings with its own employees. Negotiations in 1995 between Ontario Public Service Employees Union (OPSEU) and the government actually began before the NDP left office, but the lengthy process of developing essential service agreements delayed bargaining, and the new government immediately took up a tactic of extracting concessions from the union. The legislative end to successor rights, the planned layoff of 13,000 workers, and the provisions in the *Savings and Restructuring Act* that exempted the government from the mass-layoff provisions of the *Pension Benefits Act,* further complicated the bargaining process.[41]

Using its one positive legacy from the NDP, OPSEU launched the first-ever legal province-wide employees' strike in Ontario on February 26, 1996. The government seemed quite willing to face down the strike in the expectation that it would severely damage the union, given that not all elements in the union had been keen on getting the legal right to strike, and that the union had achieved a relatively weak strike vote before going out. Moreover, even a long and protracted strike was attractive to it for the financial savings associated with the shutdown of services. But holding off on back-to-work measures for such reasons did not mean eschewing other forms of coercion. On March 18, 1996, demonstrators at a massive rally staged at Queen's Park were met with riot police wielding billy clubs, ending in a violent confrontation in which two people were injured.[42] The violence only helped to stiffen the resolve of pickets and fuelled support from the broader labour movement. When the strike was finally ended on March 31, the union had shown that it was indeed capable of pulling off a strike relatively successfully, and actually won an agreement that gave at least "some protection against privatization, improved bumping rights for employees receiving notice of layoff, and increased benefits for those employees who eventually lose their jobs through downsizing."[43]

Up next were the province's teachers. The Harris government's determination to massively restructure the education system, centralize control of funding and curriculum, and reduce the number and autonomy of local school boards, had reached its high point in 1997. Bill 160 effectively removed 8,000 principals and vice-principals from bargaining units and eliminated teachers' right to bargain over preparation time, class sizes, teacher-to-student ratios, and the length of the workday and the school year.[44] For teachers' unions, it was a full-frontal assault, leading to an overwhelming majority voting to take strike action if necessary, and massive protests across the province, including a huge rally at Maple Leaf Gardens in Toronto.

Eventually, in an unprecedented show of unity among all the teachers' unions, over 125,000 teachers across the province walked off the job on October 27, 1997 in an attempt to prevent the passage of Bill 160. The government immediately sought an injunction on the grounds that the strike was illegal, since it took place during the term of the existing collective agreements, while also claiming for good measure that the education of the province's children was being irreparably damaged and that working parents were being inconvenienced by the strike. The irony here, as Harry Glasbeek has argued, was that "the collective bargaining law by which the teachers and their employers were bound was the very law that Bill 160 was to replace. In effect, the teachers were in breach of the technical requirements of collective bargaining law whose spirit and essence they were really trying to protect." The degree of cynicism in the government's posi-

tion was so palpable that had the injunction been granted it would, in Glasbeek's view, have brought into question "the judiciary's claim to be an independent institution."[45]

Justice MacPherson for the Supreme Court of Ontario did indeed refuse the injunction. While he agreed with the unions that their action should be interpreted as a lawful political protest rather than an illegal strike, the main basis of his ruling was the more technical one that the school boards, as teachers' direct employers, should have initiated the court action. Nor did he think that evidence of the alleged harm to the province's children and parents had yet been produced. MacPherson's comments suggested that, were a subsequent injunction sought, it might well succeed. With this possibility lurking in the face of government intransigence, several teachers' unions decided, despite widespread public support for the teachers, to return to work by the end of the second week, thus forcing the rest of the unions to follow. By the end of the year, Bill 160 was finally passed, with all of the objectionable sections intact.

Bill 160 came back to haunt the government the next year by virtue of its having set a common end of August 31, 1998 to all teachers' contracts. Efforts across the province around that time to negotiate a new collective agreement led to a series of strikes beginning in September 1998. Some high school teachers had not received a raise in eight years, but were being required to do 20 percent more work as a result of the provisions of Bill 160.[46] The strikes lasted throughout the month, and were only ended by back-to-work legislation applied to strikes in eight separate boards.[47]

The growing unpopularity of the government led the Conservatives to choose Ernie Eves to succeed Mike Harris as premier early in 2002. It was significant that the transition took place in the middle of a second OPSEU strike, with one of the central issues being the government's proposal to remove from workers the ability to control their own pension surplus.[48] Although the government initially responded to the strike by going to the courts (successfully) for injunctions to limit picketing, and to the Labour Board (largely unsuccessfully) to try restrict the number of OPSEU members who could legally be on strike, Eves attempted to distance himself from the unpopular Harris by taking a somewhat more conciliatory approach. Eves's approach led to a deal that included a wage hike of 8.45 percent over three years, and agreement by the government to allow the union to control the pension surplus.[49]

The public-sector unions would soon be tested again, this time in the municipal sector, where severe pressures from neo-liberal restructuring and flexibility finally led in the summer of 2002 to the joint strike against the City of Toronto by 6,800 members of Canadian Union of Public Employees (CUPE) Local 416 (representing outside workers) and 18,000 members of CUPE Local 79 (representing inside workers), despite some sharp and long-standing tensions between the two locals. The major sticking point in negotiations for the unions was the city's demand that job security provisions be eliminated. Mayor Mel Lastman, whose political style was akin to a side-show huckster's, was apoplectic at the strike, claiming that the workers had "pissed away their summer," and that the city was opposed to any scheme that would give "jobs for life"—even though Lastman himself had agreed to the job security clause three years prior. The provincial government added its opinion immediately, as health minister Tony Clement stated that back-

to-work legislation would be imposed if the strike by garbage collectors threatened public health and safety.[50] On this ground, after two weeks, Premier Eves resorted to back-to-work legislation on the advice of the province's chief medical officer of health.[51] Even though the underlying purpose of the legislation was ostensibly to prevent a health crisis due to uncollected garbage, not only the garbage collectors but also all the other workers in both union locals were ordered back to work. It was clear that behind the back of Ernie Eves's compassionate conservatism was still the hard fist of coercion. Old habits die hard.

The Atlantic Provinces

In all four Atlantic provinces, Liberal governments continued the assault on trade unions rights through the 1990s. In Newfoundland, this policy took shape as Bill 49, passed in February 1994 to amend the *Labour Relations Act,* removing automatic certifications from the act and making strike votes mandatory. The Newfoundland labour movement dubbed Bill 49 the "Barry Bill." accusing the government of primarily being motivated to prevent unionization at a fish processing plant owned by Newfoundland businessman Bill Barry. But the bill reflected a broader trend in the region. In the same year, The Liberal government in New Brunswick also enacted amendments to its *Labour Relations Act* and *Public Service Relations Act* (Bill 47), making it easier for employers to obtain forced ratification votes. The bill appeared more even-handed, as it retracted the old provision for automatic decertification of unions that engaged in illegal strike activity, but it left the Public Service Labour Relations Board with the discretionary power to decertify a union for this action. Meanwhile, in Prince

Edward Island, the Liberal government's strict program of fiscal austerity prompted the largest labour demonstration ever in the province in the spring of 1994 as 5,000 Island residents demanded that the Liberals put the brakes on its proposed *Public Sector Pay Reduction Act.*[52] The demonstration convinced the government to slightly soften its proposed 7.5 percent pay cut so that public-sector workers making less than $28,000 would only be required to take a 3.75 percent reduction. The Liberals never recovered from the debacle over their austerity program and were soundly defeated by the Tories in the 1996 provincial election when, for the first time in PEI history, an NDP member of the legislative assembly (MLA) was elected.

The most sparks were to fly in Nova Scotia, however, where once again the provincial government was the object of an uncharacteristically stern rebuke from the International Labour Organization (ILO). The Liberal government had passed Bill 41, the *Public Sector Unpaid Leave Act,* in November 1993, followed by Bill 52, the *Public Sector Compensation Act* in April 1994. Bill 41 forced public-sector workers to take a two percent wage rollback through unpaid leave, while Bill 52 froze all collective agreements, prohibited most wage increases until November 1, 1997, reduced wages by three percent, and essentially removed the right to strike, mediate, or arbitrate. In a 1995 decision, the ILO rejected the government's assertion that exceptional measures in a time of economic crisis could justify the use of Bills 41 and 52, and ruled that the province had violated the freedom of association convention by going far beyond the "permissible restrictions on collective bargaining."[53] The ruling went on to suggest that the Nova Scotia government allow for an ILO Advisory Mission to come to the province "in order to facilitate finding solu-

tions to the difficulties in reaching agreements in the public service."[54]

Not surprisingly, the provincial government did not take up the ILO on its offer. Instead, when the wage freeze provisions of Bill 52 expired on November 1, 1997, the Liberals attempted to transform them into a permanent three percent pay cut. After an independent arbitrator working for the Ministry of Labour ruled against the government on this, Nova Scotia Supreme Court Justice Goodfellow reversed the arbitrator's decision. But when the Nova Scotia Government and General Employees Union (NSGEU) brought the case to the Nova Scotia Court of Appeal, it sustained the union's position, and the government eventually conceded that the wages of public-sector workers ought to be readjusted to pre-rollback levels. This decision lifted the spirits of what had been a very demoralized civil service and disgruntled trade union movement, and in this context, the NDP made impressive gains in Nova Scotia in the 1998 election when both the Liberals and NDP won 19 seats.

Russell McLelland's minority Liberal government was forced to call an election again the next year, at which point the Tories were able to secure a majority government. The new premier, Dr. John Hamm, picked up where the Liberals left off. He began by legislating striking ambulance workers back to work in the fall of 1999. The *Financial Measures Act* passed in the spring of 2000 completely withdrew government funding from the arbitration process, and amendments to the *Teachers' Collective Bargaining Act* in June 2001 narrowed the range of items that could be put on the bargaining table. The Hamm government then introduced Bill 68, the *Healthcare Services Continuation Act,* sparking the most impressive example of labour militancy in Atlantic

Canada. A bitter negotiation process between the Capital District Health Authority and the nurses had ended on June 13, 2001 with a mediated settlement. But before members of the Nurses' Union of Provincial Government Employees (NUPGE) were able to cast ballots in a ratification vote, the government intervened by introducing legislation to suspend the right to strike for nurses and allow Cabinet to impose a settlement. The government's move incensed nurses, who then used the ratification vote as an opportunity to send the government a clear message about Bill 68, rejecting the tentative settlement and voting to strike instead.

A series of large demonstrations at the Nova Scotia legislature did not deter the government from pushing the bill through. However, a mass-resignation threat from the provincial nurses' unions and talk of a province-wide general strike prompted the government to announce that Bill 68 would not be brought into force.[55] On July 5, 2001 both sides agreed to end the dispute by sending all outstanding issues to final offer selection. Amidst all the defeats suffered by the labour movement in Atlantic Canada, trade unionists in Nova Scotia pointed to their successful stand against Bill 68 as proof that organized labour was alive and well. However, many in the Nova Scotia labour movement believed that Hamm put Bill 68 on the table without ever intending to implement it. The government, they argued, simply introduced the bill in order to gain the upper hand in negotiations. Removal of the bill paved the way for the unions to concede to final offer selection as an alternative to the regular collective bargaining process as a way of ending the bitter dispute. Only in an era of permanent exceptionalism can a union concession be considered a victory.

Indeed, throughout Atlantic Canada, the mere threat of back-to-work legislation has been as effective as the actual use of such legislation. For example, in March 2001 striking hospital workers in New Brunswick went back to work with a gun to their heads for fear that Premier Bernard Lord would make good on a promise to impose a substandard contract and stiff fines.[56] Four months later the Lord government essentially suspended the right to strike for nursing-home workers. Under the new regulation, no worker was permitted to reduce or withdraw services unless or until the government found alternate living arrangements for nursing-home residents. Workers in the health-care sector in Newfoundland also found themselves to be the target of anti-union legislation. Members of the Newfoundland and Labrador Nurses' Union were ordered back to work on April 1, 1999. The government followed up in May 2001 with an amendment to the *Labour Relations Act,* which increased fines for illegal strikes and lockouts.

Reform measures during this period were not unheard of—every province made minor improvements in its employment standards legislation—but there was nothing groundbreaking, and the few reforms did little to offset the negative impact of the permanent and temporary restrictive measures imposed on both private and public-sector workers. In 2001, in an effort to resolve chronic labour problems in Newfoundland and Labrador, Premier Roger Grimes, a former union leader himself, launched "a strategic partnership initiative" with business and labour. The initiative was designed to foster "a new collaborative, consensus building approach to advancing the socio-economic interests of Newfoundland and Labrador."[57] Elaine Price, president of the Newfoundland and Labrador Federation of Labour, explained that the strategic partnership was not designed to replace collective bargaining, but rather open up the lines of communication between business, labour, and the state in order to eliminate "unproductive conflict." In following this approach, she seemed to be emulating the corporatist partnerships more familiar in Quebec, although as we shall now see, these had once again achieved little to advance the interests of organized labour there in the 1990s.

Quebec's Version of Social Democracy

Corporatist arrangements between the state, business, and the Quebec labour movement were a product of the Quiet Revolution, but were particularly embedded in the Parti Québécois's (PQ) version of social democracy. The notion that all the constituent social units of the nation could come together in harmony certainly had been tarnished by the way in which the PQ governments in the 1980s had used coercive legislation so determinedly against their own main social base of public-sector employees. Nevertheless, Quebec labour was unwilling to abandon the corporatist model, opting instead to strengthen it by developing labour-sponsored investment funds.[58] The Quebec labour movement's determination to accommodate the state arguably reached a peak under PQ Premier Jacques Parizeau, a self-described social democrat. Labour leaders and the PQ closed ranks around a nation-building strategy that would lay the groundwork for a sovereign Quebec. However, the referendum loss in 1995, followed by Parizeau's resignation and Lucien's Bouchard's succession as Premier, signalled a return to the permanently exceptional coercive legislation that was so prevalent in the 1980s.

While the labour movement's nation-building project was always based loosely on social democratic principles, the PQ's vision of a sovereign Quebec was transformed significantly under Bouchard, a former Mulroney cabinet minister obsessed with achieving "winning conditions" before tackling another referendum campaign. Unfortunately for the Quebec labour movement, Bouchard seemed to think winning conditions must entail dramatic cuts in social spending, hospital closures, and the dismantling of public services. In this context, the Bouchard government arbitrarily re-opened collective agreements and slashed salaries in specific areas of the provincial and municipal public sector. And in the spring of 1998 the PQ government severely restricted the bargaining power of thousands of workers, limiting their right to strike by broadening the definition of essential public services to include the storage of gas, the transportation, collection and distribution of blood products, and forest fire protection activities. In June 1999 the PQ also suspended the right to strike for workers at the municipal housing office in Montreal by making the office an essential public service. A month later, the PQ ordered striking nurses back to work, but the nurses refused and walked the picket lines illegally for 23 days. The government fined the union roughly half a million dollars for the infraction despite the fact that nurses enjoyed overwhelming public support.[59]

The provincial election of 1999 offered little hope for workers who were tired of the PQ's anti-labour offensive. Given a choice between two former Mulroney cabinet ministers (Bouchard and Quebec Liberal leader Jean Charest), Quebeckers stuck with the devil they knew. Bouchard's eventual retirement certainly did nothing to shift Quebec politics to the left. Instead, it sent the PQ into a tailspin and opened up room for the right-wing

Action Démocratique du Québec (ADQ) to make its presence felt in provincial politics. ADQ leader Mario Dumont stole the spotlight in 2002 when his small party won a string of by-elections and topped both the PQ and the Quebec Liberals in public opinion polls throughout the year. The appeal of Dumont's party, which advocates private healthcare, a flat tax, and the repeal of Quebec's anti-scab legislation, revolves around the promise to put constitutional issues on the back burner and concentrate on concrete economic issues. Such a sharp turn to the right would deal a final blow to the Quebec labour movement's corporatist strategy.

The Prairie Provinces

The 1990s marked a significant turning point in the political and economic history of the prairie provinces, with the emergence of the regionally based Reform Party at the federal level. Its skill at using populist rhetoric (The West Wants In) to advance a neo-liberal agenda had been especially well honed in Alberta, when the 21-year Tory dynasty was handed over to Ralph Klein in late 1992. The Klein revolution had already had dramatic consequences on public and private-sector unions by the time the Harris government's own revolution in Ontario took place. Unionized public-sector workers were a particular target for the Klein government, whose determination to balance the provincial budget while also lowering taxes led it to privatize, contract out, and outsource many of the traditional services performed by public-sector workers. The provincial workforce was reduced by 23.5 percent by 1997, the single largest decline of public employees across Canada, with the Alberta Union of Provincial Employees (AUPE) losing

23.5 percent of its members in a three-year period. Public employees were also asked to take a "voluntary" five percent wage roll back, followed by a two-year wage freeze, with the government giving employers the authority to lay off workers if the wage rollbacks were not agreed to.[60] Several administrative acts opened the door for greater privatization and contracting out of public services, with the added bonus for potential contractors of not having to pay full union wages. The government also changed the structure and powers of the Labour Relations Board (LRB) and the rules for certification, bargaining rights, and grievance arbitration, in ways that disadvantaged unions.[61] As a result of these and earlier changes made throughout the 1980s, Alberta is one of only three provinces in which there are no penalties against unfair employer tactics during certification drives and no mandatory first agreement arbitration clause.

For its part, organized labour failed to build on the mobilizations during the Gainers' meat packers' strike, and again during the nurses' strike at the beginning of the decade, and never posed a serious challenge to the Klein cuts. On the few occasions, when public-sector workers did strike or attempt to challenge the government, they were dealt with harshly, as in May 2001 when a dispute between the City of Edmonton and the ambulance drivers of CUPE local 3197 threatened to disrupt emergency services in the city. In response, the government passed an amendment to the Labour Relations Code, which gave the government the power to declare emergency procedures in any labour dispute it deemed might cause undue harm, hardship, or damage to health or property, and then went on to prohibit any strike or lockout for ambulance drivers. After a series of rotating job actions and strikes by the Alberta Teachers

Association (ATA) in 2002, the Klein government passed *The Education Services Settlement Act* (Bill 12), which legislated the legally striking teachers back to work, imposed severe fines on teachers and their union in the event of a continued strike, and stripped the ATA of any reasonable form of collective bargaining. Notably, the Tories took the unusual step of changing the normal parliamentary rules in order to prevent extended discussion or debate in the legislature in order to speed the passage of Bill 12.[62]

The continued erosion of union rights by the prairie governments was not limited to Alberta or the Klein revolution. In Saskatchewan, the NDP's Throne Speech of April 27, 1992 announced an agenda of labour reform, promising changes to legislation in several areas, especially in relation to the construction industry, occupational health and safety, workers' compensation, as well as reviews of the *Trade Union Act* and the *Labour Standards Act*. But the government moved very slowly in pursuing this agenda, and meanwhile insisted that provincial employees accept a two-year wage freeze, even though their real wages had fallen by some 10 percent since 1982. The government's refusal to move from this position led to a series of rotating strikes by the Saskatchewan Government Employees Union (SGEU) throughout 1992 and 1993, and eventually to a ruling by the Labour Board that the government had failed to bargain in good faith. Ignoring the ruling, the government was ultimately successful in bludgeoning the SGEU to accede to the freeze, but in the process alienated virtually the whole of the Saskatchewan labour movement.[63]

As the government moved at a snail's pace on its labour reform agenda, little was accomplished to repair this sentiment.[64] The only concrete measure it quickly passed was Bill 93, which amended the *Construction Industry Labour Relations Act*. Designed to prohibit unionized construction companies from spinning off non-union companies as permitted by the Devine government's Bill 24 of 1983, the NDP's Bill 93 disappointed the labour movement since it did not restore the bargaining structure that had existed in the industry prior to 1983, thereby effectively leaving 80 percent of the industry non-union.[65] As a measure of any reforms still to come, this one reform gave little cause for optimism.

In fact, the Saskatchewan NDP government was revealing the limits that social democracy evinced elsewhere. While not moving as aggressively on the neo-liberal austerity policies introduced in Alberta, Roy Romanow's government was quick to assure the Saskatchewan business community that increased public spending was not on the political or economic agenda. In fact, shortly after their 1991 election, the NDP government stressed that its primary goal was the elimination of the provincial deficit, which they argued was primarily responsible for the faltering economy. The Romanow government was willing to increase corporate and business taxes by a minimal one percent in the 1994 budget, but there was also a heavy reliance on an increase in consumption taxes, such as a two percent increase in the provincial sales tax, that fell disproportionately on the working classes.[66]

The government finally introduced its long-awaited legislative package for trade unions in June 1994, with the passing of the *Trade Union Amendment Act* (Bill 54). Its concern to strike a balance between the rights of organized labour and the perceived stability of the business environment meant that long-standing union expectations for anti-scab measures and pay equity legislation were not addressed. Bill 54 did, however, ease restrictions on collective bargaining and dispute resolution by handing more power to the LRB to rule in unfair bargaining practices, loosening restrictions on first-contract arbitration and on the administration of collective agreements, and making it more difficult for employers to terminate workers during a legal strike.

With a weak Liberal opposition still unable to distance itself from the scandals of the late 1980s, the NDP secured a second majority government in the 1995 election, despite losing 13 seats. This victory allowed it to continue with limited reform measures to the province's labour laws by introducing progressive amendments to the *Health Sector Labour Relations Act* and the easing of restrictions on collective bargaining in the *Fire and Police Services Collective Bargaining Act in 1995*. But it also passed *The Balanced Budget Act* that capped public-sector wages at two percent per year, aggressively cut taxes, closed rural hospitals, and increasingly turned to public-private partnerships as a means to deliver public services.

Perhaps the most telling example of the Saskatchewan NDP's move away from its social-democratic traditions was its handling of two strikes in late 1998 and early 1999. The first involved members of the International Brotherhood of Electrical Workers Local 2067 who, having reached an impasse in bargaining with Saskatchewan Power Corporation, had taken legal strike action in October 1998. Fearing a shutdown of the province's power supply, the Romanow government introduced back-to-work legislation (Bill 65), which ended the strike by extending the previous collective agreement to December 31, 2000. The government then showed even greater contempt for the collective bargaining rights of public-sec-

tor workers when it quickly moved to end a nurses' strike through the passage of Bill 23 in April 1999. Despite being faced with $50,000 fines on the union and $2,000 a day for individual workers, the nurses vowed to resist and defied a court order to return to work.[67] With overwhelming support from the public, the nurses won, securing a collective agreement with a 13.7 percent wage increase over three years. If the New Democrats had ever expected these confrontations with public-sector unions would be electorally helpful, they were sadly mistaken, as in the 1999 election the party lost another 13 seats and fell to 38 percent of the popular vote, forcing it into a coalition government with the Liberals.

In Manitoba, the Filmon Tories' majority re-election in 1995 further inspired the radical neo-liberal reform agenda it had already been pursuing. Its inelegantly named *Balanced Budget, Debt Repayment and Taxpayer's Protection and Consequential Amendments Act* in late 1995 made individual ministers responsible for balancing the budget of their departments, and stipulated that any increase in taxes had to go before a provincial referendum.[68] The act paved the way for decentralized public services, hospital closures, and the selling off of Manitoba Telephone System. The cutbacks meant further major reductions in public-service employment, and continued the fall in real wages and benefits that had taken place each year after 1990. By 1997, the Manitoba Government Employees Union (MGEU) had lost 22 percent of its members.[69]

The government then turned its attention to the province's labour laws. Through the *Public Schools Amendment Act* (Bill 72) in late 1996, Manitoba's teachers, who had voluntarily given up the right to strike in 1956 in exchange for a system of binding arbitration, lost virtually all their bargaining rights regarding teacher selection and appointment, length of the school day, the scheduling of professional development days, classroom size, and the provisions for layoffs. Salary, benefits, preparation time, and pensions were also withdrawn from the traditional form of collective bargaining, as union members were arbitrarily subject to a form of concession bargaining by local school boards, which were able to base financial compensation on the district's ability to pay. Then, at the beginning of 1997, the government passed Bill 26 amending the *Labour Relations Act*. Among other things, the bill subjected Manitoba unions to the most restrictive measures in Canada on the use of members' dues for political purposes. It also stripped the unions of automatic certification rights and gave employers new tools to resist union drives in the workplace, eased restrictions on employers' unfair bargaining practices, and strengthened their ability to dismiss employees who had been on legal strike. Collective bargaining rights and the right to strike were further weakened when Bill 17 amended the *Government Essential Services Act*[70] in late 1996, giving the government greater unilateral ability to determine what public services were deemed essential, which workers fell outside of a collective agreement, and the conditions by which public-sector workers could strike.

The labour movement's resistance to these changes contributed in 1999 to the election of the NDP under Gary Doer. The new government moved quickly to pass Bill 44 by October 2000; this bill repealed many of the restrictive measures of the Filmon government's Bills 26 and 72, including the provisions to allow employers to dismiss workers for picket-line activity, to restrict the use of union dues for political purposes, and to eliminate teachers'

rights to collective bargaining. The Manitoba Federation of Labour was still disappointed, however, that the NDP had failed to repeal all the restrictive provisions of Bill 26 (most notably those on certification rights), and had continued the refusal of previous Manitoba NDP governments to pass anti-scab legislation.[71]

British Columbia

Like Saskatchewan, British Columbia was governed by an NDP government throughout the 1990s. Given the long and close relationship between organized labour and the party, the Mike Harcourt government elected in 1991 moved to reverse a decade of legislated restrictions imposed by the former Social Credit government. But its redress of Social Credit's infamously reactionary labour legislation did not go nearly as far as many had hoped. Beyond repealing the notoriously misnamed *Compensation Fairness Act* that had so severely undermined public-sector collective bargaining in the province, the NDP government's major legislative initiative was Bill 84, reforming the Labour Relations Code. But while it re-established many rights previously taken away by Social Credit (in particular workers' rights to engage in secondary picketing, common-site picketing, and boycotts as well as successor rights in the event of ownership changes), Bill 84 preserved many of the restrictions on the right to strike introduced by the Social Credit governments of the 1980s.[72] The bill maintained the broad definition of a strike introduced by the Socreds so that political strikes remained illegal: a vote by secret ballot (valid only for three months) still was necessary to conduct a legal strike, employers still had to be given 72 hours written notice of any strike, and the Labour Board could order a vote on the employer's last offer even during a strike. Moreover, the bill enabled the government in a manner reminiscent of the *Federal Industrial Disputes Investigation Act* of 1907 to appoint a special officer who could issue orders delaying a strike for 30 days.

Among the new reforms introduced by the bill, the most important were restrictions on the use of replacement workers, automatic access to first contract arbitration, and the removal of the prohibition on strikes during the life of a collective agreement in certain circumstances, notably where the health and safety of workers were at stake. Yet just as the Ontario NDP government had rejected many important Burkett panel recommendations, so did the BC government reject such reform proposals, including sectoral bargaining, which a majority of the advisory group on Bill 84 had recommended. The main advance involved restrictions on the use of replacement workers and not only paralleled legislation passed by the NDP in Ontario, but evinced the same broad loopholes. If anything, the BC version was less progressive, since the minister and/or the labour board were given very broad discretion to designate any facility, production or services as essential. Essential services, moreover, had to be provided "in full measure" by the union, meaning that, unlike in Ontario where essential services were merely exempted from the restrictions on the use of replacement workers, providers of these services in BC lost their right to strike.

Indeed the NDP government did not shrink from using back-to-work legislation under this rubric. Bill 31 ended a strike by Vancouver teachers in May 1993 even though the teachers had accepted the proposals of an independent mediator, which labour minister Moe Sihota acknowledged would have resulted in the "the lowest wage agreement that's been negotiated in the school sector this year."[73] This was an important testament to the role that coercion continued to occupy even within the framework of NDP reforms. The government did enact several reform amendments to the 1994 *Employment Standards Act* (Bill 29), including the introduction of more flexible arrangements in the scheduling of work, which they hoped would address many of the limitations of Bill 84 and their faltering relationship with many public-sector unions. It also passed in the same year the *Public Education Labour Relations Act* (Bill 52), which restructured the collective bargaining process for teachers so that all major decisions involving monetary compensation, classroom size, and pensions were bargained at the provincial level rather than at the level of local school boards. However, the timing of this bill was related to two recent unpopular local strikes in Surrey and Vancouver that had embarrassed the government and the British Columbia Teachers Federation (BCTF) itself. Far from being designed to strengthen the BCTF's hand in bargaining, the bill reflected the view of the schoolboard employers, Ministry of Education bureaucrats, and a range of neutrals (mediators and arbitrators) that local bargaining had made teachers too powerful at the table.

The BC NDP appeared to put its best foot forward in the process of overseeing what it called a "social contract" with three unions in the health sector. The accord was struck in March 1993, with the object of the exercise to gain the cooperation of health workers to a shift away from acute-care institutions and towards community-based care by providing for employment security and a modest wage increase alongside a government pledge to maintain the existing balance between public and private facilities. In addition, the accord specified considerable new rights and procedures for the active involvement of workers' representatives in developing proposals for new community health programs, as well as in certain areas of management and expenditure planning at local and provincial levels.[74]

Notably, it was the employers in the health sector who flatly turned down the social contract in BC. While this would appear to contrast sharply with the Social Contract experience in Ontario, from the unions' perspective the BC health sector social contract contained some of the same troubling aspects that characterized the Ontario experience, in the sense that the government's social commitment was deeply intertwined with its concern with cutting costs in the health sector. Its short-term interest in the deal was very much bound up with securing the minimal 1.5 percent wage increase and three year extension of contracts that the three unions agreed to, thereby undercutting a three percent deal the BC nurses had earlier negotiated. This lower-level increase immediately became the definition of realistic expectations for other public-sector unions in their negotiations with the government.

The BC government's concern with proving both its impartiality and its fiscal rectitude was a real problem in regard to its long-term commitment to realizing the promise of progressive health reform. Even though there was greater fiscal room to manoeuvre in BC because the recession of the early 1990s was not so severe there, one of Harcourt's first acts as Premier was to go to New York to impress the financial community with his probity. He went so far as to draw an explicit contrast between his own intentions and the large deficit run by the Rae government in its first budget. In this context, the main impetus towards community-based health care, as far as the government was concerned, was cheaper delivery. Yet the principal reason health care is cheaper when it is community-based is that community health-care wages are very low. The government's objective was clearly one of downsizing the expensive acute-care sector.

The health-care unions in BC certainly thought that they were buying into new labour relations, especially by obtaining much more input in decision-making on a cooperative basis. But the employers' resistance at first left the NDP government paralysed, and the entire process of heath-sector reform was stalled for many months after the unions signed on. In the ensuing conflicts of interpretation and implementation, the government repeatedly sided with the employers and took positions largely indistinguishable from them. This stance hardly augured well for realizing the progressive reform of the health sector. The best that could be said is that the BC social contract in this sector provided a more favourable framework for strategic union manoeuvring than was at any point on offer from the Ontario NDP.

The government also made changes in 1995 to the regulations governing public-sector employment under the *Health Authorities Act,* introducing a form of closed shop for five government-approved bargaining units in the health sector. Its commitment to strengthen collective bargaining in the health-care industry again became open to question when the government legislated an end to a health-sector dispute two days before the provincial election in April 1996. Under new leader Glen Clark, the NDP was reduced to a bare majority in the legislature. Despite his left-wing reputation and union background, Clark moved quickly to reduce fiscal expenditures, and balancing the budget became a key component of the government's discourse. The British Columbia

Government Employees' Union (BCGEU) was able to bargain around an early Clark government attempt to lay off 3,500 workers. From this time on the BC government's long-term restructuring plans did not include massive layoffs or the radical downsizing of public-sector employment as was the case in Saskatchewan, but the continuing signal from the government was that its highest priority was the reduction of costs in the public sector.

The Clark government did not shy away from coercive measures when collective bargaining measures reached an impasse. In the summer of 1998 when teachers threatened to strike over a new contract, the government passed *The Public Education Collective Agreement Act,* which effectively limited the collective bargaining rights of teachers. As the party elected Ujjal Dosanjh as leader in the wake of the scandals engulfing Glen Clark, the NDP government turned against many of its key supporters in the labour movement. It passed the *Public Education Support Staff Collective Bargaining Assistance Act* (Bill 7) in April of 2000, which imposed a collective agreement to end a CUPE strike of support workers and cleaning staff in public schools. The action so angered NDP supporters in the public-sector unions that Barry O'Neil, president of BC CUPE, called for the complete withdrawal of union support in the upcoming 2001 election for the 34 members who had voted striking workers back to work.[75] Besides alienating many in the labour movement, the passage of Bill 7 also revealed deeper splits within the Dosanjh caucus. Even the *Vancouver Sun* editorial page, never a bastion of support of the NDP, was quick to acknowledge that legislating CUPE workers back to work was a nail in the coffin for the party's key supporters in the labour movement.[76] The 2001 election proved

to be devastating to the NDP. The party was reduced to two seats in the legislature, while Gordon Campbell's Liberals, with a 77-seat majority, were finally in a position to emulate Klein and Harris.

The new government immediately undertook a massive legislative assault against labour. It first imposed a cooling-off period for striking nurses (Bill 2), and soon followed this with the *Health Care Services Collective Agreements Act* (Bill 15), forcing an end to the nurses' strike and imposing a collective agreement that a majority had earlier rejected.[77] The long Greater Vancouver Transit strike in 2001 by CAW local 111 was similarly ended by back-to-work legislation. The government then introduced major changes to the *Skills Development and Labour Statutes Amendment Act* (Bill 18). The reforms outlawed any form of sectoral bargaining in the province, changed the certification procedure in favour of the employer, and eliminated the right of teachers to strike by declaring teaching an essential service. This was followed by the *Skills Development and Fair Wage Repeal Act* (Bill 22), which relieved the requirement on employers in the construction industry performing public works to hire workers who were protected by a labour union. And in a stunning act of contempt, the government passed the *Miscellaneous Statutes Amendment Act* (Bill 16), which repealed amendments to the British Columbia Human Rights Code by the previous NDP government concerning discrimination in the payment of wages.

The new year brought a stepped-up attack on the rights of public-sector unions. Nicknamed Black Sunday by the British Columbia labour movement, January 27, 2002 recalled the worst days of Social Credit rule in the 1980s. On this date, despite holding 77 of the province's 79 seats, the government invoked closure to pass *The Education Services Collective Agreement Act* (Bill 27), *The Public Education Flexibility and Choice Act* (Bill 28), and *The Health and Social Services Delivery Act* (Bill 29). Under the terms imposed by Bills 27 and 28, the BCTF's existing contract was repealed and replaced by a new one imposed by an arbitrator appointed by the government. Bill 29 reopened the nurses' collective agreement imposed by the government a year earlier, rolled back the wages of 100,000 workers in the health sector, and gave the government greater flexibility to contract out the provision of health care. As the Health Services Minister Colin Hansen and Labour Minister Graham Bruce admitted, this legislation was designed so that government could have the flexibility to close hospitals and lay off workers.[78]

The government then turned its attention in May 2002 to passing Bill 48, a comprehensive reactionary overhaul of employment standards in the province. Bill 48, among many other things, reduced provisions for overtime benefits and the protections provided against employer abuse of overtime (maximum overtime hours would be now averaged over a four-week period as in Harris's Ontario), removed a requirement to obtain permission to employ a child under 15 years of age, and even removed the requirement for farm producers to retain copies of payroll records of farm labour contractors. Indeed, it went so far against basic democratic rights as to remove a general requirement to post a statement of employees' rights under the *Labour Relations Act* in a workplace. According to BC Federation of Labour president Jim Sinclair, the new bill represented nothing more than a bill of rights for employers.[79] In one final assault, Bill 64, *The Human Rights Code Amendment Act,* came

into force on March 31, 2003. The bill eliminated the BC Human Rights Commission and replaced it with a tribunal headed by a politically appointed chair who controls procedures and serves as judge and jury. One observer has described the new tribunal system as "velvet totalitarianism."[80] This inauspicious beginning to the new century in BC, with a government going even further against labour than Harris had dared do in Ontario, or Klein in Alberta, dashed any hope the Canadian labour movement might have had for a respite from the assault it had been facing for so long.

The Supreme Court: A Judicial Lifeline?

As they had in the 1980s, Canadian unions continued to look to the Canadian courts and the provisions of the Canadian Charter of Rights and Freedoms, as well as to the ILO Freedom of Association Committee and the international labour rights conventions signed on to by the Canadian government, for protection in the face of the continuing assault on their freedoms. Once again the complaints brought by Canadian Labour Congress (CLC) to the ILO on behalf its member unions were far more numerous than from unions in any other country in the world. In all, 35 complaints were filed between 1991 and 2001, amounting to over 80 percent of the 42 cases brought by the G7 countries. And, largely in response to the BC assault in 2001–02, half a dozen more complaints from Canada have been filed. In bringing these complaints to the ILO, however, the Canadian unions had to be aware that the tactic could only have demonstrative effects, since the federal and provincial governments had already made it clear that any endorsement of their complaints by the Freedom of Association Committee would be ignored.

Decisions by the Canadian judiciary could not be ignored by federal and provincial governments, but given the Supreme Court's endorsement of governmental restrictions on the right to bargain and strike in the 1987 labour trilogy, and other decisions in the same vein, the unions had little reason or inclination to take similar restrictions in the 1990s back to the courts. The one exception to this was the appeal of the International Longshoremen's Union against the federal government's back-to-work legislation in 1994. But its argument that freedom of association included the right to strike was peremptorily rebuffed by the Supreme Court on the ground that the approach adopted by the court in its earlier rulings "completely defeats the general argument of the appellants."[81]

The unions did indeed finally get some protection from the Supreme Court in four labour cases it heard between 1999 and 2002. By this point, the unions were in a much weaker political and economic position than at the time of the 1987 trilogy, and the language that the judges chose to describe the situation of labour organizations in this conjuncture, and

the protections that they offered, reflected this weakness. The famous Rand ruling after the Second World War had interpreted union rights in terms of balancing the interests of the great social forces of labour and capital in light of the latter's "long-term dominant position." In the 1987 trilogy, even with the freedom of association now listed in the Charter, the Supreme Court refused to find the legislative assault illegitimate. Justice McIntyre even went so far as to declare that organized labour was "an equally powerful socio-economic force" to capital. However myopic such a view was in the 1980s, by the end of the 1990s not even a Supreme Court justice could expect it to be seen as credible. And indeed, the Supreme Court was now prepared to recognize that workers' rights in Canada needed to be offered certain protections under the Charter. This view, however, did not imply that the court was overturning its trilogy stance. Freedom of association still did not include for the court the rights to bargain and strike. Further, insofar as the Court thought that a particular group of workers had, by virtue of their place

Table 15.2: Complaints of Violations of Trade Union Rights Filed with the ILO against the Group of Seven Capitalist Countries

Countries	1954–73		1974–91		1992–2001	
	No.	%	No.	%	No.	%
Canada	4	3	27	34	35	83
France	31	25	6	8	0	0
Italy	5	4	2	3	0	0
Japan	8	7	15	18	2	.04
United Kingdom	55	45	15	18	3	.07
United States	16	13	13	16	7	.04
Germany	4	3	2	3	0	0
Total	123	100	80	100	42	100

Source: *ILO Official Bulletin, Reports of the Committee on Freedom of Association*, 1985–2001; and I.U. Zeytinoğlu, "The ILO Standards and Canadian Labour Legislation," *Relations industrielles*, 42, no.2 (1987): Table 2.

in Canadian society, some degree of collective strength, there was not necessarily any right to even associate in a union. It was only insofar as they were members of a disadvantaged or vulnerable group that this right was to be given some protection.

In *Dunmore v Ontario* (2001), the court was asked to rule on whether the Ontario government's exclusion of agricultural workers from the province's collective bargaining regime was consistent with the Charter's guarantee of freedom of association.[82] Until the NDP government's *Agricultural Labour Relations Act* (ALRA), farm workers in Ontario had always been excluded from the law that protects union organizing. Their inclusion in collective bargaining legislation by the ALRA in 1994 (albeit only with a system of final offer settlement rather than the right to strike), was immediately undone in 1995 by the Harris government through its repeal of the ALRA and its further amendments to the province's *Labour Relation Act* (LRA) to prohibit farm workers from forming unions. The United Farm and Commercial Workers (UFCW), which had organized a few hundred mushroom and poultry workers in Leamington, brought an application challenging the amendments to the LRA, on the basis that it infringed their rights under Sections 2(d) and 15(1) (equality rights) of the Charter. The CLC intervened and urged the Supreme Court to reconsider the labour trilogy and read freedom of association to include collective bargaining and striking. The UFCW's position was narrower, only arguing that the exclusion of agricultural workers from labour-relations legislation violated their right to associate and participate in unions.

The Ontario government maintained before the court that the protection of the family farm was of primary importance in repealing the ALRA, in order to ensure that the labour relationship remained a private action between individual farmers and employees. How discriminatory this position was could be seen from the Supreme Court's comment that it had never before been asked to review the complete exclusion of an occupational group, other than essential public-sector workers, from collective bargaining legislation. In finding for the union, Justice Bastarache, writing for seven of his colleagues, held that there was a positive freedom to collectively associate, at the same time reaffirming that this freedom did not include the rights to bargain and strike. The court also asked whether in the age of expanding Charter values a positive obligation existed for the state to enact protective legislation for vulnerable groups in the context of labour relations. The court determined that agricultural workers represented a vulnerable section of the workforce that had been unable to associate without state protection. It also implicated the government in the failure of agricultural workers to associate. According to Bastarache, "by extending statutory protection to just about every class of worker in Ontario, the legislature has essentially discredited the organizing efforts of agricultural workers. This is especially true given the relative status of agricultural workers in Canadian society."[83]

The majority decision in *Dunmore* acknowledged that vulnerable workers have a right to associate with a union and that the state has a certain obligation not to restrict that right. It said little, however, about the limitations imposed by the state on the ability and restrictions to organize per se. In this sense, rights to collective bargaining and to strike remained clearly off the table. The fundamental basis of the court ruling (without using the group-rights provision of Section 15(1) of the Charter, as only Justice Claire L'Heureux-Dubé wanted to do) held that the vulnerability of agricultural workers in the labour market undermined their Section 2(d) freedom of association rights under the Charter. By extension, were these workers able to maintain a lasting social or economic strength, the court would not be willing to extend Charter protection to them. The court also used this rationale to explain its decision in relation to the earlier *Delisle* ruling that upheld restrictions on a Royal Canadian Mounted Police (RCMP) officer's union rights. It stated that the collective strength of the police as workers implied "there is no general obligation for the government to provide a particular legislative framework for its employees to exercize their collective rights."[84]

Moreover, the court was only willing to extend Section 2(d) to the organizational aspect of union activity rather than to the full ambit of labour relations rights which would include the collective right to bargain and strike. Its decision therefore still left vulnerable workers in a weak legal position vis-à-vis the employer and the state. Building on this contradiction, the Ontario government responded to the *Dunmore* decision with the introduction of Bill 187 on November 19, 2002, ironically entitled an *Act to Protect the Rights of Agricultural Employees*. In this bill, the government acknowledged the Supreme Court's recognition that farm workers have a legal right to associate, but stressed that those rights were not extended to the collective bargaining and strike rights enshrined in the *Labour Relations Act* (LRA). Essentially, under Bill 187 agricultural workers were allowed legal representation to an employer or an arms-length agricultural tribunal on behalf of a labour association. Bill 187 maintained the spirit of the *Dunmore* de-

cision (freedom of association) but still did not expressly give agricultural workers the same rights guaranteed to other unionized workers under the LRA, including the rights to bargain and strike.

The logic of vulnerability as the basis for the protection of workers' rights had already surfaced in a 1999 Supreme Court ruling in a case involving freedom of expression.[85] During a labour dispute with two K-Mart stores in British Columbia in which the mostly part-time women workers had been locked out for six months, the UFCW local involved had distributed leaflets at various other non-unionized K-Mart stores. The leaflets contained information on the unfair labour practices of K-Mart Ltd., informed shoppers of the labour dispute, and encouraged them to shop elsewhere. When K-Mart appealed this action to the British Columbia LRB, the tribunal found that, for the purposes of the Labour Relations Code, the union action had constituted secondary picketing, and was illegal per se.[86] The union claimed that the legislated definition of picketing was too broad and, by grouping picketing, leafleting, and boycotts in the same legal definition, violated both workers' freedom of association and freedom of expression rights.

In reviewing this case, the Supreme Court agreed with the union that the definition of picketing outlined in the Labour Code was too expansive and did infringe on freedom of association rights. The court concluded that there was a distinction between picketing, which produces a signal effect to individuals, and social protest, which is a political right of all individuals in Canada. In striking this balance, however, the court did not challenge the long-standing presumption in Canadian jurisprudence, going back to the *Hersees* case in 1963,[87] that secondary picketing was illegal per se. In finding for the workers, Justice Corry, writing for a unanimous court, came to his conclusion through a categorization of the K-Mart employees as vulnerable workers who needed to be protected alongside other disadvantaged social groups. Corry's position affirmed Chief Justice Dickson's minority dissent in the 1987 *Alberta Reference* regarding the primacy of work as a measure of an individual's self-worth in society. He found that this especially applied to vulnerable retail workers, and reinforced their need to publicly address their employer regarding matters related to working conditions. In other words, the court was willing to conceive that leafleting could, under certain circumstances, be seen as a valued means of expression insofar as organized labour was similar in its political position to other vulnerable groups in society. The court came to this conclusion through a comparison of the vulnerability of retail workers to many other non-labour groups, including new Canadians, which also address infringements in human rights actions through the use of leafleting and consumer boycotts.[88]

The court's decision rested on a delicate balance between the individual rights of vulnerable workers to political speech, and their ability to politically engage their employer through the use of a strike. Despite the narrowness of this ruling, which avoided the issue of secondary picketing being illegal per se, the UFCW expressed relief that the decision at least acknowledged the traditional right of workers to communicate their message to their communities, implying that union members have the same right to bring their issues to a public forum as everyone else.[89] As Glasbeek puts it, the court "went out of its way to make sure that the freedom that it was granting trade unions to engage in secondary actions remained under tight wraps."[90]

The legality of secondary picketing came back to the court in a similar case brought against PepsiCola in 2002. The case arose when a Retail, Wholesale, and Department Store Union (RWDSU) local in Saskatoon was locked out, leading to a bitter strike in which Pepsi brought in replacement workers. The union began picketing retail outlets that did business with the employer, dissuading the store staff from accepting Pepsi deliveries, and also picketed outside the homes of some of the management personnel. The employer argued before the court that this form of secondary picketing was illegal *per se* at common law, even though there was no legislative prohibition against it. The union countered this argument, claiming that secondary picketing is a fundamental right under Section 2(b) of the Charter.

The court now finally addressed this issue directly in terms of the constitutionality of secondary picketing, asking itself two essential questions: 1) Do the courts have the power to make the changes to the common law and rule in the secondary picketing manner in which the union advocated? 2) If so, how has the Charter affected the development of the common law? On both questions, the court argued yes, they had the jurisdiction and, more importantly, the Charter does enshrine certain values that have a fundamental influence in the extension of the common law. Although no state action was directly involved in this case, Justices McLachlin and Lebel reasoned that "common law rules ensure the protection of property interests and contractual relationships. Nonetheless, where these laws implicate Charter values, these values may be considered."[91] On this basis, the court deemed that the value of freedom of expression was of such fundamental importance to Canadian democracy that it could take primacy over common law principles developed before the implementation of the Charter.

In linking this approach to the collective action of striking workers, the court affirmed that the postwar compromise, in which Rand's formula was entrenched within the modern forms of labour law, was an important point of departure. Such a compromise recognized that certain legal rights for organized workers have entrenched "good faith negotiation as the primary engine of industrial peace and economic efficiency."[92] Workers are free to withdraw their labour and to legally picket, while employers are free, the court reasoned, to hire replacement workers. In this regard, the Court defined picketing as an organized effort of people carrying placards in a public place or near a business premises. Picketing, McLachlin and Lebel argued, is a form of free expression that the court affirmed ought to be protected, following the decision in *K-Mart*. As such, the justices acknowledged the importance that unions play in advancing social dialogue and, in particular, in bringing the debate regarding labour conditions into the public realm. While noting Justice McIntyre's reasoning in the *Dolphin Delivery* case in 1986 on the protection of "innocent third parties to labour disputes," the court affirmed that this protection is also not absolute and must be weighed against the workers' right to free expression during an industrial dispute. Although it acknowledged that the appropriate balance between employers and unions is a "delicate political matter" better left to the legislature, in the absence of a legislative scheme the court decided to treat picketing the way it treated any other non-labour forms of expression by any other social group, without assuming it would necessarily "unduly undermine the power of employers vis-à-vis employees."[93] In making this argument, the court moved farther on the issue of union speech than in *K-Mart*.

Instead of resting with Rand's class model of the centrality of labour and capital in capitalist society, the court inflected its defence of labour picketing towards a distinctly pluralist group model of society.

The Supreme Court made one other ruling in 2001, based on a narrow 5–4 vote, that could come back to haunt trade unionism in Canada. Especially important in this case was the freedom for provincial governments to legislate mandatory union membership within the construction industry, but it had wider implications in terms of whether courts in Canada would find "right to work" legislation, now common in American states, to be constitutional. André Gareau, owner of Advance Cutting and Coring Ltd., challenged the Quebec government's three-decade-old labour law that required workers in the construction industry to belong to one of five unions sanctioned by the province.[94] Central to this case was the 1991 *Lavigne* ruling by Justice Beverly McLachlin which maintained that Section 2(d) included a right "not to associate." Against this ruling, the attorney general of Quebec argued that the construction act incorporates legal rules that answer the need to set up an efficient and stable collective bargaining system in the Quebec construction industry.

In writing the decision, the newest member of the court from Quebec, Louis Lebel, argued that in the past 20 years of Charter jurisprudence and labour relations, the court had generally maintained that the judiciary is not the best arbiter of the conflicting interests at play in the field of labour relations. A hands-off policy had been adopted to dissuade those who might seek "Charter protection from the bargaining procedures and rights that have largely defined the role of unions for more than half a century in Canada."[95] Although leaving open the possibility for an evolution in the relationship between the Charter and labour law, the court acknowledged that the construction industry in Quebec was heavily regulated by the state in an effort to retain the best interests of both organized labour and the industry itself, and expressed its reluctance to question this regulation. But insofar as the court was specifically asked to determine whether a restriction on an individual's ability to not associate with a union is protected under freedom of association, it was required to revisit the *Lavigne* decision and the question of whether freedom of association was both a positive and negative freedom.

In the *Lavigne* case, the majority of the court had disagreed with Bertha Wilson's claim that freedom of association could only be construed a positive freedom, that recognition of a freedom *not* to associate would negate the nature and purpose of Section 2(d), as it was designed primarily to breathe life into associations, not take life away from them. The majority had taken the position that a right *not* to associate existed as a necessary component of the guarantee of freedom of association. On the narrower issue before them, they ruled that contemporary union dues did not violate Section 2(d), because such dues amount to compensation rendered, and did not imply ideological conformity. Now, in the *Advance Cutting* case, Lebel reaffirmed that a right not to associate does indeed exist, but that it was necessary to place limits on that right. Although the Quebec legislation did create a form of union shop, the court saw this as justified by the Quebec government's attempt to create stability in the job market. Given the contentious labour history in Quebec, the community, as well as individual workers, would benefit from the balance in the construction industry.

Most importantly, the court argued that the Construction Act did not create any mechanism to enforce an ideological conformity on union members, and also pointed out that individual workers are given the choice of five different unions to join. Lebel argued, therefore, that the questions at stake were better left to the political process. Based on this logic, if mandatory membership was found to have forced ideological conformity, it would have then violated Section 2(d) of the Charter, thus making the legislation unconstitutional. However, based on the social science evidence presented, the court concluded that clearly union members do not necessarily follow the political and social ideologies advanced by the unions themselves.

Notably, however, Lebel was really speaking for only three justices. Justice L'Heureux-Dubé had in fact gone further and taken the position that the right not to associate did not exist at all in the field of labour relations. The other five justices, however, took the opposite position. Four of them contended, in a dissenting opinion, that union membership did indeed produce ideological conformity, and that Charter values upheld the right to work as well as the freedom of conscience and expression that, in their view, union membership denied. The decision went the way it did only because of the swing vote of Justice Iacobucci. The justice agreed with the dissenters that there was a powerful right not to associate, but he was prepared to accept that the Section 2(d) protection of that right could be overridden by a Section 1 definition of what was permissible for the common good in a free and democratic society.

The court debate showed that little basis existed for trade unions in Canada to rely on the judiciary to provide any significant protection against the continuing assault on their rights. The 1987 trilogy of labour decisions had clearly warned unions off even bothering to appeal the long series of assaults on the right to bargain and strike for public-sector workers that continued through the 1990s and into the 21st century. The series of decisions made by the court between 1999 and 2002, moreover, showed that the Supreme Court stood by its earlier distinction between workers' collective right to associate and the rights to bargain and strike. The court was prepared to support trade unionism where a group of workers were particularly disadvantaged or vulnerable, or where the governments and/or employers found it in their own interest to join with unions in regulating the labour market.

This was a very narrow reed to cling to, in light of the fact that the majority of the court was clearly open to the kinds of right-to-work arguments that have been the basis of American legislation and that have devastated union membership numbers in that country.[96] Moreover, the court's concern that unions not display ideological conformity, to the point of checking whether union members voted for the parties that their unions endorsed, served to reinforce the depoliticization of trade unions at the very time when they have been severely subjected to governmental assaults on the advances workers fought long and hard to win in the political arena. The double-edged sword involved in the unions' reliance on labour law and the courts was manifest here, and it confirmed that trade unions in Canada desperately needed a new strategy to broaden and deepen their connection with their members, and indeed with working people generally, to build a political class consciousness that alone could transcend neo-liberalism.

Endnotes

1   Quoted in "Strike a Fight for Jobs," *Toronto Star,* November 21, 1997.

2   Quoted in Charles Perry, "PSAC's Rotating Strikes Set up in Moncton: Striking Government Employees Want Pay Equality with their Counterparts in the Private Sector," *Moncton Times and Transcript,* January 27, 1999.

3   "An Overview," in Gene Swimmer, ed., *Public Sector Labour Relations in an Era of Restraint and Restructuring* (Toronto: Oxford University Press, 2001), p. 1.

4   Alan Sears, "The 'Lean' State and Capitalist Restructuring: Towards a Theoretical Account," *Studies in Political Economy* 59 (1999): 91–114. This policy was foreshadowed by the Royal Commission on the Economic Union (McDonald Commission) which had emphasized Canada's failure to effectively integrate with global economic forces. See Canada, *Report: Royal Commission on the Economic Union and Development Prospects for Canada* (Ottawa: Ministry of Supply and Services, 1985) 2: 290–301.

5   See A. Jackson, et al., *Falling Behind: The State of Working in Canada 2000* (Ottawa: Canadian Centre for Policy Alternatives, 2000), 21–41.

6   Jim Stanford, "The Rise and Fall of Deficit-Mania: Public Sector Finances and the Attack on Social Canada," in L. Samuelson and W. Antony, eds., *Power and Resistance: Critical Thinking about Canadian Social Issues* (Halifax: Fernwood, 1998), 47–48.

7   Ibid, 33–35.

8   Ottawa-area Liberal candidates also declared their intention to abandon the coercive approach of the Mulroney era, in a clear bid to attract the votes of public servants living in the area. Ian Lee and Clem Hobbs, "Pink Slips and Running Shoes: The Liberal Government's Downsizing of the Public Service," in Gene Swimmer, ed., *How Ottawa Spends 1996–97: Life Under the Knife* (Ottawa: Carleton University Press, 1996), 337–8, 343.

9   Susan D. Philips, "The Liberals' Mid-Life Crises: Aspirations versus Achievements," in Susan D. Philips ed., *How Ottawa Spends 1995–96: Mid-Life Crises* (Ottawa: Carleton University Press, 1995), 11.

10 Gene Swimmer and Sandra Bach, "Restructuring Federal Public-Sector Human Resources," in Swimmer, ed., *Public Sector Labour Relations,* 189. The elimination of the increment was estimated to save approximately $400 million, but it is worth noting that "all personnel costs represent only eight percent of the [1994–95] budget. Even if the entire bureaucracy worked for free the 1994–95 federal deficit would be reduced by less than one third." Gene Swimmer, "Collective Bargaining in the Federal Public Service of Canada: The Last Twenty Years," in Gene Swimmer and Mark Thompson, eds., *Public Sector Collective Bargaining in Canada* (Kingston: IRC Press, 1995), 405.

11 Between 1993 and 1998, 53,000 positions were eliminated from the federal public service. Of those positions, the majority came from PSAC bargaining units, the union itself losing 21 percent of its membership. Professional unions, on the other hand, representing so-called "knowledge workers," were reduced in size by less than seven percent. The legislation used to facilitate downsizing suspended, for three years, key sections of the Workforce Adjustment Directive established after the 1991 strike to provide job security measures. In lieu of job security, those workers deemed to be surplus were offered buy-out packages. See Swimmer and Bach, "Restructuring Federal Public-Sector Human Resources," 179; Phillips, "The Liberals' Mid-Life Crises," 15–17; and Lee and Clem, "Pink Slips and Running Shoes," *passim.*

12 See Tony Van Alphen, "CP Rail Locks out 100 B.C. Workers: Labour Dispute Moves Closer to National Strike." *Toronto Star,* March 10, 1995; and "CAW Rejects Rotating Rail Walkouts," *Toronto Star,* March 11, 1995. On March 12, the railway settled negotiations with three smaller unions. "Rail Workers Picket for Contract," *Toronto Star,* March 13, 1995.

13 Canadian Press, "CAW Members Refuse to Cross CP Picket Lines," *Hamilton Spectator,* March 17, 1995.

14 Nicolas van Rijn, "Strike Strands Thousands: 31,000 CN, CP Rail Employees Walk Off the Job," *Toronto Star,* March 19, 1995.

15 Sandro Contenta and Tony Van Alphen, "Ottawa to End Rail Strike: Settle Quickly or Face Legislation CN, VIA Rail unions warned," *Toronto Star,* March 20, 1995.

16 David Israelson, "Economic 'Panic' Sets in: Rail Strike Called 'Severe Whammy' to Other Jobs," *Toronto Star,* March 21, 1995.

17 Edison Stewart, "Bloc Move Derails Bid for Fast End to Strike," *Toronto Star,* March 21, 1995.

18 See "Postal Union set to strike this week: Officials stick to deadline of tomorrow," *Toronto Star,* November 11, 1997; and "Canada Post Wants new union position: But CUPW dismisses crown corporation's 'posturing,'" *Toronto Star,* November 15, 1997.

19 Ottawa Bureau, "On the Picket Lines," *Toronto Star,* November 20, 1997; Chris Cobb, "Ottawa Sets Deadline for Postal Strike," *Hamilton Spectator,* November 22, 1997; Chris Cobb, "Both Sides Say Postal Pact within Reach: Charities Appeal for Early End to Revenue-Crippling Mail Strike," *Hamilton Spectator,* November 21, 1997. Cf. Russell Janzen, Jerry White, and Carla Lipsig-Mummé, "Junked Mail: The Politics and Consequences of Privatization," *Studies in Political Economy* 65 (Summer 2001).

20 See "Time Running Out in Postal Talks, Mediator Warns: Next Two Days Seen as Critical for Negotiated Settlement," *Toronto Star,* November 27, 1997.

21 Mark Dunn, "Back-to-work Legislation Tabled: Wage Settlement Imposed on Posties," *Hamilton Spectator,* December 2, 1997, B1; Rosemary Spiers, "Ottawa Hints at Ending Posties' Strike Right," *Toronto Star,* December 4, 1997.

22 *Postal Services Continuation Act, 1997.*

23 Quoted in Charles Perry, "PSAC's Rotating Strikes Set up in Moncton: Striking Government Employees Want Pay Equality with Their Counterparts in the Private Sector," *Moncton Times and Transcript,* January 27, 1999.

24 "PSAC Picketers Say Police Charged First: Police Decked out in Riot Gear before Trouble Broke Out," *Hamilton Spectator,* March 11, 1999.

25 Bill C-76 did not prevent prison guards from striking but it empowered the federal government to order workers back to work at any time and to impose a settlement. Interestingly, the guards were only in a legal strike position due to a clerical error that left certain members of the union off the designation list. The first-ever strike by federal prison guards lasted four days before the government ordered them back to their jobs, imposing a wage settlement of 2.5 percent, 2 percent and 2 percent a year in a three-year deal. See "Striking Prison Guards Ordered Back to Work: Union Leaders Condemn Government's Quick Move on Legislation," *Moncton Times and Transcript,* March 31, 1997.

26 "Legislation Passed to End PSAC Strikes: Union President Still Undecided Whether Members Will Obey Back-to-work Order or Wait Until Ratification Vote Before Abandoning Pickets," *Moncton Times and Transcript,* March 25, 1999.

27 Christopher Schenk, "Fifty Years After PC 1003: The Need for New Directions," in Cy Gonick, Paul Phillips, and Jesse Vorst, eds., *Labour Gains, Labour Pains: 50 Years of PC 1003* (Halifax: Fernwood, 1995), 199.

28 Buzz Hargrove of the CAW began a strategy of writing joint letters with large-scale employers to call for the government to rethink its strategy. On board were Chrysler, McDonnell Douglas, and Nestlé, as well as fourteen smaller enterprises, which argued that Bill 7 would end a long period of relative labour peace. Even Peel Regional Police Chief Robert Lunney questioned the wisdom of the new law considering its potential to increase the level of strike violence. See James Laxer, "Common Sense Comes from Labour Leader, not Harris," *Toronto Star,* October 8, 1995; and Thomas Walkom, "Police Uneasy over Tories' Divisive Labour Bill," *Toronto Star,* November 7, 1995.

29 The changes had their desired effects in terms of decreasing certification rates and increasing decertification rates. See Felice Martinello, "Mr. Harris, Mr. Rae and Union Activity in Ontario," *Canadian Public Policy,* 26:1 (2000).

30 William Walker, "Tories Eye Private Firms for Government Services," *Toronto Star,* October 10, 1995.

31 Sid Noel, "Ontario's Tory Revolution," in Sid Noel, ed., *Revolution at Queen's Park* (Toronto: Lorimer, 1997), 1–2.

32 Earlier that month, the OPP had shot Anthony Dudley George, an Aboriginal activist, at a land-claims protest at Ipperwash Provincial Park. There is currently a wrongful-death lawsuit pending against Harris, among others, for allegedly directing the police to use force if necessary to remove the protesters. Bill Dare, "Harris's First Year: Attacks and Resistance," in Diana Ralph, Andre Regimbald and Nerée St-Amand , eds., *Open For Business, Closed To People: Mike Harris's Ontario* (Halifax: Fernwood, 1997), 21.

33 James L. Turk, "Days of Action: Challenging the Harris Corporate Agenda," ibid., 165–76.

34 Sam Gindin, "Toronto: Days of Action, Days of Hope," *Canadian Dimension* (Jan.–Feb. 1997): 11.

35 See Joe Flexer, "Days of Action or DOA?" *Canadian Dimension* (Sept.–Oct. 1997); Marcella Munroe, "Ontario's 'Days of Action' and strategic choices for the Left in Canada," *Studies in Political Economy* 53, (Summer 1997); and Marsha Niemeijer, "The Ontario Days of Action—The Beginning of a Redefinition of the Labour Movement's Political Strategy?" Paper presented to the Fourth International Working Conference of the Transnational Information Exchange (TIE) on "The Building of a Labour Movement for Radical Change," Cologne, March 16–19, 2000.

36 Joan Kuyek, "A Celebration of Resistance in Sudbury," *Canadian Dimension* (May–June 1997): 46.

37 Gloria Galloway, "Workfare Draws Fire: Working for Benefits Without Union is Called an Outrage," *Hamilton Spectator,* June 30, 1998.

38 As with Bill 7, the changes to the industrial relations regime were rammed through without any public hearings, passing the bill in less than three weeks, much to the pleasure of building contractors and the Retail Council of Canada. Daniel Girard, "Tough labour bill approved," *Toronto Star,* June 24, 1998.

39 Labour Minister Chris Stockwell cited Statistics Canada data showing a decline in union density in Ontario from 31.7 percent in 1990 to 28.1 percent in 1999 as justification for further limits on unions. For Stockwell, the decline in union density was due to unions losing touch with people. That his government had actively and effectively used legislation to lower union density apparently hadn't occurred to the minister. Apparently, the Tories had even considered eliminating the Rand Formula. Richard Brennan, "Labour Losing its Clout in Ontario: Stockwell: Minister Cites Declining Rolls, Union Infighting," *Toronto Star,* December 29, 2000.

40 Steve Arnold, "White Paper Weakens Worker Rights," *Hamilton Spectator,* July 28, 2000, A1; Alliance of Canadian Manufacturers and Exporters, "Alliance Recommendations Re: Ontario Labour Standards," *Press Release, Canada Newswire,* August 23, 2000.

41 Jeff Rose, "From Softball to Hardball: The Transition in Labour-Management Relations in the Ontario Public Service," in Swimmer, ed., *Public Sector Labour Relations,* 76–7.

42 David Rapaport, *No Justice, No Peace: The 1996 OPSEU Strike against the Harris Government in Ontario,* (Montreal: McGill-Queen's University Press, 1999), 3–6.

43 1996 Lancaster's *Collective Agreement Reporter* quoted in Jeff Rose, "From Softball to Hardball," 80.

44 R.D. Gidney, *From Hope to Harris: The Reshaping of Ontario's Schools* (Toronto: University of Toronto Press, 1999), 246–248, 256.

45 Harry Glasbeek, "Class War: Ontario Teachers and the Courts," *Osgoode Hall Law Journal* 37:4 (1999): 813.

46 Tanya Talaga, "Who is Going to Back Down? Teachers Anxious, Not Excited as Classes Start," *Toronto Star,* September 3, 1998.

47 During a previous use of such legislation against teachers in the Lennox and Addington County Board of Education in January of 1997, Education Minister John Snobelen had publicly stated that teachers' right to strike should be banned. Ontario Secondary Schools Teachers Federation (OSSTF) president Earl Manners retorted that the law allowing teachers to strike had worked well since its inception under the Bill Davis Conservative government in the 1970s, adding, "I find it hard to believe that a law that has worked 98 per cent of the time is obsolete." Quoted by Greg Crone, "Tories Order Teachers Back to Classrooms," *Hamilton Spectator,* January 31,1997. Back-to-work measures would be used against teachers on two more occasions over the next four years, in Hamilton in 2000, and Simcoe County in 2002. A further back-to-work measure was used in the education sector in 2001 against support staff represented by CUPE in Toronto and Windsor.

48 OPSEU, "What is the Strike About?" March 12, 2002, OPSEU Web page: http://www.opseu.org/ops/bargaining/strikeabour.htm.

49 See Graeme Smith and Richard Mackie, "OPSEU and Government Preparing for Long Haul: Political Pressure Unlikely to Build Soon and Union is Supported by Large War Chest," *Globe and Mail,* March 14, 2002; Richard Mackie, "Ontario Accuses Union of Abuses: Essential Services Not in Jeopardy as Sides Prepare for Lengthy Strike," *Globe and Mail,* March 16, 2002; and Amy Carmichael, "OPSEU Strike Ends with Tentative Deal: Terms of Deal Include 8.45 Percent Raise over Three Years," *Toronto Star,* May 2, 2002.

50 Bruce Demara, "City Braces for Summer Chaos," *Toronto Star,* June 27, 2002; Kerry Gillespie, "17,000 More Poised to Join City Walkout," *Toronto Star,* June 28, 2002.

51 The legislation introduced the next day included provisions for the government to unilaterally name the mediator-arbitrator, who would use final offer selection to decide the outcome. See Paul Moloney, "Trash Cleanup Begins under City Health Order," *Toronto Star,* July 6, 2002; Theresa Boyle and Richard Brennan, "Eves Recalls MPPs to End City Strike: NDP Vows Bill Won't Get Swift Passage," *Toronto Star,* July 10, 2002; Richard Mackie, "Talks Fail, So Strike Drags on: Bid for Truce is Rejected; Back-to-work Bill May be Held up Two Weeks in Legislature," *Globe and Mail,* July 11, 2002.

52 *Summerside Journal,* May 12, 1994.

53 NSGEU summary of ILO decision against Bills 41 (1993) and 52 (1994).

54 ILO case number 1802 against the Nova Scotia government.

55 Notes for a presentation by Joan Jessome, NSGEU president, "Final Offer Selection—Assessing a new approach for breaking the impasse in healthcare negotiations," delivered to the Canadian National Summit on Labour Relations in the Health Care Sector, Toronto, January 28, 2002.

56 "N.B. Hospital Workers Reach Deal," *Globe and Mail,* March 5, 2001.

57 Newfoundland and Labrador Federation of Labour "Strategic Partnership Initiative," www.nlfl.nf.ca.

58 The Quebec Federation of Labour's Solidarity Fund was established in 1983 in order to help bail out Quebec business and save union jobs. The Confédération des syndicats nationaux developed a similar fund in 1996 called Fondaction.

59 "Supporters Beef up Picket Lines," *Montreal Gazette,* July 3, 1999.

60 Yonatan Reshef, "The Logic of Union Quiescence: The Alberta Case," in Swimmer, ed., *Public Sector Labour Relations,* 132.

61 These acts included *The Industrial Wages Security Act* (1993), *The Employment Standards Code Amendment Act* (1994), *The Labour Board Amalgamation Act* (1994), and *The Managerial Exclusion Act* (1995).

62 Kerry Williamson, "ATA Ponders Action as Bill 12 Made Law," *Calgary Herald,* March 14, 2002.

63 A. Kyle, "Unions Seek 14% Raise," *Regina Leader-Post,* February 15, 1992. See also R. Burton, "Playing Tough with Labour Strange Ploy," *Saskatoon Star Phoenix,* November 26, 1992; and "Money for Some," *Briarpatch* (February 1993): 14.

64 See M. Mandryk, "MAL Trying to Alter Trade Union Act," *Regina Leader-Post,* June 3, 1993; and A. Kyle, "Defeated Bill Incites Union Protests," *Regina Leader Post,* June 12, 1993.

65 Although it did encourage unionized contractors in large projects undertaken with public funds. See G. Manz, "Construction Spinoffs," *Briarpatch* (October, 1992): 23; M. Wyatt, "Labour Bill Placates Critics," *Regina Leader Post,* August 26, 1992; G. Brock, "Non-union Shops Worried," *Regina Leader-Post,* May 19, 1993; and K. O'Connor, "Union Hiring Debate Nasty," *Regina Leader-Post,* May 20, 1993.

66 See Jocelyne Praud and Sarah McQuarrie, "The Saskatchewan CCF-NDP from the Regina Manifesto to the

Romanow Years," in Howard A. Leeson, ed., *Saskatchewan Politics into the Twenty-First Century* (Regina: Canadian Plains Research Centre, 2001), 156–57.

67 Martin O'Hanlon, "Saskatchewan Nurses Vow to Defy NDP's Back-to-work Order," *Globe and Mail,* April 9, 1999.

68 Alex Netherton, "Paradigm Shift: A Sketch of Manitoba Politics," in Keith Brownsey and Michael Howlett, eds., *The Provincial State in Canada: Politics in the Provinces and Territories* (Peterborough: Broadview, 2001), 227.

69 Paul Phillips and Carolina Stecher, "Fiscal Restraint, Legislated Concessions, and Labour Relations in the Manitoba Civil Service, 1988–1997," in Swimmer, ed., *Public Sector Labour Relations,* 102–03.

70 Later amended on June 27, 1997 and its title changed to the *Essential Services Act* (Bill 15).

71 Manitoba Federation of Labour, *Brief to the Manitoba Legislature on Bill 44, The Labour Relations Amendment Act,* July 25, 2000.

72 D. Wilson, "B.C.'s Labour Bill Faces Easier Ride than Ontario's," *Globe and Mail,* October 28, 1992. It seems that part of the explanation for the modesty of Bill 84 (and business's muted reaction) was the accommodative stance of the BC Federation of Labour, which was "careful not to spell out a bottom line for the labour movement (and) veered away from worker rights, equality and promoting collective bargaining." Bill Zander, "Expectations of Labour Reform from B.C.'s Harcourt Run High," *Tribune,* June 8, 1992, 6. Zander also noted that the Federation really pushed cooperation, and appended three academic papers to its brief, two of which (those by Roy Adams and Thomas Cochan) were forthright appeals for tripartism. The government took the unions support so much for granted that the advisory panel on Bill 84 included only one trade unionist.

73 R. Matas, "B.C. Moves to Force Teachers Back to Work," *Globe and Mail,* May 31, 1993; and "B.C. Minister Favouring Teachers, Board Charges," *Toronto Star,* May 21, 1993.

74 See the Hospital Employees Union's *Comprehensive Report,* March 1993.

75 Petti Fong, Jim Beatty and Paul Willcocks, "CUPE Warns NDP of Lost Support," *Vancouver Sun* April 5, 2000.

76 Editorial, "Back-to-work Law Too Little, Too Late," *Vancouver Sun,* April 4, 2000.

77 Jim Beatty and Petti Fong, "Campbell Ends Strikes, Forces Deal on Nurses, Health Workers," *Vancouver Sun,* August 8, 2001.

78 Jim Beatty and Craig McInnes, "Hospitals Will Close Admits: Legislature Debates Controversial Labour Bills," *Vancouver Sun,* January 28, 2002.

79 Rod Mickleburgh, "New B.C. Labour Bill Angers Unions," *Globe and Mail* May 14, 2002.

80 James Steiger, "Out of Balance: BC Human Rights Tribunal," Society for Academic Freedom and Scholarship *Newsletter,* April 2000. www.safs.ca.

81 *International Longshoremen's and Warehouseman's Union—Canada Area Local 500 v. Canada* [1994], 1 S.C.R. 150.

82 *Dunmore v. Ontario (Attorney General)* [2001] 3 S.C.R. 1016.

83 Ibid., see paras. 42, 45,51.

84 Ibid., para. 41; and see *Delisle v. Canada (Deputy Attorney General)* [1999] 2 S.C.R. 989.

85 *U.F.C.W. Local 1518 v. K-Mart Canada Ltd.* [1999], 2 S.C.R. 1083.

86 See Michael MacNeil, "Labour Picketting and Consumer Boycotts: Judicial Ideology in K-Mart and Allsco," *Canadian Labour and Employment Law Journal,* 8 (2001): 82–4.

87 *Hersees of Woodstock Ltd.* v. *Goldstein* [1963] 38 D.L.R. (2d) 449 (Ont. C.A.).

88 *UFCW v. K-Mart,* at para. 28.

89 UFCW News Release, "Major Victory for Canadian Workers, UFCW says," September 9, 1999.

90 Glasbeek, "Class Wars," 824–5.

91 *R.W.D.S.U., Local 558 v. Pepsi-Cola Canada Beverages (West) Ltd.* [2002] SCC 8, para. 21.

92 Ibid., para.24.

93 Ibid., para. 85.

94 *R. v. Advance Cutting and Coring Ltd.,* [2001] 3 S.C.R. 209.

95 Ibid., para. 162.

96 See L. Spink, ed., *Bad Work: A review of papers from a Fraser Institute conference on "right-to-work" laws,* Working Paper No. 16, Centre for Research on Work and Society, York University, 1997.

CHAPTER 16

Canadian Labour and the Political Economy of Transformation

Sam Gindin and Jim Stanford

Introduction

THE TRADE UNION movement constitutes a central feature in the overall constellation of organizing social change in Canada. Unions reflect a large and relatively well-organized membership: close to four million Canadians are represented under collective bargaining provisions of one form or another, or about 30 percent of all paid workers. Compared to most popular organizations, unions are relatively stable and well-funded. And since they organize workers at the point of production, unions carry unique potential to exert concrete economic pressure that can be levied in the direct private interests of union members, as well as in the pursuit of broader social and political goals.

But to what extent can the labour movement be expected to act as an agent of far-reaching social transformation? (We imagine transformation as going beyond simply asking for a better deal from capital and capitalism to demanding and enforcing some form of structural change in property relationships that would democratize and socialize economic processes.) Trade unions under capitalism have traditionally reflected a dual character, serving to advance workers' demands for better treatment (both inside and outside the workplace), while also containing the militancy and activism of their members.[1] Both the traditional faith of Marxists that labour was destined to serve as the agent of revolution and the subsequent reaction by "new social movement" theorists dismissing labour as an actively progressive force overlooked the contingent nature of the process of moving beyond capitalism. The possibility of building a new society is neither inevitable nor preordained; it depends on all kinds of economic, political, and historical factors. Because of labour's central location in the capitalist order, our radical hopes depend particularly on the development of the political capacities of the working class. If the working class, with all its flaws and complex diversity, is not there, then ultimately social transformation won't happen.

> Without labour's material resources, without labour's organizational capacity and unique ability to affect the economy (while others protest, labour can shut down capital's life-lines in production and services), without the radicalization of working people and without a working class with a universal sense of social justice—without all of this no movement can sustain hopes of transforming the world. (Gindin 2002, 9)

Three particular political developments over Canada's past quarter century are useful starting points for coming concretely to grips with the potentials of, and barriers inherent in, labour's role in transformation. First, there has been a shift of leadership within progressive oppositional struggles from formal party politics to coalitions of extra-parliamentary forces, prominently including labour itself. Second, there has also been a shift over time and through consecutive campaigns and struggles in the ideological orientation of this broad opposition movement. And finally and more recently, there have emerged a number of parallel political projects aimed at developing a new politics on Canada's left—one that could unite progressive labour more closely with other mobilized social forces.

As the so-called postwar Golden Age ended and capital's search for a renewed political-economic project settled upon a neo-liberal orientation, labour's official political arm—the New Democratic Party (NDP)—began a long descent into marginalization. Major cracks in the relationship between the NDP and the labour movement opened up when the NDP (including elected provincial governments) supported wage controls in the mid-1970s. Later the NDP was uncertain in opposing free trade, ineffective in responding to the attack on the welfare state, and then staggered and demoralized by electoral setbacks in the 1990s. Meanwhile, the labour movement was increasingly taking independent initiatives in partnership with loose and evolving social coalitions to act on the major issues of our times. Even by the time of the free trade debate, it was already clear that the main opposition was not in Parliament but in the streets. Later, during the historic Days of Action protests against the Harris government in Ontario (in which several Ontario cities were essentially shut down by rotating one-day general strikes), people did not even ask why this remarkable political initiative was coming from labour and its coalition partners—rather than from the party whose raison d'être was supposedly to specialize in and lead progressive politics. A profound and exciting change in the location of left political leadership seemed to have taken place.

In its early stages, this broader oppositional constituency was rather conservative in the traditional sense of opposing change and maintaining what was. In the fight against free trade, this conservativism was commonly expressed in a romanticized vision of Canada's past and present. By the mid-1990s, however, the populist nationalism of the free trade campaigns was unevenly evolving into a focus that was internationalist, that identified corporate freedoms as undermining democratic freedoms, and that began to link a democratic orientation to an anti-capitalist one. As evidenced in more recent struggles against globalization (such as the historic events in Quebec City in April 2001), this new radicalism also reflected a generational change in the movement's energy. The positive legacy of these protests has been the combativeness, cultural rebelliousness, organizational abilities, and anti-capitalist/anti-imperialist orientation of a new youth and student movement.

In the wake of the continued weakness in the NDP and its alienation from emerging nonelectoral struggles and movements on the left, there is now a (healthy) turmoil in left politics. Greg Albo (2002) has described the emergence of three distinct political projects on the left: the expansion of nonelectoral protest movements in civil society (represented most forcefully at present in the antiglobalization campaigns); efforts to revive a more ambitious and movement-connected form of social democracy; and initial efforts to rebuild a socialist left with the explicit goal of moving beyond capitalism. Potential support for and engagement with each of these projects on the part of Canadian labour will be an important factor influencing the future trajectory of Canadian social change.

The first of these three tracks—the protest movements of civil society—reflects a general alienation from formal and electoral politics and aims to challenge state power from without. It is not interested in entering the state or capturing state power. The second strand, a revitalized and more movement-connected social democracy,[2] accepts the necessity of addressing state power, yet still expresses faith in the state as an entity that can be "captured" for progressive purposes—so long as the right people are elected. A more critical understanding of the state's inherent and structurally biased role within capitalism has yet to be developed among most of these supporters of a renewed social democracy.

The third view, influenced by traditional Marxist approaches, agrees with the fundamental importance of addressing state power but sees current state institutions as historically developed and fundamentally capitalist in nature; this state has, for example, particular hierarchical capacities to effect change from above but lacks the institutional capacities to support a more collective and democratic administration of our lives. This "rebuilding the left" movement (sometimes referred to as a structured movement against capitalism, or SMAC) consequently sees its project as developing a left politics aimed not only at taking state power but also at radically transforming the state as part of a broader effort to transform social and economic structures.[3]

Each of these three projects is in transition, because—given the nature of the present moment, both in Canada and internationally—each is necessarily experimental and unstable. That is, each confronts or will soon confront questions around which there is no ready answer and around which internal divisions exist. At present there seems to be a unique opportunity for these projects to operate in parallel fashion with relatively friendly relations and even some informal division of tasks. Over time, however, these currently separate projects—each of which has, to varying degrees, enlisted support from individual labour activists and labour organizations—will eventually have their own splits and overlaps, raising the issue of new alliances and new formations.

In addressing these issues and challenges from the perspective of labour's role, the task facing the labour movement is often posed in terms of its collective ability to form a progressive alliance with other social movements. What this formulation obscures, however, is that there is no homogeneity within labour (nor within the other social movements, for that matter) and that the process of labour's further politicization will in fact require further polarizations and divisions within the labour movement as these differences are manifested and grappled with. A myriad of ongoing debates and divisions within labour already amply attests to the contested terrain that lies ahead—including divisions over the continuing acceptance by some unions of significant bargaining concessions (like the trend toward longer-term collective agreements), ongoing disputes over organized labour's relationship to the NDP, and the expulsion from the Canadian Labour Congress in 2000, subsequently reversed, of the largest private-sector union in Canada, the Canadian Auto Workers (nominally sparked by the CAW's alleged "raiding" of members from a U.S.-based union, but actually reflecting many deeper political and organizational disputes).

Without hoping for or celebrating divisions in the labour movement, we must nevertheless recognize that apparent unity never automatically implies active solidarity. The American labour movement, for example, demonstrated great unity once its left opposition had been destroyed in the Cold War, but few would celebrate its dynamism. Any process of labour radicalization will inevitably be uneven, implying major differences and internal struggles as that radicalization occurs. Links between organized labour and the various political projects identified above are therefore not likely to occur through direct ties to labour, but rather through processes of political mediation that bring like-minded sections of each constituency together. New organizational structures will need to develop, structures that can operate within the openings that have emerged thanks to recent struggles. These structures will work to build new understandings, new

relationships, and new ways of undertaking new kinds of political tasks.

Consider, for example, the political openings created by the Ontario Days of Action.[4] It is hardly adequate to lament that a remarkable series of actions faded into a whimper because of the labour bureaucracy or labour divisions. As relevant as *those* factors were, they are part of the terrain; the more important question is why the left could only complain about but had no capacity to influence these developments. Why, for example, couldn't the left build on the momentum of the Days of Action to recruit initially hesitant unions and locals to a more activist and militant political orientation? Why, after incredible local coalitions were built to successfully organize these unprecedented actions, could the left not provide leadership to help those coalitions evolve and continue their work after the Days were over?

The problems inherent in the left's relationship with organized labour and the contingency of labour's role in evolving struggles was perhaps never symbolically clearer than in the Quebec City protests of April 2001. By bringing tens of thousands of workers out, labour (and especially labour in Quebec) showed its potential power. But by leading them on the infamous "march to nowhere" (a long parade away from the summit site to an isolated and deserted parking lot), organized labour raised questions about its ability to effectively use that potential. There were enough workers in that march—workers of every generation—who will take up the challenge of radicalizing their own unions, but this is not only a problem of labour. The students and others who played such an inspiring role in Quebec will also have to ask—together with the left more generally—how to orient their focus, their demands, and their structures with the aim of integrating

Canadian labour more solidly into their future campaigns.

This chapter will discuss the current state of Canada's labour movement and its potential transformative capacities in the context of the corresponding development of the broader political and economic environment facing the Canadian left. The first section reviews Canadian labour's uneven response to the challenges posed by the erosion of the postwar Golden Age political economy and the subsequent period of neo-liberal restructuring. The second section considers the implications of the present economic conjuncture for the traditional efforts of the labour movement to extract incremental gains and improvements (at the bargaining table and more broadly) from capital. Even the successful pursuit of this traditional reformist role for organized labour will require a far-reaching reinvention of the movement's standard practices. The final section briefly considers the prerequisites and possibilities for the labour movement, in the context of the aforementioned developments in the broader left, to pursue a more transformative political and economic vision.

Beyond Golden-Age Trade-Offs

The postwar institutionalization of labour relations in Canada (as in other developed capitalist economies) explicitly cemented the leading economic role of private employers and capital in return for an enhanced ability to bargain over the proceeds of the resulting economic growth. This trade-off was fully consistent with the politics of social democracy, which in Canada (as elsewhere) was the official political expression of the labour movement. While postwar Canadian capitalism was vibrant and growing, during the three decades of the

so-called Golden Age, Canadian unions and their members seemed to do well by this formula.[5] Union membership grew dramatically and so did the militance of union members. Important concessions were extracted (often only after tremendous and sometimes violent struggles) from individual employers and from the economic system as a whole. These victories included higher incomes (average real earnings doubled in Canada in a generation), an extension and formalization of workplace rights (including significant progress in health and safety protection), and the construction of a broader network of regulations and social policies that more generally underwrote the economic security of working people.

In the mid-1970s, however, when the dynamic of capitalist accumulation began to sputter, the mutuality of this institutionalized arrangement began to break down.[6] The further development of the labour movement and economic progress for workers (unionized or not) ran into a brick wall of slower investment, a consequent slowdown in economic and productivity growth, increased intensity of competition between firms (including international competition), and the retrenchment of public-sector programs and activities. Since unions had never tried to develop the capacity to independently challenge the economic leadership of private firms—and in particular to conceive of mechanisms through which the dominant role of private investment in initiating production could be supplemented and eventually replaced by alternative channels of accumulation—the slowdown left the labour movement naturally on the defensive, trying with varying degrees of success to preserve victories won in earlier, more vibrant times.

All of this must of course be placed in the context of Canada's unique economic integration with the United States, the imperial leader in capitalism's drive to implement the social changes subsequently identified with neo-liberalism and globalization. Among other things, this integration tied Canada to the most deregulated and unequal labour market in the industrialized world. This integration results in the strong continentalist pressures facing Canadian firms and, through them, their workers. For the labour movement, this integration is also reflected in the fact that most private-sector union members actually belong to U.S.-based unions. The labour movement's choices about how to respond to the broad U-turn in economic conditions were thus bound up with the corresponding issues of both overall Canadian sovereignty and the autonomy and democracy of Canadian unions.

After two decades of neo-liberal restructuring, the Canadian labour movement finds itself in a complex and uneasy state of affairs. Business has won obviously important victories in reshaping the political and economic environment in its favour, with negative implications for workers and their unions. The industrial relations playing field has been tilted and structured in a more business-friendly direction. Macroeconomic policy explicitly abandoned the postwar commitment to full employment, and instead—led by anti-inflation monetary authorities—began to proactively manage the labour market, with the aim of maintaining a certain desirable margin of long-run unemployment. Meanwhile, the network of public programs and services that both underwrote the economic security of working households and supplemented the consumption possibilities offered by their private money incomes came under sustained pressure for both fiscal and political reasons.

Despite this process, the Canadian labour movement—while certainly on the defensive—has not been routed. Canada is one of only a handful of countries in which the unionization rate (and therefore the organizational base of the labour movement) did not substantially decline during the 1980s and 1990s—although private-sector unionization has been declining, and, combined with the contraction of public-sector employment, this decline is now pulling down overall unionization. Many unions still demonstrate a punchy stubbornness in continuing to wage tough battles for recouping past losses and concessions in collective bargaining and for organizing unorganized workers into new unions in a wide array of industries. Strike frequency, which declined dramatically in Canada between the 1970s and the 1990s, has more recently shown some sign of a moderate rebound.

The structural dependence of the Canadian economy on the United States also informed the emergence of a firmer and eventually more radical and internationalist movement—a movement rooted in organized labour and other constituencies—against the free trade agreements and other manifestations of globalization. It became increasingly clear as North American integration proceeded that the possibility of establishing a "national capitalist" regime of Canadian accumulation rooted in an alliance between domestic property owners and an interventionist state was evaporating. Virtually all major businesses operating in Canada, including those owned by Canadians, became globally (or at least U.S.-) oriented, and the economic base for the former liberal nationalist project disappeared. Thanks to this experience, Canadian labour activists and other progressives were alerted to the dangers of corporate globalization before their comrades in most other countries. More importantly, they have become more likely to express their concerns with an internationalist, anti-corporate bent. It has become abundantly clear to most Canadian progressives that empowering and protecting private domestic firms is not the answer to globalization (since those companies have been at least as likely to undermine or lay off their Canadian workers as any foreign multinational). What are required, rather, are forms of regulated accountability for private companies and investors of any national stripe; this suggests a more internationalist and anti-capitalist politics on the part of the antiglobalization campaigners.[7]

The Labour Movement in a "Grim Economy"

There are some indications that the neo-liberal program has at least partially restored the vitality of profit-led accumulation in Canada. Business profits, investment, and job creation strengthened markedly in the latter 1990s, generating rising real incomes for the first time in two decades and contributing to a dramatic recovery in public finances. Yet the overall system remains vulnerable to external shocks and crises, and even at the best of times its profitability remains unspectacular, its sustainability uncertain. To the extent that an internally consistent regime of capitalist accumulation has indeed been restored in Canada, it certainly does not look like another Golden Age. The institutions of labour-market regulation and redistribution in Canada are presently too weak for continued economic growth to have as strong a positive impact on living conditions for the majority of Canadians as was the case in earlier decades; and at any rate, the extent

of that growth will be strictly controlled by central bankers still vigilant for any upsurge in the demands of labour—whether organized or not. We might call this regime (to the extent that it has been coherently established) a "grim economy": accumulation and growth will occur, but continuing strict limits are imposed on wages, labour activism, and public programs.

Perhaps the two-decade-long neo-liberal restructuring of Canada's economy and the subsequent and incomplete revitalization of private capital accumulation has restored some economic and political space for the pursuit of labour's traditional reformist (or "economist") goals—effected through efforts to extract concessions from individual employers, as well as initiatives to reconstruct the broader network of social protections. Even the unsure vitality that Canada's increasingly business-dominated economy began to demonstrate by the late 1990s was sufficient to open up room for some Canadian unions to shift to a more offensive position—aiming to win back some of the concessions extracted by business during the preceding two decades and capture a share of the productivity gains implied by a renewal of business investment and economic expansion. In some sectors revitalized productivity growth and business profitability, combined with sustained union mobilizing capacity, translated into significant economic gains for workers.[8] In others, like education and health, the sheer frustration of public-sector workers, coupled with understaffing resulting from past government policies, produced historically unparalleled militancy on the part of teachers, nurses, and other public-sector trade unionists.

But progress of this sort will hardly be typical across the broader labour movement, for various reasons. In the first place, the profitability and productivity demonstrated by technology-intensive, export-oriented manufacturing sectors is not representative of the economic conditions experienced by most Canadian businesses. Continuing fiscal constraints in the public sector—where over half of all Canadian union members are employed—will make it difficult for most public-sector unions even to recoup the concessions extracted by employers in the 1990s (when most public-sector workers had their wages frozen, resulting in real wage cuts averaging 10 percent), let alone to share in the fruits of a new era of growth and prosperity.

In addition, the labour movement's internal struggles became more intense as the period of neo-liberal restructuring drew to a close. Traditional jurisdictional lines within the labour movement, which had informally allocated workers in particular sectors or industries to corresponding sector-based unions, broke down in the face of several factors: stagnation in total union membership, cross-sectoral union mergers, and a more aggressive, competitive approach to organizing new members. (These factors, common in other industrialized countries, were accentuated in Canada, where the structure of unions was distorted by their American branch-plant roots: in spite of its much smaller population, Canada had as many unions as the United States, thanks to the often-small Canadian branches of U.S. unions.) Unions effectively came into direct competition with each other—both in their efforts to organize brand-new members, as well as in representation contests associated with the restructuring of various private-sector and public-sector workplaces.[9]

There were profound differences within the labour movement over how to respond to neo-

liberalism. These broader conflicts included controversies over concession bargaining, corporatist relations with business, the constitution of the Canadian Labour Congress (CLC) (especially in its effective prohibition of disaffected union members' right to change unions), and labour's respective relationships with the NDP and grass-roots movements for social change. Most private-sector unions (including all major private-sector unions except the CAW) organized an explicit caucus in the late 1990s (the so-called Pink Paper Group) to wield a focused moderating influence at conventions of the CLC and its provincial federations. Meanwhile, when action-oriented resolutions were passed at these same conventions, they were often simply ignored by federation leaders or else effectively vetoed (through non-participation or more active opposition) by key private-sector affiliates. By the late 1990s, Canada's labour centrals—the CLC and its provincial federations—had lost the effective ability to sponsor united campaigns and other initiatives.

Where rank-and-file militancy was sustained, a space was created for building a more mobilized, radicalized, and creative movement. But in the absence of a socialist current within the unions with a longer-term perspective on building working class capacities, that space was not occupied. Labour's commitment to broader initiatives—like the one-day workplace shutdowns organized as part of the Ontario Days of Action—was never complete and always contested. And even relatively successful campaigns did not translate into a more lasting and secure commitment to ongoing labour-community activism.

It is ironic, therefore, that just as the economic pendulum may be swinging back—unsteadily and unpredictably—toward a position that might allow for a resumption of forward reformist progress on the part of Canadian labour, the labour movement itself may be largely incapable of seizing the opportunity. Rank-and-file members of many unions are not engaged in union education or mobilizing initiatives; to many workers, unions are at best a service organization. And union structures have yet to adequately adapt to an economic and political environment requiring more flexibility and accountability than in the past. Yet even to win modest, reformist bargaining gains in the context of a grim economy, in which both competitive pressure and direct policy (by the central bank and other state institutions) tightly constrain the forward progress of labour, will require a far-reaching rejuvenation of union activity, starting at the level of the individual members whose loyalty has been sorely tested by the widespread passivity of many unions through the past two decades.

In other words, unions and union activists need to "think big" just to preserve the labour movement's capacity to win incremental, reformist gains for Canadian workers. Given the continued hostility of the economic and institutional environment, unions will have to become more activist, more democratic, and more radical just to rebuild their ability to fight for a better share of continued business-led expansion—let alone to fight for more fundamental, more transformative changes in Canada's economy and society. The axes along which this process of change will need to occur include the following.

Organizing the Unorganized

Union density in the public sector has been stable in Canada, but the public sector has been shrinking as a share of total employment.

Meanwhile, unionization in private-sector industries has been slowly slipping, falling below 20 percent by the end of the 1990s. Organizing success has been held back by numerous factors, including subtle but important changes in labour law (in areas such as card-check certification and other organizing procedures), sophisticated employer resistance, the broadly anti-union and individualistic influence of the mass media and popular culture, and an often-justified skepticism among many workers that joining a union can genuinely improve their working lives.[10] All this has made the already uphill struggle to organize new union members even harder.[11] The recognition that unions need to organize or die is relatively widespread in the labour movement, even among otherwise conservative unions, and the expenditure of resources on organizing drives has been significant. The results of these efforts, however, have so far been generally discouraging. Despite some efforts to be more systematic, more creative, and more representative in organizing drives; despite experiments such as the use of grass-roots and volunteer organizers (rather than professional organizing staff), community-rooted organizing campaigns (in which numerous employers in particular neighbourhoods or communities are targetted with integrated union drives), and the adoption of certification procedures that sidestep existing hostile legal requirements[12] and despite an increased sensitivity to the changing colour of the Canadian labour force and efforts to find and map communities of new immigrants—despite all of this, unions are losing many more organizing campaigns than they are winning.

If economic and labour-market conditions continue to improve in coming years, then perhaps these exciting organizing initiatives may finally bear fruit. But the most significant breakthroughs in union organization have historically come in waves and at moments of broader social conflict and mobilization. Perhaps the most important thing unions can do to rejuvenate their organizing possibilities is to contribute to building a wider oppositional movement and hence facilitate a change in the broader social climate. In other words, perhaps it is only in the context of a movement that extends beyond unions, but includes unions that are concretely participating in, if not leading, struggles against every kind of oppression and every attack on the quality of our lives, that we can really anticipate the long-sought explosion of workers organizing *themselves* into unions.

Mobilizing the Organized

The demobilization of already unionized workers during the era of concession bargaining has been at least as important as the erosion of union penetration in explaining the decline of union power in Canada. Too many unions accepted corporate demands during the period of neo-liberal restructuring (including wage and other concessions, long-term contracts, and the creation of shallow structures of "co-operation" in the workplace). Too many union leaders viewed the project of mobilizing their members with cynicism and discomfort and even as a threat rather than an asset; hence, they acted consciously to reduce the expectations and demands of their members, rather than to legitimate and give organizational expression to those expectations and demands. The creation of a demoralized, inactive, and often explicitly hostile membership base is the long-run consequence of the backward march of many Canadian unions. This is an environ-

ment that is ripe for change—a progressive, activist shift in the policies and practices of those unions, it is to be hoped, but potentially an anti-union backlash ending in widespread decertification. Transforming unions into centres of working class life—vehicles, for example, for struggling over not just wages but also issues like education reform or environmental degradation—is a way to consolidate the role of the union among all its members and a step towards the most important lesson of all: that fighting back can make a difference.

In some cases, union leaders are starting to address the need for a turnaround in the nature of unionism. But in general this change will require pressure—if not a revolt—from below. Given all the difficulties in organizing such a challenge to entrenched leadership and institutions, such revolts cannot be successful unless local activists establish horizontal links across locals and communities and call on resources from elsewhere in the broader progressive movement (including ties to activists in other unions and contacts with sympathetic academics). Indeed, even where union leaders support a more forceful membership mobilization, such local activism can take better advantage of the openings provided and constructively push progressive leaders further.

A Progressive Bargaining Agenda

Collective bargaining must clearly address the direct economic and workplace concerns of union members, but it can also address the labour movement's strategic considerations, such as linking up to organizing strategies, building labour's community base, raising political concerns, and generally building the capacities of the union and its members. Supplementing traditional goals of higher incomes for unionized workers with broader demands for inclusion, balance, and equality (through measures such as employment equity and affirmative action) can be part of demonstrating a commitment to improving the conditions of traditionally excluded groups of workers, as well as being an aid in organizing. Fighting outsourcing can be a way of proving that it is the union, rather than employers, that is defending community jobs. Putting childcare on the bargaining agenda sets the stage for a political campaign to consolidate any such gain through improvements in public programs. Negotiating paid time off for union education programs can be an effective way to enhance access to ongoing education for union members—and if those programs are union controlled, they can also serve an important union-building function.

Initiatives to redistribute working time are an especially important priority for a progressive bargaining agenda. Working time can be reduced in myriad ways, including limits on overtime, enhanced vacations, early retirement, and expanded parental and educational leaves.[13] It is not just a matter of sharing existing jobs to reduce unemployment (though working overtime when others are laid off is a particular affront to solidarity). More importantly, retrieving and controlling more of our own time are a precondition for developing ourselves as fuller human beings with time to participate within the union, the community, and in politics. The redistribution of work time also allows for more equal sharing of paid work, and flexibility over our time is essential to both a richer and more egalitarian family life (all the more so since neo-liberalism has created a worsening time crunch on families striving to supply more paid labour time in order to maintain or expand their consumption). Capturing productivity gains in the form of time off, rather than wages and consumption,

can also be seen as a progressive environmental measure (especially in developed countries).

Internal Democracy and Accountability

The issue of the accountability of unions and union leaders to their dues-paying membership cannot be separated from the challenge of mobilizing those dues-paying members more effectively. A healthy union demonstrates the highest level of rank-and-file activity during the process of collective bargaining, which involves union members in designing the bargaining agenda, electing the bargaining committee, supporting collective actions (including strikes) in support of that agenda, and then subjecting any agreement ultimately reached to the strong test of membership ratification. In this process, which members of democratic unions "own" more than any other sphere of their unions' activity, unions correspondingly enjoy the greatest level of active support from their members.[14] It is hard to imagine rank-and-file union members becoming more actively involved in any struggle, whether in collective bargaining or in other arenas, unless and until unions become more participatory, democratic, and accountable. This process of democratization will be fought on numerous different fronts: from efforts to restore active and autonomous decision-making at the local level, to developing meaningful cross-community and cross-sectoral labour forums, to the continuing need for greater autonomy (or complete independence) for the Canadian sections of international unions, to procedures allowing badly served union members more choice over their representation. Simply expanding the range of struggles the labour movement takes on can also be seen as enhancing democracy within the movement: active struggles tend to place democratic questions on the agenda because they necessitate bringing new people in, debating and explaining issues and strategies, and concretely learning how to participate in change.

Rebuilding Labour's Political Voice

Canadian union leaders have expended great energy on debates over the labour movement's relationship to the NDP, with some unions expressing deep criticisms of that party and attempting to carve out a more independent political role and others expressing more dogged support for it. Yet it has become abundantly clear that the official proclamations of union leaders, whether loyal to the NDP or not, have negligible impact on the broader political preferences and expressions of union members. Trade union members no longer generally express particularly progressive electoral opinions (if they ever did)—at least not in response to the ways left-versus-right questions are conventionally asked. And even within relatively strong and well-mobilized unions, stewards and other rank-and-file leaders do not conduct the intense consultation and educational activities that are essential if union members are to become effectively and collectively engaged in broader political struggles and campaigns.

Debates over rebuilding labour's political voice will have to confront the depth of the alienation within labour and across Canadian society from formal politics. Polls consistently show a popular desperation for getting some control over one's life—isn't this what politics should be all about? Yet the kind of empty politics offered by conventional parliamentary processes has no appeal—all the more so since globalization appears to be further restricting the scope of parliamentary decision-making. A related problem is that any such rebuilding of labour's political voice will have to address the depth of the worldwide crisis in social democracy; recent attention to the NDP's electoral failures obscures the more profound failures of vision (and the subsequent betrayals) of social democratic parties that have been electorally successful. The current absence of any radical socialist current within the trade union movement means that the range of alternative policies and politics being considered will be limited. Any "new politics" for Canadian labour will have to have as its ambition a radical change in political culture: changing the popular sense of what is possible and how politics is conducted. It is impossible to imagine unions playing the critical role this demands, unless there is also a corresponding and perhaps prior change in union attitudes and assumptions—particularly a change in perspective regarding the collective potentials of workers, both in democratically administering a new world and in developing the political capacities to get there.

Linking with other Struggles

Many Canadian unions have been relatively open to efforts to build coalitions and sponsor other joint activities with the broader social change community.[15] These generally constructive relationships, however, have not been uncontested. Some conservative union officials, like traditional social democratic leaders, tend to view the independent politics and democratic practices of the grass-roots social movements as constituting more of a challenge than an opportunity. On the other hand, many progressive trade unionists are anxious to recapture some of the creative energy and moral authority that currently characterize the work of other social movements such as the antiglobalization campaign, the student movement, and the antipoverty community. The

September 11 events and their aftermath have placed new strains on the links between unions and this broader community of activists; some segments of labour have seemed to pull back from coalition-type work in the face of the more hostile political climate that existed after September 11, just as those broader struggles (such as the antiglobalization struggles) were facing a particularly challenging moment. The struggle within labour to strengthen and develop the links to other community campaigns will obviously need to continue.

An interesting idea regarding the links between labour and other community struggles emerged during the period (2000–2001) when sanctions were imposed by the CLC on the CAW and CAW activists were consequently barred from labour council participation. The CAW prepared to establish community action groups that would be set up as an alternative to the official labour councils but that would include representation for broader community participation. The focus of these bodies would be internal and external education and solidarity support—including, in a spirit of nonsectarianism, support for any struggles involving affiliates of the official labour councils. The subsequent resolution of the dispute between the CLC and the CAW meant that these alternative councils were not established; perhaps, however, that model of labour-community organizing should instead be considered as an alternative to be generalized among the labour movement as a whole.

In all of these ways, the labour movement will need to go through a process of dramatic and wrenching internal change just to rebuild its capacity to effectively wrest a share of potential economic gains from a resurgent capitalism—and this assumes that Canadian capitalism *is* at least somewhat resurgent in

the wake of its episode of neo-liberal restructuring. It seems, then, that there can be no business as usual for the labour movement. Failing this far-reaching revitalization, unions can look forward to a rather pessimistic future of declining membership, eroding credibility with their remaining members, and continuing marginalization in the broader social and political milieus.

Toward a Transformative Vision for Labour?

Revitalizing labour's traditional reformist role might seem like an ambitious enough goal. But recent developments on Canada's left, which have variously involved portions of organized labour, indicate that the labour movement might ultimately be able to set its sights even higher, and aim to accomplish more in the long run than simply rebuilding the capacity to demand a fairer deal from a capitalist system whose authority and leadership are taken for granted. Several developing projects on Canada's left suggest an ongoing potential for revitalizing a more ambitious anti-capitalist and transformative constituency, one in which labour would need to play a central role. As noted above, these projects include the widening activism of extraparliamentary protest movements in civil society (such as the antiglobalization movement and the campaigns against the war in Afghanistan and new security legislation that were mobilized in the wake of the September 11 events); efforts to reignite a more militant and movement-connected social democracy in the wake of the deep crisis in the NDP; and efforts in several cities to organize a more explicitly socialist "structured movement." After two decades of neo-liberal restructuring and the consequent reinforcement of the dominant economic and political power of business in society, these and other important voices are now going beyond simply challenging the most painful and inhumane consequences of that restructuring to once again challenge the legitimacy of a social system so dominated by the wealth and greed of the few. This transformative vision is far from being mapped in detail, and indeed the process of defining both a thoroughgoing critique of modern capitalism and the key elements of an alternative will be a long one—and, it is to be hoped, a participatory and empowering one, too.

Despite this long-run optimism, we must, however, be honest. At present one cannot speak of a transformative project within the labour movement. The movement remains defensive. Its confidence remains shaken by the hostile political-economic environment of neo-liberalism, and it has yet to articulate a thorough critique of neo-liberalism. In fact, if anything, the labour movement has not been defensive enough, in the sense of militantly defending its past gains. The issue, however, is not to wait for renewed labour militancy and then place larger transformative issues on the agenda. Rather, issues such as what kind of political organization or what kind of party workers need must be raised alongside and in interaction with the more immediate task of mobilizing more defensive struggles. For this to happen, left activists within the labour movement need to develop independent organizations and networks extending across individual unions to raise fundamental issues and challenge their respective unions. At the same time, non-labour activists within the various progressive streams need to develop a better understanding of the centrality of labour to any serious strategy for progressive

social change and to find ways of talking to and working with labour activists that reflect the contingent but essential nature of organized labour's relationship to that process of social change. Close cooperation between left activists in various unions and their colleagues in other social movements will be required to foment and nurture a more far-reaching political stance within organized labour.[16]

Honesty about our real situation need not imply cynicism about our future prospects. Great hope is inspired in witnessing workers being infected by—rather than alienated from—the energy and direct-action techniques of the antiglobalization protestors, even by the confidence with which they have raised the banner of anticapitalism. There seems to be a growing understanding—taught so well by capital itself—that free trade agreements are primarily about protecting property rights against any democratic intervention, that a deepening of democracy and equality is a barrier to capital accumulation and therefore an enemy to capitalism, and that capital cannot live without stealing what was once held in common (things like health, education, water) and commodifying, for the purposes of profit, every aspect of our lives. Recent history has encouraged a creeping challenge to capital's authority, now that it has gotten everything it demanded but failed to deliver on its promises. In this context, even the frustrating confusion among left activists—union and non-union alike—about what to do next is positive. This confusion at least finally acknowledges that what we've being doing is inadequate and so sets the stage for debates—real debates—on what needs to be done. As painful as it is to be at such an early stage, it would truly be exciting to think that something is finally beginning.

Endnotes

1 See the papers in Gonick, Phillips, and Vorst (1995) for a consideration of the labour movement's complex and contingent role in the Canadian context.

2 The New Politics Initiative, launched in 2001 by a collective of progressives within the NDP and in nonparty social movements, represents one expression of this stream; see Davies et al. (2001) for a founding statement, and www.newpolitics.ca for ongoing discussions.

3 See Gindin (1998) for an initial expression of this view and the web page of *Canadian Dimension* magazine (www.canadiandimension.mb.ca) for a compendium of subsequent discussion.

4 Conway (2000) discusses the unique experience of the Ontario Days of Action, highlighting (among other factors) the surprising but ultimately incomplete and troubled cooperation between sections of the labour movement and other social movements.

5 While this so-called Golden Age brought about substantial improvements in both private and public living standards for most Canadian workers, the benefits of this expansionary period were obviously distributed in an unequal and uneven fashion. Within Canada women, immigrant workers, and aboriginal people all experienced this Golden Age rather differently than the largely white, male "core" workforce, and in developing countries, of course, the postwar expansion had a rather less optimistic face than it had in the First World.

6 The economic and political factors leading to the breakdown of the postwar regime and the subsequent neo-liberal response have been discussed and analyzed by many progressive scholars. The work of Brenner (1998) has sparked a lively and controversial new instalment of this ongoing discussion; among the numerous responses to Brenner, see especially the articles contained in two special editions of *Historical Materialism*, (issues 4 and 5, 2000) for a sampling of this discussion. Stanford (1999, chaps. 7–9) attempts to describe the economic dimensions of the post-Golden Age U-turn in Canada. Watkins (2003) further discusses the various political constraints and opportunities presented by the neo-liberal legacy in Canada.

7 Watkins (2003) further explores the implications of a globalized political economy for left-wing political strategies in Canada.

8 For example, the CAW's major auto contract of 1999—which provided for annual wage gains of three percent on top of inflation indexation and even more generous improvements in pensions and other non-wage benefits—was probably the richest major collective agreement signed by a Canadian union in a quarter-century and could be interpreted as a signal of the potential return to a more optimistic and effective era of trade unionism. But this same industry also demonstrates the perpetual instability of the neo-liberal era; within three years of the signing of that contract, Canadian auto assembly had plunged by over 20 percent and several assembly and parts plants were facing closure.

9 When bargaining units are amalgamated to form larger and more coherent units, any union that was represented in the initial environment has the right to compete for overall representation.

10 Yates (2000) surveys and analyzes some of these rather pessimistic results.

11 Riddell (2001) provides startling empirical evidence of the negative impact on certification success rates of the elimination of card-check certification procedures in Canada.

12 Some sections of the Hotel Employees and Restaurant Employees' union have experimented with efforts to force employers to voluntarily recognize unions through community pressure and consumer boycotts, instead of working through cumbersome and anti-union official certification processes. The grass-roots Justice for Janitors organizing drives by the Service Employees International Union in the United States similarly press employers to directly recognize unions, in actions that are completely separate from the official certification process. In a similar vein, the CAW tried numerous innovative tactics to force anti-union auto parts giant Magna International to voluntarily recognize a new union at a seat-making plant in Windsor where the union had majority support—including linking the issue to the CAW's collective bargaining at Daimler-Chrysler (the company that purchases the seats from Magna). The CAW ultimately achieved voluntary recognition at Magna, but only after agreeing that no strikes would occur during the first two collective agreements at the plant.

13 Hayden (2000) provides a useful overview of union efforts on this issue, both in Canada and internationally.

14 This is why the trend to long-term collective agreements (led by conservative private-sector unions, which have accepted employer demands for contracts of six years or even longer) is so destructive to the internal functioning of these unions. When the most important and most democratic activity within the union occurs

only every six years (or even less frequently), then internal union activity and democracy will inevitably decline. For a survey of the trend toward long-term agreements and a discussion of the dangers posed to the labour movement, see Murnighan (1998).

15 Carroll and Coburn (2003) explore dimensions of recent extraparliamentary social and political activism in Canada.

16 An interesting analogy in this regard is provided by the cooperative effort of feminists inside the labour movement and those in other feminist organizations to push the labour movement toward more progressive positions and actions on a wide range of women's issues (including traditional economic issues such as pay equity, non-economic issues such as reproductive freedom, and organizational issues such as equity and representation for women within unions). Feminist trade unionists have benefited from the knowledge and solidarity of their sisters in other constituencies; in the meantime, the broader women's movement has benefited mightily from the labour movement's adoption of feminist principles and demands—not least because of unions' potential power to realize some of those demands directly through collective bargaining.

References

Albo, Greg. 2002. "Neo-liberalism, the State and the Left: A Canadian Perspective." *Monthly Review* 53(12): 46–55.

Brenner, Robert. 1998. "The Economics of Global Turbulence." *New Left Review* 229 (May–June): 1–265.

Carroll, William K. and Elaine Coburn. 2003. "Social Movements and Transformation." In Wallace Clement and Leah F. Vosko (eds.). *Changing Canada: Political Economy as Transformation.* Montreal and Kingston: McGill-Queen's Univesity Press, pp. 79–105.

Conway, Janet. 2000. "Knowledge, Power, Organization: Social Justice Coalitions at a Crossroads." *Studies in Political Economy* 62 (summer): 43–70.

Davies, Libby, Svend Robinson, Murray Dobbin, Louise James, Judy Rebick, and Jim Stanford. 2001. "After the Labour Pains, a New NDP?" *Globe and Mail,* 22 November, A27.

Gindin, Sam. 1998. "The Party's Over." *This Magazine* November–December, 13–15.

---. 2002. "The Terrain of Social Justice." *Monthly Review* 53(9): 1–14.

Gonick, Cy, Paul Phillips, and Jesse Vorst, eds. 1995. *Labour Gains, Labour Pains: Fifty Years of PC 1003.* Halifax: Fernwood.

Hayden, Anders. 2000. *Sharing the Work, Sparing the Planet: Work Time, Consumption, and Ecology.* Toronto: Between the Lines.

Murnighan, Bill. 1998. *Long-Term Agreements: The New Concession.* Research Department, Canadian Auto Workers.

Rebick, Judy. 2000. *Imagine Democracy.* Toronto: Stoddart.

Riddell, Chris. 2001. "Union Suppression and Certification Success." *Canadian Journal of Economics* 34(2): 396–410.

Stanford, Jim. 1999. *Paper Boom: Why Real Prosperity Requires a New Approach to Canada's Economy.* Ottawa: Canadian Centre for Policy Alternatives and James Lorimer.

Watkins, Mel. 2003. "Politics in the Time and Space of Globalization." In Wallace Clement and Leah F. Vosko (eds.). *Changing Canada: Political Economy as Transformation.* Montreal and Kingston: McGill-Queen's University Press, pp. 3–24.

Yates, Charlotte. 2000. "Staying the Decline in Union Membership: Union Organizing in Ontario, 1985–1999," *Relations industrielles/Industrial Relations* 55(4): 640–74.

SECTION VIII: THE LABOUR MOVEMENT IN TRANSITION

Critical Thinking Questions

Chapter 15: Neo-Liberalism, Labour, and the Canadian State, Leo Panitch and Donald Swartz

1. Discuss some of the new legislation and practices adopted by governments in your province that have diminished the role and strength of unions. Do you believe these changes are warranted?

2. How can we explain why governments of all political stripes at the federal level and in all provinces have adopted more coercive policies and practices towards the labour movement over the course of the past quarter century?

3. Why are decisions by the Supreme Court of Canada significant for the strengthening or curtailment of workers' rights and freedoms?

Chapter 16: Canadian Labour and the Political Economy of Transformation, Sam Gindin and Jim Stanford

1. Discuss some of the key challenges faced by unions and the broader labour movement following the decline of the Golden Age of postwar capitalism in Canada.

2. How can the labour movement build on its standard reformist practices to ensure its longer-term viability?

3. Should the labour movement restrict itself to fighting for improvements to working conditions in the workplace or should it play a leading role in the broader transformation of society? How can the labour movement engage with other social movements to ensure the success of a transformative project?

Recommended Readings

Glenday, Dan. 2001. "Off the Ropes? New Challenges and Strengths Facing Trade Unions in Canada." In Dan Glenday and Ann Duffy (eds.), *Canadian Society: Meeting the Challenges of the Twenty-First Century*. Toronto: Oxford University Press. An analysis of the growth and strengthening of trade unions during the postwar period, and of their ability to survive the economic restructuring and legal setbacks of the past two decades.

Martin, Andrew and George Ross (eds.). 1999. *The Brave New World of European Labour: European Trade Unions at the Millennium*. New York: Berghahn Books. A collection of essays that examines the complex and sometimes contradictory responses of unions in six European countries to the challenges posed by economic restructuring, neo-liberal state policies, and European integration.

Moody, Kim. 1997. *Workers in a Lean World: Unions in the International Economy*. New York: Verso. An exploration of how workers and their unions struggle against the onslaught of multinational corporations intent on drastically cutting labour costs and curtailing the power of the labour movement. The book also offers a vision of hope for the international collaboration of labour movements.

Panitch, Leo and Donald Swartz. 2003. *From Consent to Coercion: The Assault on Trade Union Freedoms, Third Edition*. Aurora: Garamond Press. A detailed examination of the gradual destruction of the Canadian industrial relations system since the 1970s as federal and provincial governments embraced a neo-liberal agenda and, consequently, attacked rights and freedoms that had been won by workers in the postwar era.

Wood, Ellen Meiksins, Peter Meiksins, and Michael Yates (eds.). 1998. *Rising from the Ashes? Labor in the Age of "Global" Capitalism*. New York: Monthly Review. A series of articles that look at the challenges facing labour movements around the world, and explore the actions and strategies of workers and unions in the face of global economic restructuring and neo-liberalism.

Related Websites

Canadian Auto Workers (CAW Canada)

http://www.caw.ca/flash.html

The CAW is the largest private-sector union in Canada. Its research department provides information and statistics on wages, hours, and other conditions of employment that are needed in collective bargaining. The research department also produces general economic facts and other information, which is available online.

Canadian Labour Congress

http://www.clc-ctc.ca/web/menu/english/en_index.htm

The Congress is a national umbrella labour organization. The site includes different publications, such as a quarterly review entitled *Economy* and numerous papers on a broad range of issues relevant to labour.

Global Policy Network

http://www.globalpolicynetwork.org/

The Global Policy Network consists of policy and research institutions connected to the world's trade union movements. Its work reflects a concern with the economic, social, and political conditions of working people in both developing and developed nations. The site provides reports and other publications on a wide variety of issues relevant to the labour movement.

International Institute for Labour Studies

http://www.ilo.org/public/english/bureau/inst/

The International Institute for Labour Studies is a centre for advanced studies in the social and labour fields. It provides new perspectives for social policy, develops exchanges among labour stakeholders around the world, and familiarizes future social policy-makers with the processes of tripartite consultations and policy formulation.

International Labour Organization

http://www.ilo.org/

The International Labour Organization is the United Nations' specialized agency that formulates international labour standards in the form of conventions and recommendations setting minimum standards of basic labour rights. The site contains facts, an online magazine and other reports produced by the organization.

COPYRIGHT ACKNOWLEDGMENTS